Language and Interpretation in
the Syriac Text of Ben Sira

Monographs
of the Peshitta Institute
Leiden

Studies in the Syriac Versions of the Bible and
their Cultural Contexts

ᵞ VOLUME 16

Language and Interpretation in the Syriac Text of Ben Sira

A Comparative Linguistic and Literary Study

By

W.Th. van Peursen

BRILL

LEIDEN • BOSTON
2007

This book is printed on acid-free paper.

A C.I.P. record for this book is available from the Library of Congress.

ISSN   0169-9008
ISBN   978 90 04 16394 2

Copyright 2007 by Koninklijke Brill NV, Leiden, The Netherlands.
Koninklijke Brill NV incorporates the imprints Brill, Hotei Publishing,
IDC Publishers, Martinus Nijhoff Publishers and VSP.

PRINTED IN THE NETHERLANDS

CONTENTS

PART THREE
PHRASE STRUCTURE

PART FOUR
CLAUSE STRUCTURE

PART SIX
CONCLUSIONS

PREFACE

This monograph is a product of the project 'Computer-Assisted Linguistic Analysis of the Peshitta (CALAP)', a joint research project of
the Peshitta Institute Leiden (PIL) and the Werkgroep Informatica
Vrije Universiteit (WIVU), sponsored by the Netherlands Organization
for Scientific Research (NWO). This project has received a follow-up
in a new project called Turgama: Computer-Assisted Analysis of the
Peshitta and the Targum: Text, Language and Interpretation. This
study has benefited much from the many fruitful conversations with
the other project members: Dr Konrad D. Jenner, Professor Eep Talstra, Dr Percy S.F. van Keulen, Dr Janet W. Dyk, Constantijn Sikkel,
Hendrik Jan Bosman and Dirk Bakker.

I am very grateful to Konrad Jenner, who was always willing to discuss all kinds of issues that arose during the preparation of this monograph. He appeared to be an expert in the field of Peshitta studies as
well as a true friend.

I thank Dr Martin Baasten (Leiden) and Dr Pete Williams (Cambridge) for their valuable remarks on earlier versions of this book, Ms
Madelon Grant for her editorial assistance and Mr Mark Grundeken
for preparing the indices. I am indebted to Professor Jan Joosten
(Strasbourg) for his useful comments on an earlier version of Part
Three and to Professor Geoffrey Khan (Cambridge) and Professor Ta-
kamitsu Muraoka (Leiden) for their feedback on an earlier version of
Part Four. In my preparation of Part Five I have benefited much from
useful suggestions of Professor Arie Verhagen (Leiden). Finally, I am
thankful to Mrs Helen Richardson-Hewitt for her correction of the
English.

The present study contains six parts. Parts Three to Five contain the
results of the computer-assisted linguistic analysis of the Syriac translation of Sirach (Syr) on the levels of phrases (Part Three), clauses
(Part Four) and texts (Part Five). These parts are preceded by Part

One, which approaches Syr from a traditional philological perspective. This part discusses the text of the Syr, its place in the textual history, its character as a translation, its relationship to other texts and traditions and the translator's religious profile. It presents the philological basis for the computer-assisted research. In Parts Three to Five we frequently refer to the discussions in Part One to show how the computer-assisted analysis sheds light on or supplements the traditional philological research. This approach, which starts from traditional philological research and moves from there to the computer-assisted analysis agrees with the basic insight that the latter can fruitfully complement but never replace the former. Part Two constitutes a bridge between Part One and the other parts because it gives a description of the model of the computer-assisted analysis that has been the basis for Parts Three to Five. It also addresses the fundamentally different way in which a text is approached in a computer-assisted analysis compared with the way in which this is done in traditional philological approaches. In Part Six we summarize our results and present our conclusions.

ABBREVIATIONS AND SIGLA

Versions

Syr	The Syriac version of Sirach
Heb	The Hebrew version of Sirach (for HebI and HebII see § 2.1)
Gr	The Greek version of Sirach (for GrI and GrII see § 2.1)
Lat	The Latin version of Sirach
MT	The Masoretic Text of the Hebrew Bible
Pesh	Peshitta
A, B, C, D, E, F	Hebrew Geniza manuscripts of Sirach
M	The Sirach scroll from Masada
A^1, B^1, etc.	The first of two or three readings in a doublet or triplet in MS A, B, etc.
A(+B) etc.	The citation given comes from ms A; in B it occurs in a slightly different form, which has, however, no consequence for the subject under discussion.
A^{txt}, B^{txt}	Main text of MS A, B, etc.
A^{mg}, B^{mg}	Marginal reading in MS A, B, etc.

Grammatical terms

Ep	Enclitic pronoun
NC	Nominal Clause
NP	Noun Phrase
Pr	Predicate
Su	Subject
St.abs.	Absolute State
St.cstr.	Construct State

In some chapters we add to the quotation in Syriac font the syntactically encoded text. In this text the following symbols are used:

Transliteration alphabet: >BGDHWZXVJKLMNS<PYQRCT	
[...]	marking of phrases
{...}	marking of clauses.

For the syntactic parsing the following abbreviations are used:

\<Aj\>	Adjunct
\<ap\>	Apposition
\<Cj\>	Conjunction between clauses
\<cj\>	Phrase-internal conjunction
\<Co\>	Complement
\<Ep\>	Enclitic pronoun

\<Ex\>	Extraposition
\<eX\>	Existential particle
\<Fa\>	Fronted adjunct
\<Fs\>	Fronted subject
\<Mo\>	Modifier
\<Ng\>	Negation
\<Ob\>	Object
\<PA\>	Parallel element
\<PC\>	Nominal Complement to predication
\<PO\>	Verbal predicate with object suffix
\<Pr\>	Verbal predicate
\<Qo\>	Interrogative object
\<Qp\>	Interrogative predicate
\<Re\>	Relative particle
\<sp\>	Specification
\<Su\>	Subject
\<Ti\>	Time reference
\<Vo\>	Vocative
\<Xs\>	Existential particle with subject suffix

Example: 7:27 ܝܠܕܬܟ ܐܡܟ 'your mother who bore you'.

[L->MK [D-{[JLDTK \<PO\>} \<sp\>]]

The borders of this prepositional phrase are marked by the outer square brackets [...]. Inside there is another pair of square brackets marking the borders of the specification ܝܠܕܬܟ. This specification consists of the relative particle ܕ and the verbal predicate + object suffix ܝܠܕܬܟ. The use of decorative brackets {...} indicates that this is a predication structure.

PART ONE

SIRACH IN SYRIAC

CHAPTER ONE

THE TEXT

1.1 MANUSCRIPTS

The textual basis for the present study is the text of the Syriac version
of Sirach (= Syr) that will appear in Volume IV,1 of *The Old Testament in Syriac according to the Peshitta Version*. According to the
general policy of the Leiden edition, biblical manuscripts up to and
including the twelfth century are included. In the case of Syr this concerns the following manuscripts.

> 7a1 =MS Milan, Ambrosian Library, B. 21. Inf.
> 7h3 = MS London, British Library, Add. 12,142
> 7pk2 = MS Cambridge, University Library, T.-S. 12,743
> 8a1 = MS Paris, Bibiothèque Nationale, Syr. 341
> 9c1 = MS Paris, Bibiothèque Nationale, Syr. 372
> 10c1 = MS New Haven, Beinecke Rare Book Library, B 47b
> 10c2 = MS Rome, Vatican Library, Borgiani siriaci 93
> 10k7 = MS Damascus, National Museum of Syria, Dept. of Byzantine
>   Art, 2115/6
> 11c1 = MS London, British Library, Add. 14,440
> 12a1 = MS Cambridge University Library Oo 1.1,2
> 12h2 = MS Rome, Vatican Library, Vat. sir. 6
> 12k2 = MS London, British Library, Add. 14,730

Not included in the critical apparatus are the masoretic manuscripts
containing parts of Syr (9m1, 10m1.2.3, 11m1.2.4.5.6.7, 12m1) or
biblical manuscripts from the period after the twelfth century (13a1,
13c1, 13m1, 14c1, 15/14a1, 15a3, 15c1 and others). A description of
the manuscripts listed above will be given in the introduction to the
edition.

According to the dates of origin indicated by the sigla, the list
above contains three manuscripts from the seventh century, one from
the eighth century, one from the ninth, and seven from the tenth to

twelfth centuries.[1] For Sirach we do not have a fifth-century manuscript comparable to 5b1 for Genesis and Exodus or 5ph1 for Isaiah
and Ezekiel; nor is Sirach included in 9a1, a manuscript that is generally considered to show traces of the first attainable stage in the textual history of the Peshitta, albeit in combination with later, secondary
readings.[2]

1.2 QUOTATIONS IN EARLY SYRIAC LITERATURE

The earliest extant biblical manuscripts containing Syr date from the
sixth or seventh century AD. If we assume that Syr originated in the
second century, there is a gap of about four centuries between the origin of Syr and the earliest biblical manuscripts. It is worthwhile, therefore, investigating the Sirach quotations in Syriac literature that pre-
date these manuscripts.[3]

Quotations from Sirach occur in the works of Ephrem, Pseudo-
Ephrem, Aphrahat, *The Book of Steps* (*Liber Graduum*) and *The Life
of Eulogius the Stone-Cutter*.[4] Aphrahat quotes Sirach fourteen times.
In the other works mentioned one or two quotations occur. According
to M.M. Winter the quotations in the early Syriac literature show
traces of a pre-Peshitta translation. In his view 'the number of readings which differ from the Peshitta, in relation to the total number of
quotations, makes it probable that when first translated Sirach had a

---

[1] But the dates of origin indicated by the sigla are sometimes disputed. Thus a sixth-century origin has been advocated for 7a1, 7h3 and 8a1. Ceriani dated 7a1 in the sixth century in the *praefatio* of his facsimile edition; cf. Haefeli, *Peschitta des Alten Testaments*, 77. (On the function of 7a1 see Jenner, 'Review of Methods'; on its value as a witnesses to Syr see Schrader, *Verwandtschaft*, 19; Schrader arrives at a more positive conclusion than Smend, *Jesus Sirach*, cxlvi.) A sixth-century date of 8a1 has been argued on the basis of the iconography, see Jenner, 'Study of 8a1', 205; idem, *Perikopentitels*, 4–8; idem, 'Review of Methods', 261; Sörries, *Die syrische Bibel von Paris*. The suggestion that 7h3 dates from the sixth century can be found in Box-Oesterley, 'Sirach', 288 (cf. below, n. 29); Wright, *Catalogue* I, 97–98, ascribes 7h3 to the sixth or seventh century.

[2] On the absence of Sirach in 9a1 and its presence in other biblical manuscripts see § 6.3.

[3] For a general discussion of the use of quotations for the reconstruction of the earliest phase in the textual history of the Peshitta, see Jenner–Van Peursen–Talstra, 'Interdisciplinary Debate', 36–39, and the literature mentioned there.

[4] See Winter, *Ben Sira in Syriac*, Ch. 4 (pp. 88–108); idem, 'Ben Sira in Syriac' (Part II), 506–507; Strothmann, 'Jesus-Sirach-Zitate'; Owens, 'Early Syriac Text of Ben Sira', 48–74; McHardy, *Critical Text*, 68–78; Gilbert, 'Jesus Sirach', 890–904.

text form different from that of the Peshitta. These variants are sufficiently important to justify the use of the title Vetus Syra.'[5] R.J.
Owens has contested this claim. According to Owens the quotations in
Aphrahat's *Demonstrations* do not justify Winter's claim because in
many cases Aphrahat quotes from memory and conflates several
scriptural passages.[6] The evidence from the other early Syriac writers
is too small to support Winter's view.

Although the quotations in early Syriac literature do not allow us to
conclude that there once existed a Vetus Syra of Sirach, they may
shed some light on the earliest text of Syr. Two categories of variants
are relevant. To the first category belong cases where the quotations
seem to be closer to the Hebrew witnesses than the text in the extant
Peshitta manuscripts. Compare the following examples.

> 4:5 ܐܬܟܣܗ ܠܐ 'Do not dismiss (the request of the poor)'; Pseudo-
> Ephrem, *Sermo de admonitione et poenitia* 16 ܐܬܟܣܝ ܠܐ 'do not
> despise'[7]; Heb (MS A) אל תבזה.[8]
> 8:13 ܕܚܣܢ ܠܡܢ '(Do not become surety to) someone who is stronger
> than you'; *Life of Eulogius the Stone-Cutter* has ܠܡܢ ܕܝܬܝܪ 'someone
> who is more than you'[9]; Heb (MS A) יתר ממך.[10]
> 44:20 ܕܥܒܕ ܦܬܓܡܘܗܝ, ܕܥܠܝܐ 'who did the words of the Most High';
> Aphrahat, *Dem.* 13:8 ܕܢܛܪ ܢܡܘܣܗ 'who kept the law'[11]; Heb (MS B)
> אשר שמר מצות עליון.[12]

It is questionable, however, to conclude that these quotations reflect
an earlier text form of Syr that was closer to the Hebrew, because in
most cases alternative interpretations are possible as well. Moreover,
the complicated textual history of Sirach does not allow us to take the
Hebrew text in the mediaeval Geniza manuscripts as identical to the
source text of the Syriac translator.

---

[5] Winter, *Ben Sira in Syriac*, 108.
[6] Cf. Owens, 'Early Syriac Text of Ben Sira', 75: 'Aphrahat's text is essentially
identical to that found in the P manuscripts of the sixth to eighth centuries and later';
similarly Gilbert, 'Jesus Sirach', 894; for Aphrahat quoting scripture from memory,
see also Owens, *Genesis and Exodus Quotations*; idem, 'Early Syriac Text of Leviticus; for arguments against the notion of a Vetus Syra of the Old Testament see also
Koster, 'Copernican Revolution', 19, Weitzman, *From Judaism to Christianity*, 204–
208.
[7] Ed. Lamy I, 299.
[8] Winter, *Ben Sira in Syriac*, 104.
[9] Ed. Smith Lewis 74 (text), 21 (translation); ed. Müller-Kessler–Sokoloff 89.
[10] Winter, *Ben Sira in Syriac*, 107.
[11] Ed. Parisot 1.557, line 12.
[12] Winter, *Ben Sira in Syriac*, 94.

Another category of variants are those that agree with the linguistic profile that has been established for the earliest phase of the Peshitta. This profile is characterized by a closer resemblance to the Hebrew and forms that are typical of the earliest phase of Syriac. To the features that are well attested in the earliest Peshitta manuscripts belong the use of bipartite nominal clauses in contexts that usually require the tripartite construction and the use of the construct state in places where we would expect a construction with ܕ. These features may reflect either a tendency to imitate the Hebrew source text or an early phase of Syriac in which the features typical of Classical Syriac had not yet been crystallized.[13] In the early quotations from Sirach the following examples occur:

> 1:20a ܡܢ ܟܠܗ ܣܝܡܬܐ '(She is better to him) than all treasures'; Aphrahat, *Dem.* 20:4 ܡܢ ܟܠ ܣܝܡܐ.[14] The difference between the biblical manuscripts and Aphrahat's quotation may be related to the decline of the absolute state. In the oldest stage of Classical Syriac observable to us, the emphatic state had become the normal form of the noun, but in some 'closed syntagms' such as ܟܠ + Noun the absolute state continued to be used.[15]
>
> 2:1 ܠܕܚܠܬܗ ܕܐܠܗܐ '(If you draw near) to the fear of God'; *Book of Steps* 19:3 ܠܕܚܠܬ ܐܠܗܐ.[16] The construction with ܕ and the proleptic suffix in the biblical manuscripts may be an adaptation of an earlier reading with a construct chain reflected in the *Book of Steps*.[17]
>
> 35:12 ܡܢ ܕܝܗܒ ܠܡܣܟܢܐ ܠܐܠܗܐ ܗܘ ܡܘܙܦ 'For he who gives to the poor man lends to God'; Aphrahat, *Dem.* 20:4 ܡܘܙܦ ܠܡܣܟܢܐ

---

[13] Jenner–Van Peursen–Talstra, 'Interdisciplinary Debate', 34–35; Van Peursen, 'Response to Responses', 198–200. For the complexities involved in the application of these principles to the text-critical and text-historical study of the Peshitta, see Van Peursen, 'Language Variation'. For the development of Classical Syriac as a standard language see Van Rompay, 'Standard Language'. On the basis of the linguistic variation attested in the early Syriac manuscripts, Van Rompay concludes that Classical Syriac 'may in its beginning have been less uniform and less homogeneous than is generally assumed on the basis of later documents.' (p. 85). For the place of the language of the Old Testament Peshitta in the early history of Syriac see Joosten, 'Materials', especially his discussion of early Syriac and non-Syriac elements in the language of the Peshitta on pp. 211–218.

[14] Ed. Parisot 1.900, lines 12–14.

[15] Cf. Joosten, *Syriac Language*, 73, 145–146; Nöldeke, *Grammatik*, § 202D; Owens, 'Early Syriac Text of Ben Sira', 54; in Pesh-1 Kings ܟܠ with an absolute plural noun is not attested; Williams, *Peshitta of 1 Kings*, 42.

[16] Ed. Kmosko 454.

[17] Compare the use of the construct state in 5b1 as opposed to the construction with ܕ in later manuscripts; Wernberg-Møller, 'Scribal and Linguistic Features', 147; Koster, *Exodus*, 78; see, however, Van Peursen, 'Language Variation', § 6.

ܗܘܐ ܠܐܠܗܐ; B מלוה יי נותן אביון. It is possible that Aphrahat's quotation reflects an earlier text form that was closer to the Hebrew and that the addition of ܗܘ, ܝܬܝܪ and the enclitic pronoun served to render the text in a more 'natural' idiom.[18] Since, however, Aphrahat seems to quote almost always from memory,[19] we cannot be sure about this.[20]

In other cases the significance of quotations in early Syriac literature is text-historical rather than text-critical. Thus in the sources from the sixth and seventh centuries readings occur, which agree with 8a1 and also later witnesses against 7a1 and 7h3.

> 16:3 7a1 7h3 ܡܢ ܐܠܦ '(Because better is one who does the will) than a thousand'; other MSS, *Plerophories* 16:3 (mid-sixth century),[21] and Ishoyahb III, *Letters* (mid-seventh century)[22] ܡܢ ܐܠܦ.
>
> 41:12 7a1 7h3 ܐܨܦ ܥܠ ܫܡܟ 'Be solicitous about your name'; other MSS, Ishoyahb III, *Letters*[23] ܗܒ ܥܠ ܫܡܟ.

Another group of quotations that are interesting from a text-historical perspective occurs in the works of Philoxenus of Mabbug (AD 450–523). Philoxenus quotes Sirach four times in his *Discourses*.[24] His quotations show some remarkable differences from the text in the extant Peshitta manuscripts. The background of these quotations is a debated issue. W.D. McHardy claimed that Philoxenus used the Peshitta as it is known to us, but quoted it in a loose, free manner.[25] M.M. Winter argued that the quotations come from Philoxenus' own version.[26] McHardy's hypothesis accounts for the many differences be-

---

[18] Note the addition of the Ep in 7a1 as opposed to 5b1; Wernberg-Møller, 'Scribal and Linguistic Features', 151–152; Van Peursen, 'Response to the Responses', 199–200; idem, 'Language Variation', § 5.

[19] Cf. above, note 6.

[20] See above and compare the careful evaluation of these readings in Owens, 'Early Syriac Text of Ben Sira', 57–58: 'These are "minuses" relative to the P, and Aphrahat may be simply economizing and streamlining his text a bit as he quotes (…) However, one does notice that all three of these minuses agree with the text of a marginal clause that occurs next to 32:12 [= 35:12] in Heb MS B (…) The possibility must be considered that Aphrahat here accurately quotes a text that is slightly closer to its Heb exemplar than is P'.

[21] Ed. Nau 111. The *Plerophories* originated in the early sixth century and were translated from Greek into Syriac somewhere in the middle of the sixth century; cf. Nau's 'Introduction', 7.

[22] Ed. Duval 119, line 28 (text), 90 (translation).

[23] Ed. Duval 41, line 13 (text), 35 (translation).

[24] Edition: Wallis Budge, *Discourses*.

[25] McHardy, *Critical Text*, 69–71.

[26] Winter, *Ben Sira in Syriac*, 69–71.

tween Philoxenus' quotations and the Peshitta, but does not explain some remarkable agreements between Philoxenus' citations and the Greek version of Sirach. The problem with Winter's thesis is that it does not fit in with what we know about Philoxenus' translation activities. The *Discourses* originated in all likelihood from the early period of Philoxenus' literary activity. Quotations from Genesis, Exodus, Psalms and Isaiah that occur in the *Discourses* do not show any trace of a Philoxenian revision.[27] For this reason it is unlikely that a Philoxenian version of Sirach was available at the time in which Philoxenus wrote his *Discourses*.[28] In his *Letter to the Monks of Senun* Philoxenus quotes Sir 27:20. In this case Philoxenus' text is identical to that of the extant Peshitta manuscripts.

1.3 TRACES OF INNER-SYRIAC CORRUPTION

Since the Sirach quotations in the Syriac literature do not offer much material for a reconstruction of the earliest history of Syr, we have to resort to another source of information, namely the internal evidence of Syr: To what extent do the earliest manuscripts contain traces of the textual transmission? Are there inner-Syriac corruptions that may reveal something of the vicissitudes of Syr between the second and the sixth or seventh century AD?

This question can be answered in the affirmative. In many cases the Syriac text is the result of inner-Syriac corruptions. In a number of cases the corruption occurs in all manuscripts. This can only be explained if we assume that all extant manuscripts derive from a single ancestor in which these corruptions were already present.[29] Many cor-

---

[27] Jenkins, *Old Testament Quotations of Philoxenus of Mabbug*.

[28] See further Van Peursen, 'Sirach Quotations in the *Discourses* of Philoxenus of Mabbug'.

[29] Cf. Segal, 'Evolution', 91: 'All the extant Syriac Mss. exhibit with but slight variations one and the same text.' Compare on the Peshitta in general Weitzman, *Syriac Version*, 7: 'We may suppose that, in any given biblical book, all the extant witnesses to the Syriac text derive from a lost ancestor which already had these errors'. This assumption justifies conjectural emendation even where all extant witnesses agree. See also Weitzman, *From Judaism to Christianity*, 78. It is unlikely that one of the extant manuscripts, namely 7h3, is the parent of all the other manuscripts; *pace* Box–Oesterley, 'Sirach', 288: 'The earliest known MS. (Cod. Mus. Brit. 12142) belongs to the sixth century, but this MS. contains already a very large number of scribal errors, which point to a long previous history; it seems, however, to be the

ruptions concern the addition, omission or substitution of letters in words that are otherwise similar:[30]

4:21 ܕܐܝܩܪܗ ܛܝܒܘܬܐ '(There is a shame) the honour of which is goodness' is probably a corruption of ܕܐܝܩܪܐ ܘܛܝܒܘܬܐ 'of honour and goodness'; cf. A כבוד וחן; C חן וכבוד; Gr δόξα καὶ χάρις; Lat *adducens gloriam et gratiam*.

8:10 ܠܪܫܝܥܐ ܓܡܝܪܐ '(Be not an associate) for the wicked one who is complete'. ܓܡܝܪܐ is a reinterpretation of ܒܓܘܡܪܐ 'with coals' (בגחלת = Gr ἄνθρακας; A has בנחלת).

22:22 ܒܪ ܡܚܣܕܐ ܗܘ ܕܓܠܐ ܐܪܙܐ 'A son of reproaches is he who reveals a secret'; ܒܪ ܡܚܣܕܐ ܗܘ is probably a corruption of ܠܒܪ ܡܢ ܚܣܕܐ 'but reproach...'; cf. Gr πλὴν ὀνειδισμοῦ καὶ ὑπερηφανίας καὶ μυστηρίου ἀποκαλύψεως 'but reproach and arrogance, and betrayal of a secret'.

23:4 ܒܛܘܥܝܘܬܗܘܢ '(Do not throw me) into their erring' is probably a corruption of ܒܡܠܟܗܘܢ 'in their counsel' (Gr ἐν βουλῇ αὐτῶν = Heb בעצתם).

27:22 ܘܕܪܡܐ ܥܝܢܗ 'And he whose eye is high'. ܪܡܐ is probably a corruption of ܪܡܙ 'winks' (= Gr διανεύων).

28:13 ܕܩܛܠܐ ܣܓܝܐܐ ܐܪܡܝܬ '(The triple tongue) which has cast down many murders'. ܩܛܠܐ is probably a corruption of ܩܛܝܠܐ 'murdered, slain'; cf. Prov 7:26 ܡܛܠ ܕܣܓܝܐܐ ܕܩܛܝܠܐ ܐܪܡܝܬ.

30:7 ܢܣܪܩ ܠܒܗ '(And against all shouts) he makes his heart empty'. ܢܣܪܩ is probably a corruption of ܢܣܪܘܕ 'quakes, is terrified'; cf. Gr καὶ ἐπὶ πάσῃ βοῇ ταραχθήσεται σπλάγχνα αὐτοῦ 'And his heart is troubled at every cry'.

34:4 ܘܡܢ ܪܫ ܥܡܗ ܢܦܩ ܙܟܘܬܐ 'From the chief of his people goes out victory' is probably a corruption of ܘܡܢ ܪܫܝܥܐ ܡܢܘ ܢܦܩ ܙܟܘܬܐ 'And from the wicked man, who will bring out righteousness'; cf. Gr ἀπὸ ἀκαθάρτου τί καθαρισθήσεται; 'From an unclean thing, what can be cleaned?' The purport of the context is that something good cannot come forth from something that is wrong. Compare the following ܐܘ ܡܢܘ ܟܕܒܐ 'or who is a liar who is blameless?'[31]

35:21 ܥܠܝܗ '(Till He explores) concerning it' is probably a corruption of ܥܠܝܐ 'Most High' (= Gr ὁ ὕψιστος; B has אל).

35:22 ܥܕܡܐ ܕܢܬܒܥ 'Till He has avenged (the might of the unrighteous)'. ܢܬܒܥ is probably a corruption of ܢܬܒܪ '(till) He has broken' (= Gr συντρίψει); B has עד ימחץ מתני אכזרי.

---

parent of all other extant Syriac MSS. of Sirach, for its corruptions occur in all of them.'

[30] The examples given here are taken from the preliminary version of the English translation of Syr in *The Bible of Edessa* prepared by K.D. Jenner and the present author.

[31] Smend, *Jesus Sirach*, 305.

37:1 ܘܠܪܚܡܗ ‘And to his friend (he says, I love you)’ is probably a corruption of a ܟܠ ܪܚܡܐ ‘every friend’; cf. B^{mg}+D כל אוהב and Gr πᾶς φίλος.
38:33 ܢܬܒܘܢ ‘They (do not) sit (in the council of the people)’ is probably a corruption of ܢܬܒܥܘܢ ‘they are sought for’; cf. Gr ζητηθήσονται.
50:11 ܒܡܦܩܗ ‘When he came out (to take up songs of praise)’ is probably a corruption of ܒܡܣܩܗ ‘when he ascended’; cf. B בעלותו; Gr ἐν ἀναβάσει.
50:14b ܒܚܕܘܬܐ ܕܩܘܕܫܐ ‘(Until he had completed to serve the altar, and to serve) in holy joy’ ܒܚܕܘܬܐ ‘with joy’ is probably a corruption of ܡܕܒܚܘܬܐ ‘the altar’; cf. B מערכות עליון; Gr ἐπὶ βωμῶν.
50:16d ܠܡܒܪܟܘ ‘to bless (before all the people)’ is probably a corruption of ܠܡܕܟܪܘ ‘to mention’; cf. B להזכיר and Gr εἰς μνημόσυνον.[32]

Sometimes the graphic similarity between graphic letters accounts for the corruption. Thus confusion of ܕ and ܪ accounts for the following examples.

5:9 ܪܕܐ ‘(Do not) proceed (in every wind)’ is probably a corruption of ܕܪܐ ‘winnowing’ (= A+C זורה; Gr μὴ λίκμα).
29:28 ܟܐܬܐ ܘܪܒܝܬܐ ‘(These things are heavy to the wise man:) rebuke and usury (and the loan of the lender)’. ܪܒܝܬܐ is probably a corruption ܕܒܝܬܐ ‘of the house’; cf. Gr ἐπιτίμησις οἰκίας ‘rebuke of the house’.

In combination with the omission of another letter:

49:6 ܘܥܩܪܘ ‘And they pulled down (the Holy City)’. B ויציתו and Gr ἐνεπύρισαν suggest that ܘܥܩܪܘ is a corruption of ܘܐܘܩܕܘ ‘they burnt down’.

Perhaps graphic similarity accounts also for the confusion of ܡ and ܒ and of ܒ and ܩ:

36:31 ܢܡܘܬ ‘(In the place where he is found) he dies’ is probably a corruption of ܢܒܘܬ ‘he spends the night’; cf. B+D המרגיע ‘who finds lodging (where it becomes evening)’; Gr καὶ καταλύοντι οὗ ἐὰν ὀψίσῃ ‘he lodges (wherever he comes late)’.
40:23 ܢܬܒܪܟܘܢ ‘(A friend and a neighbour) will be blessed in time’ is probably a corruption of ܢܬܩܪܒܘܢ ‘will come near’; Gr has ἀπαντῶντες ‘meet’ (cf. ܬܬܩܪܒ in 31:22).

In combination with the omission of another letter:

[32] Syr contracts 50:13 and 50:16d, see § 3.7.2 (end).

27:14 ܡܘܗܒܬܗ 'The gift (of the wicked man makes the hair stand on end)'. ܡܘܗܒܬܗ is probably a corruption of ܡܘܡܬܗ 'his oath'; cf. Gr λαλιὰ πολυόρκου 'the talk of a man of many oaths'.

Readings that can be ascribed to confusion due to phonetic similarity are doubtful. Compare the following examples that show confusion between ܛ and ܩ and their non-emphatic counterparts.

47:6 ܩܠܝܠ '(He fought) a little' is probably a corruption of ܟܠܝܠܐ 'crown'. Perhaps a word before ܟܠܝܠܐ had been omitted, which led to the change from ܟܠܝܠܐ to ܩܠܝܠ; compare B בעטותו צניף '(he fought) while he put on the royal crown'; Gr ἐν τῷ φέρεσθαι αὐτῷ διάδημα δόξης 'when they brought him a glorious diadem' (without 'he fought').[33]

49:2 ܥܒܕܐ ܕܛܠܝܘܬܐ '(And he caused to cease) the work of childhood'. ܛܠܝܘܬܐ is probably a corruption of ܛܥܝܘܬܐ 'error, deception'; cf. B תועבות הבל; Gr βδελύγματα ἀνομίας.

Similar kinds of inner-Syriac corruptions occur in variant readings in the extant Peshitta manuscripts. Compare e.g.

2:3 ܡܛܠ ܕܬܬܚܟܡ ܒܐܘܪܚܬܟ 'So that you will become wise in your ways'. Instead of ܒܐܘܪܚܬܟ 'in your ways' 7a1 has ܒܐܚܪܝܬܟ 'in your end'.

8:10 ܕܠܐ ܬܐܩܕ ܒܫܠܗܒܝܬܐ ܕܢܘܪܗ 'Lest you burn in the flame of his fire'. Instead of ܬܐܩܕ 'burn' 9c1 has ܬܐܒܕ 'perish'.

20:1 ܐܝܬ ܡܣܟܢܘܬܐ ܕܠܐ ܝܐܝܐ 'There is a poverty that is not fitting'. Instead of ܡܟܣܢܘܬܐ 'reproof' 7a1 has ܡܣܟܢܘܬܐ 'poverty'; cf. also 50:12 where 7a1 has ܕܡܣܟܢܘܬܗܘܢ instead of ܕܡܟܣܢܘܬܗܘܢ.

24:1 ܚܟܡܬܐ ܬܫܒܚ ܢܦܫܗ 'Wisdom praises herself'. Instead of ܬܫܒܚ 'praises' 7a1 has ܬܫܟܚ 'finds'.

26:27 ܬܬܪܟܢ ܒܫܓܘܫܝܐ ܕܩܪܒܐ '(And the soul of every man that lives) submits to them in the tumult of the battle'. Instead of ܬܬܪܟܢ 7a1 has ܬܬܕܡܐ 'becomes like them'.

48:24 ܘܒܝܐ ܠܐܒܝܠܐ ܕܨܗܝܘܢ 'And he comforted the mourners of Zion'. Instead of ܠܐܒܝܠܐ 'the mourners' 12a1 has ܠܐܪܥܐ 'that land'.

In some cases multiple explanations are possible. Especially in the late nineteenth and early twentieth centuries textual corruption was adduced to explain readings that can also be accounted for in other ways. Compare the following examples.[34]

---

[33] Cf. Smend, *Jesus Sirach*, 450; Lévi, *L'Ecclésiastique* I, 123.

[34] See also Chapter 2, n. 94, on 48:16 ܬܒܘܬܐ (< ܛܒܘܬܐ?) and ibid., n. 116, on 37:13 ܬܚܝܬܗ (< ܬܚܘܬܗ?).

31:31 ܟܠܐ ܕܢܘܣܪ̈ܢܐ '(Do not speak to him) words of damage (= about what you lost?)'. According to Smend this is an inner-Syriac corruption of ܟܠܐ ܕܢܣܘܪ̈ܐ 'words of reproach'; cf. F דבר חרפה; Gr λόγον ὀνειδισμοῦ.[35] But the interpretation of this verse is difficult, and it is possible that the original Hebrew text read דבר חסר, because the root חסר can mean 'to disgrace, reproach'.[36] Moreover, confusion of חסר and חסד may also have occurred in the Hebrew transmission.[37]

33:33 ܒܐܝܪܐ ܐܝܟܐ 'And in which direction (will you find him)?' Peters emends ܐܝܟܐ to ܐܝܟܢܐ,[38] but the reading with ܐܝܟܐ is not objectionable since ܐܝܟܐ can also have the meaning of 'direction'.[39]

1.4 CONCLUSION

The earliest extant Syriac biblical manuscripts containing Sirach date from the sixth or seventh century. The external evidence (quotations in early Syriac literature) contains some indications that the earliest text of Syr was closer to Heb and that its linguistic profile was more 'Hebraizing' (whether in imitation of the Hebrew source text or as a reflection of the earliest phase of Syriac) than the BTR and the TR. But the scarcity of the material prevents us from drawing definitive conclusions. The claim that the quotations reflect a Vetus Syra should be abandoned.

The internal evidence (traces of textual transmission in the extant witnesses) includes a large number of inner-Syriac corruptions. In these cases we can emend the text to arrive at what is probably a more original reading, but other traces of textual transmission are difficult to discern. Neither the internal nor the external evidence suggests that Syr as it is represented in the extant manuscripts is the result of a revision. Although the quotations in the works of Philoxenus may reflect revision activity (but here, again, the evidence is limited and equivocal), traces of this revision in the extant Peshitta manuscripts cannot be observed. In §§ 4.3 and 4.6 we will see that the claim that other elements reflect a reworking of Syr is based on the discrepancy between the alleged original background of the Syriac translation and the

---

[35] Smend, *Jesus Sirach*, 285.
[36] Cf. Bronznick, 'Unrecognized Denotation'; Kister, 'Contribution', 337.
[37] Thus Lévi, *L'Ecclésiastique* II, 151.
[38] Peters, *Ben Sirach*, 278.
[39] Payne Smith, *Thesaurus* II, 3851; *pace* Calduch-Benages–Ferrer–Liesen, *Sabiduría del Escriba*, 202 ('and by what spirit will you find him').

views expressed in the text that has been preserved to us. Thus Winter assumes that elements that disagree with the alleged Ebionite background are the result of an orthodox Christian revision. However, if we start with the text itself, rather than with dubious hypotheses about its background, there are no ideological or theological contradictions that force us to assume that some passages reflect an original translation and other, 'contradicting' passages a later revision.

CHAPTER TWO

THE PLACE OF THE SYRIAC TRANSLATION
IN THE TEXTUAL HISTORY OF SIRACH

2.1 INTRODUCTION

Any discussion of Syr should take into account its complex relationship to the Hebrew, Greek and Latin textual witnesses.

The Hebrew witnesses are the following: one manuscript from Masada (1st century AD), containing portions of about five chapters; the tiny fragments of 2Q18 (1st century AD), containing some words from Sir 6:14–15, 20–31; the text of Sir 51:13–30 in 11QPs^a (1st century BC) and six manuscripts from the Cairo Geniza (designated A to F; 11th and 12th centuries AD).[1] Altogether about two-thirds of Sirach is extant in Hebrew. The original Hebrew book, which originated about 180 BC, has not been preserved and hence any claim about the original text is based on a scholarly reconstruction. In the literature the original text is often designated HebI (to distinguish it from HebII, see below).[2] A different use of HebI is found in J. Liesen's monograph *Full of Praise*. Liesen calls HebI a text form ('which is close to the original Hebrew from the hand of Ben Sira') rather than a text. He defines a text form as 'a certain form of the text that can be deduced from the existence of a distinct group of manuscripts', which differs from 'a hypothetical reconstruction of one supposedly original or primitive text'.[3] The advantage of Liesen's approach is that it avoids the complexities related to the notion of an 'original text',[4] and that it acknowledges the large gap of more than a century that exists between

---

[1] For details seeVan Peursen, *Verbal System*, 11–13.

[2] Thus e.g. Kearns, 'Ecclesiasticus', 547 ('HT I = the Hebrew text as it left the hand of Ben Sira'); Skehan–Di Lella, *Wisdom of Ben Sira*, 55 (HebI = 'the Hebrew original of Ben Sira').

[3] Liesen, *Full of Praise*, 7–8, 17–18. Implicitly Rüger made this distinction in his *Text und Textform*, see Liesen, ibid.

[4] Cf. Jenner–Van Peursen–Talstra, 'Interdisciplinary Debate', 14 n. 5.

the composition of the book and the oldest Hebrew witness. The Masada and Qumran manuscripts are witnesses of HebI; the Hebrew Geniza manuscripts exhibit about 90 additions of the length of one bicolon or more compared with HebI.

In the case of the Greek text we can distinguish between the original translation, made by the author's grandson in 132 BC, generally designated GrI, and the so-called 'Expanded Text' or GrII, which contains about 300 additional cola and a number of shorter additions.[5] Witnesses to GrI are the uncials A, B, C and S and the minuscules that are associated with them.[6] The main sources for GrII are the witnesses of the Hexaplaric and the Antiochene recensions,[7] but there is an irregular division of the additions over the GrII manuscripts and there is no manuscript that represents GrII as such.

The Old Latin translation (2nd century CE) has many of the additions of GrII, but also contains 75 bicola particular to itself. Jerome incorporated the Old Latin translation into the Vulgate rather than making a new translation from the Hebrew, although he tells us that he had seen a Hebrew manuscript of Sirach.

The additions in the Hebrew Geniza manuscripts, part of the Greek witnesses, the Latin version and, as we shall see below, the Syriac translation have given rise to the postulation of an expanded Hebrew text,[8] designated HebII. It has been argued that at an early stage Heb was revised and that a secondary recension of Heb was created (HebII or SirII), which is reflected in GrII and Lat and partly in Heb and Syr. Others explain the additions in terms of an ongoing process of accretion. Whereas the coherence of many additions in terms of religious perspective support the notion of a recension, the very fact that we do not find any witness containing HebII, but rather numerous diverse traces, which can also be found in rabbinic literature, supports the latter view.[9]

---

[5] For the character of GrI as a translation see Wright, *No Small Difference*.

[6] But even these manuscripts may have been influenced by GrII. To assume that they have preserved GrI in every respect is too optimistic; see Schrader, *Verwandtschaft*, 15.

[7] Ziegler's *O*-group ('Origenes-Rezension') and *L*-group ('Lukian-Rezension') respectively. Main witnesses of the *O*-group: the majuscule V, the corrector of S and the Syro-Hexapla; of the *L*-group: the minuscules 248, 493, 637; see Ziegler, *Sapientia Iesu Filii Sirach*, 57–69 for a description of these groups of witnesses and ibid., 73–75 for their importance as witnesses to GrII.

[8] The use of the designation 'Expanded Text' is widespread, but it is more correct to call HebII a text-form rather than a text, see Liesen, *Full of Praise*, 6–7 and above.

Besides Gr, Syr is the only version that goes back to a Hebrew source.[10] § 2.2 will deal with the question of what can be said about the translator's Hebrew source text. The question as to whether the Syriac translator also consulted a Greek text will be addressed in § 2.3. Syr shares with GrII about 70 of the 300 extra cola and a number of shorter additions. Since, however, many GrII readings go back to a Hebrew source, these agreements do not necessarily show the influence of a Greek version on Syr. The shared readings between Syr and GrII should be investigated in the larger context of the relation between Syr and the 'Expanded Text' (§ 2.4).

2.2 THE HEBREW SOURCE TEXT OF THE
SYRIAC TRANSLATION

2.2.1 *Methodological considerations*

A reconstruction of the Hebrew source text of Syr is difficult. If we start from the extant Hebrew manuscripts, we are hindered by the fact that these manuscripts, especially the Geniza manuscripts, show traces of a long and complex transmission process, in which the text underwent many changes. For other books of the Old Testament the assumption that the Hebrew source text of the Peshitta was more or less identical to the Masoretic Text can still serve as a working hypothesis, even though differences between the Masoretic Text and the Hebrew source text of the Peshitta cannot be ignored.[11] However, in the case of Sirach the claim that the extant Hebrew witnesses are identical or nearly identical with the source text of the Syriac translator is completely unfounded.[12]

---

[9] For details see Van Peursen, *Verbal System*, 15–19.

[10] Before the discovery of the Hebrew manuscripts at the end of the nineteenth century opinions about the question as to whether Syr was based on a Hebrew or a Greek text could still differ; cf. Schrader, *Verwandtschaft*, 16 n. 53.

[11] Cf. Jenner, 'Fille du texte massorétique?' 238–243; Gelston, *Twelve Prophets*, 111–130; idem, 'The Peshitta of the Dodekapropheton', 95–98; Weitzman, *Syriac Version*, 52–61.

[12] This claim is tacitly assumed in e.g. Smend's discussion of Syr (*Jesus Sirach*, cxxxvi–cxli); cf. the criticism by Schrader, *Verwandtschaft*, 25 n. 89.

If we start from Syr and try to reconstruct the underlying Hebrew text, we are hindered by serious problems of textual history and translation technique.[13] The first requirement for a retro-translation from Syriac to Hebrew is that we have the original Syriac translation without the changes that happened to the text in the course of its transmission. The second requirement is that the translation is consistent and literal, so that it is justified to postulate a Hebrew lexeme or construction on the basis of the Syriac text.[14] Neither requirement is met in the case of Sirach. The extant biblical manuscripts do not represent the original Syr (see § 1.3) and, as we shall see in Chapter 3, Syr appears to be a rather free translation. These two factors render it impossible to establish the exact wording of the Hebrew source text.

A further complicating factor is the status of Sirach in the Hebrew Bible and in the Peshitta Old Testament. For other biblical books that are found in the Hebrew Bible it is generally assumed that the original translation was rather literal, even to the extent that it reflects 'poor Syriac',[15] and that the text was gradually adapted to more idiomatic Syriac.[16] Whether one accepts this assumption of not,[17] it is obvious that in the case of Sirach the situation is different. Sirach is the only apocryphal book that was not translated from a Greek source but from a Hebrew one. Although already in the early Syriac tradition it constituted an undisputed part of the canon of the Old Testament,[18] it is questionable whether the Syriac translators attributed to Sirach any religious authority or canonical status.[19] Consequently, we cannot use the model of the relationship between textual history, translation tech-

---

[13] Cf. Lane, *Leviticus*, 81–86 (= 'The Hazards of Retro-Translation'); Weitzman, *Syriac Version*, 57–59.

[14] Cf. Weitzman, *Syriac Version*, 30.

[15] Cf. Pinkerton, 'Syriac Pentateuch', 39, 'The original version had the advantage of being faithful to the Hebrew, but it had the disadvantage of being in places poor Syriac'; similarly Koster, *Exodus*, 72.

[16] This had already been argued by Pinkerton, 'Syriac Pentateuch'; Koster has devoted many publications to this subject, including his *Exodus*, 'Copernican Revolution', 'The Chicken or the Egg?' and 'Translation or Transmission'.

[17] For text-historical objections against too rigid an application of this model see Jenner, 'Fille du texte massorétique?', 259–260; for linguistic objections see Van Peursen, 'Language Variation'.

[18] Beckwith, *Old Testament Canon*, 195–196; Van Kasteren, 'Canon des Ouden Verbonds'; cf. Gilbert, 'Jesus Sirach', 888–904 ('Die Christliche Rezeption des Sirach-Buches').

[19] We are inclined to think that this was not the case; cf. § 6.2.1 (B).

nique and source text that has been developed for other parts of the
Old Testament.

Although an exact reconstruction of the Hebrew source text is impossible, a comparative study of Syr and the other versions enables us
to establish a general text-historical profile of the Syriac translator's
source text. Thus we cannot establish the consistency with which Hebrew lexemes or grammatical constructions are rendered in Syriac, but
we can describe correspondences of lexemes and grammatical constructions in Heb and Syr. Likewise, although we cannot establish 'the
size of the unit of translation',[20] we can establish the size of corresponding units.

2.2.2 Inner-Hebrew variation reflected in Syr
compared with other witnesses

Sometimes we can do more than simply establishing correspondences
and we can make suggestions about the source text of the Syriac translator. Compare the following example

4:11 ܒܗ ܘܕܡܣܬܟܠܝܢ ܠܟܠ ܬܢܗܪ ܐܘ 'And she will enlighten all who consider
her closely'; Heb (A) ותעיד לכל מבינים בה 'And she admonishes all
that devote themselves to her'.

In this case the word ܬܢܗܪ in Syr corresponds to תעיד in Heb (MS A).
The easiest way to explain the relationship between the two versions
is to assume that Syr reflects תאיר instead of תעיד.[21] The confusion in
Hebrew between ד and ר, as well as that between א and ע is well
known. The former confusion is generally ascribed to the graphic
similarity between the two letters, the latter to phonetic similarity.[22]

----

[20] Brock, 'History of Syriac Translation Technique', 6; cf. Weitzman, *Syriac Version*, 5–6, 22–23; Barr, *Typology of Literalism*, 294–303. Note that in Brock's definition the 'unit of translation' is the segment of text that the translator used as his starting-point: the morpheme, the word, the phrase or the sentence. Weitzman uses 'translation unit' for 'the portion of the Bible for which a single translator was responsible';
see his *Peshitta*, 16 n. 4.
[21] The establishment of such correspondences does not say anything about the
question as to which reading is more original. In the present example we prefer the
lectio difficilior תעיד; cf. Segal, 'Evolution', 111; Smend, *Jesus Sirach*, cxxvi–cxxxvii;
and below, the end of this paragraph.
[22] Thus according to Lévi, *L'Ecclésiastique* II, 16, the Syriac translator read עיר,
which he interpreted as ܥܝܪ due to a 'confusion auriculaire'.

The explanation of graphic similarity between Hebrew letters accounts for many other examples as well.[23] Especially frequent are examples that can best be accounted for by graphic confusion between ד and ר. Thus Syr reflects עיר instead of עוד (= A) in 4:7; תסתר instead of תסוד (= A) in 7:14; יוסד instead of יוסר (= A) in 10:1; רע instead of דע 'know!' (cf. A ודע) in 12:11; בית משמר (cf. Gen 42:19) instead of בית משמד 'house of ruins' (= Gr) in 21:18; and ܒܥܒܕ̈ܝܗܘܢ 'in (their) good deeds' reflects בעבודם instead of בעבורם 'for their sakes' (= Gr) in 44:12. Confusion between ב and כ accounts for the following examples: Syr reflects שכלות instead of שבלת (= A) in 4:26; כחקר instead of בחקר (= A) in 14:22; בליל or בלילה 'in the night' instead of בכליל (= Gr) in 34:8; תשבח 'praise' instead of תשכח (= B+D) in 37:6[24]; יכין instead of יבין (= A) in 6:37; and ברוב instead of כרוב (= B) in 51:3. Confusion between ה and ח occurs in 6:19, where Syr and Gr reflect למהר instead of למחר (= A). Confusion between ו and י occurs in 30:21 and 38:18, where Syr and Gr reflect דון (or דוון) instead of דין. In 49:14 we should read with Syr and Gr כחנוך instead of כהניך (= B).

The transposition of two adjacent letters (metathesis) accounts for 4:14 ܡܥܡܪܐ 'dwelling place', which reflects ואהלו instead of ואלהו (= A[25]); 14:21 ܘܒܢܬܝܒܘܬܗ, which reflects ובנתיבותיה instead of ובתבונתיה (= A). Both metathesis and confusion between ו and י accounts for 48:7 ܒܢܣܝܘܢܗ 'in his temptation', which reflects בנסוי instead of בסיני 'at Sinai' (= B+Gr).

Variants that can be ascribed to confusion due to phonetic similarity are attested as well, though less frequent.[26] Thus ܕܓܠ ܐܓܝܪ '(a hireling who) lies' in 37:11 may reflect שקר instead of שכיר (= B^mg+D),[27] and ܦܫܪ 'interpreting' in 38:25 and 47:17 reflects פשר instead of בשיר (= B).[28]

---

[23] The examples given here are taken from the preliminary version of the English translation of Syr in *The Bible of Edessa* prepared by K.D. Jenner and the present author.

[24] It is also possible that ܬܫܒܚ is the result of an inner-Syriac corruption; compare 31:22 where 7h3 has ܬܫܒܚ instead of ܬܫܟܚ.

[25] But note that the Hebrew text is difficult.

[26] On scribal errors due to phonetic similarity see Delitzsch, *Lese- und Schreibfehler*, 136–143; Tov, *Textual Criticism*, 251–252. This type of confusion is also attested in parallel passages in the Hebrew witnesses of Sirach, see Beentjes, 'Reading the Hebrew Ben Sira Manuscripts Synoptically'.

[27] Cf. § 10.2.4 (end).

[28] This confusion is most likely to have happened in a Hebrew source with the defective spelling בשר; cf. Van Peursen, *Verbal System*, 31. The interchange of ב and פ

Other examples reflect the addition, omission or substitution of letters in words that are otherwise similar. Thus Syr reflects בכל instead of מכל (= A) in 3:18; מהלך instead of מלך 'he is king' (= A) in 10:10[29]; יכלימו instead of יעלימו 'blind (the eyes)' (= Gr) in 20:29; תשלט instead of תשלח (= Gr) in 28:23; מכפל instead of מנפל (= Gr) in 29:20; ארח instead of אח (= Gr) in 29:27; קמתי instead of קדמתי 'I advanced' (= E) in 33:17[30]; תמעד instead of תמעט 'diminish' (= Gr) in 35:10; and שכבו instead of שובו 'return' (= B) in 40:1.

It seems that such additions, omissions or substitutions sometimes took place in a manuscript with few or even very few *matres lectionis*.[31] Thus in 24:32 a defective spelling אאר may have caused the reading אמר reflected in Syr, instead of אאיר (= Gr φωτιῶ). In 30:13 Syr reflects עליו instead עולו 'his yoke' (= B), a confusion that may have occurred due to a defective spelling עלו[32]; and in 41:9 Syr reflects עם instead of עולם (= B), which may go back to a reading עלם (= M).

Other examples can be added, which sometimes combine two or more of the phenomena described above. Thus Syr reflects משמש instead of על שמש (= E+F+Gr) in 33:7; תאחר instead of תשחד (= B; cf. Gr) in 35:14; והברכה instead of ותבונה (= B) in 45:5; והשמיע instead of והשומע 'who heard' (= B; cf. Gr) in 48:7; נבראו instead of נפקדו (= B) in 49:16 (but cf. B in 49:14 [נוצר]ו).

Accordingly, many differences between Syr and the other witnesses can be ascribed to scribal or reading errors. This does not say anything about the question as to which reading is more original. The observation that Syr reflects a reading that differs slightly from that in Heb does not imply that Heb contains the original reading and Syr a secondary reading. And in those cases where Syr reflects a secondary reading, it is often uncertain whether that reading was already present in the translator's source text or whether rather the translator misread or misunderstood the Hebrew.[33] The reading reflected is sometimes also attested in Heb. Thus in 13:10 the reading reflected in Syr, תשנא, oc-

---

occurs also elsewhere in the Sirach manuscripts, see Beentjes, 'Reading the Hebrew Ben Sira Manuscripts Synoptically', 104–105, on 42:6, 43:2, 43:14.

[29] According to Smend, *Jesus Sirach*, 93, מהלך is a secondary reading due to a misunderstanding of יפול 'he falls/dies', but other commentators do not know which reading to chose; cf. Lévi, 'Notes sur les ch. VII. 29 – XII. 1 de Ben Sira', 11 ('Les deux hypotèses peuvent également se défendre'); Ryssel, 'Fragmente',VII, 351.

[30] Di Lella, *Hebrew Text of Sirach*, 54.

[31] See also above, the examples from 38:25 and 47:17, and § 3.4 (e) on 13:15.

[32] Cf. Van Peursen, *Verbal System*, 31.

curs also in MS A, but Gr reflects תנשא. In 32:17 Syr reflects איש חכם
(= B^{txt}) instead of איש חמס (= B^{mg}; cf. Gr); בשור (= B^{txt}) instead of
בשיר (= B^{mg}) in 38:25; and לדורות עולם (= B), instead of לדורותם (=
Gr) in 45:26.[34] In other cases Syr and Gr reflect the same reading differing from that in Heb. Thus in 25:7 ܐ̄ܢܫܐ 'man' reflects איש (= Gr
ἄνθρωπος) instead of אשרי 'blessed (he who)'.[35] In 5:9 Syr and Gr
reflect שביל (= C) instead of שבולת (= A).

2.2.3 Uncertainties about the Hebrew source text
of the Syriac translator

From the evidence discussed in the preceding paragraphs it follows
that in the Hebrew transmission of Sirach, as far as it can be reconstructed on the basis of the extant Hebrew witnesses and the ancient
translations, many variants originated as the result of unintentional
changes of letters or words, most often due to typical scribal errors
such as confusion of similar letters, metathesis, or variation in the use
of vowel letters. Nevertheless, we should take into account certain
restrictions in applying the notion of scribal errors. In the history of
research it has happened more than once that readings in Syr were explained as scribal errors (either in the translator's source text, or, if Syr
has preserved the preferable reading, in one of the other witnesses),
whereas at a closer look neither Syr nor one of the other witnesses
contains an error. In 3:11, for example, ܡܨܥܪ 'despises' can well be a
translation of מקלל (= A) and the emendation to מקלה on the basis of
Syr is unnecessary.[36]

In other cases we have to reject a reconstruction of the Hebrew
source text of Syr because of general considerations of translation
technique (Chapter 3). Thus the rendering of the metaphor צורו 'his

---

[33] In some cases it is even possible that the Syriac translator on purpose 'confused' Hebrew letters as a kind of *Al Tiqre* exegesis; cf. Weitzman, *Syriac Version*,
38–39; idem, *From Judaism to Christianity*, 65.

[34] For the addition of כל see § 10.2.1, esp. n. 62.

[35] Cf. Segal, *Sefer Ben Sira*, 154.

[36] Cf. Kister, 'Notes', 129–130; *pace* Smend, *Jesus Sirach*, 25; Ryssel, 'Fragmente', I, 366 and others. Another interesting example concerns the Hebrew verb חסר. For
a number of passages it has been suggested that Syr reflects חסד where חסר is found
in the Hebrew text or reflected in the Greek translation, but this suggestion does not
recognize that חסר can mean 'to disgrace, reproach', which has been pointed out by
Bronznick, 'Unrecognized Denotation'; cf. our remark on 31:31 in § 1.3 (end).

Rock' in 4:6 (A) with ܒܪܝܗ 'his creator' (= Gr) agrees with a tendency found elsewhere in Syr and does not indicate that the Syriac translator read יוצרי.[37] Similarly, because of the free character of Syr we cannot decide whether in 13:1 ܗܘ ܕܐܝܬ ܠܗ ܒܕ ܡܢ ܕܐܝܢܐ ܡܬܕܒܩ ܘܗܘ 'and he who has fellowship with the unrighteous one—he clothes himself with his ways', ܠܒܫ is a free rendering of ילמד (= A),[38] or a translation of ילבש.[39] In 49:6 ܘܐܩܠܥܘ, ܥܩܪܘ '(and they uprooted the Holy City...) in the days of Jeremiah', may be a free rendering of the difficult ביד ירמיהו (= B 49:7), rather than a reflection of a Hebrew reading בימי ירמיהו.[40]

In other cases our observations on corresponding phrase patterns argue against a suggested reconstruction of the Hebrew source text. As we shall see in Chapters 10–12, Heb and Syr correspond often at phrase level rather than at word level. Reconstructions of the translator's Hebrew source that are implicitly based on the assumption that Syr is a word-by-word translation of a Hebrew source text should be avoided. There is no justification, for example, for the assumption that in 13:17 the Hebrew source text of the Syriac translator had לאיש צדיק instead of לצדיק in MS A.[41]

The examples given thus far concern mainly word and phrase level. There can hardly be any doubt that the Hebrew source text of the Syriac translator contained many other readings that are the product of additions, omission and other alterations of phrases, clauses or even larger textual units, that occurred at some point in the transmission of the Hebrew text.[42] Thus it contained probably the additions that Syr shares with GrII as opposed to GrI and readings which it

---

[37] See § 3.2 (f); *pace* Ryssel, 'Fragmente', I, 373; Schechter–Taylor, *Wisdom of Ben Sira*. Such agreements between Gr and Syr does not show dependence of the latter upon the former; cf. § 2.3.3.

[38] Thus Peters, *Ben Sirach*, 114; Ryssel, 'Sprüche Jesus' des Sohnes Sirachs', 298; Lévi, *L'Ecclésiastique* II, 91; Peters and Ryssel refer to the idiomatic usages of ܠܒܫ mentioned in Payne Smith, *Thesaurus* I, 1887–1889.

[39] Smend, *Jesus Sirach*, 121; Matthes, 'Bemerkungen', 16; but note that Smend prefers the reading ילבש and Matthes ילמד; see also Box–Oesterley, 'Sirach', 277–288.

[40] *Pace* Smend, *Jesus Sirach*, 467, 470; cf. Skehan–Di Lella, *Ben Sira*, 541.

[41] Cf. Chapter 10, n. 10. Many other examples are given in Chapters 10–12.

[42] Cf. Segal, 'Evolution', 112: 'More often the Hebrew reading of Syr, though genuine, is not original'. Segal (ibid., p. 117–118) mentions the additions in 3:7; 11:30; 12:11c; 13:2d; 14:8; 15:20; 19:3a; 30:19; 31:6b, 13a; 35:12b. Smend, *Jesus Sirach*, cxxxix, gives the following examples. Incorrect order of the cola: 3:12b/13b; repetitions: 1:16a, 13:21b, 28:5; doublets: 7:10b, 10:6, 31:27; explanatory glosses: 26:29, 48:3.

shares with Heb as opposed to a more original reading preserved in GrI.[43]

2.3 THE RELATION TO THE GREEK TEXT

2.3.1 *Introduction*

It is commonly accepted that the Syriac translator, while translating from a Hebrew source, consulted a Greek text, especially for difficult passages.[44] Studies by R. Smend, I. Lévi, M.H. Segal and others give an overwhelming mass of evidence to support this claim. However, caution is needed, because most of the evidence consists of cases where Syr agrees with Gr and we should be aware that such evidence does not by itself prove dependency. In more general terms there are three possible sources for agreements between Syr and Gr as opposed to Heb.[45]

1. The Hebrew source text: the source texts of Gr and Syr shared a reading different from Heb. Either they share a secondary reading or they have preserved a reading that is older than the one attested in Heb.
2. The translation process.
   a. The Syriac translator consulted a Greek text.
   b. The translators of Gr and Syr came independently to the same understanding (polygenesis). This may be due to

---

[43] Cf. Segal, 'Evolution', 124 and below, § 2.4.1.

[44] Thus e.g. Lévi, *L'Ecclésiastique* I, lii; Rüger, *Text und Textform*, 112; Kearns, *Expanded Text*, 22; Schrader, *Verwandtschaft*, 17; Liesen, *Full of Praise*, 16; Segal, *Sefer Ben Sira*, 61–62; idem, 'Evolution', 110; Segal relates the use of the Greek version to the translator's limited knowledge of Hebrew (cf. § 3.4). For the relationship between the Peshitta and the Septuagint in other parts of the Old Testament and the debated issue whether the Peshitta has been influenced by the Greek text, see Weitzman, *Syriac Version*, 68–86; idem, *From Judaism to Christianity*, 181–188; Lund, *Influence of the Septuagint*; idem, 'Grecisms in the Peshitta Psalms'; Dirksen, 'Textual Criticism of the Old Testament'; Van Keulen, 'La Peshitta des Rois', 278–281. In these key publications the interested reader can find references to the vast amount of publications that has appeared on this subject; see also Jenner, 'Fille du texte massorétique?', 240 n. 6.

[45] Compare the publications by Lund, Weitzman en Van Keulen mentioned in the preceding footnote and Brock, 'Die Übersetzungen ins Syrische', 183.

similarities in translation technique or a common background of exegetical traditions.

3. The textual transmission: Later copyists of Syr altered the text under the influence of Gr or the other way round.

Evidence that can be explained in different ways cannot be put forward as compelling evidence for only one explanation. Thus cases in which Gr and Syr agree in a reading that can easily be explained in terms of translation technique do not prove the dependence of one version on the other.[46]

2.3.2 *An example: Sirach 43:1–10*

To illustrate the problems that arise when we try to determine whether Syr has been influenced by Gr we will have a look at a passage that has been put forward as an example *par excellence* of the influence of Gr on Syr, 43:1–10. It has been argued that Syr follows Gr 'almost literally'.[47] Note especially the following readings.

> 43:4 ܐܪܥܐܠ ܣܒܥܘ ܐܫܡܫ ܝܘܡܠܐ ܐܬܠܬ ܬܘ 'Three times more the sun causes the mountains to burn'. ܐܬܠܬ ܬܘ 'threefold' reflects the Hebrew שלש instead of B שולח (M [...]של) and agrees with Gr τριπλασίως. However, if the Syriac translator had a Hebrew text reading של(ו)ח, he had no reason to follow Gr; and if he had a Hebrew text reading שלש, his translation with ܐܬܠܬ ܬܘ does not indicate dependence on Gr.[48]

---

[46] Cf. Lund, *Influence of the Septuagint*, 42, 117 *et passim*; idem, 'Grecisms in the Peshitta Psalms'; Maori, 'Variant *Vorlage* and Exegesis', 119; Weitzman, *Syriac Version*, 16–17; Dirksen, 'Textual Criticism of the Old Testament'. Scholars differ about the question of whether any of the explanations given is *a priori* more likely than the others. According to Dirksen and Weitzman translation technique should be given priority over all other explanations. In Dirksen's view Lund gave too much weight to the possibility of a Hebrew variant behind a shared reading in these versions. Koster agrees with Dirksen and Weitzman that an explanation in terms of translation technique should have priority over an explanation from a shared reading of the Hebrew source text, but argues that first of all inner-Syriac changes should be taken into account.

[47] Smend, *Jesus Sirach*, 400; Lévi, *L'Ecclésiastique* I, lii, 62–70; Peters, *Ben Sirach*, 364; cf. Schlatter, *Neu gefundene hebräische Stück*, 43: 'Bei S fehlt Kap. 43 ganz. Die Verse 2–10 sind offenkundig Nachtrag aus dem Griechischen'; but note that Syr shares the omission of the rest of Chapter 43 with GrII; cf. Kearns, *Expanded Text*, 22; Halévy, 'L'Ecclésiastique', 223–226.

[48] שלש is the original reading according to Bacher, 'Hebrew Text of Ecclesiasticus', 551.

43:7 ܢܗܝܪܐ ܕܓܡܪ ܠܫܘܠܡܐ '(Because from the moon are the signs of the festivals), a luminary that ceases at the end'. ܢܗܝܪܐ agrees with Gr φωστήρ instead of B חפץ 'delight' and ܠܫܘܠܡܐ 'at the end' agrees with Gr ἐπὶ συντελείας instead of B בתקופתו 'in its circuit (completion)'.[49] However, the translation of חפץ with 'luminary' in both Gr and Syr may be a case of polygenesis. Moreover, Syr may have been influenced by ܘܡܢܗܪ in 43:4 and ܕܡܢܗܪ in 43:8. Also ܠܫܘܠܡܐ may have originated independently; compare 2 Chr 24:23 MT לתקופת השנה; Pesh ܠܫܘܠܡܗ ܕܫܢܬܐ.[50]

43:8 ܝܪܚܐ ܐܝܟ ܫܡܗ ܐܝܬܘܗܝ، ܘܡܬܪܒܐ ܡܬܕܡܪܐܝܬ ܒܫܘܚܠܦܐ 'The (new) moon is like its name, and it becomes great exceedingly in the season'; B חדש בחדשו הוא מתחדש מה נורא בהשתנותו; M חדש כשמו הוא מת[...]; Gr μὴν κατὰ τὸ ὄνομα αὐτῆς ἐστιν αὐξανόμενος θαυμαστῶς ἐν ἀλλοιώσει 'The moon is like its name; it increases considerably in its changing'. According to Smend Gr is imprecise and partly wrong and Syr follows it. Gr is bad because (a) it reflects a wrong interpunction after הוא; (b) it does not have an equivalent for Hebrew מה; (c) αὐξανόμενος is an imprecise translation of מתחדש; and (d) θαυμαστῶς reflects an incorrect adverbial interpretation of נורא. Syr follows (a) the wrong interpunction and (b) the absence of a equivalent for מה, while (c) ܡܬܪܒܐ = αὐξανόμενος and (d) ܡܬܕܡܪܐܝܬ = θαυμαστῶς.[51] However, the wrong interpunction (a) can also be a case of polygenesis and the absence of a equivalent for מה (b) may be due to a different Hebrew source text. Its occurrence in MS B is probably secondary.[52]

Some of the agreements between Syr and Gr in this passage are too easily put forward as evidence for dependence of the former on the latter. Other explanations, such as a common Hebrew source or polygenesis, are equally possible. Since the evidence for the dependence of Syr on Gr is weaker than is usually assumed, much depends on the cumulative evidence. For this reason we need to have a closer look at several patterns of agreement between Syr and Gr.

---

[49] Cf. Smend, *Jesus Sirach*, 403: 'Eigentlich ist תקופה aber die Vollendung der Lunation'.

[50] Compare the translation equivalents of תקופה in Exod 34:22 MT תקופת השנה; Pesh ܒܡܦܩܗ ܕܫܢܬܐ; 1 Sam 1:20 MT לתקופות הימים; Pesh ܠܣܘܟܐ ܕܝܘܡܬܐ; Ps 19:7 MT תקופתו, Pesh ܡܦܩܢܗ; on the Hebrew idioms used see also Driver, *Notes on the Hebrew Text of Samuel*, 16.

[51] Smend, *Jesus Sirach*, 403.

[52] Cf. 43:2 M כלי נורא; B מה נורא, Gr σκεῦος θαυμαστόν; Syr ܡܐܢܐ ܕܬܕܡܘܪܬܐ.

2.3.3 *Patterns of agreement between Syr and Gr*

Among the cases that have been put forward as evidence for the dependence of Syr on Gr the following patterns can be distinguished:

(1) Gr = Syr ≠ Heb

In the following cases Gr and Syr reflect a word different from that preserved in Heb:

> 11:17 ܠܕܚ̈ܠܘܗܝ 'to those who fear Him'; Gr εὐσεβέσιν 'the pious'; A צדיק 'the righteous one'.
>
> 31:14 ܒܠܚܐ 'in the dish' = Gr ἐν τρυβλίῳ; B בטנא 'in the basket'.
>
> 46:19 ܘܟܠܒܣܪ 'and all flesh' = Gr ἀπὸ πάσης σαρκός; B אדם 'man'.
>
> 50:12 ܐܚ̈ܘܗܝ 'his brothers' = Gr ἀδελφῶν; B בנים 'sons'.

These agreements between Syr and Gr do not demonstrate that the Syriac translator consulted Gr. They may also reflect readings—either original or secondary—that occurred in the source texts of both Syr and Gr.[53] It is possible, for example, that in the Hebrew textual transmission there was a reading אחיו in 50:12, which occurred in the source texts of both Gr and Syr. It is even possible that this reading was original, and that B's בנים is secondary.

Some claims made by earlier scholars on the relationship between Syr and Gr had to be abandoned when new Hebrew manuscripts were discovered. For 3:14 and 44:13, for example, Smend argued that in these verses Syr followed Gr,[54] but the readings reflected in Syr and Gr are now also attested in Hebrew witnesses that were discovered later on (MSS C and M respectively).

In the following cases the agreements concern more than one word.

> 47:12–13a ܘܡܢ ܒܬܪܗ ܩܡ ܡܠܟܐ ܚܣܝܢܐ ܕܝܬܒ ܒܫܠܝܐ ܫܠܝܡܘܢ 'And after him stood up a powerful king (who) dwelt quietly, Solomon'; B ובעבורו עמד אחריו בן משכיל שוכן לבטח שלמה מלך בימי שלוה 'And because of him stood up after him a discerning son, who dwelt in safety; Solomon reigned in days of quietness'; Gr Μετὰ τοῦτον ἀνέστη υἱὸς ἐπιστήμων καὶ δι' αὐτὸν κατέλυσεν ἐν πλατυσμῷ· Σαλωμὼν ἐβασίλευσεν ἐν ἡμέραις εἰρήνης 'And after him stood up a discerning son, and because of him he lived in a broad space; Solomon reigned in the days of peace'. According to Smend Syr follows but

---

[53] Cf. Reiterer, *Urtext*, 239.
[54] Smend, *Jesus Sirach*, 26, 417.

also changes the text of Gr at random.[55] However, with his remark
that Syr also changed the text Smend admits that Syr is not an exact
copy of Gr. We cannot say more than that Syr, B and Gr reflect three
interrelated but different versions; the explanation of the agreements
and the differences is equivocal.

50:2 ܪܚܬܝܘ ܒܬܐܬܪܐܘ ܪܚܠܬ̈ ܪܚܐܙ ܡܪܐܬܪܐܘ 'And the city wall (and)
the pinnacles were established and the courtyard was built'; B אשר
בימיו נבנה קיר פנות מעון בהיכל מלך; Gr καὶ ὑπ᾽ αὐτοῦ ἐθεμελιώθη
ὕψος διπλῆς, ἀνάλημμα ὑψηλὸν περιβόλου ἱεροῦ 'And under him
was constructed the elevation for the courtyard, the high fortification
for the sacred enclosure'. According to Smend Syr adopted the
courtyard from Gr to which he added the pinnacles and 'built'.[56]
Here too there are both agreements and differences between Syr and
Gr and for the agreements more than one explanation is possible.[57]

In all these cases the relation between the extant witnesses is complicated and various explanations are equally possible. They cannot be
put forward, therefore, as evidence for the dependence of Syr on Gr.

(2) Gr = Syr ≠ Heb*

Also in those parts of Sirach for which no Hebrew witness is available
(about one-third of the book), there are agreements between Gr and
Syr that have been put forward as evidence for the dependence of Syr
on Gr. An example is

18:33 ܡܨܡܕ ܠܠܘܐ ,ܐܝܘ ܚܡܚܬ ܐܬܡܘܪ ܠܪ 'Do not become poor and a
drunkard and licentious and a gossip'. According to Smend the
Greek translator inserted incorrectly γίνου πτωχός 'become poor'
and the Syriac translator followed him.[58]

In this pattern it is even more dangerous to argue that Gr has influenced Syr. Such a claim is only valid if each of the following conditions is met.

1. Gr contains a secondary reading.
2. The secondary reading does not reflect a secondary Hebrew
    source text, otherwise it may also have been present in the

---

[55] Smend, *Jesus Sirach*, 453: 'Syr. folgt dem Gr. und ändert dabei willkürlich'.
[56] Smend, *Jesus Sirach*, 480: 'Syr. übernimmt aus Gr. den Vorhof, und addiert
ἐθεμελιώθη und נבנה.'
[57] For the textual problems of this verse see further Skehan–Di Lella, *Wisdom of
Ben Sira*, 548–549.
[58] Smend, *Jesus Sirach*, 172: 'Gr. (und nach ihm Syr.) bringt ungehörig das Arm-
werden aus v. 32 hinein.'

source text of the Syriac translator, rather than in his alleged Greek source.

3. It is unlikely that the secondary reading originated independently in Syr (i.e. the agreement between Gr and Syr is not due to polygenesis).

The first condition implies that we can establish that Gr has a secondary reading even though the original reading is not attested in any source, neither Gr (if Gr reflects the original reading, Syr may go back to a Hebrew source as well, rather than following Gr), nor Syr (because Syr contains the secondary reading of Gr) nor any Hebrew source (by definition of the category under discussion). The second condition implies that the secondary character of a reading as such, however anomalous it is, does not prove that Gr influenced Syr. The third condition serves to prevent cases of polygenesis from being put forward as evidence for the dependence of Syr on Gr. We did not find any case for which we can claim with reasonable certainty that all three conditions are met. We can conclude that the evidence reflecting the pattern Syr = Gr ≠ Heb* does not provide a solid basis for the claim that the Syriac translator consulted a Greek version during his translation activities.

This conclusion applies also to two cases where Gr has a title that in Syr has become part of the running text:

18:29 ܘܒܗ ܚܟܡܬܐ ܐܝܣܘܪܐ ܕܗ ܕܝܗܒ ܘܡܠܐ ܕܡܬܠܐ ܫܘܝܐܝܬ ܘܢܕܥܘܢ ܢܦܫܐ ‘And till the end they will know the words of proverbs and the words of wisdom and the instruction of the soul’. In Gr ‘Words of Wisdom’ and ‘Instruction of the Soul’ are titles. In Syr the text and the two titles have been mixed up.[59]

20:27 ܢܘܕܥ ܢܦܫܗ ܕܒܨܝܪ ܐܝܟ ܚܟܡܬܐ ܕܡܬܠܐ ܡܠܐ ‘Who is full of proverbs of wisdom will make himself known as insignificant’. In Gr ‘Proverbs of Wisdom’ is a title.

Since section titles occur also in the Hebrew witnesses, partly parallel to those in the Greek witnesses, it is possible that the confusion of the titles took place in a Hebrew source.

---

[59] ܢܦܫܐ not in 7a1.

(3) Syr and Gr reflect the same understanding of Heb

This category comprises cases where a particular interpretation or nuance that Gr attributed to the Hebrew text is also found in Syr. However, the reasoning that is needed to take these cases as support for the claim that the Syriac translator consulted Gr is complex. On the one hand it is assumed that Gr and Syr reflect the same Hebrew reading and the same peculiar interpretation of that reading (this is given with the definition of this category). On the other hand the possibility that the steps from Heb to Gr and from Heb to Syr occurred independently is denied (this is given with the use of this category as an argument for the dependence of Syr on Gr).[60] Compare the following examples.

> 5:1 ܓܠ ܐܝܬ ܕܣܓܝ 'I have much'; Gr αὐτάρκη μοί ἐστιν; A יש לאל ידי.[61]
> 30:24 ܣܝܒܘ ܥܒܕܐ 'produces white hair'; Gr γῆρας ἄγει; B תזקין.
> 47:14 ܐܝܟ ܢܗܪܐ 'like a river'; Gr ὡς ποταμός; B כיאר 'like the Nile'.
> 48:2 ܘܐܝܬܝ ܥܠܝܗܘܢ ܟܦܢܐ 'And he brought upon them famine'; Gr ὃς ἐπήγαγεν ἐπ' αὐτοὺς λιμόν; B וישבר להם מטה לחם 'And he broke their staff of bread'.

The argument made by Smend and others that Syr follows Gr in these cases does not take into account the possibility of polygenesis. If, for example, the Greek translator decided to render 'white hair' with 'old age', why should we deny the possibility that the Syriac translator did the same independently of Gr? As we shall see in § 3.2 (a), Syr gives free renderings of idiomatic Hebrew expressions in other cases also.

Even if Gr and Syr reflect the same incorrect or imprecise rendering of Heb, it does not automatically follow that one is dependent on the other. Accordingly, polygenesis is a possible explanation even in the following cases.[62]

> 6:16 ܣܡܐ ܕܚܝܐ 'medicine of life' = Gr φάρμακον ζωῆς; A צרור חיים 'a bundle of life'.[63]

---

[60] See also above, § 2.2.3, on 4:6, where 'his Creator' in Gr and Syr corresponds to צורו 'his Rock' in A.

[61] There is no reason to assume that both the Syriac and the Greek translator read יש לו ד ד; pace Bacher, 'Notes on the Cambridge Fragments', 283; Lévi, L'Ecclésiastique II, 24.

[62] Pace Smend, Jesus Sirach, 56 (on 6:16), 117 (on 12:9), 358 (on 39:16), 446 (on 46:18).

[63] Compare the misunderstanding of צרור 22:18 (§ 3.4 [a]).

12:9 ܚܒ̈ܝܒܘܗܝ, ܚܒܠܬܐ '(In a man's prosperity) his adversaries are in sadness'; Gr οἱ ἐχθροὶ αὐτοῦ ἐν λύπῃ; A גם שונא ריע 'also the enemy is a friend'.

39:16 ܫܦܝܪ 'fitting' = Gr καλά; B טובים.[64]

46:18 ܨܘܪ 'Tyre' = Gr Τυρίων; B צר 'enemy'.

In several publications, M. Kister has discussed cases where Syr and Gr reflect a wrong interpretation of the Hebrew, sometimes followed by modern interpreters as well. Thus for 3:23 (A) תמר 'have ambition' Syr has ܐܬܥܣܩ 'be busy with' (= Gr),[65] and 7:14 (A) תפלה 'stupidity' (cf. Job 1:22) was read or interpreted as תפילה 'prayer'.[66] Kister does not use these examples to argue that Syr depends on Gr, but rather to show that Ben Sira used 'many rare words which were incomprehensible to readers as early as two or three generations after his time'.[67]

The pattern under discussion argues for the dependency of Syr on Gr only if the interpretation of the Hebrew reflected in Gr and Syr is so peculiar that polygenesis is unlikely. The following example seems to be a candidate for this qualification.

38:14 ܘܚܘܠܡܢܐ ܒܐܝܕܗ ܢܩܝܡ 'And (that) He will establish the healing through his hand'; B אשר יצלח לו פשרה 'that his diagnosis may be successful'[68] or 'that He may grant success to his diagnosis'[69], Gr ἵνα εὐοδώσῃ αὐτοῖς ἀνάπαυσιν 'that He makes them successful in (bringing) relief'. Smend and others have argued that Syr is influenced by Gr.[70] This claim is based on the usual interpretation of פשר as 'diagnosis', of which, it is argued, Gr gives an imprecise translation. However, Kister has demonstrated that פשר means 'cure' rather than 'diagnosis'.[71] In Kister's interpretation Syr can easily be understood as a translation from Hebrew rather than the result of influence of Gr.

---

[64] But note the wide range of meanings of the Hebrew טוב indicated by *HALOT* 370–371; BDB 373–375. It can also mean 'beautiful'; cf. Kister, 'Contribution', 358; see Borbone–Jenner, *Concordance* I, 814–815 for cases where Pesh-Pentateuch has a word of the root ܫܦܪ where the MT has טוב.

[65] Kister, 'Contribution', 315; see also Lieberman, 'Forgotten Meanings', 89–90; Van Peursen, *Verbal System*, 89.

[66] Kister, 'Contribution', 320.

[67] Kister, 'Contribution', 310–311; see further § 3.4 (b).

[68] Thus Skehan–Di Lella, *Wisdom of Ben Sira*, 438.

[69] Thus Smend, *Jesus Sirach*, 342.

[70] Cf. Smend, *Jesus Sirach*, 342: 'Gr. rät wohl nur ἀνάπαυσιν und danach Syr. חולמנא (Heilung).'

[71] Kister, 'Contribution', 343.

Examples belonging to this category show the opposite phenomenon
of that described above. Again Heb contains words that, at least from
the perspective of modern commentators, are difficult. But in this
category Gr and Syr have preserved the 'forgotten meanings'.[72] These
examples show that the view that the Syriac translator consulted a
Greek version is complicated not only by text-critical and text-historical issues, but also by philological and lexicographical questions.

(4) Syr = Heb + Gr

Another category comprises those cases where Syr is claimed to be a
mixture or compromise between Heb and Gr. An example is[73]

> 7:7 ܟܢܘܫܬܐ ܕܡܕܝܢܬܐ 'the community of the city'. According to Smend
> this combines 'the community of the gate' (= A בעדת שער) and 'the
> multitude of the city' (= Gr πλῆθος πόλεως).[74] Note, however, that
> the complete reading in MS A is בעדת שערי אל. According to Ryssel
> this is a combination of בעדת אל (cf. Num 27:17; Sir 24:2) and the
> original reading בעדת שער (cf. 42:11 [B^{txt+mg}]).[75] In this interpreta-
> tion Syr can be interpreted as reflecting the original Hebrew reading.

Although this category cannot be ignored in Peshitta studies,[76] as evidence for the influence of Gr on Syr these cases are often difficult.
Thus in the example quoted the change from 'gate' to 'city' may well
have originated independently in both Syr and Gr. Similar changes are
well-attested in Syr also in cases where they do not occur in Gr (cf.
§ 3.2).

2.3.4 Conclusion

An exhaustive analysis of the relationship between Syr and Gr is beyond the scope of the present study. However, if we restrict ourselves
to the material that previous scholars have put forward as evidence for

---

[72] Thus in 7:10 אל תתקצר should be interpreted with Gr and Syr as 'do not turn
away, disregard', rather than 'be not impatient' (according to the meaning of this verb
in Biblical Hebrew; thus many modern commentators); see, Kister, 'Contribution',
318–320.

[73] Other examples (cf. Smend *ad loc.*) in 3:9, 3:16, 32:18, 48:20 and 51:10.

[74] Smend, *Jesus Sirach*, 64.

[75] Ryssel, 'Fragmente', I, 392.

[76] Weitzman, *Syriac Version*, 72, speaks of cases where 'elements from both the
Hebrew and LXX are welded together inextricably'.

the commonly accepted thesis that the Syriac translator consulted Gr, especially in difficult passages, we must conclude that this evidence is not unequivocal. J.A. Lund, M.P. Weitzman and others have emphasized that agreements between two versions do not automatically demonstrate influence of one on the other. The evidence we have studied thus far is not compelling.

Moreover, the claim that the Syriac translator turned to Gr when he had difficulty with the Hebrew text, is problematic in light of those many cases in which the Syriac translator had apparently difficulty with the Hebrew, but did not follow Gr (cf. § 3.4).

2.4 SYR AS A WITNESS TO THE EXPANDED TEXT

2.4.1 *Readings and motifs that Syr shares with SirII*

Syr contains a number of readings belonging to the expanded text of Sirach (cf. § 2.2). Noteworthy are those cases where Syr shares substantial GrII readings, as in 3:25,[77] 11:15–16 (also in MS A),[78] 16:15–16 (also in MS A),[79] 25:12 (also in Lat), and 26:19–27.[80] There are also some shorter additions or slight variants in which Syr agrees with GrII against GrI,[81] including cases where GrII has preserved a more original reading.[82] In sum, the Hebrew source text of Syr contained many SirII readings.[83]

---

[77] Cf. Prato, 'Lumière', 325–332.

[78] Cf. Prato, 'Lumière', 333–334.

[79] Cf. Prato, 'Lumière', 335; Böhmisch, 'Textformen des Sirachbuches', 113–114; Philonenko 'Interpolation essénisante'; Van Peursen, *Verbal System,* 303.

[80] Cf. Kearns, *Expanded Text*, 61.

[81] See 3:1; 19:15; 20:15; 21:14; 23:14d, 20; 24:6, 15a; 25:1, 11, 15, 26; 26:2, 3, 8; 29:19; 30:2; 31:20; 38:33; 48:3 (Kearns, *Expanded Text*, 61).

[82] See 3:18; 3:19b; 6:20; 21:8; 27:10; 37:26; 38:19; 47:11; 50:10 (Kearns, *Expanded Text*, 61).

[83] Cf. Segal, 'Evolution', 113; Kearns, *Expanded Text*, 66: 'Here too, as in Heb II, we have evidence of a unity of doctrine and outlook which not only runs throughout Syr and entitles us to speak of these elements in it as belonging to *the* expanded text (or, more exactly in this case, the *edited* text); but which also coincides in all essentials with Gr II and Lat, and thus entitles us to group under one heading the whole homogeneous elaboration of Sir, as found in its Heb II (mss), Syr, Gr II and Lat witnesses, and describe it by the comprehensive term THE Expanded Text, – or Sir II.'

C. Kearns has argued that Syr contains also secondary readings that, although not attested in HebII or GrII, display the motifs and tendencies that are typical of SirII,[84] such as the good-pleasure of God[85]; 'all'[86]; promises to Israel[87]; imparting of God's gifts[88]; forgiveness of sin[89]; moral darkness[90]; divine revelation[91]; fear of the Lord; faith; hope, trust, confidence in God; self-control[92]; love of God[93]; repentance for sin[94]; commandments of God[95]; wisdom, wise, foolish[96]; patience, steadfastness[97]; ways[98]; good works[99]; just, justice, righteous[100]; holy, holiness[101]; sin, sinner, wicked, impious[102]; divine scrutiny[103]; honour, disgrace, reproach[104]; anger of God[105]; destruction of the wicked[106]; life[107]; eternal[108]; hidden[109]; spirit[110]; treasure.[111]

---

[84] Cf. Kearns, *Expanded Text*, 23: 'Syr has also characteristic variants and additions of its own, which do not coincide textually with those either of Gr II or of Heb II. And it is a striking fact that even in many of these passages a doctrinal trend can be detected which links Syr with the one or the other of these forms of Sir II.'

[85] 17:27.

[86] 1:20a, 20i; 15:13; 17:22; 28:2b; 40:26; 42:22; 50:27, 29; cf. § 10.2.1, esp. n. 62.

[87] 46:1, 7.

[88] 17:6.

[89] 3:3.

[90] 11:15, 16 (= GrII, HebII); 16:15, 16 (= GrII, HebII); 17:31

[91] 17:23.

[92] For reference to 'fear of the Lord', 'faith', 'hope' and 'self-control', see the discussions below.

[93] 15:13; 25:12 (= GrII, Lat); 46:1d.

[94] 17:24; 18:22; 48:16. In 48:16 Syr creates a contrast between the people of Israel and the remnant of Judah, see § 3.7.1; Kuhn, 'Beiträge', II, 117, considers ܪܟܐܬܘܬܐ in 48:16 an inner-Syriac corruption of ܪܟܐܬܘܬܐ (cf. B ישׁר).

[95] 1:20b; 29:19 (= GrII, Lat).

[96] 2:3b; 21:7, 15c; 50:27.

[97] 1:15, 20j; 2:4b; 22:18.

[98] 2:3; 20:25.

[99] 26:3 (= Lat).

[100] 1:20; 17:24b; 18:10; 20:18.

[101] 1:20c; 42:22; 50:11, 14; 51:12d.

[102] 11:9b, 32b; 19:22; 21:7; 41:10.

[103] 17:15, 19b; 42:18cd.

[104] 12:3; 19:7b; 22:2; 23:14c; 40:26; 50:29.

[105] 36:2. But note that in other cases the Syriac translator omitted references to God's anger; cf. § 3.3 (d).

[106] 17:24b, 27a; 27:25b; 41:10

[107] 1:20d, 20h, 20i, 20k; 23:12c; 37:13; 48:11b.

[108] 1:12, 20, 20c, 20i; 3:1b; 21:5b.

[109] 14:1; 23:18c; 42:18cd; see also below, under 'faith', the reference to the 'secret of faith' in 27:17.

[110] 1:20k.

[111] 1:20a.

In a number of cases it is likely that the secondary readings were already present in the translator's source text.[112] Accordingly, Syr can be considered as an important witness to SirII. It should be noted, however, that some of those tendencies that allegedly link Syr with SirII also connect Syr with other parts of the Peshitta. This makes the origin of a number of readings in Syr uncertain: do they reflect SirII readings in the translator's Hebrew source text (because of agreements with SirII readings in the other textual witnesses) or should they be ascribed to the Syriac translator (because of agreements with other parts of the Peshitta). Compare the following motifs.

(a) Fear of the Lord. There are some references to 'fear of the Lord' that are unique to Syr.[113] This motive is also well-attested in GrII.[114] But in 28:23 the substitution of ܕܘܚܠܬܗ ܕܐܠܗܐ '(who forsake) the fear of God' instead of Gr κύριον 'the Lord' can also be regarded as a translational ('targumic') device.[115]

(b) Faith. The prominence of this motif is not disputed, but opinions about its background differ. A. Edershcim ascribed the use of 'faith' in 1:4, 25:12 and 27:17 to a Christian hand.[116] Weitzman, although he does not deal explicitly with the Sirach passages, ascribes the 'preoccupation with faith' in the Peshitta to a non-rabbinic Jewish group.[117] Kearns considers

---

[112] Cf. Kearns, *Expanded Text*, 61: The 'directly textual evidence of a Heb II underlying both Syr and Gr II is confirmed by the many coincidences in significant words and favourite ideas between the readings peculiar to Syr and those of Gr II.'

[113] Kearns, *Expanded Text*, 62, mentions 1:20g; 2:18; 40:26; see also 38:35.

[114] Kearns, *Expanded Text*, 33.

[115] See § 3.3 (b).

[116] Edersheim, 'Ecclesiasticus', 40 (on 1:4), 133 (on 25:12) and 142 (on 27:17); similarly Peters, *Ben Sirach*, 210 (on 25:12); Joosten 'Eléments d'araméen occidental' (on 37:13); see also Margoliouth, 'Original Hebrew', 27, on 37:13 ('The Syriac [...] appears to be an alteration in furtherance of the ecclesiastical doctrine of faith') and § 5.4 on the Syriac text of 15:15, for which Lévi and Di Lella assume Christian influence. Since the connection of 'faith' and 'life' is expressed on a number of occasions, there is no reason to analyse 37:13 ܡܛܠ ܕܗܝܡܢܘܬܗ ܗܝ ܡܐܚܝܐ ܠܗ 'Because his faithfulness makes him live' as an inner-Syriac corruption; *pace* Kuhn, 'Beiträge', II, 111 (Kuhn does not mention that his emendation is supported by 7a1!).

[117] Weitzman, *Syriac Version*, 215–216 (on Chronicles), 221–222 (on other books); cf. 216: 'The rabbinic sources, although they of course value faith, generally prefer to stress observance' (i.e. פולחנא); similarly idem, *From Judaism to Christianity*, 12, 68.

the reference to 'faith' a SirII feature.[118] For 27:17 ܐܪܙܐ ܕܗܝܡܢܘܬܐ 'a secret of faith' he refers to Josephus' description of the Essenes to support his view that there is a connection between the expanded text and the Essenes.[119]

(c) Hope. This is also a central motif. In addition to its occurrence in e.g. 15:15 and 18:14 we can refer to 2:14, 17:24, 41:2, 44:10. In the latter verses references to lost hope have been omitted, perhaps because of the high value that the Syriac translator attributed to hope. This motif too relates Syr both to SirII[120] and to other parts of Peshitta.[121]

(d) Self-control. In 17:31 Syr contains a negative judgment about 'the man who does not control his own inclination' (ܒܪܢܫܐ ܕܠܐ ܟܒܫ ܝܨܪܗ) and in 11:15 the Syriac translator introduces ܢܟܦܘܬܐ 'chastity'. This motif, too, relates Syr both to SirII[122] and to other parts of Peshitta.[123]

2.4.2 *Eschatology*

To the most striking features of SirII belong the eschatological views reflected in it. The follow themes play a central role.

(a) Final divine judgment. Related to this theme are the motifs of the Day of the Lord (48:10[124]); the revelation of God as judge (17:23[125]); the exploration of human deeds before God

---

[118] Kearns, *Expanded Text*, 33; from Syr he quotes 37:13 on p. 62; similarly Böhmisch 'Haec omnia liber vitae', 168; Skehan–Di Lella, *Wisdom of Ben Sira*, 340.

[119] Kearns, *Expanded Text*, 272; cf. ibid. 55; see also Charlesworth, 'Secrecy' and compare the use of סוד אמת in the Dead Sea Scrolls.

[120] Compare the parallels from GrII in Kearns, *Expanded Text*, 34.

[121] Cf. Weitzman, *Syriac Version*, 224–225. Weitzman suggests that the non-rabbinic group that was responsible for the Peshitta had a preoccupation with hope; similarly idem, *From Judaism to Christianity*, 68–69.

[122] Cf. Kearns *Expanded Text*, 40, on parallels in GrII.

[123] H.J.W. Drijvers calls ܢܟܦܘܬܐ a 'characteristic monastic virtue' and uses it in his argument for a Christian origin of the Peshitta of Wisdom; cf. Drijvers 'Peshitta of Sapientia Salomonis', 19.

[124] Quoting Mal 3:23, see § 5.1 A (2).

[125] Syr has 'He will reveal Himself (and visit them, and He will place their transgressions on their head)' instead of Gr ἐξαναστήσεται 'He will rise up'; cf. Job 19:25 Pesh 'and I know that my redeemer lives and in the end He will be revealed (ܢܬܓܠܐ) upon the earth'; MT '... He will stand upon the earth'; cf. Weitzman, *Syriac Version*, 223. See also Kearns, *Expanded Text*, 32 on divine revelation in GrII.

(14:19[126]); the recompense for carefully recorded good and wicked deeds (9:7); the written record of bad deeds (17:20[127]).

(b) Punishment of the wicked. Related motives are the destruction of the wicked (17:24 and others); the Day of Slaughter (26:28; cf. Jer 12:3); the end of the world (23:20[128]); Hades (28:23[129]).

(c) Reward of the just.[130] Related motifs are 'the World of the Righteous' (18:10[131]); eternal life (1:12, 20, 3:1; cf. 37:26)[132]; an everlasting heritage (1:20h); the registration of names in the Book of Life (1:20i)[133]; an eternal reward and a crown (1:20c-e); eternal victory among the 'holy ones' (1:20c).[134]

The eschatological outlook of Syr differs considerably from that of the original Sirach, which does not mention retribution after death, eternal life and the world to come. References to death and Sheol have been altered or omitted accordingly in e.g. 9:12; 14:17, 19; 17:27–28; 38:21 and 44:9. This tendency is also attested elsewhere in the Peshitta.[135]

---

[126] Smend, *Jesus Sirach*, 136 ('Er denkt an das jüngste Gericht'); Edersheim, 'Ecclesiasticus', 86 ('The Syriac has here also what seems a Christian modification'); cf. Van Peursen, Review of Calduch-Benages–Ferrer–Liesen, *Sabiduría del Escriba*, 98.

[127] See § 5.3 (1) for parallels in rabbinic literature.

[128] Cf. Kearns, *Expanded Text*, 214.

[129] Syr reads 'A fire will burn and not be quenched'. Kearns does not mention this motif. Compare, however, Edersheim, 'Ecclesiasticus', 146: 'If even in the Greek wording of the first two lines (referring to the flame—although, from the context, that kindled by the tongue) raises the suspicion of a Christian modification so that the words about the flame that would burn without quenching might be understood of Hades; this suspicion is increased by the Syriac, which seems to go much further in the same direction'.

[130] For parallels in GrII see Kearns, *Expanded Text*, 73–74.

[131] Compare 'the World to Come' in Lat 24:9(14) *usque ad futurum saeculum non desinam* and 'the Holy World' in Lat 17:27(25) and 24:33(36) (Kearns, *Expanded Text* 73, 141–143) and the expression העולם הבא in *m. Abot* 4:22 (Albeck 4:17) and other rabbinic literature.

[132] This motif occurs also elsewhere in the Peshitta; see Weitzman, *Syriac Version*, 222–223. In 3:1 Syr has ܡ̈ܠܟ ܢܚܘܢ ܕܠܥܠܡ ܚܝܐ 'so that you may live an eternal life', in which 'eternal life' is a plus; for Gr σῴζω = Heb חיה see Weitzman 255–256. 37:26 ܕܠܥܠܡ ܠܦܝ ܡܒܥ ܡܐܥܡ 'and his name will stand for eternal life' is close to D ושמו עומד בחיי עולם (last word also in C) but Syr speaks of eternal life, which is not the sense of original.

[133] Similarly in Lat 24:23; cf. Böhmisch, 'Haec omnia liber vitae', 171–173, 176–177.

[134] The 'fellowship with angels in the world to come' is not attested in GrII.

[135] Weitzman, *Syriac Version*, 222; idem, *From Judaism to Christianity*, 16, 68.

2.5 CONCLUSION

The study of Syr as a translation is hindered by our lack of knowledge about the Hebrew source text of Syr. It cannot be equated with one of the extant Hebrew manuscripts. There are a number of cases where Syr presupposes a misreading in the Hebrew. We cannot determine, however, whether such errors were already present in the translator's source text or whether the translator was responsible for them.

Regarding the relationship between Syr and Gr we have challenged the commonly accepted view that the Syriac translator consulted Gr, especially for difficult verses. Our conclusions in this field are preliminary, because we did not make a complete and independent analysis of the two witnesses. We could observe, however, that the evidence put forward by previous scholars to support the dependency was not convincing.

C. Kearns and others have pointed out that Syr shares many motifs with the expanded text. It is possible that these motifs were present in the translator's source text, which seems to have contained many HebII readings. This is not to say, however, that that is necessarily the case with all so-called SirII motifs. Especially the fact that some of the motifs concerned, including the references to 'faith' and 'hope' and the eschatological tendencies, appear also elsewhere in the Peshitta indicate that it is also possible that the Syriac translator inserted them in his text. The fact that both explanations are possible for the same phenomena means that we cannot use these phenomena as proof for either of them.

APPENDIX: THE TEXTUAL HISTORY OF SIRACH

The following table indicates in a simplified form the complex textual
history of Sirach.

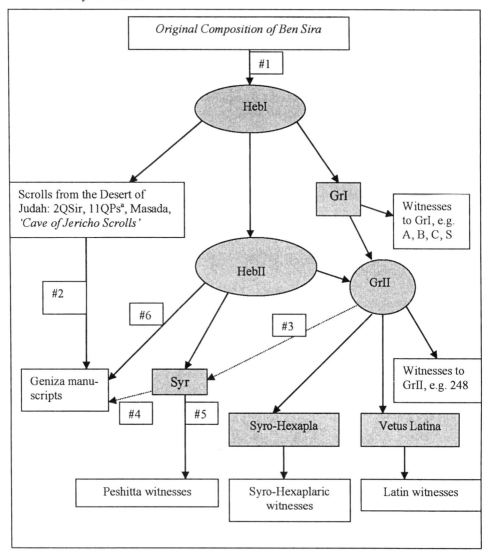

The following items have been marked:[1]

1. Extant textual witnesses (*white boxes, Roman font*). This concerns the concrete evidence of what is actually found in the manuscripts. All other items that have been marked are secondary deductions from them.[2]
2. Texts that are not preserved, but the existence of which can be postulated (*white boxes, italic font*).
3. Ancient Versions (*grey rectangular boxes*). Although one could argue that these belong to the preceding category,[3] we prefer to take them apart because of their distinctive character.
4. Text forms (*grey oval boxes*). These are certain forms of the text that can be deduced from the existence of a distinct group of manuscripts.[4]
5. Relations between the texts and the textual witnesses, marked with arrows. It should be noted that even when it is not indicated in the table, textual witnesses, rather than abstract texts are the objects of translation and transmission.

Some arrows in the diagram above are disputed:

a. The line between the original book (#1) and HebI is often ignored, because HebI is equated with the Hebrew text as it left Ben Sira's hand; cf. § 2.1.
b. The line between scrolls in the Desert of Judah and the Geniza manuscripts (#2) reflect Di Lella's historical reconstruction in which the Geniza manuscripts 'were copied from exemplars which represent a text that ultimately goes back to the caves near Khirbet Qumrân', and that they 'were based on a text that was at one time in the Essene library'.[5] In Di Lella's view the Geniza manuscripts go back to scrolls discovered in the vicinity of Jericho about AD 800.[6]

---

[1] These distinctions are not indicated in the diagram in Böhmisch, 'Textformen des Sirachbuches', 88; the table in Liesen, *Full of Praise*, 21 distinguishes between 'texts' and 'text forms', but does not distinguish between our (1), (2) and (3).

[2] On the distinction between 'texts' and 'textual witnesses', see Tov, *Textual Criticism*, 2.

[3] Thus Liesen, *Full of Praise*, 19, about GrI; Liesen does not distinguish between our (1) and (2) either.

[4] For the distinction between text and text form see § 2.1.

[5] Di Lella, *Hebrew Text of Sirach*, 78.

   c. Di Lella goes so far as to claim that the Hebrew manuscripts were lost from the middle of the fifth century,[7] until the discovery of the Jericho Cave, which denies the influence indicated by #6. However, HebII readings in the Geniza manuscripts cannot be explained if manuscripts discovered around Jericho are the sole source for the origin of the Geniza manuscripts.[8]

   d. There are some traces of the influence of Syr on Heb (#4), but the claim made by a number of scholars at the end of the nineteenth century and in the first decades of the twentieth century that the Hebrew Geniza manuscripts are translations from Syriac cannot be maintained.[9]

   e. It is generally assumed that the Syriac translation has been influenced by the Greek translation (#3), but the evidence put forward by earlier scholars is not convincing (see § 2.3).

On the complex relation between the Syriac manuscripts to the original Syriac translation (#5) see Chapter 1.

---

[6] Di Lella, *Hebrew Text of Sirach*, 78–105; idem, 'Qurmân and the Geniza Fragments of Sirach'; cf. Barthélemy–Milik, *Qumran Cave 1*, 88; Baillet–Milik–De Vaux, *Les 'petites grottes'*, 75; Kahle, 'The Age of the Scrolls', 45–48.

[7] The latest reference to the existence of a Hebrew text of Sirach is a remark by Jerome in his preface to the translation of the books of Solomon (cf. Cowley–Neubauer, *Original Hebrew*, p. x).

[8] This was already Segal's criticism of Baillet, Di Lella and Kahle in his 'Ben-Sira in Qumrân'.

[9] See Di Lella, *Hebrew Text of Sirach*; Van Peursen, 'Retroversions'; idem, 'Sir 51:13–30'; idem, *Verbal System*, 19–23.

CHAPTER THREE

THE SYRIAC SIRACH AS A TRANSLATION

3.1 GENERAL CHARACTERIZATION OF THE SYRIAC SIRACH

In the preceding chapter we have seen that any study of the character of Syr as a translation is hindered by our lack of knowledge about the translator's Hebrew source. Nevertheless, on the basis of an internal analysis of Syr and an investigation of the patterns of correspondences to other versions, it seems justified to characterize Syr as a free translation. This may be related to the status of Sirach in the community in which the translation originated. Smend argued that the character of the translation—which in his view is not only free, but also imprecise and careless[1]—indicates that the translator did not consider Sirach canonical.[2] A similar argument has been put forward for Chronicles, which too has been translated very differently from the other books of the Hebrew Bible.[3] According to some scholars the non-canonical status can also account for the poor state of the translator's Hebrew source text both in the case of Sirach and in the case of Chronicles.[4]

---

[1] Similarly Lévi, *L'Ecclésiastique* I, lii.

[2] Smend, *Jesus Sirach*, cxxxvii: 'Die Uebersetzung des Sirach ist wohl das schlechteste Uebersetzungswerk der syrischen Bibel. Es bleibt freilich in vielen Fällen unsicher, was von ihren Mängeln auf Rechnung des Uebersetzers und was auf Rechnung seiner hebräischen Vorlage oder der syrischen Textüberlieferung zu setzen ist. Es steht trotzdem fest, dass der Uebersetzer vielfach nachlässig und leichtfertig gearbeitet hat. Man kan sein Verfahren nur daraus erklären, dass das Buch ihm wie später den Jakobiten nicht für kanonisch galt.'

[3] Cf. Weitzman, *Syriac Version*, 208. Also one of the two versions of Pesh-1–2 Maccabees seems to be the product of free and sometimes inaccurate translation (Konrad Jenner, personal communication; cf. Schmidt, 'Die beiden Syrischen Übersetzungen', esp. I, p. 5).

[4] On Sirach see § 2.2.1; on Chronicles see Weitzman, *Syriac Version*, 111, 208; see, however, § 6.2.1 (A) on the validity of this argument.

3.2 EXPLANATORY AND EXPLICATIVE VARIANTS

Many free renderings are of an explanatory or explicative nature. This applies to a number of examples quoted in Chapter Two, to which we can add the following categories.

(a) Syr provides a free rendering of an idiomatic Hebrew expression.[5]

5:1 ܐ ܐܝܬ ܠܝ 'I have much'; A יש לאל ידי.[6]
5:14 ܗܠܟ ܒܬܪܬܝܢ 'walking in two (ways)'[7]; A[1+2] בעל שתים (similarly 6:1).
6:5 ܣܦܘܬܐ ܕܟܐܢܐ 'the lips of the upright'; A שפתי חן.[8]
8:16 ܓܒܪܐ ܥܘܠܐ 'an unrighteous man'; A בעל אף.[9]
9:8 ܐܦܝܟ ܠܐ ܬܚܙܝܢ ܒܐܢܬܬܐ ܕܫܦܝܪܐ 'your face should not look at a beautiful woman'; A העלם עין מאשת חן 'hide your eyes from a comely woman'.
9:16 ܐܟܠܝ ܦܬܘܪܟ 'those who eat from your table'; A בעלי לחמך.
44:5 ܘܐܡܪܝ ܡܬܠܐ 'and who say proverbs'; B נושאי משל; M ונשאי מש]ל[.
48:2 ܘܐܝܬܝ ܥܠܝܗܘܢ ܟܦܢܐ 'and he brought upon them famine'; B לחם וישבר להם מטה 'and he broke their staff of bread'.

(b) Syr explains a difficult or uncommon expression in Heb.[10]

7:12 ܠܐ ܬܐܒܕ 'do not devise (evil against your brother)'; A אל תחרוש.[11]
15:13 ܠܐ ܢܬܠ אֶܢܘܢ 'He will not give them (to those who love Him)'; A+B ולא יאננה 'He will not cause it to happen'.[12]
36:24 ܡܠܐ ܕܥܘܠܐ 'the words of the unrighteous (or: unrighteousness)'; B מטעמי כזב 'delicacies of deceit'.[13]

---

[5] Also elsewhere in the Peshitta and the Targums; cf. Weitzman, *From Judaism to Christianity*, 190.

[6] Similarly 14:11 ܐܝܬ ܠܟ; A לאל ידך. On the Hebrew idiom see Van Peursen, *Verbal System*, 63.

[7] According to Smend, *Jesus Sirach*, 52, this Syriac expression is not attested elsewhere.

[8] We consider this as a free rendering in Syr, rather than the result of a corruption of חן to כן in its Hebrew source text; *pace* Ginzberg, 'Randglossen', 615.

[9] For the examples from 8:16 and 9:8 see also § 10.1.1.

[10] Obviously, the distinction between 'Syr gives a free rendering of an idiomatic expression' (a) and 'Syr explains a difficult expression' (b) is vague, because we cannot always be sure whether a Hebrew expression is 'idiomatic' or 'difficult'.

[11] Cf. *HALOT* 357 on חרש 'plough, devise' in Biblical Hebrew.

[12] For אנהIII see BDB 58; *HALOT* 70; Daube, 'Direct and Indirect Causation', 265–266.

[13] Cf. *HALOT* 574.

37:1 ܪܚܡܐ ܕܫܡܗ ܪܚܡܐ 'a friend whose name is friend'; B^mg(+D) אוהב שם אוהב.

38:14 ܘܐܣܝܘܬܐ ܕܒܐܝܕܗ ܘܚܝܐ 'and that healing will come through his hand and life'; B ורפאות למען מחיה 'and healing that it may give life'.[14]

47:4 ܒܩܠܥ '(he moved his hand) with the sling'; B על קלע.[15]

(c) Syr simplifies a literary expression or word of Heb.

16:25a ܐܡܪ ܡܠܝ 'I will say my words'; A אביעה רוחי 'I will pour out my spirit'.

16:25b ܘܒܚܟܡܬܐ 'with wisdom'; A ובהצנע 'by measure' (cf. Mic 6:8).

23:11 ܓܒܪܐ ܕܝܡܐ ܣܓܝ ܩܢܐ ܥܘܠܐ 'a man who swears acquires transgressions'; cf. Gr ἀνὴρ πολύορκος πλησθήσεται ἀνομίας 'a man of many oaths is filled with iniquity'.

36:24 ܦܘܡܐ 'mouth'; B חיך 'palate' (= Gr φάρυγξ)

38:16 ܘܣܓܐ ܕܡܥܐ 'multiply tears'; B הזיב דמעה 'let tears flow'. הזיב is not attested elsewhere in the MT; in 1QIsa^a 48:21 it occurs instead of MT הזיל.[16]

48:22 ܘܗܠܟ ܒܐܘܪܚܬܗ ܕܕܘܝܕ 'and he walked in the ways of David'; B ויחזק בדרכי דוד 'he was strong in the ways of David'.

(d) Syr translates a common Hebrew word according to a particular meaning in a specific context.[17]

7:7 ܒܕܝܢܘܗܝ '(Do not submit yourself) to its judgments'; A בקהלה 'to its assembly'.[18]

10:20 ܣܒܐ '(Among brethren) the eldest one (is honoured)'; A ראשם 'their head'.

Sometimes, however, the Syriac translator seems to have missed a particular meaning or nuance.[19]

6:6 ܫܐܠܝ ܫܠܡܟ 'those who greet you'; A אנשי שלומך. Syr took שלום as referring to a greeting, as in 6:5 שואלו שלום (read שואלי).[20]

---

[14] Cf. Van Peursen, *Verbal System*, 365; Beentjes, 'Jesus Sirach 38:1–15', 264.

[15] Heb is difficult; cf. Van Peursen, *Verbal System*, 61.

[16] *HALOT* 266; Kutscher, *Isaiah Scroll*, 233.

[17] Similarly elsewhere in the Peshitta; cf. Weitzman, *Syriac Version*, 27; idem, *From Judaism to Christianity*, 58.

[18] Cf. *HALOT* 1079: 'juridical authority', with references to Jer 26:17, Prv 5:14, 26:26 and our Sirach passage; Segal *Sefer Ben Sira*, 45, compares Deut 33:4, Neh 5:6; in Prv 26:26 the Septuagint translates קהל with συνέδριον.

[19] Cf. Weitzman, *Syriac Version*, 34–35 on 'misguided improvements'.

[20] Cf. Ryssel, 'Fragmente', I, 384–385.

11:18 ܡܢ ܡܣܟܢܘܬܗ '(There is one who becomes rich) from his poverty'; A מהתענות. The Syriac translation misses the nuance of 'to live as a poor one'.[21]

13:3 ܡܣܟܢܐ ܚܛܐ ܘܡܨܠܐ 'The poor man sins and prays'; A ועל דל נעוה הוא יתחנן 'The poor man is wronged and yet he must beg forgiveness'.[22] ܚܛܐ corresponds to נעוא and ܡܨܠܐ with יתחנן, but Syr misses the point that is made.

15:1 ܢܗܠܟ ܒܗ '(He who learns the law) will walk in it'; A+B ידריכנה. The Syriac translation misses the nuance of 'to reach' of the Hebrew verb.[23]

30:13 ܐܠܦ ܠܒܪܟ ܕܚܠܬ ܢܦܫܐ 'Teach your son anxiety of the soul'; B יסר בנך. ܐܠܦ corresponds to יסר, but in the present context the Hebrew verb means 'to discipline, chastise'.

40:1 ܣܘܥܪܢܐ ܪܘܪܒܐ 'great things' and ܢܣܝܘܢܐ ܚܣܝܢܐ 'strong types'; B+M עסק גדול 'much occupation' and עול כבד 'heavy yoke'.

(e) Syr makes a reference to a biblical story more explicit. For examples see § 5.1.

(f) Syr explains a metaphor and substitutes the *signifiant* by the *signifié*.[24]

4:6 ܒܪܘܝܗ 'his creator' (= Gr); A צורו 'his Rock'; For 'rock' as a metaphor for 'creator', see Isa 51:1.[25]

---

[21] Smend, *Jesus Sirach*, 107: 'מהתענותו] muss hier bedeuten: daraus, dass er wie ein Armer lebt. Syr. schlecht: aus seiner Armut'. Winter, 'Ben Sira in Syriac', I, 245, translates A and Gr with 'through diligence' and explains the reading in Syr from the translator's preference for poverty, but this seems far-fetched to us

[22] Cf. Van Peursen, *Verbal System*, 350.

[23] Cf. Smend, *Jesus Sirach*, 13.

[24] Also elsewhere in the Peshitta, cf. Weitzman, *From Judaism to Christianity*, 59; Greenberg, *Jeremiah*, 61–63 (for the opposite phenomenon, i.e. retention of metaphors, cf. Gzella, 'New Ways', 411, on Isa 41:4). Peters, *Ben Sirach*, 68, discerns this phenomenon also in 7:12, where Syr has ܠܐ ܬܚܪܫ corresponding to אל תחרוש in A; but because of the frequency of the use of חרש with the meaning 'to plot, devise' in Biblical Hebrew (cf. *HALOT* 357), it seems likely that the 'metaphorical' meaning has become lexicalized. In some cases the explanation of the metaphor may already have occurred in the translator's source text; cf. 40:1 ܠܐܪܥܐ ܕܚܝܐ '(till they rest) in the land of life'; B[txt] אל אם כל חי '(till they return) to the mother of all living'; B[mg] כי ארץ ח' (Thus Beentjes' edition; the edition of the Academy of the Hebrew Language has only אל; Lévi, *L'Ecclésiastique* I, 14, prefers the reading in B[mg], but see the criticism in Bacher's review of Lévi's commentary, p. 312). In Gen 3:20 אם כל חי is a designation of Eve; its use as an epithet for the earth in Sir 40:1 is remarkable; cf. Van Peursen, *Verbal System*, 58; Vall, 'Enigma', 338–339. A reference to 'the land of life' fits in well with the eschatology of Syr, cf. § 2.4.2, n. 132.

[25] Cf. Wiegand, 'Die Gottesname צור', 85–96. Accordingly, there is no reason to assume that the Syriac translator read יוצרו instead of צורו; cf. § 2.2.3.

34:19 ܘܡܓܢ ܘܦܪܩ ܘܬܘܟܠܢܐ ܗܘ ܪܒܐ ܘܡܛܫܝܬܢܐ ܡܢ ܣܢܐܐ ܘܦܘܪܩܢܐ ܡܢ ܒܥܠܕܒܒܐ ܘܡܦܪܩܢܐ ܗܘ ܡܢ ܡܚܘܬܐ 'And He protects and saves them; and He is a great confidence and a shelter against the enemy, a saviour from adversary and a redeemer from the wound'; Gr ὑπερασπισμὸς δυναστείας καὶ στήριγμα ἰσχύος, σκέπη ἀπὸ καύσωνος καὶ σκέπη ἀπὸ μεσημβρίας, φυλακὴ ἀπὸ προσκόμματος καὶ βοήθεια ἀπὸ πτώσεως 'A mighty shield and strong staff, a shelter from the heat and a shade from the noontide-heat, a guard against stumbling'.[26]

36:31 ܐܢܬܬܐ '(the man who has no) wife'; 'wife'; B+C+D קן 'nest' (= Gr).

In 4:6 and 34:19 Syr avoids metaphors that represent God as an inanimate object. This tendency can be observed also elsewhere in the Peshitta. Thus the metaphor מגן 'shield' (cf. 34:19) is translated with ܡܥܕܪܢܐ 'helper', and צור 'rock' (cf. 4:6) with ܐܠܗܐ 'God', ܡܥܕܪܢܐ 'helper' and others.[27] The remaining example in 36:31 does not change the overall picture that Syr agrees with the other parts of the Peshitta in that it mostly retains figurative language and in this respect differs from the Targums, 'whose translators seem to have had little faith in their readers' ability to interpret figures aright'.[28]

Perhaps also the following example belongs to this category, although the metaphor in question is hardly attested elsewhere:

38:30 ܥܕ ܠܐ ܡܐܬ 'Before he dies (he is bowed down)'; Gr πρὸ ποδῶν 'before (his) feet'; According to Edersheim Syr 'took "before his feet" as a euphemism (cf. Latin *rigidas calces extendere*), scarcely to be found elsewhere.'[29] The expression *rigidas calces extendere* occurs in A. Persius Flaccus, *Saturae* 3,105,[30] where it refers to the custom of carrying away a dead person with the feet in the di-

---

[26] Cf. Edersheim, 'Ecclesiasticus', 170: 'The highly poetical metaphors of this verse are all diluted in the Syriac Version'.

[27] Weitzman, *Syriac Version*, 29, 190; cf. Barnes, 'Influence of the Septuagint', 188–189; but the contrast between the Psalms (avoiding metaphors) and the Pentateuch (retaining metaphors) is not as clear as Barnes suggested; see Weitzman, *From Judaism to Christianity*, 18.

[28] Weitzman, *Syriac Version*, 28–29; Smelik, *Targum of Judges*, 98; Van Staalduine-Sulman, *Targum of Samuel*, 108. However, the way in which metaphors are treated is not uniform and differs from Targum to Targum. On the variety of means used in the Targums to render metaphors see Kasher, 'Metaphor and Allegory'.

[29] Edersheim, 'Ecclesiasticus', 187.

[30] Cf. *Thesaurus Linguae Latinae* III, 195; Forcellini, *Lexicon Totius Latinitatis* I, 503.

rection of the door.[31] For the association of 'feet' with 'death' see also 1 Kgs 14:12, 17; Acts 5:9.[32]

(g) Syr replaces a common noun by a proper noun.

38:15 ܐܠܗܐ 'God'; B עושהו.
44:21 ܦܪܬ 'Euphrates'; B נהר.[33]
47:18 ܒܫܡܗ ܕܐܠܗܐ ܕܕܝܠܗ ܗܘ ܐܝܩܪܐ 'in the name of God whose is the honour'; B בשם הנכבד.[34]

(h) Syr replaces a pronoun by a noun or proper noun.[35]

6:20 ܟܡܐ ܥܣܩܐ ܥܠ ܣܟܠܐ ܚܟܡܬܐ 'How difficult is Wisdom for the fool'; A עקובה היא לאויל.[36]
31:7 ܡܛܠ ܕܬܘܩܠܬܐ ܗܘ ܡܡܘܢܐ ܠܣܟܠܐ 'Because Mammon is a stumbling-block for the fool'; B כי תקלה הוא לאויל.[37]
38:5 ܡܛܠ ܕܢܬܝܕܥ ܚܝܠܗ ܕܐܠܗܐ 'So that God's strength would become known'. ܚܝܠܗ ܕܐܠܗܐ corresponds to כחו in B^{txt} (= Gr τὴν ἰσχὺν αὐτοῦ) and כוחם in B^{mg}. The context argues for the reading 'his strength', in which 'his' refers to God.[38] This intended meaning is made explicit in Syr.[39]

---

31 For details see Kißel, *Aules Persius Flaccus Satiren*, 481.

32 I thank Dr P.J. Williams for these references.

33 Cf. e.g. Lévi, *L'Ecclésiastique* I, 91: 'S. commente, en traduisant נהר par "l'Euphrate".' But note that נהר as a reference to the Euphrates is already attested in the Bible (*HALOT* 677). In 39:22 (B), where נהר occurs parallel to יאר, it is also a reference to the Euphrates (cf. Bacher, Review of Lévi, *L'Ecclésiastique*, 312) but there the Syriac has twice ܢܗܪܐ (cf. below, § 3.6, on the phenomenon of repetitive parallelism in the Syriac text where Heb has two different words). According to Reiterer, *Urtext*, 107, the Syriac translation informs us about the context in which the translation originated, i.e. in an area where 'the river' was the Euphrates, rather than about the translator's interpretation of this text or the parallel passages in the Old Testament.

34 Apparently the Syriac translator applied the adjective 'glorious' to God rather than to 'the name'; cf. Van Peursen, *Verbal System*, 206 n. 27, on the interpretation of Heb as 'in the name of the Glorious One' rather than 'in the glorious name'.

35 Also 'very frequent' elsewhere in the Peshitta, according to Weitzman, *From Judaism to Christianity*, 58.

36 'Wisdom' instead of 'she' is also attested in the Latin and the Greek. Ryssel, 'Sprüche', 277, considers σφόδρα a scribal error for σοφία.

37 See below, § 3.6 for the repetition of ܡܡܘܢܐ in this passage.

38 Cf. 38:6 where B^{txt} has בגבורתו and B^{mg} בגבורתם.

39 Accordingly, we do not think that Syr changed the purport of the verse and that ܕܐܠܗܐ is 'a religious emendation on the part of the Syrian translator'; *pace* Edersheim, 'Ecclesiasticus', 184.

(i) Syr adds an explanatory word or phrase.[40]

13:2 ܡܢܐ ܓܝܪ ܬܬܫܘܬܦ ܩܕܪܐ ܕܦܚܪܐ ܠܐܘܪܐ ܕܢܚܫܐ ‘How can a pot *of the potter* have fellowship with a cauldron of *brass*?’ A מה יתחבר פרור אל סיר ‘how can a pot have fellowship with a cauldron?’[41]

15:17 ܐܬܝܗܒܘ ܓܝܪ ܠܒܢܝܢܫܐ ‘*are given* to the people’; A+B לפני אדם ‘(are) before man’.

31:30 ܡܣܓܝܐܘܬܐ ܕܚܡܪܐ ܥܒܕܬ ܠܣܟܠܐ ܬܘܩܠܬܐ ‘Abundance of wine *makes* a stumbling-block for the fool ‘; B מרבה חמר לכסיל מוקש.[42]

33:14 ܠܘܩܒܠ ܒܝܫܬܐ ܐܬܒܪܝ ܛܒܬܐ ܘܠܘܩܒܠ ܡܘܬܐ ܐܬܒܪܝܘ ܚܝܐ ܘܠܘܩܒܠ ܢܘܗܪܐ ܐܬܒܪܝ ܚܫܘܟܐ ‘Against evil good *has been created*, and against death, life *has been created*, and against light darkness *has been created*; E [...] טוב ונוכח חיים מות [...] איש [...] רשע ונוכח האור [...].[43]

36:22 ܟܠ ܕܒܣܘܦܝܗ ܕܐܪܥܐ ‘all *who are at* the end of the world’; B כל אפסי ארץ ‘all the ends of the world’.

50:22 ܡܢ ܟܪܣܐ ܕܐܡܗܝܗܘܢ ‘from *their mother’s* womb’; B מרחם ‘from the womb’.

In some cases, however, the addition misses the point:[44]

3:12 ܘܠܐ ܬܫܒܘܩ ܐܝܩܪܗ ܟܠ ܝܘܡܝ ܚܝܝܟ ‘And do not forsake *his honour* all the days of your life’ instead of A ואל תעזבהו כל ימי חייך.

4:22 ܘܠܐ ܬܒܗܬ ܠܡܘܕܝܘ ܒܬܘܩܠܬܟ ‘And be not ashamed *to confess* your offences’; A למכשוליך ואל תכשל; C ואל תבוש למכשול לך ‘Do not be ashamed so that it causes your downfall’. Compare 4:26 where Gr and Syr have ‘be not ashamed to confess your sins’ and A ‘...to draw back from our sins’.

---

[40] Examples occur also elsewhere in the Peshitta (but not as frequently as in Sirach) and in the Targums; cf. Weitzman, *Syriac Version*, 23–25; idem, *From Judaism to Christianity*, 192; Van Keulen, ‘Points of Agreement’, 220–221. For the addition of ܕ + Noun in 13:2 and 50:22 see also § 10.2.1.

[41] Cf. Smend, *Jesus Sirach*, 121: ‘Aber für die jüdischen Leser war diese zweifellos richtige Erklärung überflüssig, was allerdings für die Bedeutung der beiden Wörter von Wichtigkeit ist’.

[42] Cf. Margoliouth, ‘Original Hebrew’, 24: ‘While the terseness of the original Hebrew line requires no verb, the Syriac adds ܥܒܕܬ (maketh), thus giving a prosy aspect to the line’.

[43] Cf. Smend, *Jesus Sirach*, 299: ‘Willkürlich setzt S. zu jedem der drei hinzu: ist erschaffen.’

[44] Cf. Smend, *Jesus Sirach*, 26 (on 3:12), 44 (on 4:22).

(j) Syr makes the subject of a finite verb explicit.[45]

44:21 ܒܡܘܡܬܐ ܝܡܐ ܠܗ ܐܠܗܐ ‘God swore to him with oaths’; B בשבועה הקים לו.

45:24 ܒܡܘܡܬܐ ܝܡܐ ܠܗ ܐܠܗܐ ‘God swore to him with oaths’; B גם לו הקים חק.[46]

Note also the addition of ܐܝܣܪܐܝܠ and ܫܠܝܡܘܢ in

24:12 ܒܡܢܬܗ ܕܡܪܝܐ ܘܒܓܘ ܝܪܬܘܬܗ ܐܝܣܪܐܝܠ ‘In the Lord’s portion and in the midst of His inheritance, Israel’ and

47:14 ܟܡܐ ܚܟܝܡ ܗܘܝܬ ܒܛܠܝܘܬܟ ܫܠܝܡܘܢ ‘How wise you were in your youth, Solomon!’

(k) Syr expands on the succinct style of Heb.[47]

25:19 ܣܓܝܐܐ ܒܝܫܬܐ ܘܠܐ ܐܝܟ ܙܥܘܪܬ ܒܝܫܘܬܗ ܕܐܢܬܬܐ ‘Much evil, but not like the smallest evil of a woman’; C מעט רעה כרעת אשה.

28:10 ܟܠ ܕܬܪܡܐ ܒܢܘܪܐ ܢܐܩܕ ‘Everything that you throw in the fire will burn’; Gr κατὰ τὴν ὕλην τοῦ πυρός ‘according to the wood of the fire’.

38:13 ܒܐܝܕܗ ܡܨܠܚܐ ܐܣܝܘܬܐ ‘In his hand the cure succeeds’; B בידו מצלחת ‘in his hand is success’.

47:18 ܒܫܡܗ ܕܐܠܗܐ ܕܕܝܠܗ ܗܘ ܐܝܣܪܐ ‘in the name of God’; B בשם הנכבד.[48]

(l) Syr has an explanatory addition that covers more than a single word or phrase.

29:19 ܚܛܝܐ ܕܥܒܪ ܥܠ ܦܘܩܕܢܘܗܝ ܕܡܪܝܐ ܒܥܪܒܘܬܐ ܢܦܠ ܘܪܕܦ ܠܡܣܒܠܗ ܚܠܦܘܗܝ، ܚܛܗܐ ܢܦܠ ܒܕܝܢܐ ܚܛܗܐ ܣܓܝܐܐ ܡܝܬܝܐ ܥܪܒܘܬܐ ܘܕܡܬܐܠܨ ܡܓܢ ܘܡܫܟܚ ܕܝܢܐ ‘The sinner who transgresses the commands of the Lord will fall in surety, and he who seeks to takes sins upon himself will fall in judgment. Surety brings many sins, and he who obliges himself without expense will find judgments’; Gr ἁμαρτωλὸς ἐμπεσὼν εἰς ἐγγύην καὶ διώκων ἐργολαβίας ἐμπεσεῖται εἰς κρίσεις

---

[45] Also elsewhere in the Peshitta and the Targums, see the literature mentioned at (i), of which the present category is a subcategory, and further Greenberg, *Jeremiah*, 37–38; similarly in the Old Syriac and Peshitta Gospels, see Williams, *Early Syriac Translation Technique*, 26.

[46] On הקים ‘to swear, promise (with an oath)’, see Van Peursen, *Verbal System*, 259.

[47] Also elsewhere in the Peshitta and the Targums, cf. Weitzman, *From Judaism to Christianity*, 190. See also 37:1 and 38:14 quoted above, under (b); 30:13 quoted under (d); and the examples given under (i) and (j).

[48] Compare above, § 3.2 (g), on the replacement of common nouns with proper nouns.

'the sinner who falls in surety and pursues gain will fall into law-suits'.[49]

(m) Syr adds or omits a negation.

This is a remarkable category. It is not always clear whether the conversion is the result of a clerical error or a representative of the 'technique of converse translations', which is attested elsewhere in the Peshitta (e.g. Josh 23:4) and the Targums.[50]

18:24 ܪ‍ܒ‍ܐ ‍ ‍ ‍ 'And in the hour of distress He will not avert the face from you'; Gr καὶ καιρὸν ἐκδικήσεως ἐν ἀποστροφῇ προσώπου 'And of the time of vengeance, when He turns away His face' (cf. Deut 31:18, 32:20).[51]

21:27 ‍ ‍ ‍ 'When the fool curses him who has not sinned against him (he really curses himself)'; Gr ἐν τῷ καταρᾶσθαι ἀσεβῆ τὸν σατανᾶν 'When the godless curses his adversary'.

25:7 ‍ ‍ ‍ 'Nine things that I had not thought of I have praised, and ten that I have not said'[52]; Gr ἐννέα ὑπονοήματα ἐμακάρισα ἐν καρδίᾳ καὶ τὸ δέκατον ἐρῶ ἐπὶ γλώσσης 'Nine suppositions I called blessed in my heart and the tenth I will say with my tongue'. It seems that ܪܠܝ after ‍ is a secondary reading that enhanced the repetition of the ܪܠܝ after ‍, thus creating a strong parallelism between the two lines (cf. below, § 3.6).

31:12 ‍ ‍ '(If you sit at the table of a rich man, do not say) There is not enough for me!'; B ספוק עלי. B refers to the greedy thought 'I can take as much as I want, because there is enough', while Syr interprets it as an impolite complaint that there is not enough food on the table.

34:6 ‍ ‍ ‍ 'And if it is ordained from God (to err in the thoughts of the night, do not give them your heart)'. Instead of 'if', Gr has 'unless' (ἐὰν μή). According to Gr we should not pay heed to dreams unless they come from God, in Syr even misleading dreams may come from God, but should not be paid attention to.

---

[49] Cf. Edersheim, 'Ecclesiasticus', 150: 'The Syr. seems from its paraphrastic language to have had difficulty about this verse, and it inserts between the two clauses what reads like a later interpretation'.

[50] Weitzman, Syriac Version, 34; idem, From Judaism to Christianity, 59; Klein, 'Converse Translation'.

[51] Cf. Muraoka, Greek–English Lexicon, 61a; for ܪ‍ܒ‍ܐ ‍ as an equivalent of הסתיר פנים, see Borbone–Jenner, Concordance, 263–264.

[52] For our interpretation of ‍ ‍ ܪܠܝ as 'that I have not thought of' compare 11:5 ‍ ‍ ‍ ܪܠܝ; differently Calduch-Benages–Ferrer–Liesen, Sabiduria del Escriba, 166: '(There are) nine (things) which I have not praised in my heart'.

3.3 AVOIDANCE OF ANTHROPOMORPHISMS

Avoidance of anthropomorphisms is well-documented in Syr. The following categories can be distinguished:

(a) Addition of prepositions before references to God.

7:29 ܕܚܠ ܡܢ ܐܠܗܐ 'fear God!'; A פחד אל.

Sometimes ܩܕܡ 'before' or another preposition is inserted in a prepositional phrase.

7:4 ܡܢ ܩܕܡ ܐܠܗܐ 'from before God'; A מאל.[53]
11:15 ܡܢ ܠܘܬ ܡܪܝܐ 'from with the Lord'; A מײ 'from the Lord'.
39:5 ܡܢ ܩܕܡ ܐܠܗܐ 'from before the Lord'; Gr has two readings, one with πρός and one with ἔναντι.

Note also the preference for ܩܕܡ in the following contexts.

10:7 ܩܕܡ ܐܠܗܐ ܘܩܕܡ ܒܢܝܢܫܐ 'before God and before the people'; A לאדון ואנשים.
11:14 ܩܕܡ ܐܠܗܐ ܫܘܝܢ ܐܢܘܢ 'are equal before the Lord'; A מײ הוא 'are from the Lord'.
21:5 ܘܩܕܡ ܕܝܢܐ ܕܥܠܡܐ ܣܠܩܐ 'And it rises before the Judge of eternity'; Gr καὶ τὸ κρίμα αὐτοῦ κατὰ σπουδὴν ἔρχεται 'And his judgment comes quickly'.
35:15 ܩܕܡܘܗܝ 'Before Him (there is no partiality)'; B עמו 'with Him'.
35:21 ܘܩܕܡ ܡܪܝܐ ܕܪܒܘܬܐ ܥܐܠܐ '(The prayer enters) before the Lord of majesty'; B^{txt} ועד תגיע כי לא תנוח 'It does not rest till it reaches its goal'; B^{mg} ועד כי תגע לא תנוח; Gr καὶ ἕως συνεγγίσῃ, οὐ μὴ παρακληθῇ 'And till it draws near, he is not comforted'.

The phenomenon described here is common in the Peshitta and the Targums, but some features, such as the translation of מיהוה with ܡܢ ܩܕܡ ܡܪܝܐ, are less common in other parts of the Peshitta.[54] According to Weitzman the 'P[esh] shows a general tendency to emphasize the gulf between God and man. The preposition ܩܕܡ is often introduced as a buffer'.[55] However, as appears from the example in 10:7, the ad-

---

[53] Similarly 1:1 (cf. Gr); 15:9; 15:11; cf. 12:2 ܡܢ ܩܕܡ ܡܪܝܗ; A מײ; 16:17 ܡܢ ܩܕܡ ܡܪܝܐ; A+B מאל.

[54] Cf. Smend, *Index*, viii n. 1: 'Targumisch ist ferner das ständige ܡܢ ܩܕܡ ܡܪܝܐ (ܐܠܗܐ) für παρὰ κυρίου bezw. מיהוה, das ich in der Peshitta nur Ps. 37, 23, Prv. 20, 24, Job. 20, 29 finde. Häufig ist dagegen auch in der Peschitta ܨܠܝ ܩܕܡ ܡܪܝܐ für התפלל אל יהוה.'

[55] Weitzman, *Syriac Version*, 29.

dition of ܡܢ or another preposition is not restricted to contexts where the following noun refers to God.[56] It is questionable, therefore, whether this phenomenon is an anti-anthropomorphism at all.

(b) Replacement of references to God by references to the fear of God, etc.

> 28:23 ܕܐܠܗܐ ܕܕܚܠܬ '(who forsake) the fear of the Lord'; Gr κύριον 'the Lord'.[57]
>
> 32:13 ܫܡܗ ܕܐܠܗܐ '(bless) the name of God'; B+F עושׂךָ 'your Maker' (= Gr).
>
> 46:11 ܢܡܘܣܗ ܕܐܠܗܐ '(who did not turn from) the law of God'; B אל 'God'.

This tendency occurs also in Pesh-Chronicles,[58] but elsewhere in the Peshitta it is rare. In the Targums it is very common.[59] Even in this category, however, we cannot always be sure that all the examples can be ascribed to the Syriac translator.[60] Compare

> 32:14 ܦܘܠܚܢܗ ܕܐܠܗܐ ܕܒܥܐ 'who seeks the service of God'; B¹ דורש אל; B² דורש אל; B³ דורש חפצי אל. Where B¹ and B² have 'God', Syr has 'the service of God'. This agrees with the examples discussed above. In B³, however, there is a noun preceding 'God' also in Heb.

(c) Avoidance of references to God's ears, eyes, face and the like.

> 11:12 ܡܠܬܗ ܕܐܠܗܐ ܘܐܝܟ ܠܗ, 'The word of the Lord will be good to him'; A ועין יי צפתהו לטוב 'And the eye of the Lord watches over

---

[56] *Pace* Winter, *Ben Sira in Syriac*, 155–156; cf. Klein, 'Pseudo-Anti-Anthropomorphism'; Owens, 'Early Syriac Text of Ben Sira', 60–61 (on Sir 35:6); Maori, 'Peshitta Pentateuch and Pentateuchal Targums', 62; Van Keulen, 'Points of Agreement', 228–233 (§ 2.4); Van Keulen's discussion includes examples with ܕܚܠ (cf. Sir 7:29, quoted).

[57] 'Fear of God' is also one of the recurrent themes in GrII, cf. § 2.4.1; on דחלתא דיוי as a Targumic translation equivalent for the Tetragrammaton, see Van Keulen, 'Points of Agreement', 207.

[58] Weitzman, *Syriac Version*, 119–120; idem, *From Judaism to Christianity*, 248–249; 'Fear of the Lord' instead of 'the Lord' (cf. Sir 28:23) occurs in 1 Chr 29:18; 2 Chr 16: 9; 19:4.

[59] Cf. Van Keulen, 'Points of Agreement', 207, for a comparison between Targum Jonathan and the Peshitta of Kings.

[60] It is unlikely however, that all the examples quoted go back to a variant in the translator's Hebrew source text. As a consequence, it is incorrect to conclude that the source text read יראת יהוה etc. each time that the Syriac has ܕܚܠܬ ܐܠܗܐ etc.; *pace* Weber, 'Wisdom False and True', 355.

him for good' ('the eyes' also in Gr). Cf. Ps 18:25 MT עיניו; Targum
מימריה (but Pesh ܚܙܘܗܝ!).[61]

11:21 ܩܕܡ ܡܪܝܐ '(Because it is close) before the Lord' (i.e. 'it is in the
Lord's power'); A בעיני יי.

35:6 ܩܕܡܘܗܝ, '(Do not appear) before Him (empty-handed)'; Gr ἐν
προσώπῳ κυρίου 'in the presence of the Lord'.

35:16 ܨܠܘܬܗ ܕܡܣܟܢܐ, ܠܘܬܗ ܥܐܠܐ 'The prayer of the poor man enters before Him'; B לא ישא פנים אל דל 'He will not show partiality
(lit. raise his face) against the poor'.

This phenomenon is well attested in the Targums but not common in
the Peshitta. Bodily terms in relation to God did not in themselves
trouble the translators of the Peshitta,[62] although with Chronicles the
situation is different.[63] In this respect too Syr seems to be closer to the
Targums than to other parts of the Peshitta (cf. § 3.9).

(d) Avoidance of references to God's emotions. In some places Syr
omits a remark about God's anger. Compare e.g.

48:10 ܩܕܡ ܕܢܐܬܐ ܝܘܡܗ ܕܡܪܝܐ 'before the day of the Lord comes'; Gr
κοπάσαι ὀργὴν πρὸ θυμοῦ 'to calm the wrath (of God) before it
breaks out in fury'; B [...]להשבית אף לפנ 'to destroy wrath befor[e
...]'.[64]

(e) Replacement of active constructions in which God hears, sees and
the like, to passive constructions.[65]

16:18 ܒܓܠܝܢܗ ܕܥܠܝܗܘܢ 'at His revelation upon them'; A ברדתו עליהם
'when He descends upon them'. Compare Gen 11:5 MT ירד 'descends'; Targum Onqelos: יתגלי 'be revealed'; Pesh ܢܚܬ 'descends'.[66]
16:19 ܟܕ ܡܬܚܙܐ ܠܗܘܢ 'when He appears to them'; B בהביטו אליהם
'when He looks at them'.

---

[61] Cf. Smend, *Index*, viii n. 1; Rüger, *Text und Textform*, 113; but Rüger's sugges-
tion that Syr is dependent on the Targum to the Psalms is unlikely; on מימרא דיוי as a
Targumic translation equivalent for the Tetragrammaton, see Van Keulen, 'Points of
Agreement', 207.

[62] Weitzman, *Syriac Version*, 29; but cf. Williams, *Peshitta of 1 Kings*, 163–164,
on 'the avoidance of reference to a part of the body in connection with God' in Pesh-
1 Kings, where בעיני יהוה is translated with ܩܕܡ in each of its fourteen occurrences (cf. Sir 11:21, quoted above).

[63] Weitzman, *Syriac Version*, 119–120.

[64] Cf. Van Peursen 'Que vive celui qui fait vivre', 289.

[65] But note that the tendency to use the *passivum divinum* can also be observed in
Heb; cf. Macholz, 'Passivum Divinum', 249–250.

[66] Similarly Gen 11:7; 18:21 and others; cf. Rüger, *Text und Textform*, 113.

42:18, ‫ܡܘܬܗ‬ ... ‫ܘܟܠܗܘܢ ... ‏ ‫ܡܠܦ‬ 'and all the secrets of the people are revealed before Him like the sun'; B ‫ובכל‬ ‫מערומיהם יתבונן‬; M ‫ובמערמיהם יתבונן‬ 'and (all) their secrets He understands'.[67]

42:19, ‫ܡܘܬܗ‬ ... ‫ܡܠܦ‬ 'And everything that comes to the world is revealed before Him, those that are past and that are to come, and before Him all hidden things are revealed'; B(+M) ‫מחוה חליפות נהיות ומגלה חקר‬ ‫נסתרות‬ 'He makes known past and future things and reveals hidden secrets'. Two times the active construction in Heb has been rendered with a passive construction in Syr. By using the same construction twice, Syr introduces a repetitive parallelism.[68]

This is a significant characteristic of the Targums. In this respect Syr is closer to the Targums than to the Peshitta.[69]

(f) Avoiding typical human actions such as 'to stand'.

    17:23 ‫ܢܓܠ‬ 'He will reveal Himself'; Gr ἐξαναστήσεται 'He will rise up'. This is more than just an anti-anthropomorphism since it introduces the concept of God's revelation as judge; cf. § 2.4.2.

It can be concluded that Syr contains an anti-anthropomorphic tendency. In some respects Syr is closer to the Targums than to the rest of the Peshitta. However, in some of the examples quoted the qualification 'anti-anthropomorphism' is questionable. The use of ‫ܓܠܐ‬ may have a linguistic background and in 17:23 the notion of God's revelation as judge rather than the avoidance of anthropomorphisms may have motivated the reading in Syr.

3.4 MISINTERPRETATIONS OF THE HEBREW

In some cases Syr reflects a misunderstanding of the Hebrew source text. We can distinguish the following categories.

---

[67] Compare also the use of 'revealed before' in 17:15 ‫ܡܘܬܗ‬ ... ‫ܐܘܪܚܬܗܘܢ‬ 'and their ways are revealed before Him'; Gr αἱ ὁδοὶ αὐτῶν ἐναντίον αὐτοῦ 'their ways are before Him'.

[68] Cf. below, § 3.6; see also § 5.3 (3) for 'and everything that comes to the world'. Since the device to use a passive form is attested several times, we prefer an explanation in terms of translation technique to one in terms of a misinterpretation or misvocalization of ‫מגלה‬ as a passive; *pace* Lévi, *L'Ecclésiastique* I, 58.

[69] Cf. Van Keulen, 'Points of Agreement', 208.

(a) Confusion of homonymic roots or lexemes.[70]

19:27 ܡܢܝ ܠܐ ܟܪܐ (In the place where they do not know him) they call him upright'; Gr προφθάσει σε. As K. Weber has argued, Syr and Gr go probably back to a Hebrew text reading קרה / קרא[II] 'to meet, encounter'. Weber reconstructs קראך '(but in an unexpected place), he attacks you'. She thinks that the Syriac translator understood this verb as the Syriac ܩܪܐ 'to call', but it is also possible to think of the Hebrew קרא[I].[71]

20:3 ܡܣܬܒܚ 'praised'; Gr ὁ ἀνθομολογούμενος 'one who admits his fault'. Both Gr and Syr reflect a Hebrew source with מודה or מתודה,[72] but apparently the Syriac translator did not catch its proper, less common, meaning of 'to confess'.

22:18 ܨܖܝ ܘܚܡܪܐ 'a small bundle (on a high rock)'; Gr χάρακες ἐπὶ μετεώρου κείμενοι 'small stones lying on an open place'. Syr reflects צרור[I] 'bundle, parcel, bag' (1 Sam 25:29; cf. Sir 6:16 [A] צרור חיים); Gr reflects צרור[II] 'pebble' (2 Sam 17:13; Am 9:9).

25:15 ܠܝܠ ܖܫܐ ܕܚܘܝܐ ܡܢ ܪܝܫܐ ܕܡܪܝܪ 'There is no head more bitter than the head of a serpent'; similarly Gr οὐκ ἔστιν κεφαλὴ ὑπὲρ κεφαλὴν ὄφεως. Both versions reflect the misinterpretation of ראש as ראש[I] 'head' instead ראש[II] 'poison'.[73]

34:3 ܚܙܘܐ '(So is) a vision (and a dream of the night)'; Gr ὅρασις. According to Smend Syr and Gr reflect a misinterpretation of מראה 'mirror' as 'vision'.[74]

36:23 ܟܠ ܕܚܠܒܐ ܡܩܒܠܐ ܢܦܫܐ 'Every food the soul accepts'; ܢܦܫܐ seems to reflect a misinterpretation of נפש 'throat'; cf. B גרגרת; Gr κοιλία.

36:27 ܫܘܦܪܐ ܕܐܢܬܬܐ ܡܫܒܚ ܐܦܝܗ 'The beauty of a woman praises her face'. Syr derives יהלל (= B[mg]) from הלל[II] 'be boastful' (Qal), 'to praise' (Piel) instead of הלל[I] 'to make light up' (Qal, Hifil);[75] cf. Gr ἱλαρύνει 'gladdens'.[76]

---

[70] Sometimes the same confusion is found in Gr (see 20:3; 25:15; 34:3; 37:6), but in our view this does not indicate that Syr is dependent on Gr. Note that in other cases Syr and Gr reflect different interpretations, see § 2.3.3 (3).

[71] Weber, 'Wisdom False and True', 333, 344 n. 31; cf. Smend, *Jesus Sirach*, 179.

[72] Cf. Ps 79:13 MT נודה, Gr ἀνθομολογησόμεθα.

[73] BDB 912; *HALOT* 1167–1168. See also the discussion of this verse in § 5.1.

[74] Smend, *Jesus Sirach*, 305; compare his translation (*Jesus Sirach hebräisch und deutsch*, 58): 'Einander gleichen Spiegel und Traum: das Bild des Angesichts gegenüber dem Angesicht'; cf. *HALOT* 630–631.

[75] Cf. BDB 237; *HALOT* 248. In Isa 13:10 the MT has יָהֵל and 1QIs[a] יאירו.

[76] Margoliouth, 'Original Hebrew', 25; Ryssel, 'Fragmente', IV, 294; but as Margoliouth observes, the reading of Syr makes good sense, since ܡܫܒܚ can also mean 'decorate'; cf. Payne Smith, *Thesaurus* II, 4024.

37:6 ܒܚܡܝܘܢ 'in the neighbourhood'; Gr ἐν τῇ ψυχῇ σου 'in your soul';
B+D בקרב 'in the battle'. Syr and Gr misunderstood בקרב.[77]
37:11 ܡܚܝܘܗܝ, ܥܒܕܐ ܕܒܥܐ ܠܡܛܠܡ 'a slave who seeks to oppress his master'. ܠܡܛܠܡ reflects misinterpretation of עשק as עֹשֶׁק 'oppression'
instead of עשק, עסק 'business, occupation' (cf. 11:10, 40:1).

(b) Difficult Hebrew words that the Syriac translator did not under-stand.[78]

Indications that the Syriac translator did not understand the Hebrew
text is attested throughout the Peshitta.[79] However, their frequency in
Syr is remarkable.[80] This may be related to the linguistic character of
Heb. Gr too sometimes misinterprets Heb. According to Kister this
shows that Ben Sira was a linguistic virtuoso, who had a perfect
command of the Hebrew language. He used 'many rare words which
were incomprehensible to readers as early as two or three generations
after his time'.[81] However, the large number of misinterpretations is
not sufficiently accounted for by the linguistic nature of the Hebrew
text. They also indicate that the translator's knowledge of Hebrew was
limited.[82] Noteworthy are those cases where the Syriac translator of
Sirach seems to have misunderstood words that were interpreted correctly by the translators of other Biblical books.[83]

7:8 ܠܐ ܬܐܣܪ ܠܚܛܗܐ ܚܛܗܐ 'Do not repeat to commit sins'; A אל
תקשור לשנות חט 'Do not conspire to repeat sins'. Apparently the
Syriac translator did not understand תקשור.[84]
24:16 ܘܪܕܦܐ '(Like) an oleander (I fixed my roots)'; Gr τερέβινθος
'terebinth'. Syr is 'spectacularly wrong, introducing *rhodadaphnē*,

---

[77] Note the vocalization בְּקֶרָב in MS D, which reflects the same misinterpretation.
See further the discussion in Di Lella, *Hebrew Text of Sirach*, 75; ܚܡܝܘܢ may also be
an inner-Syriac corruption of ܒܚܡܘܬ; cf. Lévi, *L'Ecclésiastique* II, 18.
[78] Note that in this category there are no indications that the Syriac translator consulted a Greek text for these 'difficult passages'; cf. § 2.3.3 (3).
[79] Weitzman, *Syriac Version*, 36–48.
[80] But note that sometimes Syr gives a correct, 'forgotten' meaning; thus it has in
3:11 ܡܢ ܕܫܐܛ ܠ ܐܡܗ 'he who despises his mother' rather than 'he who curses his
mother' corresponding to A מקלל אמו; see § 2.2.3.
[81] Kister, 'Contribution', 310–311; see above, § 2.3.3 (3).
[82] Compare the other categories in the present paragraph and see § 6.2.2 (A).
[83] See especially the examples from 37:10 (חם), 38:30 (בער), 49:2 (חלה?), and
50:10 (גרגן). Note that the meaning of מרבק (cf. 38:26) seems to have been known to
the translator of Pesh-Jeremiah, but not to that of 1 Samuel and that of the Twelve
(see below).
[84] Smend, *Jesus Sirach*, 64. Modern interpreters are divided about the meaning of
קשר in this passage, see *HALOT* 1154.

the oleander, in a typical description of a wide-branching tree identified by Gr as the *terebinth*.'[85]

26:15 ܠܒܨܝܪܘܬ ܦܘܡܐ '(There is no weight) to paucity of the mouth'; C לצרורת פה 'the closing of the mouth'. 'Mouth' is probably euphemistic.[86]

37:10 ܒܣܢܐܟ '(Do not take counsel) with your enemy'; B עם חמיך 'with your father-in-law'; Gr τοῦ ὑποβλεπομένου σε 'him who looks at you'. According to Smend neither the translator of Syr nor that of Gr (who seems to have thought of the Aramaic root חמה) understood חמיך,[87] but note that its cognate does occur in Classical Syriac,[88] and is used for the translation of חם in Gen 38:13, 25; 1 Sam 4:19, 21.[89]

38:26 ܥܒܕܗ '(and his watching to complete) his work'; B מרבק 'fattening'. Perhaps the translator did not understand this word.[90]

38:30 ܠܡܒܢܐ ܐܬܘܢܗ 'to build his furnace'; Gr καθαρίσαι κάμινον 'to clean the furnace'. Syr is probably a wrong translation of לבער כבשן, which is a most likely reconstruction on the basis of Gr.[91]

49:2 ܐܬܛܫܝ ܡܢ ܢܣܝܘܢܐ 'He concealed himself from trials'. B נחל על משובתינו 'He grieved over our backslidings'. Apparently Syr did not understand Hebrew נחל, which should be interpreted as a Nifal of חלה (cf. Am 6:6 ולא נחלו על 'and they are not concerned about'; Pesh ܘܠܐ ܟܪܝܐ ܠܗܘܢ ܥܠ).[92]

50:8 ܘܐܝܟ ܫܒ̈ܠܐ ܕܚܩܠܐ 'and like the spikes of the field'; B כנצפענפי בימי מועד. Heb should probably be emended to read כנץ בענפי 'like the blossom on the branches…' or בענפים כנץ. Perhaps the Syriac translator did not understand the Hebrew or he had a Hebrew source text which, like the Geniza MS B, was corrupted.

---

85 Skehan–Di Lella, *Wisdom of Ben Sira*, 456.

86 Thus Skehan–Di Lella, *Wisdom of Ben Sira*, 350; they refer to 26:12 'the adulterous wife whose womb is opened to every man' and צרורת in 2 Sam 20:3; cf. *HALOT* 1058.

87 Thus Smend, *Jesus Sirach*, 329.

88 Cf. Payne Smith, *Thesaurus* I, 1300.

89 The interpretation of this verse is difficult; cf. Kister, 'Contribution', 342.

90 Cf. 1 Sam 28:24 MT עגל מרבק, Pesh ܥܓܠܐ ܡܦܛܡ. Here too the Syriac translator was perhaps unsure about the meaning of מרבק and therefore choose a word that reflected three of the four consonants in Hebrew (thus Morrison, *First Book of Samuel*, 92–93); see further Jer 46:21 MT עגלי מרבק; Pesh ܥܓܠܐ ܕܦܛܡܐ; Am 6:4 MT עגלים מתוך מרבק; Pesh ܥܓܠܐ ܡܢ ܓܘ ܒܩܪܐ; Mal 3:20 MT עגלי מרבק; Pesh ܥܓܠܐ ܕܒܩܪܐ.

91 Cf. 27:5 and see Van Peursen, *Verbal System*, 253–254. Despite its wide range of meanings, בער does not seem to have posed a problem to the translators of other parts of the Peshitta; compare the Syriac equivalents listed in the Hebrew–Syriac index in Borbone–Jenner, *Concordance*, 947.

92 Thus Skehan–Di Lella, *Wisdom of Ben Sira*, 541; Cowley–Neubauer, *Original Hebrew*, 41; Gesenius–Buhl, *Handwörterbuch*, 232a; Gr seems to have been confused by נחל as well (Skehan–Di Lella, ibid.). The reading ܐܫܬܛܝ 'he misbehaved himself' or 'he was considered foolish' in 7a1 is an error.

50:10 ܘܐܝܟ ܙܝܬܐ ܗܕܝܪܐ ܕܪ̈ܘܪܒܢ ܣܘܟ̈ܘܗܝ ‘and like a splendid olive tree with many branches’; B כזית רענן מלא גרגר ‘like a luxuriant olive tree full of berries’. Perhaps the Syriac translator did not understand ‘גרגר’, which is a *hapax legomenon* in the Hebrew Bible (Isa 17:6; here Pesh translates גרגרים with ܙܝܬܝܢ).

(c) Syr reflects a wrong vocalization of the Hebrew consonantal text.[93]

1:20e ܘܡܢܝܢ ܟܠ ܬܫܒ̈ܚܬܗ ܕܡܪܝܐ ‘And they count all the praises of the Lord’; ܡܢܝܢ seems to reflect a wrong interpretation of יספר ‘they tell’ (Piel).[94]
4:15 ܢܕܘܢ ܫܪܪܐ ‘He will judge in truth’; A ישפט אמת; ܫܪܪܐ reflects אֱמֶת, which is supported by the defective spelling in MS A, but Gr has the preferable reading ‘nations’ (ἔθνη), reflecting אֻמּוֹת (cf. Gen 25:16).
49:15 ܘܐܡܐ ܐܝܟ ܝܘܣܦ ܠܐ ܝܠܕܬ ‘And a mother did not bear like Joseph’; B כיוסף אם נולד גבר: Syr reflects אֵם ‘mother’ instead of אִם ‘if’ (i.e. ‘not’).

The confusion of רֵעַ ‘friend’ and רַע ‘evil’ occurs in the following cases.[95]

12:10 ܚܒܪܗ ‘companion’ reflects רֵעוֹ, instead of A’s רועו (= Gr ἡ πονηρία αὐτου).[96]
13:21 ܡܢ ܒܝܫ ܠܒܝܫ ‘from evil to evil’ agrees with A; but Gr has ὑπὸ φίλων ‘(thrust away) by his friends’, which reflects the preferable reading רֵעַ instead of רַע.
14:14 ܘܪܓܬܐ ܣܢܝܬܐ ܠܐ ܬܪܓ ‘And do not desire a hateful desire’; A[1] ובהלקח אח אל תעבר ‘And do not transgress when (your) brother is taken away’; A[2] וחמוד רע אל תחמוד ‘And do not desire a desirable thing of your neighbour’. A[2] is a reduplication of A[1] with רע (= רֵעַ) as an alternative for אח.[97] Syr reflects רַע instead of רֵעַ.

---

[93] Cf. Weitzman, *Syriac Version*, 20. This category is related to that mentioned under (a), but includes also examples in which words from completely different roots have the same consonants in at least one of their realizations (cf. 4:15; 49:15) and examples in which different stem formations from the same root are confused (cf. 1:20e).
[94] According to Smend this shows that the passage in 1:20a-l, which has no parallel in the other textual witnesses, derives from a Hebrew source; see Smend, *Jesus Sirach*, 14; Segal, ‘Evolution’, 111; Kearns, *Expanded Text*, 191; Böhmisch, ‘Haec omnia liber vitae’, 175; *pace* Calduch-Benages, ‘Sirácida 1’; Calduch-Benages–Ferrer–Liesen, *Sabiduría del Escriba*, 50.
[95] In 19:17 ܐܟܣ ܠܒܝܫܐ ‘Reprove someone who is evil’ Syr reflects the correct interpretation of רע whereas Gr misinterprets it as ‘a friend’; similarly in 37:4.
[96] Apparently this word was spelled without *mater lectionis* in the Syriac translator’s source text; cf. § 2.2.2.
[97] Cf. Van Peursen, *Verbal System*, 237.

37:3 ܣܢܐܐ ܘܒܥܠ 'The enemy and the wicked (why were they created?)'; B+D 'Alas! an intimate; he says, Why was I thus formed?'
Syr reflects רֵעַ instead of רָע (cf. Bmg ריע).

(d) Syr renders a Hebrew word according to its meaning in Syriac or
another form of Aramaic.

This phenomenon occurs a number of times in the Peshitta.[98] It is also
well-known from the Septuagint.[99] The examples from Syr are rare
and doubtful.[100]

13:26 ܣܓܝܐܘܬ ܡܡܠܐ 'much talking'; A ושיג ישיח (read ושיג ושיח).
Perhaps the Syriac translator thought of Syriac ܡܡܠܐ when he
found שיג in his source text.[101]

14:26 ܘܢܣܐܡ ܐܝܕܘܗܝ ܠ ܣܘܟܗ̈ 'and who lays his hands on her
boughs'; A וישים קנו בעופיה 'and who builds his nest in her foliage'.[102] Syr is difficult.[103] Smend suggests that the Syriac translator
thought of Syriac ܣܘܟܐ 'a high branch, tree-top',[104] while the Hebrew עוֹף means 'foliage'.[105] However, if Smend's explanation is
correct, one wonders why the Syriac translator did not use ܣܘܟܐ.

36:31 ܠܓܕܝܐ ܘܕܡܐ ܠܛܠܝܐ '(For who will believe) a boy who resem-
bles a deer'; B+D בגדוד צבא 'in an armed band'; C בצבא גדוד.
Apparently the Syriac translator understood גדוד in the sense of
Syriac ܓܕܝܐ.[106]

40:17 ܒܙܒܢܐ 'in time'; M כעד 'like eternity'; Gr ὡς παράδεισος 'like
Paradise'. Gr reflects כעדן. Smend suggests that the Syriac translator
read בעדן and interpreted it from Aramaic.[107] However, it is also
possible to consider ܒܙܒܢܐ as a free rendering of a Hebrew reading
such as that in MS M.

---

[98] Cf. Weitzman, *Syriac Version*, 37; idem, *From Judaism to Christianity*, 62.

[99] See Joosten, 'Aramaising renderings'; see also above, our remark on Gr 37:10.

[100] In 13:26 and 36:31 an alternative explanation is possible, namely that the
Syriac translator tried to imitate the form of the Hebrew; on this phenomenon see
Weitzman, *From Judaism to Christianity*, 62; Albrektson, *Lamentations*, 60–61; Mor-
rison, *First Book of Samuel*, 92–93; Greenberg, *Jeremiah*, 23.

[101] Cf. Taylor, 'Wisdom of Ben Sira', 623.

[102] For שים + קנו cf. Num 24:21; Ob 4; Hab 2:9.

[103] Cf. Edersheim, 'Ecclesiasticus', 87: 'But, manifestly, it is impossible to make
any good sense out of the Syr. Version'. ܐܝܕܘܗܝ can be explained in three ways: Either
it is an inner-Syriac corruption of ܝܠܕܘܗܝ 'his children' (Smend) or it reflects Hebrew
ידיו instead of ילדיו, or it is the result of a transposition of ܠ ܐܝܕܗ / κατὰ χεῖρας αὐτῆς
from 14:25 (Edersheim).

[104] *CSD* 406.

[105] Cf. Dan 4:9, 11, 18; Smend, *Jesus Sirach*, 139.

[106] Cf. Margoliouth, 'Original Hebrew', 26; Ryssel, 'Fragmente', V, 549–550; Di
Lella, *Hebrew Text of Sirach*, 70.

[107] Smend, *Jesus Sirach*, 376.

42:12 ܠܟܠ ܒܪܢܫ ܠܐ ܬܓܠܐ ܡܐ ܕܒܠܒܟ 'Do not reveal to every man what is in your heart'; M לכל זכר אל תבן תאר 'Let her not reveal her beauty to any man'; B לכל זכר אל תתן תאר. Syr related the word תאר to the Syriac word ܬܐܪܬܐ 'mind, consciousness'.[108]

(e) Syr reflects a wrong division into sense units.[109]

13:15 ܒܪܢܫܐ ܠܐܢܫܐ ܕܕܡܐ ܠܗ ܡܢ ܟܠ ܒܣܪ ܠܘܬܗ 'Man (loves) him who is like him more than any other flesh'; A וכל אדם את הדומה לו מין כל בשר אצלו 'And every man (loves) him who is like him. (16) The kind of all flesh is with it'. Syr 'from' reflects a misinterpretation of a defectively spelled מן as 'from' instead of 'sort' (= מין).[110] As a consequence of this misreading, two cola have been contracted.[111]

42:20–21 ܘܠܐ ܟܣܐ ܡܢ ܩܕܡܘܗܝ، ܟܠ ܪܐܙ ܓܒܪܘܬܐ ܘܚܟܡܬܐ ܩܕܡܘܗܝ، ܡܩܝܡܐ ܠܥܠܡ 'And not any secret of strength is concealed from Him. (21) And wisdom stands before Him for ever'; B^txt ולא חלפו כל דבר ג[בורת חכמ]תו תכן 'And not any thing escapes Him. (21) The st[rength of his wis]dom is steadfast'; B^mg חלף מנו כ׳ דבר and גבורות; M ול[א] עב[ר]ו כל דבר and (on a new line) [...גבורת חכמ[תו; Gr οὐκ ἐκρύβη ἀπ' αὐτοῦ οὐδὲ εἷς λόγος (21) τὰ μεγαλεῖα τῆς σοφίας αὐτοῦ ἐκόσμησεν 'Not any word is hidden from Him. (21) The greatness of his wisdom He has arranged'. Syr joins ܓܒܪܘܬܐ to the end of v. 20 instead of the beginning of v. 21.[112]

43:8 ܝܪܚܐ ܐܝܟ ܫܡܗ ܐܝܬܘܗܝ، ܘܡܬܪܒܐ ܡܪܘܪܒܐܝܬ ܒܫܘܚܠܦܐ 'The new moon is like its name, and it becomes great exceedingly in the season'; M חדש כשמו הוא מת[חדש] 'Like its name the new moon renews itself'; B חדש בחדשו הוא מתחדש מה נורא בהשתנותו; Gr μὴν κατὰ τὸ ὄνομα αὐτῆς ἐστιν αὐξανόμενος θαυμαστῶς ἐν ἀλλοιώσει 'the moon is like its name; it increases considerably in its changing'. Gr and Syr reflect an interpunction after הוא, perhaps because they did not understand the play on words.[113]

---

[108] Thus Owens, Review of Nelson, *Syriac Version*, 167.

[109] See the studies on unit delimitation in Syriac manuscripts mentioned in § 7.1, note 7; for the study of the delimitation markers of smaller see also the studies mentioned in § 8.8, note 23.

[110] On traces of defective spellings see also § 2.2.2.

[111] Note that in 13:16b Syr has ܠܓܢܣܗ corresponding to A מינו.

[112] On this verse see also § 4.6.

[113] Cf. Skehan–Di Lella, *Wisdom of Ben Sira*, 489: 'The reading of M and B^mg receives support from Gr and Syr, though these versions apparently had difficulty in rendering the Heb play on words'; see also § 2.3.2. Compare the retention of a play on words in 34:21 ܕܒܚܘܬܗܘܢ ܕܥܘܠܐ ܕܥܘܠܐ ܐܢܝܢ 'The sacrifices of the unrighteous are of iniquity' (thus Peters, *Ben Sirach*, 286) and the introduction of one in 8:15 ܥܡ ܓܒܪܐ ܩܫܝܐ ܠܐ ܬܐܙܠ ܒܐܘܪܚܐ ܕܠܡܐ ܢܩܫܐ ܒܝܫܬܟ 'Do not travel with a hard man, lest he makes hard your evil' (cf. Ryssel, 'Fragmente', VI, 247).

44:4d–5a ܘܫܠܝܛܢܐ ܒܨܘ ܒܬܫܒܚܬܗܘܢ ܥܠ ܐܝܕܝ ܩܝܬܪܐ ܘܟܢܪܐ 'and rulers explored in their praise upon the hands of the harps and the lyres'; B ומושלים במשמחותם (5) חוקרי מזמור על חוק; B[mg] חקו ; M משלים במ[...] (5) חקרי מזמור על קו. Syr does not reflect במשמרותם in 4d and merges 4d with 5a.

46:10–11 ܕܫܠܡ ܢܡܘܣܗ ܕܐܠܗܐ ܘܕܝܢܘܗܝ܆ ܓܒܪ ܓܒܪ ܒܫܡܗ ܟܠ ܕܠܐ ܛܥܐ ܠܒܗܘܢ '...that he had fulfilled God's law and His judgments. Each man in his name, whose heart did not err'[114]; B כי טוב אחרי ײ למלא והשופטים איש בשמו כל אשר לא נשא לבו '...that it is good to follow wholly after the Lord. (11) The judges, each one by his name, every one who did not deceive his heart'. Syr reflects והמשפטים instead of והשופטים and connects it to the preceding line.

The division of the text has an impact beyond clause or even verse level. It may affect the clause hierarchy of a complete passage and result in a textual structure that is completely different from that in Heb or Gr.[115]

3.5 OTHER DIFFERENCES WITH THE HEBREW AND THE GREEK

The differences between Syr and the other versions are considerable. In the preceding paragraph we have seen cases where difficulties or ambiguities in the Hebrew text may have caused misinterpretations. Other readings rather reflect freedom, negligence, and thoughtlessness. The following examples are only a very small selection from innumerable free, sometimes even imprecise or wrong renderings.[116]

2:17 ܘܕܫܒܩ ܠܗ ܡܚܒܠ ܪܥܝܢܗ 'And he who forsakes Him destroys his mind'; Gr καὶ ἐνώπιον αὐτοῦ ταπεινώσουσιν τὰς ψυχὰς αὐτῶν 'And they humble themselves before him'.

5:8 ܢܥܕܪܘܢܟ '(because they will not) help you (on the day of distress)'; A יועילו 'profit'.

6:12 ܢܐܙܠ ܘܢܬܛܫܐ 'He will go and conceal himself'; A יסתר 'hide'.

[114] ܒܫܡܗ not in 7a1.

[115] See the discussion on the Praise of the Fathers in Chapter 27.

[116] Compare Smend's qualifications of the readings in Syr: *ganz abweichend* (2:17), *verflachend* (5:8), *erweiternd* (6:12), *schlecht* (8:16, 22:5, 45:3, 48:25), *korrigierend* (9:15, 35:24), *unrichtig* (24:23–25), *übertreibend* (35:13), *ungenau* (38:10) and *steigernd* (39:27). If we say that the interpretation reflected in Syr is wrong, we mean that it differs from our modern understanding; cf. Weitzman, *From Judaism to Christianity*, 56–57: 'There are passages where modern scholarship would not accept those identifications, but the translators may still have been following what for them was the plain sense'.

9:15 ܓܕ̈ܫܠ ܠܐܠܗܐ 'one who fears God'; A נבון.

13:23 ܘܟܠܗܘܢ ܨܠܝ 'and they all give ear'; A הכל נסכתו 'all are silent'.

22:5 ܐܒܘܗ ܘܐܡܗ 'her father and her mother'; Gr πατέρα καὶ ἄνδρα 'her father and her husband'.

35:24 ܠܒܝ̈ܫܐ and ܚܣ̈ܝܐ, ܠܥ̈ܒܕܝ 'ܛ (till He returns to) the wicked (their reward, and to) the doers of the iniquity (their reflections)'; B לאנוש and גמול אדם.

38:10 ܫܘ̈ܩܪܐ 'falsehood'; B מהכר פנים 'partiality'.

45:3 ܘܐܩܝܡܗ ܩܕܡ ܡܠܟܐ 'And He placed him (i.e. Moses) before the king'; B ויחזקהו 'and he sustained him'.

48:25 ܟܕ ܗܘܐ ܒܥܠܡܐ 'and when he was in the world'; B עד עולם 'for ever'.

Compare further the following shortening readings.

24:9 ܡܢ ܩܕܡ ܥܠܡܐ 'from before the ages'; Gr πρὸ τοῦ αἰῶνος ἀπ' ἀρχῆς 'before the ages, from the first'.

38:9 ܒܪܝ ܐܦ ܒܟܘ̈ܪܗܢܟ ܩܕܡ ܐܠܗܐ 'My son, also in your disease pray before God'; B בני בחולי אל תתעבר התפלל אל אל 'My son, in your disease do not tarry; pray to God'.

50:16 ܒܩܪ̈ܢܬܐ 'on the horns'; B בחצרות מקשה; cf. § 9.2.

51:9 ܘܨܠܝܬ 'and I prayed'; B ומשערי שאול שועתי 'and from the gates of Sheol I called for help'. Perhaps the Syriac translator wished to avoid the expression 'the gates of Sheol'.[117]

Sometimes Syr weakens the purport of a passage.

11:12 ܡܢ ܚܦܝ̈ܐ ܘܡܢ ܩܛܡܐ '(And He will deliver him) from dust and ashes'; A מעפר צחנה 'from stinking dust'.

37:8 ܡܢ ܡܠܘܟܐ ܠܐ ܟܐܢܐ 'Be on your guard against an *unrighteous* adviser'; B(+D) מיועץ שמור נפשך.[118]

In other cases Syr strengthens it.[119]

35:13 ܪܒܘ ܪܒܘ̈ܢ 'ten thousand times ten thousand'; B שבעתים 'seventy times'.

39:27 ܠܠܘ̈ܛܬܐ '(But for the wicked they are turned) to a curse'; B לרעה 'to evil'.

The free and negligent renderings and translation or transmission errors sometimes result in a Syriac text that is hard to understand.

12:16 ܒܣ̈ܦܘܬܗ ܪܡܙ ܣ̈ܢܐܐ 'The enemy makes a sign with his lips'. We would expect that one signs with the eyes or the fingers. Cf. A בשפתיו יתהמהם צר 'The adversary speaks gently with his lips'.[120]

---

[117] Cf. Smend, *Jesus Sirach*, 500.

[118] Cf. § 4.1 (2) on 25:21 'Be not enticed by the beauty of an *evil* woman'.

[119] Cf. Smend: *übertreibend* (35:13), *steigerd* (39:27).

27:15 ܘܕܐܫܕ ܕܡܐ ܨܐܬ ܡ̈ܠܐ ܕܥܘܠܐ 'And he who sheds blood gives ear to the words of the unrighteous'.[121]

29:18 ܘܫܒܩܘ ܩܢܝܢܝܗܘܢ ܐܝܟ ܓ̈ܠܠܐ ܕܝܡܐ 'And they abandoned their possessions like waves of the sea'.[122]

37:2 ܕܠܐ ܡܛܐ ܥܕܡܐ ܠܡܘܬܐ '(A friend) who does not arrive to death'; cf. B+D 'Is it not a sorrow bringing near to death, a friend who is like oneself turning into an enemy'.[123]

39:11 ܐܢ ܨܒܐ ܒܐܠܦ ܢܫܬܒܚ ܘܐܢ ܢܫܬܘܩ ܒܥܡܐ ܙܥܘܪܐ 'If he wants, he will be praised among thousand, and if he is silent among a small people'; cf. Gr ἐὰν ἐμμείνῃ, ὄνομα καταλείψει ἢ χίλιοι, καὶ ἐὰν ἀναπαύσηται, ἐκποιεῖ αὐτῷ 'If he lives long he will leave a name more than a thousand, and if he dies he makes it complete'.

49:6 ܘܐܚܪܒܘ ܟܠܗܝܢ ܚܘܪ̈ܒܬܗ 'They made desolate all its ruins'. We expect 'ruins' as the result, rather than the object of destruction; cf. B ארחתיה.

50:11 ܒܡܣܒܗ ܠܡܣܒܠ ܬܫܒ̈ܚܬܐ 'When he came out to take up songs of praise'; cf. B בעלותו על מזבח הוד 'when he ascended the glorious altar'; Gr ἐν ἀναβάσει θυσιαστηρίου ἁγίου 'when he ascended the holy altar'.[124]

3.6 POETIC FEATURES

Heb is a highly poetic text. It is a continuation of Biblical Hebrew poetry, although it also contains some unique and innovative features.[125] Some of the poetic features got lost in the Syriac translation. The succinct style of the Hebrew with a consistent division into bicola and a relatively consistent length of individual cola,[126] had to make way for more expanded expressions in the translation. Other poetic features of the Hebrew text were retained, but we are often not sure whether or not the translator made a conscious attempt to retain poetic features. Still other phenomena cannot be explained directly from the Hebrew source text and are the work of the Syriac translator.

---

[120] Cf. Kister, 'Contribution', 325.

[121] Cf. Edersheim, 'Ecclesiasticus', 141: 'Syr. text is here confused, and seems corrupt'.

[122] Cf. Owens, 'Early Syriac Text of Ben Sira', 55–56.

[123] Di Lella, *Hebrew Text of Sirach*, 74.

[124] See also § 1.3 on ܒܡܣܒܗ, which is probably an inner-Syriac corruption of ܒܡܣܩܗ 'when he ascended'.

[125] See Reymond, *Innovations in Hebrew Poetry* (cf. our review in *Review of Biblical Literature*).

[126] Cf. Reymond, *Innovations in Hebrew Poetry*, 85–89.

The most prominent poetic features in Syr are parallelism and repetition. Repetition of words or phrases often occurs in places where Heb has different words.[127] In earlier literature such repetitions were often described as scribal errors and 'influence of adjacent lines'.[128] However, it is equally possible that the repetitions were established on purpose. From the perspective of translation technique this phenomenon can be described as 'a tendency to level the vocabulary over an extended section'.[129] From a literary perspective it can be described as a literary device to strengthen the cohesion of a textual unit. Repetition of words in parallel lines is one of the characteristics of the Aramaic-Syriac poetic tradition.[130] Both perspectives can be combined, because they share the understanding of the repetitions as an intended element in Syr rather than the result of errors. Compare the following examples.

8:1–2   ܠܐ ܬܐܬܐ ܓܒܪ ܥܡ ܓܒܪܐ ܕܥܫܝܢ ܡܢܟ ܕܠܡܐ ܬܦܠ ܒܐܝܕܘܗܝ،

ܠܐ ܬܐܬܐ ܓܒܪ ܥܡ ܕܐܝܬ ܠܗ ܕܗܒܐ ܕܠܡܐ ܢܬܩܘܠ ܬܩܘܠܟ

'Do not converse with someone who is stronger than you, lest you fall in his hands.

Do not converse with someone who possesses gold, lest he weighs out your weight'.

Syr repeats ܬܐܬܐ where A has תריב and תחרש respectively.

8:12–13   ܠܐ ܬܐܙܦ ܠܡܢ ܕܥܫܝܢ ܡܢܟ (...)

ܠܐ ܬܥܪܒ ܠܡܢ ܕܥܫܝܢ ܡܢܟ

'Do not lend to someone who is stronger than you (...)

Do not become surety to someone who is stronger than you'.

Syr has two times ܠܡܢ ܕܥܫܝܢ where A has חזק ממך and יתר ממך respectively.[131]

---

[127] The opposite phenomenon, the tendency to increase variation (cf. Weitzman, *Syriac Version*, 93), occurs far less often. An example is 32:17–18 where ܒܪܢܫܐ ܒܪܢܫܐ (...) ܥܬܝܪܐ corresponds to B[txt] איש חכם ... איש חכם (B[mg]+F איש חמס). But in this example 7a1 repeats ܒܪܢܫܐ!

[128] Cf. below, § 3.7.1; thus, for example, the commentaries of Smend and Peters on many of the examples given below. In his discussion of this phenomenon in Lamentations, Albrektson ascribes this phenomenon to the translator's 'poor vocabulary and lack of synonyms' (*Lamentations*, 211); contrast the positive evaluation of repetition and its rhetorical effect in Greenberg, *Jeremiah*, 49–51.

[129] Weitzman, *Syriac Version*, 411; Weitzman discusses the repetition of ܐܫܬܘܚܪ in Psalms 35–39, used as an equivalent for no less than six different Hebrew words.

[130] Cf. Greenfield, 'Early Aramaic Poetry', 47; see also Van Staalduine-Sulman, *Targum of Samuel*, 706, on the use of repetitive parallelism instead of synonymous parallelism.

18:20–21

'Before distress reaches you, pray (...)
Before you stumble pray and seek (...)'.

Syr repeats ܪܠ where Gr has ἐξέταζε σεαυτόν 'scrutinize yourself'
and ταπεινώθητι 'humble yourself'.

22:13

'Keep your distance from him lest he grieves you, and let him not de-
file you (...)
Keep your distance from him and you will find rest, and let him not
weary you (...)'.

Syr repeats ܐܝܢܝ ܡܢܗ where Gr has φύλαξαι ἀπ' αὐτοῦ 'beware of
him' and ἔκκλινον ἀπ' αὐτοῦ 'avoid him'.

24:32–33

'Again, I will say my instruction in the morning (...)
Again, I will say my instruction in prophecy (...)'.

Syr repeats ܐܡܪ; Gr has φωτιῶ 'enlighten'[132] and ἐκχεῶ 'pour out'.

36:4

'As you have sanctified Yourself in us before their eyes,
so before our eyes sanctify Yourself in them'.

Syr has ܐܬܩܕܫܬ and ܐܬܩܕܫ where B has נקדשת and הכבד.

38:2–3

'From God the physician becomes wise,
and from kings he receives gifts.
Because of the intelligence of the physician they exalt him,
and they make him stand before kings'.

Syr repeats ܡܠܟܐ where B has מלך and נדיבים. This reinforces the
repetitive character of these verses created by the repetition of רופא /
ܐܣܝܐ.

47:2

'For as the fat parts were lifted up from holy offerings,
so David was lifted up from Israel'.

The second ܪܡ is an addition in Syr.

---

[131] According to Peters (Ben Sirach, 79), the understanding of יתר ממך in 8:13 as
referring to a person may be due to the parallelism with 8:12; Gr ὑπὲρ δύναμίν σου
'beyond your strength' reflects and adverbial interpretation.

[132] Reflecting אאיר instead אמר, which is reflected in Syr; cf. § 2.2.2.

The repetition strengthens an antithetic parallelism in

20:7   ܘ[Syriac]

'A wise man observes the time,
but an insolent and unrighteous man does not observe the time'.
Syr repeats [Syriac]; Gr has σιγήσει ἕως καιροῦ 'is silent till the right moment' and ὑπερβήσεται καιρόν 'passes over the right moment'.

The parallelism includes a chiastic structure in

39:9   (...) [Syriac]

'And in the world his name will not be forgotten, (...)
and his name will not be forgotten from generation to generation'.
In the second line Syr has [Syriac] instead of Gr ζήσεται 'will live'.

In other cases the repetition structures a larger textual unit.[133] Thus in 1:14 and 1:16 Syr has 'in the beginning of' where Gr has different readings. The result is a threefold repetition of the same saying in 1:14–18.

(14) The beginning of wisdom is the fear of the Lord ([Syriac]), and with the faithful it is created from their mothers' womb (...)
(16) The beginning of wisdom is the fear of the Lord ([Syriac]) and with goodness she satiates from the multitude of her fruits (...)
(18) The beginning of wisdom is the fear of the Lord ([Syriac]) and she is multiplying peace and life and cure.

In 31:5–9 [Syriac] 'Mammon, riches' and [Syriac] 'to go astray' are repeated several times. They correspond to various Hebrew equivalents.[134]

(5) He who loves Mammon ([Syriac]; B חרוץ) will not be blameless, and he who pursues after possession will be led astray ([Syriac]; B ישגה) by it.
(6) For there are many who were rich and who relied upon their possessions and they were not able to deliver themselves from evil or to

---

[133] The repetition of key words is also well-attested in the Targum of Samuel; see Van Staalduine-Sulman, *Targum of Samuel*, 67.

[134] A similar repetition of a key word occurs in the poem about true and false wisdom in 19:20–30, where the Syriac root [Syriac] occurs six times; cf. Weber, 'Wisdom False and True', 333; Weber speaks of Syr's 'overfrequent use' of [Syriac].

save themselves on the day of their end.

(7) Because Mammon (ܡܡܘܢܐ; B הוא) is a stumbling-block for the fool, and everyone who goes astray (ܛܥܐ; B פותה) through it will stumble.

(8) Blessed the rich one who is found blameless (ܕܠܐ ܡܘܡܐ! B תמים) and who has not gone astray (ܛܥܐ; B נלוז) after Mammon (ܡܡܘܢܐ; B ממון).

(9) Who is he? That we may praise him, for he has performed many miracles among his people.

(10) Who is he? That we may cling to him and he has peace and it is for him to an honour. Who could go astray (ܠܡܛܥܐ; B לסור), but did not go astray (ܛܥܐ; B סר), harm to his neighbour, but did not harm?

In 34:10–12 ܢܣܐ Pael occurs three times, corresponding to three different words in Gr. The effect of the repetition is an antithetic parallelism and a close connection between the verses.

(10) He who does not put to the test (ܕܠܐ ܢܣܝ) knows little;
(11) but he who puts to the test (ܘܢܣܝ) multiplies his wisdom;
(12) I have seen much when I put to the test (ܢܣܝܬ), many things have befallen me.

In the Praise of the Fathers the remark that God swore an oath is repeated three times:

44:18 'He swore to him (i.e. Noah) oaths in truth (ܡܘܡܬܐ ܕܩܘܫܬܐ ܠܗ ܒܩܘܫܬܐ) that He would not destroy all flesh.'[135]

44:21 'Therefore God swore to him (i.e. Abraham) with oaths (ܒܡܘܡܬܐ ܝܡܐ ܠܗ ܐܠܗܐ) that in his descendants all nations of the world would be blessed.'

45:24 'Therefore God swore to him with oaths (ܒܡܘܡܬܐ ܝܡܐ ܠܗ ܐܠܗܐ) that he would build an altar for Him and that to him and his descendants should belong the high priesthood forever.'

Sometimes the repetition of lexemes creates a repetitive parallelism between two lines that are only loosely related in the source text.[136] Compare

7:2   ܐܪܚܩ ܡܢ ܒܝܫܬܐ
                                         ܘܬܬܪܚܩ ܡܢܟ

'Keep far (ܐܪܚܩ) from evil
and it will turn away (ܘܬܬܪܚܩ) from you'.

---

[135] Reiterer, Urtext, 91, assumes that the Syriac translator read בברית (instead of B's באות) in his Hebrew source.
[136] See also our comment on 42:19 discussed above, § 3.3 (e).

Heb (A) has ויט (...) הרחק. The effect of the repetition of a form of ܢܗܝ in Syr creates a contrast between 'you far from evil' and 'evil far from you'.[137]

In most cases discussed in this paragraph Syr changes a synonymous parallelism into a repetitive parallelism. The example from 7:2 is one of the very few cases where Syr creates a new parallelism that is not present in Heb.[138] An antithetic (non-repetitive) parallelism has been created in

37:4   ܪܚܡܐ ܠܦܬܘܪܐ ܪܚܝܒ ܐܝܢܐ ܒܝܫ
              ܘܒܥܕܢ ܐܘܠܨܢܐ ܡܢ ܩܕܡ ܩܐܡ

'Evil is the friend who is close to the table,
and in the time of distress he stands aloof'.

The free rendering of מביט על שלחן in the first line creates a contrast between ܪܚܝܒ 'close' and ܡܢ ܩܕܡ 'aloof'.

We can conclude that parallelism and repetition are the most prominent poetic features of Syr. Parallelism occurs mostly under the influence of the Hebrew source text, whereas repetition is most often due to the translator's treatment of lexical variation in his source.

3.7 INFLUENCE OF OTHER PASSAGES IN SIRACH

3.7.1 *Influence of adjacent lines*

In our discussion of repetition we observed the phenomenon that in Syr repetition of words or phrases occurs often in places where Heb or Gr has different words. In addition to the examples mentioned in § 3.6, we can mention the following cases.

3:13 ܚܝܘܗܝ ܝܘܡܝ ܟܠ '(And do not put him to shame) all the days of his life' (= Heb [A]!) comes from 3:12 (ܚܝܝܟ ܝܘܡܝ ܟܠ); Gr ἐν πάσῃ ἰσχύι σου 'in all your strength' (i.e. if you have still all your strength)'. Since the reading found in Syr occurs also in Heb, it is unlikely that the repetition is due to the Syriac translator.

14:17 ܕܥܠܡܐ ܘܕܪܐ 'And the generations of eternity (will certainly die)'. ܕܪܐ comes from 14:18; A וחוק עולם 'the eternal decree (is: they all will certainly die)'.

---

[137] This effect is not covered by Smend's qualification of ܡܫܘܝܐ as 'gleichmacherisch' (*Jesus Sirach*, 62).

[138] The retention of parallelisms that occur in the Hebrew is a different issue, because it does not necessarily reflect a creative effort on the part of the translator.

16:11 ܘܐܦ ܬܒܥ ܚܛܗܐ '(Because love and anger are with Him; and He forgives abundantly) but also avenges sins'; A ועל רשעים יגיה רגזו 'He causes his wrath to shine over the wicked'; Gr καὶ ἐκχέων ὀργήν 'and pours out wrath'. Gr seems to have preserved the original reading; Syr reflects influence of 16:12, A from 5:6.[139]

18:33 ܠܐ ܬܗܘܐ ܡܣܟܢ 'Do not become poor (and a drunkard and licentious and a gossip)'; similarly Gr. According to Smend 'poor' was introduced from 18:32 in Gr, which Syr followed, cf. § 2.3.3 (2).

19:2 ܢܐܒܕ '(And he who clings to a harlot) will be destroyed'; Gr τολμηρότερος ἔσται 'will become audacious'. ܢܐܒܕ offers a good transition to 19:3 ܢܦܫܐ ܚܨܝܦܬܐ ܬܘܒܕ ܡܪܗ 'a shameless soul will destroy its owner'.

19:10 ܠܐ ܗܘܬ ܓܐܪܐ ܕܬܒܙܥܟ ܘܬܡܘܬ '(Let the hearing of a word die in your heart), it is not (i.e. lest it is) like an arrow that pierces you so that you die'; Gr θάρσει, οὐ μή σε ῥήξει 'Take courage! It will not make you burst'. According to Smend 'like an arrow' is 'schlechte Vorwegnahme' of 19:12 ܐܝܟ ܓܐܪܐ 'Like an arrow (that wounds a man's thigh, so is a word in the inner parts of the fool)'.[140]

20:17/16a ܥܠ ܫܘܥܐ ܕܟܐܦܐ '(Like water poured out) on a rock of stone (so is the tongue of the unrighteous one among the righteous)'. This is a plus that entered the text from 20:16 ܐܝܟ ܫܘܥܐ ܕܟܐܦܐ '(Those who eat my bread are) like a rock of stone'; cf. Gr ὀλίσθημα ἀπὸ ἐδάφους μᾶλλον ἢ ἀπὸ γλώσσης 'A slip on the pavement is better than (a slip) of the tongue'.[141]

29:26 ܐܟܣܢܝܐ ܐܢܬ 'You are a stranger, (pass by and lay the table)' comes from 29:25; Gr πάροικε 'stranger!'

39:13 ܐܝܟ ܫܘܫܢܐ '(And your flesh will sprout) like lilies (and like the cedar planted at the water)' is an addition from from 39:14 ('Like the odour of Lebanon in its cedars and like the root of the lily of the king'), which, in turn, is influenced by Hos 14:6 and Songs 4:11.

48:25 ܚܙܐ 'He saw (the signs and the trials before they came to pass)' comes from 48:24; B הגיד Gr ὑπέδειξεν.

As we said in our introduction to § 3.6, many repetitions that have been regarded as scribal errors and 'influence of adjacent lines' are preferably considered intentional variants, which create repetitive parallelism and reflect the 'tendency to level the vocabulary over an extended section'. Cases that in our view are more likely to be intentional have been given in § 3.6, but the borderline between the exam-

---

139 Cf. Van Peursen, *Verbal System*, 223 n. 132.

140 Smend, *Jesus Sirach*, 176.

141 Cf. Smend, *Jesus Sirach*, 185: 'Ganz abweichend Syr.: (...) Aus v. 16 war in seiner Vorlage על שן סלע eingedrungen; es ist kaum denkbar, dass Sirach jenes Bild hier wiederholt hätte'.

ples given in § 3.6 and those in the present paragraph is somewhat subjective. In the following cases we are not sure whether the repetition in Syr is due to a scribal error or intentional.

27:27 ܡܢ ܐܝܟܐ ܐܬܝܐ ܥܠܘܗܝ ܒܝܫܬܐ '(And he does not know) from where evil will come upon him'. ܒܝܫܬܐ is a repetition from 27a ('He who plots evil falls through it'). It strengthens the parallelism between action and result.[142]

35:20 ܕܡܣܟܢܐ '(He hears the bitterness of the soul) of a poor man' is a plus compared with B and Gr; it comes from 35:21. The effect of the addition is that ܕܡܣ̈ܟܢܐ ܨܠܘܬܗܘܢ in 35:21 resumes ܘܨܠܘܬܗܘܢ from 35:20b and ܕܡܣܟܢܐ from 35:20a. The repetition is even reinforced in 8a1^c 9c1 11c1 12a1*fam* → where ܕܡܣܟܢܐ is also added to ܘܨܠܘܬܗܘܢ in 35:20.

48:16 ܐܝܬ ܡܢܗܘܢ ܕܥܒܕܘ ܬܝܒܘܬܐ 'There were some of them who made repentance'; B יש מהם עשו יושר. Syr is influenced by 48:15 ܘܒܟܠܗܝܢ ܗܠܝܢ ܠܐ ܬܒ ܥܡܐ 'Despite all these things the people did not repent'. The reading in Syr creates a contrast between the people of Israel and the remnant of Judah.[143]

50:14 ܠܡܫܡܫܘ ܡܕܒܚܐ ܘܠܡܫܡܫܘ ܒܚܕܘܬܐ ܕܩܘܕܫܐ '(Until he had completed) to serve the altar, and to serve in holy joy' ܠܡܫܡܫܘ in 14b comes from 14a; B has לסדר (= Gr κοσμῆσαι). The result is a repetitive parallelism, which becomes even more repetitive if we read ܡܕܒܚܘܬܐ 'the altar' instead of ܒܚܕܘܬܐ (§ 1.3).

More likely to be classified as errors are those cases where a word has moved to an adjacent line without being retained in the original place.

25:17 ܒܝܫܘܬܗ ܕܐܢܬܬܐ ܒܝܫܬܐ ܬܘܪܩ ܐܦܝ̈ ܒܥܠܗ̇ ܘܬܘܟܡ ܐܢܝܢ ܐܝܟ ܠܘܢܐ ܕܣܩܐ 'The evil of an evil wife makes pale the face of her husband, and blackens it like the colour of a sackcloth': In Syr 'his face / the face of' is part of 17b, in Gr of 17a.

48:12bc ܘܩܒܠ ܢܒܝܘܬܐ ܐܥܦܐ ܐܠܝܫܥ ܘܣܓܝܐܬ ܢܣܝܘܢܐ ܘܐܬܘܬܐ ܡܠܠ ܦܘܡܗ 'And Elisha received double of his prophetic office; and his mouth spoke many trials and signs'; B [...]ל[... פי ש[נים] אתות הרבה ע[שי]ל[א. In Syr 'twofold' is part of 12b, in Heb (MS B) of 12c.[144]

Another category consists of those cases where words or phrases in two adjacent lines have changed places.

---

[142] Cf. the example from 7:2 discussed above, in § 3.6.

[143] Alternatively we can consider ܬܝܒܘܬܐ as a corruption of ܬܘܒܬܐ; cf. § 2.4.1, n. 94.

[144] According to Lévi, *L'Ecclésiastique* I, 138, Syr conforms more to the biblical recount, because Elisha asked to receive a double portion of the prophetic spirit of Elijah (2 Kgs 2:9).

21:21 ܐܝܟ ܩܘܠܒܐ ܕܕܗܒܐ ܚܟܡܬܐ ܠܣܟܘܠܬܢܐ ܘܐܝܟ ܫܒܝܪܬܐ ܥܠ ܐܝܕܗ ܕܝܡܝܢܐ 'Like a golden bracelet is wisdom to the prudent man and like an ornament to his right hand'. G ὡς κόσμος χρυσοῦς φρονίμῳ παιδεία καὶ ὡς χλιδὼν ἐπὶ βραχίονι δεξιῷ. In Syr 'ornament' and 'bracelet' have changed places.[145]

49:8 ܘܚܙܩܝܐܝܠ ܚܘܝ، ܙܢܝ̈ܐ ܕܡܪܟܒܬܐ ܘܚܙܐ ܚܙܘܐ 'And Ezekiel made known a sort of chariot and he saw a vision'; B יחזקאל ראה מראה ויגד זני מרכבה.

3.7.2 *The wider context of Sirach*

In other cases the Syriac translator seems to have been influenced by other passages from the wider context of Sirach. In most cases we cannot establish whether Syr reflect a conscious attempt to give the Sirach more cohesion or the unconscious influence of other passages. If the former is the case, this is another feature that Syr shares with other parts of the Peshitta and the Targums.[146]

18:22 ܐܬܕܟܪ ܕܡܘܬܐ ܠܐ ܡܬܘܚܪ '(Do not waste time to return from your sins) remember that death does not tarry'; Gr μὴ μείνῃς ἕως θανάτου δικαιωθῆναι 'and do not wait till death to be released (scl. from your vow)'; cf. 14:12 ܘܐܬܕܟܪ ܕܥܕܡܐ ܠܗܫܐ ܡܘܬܐ ܠܐ ܚܙܝܬ 'And remember that until now you have not seen death (and the decree of Sheol has not been shown to you)'.

21:9 ܐܝܟ ܡܣܩܬܐ ܕܚܠܐ ܒܪ̈ܓܠܘܗܝ ܕܓܒܪܐ ܣܒܐ 'Like an ascent of sand at the feet of an old man (so is the strength of the unrighteous at the fire)'; Gr στιππύον συνηγμένον συναγωγὴ ἀνόμων 'A band of criminals is like a bundle of tow'; cf. 25:20 ܐܝܟ ܡܣܩܬܐ ܕܚܠܐ ܒܪ̈ܓܠܘܗܝ ܕܓܒܪܐ ܣܒܐ.

22:13 ܠܐ ܬܫܦܪ ܫܘ̈ܥܝܬܐ '(With a fool) do not make beautiful your talking'; Gr μὴ πληθύνῃς λόγον 'do not multiply your word'; cf. 42:12 ܠܐ ܬܫܦܪ ܫܘ̈ܥܝܬܐ '(Among women) do not make beautiful your talking'.

22:26 ܘܐܝܟ ܡܪܝܥܐ ܢܚܫܒܘܢܟ '(If your neighbour reveals to you a secret, do not bring it out, lest [...]) and they will consider you to be baneful'. This is an addition that comes from 19:9.

---

[145] Cf. Smend, *Jesus Sirach*, 194: 'Im Syr. sind Schmuck und Spange schlecht vertauscht'.

[146] See, e.g., Van Staalduine-Sulman, *Targum of Samuel*, 112–114; Smelik, *Targum of Judges*, 97, 641. Note, however, that the examples from Sirach differ from many of the 'harmonizations' discussed in this literature because they do not concern the resolution of contradictions between passages.

23:15 ܘܟܠ ܝܘ̈ܡܝ ܚܝܘܗܝ ܚܟܡܬܐ ܠܐ ܝܠܦ '(A man who learns idle words) all the days of his life he does not learn wisdom' comes from 21:14; Gr ἐν πάσαις ταῖς ἡμέραις αὐτοῦ οὐ μὴ παιδευθῇ 'All his days he will not become disciplined'.

31:13 ܡܛܠ ܕܒܝܫܘܬ ܥܝܢܐ ܣܢܐ ܐܠܗܐ 'Because God hates evil of the eye'; B רע עין שונא אל. This plus in Syr and B seems to be derived from 12:6 ܘܐܦ ܐܠܗܐ ܣܢܐ ܠܒܝ̈ܫܐ; A כי גם אל שונא רעים.

37:6 ܘܠܐ ܬܫܠܛܝܘܗܝ ܒܒܝܬܟ 'And do not give him (i.e. a friend) power in your house'; B+D ואל תעזבהו בשללך 'And do not forsake him when you distribute your spoils' (B^{mg} ונגד ערים יחזיק צנה). Instead of rendering Heb 6b, the Syriac translator provides us with a slight variation of the idea contained in 33:20 ܒܪܐ ܘܐܢܬܬܐ ܘܐܚܐ ܘܪܚܡܐ ܠܐ ܬܫܠܛ ܒܟ ܒܚܝܝܟ 'To a son, a wife, a brother or a friend do not give power over you during your life'.[147]

39:18 ܒܚܕܘܬܐ ܨܒܝܢܗ ܡܬܥܒܕ 'With joy His will is done'; Gr ἐν προστάγματι αὐτοῦ πᾶσα ἡ εὐδοκία 'When He commands, all his pleasure (is fulfilled)'; cf. 39:31 ܒܙܒܢܐ ܕܦܩܕ ܠܗܘܢ ܚܕܝܢ 'And at the time He visits them they rejoice'.

40:26 ܕܚܠܬܗ ܕܐܠܗܐ ܥܠ ܟܠܡܕܡ ܐܬܬܪܝܡܬ 'The fear of God is exalted above all these'. This is an addition taken from 25:11. The same addition occurs after 50:29.

46:12 ܐܝܟ ܫܘܫܢܐ '(May their bones be bright) like lilies'; Gr ἐκ τοῦ τόπου αὐτῶν 'out of their place'; B omits; cf. 39:14 ܘܐܝܟ ܒܪܐ ܕܫܘܫܢܬ ܡܠܟܐ However, according to Kister influence of 39:14 is questionable. The reading in Syr, and perhaps also of the translator's source text, reflects views that occur also in *Test. Simeon* 6:2.[148]

48:6 ܡܚܡܣܦ ܢܩܝܪ̈ܐ ܡܢ ܟܘܪ̈ܣܘܬܗܘܢ 'Who cast down honoured people from their thrones'. Either ܟܘܪ̈ܣܘܬܗܘܢ is an inner-Syriac corruption of ܥܪ̈ܣܬܗܘܢ 'their beds',[149] or the Syriac translator was influenced by 10:14 ܟܘܪ̈ܣܝܐ ܕܓܐܘܬܢܐ ܗܦܟ ܡܪܝܐ 'the Lord has overturned the throne of the proud', or even by Luke 1:52; see § 5.4.

50:16 ܘܗܝܕܝܢ ܝܒܒܘ ܒܢܝ̈ ܐܗܪܘܢ ܒܩܪ̈ܢܬܐ ܩܕܡ ܟܠܗ ܥܡܐ ܕܐܝܣܪܝܠ ܘܐܫܡܥܘ ܩܠܐ ܬܩܝܦܐ ܠܡܒܪܟܘ ܩܕܡ ܟܠܗ ܥܡܐ 'And then the sons of Aaron blew on the horns before all the people of Israel and caused a loud sound to be heard to bless before all the people'; B אז יריעו בני אהרן הכהנים חצצרות מקשה ויריעו וישמיעו קול אדיר להזכיר לפני עליון 'Then the sons of Aaron, the priests, sounded a blast on the trumpets of

[147] Perhaps the Syriac translator understood תעזבהו as in Gen 39:6. Note that in Heb there is a parallelism with the preceding 'do not forget your friend during the battle', for which Syr has 'do not praise a friend in the neighbourhood', in which 'praise' (ܬܫܒܚ) is the result of confusion of תשכח (= B+D) and תשבח or an inner-Syriac corruption of ܬܫܒܚ (§ 2.2.2) and 'in the neighbourhood' (ܒܩܘܪܒܐ) reflects a misunderstanding of Hebrew בקרב (§ 3.4 [a]).

[148] Kister, 'Contribution', 368–369; see also Hollander–De Jonge, *Testaments of the Twelve Patriarchs* 123–124.

[149] Cf. Smend, *Jesus Sirach*, 460.

beaten metal, yes they sounded, and caused a mighty blast to be heard, to commemorate before the most high'; cf. 50:13c ܠܡܥܗܕ ܒܟܠܗ ܥܡܐ ܕܐܝܣܪܝܠ; 50:13d נגד כל קהל ישראל; 50:16d להזכיר לפני עליון. According to Smend ܩܘܕܡ ܟܠܗ ܥܡܐ ܕܐܝܣܪܝܠ in 50:16 is a correction which follows 13c and ܠܡܕܟܪܘ (read with B and Gr ܠܡܕܟܪܘ?) ܩܘܕܡ ܟܠܗ ܥܡܐ is a contraction of 16d and 13d.[150]

50:29 ܪܘܡܐ ܕܕܚܠܬܗ ܕܡܪܝܐ ܥܠ ܟܠܡܕܡ ܐܬܬܪܝܡܬ ܐܚܘܕܝܗ̇ ܒܪܝ ܘܠܐ ܬܫܒܩܝܗ̇ 'The height of the fear of the Lord is exalted above everything; seize it, my son, and do not let it go'.[151] This is an addition in Syr; cf. 25:11–12 (...) ܕܚܠܬܗ ܕܐܠܗܐ ܥܠ ܟܠܡܕܡ ܗܝ ܐܬܬܪܝܡܬ ܐܚܘܕܝܗ̇ ܒܪܝ ܘܠܐ ܬܪܦܝܗ̇; 6:27 ܘܠܐ ܬܪܦܝܗ̇.[152]

51:1 ܘܐܫܒܚ ܫܡܟ ܡܪܝܐ ܒܟܠܝܘܡ 'And I will praise Your name, Lord, every day'; B אהללך אלהי ישעי 'I will praise you, God of my salvation'; cf. 51:11 ܐܫܒܚ ܫܡܟ ܒܟܠܝܘܡ.

3.8 'TARGUMIC' LEXICOGRAPHICAL TRADITIONS

In some cases Syr reflects a lexicographic tradition that is also attested in the Targums.[153] Compare the following examples.

6:11 ܡܬܪܚܩ '(But in your disaster) he will keep away (from you)'; A יתנדה 'He will move away'. Cf. Isa 66:5 MT מנדיכם; Tg מרחקיכון; Pesh ܡܣܬܠܩܝܢܟܘܢ; Amos 6:3 MT המנדים; Tg מרחקין אנון; Pesh ܕܡܣܬܟܝܢ.[154]

11:34 ܕܠܐ ܢܥܩܠ 'lest he distort (your way); A ויסלף 'lest he overturn'. Cf. Exod 23:8; Deut 16:19; Job 12:19 MT סלף; Tg קלקל; Pesh ܡܗܦܟ (Exod 23:8; Deut 16:19), ܥܩܠ (Job 12:19).

16:26 ܡܢ ܠܩܘܕܡܝܢ 'from the beginning'; A מראש. Cf. Isa 41:4 MT מראש; Tg מלקדמין; Pesh ܡܢ ܪܫܝܬܐ.

---

[150] Smend, *Jesus Sirach*, 487.

[151] Note the disagreement of ܪܘܡܐ and ܐܬܬܪܝܡܬ; we should omit ܕ ܪܘܡܐ or read ܐܬܬܪܝܡ. In the first emendation the parallel with 25:11 becomes even stronger.

[152] Cf. above, at 40:26, and further Prato 'Lumière', 322: 'S s'éloigne (...) de tous ces témoins (...) S est semblable à 40, 26ef et en 29b à 25, 12c; dans les deux cas, il s'agit ici d'une addition de S'; Skehan–Di Lella, *Wisdom of Ben Sira*, 557, about the addition in Syr: 'This is from the Syr of 25:11–12, the whole repeated in 40,16, with the likelihood that the last part derives in some way from the Heb of 6:27b'; similarly Smend, *Jesus Sirach*, 494: 'Er wiederholt da ungefähr, was er hinter 40, 26 nach 25, 11 zusetzt'.

[153] This phenomenon plays an important role in the discussion of the relationship between the Peshitta and the Targums; cf. Van Keulen, 'Points of Agreement', 212–218 (§ 2.1.2).

[154] Bacher, 'Notes on the Cambridge Fragments', 276–277.

40:13 ܥܢܢܐ ܩܠܝܠܬܐ 'swift clouds'; B בחזיז קולות 'thunderbolt'.[155] Cf.
Job 38:25 MT חזיז קלות; Tg ענגא; 11QtgJob ענניד קליליד. According to
Lévi the translation of חזיז with 'clouds' conforms with Targumic
tradition.[156] Note, however, that in Sach 10:1 and Job 28:26 the Targums translate differently.

Other translation equivalents, too, are well-known from the Targums.

11:5 ܟܘܪܣܝܐ ܕܡܠܟܘܬܐ 'the throne of the kingdom'; A כסא. Cf. 1 Kgs
2:4 et al. MT כסא; Tg כורסי מלכותא; Pesh ܟܘܪܣܝܐ.[157]

To these examples we could add anti-anthropomorphisms, such as

11:12 ܡܠܬܗ ܕܐܠܗܐ 'the word of the Lord'; A ועין ייי 'and the eye of
the Lord'. Cf. Ps 18:25 MT עיניך; Tg מימריה; Pesh ܥܝܢ̈ܘܗܝ.[158]
16:18 ܒܓܠܝܢܗ 'at his revelation (upon them)'; A ברדתו 'when he descends (upon them)'. Cf. Gen 11:5 et al.: MT ירד; Tg אתגלי; Pesh
ܢܚܬ.[159]

According to H.P. Rüger these examples[160] show the dependence of
Syr on the Targums,[161] but the evidence is not sufficient to support
this claim. The examples do not necessarily show that the Syriac
translator was acquainted with the rabbinic Targums of these passages. What they do show is that there are some interesting agreements between Syr and the Targums.

3.9 CONCLUSION

The general characterization of Syr given in § 3.1 is supported by a
detailed analysis of the material. Syr is a free, sometimes imprecise or

---

[155] Thus *HALOT* 302; cf. Kister, 'Contribution', 347 n. 154.
[156] Lévi, *L'Ecclésiastique* I, 21: Syr 'a commis plusieurs fautes: (1) il a rendu אדיר
"puissant" par "rempli", faisant du ב de בחזיז le complément de l'adjective "rendu
puissant par, rempli par", ce qui est contre la grammaire; (2) ne comprenant pas
l'expression de Job 38, 25, qu'emprunte Ben Sira, il a lu קלות "légers", au lieu de
קולות "voix, tonnerre". Sa traduction de חזיז par "nuées" est conforme à la tradition,
entre autre au Targoum.'
[157] Cf. Van Keulen, 'Points of Agreement', 207.
[158] Cf. above, § 3.3 (c).
[159] Cf. above, § 3.3 (e).
[160] Except for 40:13, which Rüger does not discuss.
[161] Rüger, *Text und Textform*, 112–113; similarly Winter, *Ben Sira in Syriac*, 67–
68; The existence of an Aramaic version of Sirach has also been suggested by L. Zunz
and W. Bacher; cf. R. le Déaut, *Introduction*, 147; Dalman, *Grammatik*, 37.

even incorrect translation from a Hebrew source text.[162] This indicates that the translator knew Hebrew, but this knowledge appears to be limited, because more than once he misinterpreted his Hebrew source. In many cases the explanatory character of the translation suggests that there is no one-to-one relationship at word level between Syr and its presumed source text. This suggestion is corroborated by a comparison with Heb where available. For this reason the comparative study of Syr and Heb should not be restricted to an analysis of word correspondences, but also analyse correspondences at phrase level and clause level. Syr has also many additions or omissions of one clause or more. Very often Syr expands on the succinct style of Hebrew, but it does not lose the poetic character of the text. The most prominent poetic feature of Syr is its repetitive parallelism.

Throughout the present chapter we have seen that in some respects Syr follows practices that are well known from the Targums. The 'targumic' features attested in Syr are the following.

1. The translation of two different Hebrew words in adjacent lines with the same Syriac word, thus creating repetitive parallelism.
2. The substitution of a metaphor by its *signifié*.
3. The replacement of common nouns referring to God by the word 'God'.
4. The tendency to make explicit the referents of pronouns and the subjects of verbs.
5. Avoidance of anthropomorphisms.
6. A harmonizing tendency to give more coherence to the book as a whole.
7. Shared lexicographical traditions.

The agreements between the Peshitta and the Targums play an important role in Peshitta research.[163] In some respects, especially in the avoidance of anthropomorphisms, the 'targumic' features are more

---

[162] This conclusion differs from that in Reiterer, *Urtext*, 239–240; it seems that in this respect the section analysed by Reiterer, Sir 44:16–45:26, is not representative for the whole book of Sirach.

[163] See e.g. the articles collected in Flesher, *Targum and Peshitta*; Dirksen, 'Old Testament Peshitta', 264–295; Weitzman, *Syriac Version*, 86–146; idem, *From Judaism to Christianity*, 188–204; Maori, 'Peshitta Pentateuch and Pentateuchal Targums'; De Moor–Sepmeijer, 'Peshitta and Targum of Joshua'.

prominent in Syr than in other parts of the Peshitta,[164] although an exception may be made for Chronicles.[165] They show that Syr is firmly rooted in the Aramaic translation tradition, as it is represented in Jewish-Aramaic and Syriac Bible translations.[166] They do not justify, however, the characterization of Syr as 'targumic' or even 'a targum', because there remain many differences from the translation technique, character, and function of the Jewish-Aramaic translations called Targums.[167] Nor can any dependence on an Aramaic translation of Sirach, or on Jewish-Aramaic interpretative traditions be established.[168] Moreover, some of the 'targumic' features in Syr are also found outside the

---

[164] Cf. Van Keulen, 'Points of Agreement', 207: On the basis of a comparison of the Peshitta and Targum Jonathan on Kings, Van Keulen observes that a category to which 'most notable divergences' between the two versions belong, is 'quantitative correspondence and accuracy of semantic information'. In this context Van Keulen mentions Targumic translation equivalents such as כרסי מלכותא 'throne of the kingdom' for MT כסא and מימרא דיוי 'the Word of God', and שכינתא and דחלתא דיוי for the Tetragrammaton. Some of these 'Targumic (non-Peshitta)' features or related phenomena occur in Syr; see the discussions in the preceding paragraphs and in § 5.3 (3).

[165] Already in 1868 Th. Nöldeke remarked: 'Eine besondere Stellung nimmt aber die syrische Uebersetzung der Chronik ein. Diese ist allerdings ein reines Targum. Sie zeigt vielfache Zusätze, Umschreibungen und rabbinische Ausdeutungen; die Aengstlichkeit bei der Vermeidung von Anthropomorphismen ist hier ganz wie in den Targumen (...) Bei diesem wenig gelesenen Buche haben die Syrer also ein jüdisches Targum arglos übernommen' (*Alttestamentliche Literatur*, 263–264); a similar view was advocated by S. Fraenkel in 1879; cf. Weitzman, 'Peshitta of Chronicles'.

[166] That Syr is also deeply rooted in the Peshitta tradition has been emphasized by Reiterer in his *Urtext*, see his conclusions on pp. 239–240. Reiterer points out that while there is strong evidence of the shared translation tradition, there is no evidence of literary influence of the Peshitta on Syr; cf. § 5.2.

[167] A major difference concerns the size of the translation units. Whereas in Syr the level on which correspondences between Heb and Syr can be established is usually that of the phrase, sometimes even the clause, the Targums display contradictory tendencies: on the one hand the Targums give a precise rendering in which every word of the Hebrew text is reflected (cf. Smelik *Targum of Judges*, 86–94; idem, 'Orality', 75–76); on the other hand they contain many additions and expansions. The 'interpretative' or 'free' elements in the Targums are of a different character from those in Syr; thus the omission of clauses or even larger textual units, frequently attested in Syr, is untypical of the Targums (a similar objection has been raised against the characterization of Pesh-Chronicles as a targum; cf. Weitzman, 'Peshitta of Chronicles'; see also his objection against the use of 'targum' or 'targumic' in relation to the Peshitta in *From Judaism to Christianity*, 211). For a definition of 'targumic' applied to the Peshitta, see Koster, 'The Chicken or the Egg?', 120–121. A more detailed discussion on the 'targumic' character of Syr should also take into account the diversity among the Targums, but even that would not change the general picture: We find some features, especially in the field of phraseology, lexicographical traditions and poetic conventions that also occur in the Targums, but there are also major differences.

Aramaic-Syriac Bible translations. Thus repetitive parallelism seems to have belonged to a broad and long Aramaic literary tradition and harmonizations occur in many Ancient Versions.

---

[168] On the important distinction between 'translation tradition', and 'interpretative tradition', see Maori, 'Peshitta Pentateuch and Pentateuchal Targums', 69–70; the 'interpretative tradition' is the main focus of Maori's, *Peshitta*.

CHAPTER FOUR

TENDENCIES IN THE SYRIAC SIRACH NOT SHARED BY THE 'EXPANDED TEXT'

4.1 ADAPTATIONS TO SOCIAL AND CULTURAL CONDITIONS

Although we do not know exactly what the original Hebrew book of Sirach looked like, the material available allows us to conclude that Syr differs considerably from it. This is partly due to the transmission of the Hebrew text. In the earliest centuries of its history, the Hebrew text underwent many changes and this affected the cultural and religious profile of the book. In the scholarly literature the designations 'expanded text' and 'SirII' are used for the result of this process (§ 2.1). It is likely that the Hebrew source text of the Syriac translator contained many SirII readings (§ 2.4). This is the easiest explanation for the fact that Syr not only shares about 70 readings with GrII (§ 2.1), but also contains many unique readings that reflect tendencies and opinions that are typical of the expanded text.

The SirII elements in Syr contribute to its religious profile, but if we wish to determine the translator's cultural and religious profile, we should focus on those elements for which the translator, rather than his Hebrew source text is responsible. This chapter will be concerned with some of these features, starting with adaptations that the translator made to the social and cultural conditions of his time.[1] The following paragraphs will be concerned with features that may shed light on the translator's religious profile.

(1) References to 'the neglected one of two wives' (Heb שׂנואה[2]) and 'rival wife' (Heb צרה[3]), which both imply polygamy, are avoided.

7:26 ܘܐܢ ܣܢܝܐ ܗܝ 'and if she is lawless'; A ושנואה (= Gr).

---

[1] Cf. Weitzman, *Syriac Version*, 28; idem, *From Judaism to Christianity*, 60.
[2] Cf. Gen 29:31, 33; Deut 21:15–17; Isa 60:15; Prov 30:23.
[3] Cf. 1 Sam 1:6 and Driver, *Notes on the Hebrew Text of Samuel*, 9–10.

26:6a Syr omits this half-verse; Gr 'A wife that is jealous of another wife is grief of heart and sorrow (γυνὴ ἀντίζηλος ἐπὶ γυναικί)'; ἀντίζηλος reflects צרה 'rival-wife'.

26:22 ܐܢܬܬܐ ܓܝܪܬܐ ܠܠܐ ܡܕܡ ܡܬܚܫܒܐ 'An adulterous wife is considered as nothing'. Syr has ܓܝܪܬܐ instead of Gr (GrII) μισθία, which reflects שנואה.

37:11 ܥܡ ܕܠܐ ܐܢܬܬܐ ܥܠ ܚܒܪܬܗ '(Do not take counsel) with a woman lest you commit adultery with her'; B עם אשה על צרתה 'with a woman about her rival' (= D+Gr).

(2) Ben Sira is notorious for his hostile attitude towards women. The Syriac translator slightly softens the hostile tone. Thus in some cases he adds 'evil', which restricts Ben Sira's negative remarks about women in general to 'the evil woman'.

25:17 ܒܝܫܘܬܗ ܕܐܢܬܬܐ ܒܝܫܬܐ ܡܚܘܪ ܐܦܘܗܝ ܕܒܥܠܗ, ܘܚܠܘܢܗ 'The evil of an evil wife makes pale the face of her husband'; C רע אשה (= Gr).

25:21 ܠܐ ܬܬܚܫܒ ܠܫܘܦܪܗ ܕܐܢܬܬܐ ܒܝܫܬܐ 'Be not enticed by the beauty of an evil woman'. 'Evil' is a plus compared with Gr and C (the latter fragmentary).

36:26 Gr πάντα ἄρρενα ἐπιδέξεται γυνή, ἔστιν δὲ θυγάτηρ θυγατρὸς κρείσσων 'A woman will accept any man, but one daughter is better than another daughter'; B[txt+mg] [...] כל זכר תקבל אשה אך יש אשה יפה; Syr omits this 'chauvinistic comment'.[4]

(3) Syr omits 33:27 which contains the advice to use yoke, thong, racks and tortures for a bad slave.[5]

(4) According to Winter, Syr reflects hostility towards the monarchy. He concludes this from the omission of the positive reference to kingship in 44:3.[6] One could also refer to the omission of 'king' in 50:7.

44:3 B דוי ארץ במלכותם ואנשי שם גבורתם היועצים בתבונתם 'Rulers of the earth in their royalty, and men of renown in their might, counsellors in their understanding' (= Gr); B[mg] רודי, בגבורם, יועצם; M ויעצים בתבונתם. Syr omits.[7]

---

[4] Skehan–Di Lella, *Wisdom of Ben Sira*, 431; cf. Smend, *Jesus Sirach*, 324: 'In Syr. fehlt v. 26 (wie auch v. 28) aber wohl nur deshalb, weil er an seinem derben Inhalt Anstoss nahm.'

[5] Cf. Smend, *Jesus Sirach*, cxxxiv.

[6] Winter, *Ben Sira in Syriac*, 142–143; idem, 'Ben Sira in Syriac', I, 244–245.

[7] For the absence of 44:3a-b in M, which at first sight undermines Winter's argument, see Winter, *Ben Sira in Syriac*, 143.

50:7 ܐܦܘܡܐ '(like the shining sun upon) the citadel'; B היכל המלך 'the royal palace'. According to Smend the Syriac translator avoided the reference to the '(pagan) royal palace'.[8] It is questionable, however, whether the omission of 'the king' removed the notion of kingship, since ܐܦܘܡܐ usually refers to a royal palace.[9]

4.2 SACRIFICES, PRIESTHOOD AND TEMPLE

4.2.1 *Sacrifices*

The attitude of the Syriac translator towards the temple service, sacrifices and the priesthood plays an important role in establishing the translator's religious and cultural background. Syr omits references to sacrifices in the following cases.[10]

7:31 ܠܚܡܐ ܕܩܘܕܫܐ ܘܪܝܫܝܬܐ ܕܐܝܕܝܐ 'bread of the offerings and the first-fruits of the hands'; A לחם אברים ותרומת יד זבחי צדק ותרומת קדש 'the bread of the sacrifices (אשמים), and the heave-offering of the hand, sacrifices which are due, and the heave-offering of holiness'. Heb contains a number of technical terms referring to sacrifices. Syr shortens this list, but retains the ܪܝܫܝܬܐ ܕܠܚܡܐ. In a Christian context this idiom could well be meant as a reference to the bread of the Eucharist.[11] In this sense it is used in Syriac liturgical texts.

35:1 ܐܩܝܡܬ ܦܘܠܚܢܐ '(If you do something that is written in the Law), you increase the service'. Syr has ܦܘܠܚܢܐ where Gr has προσφοράς 'offerings'.

---

[8] Cf. Smend, *Jesus Sirach*, 482 (after a quotation of B היכל המלך): אל) 'Syr las wohl ebenso, er stiess sich aber mit Recht an dem heidnischen Königspalast'.

[9] Payne Smith, *Thesaurus* I, 329–330.

[10] In the list below we have not included 14:11 ܘܐܢ ܐܝܬ ܠܟ ܐܝܬܪ ܢܦܫܟ 'And if you have something, do good to yourself'; A ולאל ידך הדשן 'And make fat (?) according to your power'; Gr 'And offer worthy sacrifices (προσφοράς) to the Lord'. According to Winter (*Ben Sira in Syriac*, 133–134; 'Ben Sira in Syriac', I, 241) Syr avoids mentioning sacrifices. However, the meaning of הדשן is disputed; *HALOT* (234) reads it as a Nifal and translates 'to make free with'; Segal (*Sefer Ben Sira*, 60) and *DCH* II, 477, interpret it as a Hitpael meaning 'to make oneself fat, be satisfied'. The context suggests that this verb refers to taking care of oneself, rather than bringing sacrifices.

[11] See Van Peursen, 'Jewish and/or Christian', 250–251, esp. n. 24.

38:11 B אזכרה ודשן ערוך בכנפי הונך […] '[…] a memorial offering and fatten the arrangement (offer a fat sacrifice) to the utmost of your means' (similarly Gr); B^{mg} אזכרתה, ערך, הונך; Syr omits.[12]

45:20–21 ܐܟ݂ܠܬܐ ܕܩܘܪܒܢܐ ܘܐܠܐܢ '(And He gave him) the holy first fruits and the rows of the bread'; B קדש נתן לו לחם [רומת]ת He gave him the sacred אשי ייי יאכלון […] חלקו ומתנה לו ולזרעו heave-offerings for bread, the fire-offerings of the Lord they shall eat, […] his portion, a gift to him and his descendants'.[13] 'First fruits' and 'showbread' are retained in Syr, but the other sacrifices are not.[14]

50:19c–21 ܘܫܒܚ ܥܡܐ ܕܐܪܥܐ ܠܐܠܗܐ 'And the people of the land praised God'; B וירנו כל עם הארץ בתפלה לפני רחום עד כלותו לשרת מזבח ומשפטיו הגיע אליו אז ירד ונשא ידיו על כל קהל ישראל וברכת ייי בשפתיו ובשם ייי התפאר וישנו לנפל שנית […א]ל מפניו 'all the people of the land shouted for joy before the Merciful One, till he had completed the service of the altar by presenting to God the sacrifice due. Then he went down and lifted his hands over all the congregation of Israel. The blessing of the Lord was upon his lips, and in the name of the Lord he glorified himself. And they fell down again a second time [...Go]d before him.' Syr omits 19c–21, which deals with sacrifices and the importance of the priestly blessing.[15]

In the following cases a positive reference to sacrifices has been substituted by a reference to prayer.[16]

35:8 ܩܘܪܒܢܝܗܘܢ ܕܟܐܢܐ ܨܠܘܬܐ ܕܦܘܡܗܘܢ ܘܥܒܕܝܗܘܢ ܠܫܡܝܐ ܒܙܥܝܢ 'The offerings of the righteous are the prayer of their mouth and their deeds pierce the heaven'; Gr προσφορὰ δικαίου λιπαίνει θυσια-στήριον, καὶ ἡ εὐωδία αὐτῆς ἔναντι ὑψίστου 'The offerings of the just man fattens the altar, and its sweet fragrance is before the Most High'.

In the following verses charity takes the place of the first-fruit offerings and tithes.[17]

---

[12] Cf. Winter, *Ben Sira in Syriac*, 133–134; idem, 'Ben Sira in Syriac', I, 241; Smend, *Jesus Sirach*, cxxxvii.

[13] In MS B the order is 20c–21a–20d–21b.

[14] Compare above on ܐܟ݂ܠ in 7:31. The conclusion that the translator avoided the reference to eating sacrifices because he was a vegetarian is far-fetched; *pace* Winter, *Ben Sira in Syriac*, 134–135; idem, 'Ben Sira in Syriac', I, 241.

[15] Cf. Winter, *Ben Sira in Syriac*, 135–137; idem, 'Ben Sira in Syriac', I, 242.

[16] For this tendency elsewhere in the Peshitta, especially in Chronicles, see Weitzman, *Syriac Version*, 214–217. On Sirach 35, which contains many of the examples quoted in the present paragraph, see Edersheim, 'Ecclesiasticus', 172; Winter, *Ben Sira in Syriac*, 127–132; idem, 'Ben Sira in Syriac', II, 238–240; idem, 'Ebionite Translation'; Owens, 'Early Syriac Text of Ben Sira', 60–63.

35:9 ܡܘܗܒܬܗ ܕܓܒܪܐ ܛܒܐ ܡܬܩܒܠܐ ܘܕܘܟܪܢܗܘܢ ܕܙܕܝܩܐ ܠܐ ܢܬܛܥܐ ܠܥܠܡ 'The gift of a good man is accepted and the memory of the righteous one will not be forgotten'; Gr θυσία ἀνδρὸς δικαίου δεκτή 'The sacrifice of a just man is acceptable'.

35:10–11 ܒܥܝܢܐ ܛܒܬܐ ܗܒ ܠܡܣܟܢܐ ܘܠܐ ܬܬܥܝܩ ܒܡܘܗܒܬܟ ܒܟܠ ܡܘܗܒܬܟ ܢܗܘܘܢ ܢܗܝܪܝܢ ܐܦܝܟ ܘܒܚܕܘܬܐ ܐܘܙܦ ܠܓܒܪ ܕܠܐ ܦܪܥ ܠܟ 'With a good eye give to the poor, and be not troubled because of your gifts; with all your gifts, let your face be shining, and with joy lend to the man who will not repay you'; B בכל מ[ע]שיך ה[א]ר [...] פנים ובששון הקדש מעשר '[...] with every deed illuminate your face, and with joy, sanctify your tithe'; Gr ἐν ἀγαθῷ ὀφθαλμῷ δόξασον τὸν κύριον καὶ μὴ σμικρύνῃς ἀπαρχὴν χειρῶν σου. ἐν πάσῃ δόσει ἱλάρωσον τὸ πρόσωπόν σου καὶ ἐν εὐφροσύνῃ ἁγίασον δεκάτην 'With a good eye glorify the Lord, and do not diminish the first-fruits of your hands; with every gift gladden your face and in joy sanctify the tithe.'[18]

In the following cases Syr gives a shortened or imprecise rendering of sacrificial terminology.[19]

45:16 ܠܡܩܪܒܘ ܥܠܘܬܐ ܘܕܒܚ̈ܐ ܘܒܣ̈ܡܐ 'to offer holocausts and sacrifices and incense'; B להגיש עלה וחלבים ולהקטיר ריח ניחח ואזכרה 'to bring near holocausts and the fat pieces and to burn a sweet savour and a memorial offering'.

45:24 ܕܢܒܢܐ ܠܗ ܡܕܒܚܐ 'that he would build an altar for Him'; B לכלכל מקדש 'that he should provide for the sanctuary'.[20]

49:1a ܐܝܟ ܦܝܪܡܐ ܕܒܣ̈ܡܐ 'like a censer of incense'; B כקטרת סמים 'fragrant perfumes'.

49:1b ܒܣܓܝܐܘܬܐ ܕܒܣ̈ܡܐ 'with an abundance of sweet spices'; B מעשה רוקח 'the work of a perfumer'.

50:13 ܩܘܪ̈ܒܢܐ 'the offerings'; B אשי ײ 'the fire-offerings of the Lord'.

50:14 ܒܚܕܘܬܐ ܕܩܘܕܫܐ 'with holy joy' (read ܡܕܒܚܘܬܐ 'the altar'? cf. § 1.3); B מערכות עליון 'the rows (on the altar) of the Most High'.

---

[17] The evaluation of good deeds and almsgiving as equivalent to cultic worship is already present in Gr 35:3–4 'He who returns kindness offers fine flour; he who gives alms makes a sacrifice of praise'.

[18] Syr seems to have been influenced by Luke 6:34, see § 5.4.

[19] Similarly elsewhere in the Peshitta; thus the sacrificial term אשם 'trespass offering' is always rendered by the 'colourless' ܩܘܪܒܢܐ; Weitzman, *Syriac Version*, 190, 218; idem, *From Judaism to Christianity*, 15, 67.

[20] Compare Levi's harsh judgment (*L'Ecclésiastique* I, 106): 'S. confirme la leçon מקדש "le temple"; mais comme ce traducteur ignorait l'histoire juive et ne connaissait que la Bible, il a parlé d' "autel" et a rendu au hazard כלכל par "bâtir".' Reiterer (*Urtext*, 222–224) argues that the Hebrew source text of Syr differed from B, although it is impossible to reconstruct it. He further observes that Phineas building an altar is not found elsewhere; but perhaps the translator was thinking of Phineas' role in Joshua 22.

Similar tendencies are attested in other parts of the Peshitta,[21] although
not as strong as in Syr. They play a role in the discussion about the
alleged Christian background of the Peshitta, but there is no consensus
on this point.[22] The translators' attitude towards sacrifices fits in well
with a Christian background, but it has been argued that Jewish
sources reflect this attitude as well. Admittedly, rabbinic sources (but
not the Targums) show a high esteem for prayer at the expense of sacrifices,[23] but unlike Syr they never reflect a rejection of sacrifices and
the temple service as such. The high esteem for prayer was stronger in
non-rabbinic circles. Philo writes about the Essenes that they 'are pre-
eminently worshippers of God, not offering animal sacrifices, but taking care to keep their minds in a state worthy of consecrated priests'.[24]
Prayer is also presented as a substitute of sacrifices in 1QS IX 4–5
ותרומת שפתים למשפט כניחוח צדק ותמים דרך כנדבת מנחת רצון 'The offering of the lips in compliance with the decree will be like the pleas-
ant aroma of justice and the perfectness of behaviour will be acceptable like a freewill offering'.[25] Moreover, some Dead Sea Scrolls reflect strong sentiments against the priesthood in Jerusalem and the
temple service. However, even in these sources the antipathy concerns
the service executed by the ruling priesthood in Jerusalem, rather than
sacrifices as such.[26]

We can conclude that the translator's attitude towards sacrifices
renders a Jewish background of Syr unlikely. For a complete refutation of the sacrificial cult there are parallels in Christian literature, including Jewish-Christian corpora such as the Pseudo-Clementine Lit-

---

[21] Cf. Weitzman, *Syriac Version*, 217–218: 'A certain negligence [regarding sacri-
fices] can indeed be detected in P's rendering of sacrificial laws. In fact, an indifferent
or even hostile attitude to sacrifice—and to the priesthood and Temple—can be traced
right through the Peshitta of the Old Testament and the Apocrypha.'

[22] Cf. Weitzman, *Syriac Version*, 10, on the nineteenth-century debate between
L. Hirzel and J. Perles and ibid., 207, on J.A. Emerton's refutation of S. Davidson's
thesis about 'an air of negligence apparent in the translation of the Levitical law, particularly in the sections concerning clean and unclean animals'.

[23] Cf. Weitzman, *Syriac Version*, 214–215 (on Pesh-Chronicles): 'It seems likely
that prayer, charity and study were all seen as replacing sacrifice. Such views are also
attested within rabbinic Judaism, albeit together with constant hope for the restoration
of sacrifice (...) R. Eliezer also declared charity superior to all sacrifice' (*b. Suk.* 49b);
see also idem, *From Judaism to Christianity*, 22–23, 67.

[24] Ed. Petit, 75 (p. 196).

[25] Cf. Chazon, 'Psalms, Hymns and Prayers', 714; translation taken from García
Martínez–Tigchelaar, *Study Edition* I, 91.

[26] Milgrom, 'Sacrifice', 807–808.

erature.[27] Even Jewish-Christian groups that adhered to circumcision and other elements of the Mosaic Law, rejected sacrifices.[28] It is likely, therefore, that the translator's negative attitude towards sacrifices reflects a Jewish-Christian or Christian background.

4.2.2 *The priesthood*

Much of what we have said in the preceding paragraph about the translator's attitude towards sacrifices applies also to his estimation of the priesthood. Especially in Chapter 45, in which Ben Sira praises the high priest Aaron, the changes are considerable.

45:7 ܐܠܗܐ ܕ ܕ ܪܝܫܐ ܘܐܩܝܡܗ 'And He set him (Aaron) to a truth of his people (?)';[29] B וישימהו לחק עולם 'and he made him to an eternal degree'. Either Syr reflects a scribal error in Hebrew (עם instead of עולם) or Syriac (ܕܥܡܐ instead of ܕܠܥܠܡ),[30] or, which we consider more likely, it contains an intentional variant, omitting a reference to the eternal decree of the priesthood.[31]

45:8–14 Syr omits the lengthy description of the liturgical vestments of Aaron (45:8c–13) and the reference to daily offerings (45:14).[32]

45:15 ܐܝܕܗ ܥܠܘܗܝ ܡܘܫܐ ܘܣܡ 'And Moses laid his hand upon him'; B [וי]מלא משה את ידו (= Gr). The idiom used in Heb, 'to fill the hand, i.e. to institute to a priestly office' (BDB 570), comes from Exod

---

[27] Cf. Stanley Jones, 'Pseudo-Clementine Literature', 719: 'The two bodies of writing differ in their attitudes toward sacrifices. In the Dead Sea Scrolls there may well be a problem with the ruling priesthood in Jerusalem and with their sacrifices (e.g., 1QpHab viii.8–17), yet there is no fundamental problem with either institution. In the Pseudo-Clementine literature the source of *Recognitions* 1.27–71 thinks that sacrifice had been endured by God for a while but is now outdated, even sinful, after the proclamation of Jesus (*Recognitions* 1.61.1), while the author of the *Homilies* (3.45) denies the genuineness of any scriptural passages promoting sacrifice.'

[28] De Boer, 'Elkesaites', 248.

[29] Cf. Calduch-Benages–Ferrer–Liesen, *Sabiduría del Escriba*, 244: 'And He constituted him for the strengthening of the people'; Smend, *Jesus Sirach*, 428: 'Und er setzte ihn zur Gewissheit (שררא = חק?) des Volkes'.

[30] Thus Lévi, *L'Ecclésiastique* I, 96.

[31] Cf. Smend, *Jesus Sirach*, 428: 'Schwerlich las er עם für עולם. Er wollte aber als Christ das ewige Hohepriestertum Aharons, das er freilich v. 15 bestehen lässt, nicht anerkennen und riet auf עם, indem er sich (ähnlich wie v. 2) durch Gr. leiten liess, der für הודו לו αὐτῷ ἱερατείαν λαοῦ hat'; similarly Winter, *Ben Sira in Syriac*, 137–138; idem, 'Ben Sira in Syriac', I, 242–243; see also Reiterer, *Urtext*, 145.

[32] Cf. Edersheim, 'Ecclesiasticus', 216: 'It seems natural to attribute this to a wish on the part of a Christian translator or emendator not to enlarge on the glories of the Jewish priesthood'; similarly Winter, *Ben Sira in Syriac*, 138–139; idem, 'Ben Sira in Syriac', I, 243.

28:14. The expression 'to lay the hand upon' is used of the consecration of Joshua in Num 27:18, but not for that of Aaron.[33]

45:16 Syr gives a shortened and imprecise translation of the Hebrew references to several types of sacrifices (see the quotations above, § 4.2.1)

45:24 ܡܕܒܚܐ 'an altar'; B מקדש 'sanctuary' (see above, § 4.2.1).

Compare also the following two cases.

46:13 ܣܡܘܐܝܠ ܕܝܢܐ ܘܟܗܢܐ 'Samuel, the judge and the priest'; B שמואל שופט וכהן 'Samuel (who) acted as judge and as priest': Heb carefully avoids saying that Samuel was a priest, but says that he acted as a priest, probably referring to the sacrifices that Samuel offered in 1 Sam 7:9 (and 10:8).[34] The Syriac translator did not bother to make this neat distinction, and saw no problem in calling Samuel a priest (cf. Ps 99:6).

50:24 ܘܢܩܘܡ ܥܡ ܫܡܥܘܢ ܚܢܢܗ ܘܐܝܟ ܝܘܡܬܐ ܕܫܡܝܐ 'And mercy will abide with Simeon, and with his descendants as the days of heaven'; B ויאמן עם שמעון חסדו ויקם לו ברית פינחס אשר לא יכרת לו ולזרעו כימי שמים 'May He establish with Simeon His mercy (or: 'may… be established'), and may He set up for him the covenant of Phineas, which will not be taken away from him and his seed, as the days of heaven' (cf. Gr); Syr omits reference to the covenant of Phineas, which according to Num 25:13 implied eternal priesthood.[35]

Note finally the following omission of the reference to the Tabernacle.[36]

24:15 ܘܐܝܟ ܡܫܚܐ ܛܒܐ ܝܗܒܬ ܪܝܚܝ 'And like choice oil I gave my odour'; Gr ὡς λιβάνου ἀτμὶς ἐν σκηνῇ 'I was as the smoke of incense in the Tabernacle'.

---

[33] Edersheim ('Ecclesiasticus', 217) saw in the Syriac idiom 'a trace of the Syrian's Christianity', but note that סמיכה is also an important concept in rabbinic Judaism. Reiterer, *Urtext*, 177, suggests that the source text of the Syriac translator had a reading different from that in B, because elsewhere in the Peshitta מלא יד is rendered with ܐܝܕܐ ܡܠܐ.

[34] Skehan–Di Lella, *Wisdom of Ben Sira*, 518.

[35] Winter, *Ben Sira in Syriac*, 140–141; idem, 'Ben Sira in Syriac', I, 244. But note that 'as the days of heaven' has been preserved in Syr.

[36] *Pace* Winter, *Ben Sira in Syriac*, 142: 'I have not found any alteration in the Syriac version which could be construed as evidence of the opposition to the temple'.

4.3 THE LAW AND THE PROPHETS

4.3.1 *The Law*

Sometimes Syr suppresses references to the Law. We can distinguish the following categories.[37]

(a) 'The Law' is replaced by another word or phrase, such as 'the ways of the Lord', 'the way', 'the fear of God', 'almsgiving and love' and 'the words of the Most High'.

9:15 ܐܘܪ̈ܚܬܗ ܕܡܪܝܐ 'in the ways of the Lord'; Gr ἐν νόμῳ ὑψίστου 'in the Law of the Most High'.

19:20 ܘܕܚܠܬܗ ܕܐܠܗܐ 'And the fear of God (is Wisdom)'; Gr ποίησις νόμου 'doing the Law'.[38]

29:11 ܒܙܕܩܬܐ ܘܒܚܘܒܐ 'with almsgiving[39] and with love'; Gr κατ' ἐντολὰς ὑψίστου '(store up your treasure) according to the commandments of the Most High'.

32:17 ܐܘܪܚܗ ܠܒܪ '(According to his will) he makes his way'; B ימשך תורה 'He distorts the Law'; B^mg למשוך; E+F למשך תורה. This use of 'the way' fits a Christian context very well,[40] but is not exclusively Christian.

32:24 ܕܢܛܪ ܐܘܪܚܗ ܢܛܪ ܦܘܩܕܢܐ ܕܐܠܗܐ 'He who keeps his way keeps the command of God'; B נוצר תורה שומר נפשו; E ה[...] נוצר נפשו; F נוצר תורה נוצר נפשו; Gr 'He who keeps the Law (νόμῳ) observes the commandments (ἐντολαῖς)'. The omission of 'the Law' may be due to the influence of Prov 16:17 שמר נפשו נצר דרכו.[41]

44:20 ܦܬܓܡܘܗܝ ܕܐܠܗܐ 'the words of the Most High'; B מצות עליון 'the commandments of the Most High'; Gr νόμον ὑψίστου 'the Law of the Most High'. Interestingly, Aphrahat's quotation of this verse in *Dem.* 13:8 has ܢܡܘܣܐ; cf. § 1.2.

---

[37] Winter, *Ben Sira in Syriac,* 181–190; idem, 'Ben Sira in Syriac', II, 494–498; similarly Weitzman, *Syriac Version,* 219: In Sirach and Wisdom 'aversion not only to sacrifice but to the law in general emerges clearly'.

[38] The reading in Syr may have been influenced by ܕܚܠܬܗ ܕܐܠܗܐ in the preceding line (= 19:20a); see § 3.7.1 on 'influence of adjacent lines' and below, § 4.3, on the addition of 'prophecy' in 19:20a.

[39] For this translation see Owens, 'Early Syriac Text of Ben Sira', 52–53.

[40] Cf. Acts 9:2; 19:9; Payne Smith, *Thesaurus* I, 375.

[41] Thus Ryssel, 'Fragmente', III, 108.

(b) Heb and/or Gr contain a reference to the Law. Syr has a completely different reading.[42]

19:17 ܘܠܐ ܠܟܠ ܡܠܐ ܬܗܝܡܢܝܘܗܝ 'And do not trust him in every word'; Gr 'and give due place to the Law of the Most High (νόμῳ ὑψίστου)'.

34:8 ܒܐܬܪܐ ܕܠܝܬ ܒܗ ܚܛܗܐ ܪܥܐ ܐܠܗܐ 'For God is pleased with the place where there are no sins'; Gr 'without deceit (scl. of dreams) the Law (νόμος) is fulfilled'.

37:12 ܕܗܢܘܢ ܕܕܚܠܝܢ ܠܡܚܛܐ ܩܕܡ ܐܠܗܐ 'who fear to sin before God'; B+D אשר תדע שומר מצוה 'whom you know to be keeping the Law' (Gr reads similar, but with ἐντολάς corresponding to מצוה).

41:8 ܕܢܩܦܐ ܡܠܘܐ ܠܗܘܢ ܥܕܡܐ ܠܝܘܡܐ ܕܡܘܬܗܘܢ 'whom misery accompanies till the day of their death'; M עזבי תורת עליון 'who forsake the Law of the Most High' (= Gr).

(c) Heb and/or Gr contain a reference to the Law. Syr omits the verse. There are two uncertain examples.

32:15 B דורש תורה יפיקנה ומתלהלה יוקש בה 'He who seeks the Law will obtain it, but the madman will be ensnared by it'. According to Winter Syr omits this verse because it contains a laudatory reference to the Law.[43] Note however, that MS F does not have this verse either!

33:2–4 Gr 'A wise man will not hate the Law (νόμον), but he who is hypocritical about it, is like a ship in a storm. A prudent man will trust the word (λόγῳ) and the Law (νόμος) is as faithful to him as the inquiry of the divine oracle. Prepare your word (λόγον) and you will be listened to, marshal your instruction and answer'. The folio of MS B that contains these verses stops at the end of 33:3. For 33:2a it has לא יחכם שונא תורה and in 3b it has ותורתו; E and F have 33:2a with שונא תורה, but 33:3 is missing. The omission in Syr can be accounted for by the distortion that apparently took place in the textual transmission. If the translator omitted these verses on purpose because of their reference to the Law, he could have resumed his translation at 33:4 rather than at 33:5.[44]

Winter suggests that Syr's negligence of the Law, if not hostility towards it, is due to orthodox Christians who revised the original trans-

---

[42] Also in 28:6 ܘܐܬܟܠ ܡܢ ܕܠܡܚܛܐ 'and refrain from sinning'; Gr 'and abide in the commandments (ἐντολαῖς)', but there the parallelism in vv. 6–7 suggests that the reading in Gr is secondary.

[43] Winter, *Ben Sira in Syriac*, 181–182; 'Ben Sira in Syriac', II, 495.

[44] Cf. Winter, *Ben Sira in Syriac*, 185—186. Note that also elsewhere in the Peshitta the Syriac translator did not understand אורים ותמים; Weitzman, *Syriac Version*, 21.

lation made by Ebionites. He considers the latter responsible for the complimentary remark about the Law in 35:4.[45]

> 35:4 ܪܚܡ̈ܘܗܝ ܢܛܪ ܕܚܢܢܐ ܘܡܢ 'And he who gives alms keeps the Law'; Gr καὶ ὁ ποιῶν ἐλεημοσύνην θυσιάζων αἰνέσεως 'And he who gives alms makes a sacrifice of praise'.

In our view, however, this example does not show that the Syriac translator held the Law in high esteem. The difference between Syr and Gr can easily be explained from a scribal error: Gr reflects תודה, Syr presupposes תורה. And even if Syr has an intentional variant, it can be interpreted as a reinterpretation of the Law, rather than an affirmation of it: Giving alms—rather than sacrifices and the like—is the fulfilment of the Law.

4.3.2 *The Prophets and prophecy*

According to Winter the Syriac translator was unwilling to quote from the Prophets. He omitted the references to Mal 4:6 in 48:10, to Jer 1:10 in 49:7, and to Ezek 14:4 in 49:9.[46] However, in 49:9 neither B nor Gr have exactly the wording of Ezek 14:4 and in 48:10 Syr has ܠܐܒܗ̈ܐ ܥܠ ܒܢ̈ܝܐ ܠܡܗܦܟܘ 'to turn the sons to the fathers' instead of 'to turn the fathers to the sons', but both phrases come from Mal 4:6. Furthermore, the Elijah passage in Sirach 48 contains some other references to the last chapter of Malachi that are retained, or even reinforced, in Syr.[47]

Other references to the Prophets are retained in Syr as well, such as that in 48:24 about Isaiah, who 'comforted the mourners of Zion' (cf. Isa 40:1–2; 49:8–13), the remark about Ezekiel, who 'made known a sort of chariot and saw a vision' in 49:8 (cf. Ezek. 1–3), and the reference to the Twelve Prophets in 49:10.

It follows that Winter's view that Syr originated in a community that cherished the Law and disregarded the Prophets should be abandoned. There are no convincing arguments to ascribe the negative atti-

---

[45] Winter, 'Ben Sira in Syriac', II, 494.

[46] Winter, *Ben Sira in Syriac*, 157–162: idem, 'Ben Sira in Syriac', I, 249–251.

[47] Compare especially in the same verse ܡܪܝ ܕܓܠܝܐ ܝܘܡܗ ܢܐܬܐ ܡܢ ܩܕܡ 'before the day of the Lord comes', which comes from Mal 3:23; see further Van Peursen, 'Que vive celui qui fait vivre', 289–290.

tude towards the Law in Syr to a later revision, because traces of an original translation reflecting a high esteem for the Mosaic Law cannot be discerned. Nor is it correct to claim that references to the Prophets are avoided. In § 5.1 we will see that in many cases Syr is influenced by passages from the Former and Latter Prophets. The view that the Prophets are an integrated part of Scripture is probably also reflected in 19:20.

> 19:20 ܐܠܟ ܢܒܝܘܬܐ ܘܟܠ ܚܟܡܬܐ 'The words of prophecy and all wisdom is the fear of the Lord'; Gr πᾶσα σοφία φόβος κυρίου 'All wisdom is fear of the Lord'. The addition of 'prophecy' in Syr probably indicates 'a desire to combine the prophetic and the "Wisdom"-books of the Old Testament as constituting the substance of true religion'.[48]

Note also the following reference to prophecy in relation to Solomon.

> 47:17 ܐܬܕܡܪ ܒܟ ܐܬܘ̈ܬܐ ܟܠܗܝܢ ܒܟܬܒܐ ܡܬܠܝ̈ ܚܟܡܬܐ ܘܒܢܒܝܘܬܐ 'Interpreting proverbs of wisdom in a book, and with prophecy you (i.e. Solomon) astonished the peoples'; B בשיר מ[ש]ל חידה ומליצה עמים הסערתה. This reference to Solomon's prophecy is remarkable. Several interpretations are possible.[49]
>
> 1. The background of the association of Solomon with prophecy is the messianic interpretation of Psalm 72 or the Christological understanding of Proverbs 8: The translator understood these passages that were ascribed to Solomon as prophecy.
> 2. The Syriac translator was thinking of extra-biblical Solomonic literature that contains 'prophetic elements' such as the *Psalms of Solomon.*
> 3. 'Prophecy' should be understood in its broad meaning of 'Scripture' rather than the restricted sense of 'prediction'.[50] Both ܡܬܠܝ̈ ܚܟܡܬܐ and ܢܒܝܘܬܐ refer to the Solomonic Wisdom literature of the Old Testament
>
> According to Lévi the association of Solomon and prophecy indicates a Christian background, because Solomon was never consid-

---

[48] Thus Edersheim, 'Ecclesiasticus', 107; but Edersheim speaks about the possibility that this reading comes from the original Sirach. Note that in the same verse a reference to the Law is omitted (see above, § 4.3.1 [a]).

[49] On ܒܝܬ corresponding to בשיר see § 2.2.2.

[50] Cf. Barton, *Oracles of God*, 154: 'Writers in that period [i.e. 'New Testament times'] seem not to have been aware of generic distinctions between the scriptural books, or if they were that awareness had few practical consequences for interpretation. On the whole they adopted some uniform model of what an "inspired" book could be expected to contain, and applied this as a hermeneutical key to whatever book they might be reading'.

ered a prophet among the Jews.[51] However, not even in early Christian literature do we find references to Solomon's being called a prophet.[52] Since, on the other hand, the understanding of all scriptural books as 'prophecy' is well attested, the third interpretation is preferable.[53]

4.4 ISRAEL AND THE NATIONS

The attitude towards Israel and the nations plays an important role in the debate on the background of Syr. A negative attitude towards Israel may reflect a Christian background; a high esteem for Israel may reflect a Jewish background.[54] Obviously, much depends on the context and the content of the translator's concept of 'Israel'.[55] In Syr a negative attitude towards Israel may account for the omission of 37:25, which speaks of the eternal existence of Jeshurun/Israel, but we cannot be certain that the omission is intentional.

In other cases Syr broadens the scope of a verse to 'all the inhabitants of the world', 'the communities' and the like. This tendency fits in well with a Christian setting, but cannot be considered as exclusively Christian.[56]

23:27 ܘܢܕܥܘܢ ܟܠܗܘܢ ܝܬ̈ܒܝ ܐܪܥܐ ܘܡܫܬܚܠܦܝܢ ܒܠ ܕܡܫܬܚܪܝܢ ܒܬܒܠ
'And *all the inhabitants of the earth* will know and all who are left over in the world will understand'; Gr καὶ ἐπιγνώσονται οἱ καταλειφθέντες 'and they that remain will know'.

---

[51] Cf. Lévi *L'Ecclésiastique* I, 129: Syr 'est étrange et semble bien chrétien, car Salomon n'a jamais été considéré comme un prophète chez les Juifs'.

[52] Contrast the understanding of David as a prophet in the New Testament, on which see e.g. Huber, 'Könige Israels', 168–171.

[53] See Barton, *Oracles of God*; Dodd, *According to the Scriptures*.

[54] Cf. Van Peursen, 'Jewish and/or Christian', 252.

[55] Cf. Weitzman, *Syriac Version*, 209–210, and *From Judaism to Christianity*, 7–8, on positive references to Israel in Pesh-Chronicles. Elsewhere in the Peshitta Weitzman detects both 'identification with the Jewish people' and 'alienation' from it (*Syriac Version*, 226–229, 231–233; *From Judaism to Christianity*, 16, 69–70).

[56] Cf. Weitzman, *Syriac Version*, 245–246: 'The combination of high regard for the nations with disdain for those Jews of differing beliefs was not unknown among Jewish groups. Indeed, it is only to be expected in a non-rabbinic group that lacked any rapport with rabbinic Judaism, which now commanded majority allegiance.' See also Drijvers, 'Peshitta of Sapientia Salomonis', 18 on positive references to the nations in Pesh-Wisdom.

31:11 ܘܐܫܬܥܝܬܗ ܢܬܠܘܢ ܟܢܘܫܬܐ 'And *the communities* will recount his praise; B קהל יספר ותהלתו: Instead of the singular קהל, Syr has a plural.[57]

39:10 ܚܟܡܬܗ ܢܬܠܘܢ ܟܢܘܫܬܐ 'The *communities* will recount his wisdom'; Gr 'the nations (ἔθνη) will declare his wisdom': According to Smend both Gr and Syr go back to a Hebrew text reading עדה, which Syr translated with ܟܢܘܫܬܐ because he was thinking of the Christian communities.[58]

4.5 VEGETARIANISM AND POVERTY

4.5.1 *Vegetarianism*

A number of the tendencies described in the preceding paragraphs point to a Jewish-Christian or Christian context, but none of them allows a precise identification of the community responsible for the translation. Winter considered the Ebionites to be the most likely candidates for the Jewish-Christian community in which Syr originated. He bases his view mainly on two characteristics: the preference for vegetarianism and the stress on the moral goodness of poverty. Winter's claim that the translator had a preference for vegetarianism is based on the following verse.[59]

19:1 ܡܣܟܢܘܬܐ ܢܐܪܬ ܒܣܪܐ ܘܪܚܡ 'And he who loves flesh will inherit poverty'; C מעוטים ובוזה [ית]ערער 'He who despises small things [will be d]estroyed' (= Gr).

It is uncertain however, what the idiom 'to love flesh' means.[60] It is also noteworthy that this verse uses 'to inherit poverty' with a negative connotation, which contradicts the alleged high esteem for poverty reflected elsewhere in Syr. In other cases the Syriac translator did not take the opportunity to change a positive statement about meat.

20:16(19) ܚܠܐ ܕܠܐ ܡܬܐܟܠܐ ܕܐܠܝܬܐ ܡܣܟܢܐ ܕܠܐ ܐܝܟܢܐ 'As a fat tail cannot be eaten without salt (so a word that is not said in the proper

---

[57] Cf. Smend, *Jesus Sirach*, 276: 'Syr. Plural (christlich)' (without further comment).

[58] Cf. Smend, *Jesus Sirach*, 355: 'Die Eitelkeit des Uebersetzers setzt 44,15 für עדה fälschend λαοί (vgl. λαός = עדה 45,7), ebenso hier ἔθνη (...). Syr. hat für עדה hier כנושתא indem er an die christlichen Gemeinden denkt'.

[59] Winter, *Ben Sira in Syriac*, 141–142; idem, 'Ben Sira in Syriac', I, 244

[60] Cf. Van Peursen, 'Jewish and/or Christian?', 258.

time)'. This is a plus in Syr compared with Gr. Compare 1 Sam 9:24, where Samuel reserves the fatty tail for Saul. The plus is probably original. In Gr or its Hebrew source 'that text has been obscured (...) because of a seeming conflict with the laws of sacrifice in Exod 29:22; Lev 3:9; 7:3; 8:25; 9:19.'[61]

Should Winter's hypothesis be correct, we would also aspect a negative attitude towards wine, but there are no variants reflecting that.

4.5.2 Poverty

Winter adduces a number of examples to support his argument that Syr reflects a high esteem for poverty.[62] In some cases Syr inserts a positive reference to poverty.

> 11:14 ܫܠܝܐ ܡܟܣܟܬܐ ܡܬܡ ܐܠܗܐ ܙܥܘܪ ܐܦ ܥܬܝܪ 'The rich one and the poor one are equal before the Lord'; A ריש ועושר מיי הוא 'Poverty and wealth are from the Lord' (= Gr). According to Winter Syr 'has all the signs of a deliberate alteration, whose motivation would seem to be a high regard for the state of poverty'[63]; the change in Syr 'is best understood as a way of vindicating the dignity of poverty'.[64]

> 49:12 ܘܒܡܣܟܢܘܬܗܘܢ ܐܩܝܡܘ ܡܕܒܚܐ '(And also Joshua, the son of Jozedek) who in their poverty established the altar and built the temple which was prepared for eternal glory; B+Gr have 'in their days' instead of 'poverty'. According to Winter, 'it is hard to see why these words should be inserted, unless the translation was made by somebody who had an unusual esteem for poverty'.[65]

In other cases Syr avoids a negative reference to the state of poverty.

---

[61] Thus Skehan–Di Lella, *Wisdom of Ben Sira*, 298; cf. Peters, *Ben Sirach*, 167: 'Wahrscheinlich hat Syr das ursprüngliche erhalten mit: *Wie ein Fettschwanz* (der Leckerbissen vom morgenländischen Fettschwanzschafe; vgl. 1 Sm 9, 24 wo אַלְיָה zu lesen ist) *nicht ohne Salz gegessen werden kann,* | *so ist ein Wort, das nicht zu seiner Zeit gesprochen wird.*'

[62] Winter, *Ben Sira in Syriac*, 143–151; similarly Nelson, *Syriac Version*, 123–125.

[63] Winter, 'Ben Sira in Syriac', I, 245.

[64] Winter, *Ben Sira in Syriac*, 144.

[65] Winter, *Ben Sira in Syriac*, 151; idem, 'Ben Sira in Syriac', I, 248–249. Compare also the references to poverty in relation to David's concern for the building of the temple in Ps 132:1 כל ענותו and 1 Chr 22:14 בעניי (Smend, *Jesus Sirach*, 473). According to Peters, *Ben Sirach*, 422, the reading 'poverty' may be original.

13:20 A תועבת גאוה ענוה ותועבת עשיר אביון 'An abomination to the proud is humility and an abomination to a rich man is a poor man' (= Gr); Syr omits this uncomplimentary comment about the poor.[66]

40:28 ܐܠܐ ܗܘ، ... 'My son, do not refuse him who asks you, and be not good to kill but good to keep alive';[67] B בני חיי מתן אל תחי טוב נאסף ממסתולל 'My son, do not lead a beggar's life ('a life of gifts'), better to be dead than to beg' (= Gr; cf. M). Syr keeps the theme of begging, but removes suggestions that the poor man is despicable.[68]

In other cases the Syriac translator did not change the text. Thus the (probably secondary[69]) reading in 18:33 ܠܐ ܬܗܘܐ ܡܣܟܢ 'do not become poor' has been retained. In still other cases Syr introduces a negative remark about riches.

37:14 ܗܢܘ ... 'A man's heart rejoices in his way) more than riches of the world that do not profit'; B[txt/mg](+D) משבעה צופים על שן 'more than seven watchmen on a watchtower' (= Gr).[70]

38:21 ... 'And do not rely upon riches, because in them there is no hope. For like a bird of heaven that flies and settles, so are riches before the people: it gladden you, but it does evil to someone else'; B אל תזכרהו כי אין לו תקוה מה תועיל ולך תריע 'Do not remember him (i.e. the dead person) because there is no hope for him. It does not profit him, and to you it causes pain'. 'The pessimistic thought that there was no hope for the dead would motivate a Christian to alter it. The notions of profit and pain have been retained, and they have been reworked ingeniously into strictures against wealth'.[71]

40:8/9 ... 'With all the men of flesh, care is with them) and riches drive away their sleep'; B שד ושבר רעה ומות 'violence, destruction, evil and death'; Gr καὶ ἐπὶ ἁμαρτωλῶν ἑπταπλάσια πρὸς ταῦτα 'and seven times more for the sinners'. Syr has a hostile reference to wealth not found in B and Gr.[72]

---

[66] Winter, *Ben Sira in Syriac,* 145; idem, 'Ben Sira in Syriac', I, 245–246.

[67] Instead of ܗܘ 7a1 has ܗܘܬ, cf. § 23.2.2 (end).

[68] Winter, *Ben Sira in Syriac,* 149; idem, 'Ben Sira in Syriac', I, 248.

[69] Cf. §§ 2.3.3 (2), 3.7.1.

[70] Winter, *Ben Sira in Syriac,* 147; idem, 'Ben Sira in Syriac', I, 246–247; for 'riches of the/this world' compare Pesh-1 Chr 29:28 (Weitzman, *Syriac Version,* 226).

[71] Thus Winter, 'Ben Sira in Syriac', I, 247; see also idem, *Ben Sira in Syriac,* 147–148.

[72] Winter, *Ben Sira in Syriac,* 148; idem, 'Ben Sira in Syriac', I, 247.

Some of the examples put forward by Winter are open to other explanations as well.

11:18 ܐܝܬ ܕܥܬܪ ܡܢ ܡܣܟܢܘܬܗ 'There is one who becomes rich from his poverty'. ܡܢ ܡܣܟܢܘܬܗ corresponds to A מהתענות. The Syriac translator missed the particular meaning of מהתענות (§ 3.2 [d]). We cannot be sure that his translation reflects an intentional alteration of the text.

29:28 ܠܒ ܠܒ ܗܒ ܗܘ ܠܡܣܟܢܐ ܘܡܢ ܡܐ ܕܒܐܝܕܝܟ ܐܘܟܠܝܘܗܝ، ܘܐܢ ܥܪܛܠܝ ܗܘ ܐܠܒܫܝܗܝ، ܡܛܠ ܕܒܣܪܟ ܐܢܬ ܡܟܣܐ ܘܠܐܠܗܐ ܗܘ ܡܘܙܦ ܐܢܬ ܘܗܘ ܦܪܥ ܠܟ ܚܕ ܒܫܒܥܐ 'Much, give much to the poor man and nourish him from what is in your hand; and if he is naked, clothe him, because you cover your own flesh and you lend to God, and He will repay you sevenfold': This is a plus in Syr. Winter considers it an 'addition from the pen of one who felt strongly about the moral goodness of poverty'.[73] According to Smend, however, it originated from a secondary Hebrew text; cf. Isa 58:7 and Sir 35:13.[74] But even if the Syriac translator is responsible for the addition, it reflects his appreciation of charity, which is not identical to a high esteem for poverty.[75]

32:1 ܘܒܪܝܫ ܥܬܝܪܐ ܠܐ ܬܣܬܡܟ '(If they have appointed you as the chief, be not exalted) and at the head of the rich do not recline'. This is a plus compared with B and Gr. Winter considered it an addition by the Syriac translator, reflecting hostility to wealth,[76] but the reading is now also found in MS F!

44:6 ܘܡܣܬܡܟܝܢ ܚܝܠܐ 'and at those who are sustained with strength'; B+M אנשי חיל וסמכי כח (B סומכי). Winter argued that the Hebrew חיל means 'wealth', a notion that has been omitted in Syr,[77] but this is not certain.

We can conclude that the devotion to poverty is indeed present in Syr, although not as pervasive as suggested by Winter. Moreover, an appreciation of charity should not be confused with a high esteem for poverty (cf. 29:28). Thus rabbinic sources reflect an admiration for charity but not for poverty. The latter is found, however, in several New Testament passages and in non-rabbinic Jewish sources, such as the Dead Sea Scrolls. Since it is not exclusively Ebionite, it cannot be used as an argument for an Ebionite background of Syr. Disdain for

---

[73] Winter, 'Ben Sira in Syriac', I, 246; see also idem, *Ben Sira in Syriac*, 145–146.

[74] Smend, *Jesus Sirach*, 263.

[75] Charity was also an important value for the translator of Pesh-Chronicles. Thus in 2 Chr 31:10 the Peshitta adds 'and give to the poor and the needy'; Weitzman, *Syriac Version*, 14.

[76] Winter, *Ben Sira in Syriac*, 146; idem, 'Ben Sira in Syriac', I, 246.

[77] Winter, *Ben Sira in Syriac*, 150; idem, 'Ben Sira in Syriac', I, 248.

earthly wealth occurs also in the Peshitta of Proverbs, Qoheleth, Chronicles and Wisdom.[78]

4.6 THE CREATION OF WISDOM

In four passages Syr seems to avoid references to the creation of Wisdom, namely 1:4, 9; 39:32; 42:21. Winter attributed this to a post-Arian revision of Syr by orthodox Christians. Since Wisdom was identified with Christ, references to its creation were considered blasphemous.[79] According to Owens the material does not support Winter's claim.[80]

1:4 ܚܟܡܬܐ ܡܢ ܟܠܗܘܢ ܗܠܝܢ ܣܓܝܐܐ 'Wisdom is more than all these'; Gr προτέρα πάντων ἔκτισται σοφία 'Wisdom was created before all things'. Syr may also be the result of a confusion of נברא and רבא in Heb; the context allows both.[81]

1:9 ܒܨܗ 'He explored her'; Gr κύριος αὐτὸς ἔκτισεν αὐτήν 'The Lord himself created her'. It is certainly possible that both Gr and Syr go back to a Hebrew text that had חלקה.[82]

39:32 ܡܛܠ ܕܡܢ ܪܫܐ ܒܪܝܢ ܐܢܘܢ 'Because from the beginning they are created'; B על כן מראש התיצבתי 'Therefore from the beginning I stood firm'; Gr διὰ τοῦτο ἐξ ἀρχῆς ἐστηρίχθην 'Therefore from the beginning I was established'. According to Winter, 'the Hebrew word התעכבתי [his reading instead of התיצבתי] is very rare (...) it is possible that the Syrian translator was about to render it as ܐܬܥܟܒ Possibly he realized that this could imply the creation of wisdom, and altered one letter to make it refer to the whole of creation.'[83] But Winter's reading is complicated and based on a faulty reading of Heb.[84]

42:21 ܣܗܕܘܬܐ ܕܚܟܡܬܐ, ܘܣܗܡܘ ܠܥܠܡ 'And wisdom stands before Him for ever'; B[txt] ג.[...]תו תכן; B[mg] גבורת; M גבורת חכמ[תו]; Gr τὰ μεγαλεῖα τῆς σοφίας αὐτοῦ ἐκόσμησεν 'And the greatness of his wisdom He

---

[78] Weitzman, *Syriac Version*, 225–226.

[79] Winter, *Ben Sira in Syriac*, 164–176; idem, 'Ben Sira in Syriac', II, 501–505; similarly Nelson, *Syriac Version*, 116–119.

[80] Owens, 'Early Syriac Text of Ben Sira', 42–48; idem, Review of Nelson, *Syriac Version*, 166.

[81] Owens, 'Early Syriac Text of Ben Sira', 45; cf. Smend, *Jesus Sirach*, 7; *pace* Winter, *Ben Sira in Syriac*, 165–166; idem, 'Ben Sira in Syriac', II, 501.

[82] Owens, 'Early Syriac Text of Ben Sira', 49; cf. Van Peursen, *Verbal System*, 72; *pace* Winter *Ben Sira in Syriac*, 165; idem, 'Ben Sira in Syriac', II, 502.

[83] Winter, *Ben Sira in Syriac*, 166–168 (quotation from p. 167); idem, 'Ben Sira in Syriac', II, 502–503.

[84] Cf. Owens, 'Early Syriac Text of Ben Sira', 44–45.

has arranged'. According to Winter Syr altered the text for fear of giving the impression that God's establishing Wisdom might seem to imply that He had created it.[85] But this interpretation is forced. Syr is entirely explainable as the result of the reading of the Hebrew verb as תִּכֵּן.[86]

In this context we should also mention another reference to Wisdom that according to Edersheim has been altered by a Christian translator.

> 24:5 ܐܝܟ ܐܢܫܐ ܥܡܗ ܒܫܡܝܐ 'I dwelt together with Him in heaven'; Gr γῦρον οὐρανοῦ ἐκύκλωσα μόνη 'Alone I encompassed the circuit of heaven'. According to Edersheim the background of the reading in Syr may be the Christian identification of 'Wisdom' with Christ. He refers to John 1:1, where it is said that the Logos was with God. [87] Note, however, that ܥܡܗ and ܐܢܫܐ occur neither in the Peshitta of John 1:1, nor in that of Prov 8:30. In John 1:1 the Peshitta and the Curetonian have ܠܘܬ; Pesh-Prov 8:30 has ܡܬܩܢܐ,.

4.7 CONCLUSION

In the present chapter we have encountered a lot of evidence that is relevant to the translator's religious profile. However, since this will be the subject of Chapter Six, we will restrict ourselves here with a short summary of our findings.

(1) The translator had an indifferent, if not hostile attitude towards the sacrificial temple service. This appears from the omission of references to sacrifices, priesthood and temple, the substitution of references to sacrifices by remarks about prayer or charity, and the imprecise or shortened rendering of sacrificial terminology.

(2) The translator did not bother to retain references to 'the Law', and even tends to omit them. Winter's suggestion that the

---

[85] Winter *Ben Sira in Syriac*, 168-171; idem, 'Ben Sira in Syriac', II, 504.

[86] Thus Owens, 'Early Syriac Text of Ben Sira', 43–44; see already Lévi, *L'Ecclésiastique* I, 58.

[87] Cf. Edersheim, 'Ecclesiasticus', 126: 'Remembering that the ancient Christian writers identified "Wisdom" in Ecclus. with Christ, it suggests a Christian hand (...) In any case the expression "together with Him" goes much beyond the language of Prov. viii. 30, in which Wisdom presents herself as 'an artificer by His side' (אֶצְלוֹ— certainly not = "together with Him").'

translator had a high esteem for the Law and rejected the Prophets should be abandoned.

(3) Syr omits a remark about the eternity of Israel and inserts references to 'the nations'. However, we do not know whether the omission was intentional, and the remarks about the nations do not exceed what we find in, for example, Deutero-Isaiah.

(4) Winter argued that Syr reflects a high esteem for vegetarianism and poverty, two features that were typical of the Ebionites. The high esteem for poverty is indeed well-attested in Syr, although we should not confuse it with another notion, namely that of charity towards the poor (Winter does not distinguish between them). There are no convincing arguments for the translator's alleged vegetarianism.

(5) Winter's hypothesis that the Syriac translator avoided references to the creation of Wisdom is unfounded. The four cases that allegedly reflect this tendency are open to other, in most cases preferable, explanations.

CHAPTER FIVE

INTERTEXTUAL ANALYSIS

5.1 INFLUENCE OF THE OLD TESTAMENT

Syr did not originate in a vacuum. In Jewish and Christian movements oral traditions and written documents were cultivated, cherished and transmitted. But can we establish the sources with which the translator was in touch? Was he acquainted with the Hebrew Bible, the New Testament or rabbinic literature? Parallels with these corpora may assist us in establishing the translator's religious background, but before we can use the parallels for this purpose, our first task is a formal registration of them. This means that we have to investigate whether it is possible to identify phrases or idioms in Syr that seem to be due to the influence of passages in one of these corpora. The original Sirach already contained biblical references, but since our concern is the translator's work, we will restrict ourselves to parallels that are secondary, as far as a comparison with the other textual witnesses can tell us. And even the secondary parallels are not necessarily due to the translator. We will take into account the possibility that some parallels were already present in the translator's source text and that others have entered the text during the textual transmission of Syr.

The present paragraph will be concerned with parallels with the Old Testament in general. One of the questions that will concern us is the question of whether Winter's claim that the translator avoided references to the Prophets (cf. § 4.3.2) is correct. § 5.2 will deal with the more specific question of whether these parallels reveal any influence of the Peshitta version of the Old Testament. This question is relevant for gaining insight into the milieu in which the Peshitta originated and the character of the sources that the translator had at his disposal.[1] In § 5.3 the parallels with rabbinic sources and other affinities with rab-

---

[1] H.P. Rüger's unlikely hypothesis that the translator of Syr was dependent on the Targums has been discussed in § 3.8.

binic literature will be investigated and § 5.4 will be concerned with parallels with the New Testament.

In the present paragraph we will distinguish between the following categories: (A) Syr gives a free rendering containing words or phrases that occur also in other parts of the Old Testament and seem to have been borrowed from them; (B) Syr adds phrases or even whole verses taken from the Old Testament; (C) Heb or Gr contains a reference to a biblical passage which has been strengthened in Syr; (D) Syr introduces allusions to biblical stories. Finally we will have a look at (E) the tendency to make references to biblical stories in the Praise of the Fathers more explicit by introducing biblical phraseology.

The establishment of parallels is based on the observation of formal similarities, but it is sometimes difficult to determine what degree of similarity is significant enough to speak of parallels. Moreover, if parallels can be established, their background often remains obscure. Did the translator possess manuscripts with the Hebrew or Syriac text of the Old Testament? Or did he know parts of them by heart? Or did he have a general acquaintance with biblical phraseology and ideas? His use of 'in the expanse of heaven' in 26:16 (see below), for example, suggests that he was acquainted with this expression, but does not show that he wished to refer to the creation story, and the combination of 'enmity', 'the head of the serpent' and 'the wife' in Sir 25:15 (see below) does not necessarily show dependence on the text of Genesis 3.

A. In the following cases Syr gives a free rendering containing words or phrases that occur also in other parts of the Old Testament and seem to have been borrowed from them.[2]

(1) From the Pentateuch

> 26:16 ܒܪܩܝܥܐ ܕܫܡܝܐ 'in the expanse of heaven'; Gr ἐν ὑψίστοις κυρίου 'in the Lord's highest'. Cf. Gen 1:15 MT ברקיע השמים; Pesh ܒܪܩܝܥܐ ܕܫܡܝܐ.
>
> 30:8 ܗܟܢܐ ܗܘ ܒܪܐ ܡܪܘܕܐ ܕܠܐ ܫܡܥ ܠܐܒܘܗܝ 'Thus is a rebellious son who does not listen to his father'; Gr καὶ υἱὸς ἀνειμένος ἐκβαίνει προαλής 'And a son who is left to himself turns out precipitous'. Cf. Deut 21:18 MT בן סורר ומורה איננו שמע בקול אביו ובקול אמו 'a stubborn and rebellious son who does not listen to the voice of his father

---

[2] Cf. Weitzman, *Syriac Version*, 43.

and his mother'; Pesh ܒܪܐ ܡܒܙܪܐ ܘܡܨܥܪܢܐ ܘܠܐ ܥܒܕ ܠܐܒܘܗܝ ܘܠܛܐ ܐܡܗ.

34:2 ܡܢ ܕܡܗܝܡܢ ܠܚܙܘܐ ܕܠܠܝܐ 'who trusts in a vision of the night'; Gr ὁ ἐπέχων ἐνυπνίοις 'who takes notice of dreams'. Cf. Gen 46:2 MT במראת הלילה 'in the visions of the night'; Pesh ܒܚܙܘܐ ܕܠܠܝܐ.

35:17 ܘܨܠܘܬܐ ܕܐܪܡܠܬܐ ܫܡܥ '(He does not reject the groan of the orphans) and He hears the prayers of the widows'; B ואלמנה כי תרבה שיח. Cf. Exod 22:21–22 MT כל אלמנה ויתום (...) שמע אשמע צעקתו 'any widow or orphan (...) I will certainly hear their cry'; Pesh ܘܟܠ ܐܪܡܠܬܐ ܘܝܬܡܐ (...) ܡܫܡܥ ܐܫܡܥ ܩܠܗܘܢ.

36:17 ܥܡܟ ܕܐܬܩܪܝ ܫܡܟ ܥܠܘܗܝ 'Your people, who are called by Your name'; B עם נקרא בשמך (= Gr). Cf. Deut 28:10 MT כי שם יהוה נקרא עליך 'That you are called by the name of the Lord'; Pesh ܕܫܡܗ ܕܡܪܝܐ ܐܬܩܪܝ ܥܠܝܟ.[3]

Several factors are involved in the parallel to Genesis 3 in 25:15.

25:15 ܠܝܬ ܪܫܐ ܡܪܝܪܐ ܡܢ ܪܫܗ ܕܚܘܝܐ ܘܠܝܬ ܒܥܠܕܒܒܘܬܐ ܕܡܪܝܪܐ ܡܢ ܕܐܢܬܬܐ 'There is no head more bitter than the head of a serpent, and there is no enmity more bitter than that of a wife'; Gr οὐκ ἔστιν κεφαλὴ ὑπὲρ κεφαλὴν ὄφεως, καὶ οὐκ ἔστιν θυμὸς ὑπὲρ θυμὸν ἐχθροῦ 'There is no head above the head of a serpent, and there is no wrath above the wrath of an enemy'. In the first half of this verse both Gr and Syr misunderstood ראש 'poison' as 'head' (§ 3.4 [a]); in the second half Syr has 'wife' instead of 'enemy'. The latter change is a consequence of the former, because the 'head of the serpent' reminds of Genesis 3 and 'the bitterness of a woman' strengthens this link. Compare especially Gen 3:14–15, where enmity (ܒܥܠܕܒܒܘܬܐ), the head (ܪܫܐ) of the serpent (ܚܘܝܐ), and the wife (ܐܢܬܬܐ) occur together. The change from 'enemy' to 'woman' also fits the context, because the following passage deals with the evil of women. According to Edersheim the Syriac translator intentionally altered the text to make the text allude to the Christian doctrine of the fall of man.[4] Compare Wisdom 16:10 ܒܢܝܟ ܕܝܢ ܠܪ̈ܫܘܬܐ ܕܬܢܝܢܐ ܘܠܫܢܝܗܘܢ ܐܦ ܙܟܘ 'Your sons, however, overcame the teeth and the heads of the dragons'; Gr τοὺς δὲ υἱούς σου οὐδὲ ἰοβόλων δρακόντων ἐνίκησαν ὀδόντες 'And the teeth of venomous serpents did not overcome your sons'.[5] There are no compelling reasons, however, to

[3] Smend, *Jesus Sirach*, 321.

[4] Edersheim, 'Ecclesiasticus', 134: 'We have little doubt that the Syr. here purposely altered the original Hebrew, which was correctly given by the Greek, and the alteration is the more cunning that it fits so well into the context of the following verses. But what was the purpose of the alteration? We cannot help suspecting that it was intended to allude to the doctrine of the fall of man.'

[5] Cf. Drijvers's comment on this verse in his 'Peshitta of Sapientia Salomonis', 25: 'In this translation the text refers to Gen 3:15 and symbolizes man's victory over the serpent or dragon, i.e. mortality; this is a very common motif in early Syriac the-

think that the reference to Genesis 3 in Sir 25:15 is from a Christian hand. It is already implied in Sir 25:24 ‘From a woman sin started, and because of her we all will die’.

(2) From the Latter Prophets

18:10 ܐܝܟ ܕܠܡܡܠܐ ܓܘܪܐ ܡܢ ܝܡܐ ‘as to fill a jar from the sea’; Gr ὡς σταγὼν ὕδατος ἀπὸ θαλάσσης ‘like a drop of water from the sea’. According to Smend the ‘jar’ has entered the text under the influence of Isa 40:15 MT כמר מדלי ‘(Behold, the nations are) like a drop from the jar’ (Pesh ܐܝܟ ܩܛܪܬܐ ܡܢ ܕܘܠܐ).[6]

23:19 ܡܢܐ ܕܒܚܫܘܟܐ ܡܡܠܠܐ ܥܒ̈ܕܝܗܘܢ ‘(And he considers closely) what in the darkness is the appearance of their works’; Gr εἰς ἀπόκρυφα μέρη ‘in the hidden parts’. Cf. Isa 29:15 MT והיה במחשך מעשיהם (Woe to those…) and whose work are in darkness’; Pesh ܘܗܘܝܢ ܒܚܫܘܟܐ ܥܒ̈ܕܝܗܘܢ.

26:28 ܐܫܠܡܝܗܝ، ܠܝܘܡܐ ܕܩܛܠܐ ‘Deliver him on the day of slaughter!’; Gr ὁ κύριος ἑτοιμάσει εἰς ῥομφαίαν αὐτόν ‘The Lord makes him ready for the sword’. Cf. Jer 12:3 MT והקדשם ליום הרגה ‘Set them apart for the day of slaughter’; Pesh ܘܩܕܫ ܠܝܘܡ ܕܩܛܠܐ.

36:17 ܘܚܕܝ، ܥܠ ܥܡܟ ‘And rejoice in Your people’; B רחם על עם (= Gr). cf. Isa 65:19 MT וגלתי בירושלם וששתי בעמי ‘I will be glad about Jerusalem and rejoice in My people’; Pesh ܘܐܚܕܐ ܒܐܘܪܫܠܡ ܘܐܪܘܙ ܒܥܡܝ.

(3) From the Writings

18:26 ܘܟܠܗܘܢ ܗ̈ܠܝܢ ܫܦܝ̈ܪܢ ܐܝܟ ܩܕܡ ܐܠܗܐ ‘And they are all beautiful before God’; Syr has ‘beautiful’ where Gr has ταχινά ‘quick’; cf. Qoh 3:11 MT את הכל עשה יפה בעתו ‘He has made everything beautiful in its time’; Pesh ܟܠ ܕܥܒܕ ܕܫܦܝܪ ܒܙܒܢܗ.

21:11 ܘܕܕܚܠ ܠܐܠܗܐ ܠܐ ܢܣܬܢܩ ܠܗ ܡܕܡ ‘And he who fears God, he will lack nothing’; Gr καὶ συντέλεια τοῦ φόβου κυρίου σοφία ‘And the completion of the fear of the Lord is wisdom’. Cf. Ps 34:11 MT ודרשי יהוה לא יחסרו כל טוב ‘But those who fear the Lord will lack no good thing’; Pesh ܘܐܝܠܝܢ ܕܠܡܪܝܐ ܒܥܝܢ ܠܐ ܢܬܒܨܪ، ܠܗܘܢ ܛܒܬܐ.

28:6 ܘܠܫܝܘܠ ܘܠܐܒܕܢܐ ‘and (to) Sheol, and (to) destruction’; Gr καταφθορὰν καὶ θάνατον ‘destruction and death’. Cf. Prov 15:11, 27:20 MT שאול ואבדון and שאול ואבדה ‘Sheol and destruction’; Pesh ܫܝܘܠ ܘܐܒܕܢܐ.

---

ology and a central element in the famous Hymn of the Pearl in the apocryphal Acts of Thomas.’

6 Smend, *Jesus Sirach*, 164: ‘Der Schlauch des Syr. beruht wohl auf Glossierung seiner Vorlage nach Jes. 40, 15 (מר מדלי)’.

28:13 ܩܛܝܠܐ ܣܓܝܐ̈ܐ ܐܚܬܬ 'It [i.e. the triple tongue] has brought down many slain [ܩܛܝܠܐ]'; Gr πολλοὺς γὰρ εἰρηνεύοντας 'many peaceable men'. Cf. Prov 7:26 MT כי רבים חללים הפילה 'For she has brought down many wounded'; Pesh ܡܛܠ ܕܣܓܝܐܐ ܕܩܛܝܠܐ ܐܦܠܬ.

31:23 ܥܝܢܐ ܛܒܬܐ ܥܠ ܠܚܡܐ ܡܒܪܟܐ 'A generous eye over the bread is blessed'; B טוב על לחם תברך שפה 'Him who is generous over the bread the lip will bless'. Cf. Prov 22:9 MT טוב עין הוא יברך 'He who has a generous eye will be blessed'; Pesh ܡܢ ܕܛܒܬܐ ܥܝܢܗ ܗܘ ܢܬܒܪܟ.

36:22 ܐܝܟ ܨܒܝܢܐ ܕܥܡܟ 'according to the will of Your people'; B כרצונך על עמך (B^mg ברצונך). Cf. Ps 106:4 MT רצון עמך 'the favour (that You have shown to) Your people'; Pesh ܒܨܒܝܢܗ ܕܥܡܟ.

The following is a complicated example:

35:20 ܘܨܠܘܬܗܘܢ ܥܢܢ̈ܐ ܡܚܬܐ 'And their prayer brings down the clouds'; B וצעקה ענן חשתה (mg[1] וצעקתיה; mg[2] צעקתה) 'And the cloud has retained the sigh (i.e. restrained it from reaching God)'[7] or 'her cry hastens to the clouds'.[8] Cf. Ps 18:10 MT ויט שמים וירד 'He bowed the heavens and came down'; Pesh ܘܐܪܟܢ ܫܡܝܐ ܘܢܚܬ. Syr 'seems to reverse the imagery of Ps 18:10'.[9] Compare 35:21 ܨܠܘܬܗܘܢ ܕܡܣܟܢ̈ܐ ܠܥܠ ܡܢ ܥܢܢ̈ܐ ܣܠܩܐ 'The prayer of the poor rises up above the clouds'.

Our argument given above that some of the secondary parallels in Syr may already have been extant in the translator's Hebrew source is supported by cases where both Syr and Heb share such a secondary parallel, as in[10]

36:10 ܡܛܠ ܕܠܝܬ ܕܢܐܡܪ ܠܟ ܡܢܐ ܥܒܕ ܐܢܬ 'So that there is no-one who can say to You, What are you doing?' B כי מי יאמר לך מה תעשה; Gr καὶ ἐκδιηγησάσθωσαν τὰ μεγαλεῖά σου 'And let your mighty deeds be proclaimed'; Syr and B contain a borrowing from Job 9:12 MT מי יאמר אליו מה תעשה 'Who says to him, What are you doing?' Pesh ܘܡܢܘ ܢܐܡܪ ܠܗ ܡܢܐ ܥܒܕ ܐܢܬ.

Sometimes only part of the Hebrew witnesses agrees with Syr.

32:21 ܥܠ ܐܘܪܚܐ ܕܥܘ̈ܠܐ '(Be not confident) on the way of the unrighteous'; B[2]+E+F בדרך רשעים; B[1] אל תבטח בדרך מחתף 'Do not

---

7 Thus Yadin, *War of the Sons of Light*, 108–109 n. 4; cf. Van Peursen, *Verbal System*, 257.

8 Cf. Schechter–Taylor, *Wisdom of Ben Sira*, xli, 59.

9 Skehan–Di Lella, *Wisdom of Ben Sira*, 415; Smend, *Jesus Sirach*, 315, calls the reading in Syr 'sinnlos'.

10 Compare Smend's comment on 18:10, quoted above, note 6, and Reiterer's analysis of 45:8 mentioned below, in note 22.

trust the road, because of bandits'; B^mg (to B[1]) רשעים. Heb reflects two readings, one with מחתף (B[1]; cf. 50:4; Prov 23:28) and another with רשעים (B[2], B^mg, E, F). Syr agrees with the second. מחתף is preferable because in the following 'the way' is not referring to the way of the wicked.[11] The reading רשעים is perhaps influenced by Ps 1:1 MT בעצת רשעים ובדרך חטאים 'in the counsel of the wicked and the way of the sinners'; Pesh ܒܐܘܪܚܐ ܕܥ̈ܘܠܐ (...) ܘܒܪܚܡܐ ܕܫ̈ܛܝܐ.[12]

B. Sometimes Syr adds phrases or even whole verses taken from the Hebrew Bible.

(1) From the Prophets

36:2 ܘܐܝܬܐ ܪܘܓܙܟ ܥܠ ܥܡܡ̈ܐ ܕܠܐ ܝܕܥܘܢܟ 'And bring anger upon the nations who do not know You'; B [וש]ים פחדך על כל הגוים. Cf. Jer 10:25 MT שפך חמתך על הגוים אשר לא ידעוך; Pesh ܐܫܘܕ ܚܡܬܟ ܥܠ ܥܡܡ̈ܐ ܕܠܐ ܝܕܥܘܢܟ.

(2) From the Writings

27:20 ܐܝܟ ܛܒܝܐ ܡܢ ܢܫܒܐ ܘܐܝܟ ܨܦܪܐ ܡܢ ܦܚܐ '(Because he has escaped) like a deer from the net and like a bird out of the snare'. ܘܐܝܟ ܨܦܪܐ ܡܢ ܦܚܐ is an addition taken from Prov 6:5 MT הנצל כצבי מיד וכצפור מיד יקוש; Pesh ܕܬܬܦܨܐ ܐܝܟ ܛܒܝܐ ܡܢ ܢܫܒܐ ܘܐܝܟ ܨܦܪܐ ܡܢ ܦܚܐ.

36:31 ܠܥܠܘܕܐ ܕܕܡܐ ܠܛܒܝܐ '(For who will believe) a boy who resembles a deer'; B+D בגדוד צבא 'in an armed band'; C בצבא גדוד. The Syriac translator understood גדוד in the sense of Syriac ܥܠܘܕܐ (§ 3.4 [d]) and צבא as 'gazelle' (cf. the א in צבאים in 1 Chr 12:9 and צבאות in Cant 2:7; 3:5). He connected these words with ܕܕܡܐ ܠ, which comes from Cant 2:9 MT דומה דודי לצבי; Pesh ܕܡܐ ܕܕܝ ܠܛܒܝܐ.[13]

39:13–14 ܘܐܝܟ ܒܣܡ̈ܐ ܛܒܐ ܢܒܣܡ ܪܝܚܟܘܢ ܐܝܟ ܪܝܚܐ ܕܠܒܢܢ ܒܐܪ̈ܙܘܗܝ, ܘܐܝܟ ܥܩܪܐ ܕܫܘܫܢܬܐ ܡܠܟܐ 'And like sweet incenses your odour will be sweet, like the odour of Lebanon in its cedars and like the root of the lily of the king'; Gr καὶ ὡς λίβανος εὐωδιάσατε ὀσμὴν καὶ ἀνθήσατε ἄνθος ὡς κρίνον 'And as frankincense give a sweet odour and put forth flowers as a lily'.[14] Syr reflects influence of Hos 14:6 ('lily' and 'Lebanon') and Cant 4:11 ('odour of Lebanon').

---

[11] Smend, *Jesus Sirach*, 295.
[12] Skehan–Di Lella, *Wisdom of Ben Sira*, 395.
[13] Di Lella, *Hebrew Text of Sirach*, 70; Smend, *Jesus Sirach*, 326.
[14] Gr λίβανοι may go back to לבנון (cf. 50:8c, 12d) or לבונה 'incense' (cf. 50:9a). The latter reading is preferable because of the following 'odour'.

In this category too it is difficult to determine what additions were already present in the translator's Hebrew source text. Again, we can adduce examples where the addition is also attested in Heb.

14:16 ܘܟܠ ܡܕܡ ܕܫܦܝܪ ܠܡܥܒܕ ܩܕܡ ܐܠܗܐ ܥܒܕ 'And everything that is beautiful to do, do it before God'; A וכל דבר שיפה לעשות לפני אלהים עשה; not in Gr. This is an addition in A and Syr in the spirit of Qoh 9:10, 11:9.

16:17 ܐܘ ܡܢܐ ܗܝ ܢܦܫܝ ܒܝܬ ܪ̈ܘܚܬܐ ܕܟܠܗܘܢ ܒܢܝ̈ܢܫܐ 'Or what is my soul among the spirits of the people?'; A ומה נפשי בקצות רוחות כל בני אדם. This is a gloss based on Num 27:16.

31:6 ܘܠܐ ܐܫܟܚܘ ܠܡܦܨܝܘ ܐܢܘܢ ܡܢ ܒܝܫܬܐ ܐܦܠܐ ܠܡܦܪܩ ܐܢܘܢ ܒܝܘܡܐ ܕܣܘܦܗܘܢ 'And they were unable to deliver them from evil or to save them on the day of their end'; B[txt] ולא מצאו להנצל מרעה וגם ולהושע ביום עברה; B[mg] ולא מצאו להנצל ביום עברה ולהושיע ביום רעה. This is a gloss in B and Syr. Because it cuts 31:6 away from 31:7, it is evidently an addition, due to the influence of Prov 11:4 MT לא יועיל הון ביום עברה וצדקה תציל ממות; Pesh ܠܐ ܡܘܬܪܐ ܩܢܝܢܐ ܒܝܘܡܐ ܕܪܘܓܙܐ. ܙܕܝܩܘܬܐ ܕܝܢ ܡܦܨܝܐ ܡܢ ܡܘܬܐ.

Sometimes the Hebrew evidence is divided.

35:12 ܡܢ ܕܝܗܒ ܓܝܪ ܠܡܣܟܢܐ ܠܐܠܗܐ ܗܘ ܡܘܙܦ ܡܢܘ ܓܝܪ ܦܪܘܥܐ ܐܠܐ ܐܢ ܗܘ 'For he who gives to the poor man lends to God, for who is a rewarder if not He?' This is a plus that is also found in B[mg], but not in B[txt] or Gr. It is a gloss based on Prov 19:17.[15]

C. Sometimes Heb or Gr contains a reference to a biblical passage which has been strengthened in Syr. Especially in the Praise of the Fathers there is a tendency to make references to biblical stories explicit.

(1) Stories from the Pentateuch

44:17 ܢܘܚ ܙܕܝܩܐ ܐܫܬܟܚ ܒܕܪܗ ܫܠܡ ܒܥܕܢܐ ܕܛܘܦܢܐ ܗܘܐ ܚܘܠܦܢܐ ܠܥܠܡܐ ܘܡܛܠܬܗ ܗܘܬ ܫܘܙܒܘܬܐ ܘܝܡܐ ܠܗ ܐܠܗܐ ܕܠܐ ܢܗܘܐ ܬܘܒ ܛܘܦܢܐ

[15] According to Winter the gloss originated in Syr as an Ebionite addition, which was later retroverted into Hebrew, but this is unlikely. Owens gives the following objections against Winter's interpretation: (1) It cannot explain why the Hebrew translator rearranged the word-order. (2) It cannot explain why the Hebrew scribe did not translate Syriac ܦܪܘܥܐ as literally as possible, using the participle גומל or the phrase that already lay before him in v. 13, אלוה תשלומות. (3) The Hebrew text 'presents precisely the sort of slight reworking of a Proverbs saying that is so characteristic of Ben Sira'. The plus occurs also in Aphrahat's quotation of this verse in *Dem.* 20:4, cf. § 1.2; Winter, 'Ben Sira in Syriac', I, 506; idem, *Ben Sira in Syriac*, 240; Owens, 'Early Syriac Text of Ben Sira', 56–60 (quotation from p. 58).

'Noah the righteous one was found perfect in his generation. In the time of the flood he was a substitute. And for his sake there was redemption and God swore to him that there would be no flood again';[16] B [נ]ח צדיק נמצא תמים לעת כלה היה תחליף בעבורו היה שארית ובבריתו חדל מבול 'Noah the righteous one was found perfect. At the time of destruction he became a substitute. For his sake there was a remnant and through his covenant the flood ended'. ܒܕܪܗ is a plus under the influence of Gen 6:9; ܒܛܒܥܐ ܕܠܡܒܘܠܐ strengthens the reference to the flood;[17] and ܘܝܡܐ ܠܗ ܐܠܗܐ ܕܠܐ ܢܗܘܐ ܬܘܒ ܠܡܒܘܠܐ may be due to the influence of Gen 9:11.[18]

(2) Stories from the Former Prophets

48:14 ܘܒܡܘܬܗ ܐܚܝ ܡܝܬܐ 'And in his death he gave life to a dead person'; B ובמותו תמהי מעשה 'And in his death (he did) marvellous works'. Syr makes the reference to 2 Kgs 13:21 more explicit.

D. Sometimes the translator introduces allusions to biblical stories.

33:30 ܐܫܠܛܝܗܝ ܒܒܝܬܟ 'Entrust him in your house'; Gr ἔργασαι 'Give (him) work to do'; Syr is reminiscent of Gen 39:4 MT ויפקדהו על ביתו; Pesh ܘܐܫܠܛܗ ܥܠ ܒܝܬܗ.[19]

34:26 ܕܩܛܠ ܚܒܪܗ ܝܪܬ ܢܟܣܘܗܝ 'He who kills his neighbour inherits his possessions'; Gr φονεύων τὸν πλησίον ὁ ἀφαιρούμενος ἐμβίωσιν 'He who seizes his neighbour's living murders him'. Syr is reminiscent of 1 Kings 21.

47:16 ܘܨܒܝܢ ܠܫܡܥܟ 'And they wanted the report about you'; Gr καὶ ἠγαπήθης ἐν τῇ εἰρήνῃ σου 'And you were loved in your peace'. Syr is reminiscent of 1 Kgs 10:24; cf. also Job 29:21–23 and Isa 42:4.

48:13 ܐܬܟܣܝܬ ܡܢܗ '(Nothing) was hidden from him (i.e. Elijah)'; B נפלא ממנו 'too wonderful for him'. Syr is reminiscent of 2 Kings 1.

E. Especially in the Praise of the Fathers we see a tendency in Syr to introduce biblical phraseology, most often taken from a context dealing with the same subject matter as the Sirach passage.

(1) From the Pentateuch

44:21b ܠܟܠܗܘܢ ܥܡܡܐ ܕܐܪܥܐ 'All nations of the world'; B גוים. Cf. Gen 22:18 כל גויי הארץ.[20]

---

16 Instead of ܗܘܐ 7a1 reads ܗܘܬ; see Owens, 'Early Syriac Text of Ben Sira', 68.
17 Cf. e.g. Gen 7:6 and Payne Smith, *Thesaurus* I, 1446.
18 Cf. Reiterer, *Urtext*, 90.
19 Thus Skehan–Di Lella, *Wisdom of Ben Sira*, 404.

44:21c ܐܝܟ ܚܠܐ ܕܝܡܐ 'like the sand of the sea'; Gr ὡς χοῦν τῆς γῆς (not in MS B). Cf. Gen 22:17.[21]

44:23 ܕܩܪܝܗ ܒܪܝ ܒܘܟܪܝ ܐܝܣܪܝܠ '(Israel) whom He called My son, My first-born, Israel'; B ויכוננהו בברכה 'And He established him with a blessing'; B[mg] ויכנהו בבכורה 'And He gave him the title of first-born'. Cf. Exod 4:22 MT בני בכרי ישראל 'Israel is my first-born son'; Pesh ܒܪܝ ܒܘܟܪܝ ܐܝܣܪܝܠ, and Sir 36:17 B עם נקרא בשמך 'the people called by your name'; Syr: ܥܡܟ ܕܐܬܩܪܝ ܫܡܟ ܥܠܘܗܝ.

45:8 ܢܚܬܐ ܕܬܟܠܬܐ 'garments of purple'; B כליל תפארת; According to Lévi Syr reflects כליל תכלת; cf. Exod 28:31 MT כליל תכלת (but Pesh ܡܥܝܪܐ ܕܬܟܠܬܐ).[22]

46:5 ܘܟܒܪܝܬܐ ܡܢ ܫܡܝܐ ܐܚܬ 'And sulphur He sent down from heaven'; B [...]ל[...] באבני; Gr ἐν λίθοις χαλάζης δυνάμεως κραταιᾶς 'with hailstones of mighty power'. Cf. Gen 19:24 MT ויהוה המטיר על סדם ועל עמרה גפרית ואש מאת יהוה מן השמים 'And the Lord rained down sulphur and fire over Sodom and Gomorrah from the Lord out of heaven'; Pesh ܘܡܛܪܐ ܐܚܬ ܥܠ ܣܕܘܡ ܘܥܠ ܥܡܘܪܐ ܟܒܪܝܬܐ ܘܢܘܪܐ ܡܢ ܩܕܡ ܡܪܝܐ ܡܢ ܫܡܝܐ.

(2) From the Latter Prophets

47:18 ܘܣܐܡܐ ܐܝܟ ܥܦܪܐ '(And you gathered gold like lead) and silver like dust'; B וכעפרת הרבית כסף; Syr reflects כעפר instead of כעפרת; cf. Zech 9:3 MT ותצבר כסף כעפר 'She has heaped up silver like dust (and gold like the dirt of the streets)'; Pesh ܘܟܢܫܬ ܣܐܡܐ ܐܝܟ ܥܦܪܐ; Job 27:16 MT אם יצבר כעפר כסף; Pesh ܐܢ ܢܟܢܘܫ ܟܣܦܐ ܐܝܟ ܥܦܪܐ.

48:10 ܩܕܡ ܕܢܐܬܐ ܝܘܡܗ ܕܡܪܝܐ 'before the day of the Lord comes'. Cf. Mal 3:23 MT לפני בוא יום יהוה; Pesh ܩܕܡ ܕܢܐܬܐ ܝܘܡܗ ܕܡܪܝܐ. B and Gr have a completely different reading.[23]

(3) From the Writings

45:23 ܘܨܠܐ ܥܠ ܐܝܣܪܝܠ 'And he (i.e. Phinehas) prayed for Israel'; B ויכפר על בני ישראל. Syr is reminiscent of Ps 106:30 MT ויעמד פינחס ויפלל 'And Phinehas stood up and prayed'; Pesh ܩܡ ܦܝܢܚܣ ܘܨܠܝ.

47:18 See above, under 'From the Latter Prophets'.

The phenomena described in this paragraph occur throughout Syr. There can hardly be any doubt that the translator was well acquainted

---

[20] But ܕܐܪܥܐ does not occur in the Nestorian manuscripts 9c1, 10c1.2, 11c1 and others.

[21] Cf. Schrader, *Verwandtschaft*, 36

[22] Lévi, *L'Ecclésiastique* I, 98; according to Reiterer, *Urtext*, 152, the Hebrew source text of Syr had בגדי תכלת.

[23] Cf. Van Peursen, 'Que vive celui qui fait vivre', 289–290.

with the other parts of the Bible. Winter's suggestion that he avoided references to the Prophets (§ 4.3.2) is overtly incorrect.

5.2 INFLUENCE OF THE OLD TESTAMENT PESHITTA?

In the preceding discussion we have not touched upon the question as to the translator's Old Testament source: Did he use a Hebrew text, a Syriac version or even a Targum? In § 3.8 we have argued that Rüger's claim that the translator was acquainted with the Targums to the Old Testament is not convincing. The question of whether he used a Hebrew or a Syriac source is more difficult to answer. In many cases there are verbal similarities between Syr and a parallel passage in the Peshitta, but that evidence does not indicate that Syr depends on it. If the relevant Peshitta passage does not give an unusual rendering of the Hebrew, the passage in Syr that parallels it can have been influenced either by the Peshitta or by the Hebrew text of the Old Testament. Thus the use of ܐܡܬܐ ܕܐܪܥܐ in Syr 26:16 and Pesh-Gen 1:15 or that of ܫܘܡ ܕܓܠܠܐ in Syr 34:2 and Pesh-Gen 46:2, discussed in the preceding paragraph, does not demonstrate that the Syriac translator of Sirach consulted the Peshitta. It is possible that he had in mind the Hebrew phrases ברקיע השמים and במראת הלילה and arrived at his Syriac rendering independently of the Peshitta. Even renderings that are less obvious do not prove the dependence of Syr on the Peshitta, because they may reflect the Aramaic/Syriac translation tradition with which the translator was acquainted.[24]

Some parallels even argue against Peshitta influence. Thus ܟܘܝܠܐ ܡܢ ܐܠܗܐ in Syr 18:10 is reminiscent of Isa 40:15 כמר מדלי, but differs from Pesh-Isa 40:15 ܢܘܩܠܬܐ; similarly 23:19 ܡܚܫܟܬܐ ܘܬܒܘܥܬܐ ܐܠܐ ܚܒܘܫܐ reflects the influence of Isa 29:15 MT והיה במחשך מעשיהם, but Pesh-Isa 29:15 has ܘܗܡܣ ܒܚܘܫܟܐ ܚܒܘܫܐ.[25] For the following

---

[24] Cf. § 6.2.3 (A) and Weitzman, *From Judaism to Christianity*, 194, quoted there (note 15).

[25] For details and other examples see § 5.1. Our observations agree with Reiterer's conclusion based on his analysis of 44:16–45:26. In this section the Hebrew text contains many parallels with other parts of the Old Testament, but in most cases the Syriac translation is clearly independent of the Peshitta to these parallel passages; in other cases dependence cannot be established because both Syr and the Peshitta render in a 'usual' way; see the extensive discussion of each colon in this section in Reiterer, *Urtext*, 82–234 and the conclusions on p. 240. Reiterer frequently draws conclu-

passages, however, it has been argued that the Syriac translator was influenced by the Peshitta.

6:37 ܘܗܘ ܢܚܠܡ ܐܘܪܚܬܟ 'and He will make firm your ways'; A והוא יבין לבך 'And He will make firm (יכין) your heart'. Cf. Prov 21:29 MT הוא יכין דרכיו; Pesh ܗܘ ܡܚܠܡ ܐܘܪܚܬܐ ܕܢܦܫܗ. Syr differs from A in that it has 'your ways' instead of 'your heart'. According to Rüger Syr has been influenced by Pesh-Prov 21:29,[26] but it is not clear why the influence should have come from the Peshitta of this passage rather than from the Hebrew text. Moreover, Sir 6:37 and Prov 21:29 differ in that in Proverbs the upright person is the subject of הכין / ܡܚܠܡ, whereas in Sirach it is God. If we were to assume the influence of the Peshitta, a better parallel is Gen 24:56 ܘܡܪܝܐ ܐܚܠܡ ܐܘܪܚܝ 'the Lord has confirmed my way' (MT ויהוה הצליח דרכי; similarly Gen 24:40; cf. also 24:42). However, since both הכין + לב and הכין + דרך are well-attested in the Hebrew Bible,[27] we do not have to resort to the influence of the Peshitta to explain the confusion of the two idioms.

10:17 ܘܒܛܠ ܡܢ ܒܢܝܢܫܐ ܕܘܟܪܢܗܘܢ 'And He effaced their memory from the people'; A וישבת מארץ זכרם 'And He effaced their memory from the earth'. Cf. Deut 32:26 MT אשביתה מאנוש זכרם; Pesh ܐܒܛܠ ܡܢ ܒܢܝܢܫܐ ܕܘܟܪܢܗܘܢ. According to Rüger Syr has been influenced by Pesh-Deut 32:26.[28] However, the rendering 'from the people' instead of 'from the earth' can also be due to the influence of the Hebrew text of Deut 32:26.

15:17 ܐܬܝܗܒܘ ܓܝܪ ܠܒܢܝܢܫܐ ܚܝܐ ܘܡܘܬܐ ܕܢܓܒܘܢ ܚܝܐ ܘܢܫܒܩܘܢ ܡܘܬܐ 'For life and death are given to the people, so that they choose life and abandon death'; A(+B) לפני אדם חיים ומוות אשר יחפץ יתן לו 'Before man are life and death; what he desires is given to him'. Cf. Deut 30:19 MT החיים והמות נתתי לפניך הברכה והקללה ובחרת בחיים למען תחיה אתה וזרעך 'I have given before you life and death, blessing and curse. Therefore choose life, so that you and your descendants will live'; Pesh ܕܚܝܐ ܘܡܘܬܐ ܝܗܒܬ ܩܕܡܝܟܘܢ ܒܘܪܟܬܐ ܘܠܘܛܬܐ ܓܒܝ ܠܟ ܚܝܐ ܘܬܐܚܐ ܐܢܬ ܘܙܪܥܟ. Some scholars think that Syr has been influenced by Pesh-Deut 30:19. It is true that the addition of 'are given' (ܐܬܝܗܒܘ) and the expression 'that they may choose life' (ܕܢܓܒܘܢ ܚܝܐ) in Syr 15:17 are reminiscent of Pesh-Deut 30:19.[29] Since, however, ܝܗܒ is the usual equivalent of Hebrew נתן and ܓܒܐ

---

sions such as 'Aus dem Übersetzungsvergleich wird deutlich, daß Syr-Sira in der Tradition der Peschitta steht. Eine Zitatsübernahme liegt nicht vor.' (p. 133).

[26] Rüger, *Text und Textform*, 113; similarly Winter, *Ben Sira in Syriac*, 68.

[27] Cf. *HALOT* 465; *DCH* IV, 375.

[28] Rüger, *Text und Textform*, 114; similarly Winter, *Ben Sira in Syriac*, 68.

[29] The Hebrew text of Sir 15:17 itself is reminiscent of Deut 30:19 as well, but in Syr the parallel has been strengthened; cf. Segal, *Sefer Ben Sira*, 88.

that of בחר, these parallels do not prove that Syr has been influenced by the Peshitta version of Deut 30:19.

16:11 ܘܡܣܓܐ ܠܡܚܣܐ 'And He forgives abundantly'; A ונושא וסולח 'He forgives and pardons'. Cf. Isa 55:7 MT כי ירבה לסלוח 'For He will forgive abundantly'; Pesh ܣܓܝ ܠܡܚܣܐ. According to Rüger Syr has been influenced by Pesh-Isa 55:7.[30] We agree that influence of Isa 55:7 may account for the reading in Syr, but there is no compelling argument for assuming that it comes from the Peshitta version.

Sometimes there are additional text-critical observations that render it unlikely that the Syriac translator was influenced by the Peshitta.

33:11 ܥܒܕ ܐܢܘܢ ܥܡܘ̈ܪܐ ܕܐܪ̈ܥܬܐ 'And He made them inhabitants of the world'; E¹ [ץ]וישם אותם דרי הא[ר] 'And He made them inhabitants of the world'; E² [ה]וישנ את דרכיהם 'And in different paths He made them walk' (= Gr). Cf. Dan 4:32 MT וכל דארי ארעא כלה 'And all inhabitants of the world'; Pesh ܘܟܠܗܘܢ ܥܡܘ̈ܪܐ ܕܐܪ̈ܥܐ. Segal thought to discern the influence of Pesh-Dan 4:32 in Syr 33:11.[31] It is true that the reading in Syr and E¹ is the most likely candidate to be secondary (cf. Gen 11:8), but there is no reason to assume the influence of Pesh-Daniel rather than from MT–Daniel (even apart from the question of whether the Daniel passage has influenced the Sir 33:11 at all), nor is it likely that the variant is due to the Syriac translator, now that it is also found in Heb.

The argument for the influence of the Peshitta is relatively stronger in the following cases, but again, it is hard to establish whether they demonstrate Syr's dependence on the Peshitta or rather the translator's acquaintance with phrases that we are inclined to consider biblical phraseology, such as 'creeping worms' (10:9), 'the will of Your people' (36:22), or 'a help like you' (36:29).

10:9 ܕܒܚܝܘܗܝ ܪܚܫܐ ܬܘܠܥܐ 'in whose life worms are (already) creeping'; A אשר בחייו ירם גויו 'in whose life his body decays'. Cf. Exod 16:20 MT וירם תולעים 'and it decayed (i.e. was full of) worms'; Pesh ܘܐܪܚܫ ܬܘܠܥܐ 'and it made creep worms'. According to Rüger Syr has been influenced by Pesh-Exod 16:20.[32] Although the association of רמם Hofal with worms may also be due to the Hebrew text of Exod 16:20, the combination of ܪܚܫ and ܬܘܠܥܐ argues for Rüger's interpretation.

---

[30] Rüger, *Text und Textform*, 114; similarly Winter, *Ben Sira in Syriac*, 68.
[31] Segal, 'Evolution', 125; similarly Winter, *Ben Sira in Syriac*, 68.
[32] Rüger, *Text und Textform*, 114; similarly Winter, *Ben Sira in Syriac*, 68.

22:24 ܩܕܡ ܢܘܪܐ ܥܛܪ ܬܢܢܐ 'Before fire is vapour of smoke';[33] Gr πρὸ πυρὸς ἀτμὶς καμίνου καὶ καπνός 'before fire is the vapour of the furnace and smoke'. Cf. Joel 3:3 (2:30) MT דם ואש ותימרות עשן 'blood and fire and pillars of smoke'; Pesh ܕܡܐ ܘܢܘܪܐ ܘܥܛܪܐ ܕܬܢܢܐ 'blood and fire and vapour of smoke'; Cant 3:6 MT כתימרות עשן 'like pillars of smoke'; Pesh ܐܝܟ ܥܛܪܐ ܕܬܢܢܐ 'like vapour of smoke'. In Gr the smoke comes from an oven. Syr suggests the language of Pesh-Joel 3:3 and Pesh-Cant 3:6.[34]

36:22 ܐܝܟ ܨܒܝܢܐ ܕܥܡܟ 'according to the will of Your people'; B[txt] כרצונך על עמך; B[mg] ברצונך Cf. Ps 106:4 MT ברצון עמך 'according to the favour [that You bears to] Your people'; Pesh-Ps 106:4 ܒܨܒܝܢܗ ܕܥܡܟ. According to Ryssel Syr reflects the influence of Pesh-Ps 106:4. Whereas the Hebrew text of Ps 106:4 and Sir 36:22 refers to God's favour over His people, in the Syriac text it refers in both cases to 'der Herzenhingabe (an Gott) und Glaubensbethätigung'.[35]

36:29 ܥܕܪܐ ܗܝ ܥܒܕ ܐܟܘܬܟ 'For she (i.e. a good wife) is a help like you'; B עזר ומבצר; B[mg]+D עיר מבצר. Cf. Gen 2:20 MT עזר כנגדו; Pesh ܡܥܕܪܢܐ ܐܟܘܬܗ. Syr is reminiscent of Pesh-Gen 2:20.[36]

46:2 ܟܕ ܡܪܝܡ ܟܘܢܬܐ ܕܒܐܝܕܗ 'when he raised the javelin which was in his hand'; B בנטותו יד 'when he stretched out his hand'. Cf. Josh 8:18 MT נטה בכידון אשר בידך אל העי (...) ויט יהושע בכידון אשר בידו אל העיר 'Stretch out the javelin which is in your hand (...) and Joshua stretched out the javelin which was in his hand'; Pesh ܐܪܝܡ ܟܘܢܬܐ ܕܒܐܝܕܟ (...) ܘܐܪܝܡ ܝܫܘܥ ܟܘܢܬܐ ܕܐܝܬ ܗܘܐ ܒܐܝܕܗ; Josh 8:26 MT אשר נטה בכידון; Pesh ܕܐܪܝܡ ܗܘܐ ܟܘܢܬܐ. Syr translates 46:2 according to Pesh-Josh 8:18, 8:26.[37]

Accordingly, there are some cases that seem to support the assumption that the Syriac translator was acquainted with the Peshitta and has been influenced by it. In other cases, however, he seems to have been influenced by a passage from the Old Testament in another way, not through the Peshitta version. Moreover, the evidence for the translator's dependence on other parts of the Peshitta is very small, espe-

---

[33] Thus Smend (*Jesus Sirach*, 202), who translates ܥܛܪ ܬܢܢܐ with 'Rauchqualm'. Calduch-Benages, Ferrer and Liesen (*Sabiduría del Escriba*, 152) take ܥܛܪ as a verb and translate 'From a fire smoke rises up'.

[34] Cf. Segal, 'Evolution', 125; Winter, *Ben Sira in Syriac*, 68.

[35] Ryssel, 'Fragmente', IV, 289.

[36] But it is also possible that his Hebrew source (and that of Gr, which has here the same translation as in Gen 2:20) read עזר כנגדו; cf. Margoliouth, 'Original Hebrew', 25; Lévi, *L'Ecclésiastique* II, 175.

[37] Thus Smend, *Jesus Sirach*, 440. Note that in Syr 'the javelin' has moved from 2b (B בהניפו כידון על עיר; Syr ܘܟܕ ܡܢܝܦ ܥܠ ܡܕܝܢܬܐ) to 2a; cf. Smend, ibid.: 'Syr. zieht כידון aus b [= v. 2b] herüber und übersetzt nach Pesch.'

cially if one takes into account alternative explanations such as the influence of the Aramaic/Syriac translation tradition and an acquaintance with biblical phraseology.

5.3 AFFINITIES WITH RABBINIC LITERATURE

In Peshitta research the question as to whether the translators were acquainted with Jewish sources and traditions plays an important role. Numerous parallels with rabbinic sources[38] have been put forward as evidence for a Jewish or Jewish-Christian background to the Peshitta; parallels with Jewish Bible translations have even led to the assumption that the Peshitta derived from a Targum.

Syr too has a 'rabbinic flavour'. According to Segal there are a number of cases where the translator gives a translation 'in the spirit of the tradition and the oral law'.[39] We can distinguish the following categories.

(1) Parallels with rabbinic literature

There are some parallels between unique readings in Syr and rabbinic sources.[40]

> 9:9 II° ܐܢܬܬ ܓܒܪܐ ܠܐ ܬܡܠܠ ܣܓܝ ܘܠܐ ܬܣܓܐ ܡܡܠܠܟ ܥܡܗ ܘܕܘܥܬܟ
> 'With a married woman do not speak much, and do not multiply your conversation with her'; A עם בעלה אל תטעם וא[ל ת]סב עמו שכור. Cf. *m. Abot* 1:5 'Do not multiply your conversation with a woman (אל תרבה שיחה עם האשה). This applies to one's own wife; how much more then, to the wife of one's neighbour (אשת חברו); hence the Sages say, Every time a man multiplies his conversation with a woman (מרבה שיחא עם האשא) he brings evil upon himself and neglects the words of the Torah, and his end will inherit Gehinnom.'

> 17:20 ܐܠܗܐ ܕܚܛܗܐ ܕܟܠܗܘܢ ܥܡܡܐ ܪܫܝܡܝܢ ܠܩܘܕܡܘܗܝ 'And the sins of all the people are written down before Him'. 'Written down' is a plus com-

---

[38] See e.g. Weitzman, *Syriac Version*, 149–169.

[39] Segal, *Sefer Ben Sira*, 61. Segal mentions 8:8, 9:5, 11:18, 15:17, 17:20 and 41:20, but elaborates on only some of them in his commentary, which makes it sometimes difficult to see what he has in mind.

[40] Compare Pesh-1 Chr 29:19, where the Syriac translator appears to be acquainted with the Qaddish prayer. Weitzman, *Syriac Version*, 43, 212–213; idem, 'Qaddish Prayer'.

pared with Gr. Cf. *m. Abot* 3:20 (Albeck 3:16) הפנקס פתוח והיד
כותבת 'The book of (God's) accounts lies open, and the hand
writes'.[41]

18:10 ܐܠܐ ܓܒܪ ܡܢ ܐܠܦ ... 'Thousand years of this world—they are not like one day in
the World of the Righteous'; Gr οὕτως ὀλίγα ἔτη ἐν ἡμέρᾳ αἰῶνος
'So are these few years among the days of eternity'. Cf. *m. Abot* 4:22
(Albeck 4:17) ויפה שעה אחת שלקורת רוח בעולם הבא מכל חיי העולם
הזה 'Better is one hour of satisfaction in the world to come than the
whole life of this world'.[42]

25:3 ܐܢ ... 'If you
have not gathered wisdom in your youth, how will you find it in your
old age?'. 'Wisdom' is a plus vis-à-vis Gr. Cf. *Abot R. Nat.* 24 אם
בנעורתיך לא חפצתם איך תשיגם בזקנותיך 'If you did not desire them in
your youth, how shall you attain them in your old age?'[43]

41:12–42:8 ... 'Be solicitous about your name, for it will
accompany you more than thousands of treasures of villainy, because
it causes gifts and covenants to cease. Everyone whom they greet
and he is silent, he is a great spoiler. The greeting you give him he
will not return to you, and the deposit you give him, how will he return it to you?' Cf. *b. Ber.* 6b (bottom) (...) ליתן לו שלום (...) ואם נתן לו ולא
גזלן נקרא החזיר 'To greet him (...) And if one greets him and he does
not answer, he is called a spoiler'. The first lines of 41:12 are also attested in B and M,[44] but from the following 'Instruction about
Shame' (41:12–42:8) Syr translates only 41:19b (M מהפר אלה
וברי]ת) and 41:20a (M משאל שלום החריש), followed by a 'rabbinic
addition',[45] with which one can compare the saying of R. Huna in *b.*

---

[41] Thus Jastrow, *Dictionary*, 1165b; cf. also *b. R.H.* 16b and see Segal, 'Evolution', 124. The addition 'written down' fits in well with the eschatology of SirII, cf.
§ 2.4.2.

[42] Cf. Jub 4:29, 30; 23:27, quoted in Kearns, *Expanded Text*, 212, as 'less close
parallels' to 'a thousand years (...) are not as one day (...)'; and note the 'close parallel' in Ps 84:10; see further § 2.4.2, n. 131.

[43] Ed. Schechter 78; cf. Edersheim, 'Ecclesiasticus', 132 (on 25:3): 'Similar sentiments are expressed in Talmudic writings, the most closely resembling that of the
Son of Sirach being the following [i.e. *Abot R. Nat.* xxiv] quoted as a proverb'.

[44] But ܚܒܐ instead of חכמה (B[txt]) or חמדה (B[mg]) does not fit the context. Cf.
Lévi, *L'Ecclésiastique* I, 38–39: 'עתא correspond quelquefois dans la Peschito à חנם,
il n'est donc pas impossible qu'ici חמדה ait été lu חנם; mais ce mot traduit aussi מרמה
"tromperie". Peut-être aussi S. a-t-il été le jouet d'une reminiscence de אוצרות רשע
"les trésors de méchanceté" (Prov., 10, 2).'

[45] Smend, *Jesus Sirach*, cxxxviii.

Ber. 6b.[46] Note that not only the addition in Syr, but also the Hebrew text of 41:12 has close parallels in rabbinic literature.[47]

(2) Rabbinic concepts and ideas

Sometimes the rabbinic flavour does not consist of literary parallels, but rather of the expression of certain concepts or views. Rabbinic ideas possibly constitute the background of the following readings.

18:13 ܩܪܝܒ ܒܣܪܗ '(A man's mercies are on) his kinsman'; Gr τὸν πλησίον αὐτοῦ 'his neighbour'. According to Edersheim Syr is 'in accordance with rabbinic usage and ideas'.[48] He does not give references, but perhaps he has in mind usages of קרוב such as those listed in Levy's dictionary.[49] According to Smend Syr reflects perhaps the original text. He refers to Pesh-Lev 18:6, 25:49 where the Peshitta has ܩܪܝܒ ܒܣܪܗ for שאר בשרו 'his blood-relation',[50] but in Sir 18:13 Gr reflects רע rather than שאר בשרו or something similar.

23:9 ܠܡܘܡܬܐ ܠܐ ܬܐܠܦ ܦܘܡܟ ܘܒܝܬ ܕܝܢܐ ܠܐ ܬܗܘܐ ܝܬܒ 'Do not teach your mouth oaths, and among judges be not sitting'; Gr καὶ ὀνομασίᾳ τοῦ ἁγίου μὴ συνεθισθῇς 'Do not become too familiar with the Holy Name'. The reading reflected in Gr may have been too harsh for a Jewish readership: 'The Syr. seems to have thought such a light use of the Holy Name impossible, and hence applies the passage to judicial investigations'.[51]

(3) Rabbinic idioms

Rabbinic idioms in Syr are allegedly reflected in the expressions ܥܠܡܐ ܕܙܕܝܩܐ 'the World of the Righteous' (18:10),[52] ܠܫܢܐ ܬܠܝܬܝܐ 'the triple tongue' (28:13), ܣܠܩ ܥܠ ܦܓܪܗ 'go up in his body' (30:24), ܡܫܟܢܬܟ 'Your habitation, Shechinah' (36:18) and ܟܠ ܕܐܬܝܢ ܠܥܠܡܐ 'all that come to the world' (42:19).

28:13 ܠܫܢܐ ܬܠܝܬܝܐ 'the triple tongue'; Gr 'the whisperer and double tongued'. The 'third tongue' is a post-biblical Jewish usage. It means the calumnious, babbling tongue. According to Edersheim, 'the Syr. translator seems to have had this in mind in his paraphrastic render-

---

46 Cf. Segal, 'Evolution', 125; Rüger, *Text und Textform*, 114.
47 Cf. e.g. *m. Abot* 6:9; see Van Peursen, *Verbal System*, 111.
48 Edersheim, 'Ecclesiasticus', 101.
49 Levy, *Wörterbuch*, IV, 396; under בשר (I, 274) Levy does not give parallels to the idiom under discussion.
50 Ryssel, 'Sprüche Jesus' des Sohnes Sirachs', 320; Smend, *Jesus Sirach*, 165.
51 Edersheim, 'Ecclesiasticus', 122.
52 Discussed above, in § 5.3 (1).

ing of the verse'.[53] However, the reference to the 'triple tongue' is also present in 28:14 (Gr and Syr). Accordingly, the Syriac translator may have taken this idiom from the following verse, rather than having been influenced by rabbinic phraseology.

30:24 ܣܠܩ ܠܗ ܒܓܘܗ '(And everything he eats) goes up in his body'. According to Edersheim this phrase reflects the rabbinical expression עלים על גופו.[54]

36:18 ܐܬܪܐ ܕܬܫܪܝܬܟ 'the place of your Shechinah'; B מכון שבתך. This designation is well-attested in rabbinic sources.[55] In the Targums שכינתא is often used to translated the Tetragrammaton.[56] Note, however, that in Sir 36:18 it does not translate a reference to God, but one to His habitation.

42:19 ܠܗ ܕܐܬܝܢ ܠܥܠܡܐ 'all that come to the world' represents כל באי עולם, which is a standing expression in Rabbinic Hebrew (see e.g. *m. R.H.* 1:2).

(4) Halakhic traditions

Acquaintance with Halakhic traditions is possibly responsible for the following readings.

9:5 ܕܠܡܐ ܬܬܚܝܒ ܕܬܦܪܘܥ ܐܥܦܐ '(Be not tempted by a virgin) lest you owe to pay a double bride-price'; A פן תוקש בעונשיה 'lest you are ensnared by her penalties'; Gr μήποτε σκανδαλισθῇς ἐν τοῖς ἐπιτιμίοις αὐτῆς 'lest you take offence at the penalties for her'. The Syriac ܡܗܪܐ is used both for the price paid to the father of the bride (Hebrew מהר; in the Peshitta rendered with ܡܗܪܐ[57]) and, less frequently, for the portion brought by the bride from her father's house (in 1 Kgs 9:16 called שִׁלֻּחִים; Peshitta: ܡܫܕܪܬܐ).[58] The latter interpretation, i.e. 'you have to give twice as much as the gift that she brings with her' is preferred by Bar Hebraeus.[59] In the former interpretation the background of this passage may be sought in Exod 22:15 or Deut 22:29.[60] According to Exod 22:15 a man who seduces

---

[53] Edersheim, 'Ecclesiasticus', 145; see further Smend, *Jesus Sirach*, 253 (on 28:14); Segal, *Sefer Ben Sira*, 164 (idem); Levy, *Wörterbuch* II, 530b.

[54] Edersheim, 'Ecclesiasticus', 154; cf. *Abot R. Nat.* 26 האוכל אוכלין שאינם עולים על גופו 'If a man eats food which is unsuitable for his constitution (he transgresses three commandments)' (ed. Schechter 83; translation: Cohen, *Minor Tractates* I, 131.)

[55] Cf. Séd, 'Shekhinta'.

[56] Van Keulen, 'Points of Agreement', 207.

[57] Gen 34:12; Exod 22:16; 1 Sam 18:25.

[58] *CSD* 462; Payne Smith, *Thesaurus* II, 3268.

[59] Ed. S. Kaatz 9 (text), 23 (translation; see the comment in his n. 23); cf. Peters, *Ben Sirach*, 82.

[60] Thus, e.g. Segal, *Sefer Ben Sira*, 56.

a virgin is obliged to pay the full bride-price (מהר ימהרנה); if the
virgin's father refuses to give her, the man has to pay him in silver a
sum equal to the bride-price for virgins. In Deut 22:29 it is stated that
a man who has intercourse with a virgin should pay fifty pieces of
silver to her father. Extra fines are discussed in rabbinic literature.[61]
However, neither these rabbinic passages, nor the fifty pieces of silver give us a clue to the double ܦܘܝܬܐ in our text. If ܦܘܝܬܐ refers
indeed to the bride-price, it can be derived from a rabbinic exegesis
of Exod 22:15 in two ways. Either (1) the absolute infinitive in the
construction מהר ימהרנה was interpreted as an indication that something more than just one bride-price had to be paid, from which it
was concluded that the man in question had to pay a double bride-
price[62] or (2) the remark to pay the bride-price even if the virgin's father refuses to give her implies that the seducer had to pay an extra,
and hence a double bride-price. Whatever the exact background of
the double bride price is, it is evident that the reference to the double
dowry is much more specific than the general expressions in Heb
and even more specific than Gr. Such a specific reference may go
back to halakhic rules about intercourse with a virgin, but to our best
knowledge such a halakhic rule is not attested in rabbinic literature.
It is imaginable, therefore, that the reading in Syr reflects a so-called
'pseudo-halakha'. Pseudo-halachot are 'guesses ventured by the
translator where the context happened to be legal'. These renderings
'suggest indifference to rabbinic halachah' and are 'pseudo-halachot
(...) rather than hard evidence of non-rabbinic practice'.[63]

25:26 ܘܐܠܐ ܐܬܬܟ ܐܝܟ ܟܦܗ ܗܝ ܡܦܣ ܡܢܗܝ ܩܨ ܡܢ ܒܣܪܟ ܠܗ ܦܝܠܬܐ ܗܘ
ܒܫܠܐ 'And if she is not following you, cut off your flesh, give her
(scl. a bill of divorce), and dismiss her from your house'. 'Give her'
is an addition.[64] It reflects the Jewish custom of sending a bill of divorce (Deut 24:1) and represents a Jewish rather than a Christian
background (cf. Mark 10:4).

The rabbinic flavour of Syr is undeniable. The question is how we
should account for these data. The parallels with rabbinic sources led
some scholars to the assumption of a Jewish or Jewish-Christian
background.[65] Others argued that the parallels with rabbinic sources

---

[61] See *m. Ket.* 3:4; *b. Ket.* 38b ; cf. Segal, *Sefer Ben Sira,* 56; idem, 'Evolution',
124.

[62] Cf. Van der Heide, 'Reception of a Linguistic Statement', 257–258.

[63] Weitzman, *Syriac Version,* 219.

[64] Compare the addition δίδου καὶ ἀπολύσον in Gr MS 248.

[65] Thus e.g. Edersheim, 'Ecclesiasticus', 29: 'We infer the Jewish origin of the
translation from the occasional occurrence of expressions in Rabbinic usage'.

were already present in the translator's source text.[66] It is likely that at least some of the rabbinic elements in Syr was present in the translator's Hebrew source text, because affinities with rabbinic literature are not restricted to unique readings in Syr. The same rabbinic elements that we encounter in Syr are attested in Heb. It contains numerous parallels with rabbinic literature;[67] rabbinic idioms such as בית מדרש,[68] כיוצא בו,[69] and מה...כן/כך and מה...אף;[70] and passages reflecting rabbinic exegesis, such as the designation of Samuel as *nazir*.[71] In some cases a parallel that we discovered in Syr is also present in Heb, although less explicit.[72]

The assumption that rabbinic paraphrases and additions entered the Hebrew text in the course of its transmission, even before Syr was made, is corroborated by the loose transmission of the Hebrew text. In this context it should be recalled that the transmission of Sirach and the relationship between the Hebrew and the Syriac witnesses is very different from the situation with the books belonging to the Hebrew Bible. The transmission of the Hebrew text was very fluid and receptive to all kinds of changes and additions. The fluidity appears from the following phenomena:

1. The way in which Sirach is quoted in rabbinic literature. There are rabbinic quotations from Sirach in a form that is very different from that in the extant textual witnesses of the book.[73] Moreover, there are rabbinic quotations in the name of

---

[66] Thus e.g. Segal, 'Evolution', 123: 'Syr. is based upon a Hebrew text which embodied popular paraphrases of certain verses originally current orally in Jewish circles of the talmudic period'.

[67] See the lists in Cowley–Neubauer, *Original Hebrew*, xix–xxx ('Ben Sira's Proverbs Preserved in Talmudic and Rabbinic Literature'); Segal, 'Evolution', 133–134 (addenda to Cowley–Neubauer); idem, *Sefer Ben Sira*, 37–42; Smend, *Jesus Sirach*, xlvi–lvi; Gnan, *Nachklänge des Buches Jesus Sirach*, 24–61 (= 'Beiträge zur Rezeptionsgeschichte des Buches Ben Sirach im Judentum').

[68] Sir 51:23 (B); cf. Van Peursen, 'Sirach 51:13–30', 369–370.

[69] Sir 10:28 (A), 38:17 (B); cf. Van Peursen, *Verbal System*, 390.

[70] Sir 12:13–14 (A), 13:17 (A), 30:19 (B^mg); 38:25–27 (B); cf. Kister, 'Notes', 132–133; idem, 'Additions', 43; Van Peursen, *Verbal System*, 387–388; see further Schechter–Taylor, *Wisdom of Ben Sira*, 33–34; some of the examples given by Schechter and Taylor are merely linguistic variants, showing Ben Sira's affinity with Late Biblical Hebrew and Post Biblical Hebrew, but others reflect rabbinic idioms.

[71] Sir 46:13 (B); cf. Schechter–Taylor, *Wisdom of Ben Sira*, 29–32.

[72] See above, the discussion of 25:3, 41:12–42:8.

[73] See the lists given in note 67; cf. Segal, 'Evolution', 136: 'The text of the quotations in the Talmud and Midrash differs in most cases more or less widely from

Ben Sira of proverbs that do not belong to his book, as well as citations from Sirach in the name of other sages.[74]

2. The general character of the Geniza manuscripts, containing many doublets, paraphrases and alterations, which shows that the Hebrew text was reworked over and over again.[75]

3. The existence of witnesses that are loosely related to Sirach, such as the Geniza MS C, which can be called a *florilegium*, the so-called *prosodic version of Ben Sira* in MS Adler 3053,[76] and a Geniza Fragment published by S. Schechter.[77] The fact that MS C is treated as a witness to the book of Sirach and is included in text editions, while the others are not, should not blind us to the variety of ways in which this book or parts of it were transmitted.

We can conclude that the textual transmission of the Hebrew text of Sirach provided the opportunity for all kinds of rabbinic parallels to be included in the text. It is likely, therefore, that the parallels attested in Syr were already present in the translator's source text. Although we should leave open the possibility that the translator himself is responsible for some of the rabbinic elements, we cannot use them as evidence for a Jewish-rabbinic background.

Heb. and the versions. Their diction is as a rule in the late and mishnaic Hebrew of the Rabbis, instead of the classical diction of our Heb.'

[74] See the literature mentioned in the preceding footnote and further Segal, 'Evolution', 134–135; Leiman, *Canonization of Hebrew Scipture*, 96–97; Leiman discusses the broader context of the quotation formulae used to introduce verses from Sirach and their relevance for the status of Sirach in rabbinic Judaism.

[75] Lévi, *L'Ecclésiastique* II, xxvii-xxxiii; Rüger, *Text und Textform*.

[76] Marcus, 'A Fifth MS. of Ben Sira', 225–226, 238–240 (= idem, *Fifth Manuscript*, 9–10, 26–28)'; cf. Segal, 'Evolution', 116: 'Of special interest are the agreements between Syr. and the Hebrew text underlying the mediaeval Hebrew rhymed version of Ben Sira, a fragment of which was published by Rabbi Marcus (...), corresponding to 22.22–23, 9'.

[77] Schechter, 'Further Fragment of Ben Sira', 459–460: '[The fragment is] a collection of proverbs and sayings. The style is highly Paitanic and it is composed in rhymes. I am unable to identify it, but it can hardly be doubted that the author was acquainted with the Wisdom of Ben Sira. This will easily be seen by a comparison of the page given here with the contents of Ben Sira xii. 2–5 and xiii'.

5.4 PARALLELS WITH THE NEW TESTAMENT

Influence of the New Testament has been claimed for the following passages.

3:22 ‏ܘܠܝܬ ܠܟ ܬܘܟܠܢܐ ܥܠ ܟܣܝܬܐ‎ 'And there is no confidence for you over what is hidden'; A ‏ואין לך עסק בנסתרות‎ 'You should have no business in hidden things'; C ‏ועסק אל יהי לך בנסתרות‎. Cf. 1 Tim 6:17 ‏דܠܝܬ ܥܠܝܗ ܬܘܟܠܢܐ‎ 'over which there is no confidence'.[78]

15:15 ‏ܘܐܢ ܬܬܟܠ ܒܗ ܐܦ ܐܢܬ ܬܚܐ‎ 'And if you trust in Him, also you will live'; A (b)' ‏ותבונה לעשות רצונו אם תאמין בו גם אתה תחיה‎ And insight is the doing of His will.[79] (c) And if you trust in Him, also you will life'; B ‏ואמונה לעשות רצונו [ואם] ת[א]ה [םם] ת[א]מין ג[ם] את[ה]‎; ‏תח[יה‎[80] B[mg] ‏ותבונה לע' רצונו‎. Syr corresponds to the second line (15c) in Heb, but it has been argued that it translates 15b of Heb and that Heb 15c is a retroversion of it. In that case, one might argue that the Syriac text has been prompted by John 11:25.[81]

18:13 ‏ܘܡܕܒܪ ܠܗܘܢ ܐܝܟ ܪܥܝܐ ܛܒܐ ܕܪܥܐ ܠܓܙܪܗ‎ 'And He leads them like a good shepherd who shepherds his flocks'. The epithet 'good', not found in Gr, is probably due to the influence of John 10:11.[82]

25:8 ‏ܛܘܒܘܗܝ, ܠܒܥܠܗ ܕܐܢܬܬܐ ܛܒܬܐ܂ ܘܠܐ ܕܒܪ ܗܘ ܒܬܘܪܐ ܐܟܚܕܐ ܘܒܚܡܪܐ‎ 'Blessed is the husband of a good wife, who does not plough with bullock and ass combined'; C ‏[...] בעל אשה מ[... ...]חורש‎ ‏[...כשור]‎ '[...] husband [...] one ploughing as (with) a bull [...]'; Gr μακάριος ὁ συνοικῶν γυναικὶ συνετῇ 'Blessed is he who is married to a prudent wife'. Cf. Deut 22:10 ‏לא תחרש בשור ובחמר יחדו‎; 2 Cor 6:14 'be not unequally yoked together with unbelievers'. Before the discovery of the Hebrew text of this verse, the relationship between Syr 25:8 and 2 Cor 6:14 was difficult to establish: Did Syr reflect influence of 2 Corinthians, or did 2 Cor 6:14 derive from a Jewish proverb, preserved in Syr?[83] Now that the 'bull' in the context of

---

[78] Rüger, *Text und Textform*, 113.

[79] For alternative interpretations see Van Peursen, *Verbal System*, 253.

[80] The reading in the manuscript is not very clear. Beentjes' edition has only ‏יה[...]‎.

[81] Cf. Di Lella, *Hebrew Text of Sirach*, 125–129; Van Peursen, 'Retroversions', 66–67.

[82] Winter, *Ben Sira in Syriac*, 176–177; idem, 'Ben Sira in Syriac', II, 498–499.

[83] Cf. Edersheim 'Ecclesiasticus', 133: 'To the first clause of the verse there are many parallels in Rabbinic writings. But the Syr. addition to this clause is, so far as we remember, the only source of what is an undoubtedly Jewish simile for an ill-assorted marriage. (...) May the apostolic injunction (2 Cor. vi. 14) (...) have been derived from a Jewish proverb, preserved in this Syr. rendering, rather than from Lev. xix. 19; Deut. xxii. 10? Or is the opposite the case, and did the Syr. derive its simile

marriage is attested not only in Syr, but also in MS C, the latter option is preferable, although the relation between these and related passages is complex.[84] It could be argued, for example, that the Sirach passage (at least in the Hebrew) refers to a man married to two incompatible women (the farmer is a metaphor for the man, the two animals for the wives), while the Corinthians passage concerns rather the advice not to be yoked together with an unbeliever.[85]

35:11 ܘܒܚܕܘܬܐ ܐܘܙܦ ܠܡܢ ܕܠܐ ܦܪܥ ܠܟ '(With all your gifts, let your face be shining), and with joy lend to him who will not repay you'; B ובששון הקדש מעשר 'And with joy, sanctify your tithe'. The reading in Syr is reminiscent of Luke 6:34 ܘܐܢ ܡܘܙܦܝܢ ܐܢܬܘܢ ܠܡܢ ܕܡܣܟܝܢ ܐܢܬܘܢ ܕܬܬܦܪܥܘܢ ܡܢܗ 'And if you lend to him from whom you expect that he will repay you (what is your goodness?)'.[86]

38:24 ܘܕܠܐ ܡܦܢܐ ܣܘܪܩܘܬܐ 'And who is not distracted with vanities'; Gr ὁ ἐλασσούμενος πράξει αὐτοῦ 'Who is free from business'. Cf. 1 Tim 5:13 ܘܡܦܢܝܢ ܣܘܪܩܘܬܐ 'And they are distracted with vanities'.[87]

40:15 ܥܩܪܗܘܢ ܓܝܪ ܕܚܛܝ̈ܐ ܐܝܟ ܫܒܠܐ ܕܢܒܬ ܥܠ ܫܢܐ ܕܫܘܥܐ 'For the root of sins is like a spike that springs up on the tooth of a rock'; B כי שורש חנף על שן סלע 'For the root of the godless is like a tooth on a rock; B^mg ושורש חנף ען שן צור; Gr καὶ ῥίζαι ἀκάθαρτοι ἐπ' ἀκροτόμου πέτρας 'and impure roots on a sharp edged rock': According to Edersheim the Syriac reading 'a spike that springs up on the tooth of a rock' instead of 'a tooth on a rock' seems to indicate that the Syriac translator was thinking of the parable in Matthew 13.[88]

40:28 ܒܪܝ، ܡܢ ܕܫܐܠ ܠܟ ܠܐ ܬܟܠܝܘܗܝ، 'My son, do not refuse him who asks you'; B בני חיי מתן אל תחי 'My son, do not lead a beggar's life

---

from 2 Cor. vi. 14?' (Edersheim wrote this before the discovery of the Hebrew manuscript!); similarly Ryssel, 'Sprüche Jesus' des Sohnes Sirachs', 359.

[84] For the relationship between 2 Cor 6:14 and Deut 22:10 see also Derrett, 'Midrash on Dt 22,10'; Derrett does not refer to Sir 25:8, but he notes some interesting parallels between 2 Corinthians 6 and Sirach 13.

[85] Cf. Skehan–Di Lella, *Wisdom of Ben Sira*, 340: '[Syr has] the normal allusion to Deut 22:10. The allusion in the context of Sirach is certainly to an incompatible marriage; here it is being understood of one man married to two incompatible woman (compare 37:11a). That the incompatible pair should be husband and wife is an application that has been made (viz., to Dinah and Shechem, Genesis 34; see Segal); since the terms more precisely mean "with a bull and a jackass combined", such an application multiplies incongruities to the straining point.'

[86] Cf. Winter, 'Ben Sira in Syriac', I, 240:'Verse 9b [= 11b; WP] is so clearly reminiscent of Luke vi, 34–35, that one can hardly avoid ascribing it to the pen of a Christian of some shade or other'; similarly Smend, *Jesus Sirach*, 312.

[87] Smend, *Jesus Sirach*, 346; Segal, 'Evolution', 125; Winter, *Ben Sira in Syriac*, 68.

[88] Edersheim, 'Ecclesiasticus', 195; note however, that there is no lexical parallel between the parable in Matthew (in the Peshitta or Vetus Syra) and the Syriac translation of Sir 40:15.

(a life of gifts)' (= Gr). Cf. Matt 5:42 ܡܢ ܕܫܐܠ ܠܟ ܗܒ ܠܗ ܘܡܢ ܕܒܥܐ ܕܢܙܕܝܦ ܡܢܟ ܠܐ ܬܟܠܝܘܗܝ 'Give to him who asks you and do not refuse him who wants to borrow from you'.[89]

48:6 ܡܣܚܦ ܝܩܝܪܐ ܡܢ ܟܘܪܣܘܬܗܘܢ 'Who cast down honoured people from their thrones'; B המוריד מלכים על שחת ונכבדים ממטותם 'Who brought down kings to the pit, and honoured people from their couches'; Gr ὁ καταγαγὼν βασιλεῖς εἰς ἀπώλειαν καὶ δεδοξασμένους ἀπὸ κλίνης αὐτῶν 'Who sent kings down to destruction, and famous men from their sickbeds'. The Syriac ܟܘܪܣܘܬܗܘܢ may be an inner-Syriac corruption of ܐܪܣܘܬܗܘܢ, or the result of influence of Sir 10:14 ܟܘܪܣܝܐ ܕܓܐܘܬܢܐ ܡܣܚܦ ܡܪܝܐ 'The Lord has overturned the throne of the proud', or Luke 1:52 ܫܕܐ ܥܫܝܢܐ ܡܢ ܟܘܪܣܘܬܐ 'He cast down strong people from their thrones'. Accordingly, influence of the New Testament is possible, but other explanations can account for Syr as well.

48:10a (7a1 ܕܥܬܝܕܐ) ܘܗܘ ܥܬܝܕ ܠܡܐܬܐ 'And he is destined to come'; B הכתוב נכון לעת 'who is written as destined at the appointed time'; Gr ὁ καταγραφεὶς ἕτοιμος εἰς καιρούς who is written to be ready to the appointed time'. Cf. Matt 11:4 ܐܠܝܐ ܕܥܬܝܕ ܠܡܐܬܐ 'Elijah, who is prepared to come'.[90]

48:10d ܘܠܡܣܒܪܘ ܠܫܒ̈ܛܐ ܕܝܥܩܘܒ '(Elijah is prepared to come) to bring good tidings to the tribes of Jacob'; B להכין ש[בטי ישרא]ל 'to establish the tribes of Israel'; Gr καὶ καταστῆσαι φυλὰς Ιακωβ 'and to establish the tribes of Jacob'. Cf. Luke 3:18 (on John the Baptist) 'With many other exhortations he preached good tidings (ܡܣܒܪ) to the people'.[91]

48:11 ܛܘܒܘܗܝ ܠܡܢ ܕܚܙܟ ܘܡܝܬ ܘܠܐ ܡܐܬ ܐܠܐ ܡܚܐ ܢܚܐ 'Blessed is he who sees you and dies. Yet he will not die, but giving life he will give life' (interpreting ܢܚܐ as an Aphel) or: '...but he will surely live (interpreting ܢܚܐ as a Peal)'; B ך[...]; [... ...]יה; Gr μακάριοι οἱ ἰδόντες σε καὶ οἱ ἐν ἀγαπήσει κεκοιμημένοι· καὶ γὰρ ἡμεῖς ζωῇ ζησόμεθα 'Blessed are those who saw you and were adorned with love; for we also shall surely live'. For the interpretation of ܢܚܐ as an Aphel compare John 5:21; 12:47; 1 Cor 15:22, 45; for the Peal interpretation compare Rev 1:18; 2:8.[92]

---

[89] Joosten, 'Eléments d'araméen occidental'.

[90] Winter, *Ben Sira in Syriac*, 177–178; idem, 'Ben Sira in Syriac', II, 499; Van Peursen, 'Que vive celui qui fait vivre', 293.

[91] Winter, *Ben Sira in Syriac*, 177–178; idem, 'Ben Sira in Syriac', II, 499; Van Peursen, 'Que vive celui qui fait vivre', 291–293. Compare the introduction of ܣܒܪܬܐ 'good news' in Pesh-Ps 19:5, 68:11; Weitzman, *Syriac Version*, 225.

[92] Winter, *Ben Sira in Syriac*, 178–181; idem, 'Ben Sira in Syriac', II, 499–501; Van Peursen, 'Que vive celui qui fait vivre', 299–300.

In 3:22, 18:13, 35:11, 38:24, 40:28 and especially in 48:10, 11 the argument for the influence of the New Testament is rather strong. In 15:15, 25:8, 40:15 and 48:6 it is uncertain. Even in those cases that reflect the influence of the New Testament, it is possible that the parallels are the result of a later Christian revision and that there once existed a Peshitta version that did not have these parallels. Because of the uncertainty about the earliest textual history of Syr, we cannot rule out this possibility. However, the text itself does not give any indication that the New Testament parallels are secondary.

5.5 CONCLUSION

In a number of cases Syr has a free rendering containing words or phrases that have been borrowed from or are reminiscent of passages in the Old Testament. This phenomenon is also attested in the other versions of Sirach, especially Heb, and in many cases it cannot be decided whether the Syriac translator is responsible for them or his source text, or perhaps later scribes. Sometimes a reference to a biblical passage in Heb or Gr has been strengthened in Syr. In a very few cases Syr seems to reflect the influence of a Syriac version of the Old Testament. There is no evidence for the assumption that the Syriac translator was acquainted with the Targums. Syr contains rabbinic idioms, parallels with rabbinic literature, and passages that reflect acquaintance with halakhic traditions. It has also some interesting parallels with New Testament passages.

Because of the uncertainties about the sources of the parallels (Hebrew source text, translation or transmission), we cannot draw firm conclusions about the translator's religious background. This applies especially to the parallels for which there are only a few examples (parallels with the Old Testament Peshitta and with the New Testament). The parallels with rabbinic sources are more pervasive throughout Syr, but since it is likely that the translator's source text had already a strong rabbinic flavour, we cannot conclude that the translator had a rabbinic-Jewish background.

CHAPTER SIX

THE RELIGIOUS PROFILE OF THE SYRIAC SIRACH

6.1 INTRODUCTION

In the preceding chapters we have made a distinction between features that can be ascribed to the translator's activity and elements that in all likelihood were part of his source text. This distinction is relevant if we endeavour to describe the translator's religious profile. For this purpose we need to distinguish between the profile of the translation and that of the translator. The first includes the complete picture of religious thoughts, ideas, tendencies and world view to which the text bears witness. The second is based only on those elements for which the translator is responsible. Elements in the translation that were already present in the translator's source text do not necessarily reflect the translator's opinions and beliefs. If we wish to establish the cultural and religious context in which Syr originated, we are interested in the translator's cultural and religious profile rather than in that of the translation. However, to establish the translator's profile, we should start with the profile of the text as a whole. After we have charted the profile of the text, we can isolate features that shed light on the translator's profile.

The differences between the translator's profile and that of the translation may be less than in the case of other biblical books. We have seen a number of cases where the translator appears to have omitted words, verses or even whole passages, that did not concur with his own theological perspective, or that reflected an interest that was not his, such as the praise of Aaron in Chapter 45. If the translator took on himself the freedom to change the text or omit parts of it, we may suspect that those passages that he did not change or omit agreed with his own religious thoughts and beliefs. But even if this is true, the distinction between the elements for which the translator is responsible and those that are due to his source text is useful, because it is particularly in the former that the translator's own main concerns and interests can be detected.

6.2 CHARACTERISTICS OF THE RELIGIOUS PROFILE OF THE TRANSLATOR AND THE TRANSLATION

6.2.1 *Text-critical issues*

A. The poor state of the translator's source text

It seems that the Hebrew text used by the Syriac translator was full of mistakes (Chapter 2), even though some of the examples adduced may be due to misreadings by the translator rather than to errors in his source text. The poor state of the translator's Hebrew source text has been taken as evidence for the non-canonical status of Sirach in the community in which Syr originated (§ 2.2.1).[1] It is questionable, however, to what extent we can apply the dichotomy of 'canonical' and 'non-canonical' books to a largely unknown second- or third-century Syriac community. Moreover, the text-critical profile of the translation and its source text does not inform us about their religious profile.[2] A text that has a low authority from the perspective of the text-critical scholar may have been cherished as authoritative in a religious community. This is what happened, for example, to the Masoretic Text of Samuel. The poor state of this text did not affect its status in communities that considered the Hebrew Bible as authoritative.[3]

B. The character of the translation

Smend characterized Syr as the worst piece of translation of the Syriac Bible.[4] The character of the translation is without parallel, except per-

---

[1] Weitzman has put forward a similar argument for Pesh-Chronicles, see § 3.1.

[2] For a somewhat different view see see Weitzman, *Syriac Version*, 111, 208; cf. § 3.1.

[3] Cf. Barthélemy, 'Qualité du texte massorétique', 43: 'Le T[exte] M[assorétique] de Samuel a subi un certain nombre d'accidents (mutilations ou corruptions) et quelques retouches théologiques. Sous ces deux aspects, il semble avoir été plus mal conservé que le TM de la plupart des autre livres de la Bible'; see also Tov, *Textual Criticism*, 161.

[4] Smend, *Jesus Sirach*, cxxxvii (quoted in Chapter 3, n. 2); similarly Owens, Review of Nelson, *Syriac Version*, 166.

haps for Chronicles and 1–2 Maccabees. Especially the omission of large parts of the book and the thoughtlessness or negligence with which the translator seems to have done his work (cf. § 3.5) suggest that for him Sirach did not have a canonical status (§ 3.1).[5] However, as we said above, it is questionable to what extent we can apply the dichotomy of 'canonical' and 'non-canonical' books to a largely unknown second- or third-century Syriac community. However carelessly the translator has done his work, he considered the book of Sirach worthy of spending his time and expertise on.

6.2.2 *The translator's knowledge of languages*

A. The translator's knowledge of Hebrew

It is unquestionable that Syr was derived from a Hebrew source (§§ 2.1–2.2). This indicates that the translator knew Hebrew and that he considered a Hebrew source text appropriate for his purpose of producing a Syriac translation. At first sight the translator's knowledge of Hebrew indicates a Jewish or Jewish-Christian background, since there is hardly any evidence for knowledge of Hebrew outside Jewish or Jewish-Christian groups in the first three centuries of the Common Era.[6] However, the term 'Jewish-Christian' is used in different ways. It can be used in a genetic sense, as referring to Jews who converted to Christianity, or in a praxis-based definition, as referring to people who accepted the messianic status of Jesus but felt it necessary to keep, or perhaps adopt, practices associated with Judaism such as circumcision, the observance of the Sabbath and the keeping of food laws.[7] The translator's knowledge of Hebrew argues in favour of a Jewish-Christian background if this term is used in the genetic sense, but does not indicate a Jewish-Christian background in the praxis-based definition. Since, however, the Jews who became Christian represented a large variety of opinions, the designation 'Jewish-Christian' in the genetic sense does not define anything specific at all and therefore it is not very useful in a discussion about the translator's religious

---

[5] In this case too Weitzman has put forward a similar argument for Chronicles; see § 3.1; see ibidem note 3 for 1–2 Maccabees.

[6] Van Peursen, 'Jewish and/or Christian', 246.

[7] Cf. Carleton Paget, 'Jewish Christianity'.

background.[8] Moreover, the claim that the translator knew Hebrew should be modified by the observation that his knowledge of this language was limited.[9]

A different issue is raised by the question of why the translator chose a Hebrew source as the basis for his translation. Sirach is the only book of the Apocrypha that was translated from a Hebrew rather than a Greek source. This has been observed by earlier scholars,[10] but is still in need of a satisfying explanation. It suggests that the Syriac translator of Sirach did not consider this book as Scripture. In the second and third centuries AD it is only in Christian groups that Sirach had canonical status, but should the production of Syr have been part of a project to translate the Christian Scriptures into Syriac, one would have expected that for Sirach, as for the other Apocrypha, a Greek source had been used.

B. The translator's knowledge of Greek

The generally accepted view that the translator consulted the Septuagint cannot be proved (cf. § 2.3). Even if this were the case, the translator's apparent knowledge of Greek does not help us specify the translator's cultural and religious background, because in the first centuries of the Common Era the use of Greek was widespread.

Another question, already raised above, is why Syr is not based on a Greek source. Even if the Septuagint played a role in the production of Syr, this was only a subordinate role. In Weitzman's discussion of the Peshitta as a whole, he considers the subordinate role of the Septuagint in the making of the Peshitta an argument in favour of a Jewish rather than a Christian origin, because 'the church did not yet fully appreciate the *Hebraica veritas*, and cherished LXX as its Old Testament. It is hard to see why Christian translators should instead have

---

[8] Cf. Carleton Paget, 'Jewish Christianity', 733–734. Perhaps the translator was not raised in a Hebrew-speaking environment, but his parents, or only one of them, used Hebrew. This is of course all speculation, only to indicate that we should be very careful with the step from 'Hebrew' to 'Jewish'.

[9] See Chapter 3, esp. § 3.4. Accordingly, the observation that the Peshitta 'betrays an excellent knowledge of the [Hebrew] language' (Ter Haar Romeny, 'Development of Judaism and Christianity', 25 = idem, 'Syriac Versions', 90) does not hold true for Sirach. For Pesh-Chronicles too it has been argued that the translator's knowledge of Hebrew was poor; see especially Fraenkel, 'Chronik', I, 757.

[10] Cf. e.g. Haefeli, *Peschitta des Alten Testaments*, 8; Van Kasteren, 'Canon des Ouden Verbonds', I, 391; Beckwith, *Old Testament Canon*, 21.

given primacy to the Hebrew and thereby produced a version often at odds with LXX.'[11] However, in the case of Sirach this argument can be countered by the observation that Sirach was not part of the Hebrew Bible. Accordingly, it is very unlikely that the translation of Sirach into Syriac was part either of a Jewish project to translate the Hebrew Scriptures (because Sirach did belong to it) or of a Christian project to translate the corpus of the Apocrypha as a supplement to the translation of the Hebrew Bible (because in that case we would have expected the use of a Greek source text, as in the case of the other Apocrypha).[12]

C. The translator's knowledge of Syriac

Apparently the motivation to make a Syriac translation of Sirach arose in a Syriac-speaking community. We have no reason to question the translator's proficiency in this target language. He was even able to introduce poetic features into his Syriac translation (§ 3.6). That his translation sounds sometimes incomprehensible (§ 3.5, end) should be ascribed to his free and negligent way of translation, rather than to a poor command of the Syriac language.

6.2.3 *Translational features*

A. The targumic features of the translation

Syr has much in common with the Jewish Aramaic Bible translations (Chapter 3, esp. § 3.9). Some 'targumic features' are more prominent in Syr than in other parts of the Peshitta, but it should be recalled that also in other parts of the Peshitta there is diversity with regard to the 'targumic flavour'.[13] Moreover, the so-called targumic features appear still relatively infrequently compared with their occurrences in the Targums.[14] The targumic elements show that the translation stands in the Aramaic-Syriac translation tradition and suggests an educated

---

[11] Weitzman, *Syriac Version*, 245.

[12] For the view that the Apocrypha were translated somewhat later than the books of the Hebrew Bible see the literature mentioned in note 10.

[13] Cf. Weitzman, *Syriac Version*, 111, on Pesh-Chronicles.

[14] Cf. Van Keulen, 'Points of Agreement', 234, on the Pesthitta and Targum Jonathan to Kings: 'Several types of differences from the MT that are common to P and TJ are more consistently exhibited in TJ than in P'.

translator, who had received training in the main principles of this tradition,[15] but they do not necessarily reveal a Jewish background.[16]

B. Avoidance of anthropomorphisms

The avoidance of anthropomorphisms (§ 3.3) is also a characteristic
feature of the Aramaic translation tradition. Accordingly, what we
have said about 'targumic features' applies here as well. Some alleged
anti-anthropomorphisms may be motivated by other considerations
than the avoidance of anthropomorphisms as such. Thus a typical example such as the substitution of 'the Lord' by 'fear of the Lord' may
be due to an emphasis on the concept of 'fear' (cf. § 2.4.1) rather than
a wish to make the reference to 'the Lord' less direct, and the preference for using ܩܕܡ before references to God may have a linguistic
background, which would explain why it is also inserted before references to human beings.

6.2.4 *Religious and cultural views reflected in the translation*

A. Motifs shared with the Expanded Text of Sirach (SirII)

Syr shares many motifs with SirII, such as 'love of God', 'repentance', 'faith', 'hope' and 'fear of the Lord' (§ 2.4.1). The fact that the
same motifs are also found in other witnesses of SirII suggests at first
sight that they were already part of the SirII readings in the Hebrew
source text of Syr (cf. § 2.1) and that they cannot be ascribed to the
Syriac translator. However, the same motifs occur also in other parts
of the Peshitta, and in those parts it is highly unlikely that the source
text is responsible for them. This suggests the possibility that the
translator of Syr, like the translators of other parts of the Peshitta, was
responsible for these motifs. In other words, there are a number of motifs shared by both other witnesses to SirII and other parts of the

---

[15] Cf. Weitzman, *From Judaism to Christianity*, 194: 'The schoolhouse and the
synagogue together gave rise to a fund of Aramaic renderings for individual words or
phrases, which was passed down as part of the exegetical tradition, and so was acces-
sible to P.'
[16] Accordingly, to discuss a 'targumic' feature such as the 'emphasis on the gulf
between God and man' under 'elements inherited from a Jewish background' may be
misleading; *pace* Weitzman, *From Judaism to Christianity*, 72. See also our conclusions at the end of Chapter 3.

Peshitta, which makes it impossible to determine whether they go back to the translator's source text (reflecting SirII) or his own translation activity (as in other parts of the Peshitta).

B. Eschatology

The eschatological outlook of Syr differs considerably from the original book of Sirach because of its introduction of final divine judgment, punishment of the wicked, and reward of the just (§ 2.4.2). This eschatology is typical of SirII and what has been said about motifs shared with SirII applies here as well. In many we cases we do not know to what extent the new eschatological features were already present in the translator's source text and to what extent the translator is responsible for them. Even if we were to be able to ascribe them to the translator, we should have to bear in mind that they reflect changes in religious thought that affected large segments of the broad spectrum of Jewish, Jewish-Christian and other Christian groups. Attempts by Edersheim, Smend and others to put forward the eschatology of the translation as evidence of a Christian background are unconvincing.[17]

C. Sacrifices, priesthood, temple

The omission of references to sacrifices, priesthood and temple, the substitution of references to sacrifices by remarks about prayer or charity and the imprecise or shortened rendering of sacrificial terminology, strongly suggest that the translator was indifferent, if not hostile, to sacrifices and the priesthood (cf. § 4.2). Since this attitude concerns the institutions as such, rather than only the contemporary priestly service in Jerusalem (as in e.g. some Dead Sea Scrolls), it is hard to reconcile it with a Jewish background, but it fits in well with a Christian or Jewish-Christian background.

D. The Law and the Prophets

The Syriac translator was familiar with all parts of the Hebrew Bible and was influenced by them in his translation. Winter's claim that he was unwilling to quote from the Prophets is not supported by the data (§ 5.1). Likewise, Winter's distinction between an original translator

---

[17] See their commentaries on passages where Syr introduces eternal life, judgment, etc., mentioned in § 2.4.2.

who had a high esteem for the Law and a later editor who had a hostile attitude to it cannot be maintained. In the text we discern a certain carelessness about references to the Law, and sometimes these references are even omitted (§ 4.3.1). Traces of an original translation reflecting a high esteem for the Law cannot be observed.

E. Israel and the nations

There is one striking example in which Syr omits a remark about the eternity of Israel, in 37:25, but we cannot be sure that this omission was intentional. In other cases Syr introduces references to 'the nations', which would go well with a Christian background. However, since the remarks do not exceed what can be found in the Hebrew Bible, especially Deutero-Isaiah, this tendency does not tell us much about the translator's religious ('Jewish or Christian') background (§ 4.4).

F. Poverty

The translator appears to have had a high esteem for poverty and charity (§ 4.5.2). Winter, who does not distinguish between the two, ascribed these tendencies to the translator's alleged Ebionite background. However, the devotion to poverty is not exclusively Ebionite. It is also reflected in non-rabbinic Jewish sources, including the Dead Sea Scrolls, and in several New Testament passages. A positive assessment of charity is also found in rabbinic sources. Other parts of the Peshitta too reflect a high esteem for both poverty and charity.

G. Others?

Some tendencies that in the history of research have been attributed to Syr are in reality not reflected in it. Thus the translator's alleged vegetarianism, which plays an important role in Winter's hypothesis of an Ebionite background, is not corroborated by the data (§ 4.5.1). His claim that Syr reflects an unwillingness to refer to the creation of Wisdom, which allegedly reflects a post-Arian orthodox Christian revision, cannot be maintained either (§ 4.6). Nor is Edersheim's claim that Syr reflects the Christian doctrine of the fall of man in 25:15 compelling (§ 5.1).

6.2.5 *Parallels with other sources*

A. The Old Testament

The translator introduced parallels to all parts of the Old Testament (§ 5.1). Winter's claim that the translator avoided references to the Prophets should be abandoned (above, § 6.2.4 [D]). In some cases the influence seems to come from Old Testament Peshitta, but in other cases Syr seems to have been influenced in another way, i.e. not from the Peshitta version (§ 5.2). One could tentatively argue that the Syriac translator was acquainted with both the Hebrew Old Testament[18] and the Peshitta, but the evidence for the translator's dependence on other parts of the Peshitta is very small, especially if one takes into account alternative explanations such as the influence of the Aramaic/Syriac translation tradition and acquaintance with biblical phraseology (§ 5.2, end).

B. Rabbinic Literature

Syr contains many parallels with rabbinic sources. Sometimes the reading in Syr seems to be due to the influence of a rabbinic source; in other cases Syr reflects acquaintance with halakhic traditions, rabbinic exegetical methods or typical rabbinic idioms (§ 5.3). We have found many interesting examples, and this feature deserves further study. However, on the basis of our present knowledge of the textual transmission of Sirach, it is likely that the rabbinic flavour was already present in the translator's source text, and not the result of his translation activity.

C. New Testament

In five cases Syr contains a parallel with a New Testament passage. Four other cases for which New Testament influence has been claimed are uncertain (§ 5.4). Since the number of examples is limited, they alone do not provide a solid base for a Christian or Jewish-Christian background of Syr. One could argue that later scribes, rather than the original translator are responsible for them. However, the text itself does not show any trace of the New Testament parallels being secondary and especially the most obvious example, namely the reformula-

---

[18] For the implications of the translator's knowledge of Hebrew see § 6.2.2 (A).

tion of 48:10–11, is well-integrated in its context. Taken together with some other features, especially the attitude towards sacrifices, priest-hood and temple (§§ 4.2, 6.2.4 [C]), the New Testament parallels can be considered part of the cumulative evidence of the Christian or Jew-ish-Christian background of Syr.

6.3 SYR IN THE SYRIAC TRADITION

In the preceding paragraphs we have occasionally touched upon the question as to the translator's attitude to the book he was translating. Some features of Syr can be taken as evidence that the translator of Sirach did not regard this book as Scripture, especially the negligent way in which the translation was made (§ 6.2.1 [B]) and the fact that it was translated from Hebrew (§ 6.2.2). At first sight the textual history of Syr indicates that also after the production of the translation it did not quickly acquire a canonical status, because in the early phase of its textual history Syr was not transmitted very carefully (§ 1.3). How-ever, the textual corruptions that originated in this phase do not argue against the authoritative status of Sirach. They suggest that those re-sponsible for the transmission 'did not regard the Syriac text before them as letter-perfect',[19] but they do not indicate that Sirach was not held in high esteem. Traces of inner-Syriac corruptions are attested throughout the Peshitta.[20] They cannot be used to identify books that had a lower status as Scripture.

Other evidence points out that if Sirach did not have a canonical status when it was translated, it soon acquired one (cf. § 2.2.1). It oc-curs in a number of biblical manuscripts,[21] including the complete Bi-ble manuscripts 7a1 and 8a1 (§ 1.1),[22] and is quoted as Scripture by, for example, Aphrahat, the author of the *Book of Steps* and Philoxenus

---

[19] Weitzman, *Syriac Version*, 300–301; Weitzman discusses here the background of intentional changes, but his remark is also useful for explaining changes that were not intentional.

[20] Cf. Weitzman, *Syriac Version*, 7.

[21] One could object that a book's inclusion in a 'biblical' manuscript does not prove its canonical status, since Josephus' *Jewish War* too is included in 7a1. But whereas the *Jewish War* occurs at the end, as a kind of appendix, Sirach occurs in the middle of the manuscript, between other 'canonical' books.

[22] Cf. Beckwith, *Old Testament Canon*, 195–196; Beckwith's explanation for the absence of Sirach in 9a1 is that it has been part of 9a1 at the lost end of the manu-script.

(§ 1.2).[23] It is listed as one of the canonical books in the *catalogus si-naiticus*, a list of sacred books ascribed to Irenaeus found in the monastery on Mount Sinai.[24]

Sometimes readings from Syr occur in Syriac liturgies. Thus there are two readings from Syr in the fifth- or sixth-century index of scriptural readings called 'COMES' (B.M. Add. 14,528): Sir 44:1–49:6 is read on Thursday in the Week of Rest, (i.e. the week after Easter) in Commemoration of Bishops, and Sir 44:1–45:26 is given as a reading for the Commemoration of Martyrs.[25] In the liturgy of the Upper Monastery the prayer for God's mercy in Sir 36:1–17 is part of the liturgy for the Rogation of the Ninevites,[26] and the opening of the Praise of the Fathers in 44:1–45:4 (variant: 44:1–23) is read at one of the Fridays of the Saints.[27] A reading from Sirach 50 occurs twice in the lectionary system of the Church of Kokhe, at the sixth and eight Fridays of Epiphany, commemorating the Syrian Doctors and the Catholic Fathers respectively.[28]

6.4 CONCLUSION

The features discussed in the preceding chapters and summarized and evaluated in the present chapter are the main characteristics of the religious profile of Syr. To establish the cultural and religious background in which Syr originated on the basis of these features is not an easy task. As we said in § 6.1, a distinction should be made between the profile of the text and that of the translator. Elements that were already present in his source text (about which we cannot say more than that the translator did not remove them) or elements that were inserted by later scribes may have contributed considerably to the

---

[23] Cf. Van Kasteren, 'Canon des Ouden Verbonds', I, 391–392.

[24] Ed. Smith Lewis, 4–16. The manuscript can be dated in the ninth century, but for the list itself an earlier date, in the fourth century, has been argued; cf. Van Kasteren, 'Canon des Ouden Verbonds', I, 395–403.

[25] Burkitt, 'Early Syriac Lectionary System', 311, 313; Jenner, *Perikopentitels*, 460; on the status of COMES in the history of the Syriac liturgy see Jenner, *Perikopentitels*, 11–20; idem, 'Syriac Lectionary Systems'.

[26] Baumstark, 'Nichtevangelische Syrische Perikopenordnungen', 62, 64.

[27] Baumstark, 'Nichtevangelische Syrische Perikopenordnungen', 52–54.

[28] Macomber, 'Chaldean Lectionary System', 500–501. According to one manuscript these are the fifth and seventh Fridays of Epiphany.

theological profile of the text, but do not tell us much about the trans-lator's religious background.

In addition, there are two other complicating factors. In the first place the Jewish-Christian spectrum in the first centuries of the Common Era was more diverse than a bipartite division in 'Jewish' and 'Christian', or even a tripartite division, including 'Jewish-Christian', suggests. In the second place there are a number of features that do not belong exclusively to a particular group. Features that in the history of research have been put forward as revealing a Christian background, such as the references to 'faith' or the eschatological views are not exclusively Christian. Even less convincing are attempts to identify the community in which Syr originated with a specific Jewish, Jewish-Christian or Christian group, such as Winter's Ebionite hypothesis.

Elsewhere we have investigated how we can improve on the very general observation that Syr originated somewhere within the broad spectrum of Jewish-Christian groups in the second or third century CE.[29] There are both elements that point to a Jewish background, such as the occurrence of rabbinic quotations and the use of a Hebrew source text, and elements that suggest a Christian background, such as the translator's negative attitude towards sacrifices, priesthood and temple. The combination of 'Jewish' and 'Christian' elements at first sight suggests a Jewish-Christian background, but a closer look at the material reveals that some of the 'Christian' elements, such as the in-difference or even hostility towards 'the Law' cannot be accounted for if we assume a Jewish-Christian background of Syr. Moreover, the arguments for the 'Jewishness' of the translation are not compelling. The argument that Syr contains parallels with rabbinic literature is not valid because these parallels may have been part of the translator's source text (§ 6.2.5 [B]). The argument that only a Jew can be ex-pected to use a Hebrew source text, may suggest that the translator was raised in a Jewish/Hebrew context, but does not inform us about his religious profile at the time he produced Syr (§ 6.2.2 [A]). It is possible that the translator was a Jew who converted to a type of Christianity, and hence that he was a Jewish-Christian in the genetic sense (cf. above § 6.2.2 [A]). Since, however, the genetic definition of Jewish-Christian is not very useful if we wish to establish the transla-tor's religious background, this does not help us much.[30]

---

[29] Van Peursen, 'Jewish and/or Christian'.

What we can say about the translator, for example concerning his attitude towards poverty, is helpful for describing his religious profile but does not assist us in identifying the community in which Syr originated with any known religious group from the second or third century CE.

---

[30] Our conclusions agree to a large extent with Smend's view that the translator's knowledge of Hebrew indicates that he was probably born a Jew, but that his translation reflects an anti-Judaistic tendency. See Smend, *Jesus Sirach*, p. cxxxvii: 'Zugleich tritt aber bei dem Verfasser, der nach seiner hebräischen Sprachkenntnis wahrscheinlich ein geborener Jude war, hier eine gewisse antijüdische Tendenz zu Tage'. However, even though we agree with Smend's conclusion, we do not agree with many of his arguments; see our 'Jewish and/or Christian', 249–250, 262.

PART TWO

METHODOLOGY OF THE
COMPUTER-ASSISTED LINGUISTIC
ANALYSIS

CHAPTER SEVEN

THE CALAP MODEL OF TEXTUAL ANALYSIS

7.1 INTRODUCTION

In the CALAP project, of which the present monograph is a product, we have developed a model of linguistic analysis and text interpretation, in which both insights from linguistics, especially computer linguistics, and text-critical and text-historical considerations are taken into account.[1] The present chapter will be concerned with the characteristics of this model and its underlying assumptions concerning languages and texts. We will also discuss the implications of this model for the analysis of texts and translations.

The way in which a text is approached in a computer-assisted analysis differs considerably from that in the traditional philological analysis. From a computer-linguistic perspective a text is a one-dimensional sequence of characters. Behind this string of characters several layers or dimensions[2] of information can be added. It is also possible to mark relationships between non-sequential elements,[3] or to take into account several witnesses of one text as parallel sequences of characters.[4] However, the understanding of the text as a one-dimensional entity remains radically different from the philological understanding of the text as an abstraction, a scholarly construct on the basis of the extant manuscripts and quotations, which are the result of a long and complicated transmission history.[5]

---

[1] CALAP stands for Computer-Assisted Linguistic Analysis of the Peshitta. For more details about this project see www.leidenuniv.nl/gg/calap. For its background and methodology see Van Keulen–Van Peursen, *Computer Linguistics and Textual History*. See also preface to the present study.

[2] Cf. Kroeze, 'Multidimensional Linguistic Database'.

[3] The database model used in CALAP is a further development of C.-J. Doedens' Monads dot Feature (MdF) model, described in his *Text Databases*; see also Petersen, 'Emdros'.

[4] Cf. Bosman–Sikkel, 'Response to Pier G. Borbone', 120–121.

[5] Cf. Borbone, 'Response to Hendrik Jan Bosman and Constantijn J. Sikkel'.

The understanding of a text as a one-dimensional sequence of characters differs also from the paleographical and codicological notion of a text as a two-dimensional entity, in which the *mise-en-page* entails not only 'the text' as a sequence of graphemes, but also the various ways in which graphs represent the graphemes, page layout, delimitation markers of larger and smaller units, spaces[6] and illuminations.[7] Even written words or sentences may in some cases belong to the non-textual or meta-textual data, such as marginal notes, titles of pericopes and colophons.[8]

Both the notion of 'the text' as an abstraction from the extant textual witnesses, and that of 'textual witnesses' as documents with their own codicological and paleographical peculiarities differ from the understanding of the text as a sequence of graphemes as is current in computer linguistics. This poses challenges to the computer-assisted interdisciplinary analysis of the Peshitta. In the CALAP project we have tried to develop a procedure of computer-assisted analysis that accounts for issues that from a philological perspective belong to the exigencies of a sound textual analysis. To do justice to the philological notion of 'the text', our digitized texts that constitute the starting-point for the textual analysis, contain variant readings and the possibility of retrieving, analysing and comparing various textual witnesses.[9] As a first step to do justice to the *mise-en-page* and related phenomena, we have paid attention to delimitation markers in the manuscripts and their relation to the syntactic organization of the text.[10]

---

[6] Even the regular spaces between words can be considered as a matter of layout, rather than elements with grapheme status.

[7] For this perspective on textual analysis, see Jenner, *Perikopentitels*, 21–23, 157–275; idem, 'Review of Methods'; idem, 'Study of 8a1'; idem, 'Unit Delimitation in the Syriac Text of Daniel'; cf. on Hebrew textual witnesses idem, 'Tools for Interpretation or Matter of Lay-Out?' The *mise-en-page* is often ignored in text-critical and text-historical studies of the Peshitta; cf. Jenner, 'Study of 8a1', 205. For the Syriac witnesses to Sirach see Jenner–Van Peursen, 'Unit Delimitation and the Text of Ben Sira'. Unfortunately, codicological and paleographical studies do not receive due recognition as part of the discipline of textual criticism and textual history. The little attention that E. Tov in his otherwise very valuable introduction to the textual criticism of the Old Testament (*Textual Criticism*) pays to them is representative of the situation in this area of scholarship.

[8] Compare e.g. the occurrence of ܗܘ in 7a1 in 22:1, 28:22 and 51:22, which the scribe apparently added to fill up the line. (Why the scribe used this device to fill up the line, rather than, for example, the use of extended letters, is not clear).

[9] See Bosman–Sikkel, 'Response to Pier G. Borbone'; Jenner–Van Peursen–Talstra, 'Interdisciplinary Debate', 41.

In a philological approach much depends on the scholar's intuition. The *master's eye*[11] plays a crucial role in the decision as to what data are to be considered important. An example may illustrate this. In § 5.4 we discussed the addition of the adjective 'good' in 18:13 'a good shepherd'. For the human scholar this addition is exciting because it may shed light on the translator's religious background, since it is reminiscent of an expression in the Gospel of John. However, the pattern in which Noun + Adjective in Syr corresponds to a single noun in Heb is not unique. And semantically there is little difference between 'a shepherd who shepherds his flocks' and 'a good shepherd who shepherds his flocks'. If we were unaware of the parallel in the Gospel of John, we would certainly have categorized this example under 'Syr adds an explanatory word or phrase' (§ 3.2 [j]). If we were investigating the 'faithfulness' of the translation, we would probably pay more attention to cases in which the addition of an adjective changes the purport of the verse, as in 25:21, where a warning against women has become one against 'evil women' (§ 4.1 [2]). Whatever the goal of our research may be, much depends on the scholar's intuition and this intuition is selective. This intuitive selective mechanism, however, is completely absent from the computer program that establishes correspondences at phrase level between two texts. It makes a systematic registration of all cases where Noun + Adjective in Syr corresponds to a single noun in Heb. It lacks, so to speak, the excitement if a parallel with the New Testament can be established, and it does not become inattentive or bored if the addition of an adjective is 'nothing special'.[12]

---

[10] See e.g. § 27.3 (end), and Van Peursen, 'Clause Hierarchy and Discourse Structure', 137.

[11] This expression is the title of R.W. Jongman's PhD dissertation (*Het oog van de meester*) about an experimental psychological investigation of the way in which chess players think and evaluate positions. It is tempting to elaborate further on the analogy between chess games and linguistic research. In both cases the human thinking is characterized by a selective mechanism in which pattern recognition plays an important role. And in both cases the difference between an elementary level and an advanced level is closely related to the ability to recognize patterns. The computer lacks this selective mechanism (although in chess computing there are attempts to repair this lack), but compensates for it by its being much stronger than human beings in systematic registration and calculation.

[12] On the addition of adjectives see further § 10.1.1; see also § 10.2.1 for similar considerations applied to cases where Noun *d*-Noun in Syriac corresponds to a single noun in Hebrew.

In this introduction we have indicated some differences between a computer-assisted approach and traditional philological approaches. It would be incorrect, however, to describe 'the computer-assisted approach' and 'the philological approach' as two opposed monolithic entities. In the following we shall see that some 'philological approaches' agree with the perspective of the computer-assisted textual analysis described here in that they emphasize the need of a formal description of languages and texts and of a systematic registration of the data.

7.2 FORM TO FUNCTION

7.2.1 The form-to-function approach in Semitic linguistics

A first characteristic of the CALAP-model of linguistic analysis is its form-to-function approach. This approach implies that (a) a clear dichotomy is drawn between the structure of a syntactic construction on the one hand and its function on the other and that (b) the analysis starts with observations of regularities in form, before any functions are assigned. Accordingly, the aim of the analysis is to seek the function that is performed by a given morpheme, word or structure, rather than to look for the morpheme, word or structure that performs a given function.[13] Thus at word level, a distributional analysis of morphemes is accomplished before any conclusions are drawn about their function; at clause level, a distributional analysis of clause patterns is made, before these clauses are labelled according to their function, etc.

In the field of Biblical Hebrew studies, the form-to-function approach has been advocated by J. Hoftijzer and W. Richter. It has also been one of the basic assumptions of the computer-assisted research of Biblical Hebrew of E. Talstra and his colleagues at the Free University.[14] A student of Hoftijzer, M.L. Folmer, has applied the form-to-function approach to the study of the Aramaic language in the Achaemenid period.[15] In Syriac and general Semitic studies, a prominent advocate of the form-to-function approach is G. Khan. In his

---

[13] Khan, *Studies in Semitic Syntax*, xxvii.

[14] For a survey of both form-to-function approaches and functional approaches in the field of Biblical Studies, see Van der Merwe, 'Discourse Linguistics', 16–20.

[15] Folmer, *Aramaic Language in the Achaemenid Period*.

Studies in Semitic Syntax it is this method that he follows in his analysis of extraposition and pronominal agreement in several Semitic languages.[16] We are not aware, however, of any other attempt to apply a strict form-to-function approach to the study of Classical Syriac.

There are mainly two arguments to proceed from a formal analysis to a functional one rather than *vice versa*. The first argument concerns a general linguistic observation. In languages there is usually not a one-to-one relation between forms and functions. This means that the study of forms and their functions is a complex undertaking, in which one has to establish either the various and often diverse functions performed by a given form, or the various forms and structures that perform a given function. A reason to start the analysis at the formal level is that this level consists of a limited number of elements that build up a larger, but still limited number of structures. Hence the formal analysis, however complex it may be, is relatively easier and more unequivocal than the analysis of the level of functions and meaning, which include nuances that are often very hard to grasp.[17] Whereas in natural languages there is a lot of fuzziness and opacity at the functional level,[18] at the formal level there is much more clarity and consistency.

An example may illustrate this argument. A debated issue in Syriac linguistics is the function of the enclitic pronoun (Ep) in tripartite nominal clauses: Does it function as a copula (Khan), as a 'lesser subject' in a bipartite clause core, referring to a subject in fronted or rear extraposition (Goldenberg), or as an emphatic particle, giving prominence to the preceding element (Muraoka). If it is a copula, the tripartite nominal clause is an unmarked construction and functionally equivalent to the bipartite nominal clause. If it fulfils another syntactic or emphatic function, it is marked. Elsewhere we have argued that the tripartite nominal clause was originally a marked construction (as it is

---

[16] For the definition of 'extraposition' and 'pronominal agreement', see § 21.1.

[17] Cf. Richter, *Grundlagen* I, 11: 'Die Ausdrucksseite baut sich aus einer begrenzten Zahl von Zeichenelementen auf; ihre Analyse ist einfacher und eindeutiger. Deshalb setzt die Beschreibung der Sprache bei ihr an und schreitet zur Deutung der Funktion weiter'; see also Fohrer *et al.*, *Exegese des Alten Testaments*, 59.

[18] Much of the fuzziness is due to the fact that languages undergo diachronic developments. Cf. Khan, 'Response to Janet Dyk', 155: 'Historical change in language does not take place in a clear shift from one state to another but rather it typically involves a transitional period in which there is opacity and fuzziness in grammatical parsing and category assignment'.

in Biblical Hebrew), but that in Classical Syriac it is unmarked in many cases. Since the transition from a marked to an unmarked construction in languages takes place gradually, we can expect that at a certain stage cases where the construction with the Ep is unmarked and cases where it is marked occurred side by side.[19] All this means that there is a lot of fuzziness and opacity at the functional level, even apart from the confusion due to different usages of terms such as 'Subject', 'Predicate' and 'emphasis'. At the formal level however, one can describe the clause patterns in which the Ep occurs irrespective of one's position in this debate.

The second argument for the form-to-function approach concerns the corpus that we investigate. An approach that proceeds from a functional analysis to a formal one is only possible if one knows the functions that are relevant to the distinction between different forms. This is often not the case if we are dealing with ancient texts. For this reason the safest way is to start with the data that we have at our disposal and that can be studied in a descriptive way: the formal structures that occur in the corpus under investigation.[20]

7.2.2 *Implications of the form-to-function approach: an example*

An example may illustrate the implications of the form-to-function approach. The Syriac conjunction ܘ and its compounds fulfil a number of functions. A form-to-function approach, however, does not start with the alleged functions of the clauses introduced by ܘ and its compounds (causal, final, temporal, etc.), but with a formal distributional analysis of the clause patterns attested.[21] Compare e.g.

---

[19] Van Peursen, 'Three Approaches', 163.

[20] See Hoftijzer, 'Nominal Clause Reconsidered', 477: 'In the study of languages of which we cannot [achieve] a real degree of competence, as we can have with modern languages, the safest way is to start with formal criteria and with formal oppositions. For in such a case it is easier to get a reasonable grip on these phenomena than on functional, semantic and other ones'; see also ibid. 452–453 and idem, *Search for Method*, 1–2 n. 1: 'In the study of languages like classical Hebrew which have not been spoken any more for centuries, it is preferable to start one's study with formal criteria and formal oppositions, and not with functional/semantic ones, because in these fields no-one possesses the necessary native-speaker *competence*, as is the case for modern Western-European languages'; cf. also Talstra, 'Hierarchy of Clauses', 93.

[21] Cf. Talstra, 'Text Grammar', I, 172 on Biblical Hebrew.

2:3 ܡܟܠ ܕܠܐ ܬܫܒܩܝܘܗܝ ܘܒܗ ܐܬܕܒܩ '(Cling to Him and do not leave Him), so that you will become wise in your ways'.

2:5 ܡܟܠ ܕܒܗܝ ܐܝܟܢ ܕܗܘ ܐܘܪܚܟ ܢܬܪܨ ܘܗܘ ܕܘܒܪܟ ܐܬܬܟܝܠ '(Put your trust in Him and He will make straight your ways), for gold is tried in the fire and people in the furnace of poverty'.

Taking function as point of departure, one can attach a final function to ܡܟܠ ܕ in 2:3, and a causal function to the same compound conjunction in 2:5. However, starting from the form, there is no difference between ܡܟܠ ܕ in 2:3 and ܡܟܠ ܕ in 2:5. Accordingly, rather than giving the conjunction two different labels on the basis of our understanding of the clauses, we should make a distributional analysis of the clause patterns in which it occurs.

In the form-to-function approach, as its very name indicates, functional distinctions are not assigned before formal differences have been described. The starting-point for an analysis of the constructions under discussion is an inventory of all the occurrences of ܡܟܠ ܕܥ rather than one of final constructions, causal conjunctions, and the like. In this context it should be recalled that logically final and consecutive clauses can be considered as a subcategory of causal clauses, because they indicate a situation that constitutes the basis for another situation. What can be said about the examples quoted is that the clauses introduced by ܡܟܠ ܕܥ introduce the logical antecedence of the preceding clauses, without specifying the nature of the logical relationship.[22] In this way it is possible to cover in one description what at first sight seem to be different functions of the form ܡܟܠ ܕܥ.

Another implication of this approach is that it is not decided *a priori* on which level functions should be assigned. Thus the examples quoted do not differ in the form of the conjunction, but they do differ in the pattern of the clause as a whole (ܡܟܠ ܕܥ + imperfect + prepositional phrase versus ܡܟܠ ܕܥ + prepositional phrase + participle). Further investigations should point out whether a functional difference can be assigned to this formal difference in clause pattern.

---

[22] Cf. Van Peursen, *Verbal System*, 376.

7.2.3 *Formal syntactic analysis and the assignment of*
semantic functions

The concentration on the formal properties of a language implies that
the syntactic analysis of forms and patterns comes prior to the functional analysis of their semantic relations.[23] It should be noted, however, that the formal syntactic analysis and the assignment of semantic
functions are often closely related. In many cases the syntactic structures are multivalent and semantic information is needed to resolve the
ambiguity. Compare e.g.

> 24:13 ܐܝܟ ܐܝܠܢ ܕܡܫܚܐ ܒܣܢܝܪ 'like a tree of oil on the Senir', and
> 50:9 ܐܝܟ ܪܝܚ ܠܒܘܢܬܐ ܥܠ ܦܝܪܡܐ 'like the odour of frankincense
> upon the censer'.

On the formal level both phrases have the same structure: a head consisting of a preposition and a noun, followed by two specifications,
namely a *d*-phrase and a prepositional phrase. However, in the first
example we consider the prepositional phrase ܒܣܢܝܪ a specification of
the head of the phrase ܐܝܟ ܐܝܠܢ (or rather to the preceding
construction as a whole); in the second example we analyse the
prepositional phrase ܥܠ ܦܝܪܡܐ as a specification of the preceding
ܠܒܘܢܬܐ, rather than ܪܝܚ. Accordingly, the phrases quoted represent
two different patterns, namely

> [Noun [D-noun <sp>] [Prep-Noun <sp>]] (24:13) and
> [Noun [D-noun [Prep-Noun <sp>] <sp>] (50:9).

The observation that the two phrases reflect different patterns is not
based on a formal analysis, but on a rather complex process of interpretation: we know that the Senir is a mountain and that mountains
may be covered by trees, rather than by oil. For this reason we prefer
to regard 'on the Senir' as a specification of 'a tree of oil', rather than
'oil on the Senir' as a specification of 'a tree'. We also know that
frankincense is put in a censer, and that it may spread a nice smell.
From this knowledge we conclude that it is the frankincense, rather
than the odour that is located in the censer.[24] Interestingly enough,

---

[23] Cf. Talstra, 'Text Grammar', I, 169.

[24] Cf. Polak, 'Bottom-Up Structuring', 128–129, for some examples from Biblical
Hebrew. Polak argues that the translation of Exod 21:12 מכה איש ומת מות יומת with
'who smites a man so that he dies, shall certainly be put to death' rather than 'who
smites a man and dies, shall certainly be pronounced dead' is based on general as-

however, the larger the corpus under investigation, the more so-called extra-textual information becomes inter-textual. Thus the information that 'of the Senir' specifies the tree rather than the oil can also be retrieved if we have other textual evidence for the connection between a tree and a mountain (cf. 50:8 ܕܠܒܢܐ ܐܝܟܠܐ ܐܝܟ) and between frankincense and a censer.

In the preceding we pointed out that in our approach the syntactic analysis of forms and patterns comes prior to the functional analysis of their semantic relations. However, in the light of the fact that multivalent syntactic structures are rather frequent, we wish to emphasis our 'comes prior to': We consider making an inventory of forms as the *first step* in the linguistic analysis, but it is not our intention to claim that a formal description *alone* is sufficient to come to a coherent linguistic analysis.

7.3 TEXT LINGUISTICS

Having decided that a linguistic analysis of ancient texts should start with a formal, distributional description of linguistic elements, we have to establish the scope of this description and the extent to which linguistic analysis can be applied to texts.

In older linguistic theories, the sentence was considered the largest unit of grammatical description.[25] The problem with this traditional approach is twofold. First, many elements that occur at sentence level can only be understood if the sentence is taken as an element in the larger structure of the text. This concerns, for example, pronominal elements that refer to nouns or pronouns in preceding sentences, and elliptical constructions. Secondly, the arrangement of sentences within the text, just like the organization of phrases within the sentence, follows certain rules that are part of the language system.

Dissatisfaction with the traditional sentence-oriented approach in the nineteen-sixties gave rise to a new approach, which is called Text Linguistics. This approach aims at a grammatical analysis on the basis

---

sumptions and non-linguistic considerations. On purely syntactic grounds both translations are equally possible.

[25] Cf. Lyons, *Theoretical Linguistics*, 172–173; Richter, *Grundlagen* I, 20; Waltke–O'Connor, *Biblical Hebrew Syntax*, § 3.3.4d.

of texts rather than on the basis of sentences.[26] Texts are viewed as coherent structures in which linguistic phenomena constitute the relations in the textual structure. To these linguistic phenomena belong forms that refer to other words or phrases in the text (pronouns), forms that indicate the relationship between clauses (particles, conjunctions), and forms that refer to relations between text segments (macrosyntactic signs).[27]

In the seventies and eighties some attempts were made to apply the text-linguistic theoretical framework to biblical studies.[28] To these attempts belong the works of W. Schneider, E. Talstra and A. Niccacci.[29] These scholars were inspired by a study that appeared in the mid-sixties, namely H. Weinrich's *Tempus. Besprochene und Erzählte Welt*.[30] In the nineteen-nineties many studies appeared which under labels such as 'text linguistics', 'text grammar', 'discourse grammar' or 'narrative syntax' continued the work of these pioneers. A collection of essays that gives a good overview of the diversity of approaches is the volume *Biblical Hebrew and Discourse Linguistics* edited by R.D. Bergen.[31]

The implications of the text linguistic approach concern not only the view of the language system, but also the interpretation of texts. In traditional studies everything up to the sentence level was an object of grammatical study; the organization of a text beyond sentence level

---

[26] Cf. Talstra, 'Text Grammar', I, 169; idem, 'Hierarchy of Clauses', 86.

[27] Cf. Talstra, 'Text Grammar', I, 172. For further details see § 26.5.

[28] We are not aware of studies in which this framework has been applied to Syriac, but consideration to discourse phenomena is given in e.g. G. Khan's *Studies in Semitic Syntax* (cf. especially his 'span of discourse'), cf. § 21.3.2.

[29] See Schneider, *Grammatik*; Talstra, 'Text Grammar'; Niccacci, *Syntax of the Verb*.

[30] Weinrich, *Tempus. Besprochene und Erzählte Welt*.

[31] Bergen, *Biblical Hebrew and Discourse Linguistics*. It is remarkable that in biblical studies the most influential reference point for Text Linguistics is still H. Weinrich's 1967 monograph. Many biblical scholars seem to be unaware of developments in the field of Text Linguistics in the last decades of the twentieth century. We can mention here the Rhetorical Structure Theory (see Mann–Thompson, 'Rhetorical Structure Theory'), further developed in the model of Coherence Relations (see Sanders–Spooren–Noordman, 'Coherence Relations'), the Procedure for Incremental Structure Analysis (see Sanders–Van Wijk, 'PISA'), and the distinction between hypotaxis and embedding from the perspective of discourse analysis (Matthiessen–Thompson, 'Structure of Discourse'; further elaborated upon in Verhagen, 'Subordination and Discourse Segmentation'). Positive exceptions to the rule are Winther-Nielsen, *Functional Discourse Grammar*, and Van der Merwe, 'Narrative Syntactic Approaches'; see further Chapter 26 and Van Peursen, 'Clause Hierarchy and Discouse Structure'.

was considered another field of study, which could be labelled stylistics and rhetorical analysis.[32] However, if one recognizes the linguistic factors that play a role beyond sentence level, the purpose and possibilities of stylistic and rhetorical analysis should be redefined as well. Syntactic forms are 'the linguistic forms that conduct the process of communication'. They constitute the 'frame' of a text and give 'a preliminary and rather rough outline' of the text or the communication process.[33] This means that in any oral or written utterance, syntax concerns the frame given, while stylistics and rhetoric relate to the way in which this given setting or frame is treated. Accordingly, the border between linguistics and text analysis does not lie between two levels of description (i.e. sentence level and the level beyond), but between the given setting of the language system and the way in which this setting is used.

7.4 THE PLACE OF SYNTAX IN THE ANALYSIS OF TEXTS AND TRANSLATIONS

7.4.1 *A 'shift of priorities in exegetical practice'*

The text linguistic approach not only leads to a redefinition of the border between syntactic analysis and rhetorical and stylistic analysis, it also gives the former priority over other activities involved in textual analysis, which includes literary critical, form critical, and semantic approaches. First of all, 'one has to exploit as far as one can get the information to be derived from [the] linguistic system and from the textual composition, in searching for the way they are marked in a particular text'.[34]

The priority given to linguistic analysis is based on the conviction that a proper analysis of texts should proceed from the given syntactic frame to the way in which this frame is used, from the linguistic restrictions of an utterance to the way in which the utterance is modelled within these constraints, from general linguistic features to the unique text, in short, from the general to the particular. This means a 'shift of

---

[32] Cf. Talstra, 'Hierarchy of Clauses', 86.

[33] Talstra, 'Text Grammar', I, 169, referring to Weinrich, *Tempus*, 29 and Schneider, *Grammatik*, 232–234.

[34] Talstra–Van der Merwe, 'Analysis, Retrieval, Data', 51.

priorities in exegetical practice',[35] because earlier scholarship focused much more on 'the particular'. Thus linguistic analysis was often subordinate to historical critical or form critical questions. One tried to find linguistic characteristics of authors, sources, or genres. Such characteristics, however, can only be traced if one starts with an analysis of the general linguistic features. Only if one has established what belongs to 'the general' (linguistic features) can one decide what should be attributed to 'the particular' (unique features that are characteristic of a certain author or genre).[36]

The procedure of analysis from the 'general' to the 'particular' is not unidirectional. In the case of ancient texts, we have no other sources of information about the language system (*la langue*) than its manifestations in unique concrete texts (*la parole*). As a consequence, we do not know *a priori* what is 'general', but have to establish it on the basis of a large number of 'particular' texts. To overcome this problem, our linguistic and textual analysis should take place in an interaction of two procedures: (1) a description of the language system on the basis of a linguistic analysis of a corpus and (2) an analysis of particular texts within that corpus. On the one hand the first procedure provides the basis for the second one, since the knowledge about the language system gained in the first procedure plays an important role in the textual analysis. On the other hand the second procedure functions as a feedback mechanism for the first one, since it is only on the basis of the text itself that the language reflected in it can be described. Any further analysis of the text, therefore, will lead to refinements, adaptations or corrections of the description of the language system. For this reason there should be a constant interaction between the two procedures.

---

[35] Talstra–Van der Merwe, 'Analysis, Retrieval, Data', 76.

[36] Cf. Talstra, 'Singers and Syntax', 12: '[On the basis of] the assumption that a linguistic analysis referring to language as a *system* comes prior to a stylistic analysis referring to the phenomena that mark the structure of a *specific* textual composition, it is my view that observations on the level of grammar and lexicon should have priority over observations in terms of semantics or stylistics'.

7.4.2 *The role of language and linguistics in the interpretation of texts*

Since the nineteen-seventies the importance of language and linguistics in textual analysis has been emphasized not only by linguists, but also by Old Testament exegetes.[37] The language-oriented approaches that accompany this emphasis on linguistics often showed a tendency to focus on the text. It is not without reason that Oeming in his study on biblical hermeneutics discusses 'linguistic-structuralistic' approaches as a subcategory of text-oriented methods ('an den Texten und ihren Welten orientierte Methoden').[38] The focus on the general linguistic features of texts, rather than unique features that are characteristic of certain authors or genres, implies that it is in the first place the text, which is the object of investigation.[39]

The linguistic approaches that originated in the high days of Structuralism often show a focus on syntactic structures in the text. In recent years, however this focus on syntax has been questioned. An example of a post-structuralistic approach that challenges this focus is Cognitive Linguistics.[40] This approach advocates a shift from syntax to semantics, from language as a system in itself, to its referential se-

---

[37] See e.g. Richter, *Exegese als Literaturwissenschaft*, 29–30, 42–43 *et passim*; Schweizer, *Biblische Texte verstehen*; compare also Fohrer *et al.*, *Exegese des Alten Testaments*, 57–63, but note that in the view of Fohrer *et al.* the linguistic analysis comes after the literary-critical analysis. This means that they give priority to the analysis of 'the particular', which is the basis of the literary-critical analysis, over 'the general', that is, the linguistic analysis; in our view this procedure is incorrect; see above, § 7.4.1. See further Oeming, *Hermeneutik*, 66.

[38] Oeming, *Hermeneutik*, 63–69. Cf. p. 63: 'Der Text kann und muß *als Text, als Sprachwelt, als Welt der Sprache* für sich allein bestehen'. The other categories Oeming distinguishes are 'an den Autoren und ihren Welten orientierte Methoden', 'an den Lesern und ihren Welten orientierte Methoden' and 'an der Sache und ihrer Welt orientierte Methoden'.

[39] The importance of language in the interpretation of texts has been stressed not only in the linguistic-structuralistic methods, but also in other, more philosophical oriented approaches. See the section 'Schriftauslegung als Sprachgeschehen und Wortereignis' in Oeming, *Hermeneutik*, 82–88, on the attempts made by E. Fuchs, G. Ebeling, A.H.J. Gunneweg and others to apply M. Heidegger's language theory and H.-G. Gadamer's model of hermeneutics to the interpretation of the Bible. For these approaches hermeneutics concerns not only the interpretation of texts, but the understanding of being. Language is not just a medium of communication, it is 'das Haus des Seins' (Heidegger): 'Alles Sein, das verstanden werden kann, ist Sprache' (Gadamer).

[40] For the application of Cognitive Linguistics to biblical studies, see the papers collected in Van Wolde, *Cognition in Context*.

mantics, and from the text to the context.[41] In our view, however, the re-appreciation of semantic analysis does not impinge on the primary importance of syntactic analysis, since a thorough description of syntactic structures is a *sine qua non* for any sound semantic, literary or literary critical analysis of the text.[42]

7.4.3 *The role of syntactic analysis in the study of the Ancient Versions*

In our analysis of the Peshitta, it is assumed that the translator made his translation within the given frame of the language system of his target language. Accordingly, conclusions about the relationship of the translation with its source text and about the translator's interpretational or exegetical activities cannot be drawn if the Syriac language system is not taken into account. In the past few decades there has been a shift in the study of the Ancient Versions from a philological, text-critical approach to an exegetical, interpretative orientation. However, without taking into account the constraints of the target language, one runs the risk of ascribing to the translators' rhetorical or exegetical strategies elements of the translation that are in reality enhanced by the constraints of the target language.[43]

Two examples from recent studies on respectively the Peshitta and the Targum to the Books of Samuel may suffice to show that this danger is not imaginary. In C.E. Morrison's study on the Peshitta of 1 Samuel, we read that the translation of שאול ליהוה with ܝܗ ܠ ܫܐܠܬܗ ܡܪܝܐ in 1 Sam 1:28 is a 'highlighting of Hannah' because of the addition of ܠ + pronominal suffix.[44] However, in the light of the differences between Hebrew and Syriac regarding the use of constructions with suffix pronouns, it seems easier to explain the formal difference between the Hebrew and the Syriac text from the requirements of the

---

[41] Cf. Van Hecke, 'Cognitive-Semantic Approach', 143: 'In contrast to the structuralist approach to language, with its stress on language-internal paradigmatic and syntagmatic relations, the cognitive approach to linguistics explicitly studies language against the background of human cognition'.

[42] Compare our remark at the end of § 7.2.3.

[43] For an application of this principle to the study of an ancient version see Van der Louw, *Transformations*, 78.

[44] Morrison, *First Book of Samuel*, 23.

Syriac language system, rather than from a conscious attempt to modify the presentation of one of the characters in the narrative.

In her extensive commentary on Targum Samuel, E. van Staalduine-Sulman suggests that in 2 Sam. 3:34 and others the translators of Targum Jonathan rendered Hebrew עולה בני with Aramaic גבריא רשיעיא in order to avoid personification.[45] In our view, however, it is more likely that linguistic factors rather than exegetical or theological motives are responsible for the translation equivalents that occur in the Targum.[46]

More examples can be adduced from other corpora. In a number of publications P.J. Williams has demonstrated how disregard for linguistic aspects has led to incorrect text-critical use of the Peshitta to the New Testament, even in such a standard work as the 27th Nestle–Aland edition. This edition incorrectly refers to ܠܚܡܐ as supporting the singular ἄρτος instead of the plural ἄρτοι,[47] and to ܦܐܪ̈ܐ as evidence of the plural καρποί instead of the singular καρπός.[48] It also refers erroneously to the Peshitta reading ܣܛܢܐ as reflecting σατανᾶς instead of διάβολος,[49] and to ܗܠܝܢ ܟܠܗܝܢ as supporting the reading ταῦτα πάντα instead of πάντα ταῦτα, which ignores the fact that ܗܠܝܢ ܟܠܗܝܢ is always the preferred order in the New Testament Peshitta.[50] In another publication Williams discusses an issue from the Old Testament Peshitta: In fourteen cases where the MT has כל the *Biblia Hebraica Stuttgartensia* suggests that the Peshitta reflects a different reading because of the lack of formal correspondence with the MT. Since, however, the Peshitta appears to avoid a literal translation of כל, this suggestion is incorrect.[51]

---

[45] Van Staalduine-Sulman, *Targum of Samuel*, 85; See our review of this book in *ANES* 40 (2003), 270–272, where we also question the labelling of phenomena such as asyndeton, polysyndeton, parataxis and 'departure from normal word order', as rhetorical devices (Van Staalduine–Sulman, ibid., 70, 72–73).

[46] See our observations in § 10.1.1.

[47] Williams, 'Bread in the Peshitta'.

[48] Williams, 'Early Syriac Versions', 538–539.

[49] Williams, 'Early Syriac Versions', 541–542.

[50] Williams, 'Early Syriac Versions', 539–540. For other examples see idem, *Early Syriac Translation Technique*; Brock, 'Limitations'; Falla, 'Questions', 93–94.

[51] Williams, 'According to All'.

7.5 CLAUSE HIERARCHY

An important insight of Text Linguistics, Discourse Analysis and related approaches is that in the grammatical analysis of sentences due attention should be paid to the place of the sentences in the larger structure of a textual unit. Opinions differ, however, about the question of *how* we can describe this place. One respect in which our model differs from other text linguistic models such as those of Niccacci and Longacre, is its 'form-to-function' approach.[52] Our approach does not start with the labelling of clauses as 'circumstantial clause', 'background information', 'climax' and the like, but with a distributional analysis of the clause patterns attested.[53]

Another distinctive feature of our model concerns the concept of clause hierarchy. In Text Linguistic studies on Biblical Hebrew there is a strong tendency to treat, for example, clause types as more or less independent linguistic elements with some well-defined functions (e.g. *wayyiqtol* presents the story line of a narrative, *w*-X *qatal* gives background information). However, such general statements on clause types and their syntactic functions do no justice to the fact that a syntactic construction may occur at different levels. The model we have followed in our analysis tries to avoid such general statements by taking a hierarchical approach (which Talstra developed for Biblical Hebrew) rather than a sequential approach (advocated by, for example, A. Niccacci and R.E. Longacre).[54]

The basic assumption of the hierarchical approach is that every clause is grammatically related to one preceding it. It is either parallel to or dependent on this preceding clause. A clause is not necessarily related to the directly preceding clause. As a consequence, sometimes more than one clause is dependent on the same preceding clause. A hierarchical analysis tries to establish the relationship between clauses, that is to say, it determines for each clause to which preceding clause it is related and whether this relationship is one of coordination or subordination. Unlike the sequential approaches, the hierarchical ap-

---

[52] Cf. Van der Merwe, 'Narrative Syntax', 13.

[53] See further above, §§ 7.2.1–7.2.2.

[54] Cf. Talstra, 'Clause Types and Textual Structure', 166; idem, 'Hierarchy of Clauses', 101: 'A further challenge is the fact that paragraph markers can be used *recursively* with the effect that paragraphs in a text do not appear sequentially, but can be embedded in higher level paragraphs'.

proach takes not only clause types into account to establish the relationship between clauses, but also other linguistic elements that have connective effects, such as morphological and lexical correspondences, syntactic marking of paragraphs, and the set of actors in the text.[55]

The text-hierarchical analysis gives us insight into the syntactic structure of a text. A study of the thematic or stylistic organization of a text that ignores this structure runs the risk of overruling linguistic information. [56] Thus the understanding of the Praise of the Fathers (Sirach 44–50) as a *Beispielreihe* is based on a thematic division of the text that ignores its text-hierarchical structure.[57]

7.6 BOTTOM-UP APPROACH

The procedure of the computer-assisted analysis follows basically a bottom-up approach, starting from the level of graphemes and ending with text linguistics.[58] However, in the CALAP model of textual analysis the bottom-up strategy concerns not only the procedure of the computer-assisted analysis: It is also an important methodological feature of the text-hierarchical analysis. Rather than interpreting smaller elements by positing them into larger, more abstract pattern frames such as 'paragraphs' (which would be a top-down approach), the CALAP model starts with the smaller units from which larger patterns are constructed.

Related to this approach is the insight that linguistic elements occur at several levels. They entertain relations with elements of the same level, but also with elements of the lower and higher levels. Thus 'words are *composed* of morphemes, while they are *integrated* into sentences, and so on'.[59] The *form* of a linguistic element is determined by its relation to lower-level elements, its *function* is determined by its

---

[55] Talstra, 'Clause Types and Textual Structure', 170; idem, 'Hierarchy of Clauses', 89.

[56] Cf. Talstra–Van der Merwe, 'Analysis, Retrieval, Data', 76.

[57] See §§ 27.2, 27.3.

[58] See Chapter 8, 'The procedure of the CALAP analysis'.

[59] Thus Joosten, 'Indicative System', 53, following Benveniste, 'Niveaux'. Joosten applies this insight to the verbal system: verb forms do not function at the text level, but verb forms function at the sentence level, sentences function at text level. See also Van Wolde, 'Introduction', viii-ix.

relation to higher-level elements. There can be no direct relation between elements of non-contiguous levels: morphemes do not function
at phrase level, words do not function at clause level.[60] This means
that an analysis on a certain level should integrate the analyses of the
preceding level. Accordingly, one should start at the lowest level and
elaborate the analysis on the subsequent levels.

7.7 MULTILINGUAL COMPARATIVE ANALYSIS

7.7.1 *Multilingual comparative analysis of the Ancient Versions*

The CALAP model concerns a refinement of the computer-assisted
linguistic analysis that in the WIVU has been developed for Biblical
Hebrew and its adaptation to the study of Syriac. This enabled the
creation of 'parallel' databases that could be used in a comparative
analysis of the Hebrew and the Syriac witnesses. In CALAP this has
first been done for the books of Kings.[61] The analysis of Sirach, which
resulted in the present monograph, was the second project. The textual
evidence for Sirach differs from that of Kings in that the extant Hebrew manuscripts cannot be considered as more or less identical to the
presumed *Vorlage* of the Syriac text.[62] Nevertheless, the comparative
analysis of the Hebrew and Syriac textual witnesses is valuable for
both linguistic and text-critical studies. A contrastive linguistic analysis can reveal the agreements and differences between the Hebrew and
Syriac language systems. And the text-critical study of patterns of
agreement and disagreement can shed more light on the relationship
between these textual witnesses, and provide data that may help us
determine what parameters in Syr should be taken into consideration
for constructing a model of the Hebrew text that formed its basis.

In biblical studies, the use of the computer for a comparative analysis of the Hebrew text and the Ancient Versions is not new. Especially
in the field of Septuagint studies, some useful tools have become

---

[60] We do not deny, of course, the possibility that a phrase consists of one word
(which may also be an enclitic word, such as a pronominal suffix) or that a word consists of one morpheme.

[61] Cf. Dyk–Van Keulen, *Peshitta of Kings*.

[62] But also in the case of Kings the differences between the Masoretic Text and the
Hebrew source text of the Peshitta cannot be ignored, see § 2.2.1.

available, such as E. Tov's CATSS database, which gives the MT and the Septuagint in parallel alignment. Moreover, the inclusion of the text of the Septuagint, the Targums and other versions in software packages such as Bible Works, Logos and Accordance has been profitable to many scholars. These tools mark a step forward in Septuagint studies, because they facilitate, for example, the research on complicated patterns of correspondences on word level or the retrieval of statistical data. There is a danger, however, that these tools also mark a step backwards. In a survey of computer-assisted investigations in the Septuagint, J. Lust observes that 'the machine threatens to impose its way and methods, influencing the choice of problems to be dealt with, as well as their formulation, and solutions'.[63] In the study of the Ancient Versions considerable progress has been made in the last decades. This concerns, among others, the insight that the textual witnesses are literary compositions that deserve to be studied for their own sake. For this reason, an 'atomistic' linguistic or text-critical analysis of variant readings should be complemented by a 'contextual' analysis of the actual context in which these variants occur.[64] However, if scholars are tempted to stick to a word-by-word comparison of the MT and the Septuagint, because of the useful computerized tools that are available for this purpose, the result is a step backwards in Septuagint studies, rather than a step forward.

The models of computer-assisted analysis of the Ancient Versions mentioned above mainly concern the Septuagint, although some software packages also include other Ancient Versions.[65] An innovative aspect of the CALAP model of computer-assisted analysis is that it enables a comparative analysis of Hebrew and Syriac sources. Moreover, we have tried to develop a model that overcomes the problems indicated above. In our model the computer not only presents the data

---

[63] Lust, 'Rekenaar', 366–367.

[64] In many publications A. van der Kooij has discussed the necessity of a contextual analysis of variant readings in the Ancient Versions, as well as the procedure that should be followed in such an analysis, see e.g. his 'Accident or Method?', 369; 'Contextual Approach', 569–570; 'Old Greek of Isaiah', 204–207; *Oracle of Tyre*, 15–19. For a refinement of this model see Van der Louw, *Transformations*, 78. In Van der Louw's model the linguistic study of 'transformations' is a separate step in the analysis, preceding the text-critical and text-historical study of 'deviations' in a passage. See also Gzella, 'New Ways', 388.

[65] In the *Peshitta Electronic Text Project*, directed by the present author, the text of the complete Old Testament Peshitta will be digitized to make it available in, among others, these software packages.

(as in most of the software packages available), but also plays an important role in their analysis. Further, unlike other systems of computer-linguistic analysis, we do not restrict ourselves to a comparison at word level, but have developed a model that enables a multi-layered comparison of different texts.

7.7.2 *The procedure of the comparative analysis*

In the CALAP model the analysis of the separate witnesses follows a bottom-up approach.[66] The comparative analysis of two parallel texts, however, follows a top-down approach. This means that this analysis proceeds from corresponding texts to corresponding sentences, from corresponding sentences to corresponding phrases and from corresponding phrases to corresponding words. This comparative analysis at different levels is necessary because a linear approach that starts with a word-by-word comparison does not suffice in establishing the relationship between textual witnesses if the witnesses do not correspond at word level. This is especially true for those translations that do not give a literal word-to-word translation. The level on which correspondences between a source text and its translation can be established has a strong impact on the character of the translation. This may be word level, but also phrase or even sentence level.[67] In Kings, for example, there is fairly often a one-to-one relation between the clause constituents in the MT and the Peshitta, while in their internal structure these constituents differ considerably.[68] In the case of Sirach even a comparison at sentence level does not suffice to establish the relationship between the Hebrew and Syriac witnesses and a comparative analysis at the level of larger textual units is required.

---

[66] See the description of the analytical procedure in Chapter 8.

[67] In translations from Greek into Syriac up to the early eighth century we see a continuous reduction in the size of the unit of translation; cf. Brock, 'History of Syriac Translation Technique', 6: 'Thus in very general terms one can say that most sixth-century translators adopt the sentence or phrase as the unit, while seventh-century ones reduced this to the word (and often segment even below word level)'. See also Weitzman, *Syriac Version*, 22–23; Aland–Juckel, *Neue Testament in syrischer Überlieferung* I, 103; Barr, *Typology of Literalism*, 294–323.

[68] Cf. Dyk, 'Data Preparation', 151. It would be interesting to compare this with the Targum on Kings, which at first sight seems to reflect much more phrase-internal similarities with the Hebrew text, probably because of its liturgical function; cf. Smelik, 'Orality', 75–76.

The implications of our approach may be illustrated by the following examples.

9:16 ܐܢܫܐ ܟܐܢܐ ܢܗܘܘܢ ܐܟ̈ܠܝ ܦܬܘܪܟ 'Let upright people be those who eat from your table'; A אנשי צדק בעלי לחמך.

It is incorrect to say that the word ܐܟ̈ܠܝ corresponds to בעלי and ܦܬܘܪܟ to לחמך. The Syriac phrase ܐܟ̈ܠܝ ܦܬܘܪܟ as a whole corresponds to the Hebrew בעלי לחמך. Accordingly, the two witnesses correspond at phrase level.

48:1–2 ܥܕܡܐ ܕܩܡ ܢܒܝܐ ܕܕܡܐ ܠܢܘܪܐ 'Until there arose a prophet who was like fire'; B עד אשר קם נביא כאש.

On clause level both Syr and Heb have the same structure, i.e. <Cj> <Pr> <Su> <sp>. For the first three constituents the internal phrase structure runs parallel as well: ܥܕܡܐ ܕ corresponds to עד אשר, ܩܡ to קם, and ܢܒܝܐ to נביא. However, in the specification of this noun the two versions display different internal phrase structures, which can be rendered as follows.[69]

Syr [<DM> D- <Cj>] [QM <Pr>] [NBJ> [D -{[DM> <Pr>] [L-NWR> <Co>]} <sp>] <Su>]
B [<D >CR <Cj>] [QM <Pr>] [NBJ> [K->C <sp>] <Su>]

Where Heb has a prepositional phrase, Syr has an embedded relative clause. To say that ܕܕܡܐ is a plus in Syr does no justice to the fact that ܠܢܘܪܐ functions differently from כאש. It is more appropriate to describe ܕܕܡܐ ܠܢܘܪܐ as the equivalent of כאש, both elements having the same function at clause level, but displaying different internal phrase structures.

Sometimes, however, Syr and Heb do not correspond at phrase level but at clause level, as in the following example.

42:18 ܘܟܠܗܝܢ ܬܐܪ̈ܬܗܘܢ ܕܒܢ̈ܝܢܫܐ ܐܝܟ ܫܡܫܐ ܓܠܝܢ ܩܕܡܘܗܝ 'And all the secrets of the people are revealed before Him like the sun'; B ובכל מערומיהם יתבונן 'And all their secrets He understands'; M ובמערמיהם יתבונן.

48:2 ܘܐܝܬܝ ܥܠܝܗܘܢ ܟܦܢܐ 'And he brought upon them famine'; B וישבר להם מטה לחם 'and he broke their staff of bread'.[70]

---

[69] For the transliteration and symbols used see the 'Abbreviations and Sigla' on pp. xv-xvi.

[70] On 42:18 see also § 3.3 (e) and on 48:2 see § 3.2 (a).

7.8 CONCLUSION

The basic assumptions of the CALAP model of linguistic analysis can be summarized as follows.

1. A proper linguistic analysis should start with the distribution of forms, rather than with the functions that these forms fulfil. Because of this assumption our model can be characterized as distributional rather than functional, as form-to-function instead of function-to-form.

2. Because syntax is considered the framework of the text, it is given priority over other areas of linguistic analysis, such as semantics. For the same reason it has priority over literary or rhetorical analysis.

3. A text is considered as a structure in itself, rather than a collection of sentences. Grammatical description should not stop at sentence level. This insight we share with those approaches that are often labelled Text Linguistics or Discourse Analysis.

4. Unlike other Text Linguistic approaches, our approach is hierarchical rather than sequential. This means that all the linguistic elements that have connective functions are taken into account for establishing the relationship between clauses, not just the repetition or change of clause patterns.

5. The comparison of two 'parallel' text-corpora in different languages adds a new dimension to this analysis. In contrast to some other attempts to subject the Ancient Versions to a computer-assisted analysis, our model aims at a comparison at different linguistic levels, because it cannot be established *a priori* at which level a comparison between the two texts is most fruitful.

CHAPTER EIGHT

THE PROCEDURE OF THE CALAP ANALYSIS

8.1 INTRODUCTION

In the preceding chapter we have described the model of linguistic and textual analysis that has been applied in the present study. In the present chapter we will elaborate on the procedure of the computer-assisted analysis and the computer-programs used in this analysis.

Some of the computer programs were developed in the CALAP project, others were adaptations of programs that had been used previously in the WIVU for the linguistic analysis of Biblical Hebrew texts.[1] Although the adaptation to Syriac could have been done more directly by substituting the Syriac linguistic data for the Hebrew data, one of the aims of the CALAP project was to do more than that. Both from a methodological view and because of practical considerations, we thought it more appropriate to develop language-independent tools for linguistic analysis. This explains why in the following paragraphs a clear distinction is made between language-specific auxiliary files—such as description of the morphology or a lexicon—and language-independent programs that use these auxiliary files in the linguistic analysis.

The use of auxiliary files or language-definition files, which contain grammatical and lexical information, is one of the main characteristics of the CALAP procedure of linguistic analysis. Thus rather than tagging a 'perfect 3rd pers. masc. sing. Pael', it is the computer program that produces such an analysis on the basis of a combination of grammatical information from the auxiliary files and the encoded text. As a consequence, the observations that led to a certain analysis can always be retrieved.

The auxiliary files are used in the analysis of documents containing the text in question and the results of the analyses at earlier stages.

---

[1] For a description of these programs see Talstra–Sikkel, 'WIVU-Datenbank'.

Accordingly, for each program the input contains files that are the output of preceding steps in the analysis. Even though each program generates new data, the old information from earlier analyses is preserved. This makes it possible at each phase of the analysis process to reconsider decisions made previously.

8.2 THE GRAPHIC TEXT

The first step in the analysis of a written text is the abstraction of the graphs that occur in the actual manuscripts or editions towards the graphemes they represent. Graphs are the written or printed realizations of graphemes. The realizations may differ, for example, in the script used (thus ، and ؛ represent the same grapheme in respectively an Estrangelo and a Serto font) or in their conventional form according to the place in a word (compare the Kaph in ܠܝ, ܟܠ and ܐܠܚ).

The subsequent steps in the textual analysis require the preparation of a text that contains unique and unequivocal representations of each grapheme. In the CALAP project this is done with the computer program 'pil2wit'.

The input for this program is the so-called 'running text', in the case of Sirach the Syriac text from the Leiden edition (in preparation for publication) in electronic form (file-name: 'sirach'). It contains the consonants in transliteration, diacritics and interpunction, variant readings and instructions regarding the variant readings which should be accepted in the main text, and comments from the researcher (optional). For example, the running text of Sir 48:1 in 'sirach' is[2]

```
1  `dm' dqm nby' ddm^' lnwr'. wmlth yqd' 'yk tnwr': dm$tgr
   [dm$tgr / + 7a1]
```

In the printed Leiden edition this will appear as

ܕܢܘܪ ܡܢ ܩܡ ܕܡ ܕܡܐ܂ ܢܒܝܐ ܠܘܢ ܡܬܠܘܗ ܐܝܟ ܢܘܪܐ ܕܐܝܬ ܐܝܟ ܬܢܘܪ ܀

The output of pil2wit is the 'graphic text' (file-name: 'BenSira'). This is a transliterated text according to an established format that enables

---

[2] The caret marks a point over the preceding letter. The semicolon marks the end of the verse. 7a1 repeats ܐܝܟ ܬܢܘܪ. Such a dittography occurs eight times in Syr in 7a1. The repetition will not be selected as the main text and in the Leiden edition it will appear in the first critical apparatus.

the subsequent steps in the analysis. In this text the instructions in the running text to select variants are executed and markers of book, chapter and verse are added.[3] Thus the graphic text of 48:1 in 'BenSira' is

48,01 <DM> DQM NBJ> DDM> LNWR> WMLTH JQD> >JK TNWR> DMCTGR[4]

8.3 MORPHOLOGICAL SEGMENTATION

The next step in the analysis is the segmentation of Syriac words into morphemes, that is, the insertion of morpheme markers. A morpheme is the base unit in the composition of words, with its own grammatical or lexical relevance. Morphemes are abstractions of morphs. The latter are the realizations of morphemes in the actual text. The marking of the morphemes may be illustrated by the following example.

> 48:1 ܐܝܟ ܠܗܢܐ ܕܕܡܐ ܢܒܝܐ ܕܩܡ ܥܕܡܐ 'Until there arose a prophet who was like fire'

The graphic text is

<DM> DQM NBJ> DDM> LNWR>

This is encoded as

<DM> D-Q(WM[NBJ/~> D-DM>[L-NWR/~>

The explanation of this line is as follows. ܕܩܡ is encoded as D-Q(WM[. The form ܩܡ comes from the lexeme ܩܘܡ. Accordingly, the ܘ is encoded as a paradigmatically expected, but actually absent letter, indicated by the round bracket (.[5] The square bracket [is the marker of a verb ending. In this example the verb ending is zero; 'you arose' would have been Q(WM[T. The hyphen between D and Q(WM[splits the word D-Q(WM up into two lexemes which in the surface form are connected.

The lexeme of NBJ/~> is ܢܒܝ. The slash / marks the nominal ending. ~> is the marker of the emphatic state ending. The tilde marks the dif-

---

[3] For further details see Talstra–Jenner–Van Peursen, 'Linguistic Data Types', 62–63.

[4] For the transliteration alphabet see the 'Abbreviations and Sigla' on pp. xv-xvi.

[5] This representation enables the computer to analyse ܩܡ automatically as derived from ܩܘܡ. Accordingly, 'paradigmatically expected' should be understood here in a mechanical sense of the word. It does not deny that even a student who has only an elementary training in Syriac will not 'expect' the second radical in this context.

ference from NBJ/>, which would be an absolute state feminine. The same analysis applies to the noun NWR/~> .[6]

In the CALAP project the existing paradigm of Hebrew morphology developed at the WIVU was very helpful for the development of the Syriac paradigm, but it will be evident that a number of issues needed thorough reconsideration. Thus the Hebrew paradigm distinguishes between the following morpheme markers for the *binyanim*.

| | A vertical stroke for the Piel and related stems such as the Pilpel |
|]...] | Two square brackets open to the left for the preformatives of the Hifil, Nifal, and Hitpael, i.e.]H],]N] and]HT] |

In Syriac the Nifal does not occur, while each of the three patterns Peal, Pael and Afel has a corresponding form with the ܐܬ prefix. Expanding the Hebrew paradigm by the addition of two reflexive stems would not do justice to the 'much neater and more symmetrical scheme'[7] in Syriac. Peal, Pael and Aphel are three mutually exclusive categories, but the reflexive-passive ܐܬ prefix does not exclude one of these three verbal stems. Therefore in the Syriac analysis the ܐܬ prefix is taken apart: We have the three verbal stems Peal, Pael and Aphel, and each of them can be combined with the reflexive-passive morpheme ܐܬ.

The insertion of morpheme markers in the text is done with the computer program 'analyse'. The input of this program is the graphic text; the output is an analysed text called xxx.an.[8] The program uses an auxiliary file, called the analytical lexicon ('anzb'). This is a file containing all previous analyses of words. On the basis of this list the program makes suggestions in an interactive analysis.

An example may illustrate this procedure. Let us assume that we start with an empty analytical lexicon, that Syr is the first Syriac text to be analysed and the analysis starts with chapter one.[9] At a certain point the analysis arrives at ܠܛܐ in 1:20 ܡܗܝ܂ ܠܛܐ ܗܢܐ ܡܢ ܟܕ ܗܘܐ ܡܫܒܚܐ

---

[6] For more details see Van Peursen, 'Progress Report', 367–368.

[7] Muraoka, *Classical Syriac for Hebraists*, § 33.

[8] 'xxx' can be replaced by each book name and chapter number, e.g. Ben-Sira01.an, BenSira02.an, etc.

'For she is better to him than all treasures'. Since we did not encounter this word before, the program cannot make a suggestion. The human researcher has to decide that it is a feminine nominal form in the absolute state and (s)he will add a slash before the feminine ending: VB/>. For all subsequent occurrences of ܛܒܐ, the computer will suggest the analysis VB/>. The human researcher can accept or reject the suggestion. When the analysis arrives at 3:6 ܛܒܐ ܣܝ̈ܡܬܐ, (s)he will reject the suggestion, because this is an emphatic state masculine plural, which according to the paradigm should be encoded as VB/(J~>. From now on, wherever a form ܛܒܐ occurs, the computer program will offer two suggestions: VB/> and VB/(J~> and the human researcher has to make a disambiguing decision. When the analysis comes to 12:7 ܛܒܬܐ ܐܛܐܒ 'Do good to the good one', the human researcher will reject both suggestions because here ܛܒܐ is an emphatic state masculine singular, which should be encoded as VB/~>. This analysis too is stored in the database and from now on the program will make three suggestions whenever ܛܒܐ occurs. In this way a large database of all the words analysed is gradually built up.[10]

For Syriac, our database contains now all the materials from Sirach and Kings. The Hebrew analytical lexicon, which has a longer history, contains all forms attested in the Hebrew Bible. The interactive analysis and the retrieval of previous analyses in the segmentation process contribute significantly to the consistency of the analysis and make it more and more efficient.

8.4 MORPHOLOGICAL ANALYSIS

The segmentation of words into morphemes described in the preceding paragraph is followed by the deduction of grammatical functions. This concerns the calculation of the grammatical functions of the segments. To return to the example given above: The morpheme segmentation resulted in

  48:1 <DM> D-Q(WM[NBJ/~> D-DM>[L-NWR/~>

---

[9] It follows that 'analyse' in its present form is basically a matching program. It matches the forms that occur in the text with forms from the analytical lexicon.

[10] In reality, when I started my research on Sirach, the analytical lexicon already contained many results from the analysis of Kings carried out by my colleagues Janet Dyk and Percy van Keulen.

A computer program called 'at2ps' retrieves grammatical functions from this encoded text. The input of this program is called xxx.at. This is a selected and reformatted chapter (e.g. BenSira01.at) from the xxx.an file (e.g. BenSira.an).[11] The program uses four auxiliary files: the 'alphabet', the 'word grammar', the 'lexicon' and the so-called 'ps-definition file'. The first language-definition file, the 'alphabet' contains a description of all graphemes of a language (in this case Syriac). The 'ps-definition' file describes the way in which the output of 'at2ps', the xxx.ps2 files (see below), are organized.

The 'word grammar' is the established morphological paradigm in a format that can be read by the computer. It is based on grammars of Classical Syriac and other studies, especially on Nöldeke's classic grammar. It contains, for example, the information that a verb form with an empty verb ending and without a prefix should be analysed as a perfect third person masculine. With this information the program can calculate that the word Q(WM[is a perfect 3rd pers. masc. sing. This calculation is performed automatically.[12] It is possible to revise the morphological paradigm if the results of the linguistic analysis give reason to do so.[13]

The 'lexicon'[14] contains grammatically relevant lexical information, such as part of speech, lexical set, the gender of nouns, and others.[15] It contains, for example, the information that the lexeme ܩܡ is a verb and ܝܕ a noun.[16] Sometimes the word grammar and the lexicon provide contradictory information. This happens, for example, with masculine words that have a feminine plural ending, such as ܐܒܗܬܐ 'fathers'. In this case the information from the lexicon (i.e. ܐܒ and its plural ܐܒܗܬܐ are masculine) overrules the information from the word grammar (i.e. ܬܐ is a feminine ending).

The output of at2ps is called 'xxx.ps2'. This is an analysed text containing morphological information such as the encoded mor-

---

[11] Note, however, that also for the morphological segmentation it is possible to select a chapter (with the program 'get_chapter'), carry out the interactive analysis, and make an updated version of the xxx.an file. In other words, one does not need to complete the morphological segmentation of the whole book before the functional analysis of a selected chapter can start.

[12] See further Dyk, 'Data Preparation' 135–139.

[13] Cf. Van Peursen, 'Progress Report', 368.

[14] Not to be confused with the 'analytical lexicon' discussed in § 8.3.

[15] The information about the gender of a word is given only if it is not determined morphologically.

[16] See further Dyk, 'Data Preparation', 134.

phemes and the functions that can be derived from them, and lexical information such as parts of speech. On request the program can also produce a data description in human readable form ('xxx.dmp').

The model of a morphologically encoded text read by the computer program with the help of a grammar and a lexicon is in principle language-independent. It can be implemented for all languages for which the language-definition files are available.[17] At the moment this is the case for Classical Hebrew, (Biblical) Aramaic and Classical Syriac.[18]

The procedure in which the encoded text is analysed with the help of a word grammar and a lexicon, has two advantages over an approach that uses the more common procedure of 'tagging'. The first is that this procedure guarantees consistency in the analysis of morphemes, because this analysis is produced automatically. The second advantage is that not only the interpretation of a word but also the data that led to a certain interpretation can be retrieved, whereas the motivation behind a tagging cannot be made visible.[19]

8.5 PHRASE SEGMENTATION AND MORPHOSYNTACTIC ANALYSIS

After the morphological segmentation of words, the analysis entails the combination of words into phrases. This is an interactive process in which a computer program called 'syn03' offers suggestions for the combination of words into phrases. The way in which the program arrives at its suggestions is similar to that in which the program 'analyse' makes suggestions as to word segmentation with the help of the analytical lexicon. In the phrase level analysis syn03 uses a file called

---

[17] That the present state of the computer programs will not suffice to handle all kinds of language-specific auxiliary files does not deny the language-independent applicability of the model.

[18] The results gained from a morphological analysis may differ from language to language. Till now we have applied the analytical procedure to languages with a rich morphology. Were it to be used for languages with a poor morphology such as English, it is to be expected that relatively less information can be retrieved form the morphology and more information will come from the lexicon and the syntactic analysis at higher linguistic levels.

[19] Admittedly, the motivation behind a tagging decision can be retrieved if the considerations of the human researcher who performs the tagging are well-documented; but we are not aware of any tagging project of the Bible for which such documentation exists.

'phraseset'. This file contains all phrases accepted in earlier analyses (e.g. 'construct noun + noun in the emphatic or absolute state'). Another auxiliary file, called 'morfcond', describes word functions that define grammatical functions.

In addition to the delimitation of phrases, the interactive analysis concerns phrase-internal relations (e.g. *regens–rectum*, head–attribute) and the morphosyntactic analysis. In the latter analysis, a distinction is made between the 'default' part of speech found in the lexicon and the phrase-dependent part of speech. With this distinction we can handle systematic adaptations of word classes in certain environments (e.g. adjectives functioning as nouns).

The input of syn03 includes the xxx.ps2 files. The output is a morphosyntactically analysed text called 'xxx.ps3', which includes the lexicographical analysis (determination of the lexical class), the morphosyntactic analysis (including the part of speech and the phrase-dependent part of speech), and the analysis of phrase-internal relations.

In the analysis of phrase level a number of questions are involved about, for example, the definition of phrases, the distinction between phrase atoms and extensions and the description of complex internal phrase structures. These questions will be discussed in Part Three of this monograph.

It should be noted that some decisions about the parsing of words cannot be made in the word level analysis and can be solved only at phrase level. Thus the question as to whether a noun is in the absolute state or the construct state can in some cases be answered at word level on the basis of morphemes marking the construct state or the absolute state, but in other cases only at phrase level. In any Syriac grammar one will find that the absolute state masculine singular is ܟ݂ܬ, the construct state masculine singular ܟ݂ܬ, the absolute state masculine plural ܟܬܒ and the construct state masculine plural ܟܬܒ. However, what is presented in the traditional grammars as morphological information is sometimes insufficient for the parsing process at word level. Compare e.g.

48:10 ܟ݂ܡܘܡܚ ܩܛܠ݂ܘ L-CBV/J J<QWB/
47:25 ܟܠܬܐ ܟ݂ܠ ܟ݂ܠ <L KL/ BJC/T~>

In the first example the analysis of ܩܛܠ݂ܘ as a construct noun is made at word level, because of the construct ending /J. The analysis of ܟ݂ܠ as a construct noun in 47:25 is made on phrase level, because at word level it cannot be decided whether it is in the absolute or the construct state. That both ﺳﻔﻴﻨ and ﺟﺎ are part of a construct chain is undisputed. The only difference concerns the linguistic markers of this relationship. In the case of ﺟﺎ it is marked only syntactically, in the case of ﺳﻔﻴﻨ it is also signalled morphologically.

8.6 CLAUSE SEGMENTATION

The xxx.ps3 file contains the segmentation of the text into phrases as well as the morphosyntactical analysis. The next step concerns the combination of phrases to form clauses. This too is an interactive process in which a computer program called 'syn04' offers suggestions for the combination of phrases into clauses. The procedure of the interactive analysis is similar to what we have seen with the programs 'analyse' and 'syn03': 'Syn04' uses a file called 'clset'. This file contains all the clause patterns accepted in earlier analyses (e.g. conjunction + verb + determinate noun phrase + prepositional phrase). Two auxiliary files, called 'lexcondcl' and 'morfcondcl' describe lexical and morphological conditions that further specify acceptable patterns of clauses.

Each construction in which predication occurs is considered a clause. Compare e.g.

48:1 ܥܠܝܐ ܕܢܗܘܐ ܢܒܝܐ ܕܕܡܐ ܠܢܘܪܐ. ܘܡܠܬܗ ܕܡܠܬܗ ܝܩܕܐ ܐܝܟ ܐܬܘܢܐ ܕܢܗܪ
'Until there arose a prophet who was like fire and whose word was burning like a furnace that glows'.

This verse contains four clauses:

ܥܠܝܐ ܕܢܗܘܐ || ܢܒܝܐ ܕܕܡܐ ܠܢܘܪܐ || ܘܡܠܬܗ ܝܩܕܐ ||. ܐܝܟ ܐܬܘܢܐ ܕܢܗܪ

This example is relatively straightforward. The situation may be more complex. Although language is expressed in a linear, unidirectional manner, a text is not a chain of subsequent complete and uninterrupted predication structures, each one directly connected to the preceding one. The isolation of predication structures may result in clause atoms that by themselves do not constitute a clause.[20] This happens in e.g.:

---

[20] Cf. Talstra–Sikkel, 'WIVU-Datenbank', 40: 'Zunächst ist der Text linear zu segmentieren, auch wenn dabei vorläufig unvollständige Sätze auftreten (…); anschlie-

48:8 ܡܝܟܐ ܗܘܐ ܘܢܒܝܐ ܫܘܬܦ ܠܡܦܪܥ ܡܠܟܐ ܕܡܫܚ 'Who anointed kings for retribution and a prophet who would succeed him'

If we isolate ܠܡܦܪܥ ܡܠܟܐ and ܡܝܟܐ ܗܘܐ as two distinct clauses, we get four segments:

ܡܝܟܐ ܗܘܐ ‖ ܘܢܒܝܐ ‖ ܠܡܦܪܥ ܡܠܟܐ ‖ ܕܡܫܚ

However, the segment ܘܢܒܝܐ is not a clause, but a parallel element to ܕܡܫܚ. Such relations are accounted for at sentence level.[21]

The output of syn04 is a file named 'xxx.ps4', a syntactically analysed text containing clause segmentation.

8.7 CLAUSE PARSING

The next step in the analysis is the assignment of syntactical functions such as predicate, subject, complement and adjunct. While syn03 and syn04 concern mainly the distribution of elements (the determination of phrase and clause boundaries), in this step of the analysis functional categories are introduced. Like the previous steps, it concerns an interactive analysis. The input of the computer program used, 'Parse-Clauses', includes xxx.ps4 files as well as four auxiliary files:

1. VerbvalList: List of previously accepted valency patterns.
2. VerblessList: List of previously accepted patterns of elements occurring in verbless clauses.
3. Loc.ref: List of previously accepted patterns that function as locative expressions.
4. Time.ref: List of previously accepted patterns that function as time expressions.

ßend sind die gewonnen (Teil-)Sätze nach funktionalen Kriterien zu kombinieren'. It follows that a 'clause atom' is not a 'minimal clause', because it does not necessarily contain a predication structure. It is rather the result of a segmentation procedure. Accordingly, a clause atom is either (a) a combination of phrases containing predication, or (b) a phrase or combination of phrases that does not contain predication but becomes part of a predication structure if it is taken together with other non-adjacent clause atoms, or (c) an element that never reaches the status of a clause (e.g. elements in extraposition). Cf. Lyons, *Theoretical Linguistics*, 172, on 'incomplete sentences' and other utterances that do not constitute a sentence.

[21] See below, § 8.8. For the problems involved in clause segmentation, see also Andersen–Forbes, 'Clause Boundaries'.

With the help of these files the program makes suggestions for the clause parsing. With the help of the VerbvalList, for example, it can recognize patterns that in previous analyses have been labelled as 'verb + complement'. Thus if ܪܝܫܐ in ܪܝܫܐ ܕܡܢ is analysed as a complement, the next time the verb ܕܡܢ and a prepositional phrase with ܠ occur in the same clause, the program will suggest analysing the prepositional phrase as a complement.

The output of ParseClauses is twofold. On the one hand it produces 'xxx.ps4.p', a syntactically analysed text, including all the information of the previous steps in the analysis. On the other hand it produces 'xxx.ct4.p', a syntactically analysed surface text, which contains, for example, the following lines:

SIRA 48:1 [<DM> D-<Cj>] [QM <Pr>] [NBJ> <Su>]
SIRA 48:1 [D-<Re>] [DM> <Pr>] [L-NWR> <Co>]
SIRA 48:1 [W-<Cj>] [MLTH <Su>] [JQD> <PC>] [>JK TNWR> <Aj>]
SIRA 48:1 [D-<Re>] [MCTGR <Pr>]

8.8 SENTENCES

Clauses are combined to form sentences. In traditional grammars sentences are the largest units of linguistic description (cf. § 7.3). Sentences may consist of one clause or a combination of clauses. The definition of 'sentences' in Hebrew and Syriac is a debated issue, and even more controversial than that of clauses (cf. § 8.7).[22] Because of the absence of graphical markers such as capitals and periods, the combining of clauses into sentences can be based only on syntactic criteria.[23] However, there is no satisfying theory about the syntactic

---

[22] See § 8.7; cf. Den Exter Blokland, *Text Syntax*, 19, on Andersen's study on the sentence in Biblical Hebrew: 'In the end, however, one does not come away with a Hebrew sentence as a regular surface structure text constituent, but rather with what may perhaps be termed deep structure sentences: any set of two or more constituents that display a notional relationship characteristic of this deep structure sentence'. On the definition of 'sentence' in Biblical Hebrew see also Van Peursen, *Verbal System*, 347 n. 1 and the literature mentioned there.

[23] The study of delimitation markers of smaller units in Syriac biblical manuscripts is still in its infancy; cf. Korpel–De Moor, *Structure of Classical Hebrew Poetry*, 7–8; Korpel, 'Introduction to the Series Pericope', 15; De Moor, 'Unit Division'. It is interesting to compare the division of the text suggested by the delimitation markers with the division based on a syntactic analysis, but the former cannot serve as the point of departure for the latter.; cf. §§ 7.1, 27.3 (end).

basis on which some clauses should be regarded as combining to sentences and others not. The notion of 'sentence' may be helpful to indicate the logico-semantic relationship between clauses (e.g. 'conditional sentence'), but such a qualification is not based on syntactic criteria (compare e.g. conditional sentences without a linguistic marker of the conditional relationship). For this reason in our procedure of syntactical analysis the clause parsing is directly followed by the analysis of the combining of clauses in the hierarchical structure of the text, to be discussed in § 8.9.

Our preceding remarks in no way deny that in some cases it is preferable to make explicit the complex structure of clauses (whether we call the complex clauses sentences or not). Thus for the comparison of the Hebrew and Syriac textual witnesses of Sirach it is important to acknowledge embedded clauses (relative clauses, and subject and object clauses) as clause constituents in their host clauses.[24] This helps us make visible some recurrent correspondences such as that between Noun + Adjective in Hebrew and Noun + א + Adjective in Syriac that occurs, for example, in 48:1. At the end of the preceding paragraph we have quoted the four clauses that occur in Syr. In Heb (B) there are only two clauses:

[<D >CR <Cj>] [QM <Pr>] [NBJ> [K->C <sp>] <Su>]
[W-Cj>] [DBRJW <Su>] [K-TNWR <Aj>] [BW<R <PC>]

The differences between Heb and Syr do not concern the addition or omission of clauses, but rather linguistic differences in internal sentence structure. This can be made visible if the two relative clauses introduced by א in Syr are taken as specifications of their respective heads, which results in the following analysis:[25]

[<DM> D-<Cj>] [QM <PC>] [NBJ> [D -{[DM> <Pr>] [L-NWR> <Co>]} <sp>] <Su>]
[W-<Cj>] [MLTH <Su>] [JQD> <PC>] [>JK TNWR> [D -{[MCTGR <PC>]} <sp>] <Aj>]

8.9 TEXT HIERARCHY

After the analysis of the internal structure of clauses and sentences comes the analysis of clause relations. This is done in an interactive

---

[24] Compare § 26.2 for the distinction between embedding and hypotaxis.
[25] The decorative brackets mark an expansion containing predication.

analysis with the program 'syn05'. The basic assumption in the analysis is that each clause is connected to a preceding clause. On the basis of a number of parameters such as morphological correspondences and clause types, the progam suggests for each clause to which clause it is connected and whether it is parallel to that clause or dependent on it. The input of syn05 includes the xxx.ps4.p files and an auxiliary file called 'ArgumentsList' (also: 'Arglist'), which contains a list of grammatical and lexical arguments such as those mentioned above (morphological correspondences, clause types, etc.). This file too is built up gradually on the basis of previous analyses.

For each clause the distance to the governing clause and the type of the clause connection are registered in the output of syn05, 'xxx.PX'.[26] Accordingly, the xxx.PX files include, in addition to the information available in the xxx.ps4.p files, information about clause types and clause connections (e.g. 'adjunct clause connection'). Syn05 creates also the 'xxx.CTT' files. These are human readable texts, in which indenting marks the place of each clause in the hierarchy; vertical strokes indicate connections between clauses at a distance larger than one line.[27] The instructions for the indentation are stored up in a file called 'xxx.usertab'.

8.10 COMPARISON OF TWO TEXTS

In the preceding paragraphs we have described the procedure of a computer-linguistic bottom-up analysis of a Syriac text or corpus. The same procedure can, *mutatis mutandis* be applied to a part of the Hebrew text. To distinguish the Syriac and the Hebrew data files, we call the Syriac files 'BenSira' and the Hebrew data files 'Sira'. Accordingly, an independent analysis of the Syriac and the Hebrew text up to the level of text hierarchy results in the two xxx.PX data files (e.g. BenSira48.PX and Sira48.PX). After the independent analysis of the two texts, a comparison can be made.

The first step is the reformatting of the Syriac and Hebrew data in such a way that a comparison of the data of a particular chapter is possible. This reformatting is done by the program 'Prepare' (also: 'Prep-

---

[26] Cf. Talstra–Jenner–Van Peursen, 'Linguistic Data Types', 46–48, 58–59.
[27] Further details in Talstra–Jenner–Van Peursen, 'Linguistic Data Types', 47.

Syr'). The input includes the xxx.PX files. The output is called 'xxx.ParalData'. The ParalData files contain five lines of information: (1) surface text with reference; (2) lexical entries of forms in the surface text; (3) phrase types and internal phrase structures; (4) parsing label of phrases; (5) clause type label.[28]

The second step is the comparison of the Syriac and Hebrew ParalData files with the help of a computer program called 'Synopsis'. This program makes suggestions as to which clauses in the Syriac and Hebrew texts are parallel. The output of this analysis is twofold: synoptic data files, called 'xxx.ParalText', and files containing a human readable presentation of the data, called 'xxx.Synops'. Since these files contain the data from both the Syriac and Hebrew ParalData files mentioned above, it is now possible to compare the Syriac and Hebrew data in terms of words, lexemes, but also grammatical features such as phrase types and internal phrase structure.

The programs used in the synoptic analysis have been developed in the CALAP project. In CALAP they have been used for the analysis of Kings. It turned out, however, that for a comparative analysis of the Syriac and Hebrew texts of Sirach the programs had to be adapted because of the large differences between the two sources. Fairly often a clause in Heb does not correspond to one clause in Syr. And if corresponding clauses can be established, they may appear in a different order.[29]

8.11 DATA RETRIEVAL AND TOOLS FOR LINGUISTIC AND COMPARATIVE ANALYSIS

The analyses described in the preceding paragraphs provide a wealth of information at various linguistic levels as well as valuable comparative data. Several programs are used to select and sort the data for purposes of linguistic and comparative analysis.

---

[28] For the set of labels for clause types in Biblical Hebrew see Talstra, 'Clause Types and Clause Hierarchy'; idem, 'Clause Types and Textual Structure'. For Syriac such a set still has to be developed.

[29] Our experiments with the program Synops to deal with parallel texts with a complex relationship appeared also to be useful for a computer-assisted analysis of inner-biblical parallels in Kings, Isaiah and Chronicles, see Van Peursen–Talstra, 'Parallel texts'.

At morphological level the data can be sorted with the program 'sort' according to nominal and/or verbal categories such as number, gender, state, person, root, *binyan* and tense. These data can be employed, for example, in an analysis of the use of the absolute state or in a study of the *binyanim* system in Syriac. At phrase level the data can be sorted, also with the program 'sort', according to simple and complex patterns. These data can be used, for example, for a description of the internal structure of complex phrases.[30] At clause level the data can be sorted according to lexical and grammatical characteristics such as clause pattern, word order, and internal structure of clause constituents. The program used, called 'TestclausesSyr', is able to handle complex instructions such as 'select all clauses containing the negative ܠܐ in first position and a finite form of the verb ܗܘܐ' (cf. § 23.2.4). These data can be used, for example, for a distributional analysis of all clauses containing the enclitic personal pronoun or existential clauses.[31]

The data of the synoptic analysis can be sorted according to clauses, phrases or lexemes with the program 'Compare'. With these data it is possible, for example, to analyse the frequency of 'cognate' translation equivalents or to make a contrastive analysis of internal phrase structure in Syriac and Hebrew.[32]

8.12 CONCLUSION: CALAP AND OTHER SYSTEMS OF COMPUTER-ASSISTED ANALYSIS

The procedure of a computer-assisted analysis described in this chapter has some characteristics that distinguish it from other models of computer-assisted linguistic and textual analysis.

First, the analysis concerns encoding rather than tagging. The encoding takes place in an interactive procedure in which the computer makes suggestions on the basis of previous analyses. As we have pointed out in § 8.4 (end), this has two advantages. The first advantage is the consistency. The consistency in the formal encoding is due to the fact that the computer programs always resort to analyses made previously. The consistency in the functional analysis is guaranteed by

---

[30] See Part Three.
[31] See Part Four.
[32] See Dyk, 'Hierarchical Approach'; idem, 'Lexical Correspondence'.

the fact that the deduction of functions is done automatically. The second advantage is that the choices that led to a certain analysis can be retrieved and, if necessary, corrected.

In the interactive analysis, most programs function as matching programs. That is to say, the programs seek to match forms or patterns that occur in the text to be analysed with forms of patterns that have been accepted in previous analyses. This matching procedure itself plays an important role in checking the consistency of the human researcher and helps collect data in an efficient way.[33]

Related to this first characteristic is the second one, namely that the distinction between abstract linguistic entities and their realizations plays an important role. Graphs are analysed as realizations of a certain grapheme, morphs are regarded as realizations of a certain morpheme, etc.[34] Both the realizations at surface level and the abstract linguistic entities they represent are stored in the database.

Thirdly, the analysis follows basically a bottom-up approach, starting on the level of graphemes (an abstraction of the actual graphs in a manuscript or printed document) and ending on the level of the text. The levels described in the present section are analysed in the order indicated, and the analysis on a subsequent level can only start when the analysis of the preceding level is completed. However, at each stage of the analysis it remains possible to reconsider decisions that have been made at a lower level.

Fourthly, the decisions that on each level are made by the human researcher, are defined as working assumptions, which can be reconsidered or reformulated, for example on the basis of the analysis of the higher levels. Formulating the interaction between the computer and the human researcher in this way, we try to avoid both the danger of

---

[33] We hope that in the future it will be possible to develop the programs further so that they can be used not only for matching procedures, but also for analytical procedures. This concerns, for example, the development of the program 'analyse' (§ 8.3) into a more sophisticated program that can make suggestions for the analysis of words that have not been analysed previously. To achieve this aim the program should be able to calculate possible morpheme segmentations on the basis of the information from the 'word grammar' (§ 8.4) about the paradigmatic forms of the morphemes. For this step the integration of Finite State Morphology looks promising (cf. Kiraz, *Computational Nonlinear Morphology*). A next step would be the inclusion of statistical data so that the program can calculate the most probable analysis if more than one morphological segmentation is possible.

[34] Bosman–Sikkel, 'Reading Authors', 114; idem, 'Discourse on Method', 104–105; idem, 'Worked Examples', 272.

overestimating the possibilities of the computer and the danger of re-
ducing its role. The possibilities of the computer are overestimated if
it is described (explicitly or implicitly) in terms of artificial intelligence, that is, as an instrument that can make decisions if human re-
searchers fail. The function of the computer is underestimated, however, if it is reduced to an advanced search engine or concordance,
which would imply that a computer-assisted analysis is not basically
different from an analysis without the computer.[35] We have tried to
develop a model that shows awareness of both the opportunities and
the limitations of a computer-assisted analysis.

In the following chapters we will focus on the linguistic analysis at the
levels of phrases (Part Three), clauses (Part Four) and texts (Part
Five). The results of the synoptic analysis will be integrated into these
chapters.

---

[35] See Talstra–Dyk, 'The Computer and Biblical Research'.

APPENDIX: COMPUTER PROGRAMS
USED IN THE CALAP ANALYSIS

A. PROGRAMS USED IN THE BOTTOM-UP LINGUISTIC ANALYSIS

Program:	Pil2wit.
Description:	Transformation of the input text into a transliterated text according to an established format that enables the subsequent steps in the analysis.
Input:	'Running text', e.g. 'sirach', i.e. the Syriac text from the Leiden edition: consonants in transliteration; diactritics encoded; interpunction encoded; instructions to select variant readings; comments.
Output:	'Graphic text', e.g. 'BenSira'[1]: the Syriac text from the running text, with the instructions to read variants executed, comments omitted, and markers of book, chapter and verse added.

Program:	Analyse.
Description:	Segmentation of the Syriac words into morphemes, i.e. insertion of morpheme markers. The program makes suggestions on the basis of the analytical lexicon.
Input:	Selected chapter from graphic text (e.g. BenSira01).
Auxiliary file:	Analytical lexicon ('anzb'): list of all encodings made in previous analyses.
Output:	Analysed text, e.g. BenSira.an.

Program:	Genat.
Description:	Selection of chapter and reformatting (textual reference, line format).
Input:	BenSira.an.
Output:	xxx.at (e.g. BenSira01.at).

Program:	at2ps.
Description:	Deduction of functions at word level from the xxx.at files.
Input:	xxx.at.
Auxiliary files:	Alphabet.
	Word morphology ('word grammar').
	Lexicon.

---

[1] The distinction between 'sirach' (running text) and 'Ben Sira' (graphic text) is just a matter of convention. The different names have no other function than to keep the two files apart.

	ps-definition file: organization of output files.
Output:	xxx.ps2: registration of morphemes and the functions that can be derived from them (person, number, gender) + information from the lexicon (part of speech, lexical sets).
	xxx.ct: encoded surface text.
	xxx.dmp: data description in human readable form (on request).

Program:	Syn03.
Description:	Phrase segmentation i.e. words are combined to phrases. The program makes suggestions on the basis of Phrset.
Input:	xxx.ps2.
Auxiliary files:	Phrset: list of phrase structures accepted in previous analyses.
	Morfcond: word functions that define grammatical functions.
Output	xxx.ps3: morphosyntactically analysed text (phrase atoms).

Program:	Syn04.
Description:	Clause segmentation, i.e. phrases are combined into clauses.
Input:	xxx.ps3.
Auxiliary files:	Clset: list of accepted clause patterns, based on previous analyses.
	Lexcondcl: lexical conditions for acceptable clause patterns.
	Morfcondcl: morphological conditions for acceptable clause patterns.
Output:	xxx.ps4: syntactically analysed text (clause atoms).

Program:	ParseClauses.
Description:	Clause parsing: Syntactical functions are assigned (subject, predicate etc.)
Input:	xxx.ps4.
Auxiliary files:	Verbvallist: list of previously accepted valency patterns.
	Verblesslist: list of previously encountered patterns of elements occurring in verbless clauses.
	Loc.ref: list of patterns that function as locative expressions.
	Time.ref: list of patterns that function as time expressions.
Output:	xxx.ps4.p: syntactically analysed text (clause constituents).
	xxx.ct4.p: syntactically analysed surface text.

Program:	Syn05.
Description:	Establishing of clause relations and text hierarchy.
Input:	xxx.ps4.p.

Auxiliary file: 'Arglist': list of grammatical and lexical arguments.
Output: xxx.PX: syntactically analysed text including information
                   about clause connections (type, distance).
                   xxx.CTT: hierarchically analysed text in human readable
                   form.
                   xxx.usertab: instructions for indenting in the xxx.CTT files.

B. PROGRAMS USED FOR THE COMPARISON OF
SYRIAC AND HEBREW DATA

Program: Prepare (= PrepSyr).
Description: Reformatting of the Syriac and Hebrew data to enable a
                   comparison; arrangement of the data in five lines of infor-
                   mation: (1) surface text with reference; (2) lexical entries of
                   forms in the surface text; (3) phrase types and internal
                   phrase structures; (4) parsing labels of phrases; (5) clause
                   type labels.
Input: xxx.PX (e.g. BenSira48.PX [Syriac] and Sira48.PX [He-
                   brew]).
Output: xxx.ParalData: format for comparison.

Program: Synopsis.
Description: Combination of the Hebrew in Syriac xxx.ParalData files.
                   The program uses the parsing labels (see Prepare) to make
                   suggestions as to which clause atoms are parallel within a
                   verse.
Input: xxx.ParalData (e.g. BenSira48.ParalData [Syriac]).
                   xxx.ParalData (e.g. Sira48.ParalData [Hebrew]).
Output: xxx.ParalText : combination of Hebrew and Syriac data.
                   xxx.Synops: human-readable bilingual synops of the He-
                   brew and Syriac data.

C. OTHER PROGRAMS FOR RETRIEVAL AND SORTING OF DATA

Program: Sort.
Description: Sorting of the morphological data according to nominal
                   and/or verbal categories such as number, gender, state, per-
                   son, root, *binyan* and tense; sorting of phrases according to
                   internal structure.
Input: This is a general unix application that can be used for any
                   selected file or collection of files.

Output:	Files with lines of the input files sorted according to one or more sort keys.
Program:	TestclausesSyr.
Description:	Sorting of clauses according to grammatical and lexical characteristics.
Input:	xxx.PX.
	xxx.ct4.p.
Output:	xxx.ClPattern.
Program:	PrepareCC1.
Description:	Production of concordances and frequency lists (first step)
Input:	xxx.PX.
	xxx.ct4.p.
Output:	xxx.LEX: list of lexemes and their context in text order.
Program:	PrepareCC2.
Description:	Produces concordances and frequency lists (second step)
Input:	xxx.LEX.
Output:	xxx.FRQ: Frequency list.
	xxx.CONC: Concordance: sorted list of lexemes and their context.
Program:	Compare (= CompSyr).
Description:	Comparison of the Hebrew and Syriac data at the level of clauses, phrases or lexemes.
Input:	xxx.ParalTxt.
	xxx.Synops.
Output:	ParalPh: list of corresponding phrases in Syriac and Hebrew.
	ParalCl: list of corresponding clauses in Syriac and Hebrew.
	ParalLex: list of corresponding lexemes in Syriac and Hebrew.

PART THREE

PHRASE STRUCTURE

CHAPTER NINE

PRELIMINARY REMARKS ON PHRASE STRUCTURE

9.1 INTRODUCTION

A phrase is a word or a group of words that makes up a part of a clause, but does not constitute a clause in itself,[1] that is to say that it does not express predication.[2] It consists of a 'main word' together with its obligatory or optional expansions. This 'main word' may be called the 'head': A head is a single element in a phrase that characterizes the phrase as a whole.[3] A phrase is the largest unit that has one word as its head;[4] it is the maximal projection of that head.[5]

In our investigation the concept of 'phrase atoms' or 'minimum units' plays an important role. We define phrase atoms as the smallest indivisible units of a phrase, i.e. those elements that cannot be subdivided into smaller units.[6] Phrase atoms, like physical atoms, can have a complex internal structure. Thus there are phrase atoms of the type [Preposition–Noun] or [CstrNoun–Noun].[7] The atoms are the smallest elements out of which larger constructions are built.

Phrase atoms can be extended by specifications or by other phrase atoms that are juxtaposed. This may lead to rather complex structures of phrases, consisting of one or more phrase atoms, specifications and parallel elements. On the basis of formal criteria we distinguish the following types of phrase extensions.[8]

---

[1] On phrases that are not part of a clause see § 8.6; for the definition of 'clause' see § 16.1.

[2] Even though it may contain embedded predication structures; cf. § 26.2.

[3] Thus Matthews, *Dictionary*, 158.

[4] Thus Matthews, *Dictionary*, 279.

[5] Cf. Trask, *Dictionary*, 208.

[6] Cf. Talstra–Sikkel 'WIVU-Datenbank', 47–48: 'Mit diesem Begriff werden zwei Sachverhalte gekennzeichnet: zum einen sind Atome auf ihrer linguistischen Ebene nicht weiter teilbar; zum anderen sind sie – einzeln oder in Kombination – Bausteine höherer funktionaler Einheiten.'

[7] Square brackets indicate the boundaries of a phrase atom.

[8] Compare Dyk, 'Data Preparation', 146–147. Unlike Dyk, we prefer to keep apart phrases with גּ and prepositional phrases (cf. § 14.1) and to treat demonstratives as a

1. Adjective, e.g. 7:21 ܚܟܝܡܐ ܥܒܕܐ 'a wise servant'.
2. *d*-phrase, e.g. 17:11 ܕܚܝܐ ܢܡܘܣܐ 'the law of life' or 7:27 ܝܠܕܬܟ ܐܡܟ 'your mother who bore you'.
3. Noun, e.g. 51:1 ܡܠܟܐ ܡܪܝܐ 'Lord, king'.
4. Demonstrative, e.g. 50:27 ܗܢܐ ܒܟܬܒܐ 'in this book'.
5. Prepositional phrase, e.g. 42:11 ܒܥܡܐ ܡܬܚܪܝ 'gainsaying among the people'.
6. Parallel element, e.g. 6:28 ܘܛܒܬܐ ܢܝܚܐ 'rest and good cheer'.

By '*d*-phrase' we refer to phrases introduced by ܕ. There are two types: one in which ܕ is followed by a noun and another in which it introduces a construction in which predication occurs. These types are related diachronically and the functions of the ܕ in each of them can be covered by the single term *translatif*,[9] but syntactically they show different behaviour.[10]

One could argue that attributively used demonstratives belong to the first category, that of adjectives. Most Syriac and Hebrew grammars speak of the adjectival or attributive use of demonstratives (in contrast to their independent use), qualifying or determining a noun.[11] Since, however, our main criterion for distinguishing types of phrase extensions is their form, we prefer to keep 'demonstrative' apart as a separate type, without denying the syntactic similarities between the adjective and the attributively used demonstrative.

The parallel element constitutes a separate category, because it concerns the addition of another element (phrase atom), rather than a modification of the head of the phrase.

---

separate category. In the CALAP encoding system the specification consisting of a noun is marked with <ap> (= 'apposition'), the parallel element with <PA>, and the other extensions by <sp> (= 'specification'). Accordingly, in the present system there is not a one-to-one relation between the types of extensions and the labels attached to them. In the future we hope to develop the encoding system further. Our grammatical description argues on the one hand for a more general label such as 'extensions', indicating the relation to a preceding head, and on the other hand for a more precise subdivision of this label on the basis of the forms of the extensions.

[9] Wertheimer, 'Functions'; see further § 14.1.
[10] See especially § 12.6.
[11] Thus e.g. Nöldeke, *Grammatik*, § 226; Joosten, *Syriac Language*, 36 n. 9; Joüon–Muraoka, *Grammar*, § 143*h*; Waltke–O'Connor, *Biblical Hebrew Syntax*, § 17.1*a*. According to Dyk, 'Data Preparation', 146, the demonstrative may also function as an apposition.

The aim of Part Three is to describe the way in which phrase atoms and extensions are combined to constitute phrases. This approach has three innovative aspects.

Firstly, we take phrase atoms, rather than nouns, as the nuclei of phrases. In Syriac grammars one often finds a section on the way in which a noun can be extended by, for example, a genitive or an apposition, without a distinction being made between those cases where this extension is an obligatory element that is necessary to make up a phrase atom (e.g. a 'genitive noun') and those where it is an optional specification (e.g. a *d*-phrase).[12] The difference between obligatory and optional expansions is also visible if we compare textual witnesses. Whereas optional elements can be omitted or added, obligatory elements cannot. Compare the following cases of inner-Syriac variation related to these optional specifications:

18:29 ܪܕܝܘܬܐ 'and instruction'] *add* ܢܦܫܐ 'of the soul' 7h3 8a1 9c1 10c1.2 11c.1 12a1*fam* →
26:16 ܫܘܦܪܗ ܕܐܢܬܬܐ 'the beauty of a woman'] *add* ܛܒܐ 'good' 9c1 10c1.2 11c1 12a1*fam* →
35:20 ܘܨܠܘܬܗܘܢ 'and their prayers'] *add* ܕܡܣܟܢܐ 'of the poor' 8a1ᶜ 9c1 11c1 12a1*fam* →
44:21 ܟܠܗܘܢ ܥܡ̈ܡܐ ܕܥܠܡܐ 'all the peoples of the world'] *om* ܕܥܠܡܐ 'of the world' 9c1 10c1.2 11c1 *fam* →

Secondly, our main criterion for distinguishing several types of specification is formal. This leads to a division of the data that in some respects differs from that in traditional grammars, in which functional and formal considerations intervene. Thus whereas in traditional grammars cardinals are often taken together with ordinals in a paragraph on numerals,[13] we analyse them as a subgroup (lexical set) of the noun and hence their combination with another noun is discussed under 'apposition'.

Thirdly, our main concern is the way in which the combination of phrase atoms and their extensions are structured to build up phrases. Many grammars discuss subsequently several types of modifiers, but pay little attention to the question of how these elements are organized

---

[12] Thus we find in Muraoka, *Basic Grammar*, § 91 under the heading 'noun phrase expanded': attributive adjective, demonstrative pronoun and cardinal numbers, but also the so-called genitive noun.

[13] Thus in Muraoka, *Basic Grammar*, apposition is not discussed in the section 'noun phrase expanded' (§ 91), but receives its own paragraph elsewhere (§ 95), and cardinals are discussed under the former (see our preceding footnote).

if they occur together and whether we can discern rules that determine the order and number of the extensions.[14]

9.2 INTERNAL STRUCTURE OF PHRASE ATOMS

It follows from our definitions given in § 9.1 that a phrase atom may consist of more than one noun. Words that need other words to make up a phrase atom are prepositions and nouns in the construct state. In the case of noun phrases the boundary of a phrase atom is an absolute or emphatic state ending (noun or adjective) or a pronoun (suffix pronoun or independent pronoun). In some cases a construct noun is followed by another construct noun. Accordingly, there are phrase atoms with the pattern [CstrNoun–Noun],[15] such as

2:14 ܚܝܠܐ, ܬܘܟܠܢܐ 'heroes of confidence'.
26:22 ܐܢܬܬܐ ܓܒܪܐ 'a man's wife'.

And with the pattern [CstrNoun–CstrNoun–Noun], such as

1:19 ܒܝܬ ܣܡܟܐ ܬܫܒܘܚܬܐ 'a house of support of praise'.[16]

The other attestations of the pattern [CstrNoun–CstrNoun–Noun] in Syr are with ܒܪ ܐܢܫ and/or ܟܠ:

1:29 ܒܥܝܢܝ ܒܢܝ ܐܢܫܐ 'in the eyes of men'.[17]
3:12 ܟܠ ܝܘܡܬܐ ܕܚܝܝܟ 'all the days of your life'.[18]
8:19 ܠܟܠܒܪܢܫ 'to every man'.[19]

---

[14] Cf. § 15.1 for a similar tendency in studies on sentence structure.

[15] Cases where the *nomen rectum* takes a parallel element will be discussed in § 10.2.2 (7). For an exceptional case where the *nomen regens* has a parallel element, see Nöldeke, *Grammatik*, § 208A (end).

[16] Winter (*Concordance*, 392) interprets ܣܡܟܐ as a participle of the Pael. This interpretation is also reflected in the translation made by Calduch-Benages, Ferrer and Liesen (*Sabiduría del Escriba*, 68–69: 'a mansion which sustains glory'; 'casa que sostiene la gloria'). Payne Smith, Smend and Peters however, consider ܣܡܟܐ as a noun; see Payne Smith, *Thesaurus* II, 2662; Smend, *Jesus Sirach*, 13 ('eine Stütze von Herrlichkeit'); Peters, *Ben Sirach*, 15. The advantage of the latter interpretation is that it accounts for the construct state ܒܝܬ (in the former interpretation both ܒܝܬ and ܣܡܟܐ should be regarded as being in the absolute state) and that it better fits the parallelism with ܫܘܠܛܢ ܥܘܫܢܐ 'sceptre of strength'.

[17] Other examples with ܒܪ ܐܢܫ occur in 31:31 and 45:1.

[18] Other examples with ܟܠ occur in 3:13; 21:14 (ܟܠ ܝܘܡܝ ܚܝܘܗܝ; but 7a1 ܟܠܗܘܢ ܚܝܘܗܝ); 22:12; 23:15; 38:29.

[19] Other examples with both ܒܪ ܐܢܫ and ܟܠ occur in 11:29 and 23:10.

Longer chains of construct nouns do not occur. Accordingly, the maximum matrix[20] of phrase atoms can be rendered as

[Preposition–CstrNoun–CstrNoun–Noun][21]

There are only seven examples in which all the slots of this matrix are filled. Without preposition, but with two construct nouns, there occur another six examples. Of this total of thirteen examples, twelve contain ܟܠ and/or ܒܪ ܐܢܫ. Regarding ܒܪ ܐܢܫ we can conclude that the combination of these two lexemes became to be treated as a single word. One can compare the situation in Neo-Aramaic dialects, where ܒܪ and some other nouns no longer function as separate nouns.[22] About ܟܠ we can observe that it behaves somewhat differently from other nouns. In other phrase patterns too [CstrNoun–Noun] is more frequent with ܟܠ than with other nouns.[23]

In Heb the chain with two construct nouns is more frequent,[24] and longer chains are attested as well, e.g.

16:17 (A) בקצות רוחות כל בני אדם 'in the totality of the spirits of all men'.[25]

---

[20] On the concept of a 'maximum matrix', see further Chapter Fifteen.

[21] The final noun of the phrase atom may be in the absolute or emphatic state or take a suffix pronoun. It is true that [CstrNoun–Noun] may be transformed into [Noun+suffix] (e.g. ܟܬܒܗ ܕܢܒܝܐ 'the book of the prophet' → ܟܬܒܗ 'his book'; cf. Muraoka, *Basic Grammar*, § 91f; Goldenberg, 'Attribution', 3), but in the syntactic combining of words to phrases the two constructions behave differently. It seems that the presence of a suffix pronoun does not influence the number of other elements in the phrase atoms. Otherwise we would have expected, for example, to find the pattern
[CstrNoun–CstrNoun–CstrNoun–NounAbs/Emph]
because the 'equivalent' pattern
[CstrNoun–CstrNoun–Noun+suffix]
is attested as well.

[22] Cf. Khan, *Neo-Aramaic Dialect of Qaraqosh*, 211.

[23] Note the frequency of ܟܠ in the following patterns: [Noun$_1$ [*d-kl* CstrNoun–Noun$_2$ <sp>]] (CstrNoun = ܒܝܬ; Noun$_2$ = ܐܠܗܐ or ܫܡܝܐ; § 10.2.1 [1]); [*kl* Noun [*d*-Noun <sp>]] (§ 10.2.1 [2]); [Noun [*d-kl*+suffix [Noun <ap>] <sp>]] (§ 10.2.2 [1]); [*kl* [Noun *w*-Noun] and even [*kl* [Noun *w*-Noun *w*-Noun]] (§ 10.2.2 [7]); [*kl* [*d*-{[Adjective <PC>]} <sp>]] (§ 10.2.3 [3]); [*kl*+suffix [CstrNoun–Noun <ap>]] (§ 10.3.1); [CstrNoun–*kl*+suffix [Noun <ap>]] (§ 10.3.1); [CstrNoun–Noun [*kl*+suffix <ap>]] (§ 10.3.1); [*kl*+suffix [Noun [*d*-Noun <sp>] <ap>]] (§10.3.2 [2]); [*klhyn* [*hlyn* <sp>]] and *hlyn* [*klhyn* <sp>]] (§ 10.4).

[24] See § 10.2.1 for cases where the Hebrew [CstrNoun–CstrNoun–Noun] occurs parallel to [Noun [*d*-CstrNoun–Noun <sp>]] or [CstrNoun–Noun [*d*-Noun <sp>]] in Syr; § 10.2.2 (3) for cases where it occurs parallel to [Noun [*d*-Noun [*d*-Noun <sp>] <sp>]]; and § 10.3.2 (2) for occurrences parallel to [Noun [Noun [*d*-Noun <sp>] <ap>]] (one of the three nouns being ܟܠ).

[25] Syr has ܪܘܚܬܐ ܕܟܠܗܘܢ ܒܢܝ ܐܢܫܐ, see § 10.2.2 (1).

with the pattern

[Preposition–CstrNoun–CstrNoun–CstrNoun–CstrNoun–Noun].

When we compare Heb and Syr, there are a number of cases where a phrase atom in Syr corresponds to one in Heb, although the internal structure is different. Thus [CstrNoun–Noun] in Syr corresponds to a single noun in Heb in

7:10 ܡܠܝ ܨܠܘܬܟ 'in the words of your prayer'; A בתפלה.
11:31 ܡܐܢܝ ܪܓܬܐ 'with vessels of desire'; A ובמחמדיך.[26]
41:1 ܒܟܠ ܙܒܢ 'at every time'; B+M בכל.[27]
50:22 ܒܢܝ ܐܢܫܐ 'sons of man'; B אדם.

[CstrNoun–Noun] in Syr corresponds to a single noun in Gr (Heb not extant) in

18:30 ܒܬܪ ܪܓܬ ܢܦܫܟ 'after the desires of your soul'; Gr ὀπίσω τῶν ἐπιθυμιῶν σου.
25:6 ܣܘܓܐܐ ܕܡܠܟ 'the abundance of deliberation'; Gr πολυπειρία.
26:26 ܠܟܠ ܐܢܫ 'to every man'; Gr πᾶσι.

[CstrNoun–Noun] in Syr corresponds to [Noun+suffix] in Heb in[28]

25:18 ܒܥܠܗ ܕܐܢܬܬܐ 'the husband of a foolish woman'; C בעלה.[29]
38:5 ܚܝܠܐ ܕܐܠܗܐ 'God's strength'; B^txt כחו; B^mg כוחם.[30]

Compare cases where Syr has [Noun+suffix] corresponding to a single noun in Heb:[31]

8:16 ܕܡܟ 'your blood'; A דמים.

---

[26] But Smend, *Jesus Sirach*, 112, thinks that the מחמדים in Heb are virtues, rather than precious vessels, and according to Skehan–Di Lella, *Wisdom of Ben Sira*, 245, מחמדיך 'refers to the injured person's good name and reputation'. Segal, *Sefer Ben Sira*, 67, thinks that the combination with קשר יתן suggests that מחמדיך refers to persons, i.e. '(He will make) those who are dear to you (plot against you)'.

[27] Cf. Lévi, *L'Ecclésiastique* I, 32: 'S. ajoute à la fin le mot עת "temps", qui est inutile'. Note that ܒܟܠ ܙܒܢ also occurs in the parallel line in 41:2, where Heb (B^txt+mg) also has בכל.

[28] On the functional equivalence of [CstrNoun–Noun] and [Noun+suffix], see note 21.

[29] Since the pattern of correspondence is not anomalous, there is no reason to omit ܕܐܢܬܬܐ; nor is it necessary that it was added under the influence of 'sin' in 25:19 (cf. § 3.7.1 on the 'influence of adjacent lines'); *pace* Ryssel, 'Fragmente', VII, 393.

[30] Cf. § 3.2 (h).

[31] See also the examples from Sir 44:16–45:26 in Reiterer, *Urtext*, 52 and the remark on p. 53: 'Die das Syrische insgesamt charakterisierende Vorliebe für die Verwendung von s[uffix] P[ronomen] hat auch den vorliegenden Übersetzer nicht unberührt gelassen.'

36:3 ܐܝܕܟ 'your hand'; B יד.[32]
47:22 ܠܛܝܒܘܬܗ 'his goodness'; B חסד.[33]

Vice versa there are cases where a single word in Syr corresponds to [CstrNoun–Noun] in Heb:

4:1 ܠܡܣܟܢܐ 'to the poor one'; A נפש עני.
4:20 ܙܒܢܐ 'the time'; A עת המון.[34]
9:1 ܐܢܬܬܟ 'your wife': A את אשת חיקך.
10:5 ܟܠ 'everything'; A כל גבר.
30:24 ܠܒܐ 'a good heart'; B שנות לב טוב.[35]
35:13 ܦܘܪܥܐ 'a rewarder'; B[mg] בעל גמולות.[36]
37:3 ܐܪܥܐ 'the earth'; B פני תבל.
38:10 ܫܘܩܪܐ 'falsehood': B מהכר פנים.[37]
42:11 ܡܠܠܘܬܐ 'talking'; B+M דבת עיר.
42:11 ܡܦܩܐ 'exit'; B מבוא סביב.[38]
42:21 ܘܚܟܡܬܐ 'and wisdom'; B[txt] תכן […]תו; ג; B[mg] גבורות; M גבורת גבורה; [חכמ]תו.[39]
45:18 ܒܚܝܠܐ 'in strength'; B בעזוז אפם.[40]

---

[32] Ryssel, 'Fragmente', IV, 281, suggests that the source texts of Syr and Gr had יד, but that is not necessary; nor is it correct to claim that the absence of a suffix in Heb is 'grammatically wrong'; *pace* Buttenwieser, 'Maccabean Psalms', 227–228, *Psalms*, 12–13; cf. Van Peursen, *Verbal System*, 61. According to Brock the Syriac idiom virtually demands the use of the suffix with words denoting parts of the body. The attachment of suffixes to parts of the body and other inalienable possessions (cf. also the example from 8:16) is well documented in the Old Syriac and Peshitta Gospels; see Brock, 'Limitations', 95–96; Williams, *Early Syriac Translation Technique*, 69–87.

[33] Here too the conclusion that the Syriac translator read חסדו with a suffix in his source text is more than the evidence allows us; *pace* Lévi, *L'Ecclésiastique* I, 131.

[34] Schechter and Taylor (*Wisdom of Ben Sira*, 41) emend וזמן עת (cf. Qoh 3:1); Ryssel ('Fragmente', I, 375) proposes to read עת הזמן; Peters (*Ben Sirach*, 48) suggests that המון means agitation of the inner parts as in Isa 63:15 (read this instead of Peters' Ps 63:15), and refers to the agitation that arouses a feeling of shame. He thinks that המון is an explanatory gloss to עת, or perhaps only a variant (המון > הזמן) to it.

[35] According to Peters, *Ben Sirach*, 251, שנות 'sleep' is secondary, because it 'überlastet den Stichos'; similarly Lévi, *L'Ecclésiastique* II, 135; but Smend, *Jesus Sirach*, 272, prefers to retain it; he compares 31:20 and Prv 6:10; 24:33.

[36] ܦܘܪܥܐ repeats ܦܘܪܥܐ in 35:13 (in Syr 35:13 precedes 35:12), where ܐܠܗܐ ܗܘ ܦܘܪܥܐ corresponds to אלוה תשלומות הוא in B; see § 3.6 on repetitive parallelism.

[37] This may be a free rendering of Heb; it is not necessary to assume that the Syriac translator could not read or understand his Hebrew text; *pace* Ryssel, 'Fragmente', V, 583.

[38] For the expression used in Heb Kister ('Notes', 140) refers to מבאת סבבת in the Amman Citadel Inscription (Aufrecht, *Ammonite Inscriptions*, 54; cf. Ahituv, *Ancient Hebrew Inscriptions*, 220).

[39] But note that Syr has ܓܢܒܪܘܬܐ at the end of v. 20 (§ 3.4 [e]). This verse in Sirach is based on Isa 40:13–14; [גבורת חכמ]תו corresponds to רוח יהוה in Isaiah; cf. Kister, 'Contribution', 356–357; see also ibid. n. 196 on the combination of חכמה and גבורה.

45:19 ܒܢܘܪܐ 'in fire'; B בשביב אשו.
46:13 ܢܙܝܪܐ 'the Nazirite'; B יי נזיר.
47:3 ܐܝܟ ܐܡܪܐ 'like lambs'; B כבני בשן.[41]
49:4 ܢܡܘܣܐ 'the law'; B עליון תורת.
50:7 ܥܠ ܒܝܪܬܐ 'over the citadel'; B אל היכל המלך.[42]
50:13 ܩܘܪܒܢܐ 'the offerings'; B יי ואשי.[43]
50:16 ܒܩܪܢܬܐ 'on the horns'; B מקשה בחצצרות.

And cases where a single noun in Syr corresponds to [Noun+suffix] in Heb:[44]

38:8 ܥܒܕܐ 'the work'; B מעשהו.
50:24 ܚܣܕܐ 'mercy'; B חסדו.[45]

[Noun [d-Noun <sp>]] corresponds to [CstrNoun–CstrNoun–Noun] in Heb in[46]

7:7 ܒܟܢܘܫܬܐ ܕܣܓܝܐܐ 'in the community of the city'; A בעדת שערי אל.[47]

Although in some cases the Syriac translator may have had a different *Vorlage*, the frequency of the examples suggests that Syr is not a translation at word level, but at least at phrase level. It is dangerous, therefore, to draw conclusions about the translator's Hebrew source text or about his use of a Greek text (cf. note 47) on the basis of these correspondences.

A more precise characterization of the translation can only be made after the analysis of phrase structure and clause structure in the following chapters.

---

[40] Cf. Reiterer, *Urtext*, 197–198. According to Lévi, *L'Ecclésiastique* I, 103, Syr reflects בעזוז.

[41] Read בני כבשים? Cf. Smend, *Jesus Sirach*, 449; Peters, *Ben Sirach*, 402; Skehan–Di Lella, *Wisdom of Ben Sira*, 524.

[42] Cf. § 4.1 (4).

[43] Cf. § 4.2.1.

[44] See also the examples from Sir 44:16–45:26 in Reiterer, *Urtext*, 53. Since the Syriac translator tends to add pronominal suffixes rather than to omit them, Reiterer assumes that where there is no suffix in Syr, it was not present in its Hebrew source text either; thus e.g. *Urtext*, 190 (on 45:17), 218 (on 45:23).

[45] Perhaps the Syriac translator tried to avoid confusion about the referent of the suffix; cf. Ryssel, 'Fragmente', VI, 207.

[46] The correspondence of [Noun [d-Noun <sp>]] in Syr with [CstrNoun–Noun] in Heb is frequent; cf. § 10.2.1

[47] According to Smend the Syriac translator combined 'the community of the gate' (= A) and 'the multitude of the city' (= Gr); according to Ryssel MS A reflects a combination of an original reading שער בעדת and the expression בעדת אל; see the references given in § 2.3.3 (4).

CHAPTER TEN

PHRASES WITH ONE EXTENSION

In § 9.1 we have mentioned the types of extensions that a phrase atom can take. The present chapter will be concerned with those phrases that consist of a phrase atom and one extension. The extension itself may take other extensions.

10.1 ADJECTIVE

10.1.1 *Basic patterns*

The basic pattern is

[Noun [Adjective <sp>]]

This pattern is abundantly attested, e.g.:

7:21 ܥܒܕܐ ܚܟܝܡܐ 'a wise servant'.
14:10 ܥܝܢܐ ܒܝܫܬܐ 'an evil eye'.
26:7 ܐܢܬܬܐ ܒܝܫܬܐ 'an evil wife'.

Sometimes [Noun [Adjective <sp>]] corresponds to a single noun in Heb, e.g.:[1]

9:1 ܚܫܒܬܐ ܒܝܫܬ 'an evil scheme (wisdom)'; A רעה.
9:9 ܕܡܐ ܚܝܒܐ 'with guilty blood (i.e. with blood-guilt)'; A בדמים.[2]
10:1 ܕܝܢܐ ܚܟܝܡܐ 'a wise judge'; A שופט.[3]
13:17 ܠܓܒܪܐ ܙܕܝܩܐ 'with a righteous man'; A לצדיק.

---

[1] Some examples belong to the category 'Syr provides a free rendering of an idiomatic Hebrew expression' (§ 3.2 [a]), but in the present chapter the selection of corresponding phrase patterns is based on formal criteria rather than the selection of 'idiomatic Hebrew expressions'.

[2] Syr gives two renderings of this verse, one before and one after 9:8; the other rendering has ܚܝܒ ܡܘܬܐ 'guilty of death (you descend to Sheol)'.

[3] But note that in A it is followed by the *nomen rectum* עם (cf. the following יוסד עמו); cf. Peters, *Ben Sirach*, 87 on this verse: 'Gemeint is jedenfalls der *Weise* als Herrscher; vgl. 9, 17. Deshalb ist mit Gr und Syr חָכָם hinzuzufügen (…) In T [= MS A] ist es durch ein überschüssiges עָם verdrängt.'

20:7 ܓܒܪܐ ܚܟܝܡܐ 'a wise man'; C חכם.
31:28 ܘܥܕܢܐ ܛܒܐ 'and good seasons'; B עדוי; F יעדוי.[4]
37:8 ܡܢ ܡܠܘܟܐ ܒܝܫܐ 'a wicked counsellor'; B מיועץ.
38:5 ܡܝܐ ܡܪܝܪܐ 'the bitter water'; B מים.
41:1 ܠܓܒܪܐ ܥܬܝܪܐ 'to the rich man'; B+M לאיש.
44:23 ܓܒܪܐ ܙܕܝܩܐ 'to righteous men'; B איש.[5]
48:15 ܡܢ ܥܒܕܝܗܘܢ ܒܝܫܐ 'from their evil deeds'; B מחטאתם.
50:1 ܟܗܢܐ ܪܒܐ 'the High Priest'; B הכהן.
51:12 ܫܡܗ ܩܕܝܫܐ 'His holy name'; B שם ײ.[6]

[Noun [Adjective <sp>]] corresponds to a single noun in Gr (Heb not extant) in

18:13 ܪܥܝܐ ܛܒܐ 'a good shepherd'; Gr ποιμήν.
21:16 ܛܥܢܐ ܝܩܝܪܐ 'a heavy burden'; Gr φορτίον.
24:4 ܒܡܪܘܡܐ ܥܠܝܐ 'in the most high places'; Gr ἐν ὑψηλοῖς.
34:28 ܥܡܠܐ ܣܪܝܩܐ 'worthless labour'; Gr κόπους.
44:12 ܒܥܒܕܐ ܛܒܐ 'in their good deeds' (translating Hebrew בעבודם?); Gr δι' αὐτούς (=בעבורם).[7]

In some cases the Hebrew evidence is divided:

31:12 ܥܠ ܦܬܘܪܗ ܕܓܒܪܐ ܥܬܝܪܐ 'at the table of a rich man'; B^txt על שלחן גדול; B^mg איש.[8]

[Noun [Adjective <sp>]] corresponds to [Noun [Adjective <sp>] [Adjective <sp>]] in Heb in

49:5 ܠܥܡܐ ܢܘܟܪܝܐ 'to a foreign people'; B לגוי נבל נכרי.[9]

In the example from 37:8 the adjective in Syr can be regarded as a plus compared with Heb. The addition of the adjective changes the purport of the verse considerably. In Syr one is advised to be on his guard for a wicked counsellor, which is less radical than Heb, which

[4] Ryssel, 'Fragmente', III, 90, emends עדנים in Heb and comments: 'Eine Bestätgung hierfür liegt in dem von S gewählten Ausdrucke עִדָּנָא טָבָא "gute Zeiten", insofern S das hebr. עדנים i. S. v. syr. עדנא "Zeit" faßte (und darum, zur Erzielung eines passenden Sinnes, das Adj. ܛܒܐ beifügte).' On cases where Syr renders a Hebrew word according to its meaning in Syriac or another form of Aramaic, see § 3.4 (d).

[5] For arguments to reconstruct an adjective in Heb as well, see Smend, *Jesus Sirach*, 426; Reiterer, *Urtext*, 118.

[6] For the equivalence of CstrNoun+suffix and CstrNoun + (Proper) Noun, see § 9.2 (n. 21).

[7] Cf. § 2.2.2.

[8] The adjective modifies the *nomen rectum*, cf. § 10.2.2 (2); Gr seems to have taken גדול as an adjective to שלחן instead of a genitive (Peters, *Ben Sirach*, 255).

[9] According to Skehan–Di Lella, *Wisdom of Ben Sira*, 541, נבל is a gloss based on Deut 32:11; cf. also Sir 50:24.

says that one should not trust any counsellor at all. The same applies to the plus ܣܓܝ in 10:1, but in this case it is generally agreed that the reading in Heb is secondary. In 18:13 the addition of the adjective is probably due to the influence of John 10:11 (§ 5.4). It hardly affects the meaning of the verse as a whole, which speaks of 'a (good) shepherd who shepherds his flocks'. The same holds true for 'His holy name' instead of 'the name of the Lord' in 50:12. In 13:17 and 20:7 the noun rather than the adjective is a plus.[10] At first sight 'the water' in 38:5 (B) differs from 'the bitter water' (Syr), 'a man' in 41:1 (B+M) from 'a rich man' (Syr), and 'a man' in 44:23 (B) from 'righteous men' (Syr) but in these cases the adjective expresses a meaning that is clearly understood in the context.[11]

In other cases, however, [Noun [Adjective <sp>]] as a whole corresponds to the noun in Heb and the interpretation of the adjective as a plus can be challenged. In 9:1 the adjective ܒܝܫܬܐ rather than the noun ܡܚܫܒܬܐ transfers the meaning of רעה. In 48:15 ܚܛܗܐ ܣܓܝܐܝܢ—not only ܣܓܝܐܝܢ—is the equivalent of חטאתם. And in 50:1 ܪܒ ܟܗܢܐ—not only ܟܗܢܐ—corresponds to הכהן. The Syriac translator added an adjective to make the meaning of הכהן explicit.[12] That also the Hebrew הכהן refers to the High Priest or הכהן הגדול can be argued on the basis of the following observations: (a) In the Hebrew Bible הכהן 'is frequently used to designate the priest who was at the head of priestly affairs',[13] and thus equivalent to הכהן הגדול.[14] (b) The Hebrew expression גדול אחיו, which opens 50:1 in MS B, is reminiscent of Lev 21:10 הכהן הגדול מאחיו.[15] (c) Heb alludes to the expression הכהן הגדול by the inclusion הכהן ... גדול. Syr, which has ܪܒ ܟܗܢܐ ... ܒܪ ܟܗܢܐ, (with the inclusion of ܒܪ ... ܒܪ) is more explicit.

---

[10] In the light of the correspondences between [Noun [Adjective <sp>]] in Syr and a single noun in Heb, there is no need to assume that the Hebrew source text of the Syriac translator read לאיש צדיק instead of לצדיק (= A) in 13:17 (*pace* Bacher, 'Notes on the Cambridge Fragments', 283) or איש חכם instead of חכם (= C) in 20:7 (*pace* Lévi, *L'Ecclésiastique* II, 123).

[11] In 41:1 the complete phrase is 'the (rich) man who sits on his possessions'; 38:5 deals with the water that was made sweet (Exod 15:23–26); and in 44:23 'a (righteous) man' refers to Moses.

[12] Similarly Gr ἱερεὺς ὁ μέγας.

[13] BDB 464.

[14] The adjective הגדול first appears of Jehoiada in 1 Kgs 2:11; the Priestly Code uses it of Aaron (BDB 464).

[15] Cf. Mulder, *High Priest*, 105–107.

The opposite phenomenon, i.e. Heb has [Noun [Adjective <sp>]] where Syr has a single noun occurs in

39:35 ܫܡܗ 'his name'; B[txt] את שם הקדוש; B[mg] קדשו.[16]
45:26 ܐܠܗܐ 'God'; B את יי הטוב.[17]
46:1 ܦܘܪܩܢܐ 'salvation'; B תשועה גדלה.[18]

A single noun in Syr corresponds to Noun + Adjective in Gr (Heb not extant) in

2:5 ܒܢܝܢܫܐ 'man'; Gr ἄνθρωποι δεκτοί.

The Hebrew evidence is sometimes divided:

9:3 ܙܢܝܬܐ 'a harlot'; A[1] אשה זרה; A[2] זונה.[19]
10:30 ܥܬܝܪܐ 'a rich one'; B איש עשיר; A נכבד.[20]

In the following example a substantivized adjective in Syr corresponds to [Noun [Adjective <sp>]] in Heb:

37:11e ܥ�m ܒܝܫܐ 'with a wicked one'; B+D עם איש רע.[21]

In this case the *Leitwort allgemeiner Bedeutung*[22] איש is left untranslated in Syr.[23]

A number of times [Noun [Adjective <sp>]] corresponds to [CstrNoun–(Abstract) Noun] in Heb,[24] e.g.:

8:16 ܓܒܪܐ ܚܡܬܢܐ 'a wicked man'[25]; A בעל אף.[26]

---

[16] The use of שם as a divine title may be the background of this structure; see Elwolde, 'Use of *ēt*', 172.

[17] הטוב is considered secondary by Peters, *Ben Sirach*, 392–393; Reiterer, *Urtext*, 229; whether the scribe who added הטוב was influenced by 2 Chr 30:18 (cf. Smend, *Jesus Sirach*, 438) cannot be established; cf. Reiterer, ibid.

[18] According to Lévi, *L'Ecclésiastique* I, 110, Gr μέγας ἐπὶ σωτηρίᾳ reflects גדול בישועה.

[19] According to Peters, *Ben Sirach*, 82, the reference to a harlot, although supported by Gr, Syr and A² is secondary: in the present verse אשה זרה is just a wife other than one's own wife (cf. 9:1–2). Only in 8:6 does the harlot appear.

[20] Cf. Schrader, *Verwandtschaft*, 30–32.

[21] Perhaps we should interpret איש רע as elliptical for איש רע עין. For the phrase רע עין see Van Peursen, *Verbal System*, 213; for the elliptical construction see ibid., n. 77.

[22] Cf. Brockelmann, *Hebräische Syntax*, § 63a; cf. Van Peursen, *Verbal System*, 230.

[23] For the opposite phenomenon, where Syr adds ܓܒܪܐ, see above, the beginning of this paragraph.

[24] We regard this as a linguistic phenomenon, rather than an exegetical or interpretative one; cf. § 7.4.3; see also Avinery, *Syntaxe*, 193–194; Weitzman, *Syriac Version*, 25.

9:16 ܐܢܫܐ ܟܐܢܐ 'upright men'; A אנשי צדק.
15:12 ܒܒܪ ܐܢܫܐ ܥܘܠܐ 'in a wicked man'; A+B באנשי חמס.[27]
16:1 ܕܒܢ̈ܝܐ ܚܛ̈ܝܐ 'of sinful sons'; A נערי שוא.
16:9 ܥܡܐ ܚܪܡܐ 'the accursed people'; A גוי חרם.[28]

[Noun [Adjective <sp>]] corresponds to a genitive construction in Gr (Heb not extant) in

23:15 ܡ̈ܠܐ ܒ̈ܛܠܬܐ 'idle words'; Gr λόγοις ὀνειδισμοῦ (= דברי חרפה[29]).

With ܕ + Adjective (cf. § 10.2.3) we find

9:8 ܒܐܢܬܬܐ ܕܫܦܝܪܐ 'at a beautiful woman'; A אשת חן.

Sometimes the Syriac construction [Noun [Adjective <sp>]] has a different meaning from the genitive construction in Heb or Gr, e.g.:

31:23 ܣܗܕܘܬܐ ܛܒܬܐ 'a good testimony'; B עדות טובו; Gr ἡ μαρτυρία τῆς καλλονῆς αὐτοῦ 'the testimony of his goodness'.[30]

Syr does not have [Noun [Adjective <sp>]] in each case where Heb has [CstrNoun–(Abstract) Noun]. The 'regular' correspondence of [CstrNoun–(Abstract) Noun] in Heb with [CstrNoun –Noun] or [Noun [*d*-Noun <sp>] in Syr is attested in

5:8 ܥܠ ܢܟ̈ܣܐ ܕܥܘܠܐ 'upon wealth of iniquity'; A על נכסי שקר.[31]
15:2 ܘܐܝܟ ܐܢܬܬ ܥܠܝܡܘܬܐ 'and like a youthful wife'; A+B וכאשת נעורים.

---

[25] Thus 7a1 7h3 and 8a1*; ܓܒܪܐ does not occur in 9c1 10c1.2 11c1 12a1*fam* →.

[26] Cf. § 3.1 (a). Note that what has been characterized there as 'Syr provides a free rendering of an idiomatic Hebrew expression' appears to belong to a more widespread pattern of corresponding phrase structures. There is no need to assume that the Syriac translator's *Vorlage* was difficult to read; *pace* Ryssel, 'Fragmente', VI, 248.

[27] Cf. § 3.1 (a). Note that what has been characterized there as 'Syr provides a free rendering of an idiomatic Hebrew expression' appears to belong to a more widespread pattern of corresponding phrase structures. There is no need to assume that the Syriac translator's *Vorlage* was difficult to read; *pace* Ryssel, 'Fragmente', VI, 248.For ܒܪ ܐܢܫܐ corresponding to אנש cf. § 9.2.

[28] Cf. also 15:8 ܘܐܡܪ̈ܝܢ ܒܝܫܬܐ 'and those who speak evil' corresponding to אנשי כזב in MS A. Since the pattern [CstrNoun – (Abstract) Noun] is resolved quite frequently, there is no compelling reason to assume that in this case the Syriac translator had a different Hebrew source text (reading ודוברי רע); *pace* Ginzberg, 'Randglossen', 622.

[29] Thus Smend, *Jesus Sirach*, 209; Peters, *Ben Sirach*, 189.

[30] Segal (*Sefer Ben Sira*, 199) suggests that the Syriac translator read טובה instead of טובו. Ryssel ('Fragmente', II, 85) thinks that the reading in Syr is the result of an inner-Syriac corruption.

[31] Schechter and Taylor (*Wisdom of Ben Sira*, xix) refer to ܡܡܘܢܐ ܕܥܘܠܗ in Luke 16:9–11.

There are even some examples of the opposite phenomenon, i.e.
[CstrNoun–(Abstract) Noun] or [Noun [*d*-(Abstract) Noun <sp>]] in
Syr corresponds to [Noun [Adjective <sp>]] in Heb:[32]

43:2 ܐܢܐܕ ܕܓܐܡܗܬܐ 'a marvellous vessel (a vessel of marvel)'; M כלי
נורא.

Other patterns of correspondence are attested as well. Thus [Noun
[Adjective <sp>]] in Syr corresponds to [Noun [*w*-<cj>] [Noun
<PA>]] in Heb in

40:20 ܚܡܪܐ ܥܬܝܩܐ 'old wine'; B יין ושכר.[33]

And to [CstrNoun–Noun [*w*-<cj>] [CstrNoun–Noun <PA>]] in

4:1 ܠܚܫܘܟܐ ܣܘܕܐ 'a poor and obscure man'[34]; A נפש עני ומר נפש.[35]

Sometimes the Hebrew evidence is divided. Thus one Hebrew manuscript has [Noun [*w*-<cj>] [Noun <PA>]] and another [Noun [Adjec-
tive <sp>]] in

10:22 ܬܘܬܒܐ ܢܘܟܪܝܐ 'a foreign sojourner'; A גר וזד; B גר זר.[36]

If the adjective follows a head consisting of [CstrNoun–Noun], it always modifies the head as a whole, not just the second element, e.g.:

16:4 ܕܒܢܝܢܫܐ ܥܘܠܐ 'of wicked sons of man'.
19:15 ܡܐܟܠܬܐ ܕܦܪ̈ܬܐ ܣܪ̈ܝܬܐ 'worthless slandering (lit. eating of broken morsels)'.

---

[32] Compare also 50:6 ܐܝܟ ܟܘܟܒܐ ܕܢܘܓܗܐ, corresponding to B ככוכב אור. In this example אור can be interpreted either as 'genitive' noun (cf. Ps 148:3 כוכבי אור and Job 38:7 כוכבי בקר) or as an attributive participle. Gr (ὡς ἀστὴρ ἑωθινός) and Syr understood it in the first way, but the second interpretation is possible as well, compare 13:26 (A) פנים אורים; Smend (*Jesus Sirach*, 482) and Peters (*Ben Sirach*, 428) prefer the latter interpretation.

[33] יין ושכר also occurs in 40:18 in MS B, where M has יתר שכר in a line that is missing in Syr; cf. Kister, 'Contribution', 348–349; in Pesh-Num 28:7 ܚܠܐ corresponds to שכר in MT.

[34] Thus *CSD* 162.

[35] According to Peters, *Ben Sirach*, 38, the repetition of נפש is strange, and the first נפש should be omitted with Gr and Syr. However, it cannot be concluded from Syr that the translator's source text did not contain the first נפש; cf. § 9.2; for the expression מר נפש, see Van Peursen, *Verbal System*, 213.

[36] Ginzberg, who had only MS B, suggested that Syr read וזד and explained it according to Prov 21:8 איש וזר; Ginzberg, 'Randglossen', 620; it is a disputed issue whether in Prov 21:8 וזר is the conjunction ו + זר (thus Ehrlich, *Randglossen*, VI, 22) or an adjective וזר (cf. *HALOT* 259).

Accordingly, there are no examples where, for example, 'the beauty of a good woman' is expressed by *ܫܘܦܪ ܐܢܬܬܐ ܛܒܬܐ (cf. 26:16 ܫܘܦܪܗ ܕܐܢܬܬܐ ܛܒܬܐ, quoted below, § 10.2.2 [2]).

10.1.2 *Adjective preceding the head*

Sometimes the adjective precedes the noun. In Syr there occur three examples with ܣܓܝ.[37]

11:5 ܣܓܝܐܐ ܫܝܛܐ 'many despised'.
11:6 ܣܓܝܐܐ ܡܠܟܐ 'many kings'.
29:4 ܣܓܝܐܐ ܓܝܪ ܝܙܘܦܐ 'many borrowers'.

Since ܣܓܝܐܐ in 29:4 has the emphatic state, it is preferable to analyse it as a modifier to ܝܙܘܦܐ rather than the predicate of a clause of which ܝܙܘܦܐ is the subject.[38] The whole verse runs as follows:[39]

29:4 ܣܓܝܐܐ ܓܝܪ ܝܙܘܦܐ ܕܒܥܘ ܝܙܦܬܐ ܘܐܗܪܘ ܠܡܘܙܦܢܝܗܘܢ
[SGJ>> <sp>] [GJR <Cj>] [JZWP> <Su>]]
[D-<Re>] [B<W <Pr>] [JZPT> <Ob>]
[W-<Cj>] [>HRW <PC>] [L-MWZPNJHWN <Co>]
'For there are many borrowers who have asked a loan and did harm[40] to their lenders.'

In 11:5 and 11:6 too we find 'there are many…':

11:5 ܣܓܝܐܐ ܫܝܛܐ ܕܝܬܒܘ ܥܠ ܟܘܪܣܝܐ ܕܡܠܟܘܬܐ
[[SGJ>> <sp>] CJV> <Su>]
[D-<Re>] [JTBW <Pr>] [<L KWRSJ> [D-MLKWT> <sp>] <Aj>]
'There are many despised who sit on the royal throne.'

11:6 ܣܓܝܐܐ ܡܠܟܐ ܕܐܨܛܥܪܘ ܐܝܟ ܚܕܐ
[[SGJ>> <sp>] MLK> <Su>]
[D-<Re>] [>YV<RW <Pr>] [>JK XD> <Aj>]
'There are many kings who have suffered dishonour together.'

---

[37] Cf. Nöldeke, *Grammatik*, § 211B; Muraoka, *Classical Syriac for Hebraists*, § 76.

[38] In Syr the predicative ܣܓܝ has always the absolute state, e.g.: 3:19 ܡܛܠ ܕܣܓܝܐܝܢ ܐܝܟ ܪ̈ܚܡܘܗܝ ܕܐܠܗܐ. Other examples in 3:24; 6:6; 11:29; 11:30; 13:22; 16:5; 16:12; 17:29; 28:18; 30:24; 36:25; 39:20. See further § 20.1.

[39] For the intervening ܓܝܪ see § 13.2 (4).

[40] We interpret ܐܗܪܘ as an Aphel of ܗܪܪ; Winter (*Concordance*, 392) analyses it as an Aphel of ܢܗܪ (= 'to enlighten or shine brightly').

Compare 34:7, where ܣܓܝܐܐ is not followed by a noun:

34:7 ܣܓܝܐܐ ܓܝܪ ܛܥܘ ܒܚܠܡܝܗܘܢ ܘܐܫܪܘ ܘܗܠܟܘ ܒܫܒܝܠܝܗܘܢ

[SGJ>> <PC>] [GJR <Cj>]

   [D-<Re>] [B-XLM> <Aj>] [V<W <Pr>] [>WRX> <Ob>]

     [W-<Cj>] [>TTQLW <Pr>] [B-CBJLJHWN <Aj>]

'There are many who have erred through dreams and they stumbled on their roads.'

In 11:5 and 11:6 Heb is available in MS A. In both cases the adjective רבים precedes the noun as well.[41]

In addition to the three examples in which ܣܓܝ precedes its head, there are thirteen cases where it follows the noun.[42] Thus even with this adjective the post-position is more frequent.

In Classical Syriac also the adjective ܐܚܪܝܢ often precedes the noun it modifies. In Syr it occurs once as a modifier of a noun, in which case it follows the noun:

42:10 ܒܬܪ ܓܒܪܐ ܐܚܪܢܐ 'after another man'.

In this respect Syr agrees with the situation in the Old Syriac versions of Matthew, in which the ante-position of ܣܓܝ is well-attested, but that of ܐܚܪܝܢ is rare. The ante-position of ܐܚܪܝܢ is more frequent in the Peshitta of Matthew.[43] There is also one example with undeclined ܩܠܝܠ preceding the noun,[44] namely in

11:32 ܡܢ ܩܠܝܠ ܣܝܘܡܐ 'from a little tow'.

---

[41] Cf. Van Peursen, *Verbal System*, 282 n. 31.

[42] 2:12; 16:3; 16:17; 24:32; 27:3; 29:5; 29:19; 29:22; 32:16; 34:12; 34:13; 37:29; 37:31.

[43] Joosten, *Syriac Language*, 73–75, 147. See also idem, 'Ante-Position of the Attributive Adjective'; in this article Joosten demonstrates that in both Classical Syriac and Biblical Hebrew the adjective may be positioned before the substantive if the latter has little or no informative value; cf. below, § 10.1.1 on the use of a *Leitwort allgemeiner Bedeutung* (Brockelmann); on Biblical Hebrew see Waltke–O'Connor, *Biblical Hebrew Syntax*, § 14.3.1b. In the Peshitta to the Pentateuch ܣܓܝ always follows the noun, see Avinery, *Syntax*, 200–201; Borbone–Jenner, *Concordance* I, 583.

[44] Cf. Nöldeke, *Grammatik*, § 215: ܣܓܝ and ܩܠܝܠ 'bleiben oft, vor- oder nachstehend, adverbial unverändert'. For examples from the Peshitta to the Pentateuch see Avinery, *Syntax*, 201; Borbone–Jenner, *Concordance* I, 743.

10.1.3 *Adjective extended*

The adjective may be extended by the following elements.

1. A parallel element:

> 25:2 ܣܒ ܣܟܠܐ ܘܚܣܝܪ ܪܥܝܢܐ 'an old man who is foolish and void of understanding'.
> 26:8 ܐܢܬܬܐ ܪܘܝ ܘܡܫܢܝܐ 'a drunken and roaming wife'.

In our corpus we find no other patterns in which the attributive adjective takes an extension (e.g. [Noun [Adjective [Adverb <sp>] <sp>]]). There are cases, however, where a predicative adjective is followed by a specification. Accordingly, the sections 2 to 5 below contain only examples with predicative adjectives.

2. An adverb:

> 22:14 ܡܢ ܐܒܪܐ ܝܬܝܪ ܣܓܝ ܝܩܝܪ 'much heavier than lead'.
> 22:18 ܘܡܕܡ ܕܩܠ ܠܗ 'and what is very light'.

3. A prepositional phrase:

> 38:18 ܚܝܝ ܡܢ ܡܘܬܐ 'more than death'.[45]

4. A preposition with an infinitive:

> 14:16 ܠܗ ܟܠ ܕܫܦܝܪ ܠܡܥܒܕ 'everything that is beautiful to do'.

5. An interrogative modifier:

> 41:1 ܡܐ ܒܝܫ 'how evil!'
> 48:4 ܡܐ ܕܚܝܠ 'how awesome!'[46]

It is remarkable that there are so few examples of Noun + Adjective + Specification. A possible explanation for the low number of examples may be the fact that if the adjective has further specifications the construction with ܕ + adjective is more frequent (§ 10.2.3).

---

[45] The construction with ܡܢ expresses the comparative degree; Muraoka, *Basic Grammar*, § 96c.

[46] Other examples in 25:5; 37:9; 41:2; 46:2; 47:14; 50:5.

10.2 *d*-PHRASE

10.2.1 *Basic patterns*

The basic pattern is

[Noun [*d*-Noun <sp>]]

This pattern is abundantly attested, e.g.:

17:2 ܡܢܝܢܐ ܕܝܘܡܬܐ 'the number of days'.
17:11 ܢܡܘܣܐ ܕܚܝܐ 'the law of life'.

In many cases [Noun [*d*-Noun <sp>]] in Syr corresponds to [ConstrNoun–Noun] in Heb,[47] but other patterns of correspondence are attested as well. Thus [Noun [*d*-Noun <sp>]] corresponds to a single noun in Heb in, e.g.:[48]

11:5 ܥܠ ܟܘܪܣܝܐ ܕܡܠܟܘܬܐ 'on a royal throne (a throne of kingdom)'; A על כסא.

13:2 ܡܐܢ ܕܦܚܪܐ 'a pot of earth ware'; A פרור.

13:2 ܠܩܕܣܐ ܕܢܚܫܐ 'to a cauldron of brass'; A אל סיר.

16:17 ܒܪܘܡܐ ܕܫܡܝܐ 'in the height of heaven'; A ובמרום.

32:13 ܫܡܗ ܕܐܠܗܐ 'the name of God'; B+F עושך.

33:16 ܐܝܟ ܡܒܬܟܢܐ ܕܟܪܡܐ 'like a gleaner of the vineyard'; E וכמו עולל.

36:20 ܣܗܕܘܬܐ ܕܥܒܕܐ 'the testimony of year servants'; B עדות.[49]

37:29 ܡܐܟܠܬܐ ܕܦܐܩܘܬܐ 'luxurious food (food of luxury)'; B^{bxt+mg}+D תענוג.[50]

40:3 ܟܘܪܣܘܬܐ ܕܡܠܟܐ 'the thrones of kings'; B כסא.

46:11 ܡܢ ܢܡܘܣܐ ܕܐܠܗܐ 'from the Law of God'; B מאחרי אל.

50:22 ܡܢ ܟܪܣܐ ܕܐܡܗܘܢ 'from their mother's womb'; B מרחם.

---

[47] Cf. Reiterer, *Urtext*, 55–56; Avinery, 'Influence of Hebrew on the Peshitta Translation', discerns a tendency to translate [CstrNoun–Noun] with [CstrNoun–Noun] on its first occurrence, but thereafter with [Noun [*d*-Noun <sp>]], but we did not find any examples of this phenomenon in Sirach. See also Weitzman, *Syriac Version*, 31. Variation between [CstrNoun–Noun] and [Noun [*d*-Noun <sp>]] in Syriac manuscripts occurs in 4:6, 9:13, 28:10, 36:27 and 50:11, but we cannot discern a tendency that a certain manuscript or text type prefers one construction to the other.

[48] Note also the examples given under § 3.2 (i) 'Syr adds an explanatory word or phrase'.

[49] Cf. Ryssel, 'Fragmente', IV, 286–287: 'Was S dafür hat, erklärt sich am einfachsten so, daß dieser עֵדוּת konkret faßte, indem er zugleich dem Worte kollektive Bedeutung beilegte oder auch vielleicht schon das hebr. Textwort als plur. עֵדְוֹת las, und auf die Bezeugungen Gottes durch die Propheten, "seine Knechte" (...), bezog.'

[50] Cf. מאכל תענוג in 37:20 (B+D).

[Noun [*d*-Noun <sp>]] corresponds to a single noun in Gr (Heb not extant) in

27:9 ܦܪܚܬܐ ܕܫܡܝܐ 'a bird of heaven'; Gr πετεινά.
28:23 ܕܚܠܬܗ ܕܐܠܗܐ 'the fear of God'; Gr κύριον.

The examples given here include a number of phenomena discussed in various places in Part One, but all belonging to the same pattern of correspondence between Heb and Syr. The addition of 'of earthenware' and 'of brass' in 13:2 may have had the function of making explicit what kind of vessels were meant, but it does not add information that is not implicit in the words used (§ 3.2 [i]); 'bird of heaven' (27:9) does not give additional semantic information compared with 'bird', nor does 'their mother's womb' (50:22) compared with 'the womb'. 'Royal throne' as a translation of 'throne' (11:5; 40:3) is a so-called targumic feature (§ 3.8), but the pattern of correspondence does not differ from the other examples. The same applies to the 'anti-anthropomorphisms' in 28:23, 32:13 and 46:11, where a reference to God has been replaced by one to his fear, his name or his law (§ 3.3 [b]).[51]

Occasionally Syr reflects a wrong interpretation of an ambiguous construction in Heb, e.g.:

36:24 ܠܒܐ ܕܚܟܝܡܐ 'the heart of the wise'; B לב מבין 'an understanding heart'.[52]

In other cases Syr has [Noun [*d*-Noun <sp>]] where Heb has two parallel nouns:

13:26 ܣܘ ܣܓܐܬ ܕܡܡܠܠܐ 'much talking'; A ושיג ישיח (read ושיג ושיח).[53]
45:8 ܠܒܘܫܐ ܕܥܘܫܢܐ 'vestments of strength'; cf. Gr σκεύεσιν ἰσχύος; B בכבוד ועוז.[54]

---

[51] For inner-Syriac variation where some witnesses have a specification of the type *d*-Noun that does not occur in other witnesses, see § 9.1.

[52] The opposite phenomenon is attested as well: In 41:6 ܡܢ ܒܪ ܥܘܠܐ 'from an unrighteous son', the Syriac translator missed the construct state in מבן עול 'from a son of an unrighteous one' (thus Smend, *Jesus Sirach*, 324).

[53] Perhaps the Syriac translator interpreted שיג according to Syriac ܣܘܐܬ, cf. § 3.4 (d).

[54] Bacher, 'Hebrew Text of Ecclesiasticus', 553, prefers the reading of Gr and Syr. According to Reiterer, *Urtext*, 154–156, the Syriac translator read כלי instead of B's כבוד in his Hebrew source.

[Noun [*d*-Noun <sp>]] corresponds to [Noun [Adjective <sp>]] in Heb in

48:24 ܒܪܘܚܐ ܕܓܢܒܪܘܬܐ ‘in the spirit of strength’; B ברוח גבורה.[55]

Since we take phrase atoms rather than words as the minimal building blocks of phrases (§ 9.1), structures with phrase atoms consisting of more than one word belong here as well. This concerns those cases where either the *d*-phrase or the element modified by the *d*-phrase contains a construct chain. Both structures occur in our corpus.

1. The *d*-phrase contains a construct chain,[56] i.e.

[Noun [*d*-CstrNoun–Noun <sp>]]:

2:11 ܠܩܠܐ ܕܥܒ̈ܕܝ ܨܒܝܢܗ ‘to the voice of those who do His will’.
35:16 ܒܥܘܬܐ ܕܟܪܝܗܝ ܪܘܚܐ ‘the request of the grieved of spirit’.
39:14 ܘܐܝܟ ܥܩܪܐ ܕܫܘܫܢܬ ܡܠܟܐ ‘and like the root of the lily of the king’.
49:4 ܡ̈ܠܟܐ ܕܒܝܬ ܝܗܘܕܐ ‘the kings of the house of Judah’.

A numbcr of times the construction [Noun [*d*-CstrNoun–Noun <sp>]] corresponds to a chain with two construct nouns in Heb:

3:24 ܪ̈ܢܝܗܘܢ ܕܒܢ̈ܝܢܫܐ ‘the thoughts of men’; A עשתוני בני אדם.

In other cases the Syriac construction corresponds to a chain with one construct noun in Heb, e.g.:

41:11 ܫܡܐ ܕܥܒ̈ܕܝ ܛ̈ܒܬܐ ‘the name of those who do good things’; B+M שם חסד.

With ܟܠ and ܒܪ ܢܫܐ there occur chains with two construct nouns (§ 9.2), i.e.

[Noun [*d*-CstrNoun–CstrNoun–Noun <sp>]]:

23:19 ܐܘܪ̈ܚܬܐ ܕܟܠ ܒܢ̈ܝܢܫܐ ‘the ways of all men’.
39:19 ܥܒ̈ܕܝܗܘܢ ܕܟܠ ܒ̈ܢܝ ܒܣܪܐ ‘all the works of the men of flesh’.

---

[55] Contrast those cases where Syr has [Noun [Adjective <sp>]] corresponding to [CstrNoun–(Abstract) Noun] in Heb (§ 10.1.1). On the expression used in Heb, see Kister, ‘Contribution’, 371–372; in 2 Chr 20:14 ܪܘܚܐ ܕܓܢܒܪܘܬܐ ܡܢ ܩܕܡ ܡܪܝܐ corresponds to רוח יהוה in the Hebrew; see Kister, ibid.

[56] Noun phrases with the pattern [Noun [*d*-CstrNoun–Noun <sp>]] also occur in 15:19 and 42:18, where they stand in apposition to another word; see § 10.3.2 (2).

In 23:19 the Hebrew text is not available. In 39:19 MS B has a chain with two construct nouns: מעשה כל בשר.

2. The head that is modified by the *d*-phrase contains a construct chain, i.e.

[CstrNoun–Noun [*d*-Noun <sp>]]:

25:12 ܪܝܫ ܕܕܚܠܬܗ ܕܡܪܝܐ 'the beginning of fear of the Lord'.
38:25 ܐܚܝܕ ܚܪܒܐ ܕܦܕܢܐ 'one who holds the ploughshare'.[57]
40:3 ܡܢ ܝܬܒܝ ܟܘܪܣܘܬܐ ܕܡ̈ܠܟܐ 'from those who sit on royal thrones'. [58]

This pattern occurs a number of times with ܟܠ:

1:20e ܟܠ ܬܫܒܘܚܬܗ ܕܡܪܝܐ 'all the praise of the Lord'.
16:1 ܟܠ ܒ̈ܢܝܐ ܕܫܘܩܪܐ 'all sons of falsehood'.
16:27 ܠܟܠ ܕܪ̈ܐ ܕܥܠܡܐ 'to all the generations of the world'.
39:2 ܕܟܠ ܐܢܫܐ ܕܥܠܡܐ 'of every man of the world'.[59]
45:26 ܠܟܠ ܕܪ̈ܐ ܕܥܠܡܐ 'to all the generations of the world'.[60]
50:27 ܟܠ ܡܬܠܐ ܕܚܟ̈ܝܡܐ 'all the proverbs of the wise'.[61]

In 1:20 there is no corresponding text in either Heb or Gr. In 16:27 and 39:2, where there is no corresponding Hebrew text, ܟܠ is a plus compared with Gr. In 16:1, 45:26 and 50:27 ܟܠ is a plus vis-à-vis Heb as well as Gr.[62]

In the pattern [CstrNoun–Noun [*d*-Noun <sp>]] the *d*-phrase modifies the *nomen rectum* rather than the complete head. This is evident in 25:12, 29:21, 38:25, 40:3 and the examples with ܟܠ, and it is likely in the other examples. Accordingly, both

[CstrNoun–Noun [*d*-Noun <sp>] and
[Noun [*d*-CstrNoun–Noun <sp>]]

---

[57] Heb (B) has only תומך מלמד.
[58] Heb (B) has מיושב כסא לגבה 'who sits on the throne in exultation'.
[59] Preceded by ܫܘܥܝ̈ܬܐ; see below, § 10.2.2 (3).
[60] Heb (B) has לדורות עולם, but Gr reflects לדורותם, see § 2.2.2 (end).
[61] Followed by ܘܐܘܚ̈ܕܬܗܘܢ; see below, at the end of this paragraph.
[62] According to Kearns the emphasis on *all* people etc., is a typical feature of SirII; see his *Expanded Text*, 29 (on GrII) and 61–62 (on Syr); cf. § 2.4.1. Note also the addition of ܟܠ in 42:18 in B (also in Syr; M does not have it). The examples from Gr and Heb suggest that the addition of 'all' is not characteristic of Syr, but rather of SirII. However, for the addition of ܟܠ in e.g. ܟܠܗ ܐܝܣܪܝܠ '*all* Israel' (45:16; B בני ישראל) there are some parallels in other parts of the Peshitta; cf. Weitzman, *From Judaism to Christianity*, 98. Accordingly, this phenomenon belongs to the features that Syr shares both with SirII and with other parts of the Peshitta (§ 2.4.1).

are used to say 'A of B (modifying A) of C (modifying B)'.[63] From this observation it seems justified to consider both constructions as equivalent to the Hebrew construction

[CstrNoun–CstrNoun–Noun]

However, in our corpus there occur only examples where this Hebrew construction corresponds to the pattern [Noun [d-CstrNoun–Noun <sp>]]. There are also instances of the pattern [CstrNoun–Noun [d-Noun <sp>]] in Syr, but as far as it occurs in passages for which the Hebrew text is also extant, Syr has a plus vis-à-vis Heb.[64]

When two nouns are modified by the same d-phrase, the d-phrase follows the first noun, and is resumed by a suffix attached to the second noun, e.g.:

    46:10 ܡܘ̈ܗܝ ܪܡܠܐܪܝ ܡܘ̈ܗܝ 'God's law and His judgments'.
    50:27 ܘܐܘܚܕܬܗܘܢ ܕܚ̈ܟܝܡܐ ܟܠܗ ܡܬ̈ܠܐ 'all the proverbs of the wise and their riddles'.
    51:8 ܘܛܝܒܘܬܗ ܕܡܪܝܐ ܚܢܢܗ 'the mercy of the Lord and His goodness'.

A similar construction is found in Hebrew when two nouns are modified by the same 'genitive', e.g. 51:8 (B). רחמי ייי וחסדיו. With this pattern one can contrast the pattern

[CstrNoun–Noun] [w-<cj>] [Noun [d-Noun <sp>] <PA>]:

    36:11 ܕܥܡܐ ܫ̈ܠܝܛܐ ܘܪܝܫ̈ܐ ܟܠ 'all the leaders and rulers of the people'.

In the light of the data presented above, we analyse ܕܥܡܐ as a specification of ܫ̈ܠܝܛܐ rather than one to both ܪܝܫ̈ܐ and ܫ̈ܠܝܛܐ.

---

[63] Cf. Nöldeke, *Grammatik*, § 205D, on examples in which several types of 'genitive connections' occur together ('Beispiele, in denen mehrere Arten der Genitivverbindung zusammenstehen'). We shall see below, in § 10.2.2 (3), that the pattern [Noun [d-Noun [d-Noun <sp>] <sp>]] fulfils the same function.
[64] A number of those pluses concern the addition of ܟܠ, which may have theological significance; cf. above, note 62.

10.2.2 d-*phrase extended*

The *d*-phrase may itself be extended by an apposition, an adjective or a *d*-phrase.

1. Apposition.[65] The basic pattern is

[Noun [*d*-Noun [Noun <ap>] <sp>]]:

47:5 ܩܪܢܐ ܕܥܡܗ ܐܝܣܪܝܠ 'the horn of his people Israel'.[66]

To this pattern also belong constructions with ܟܠ + suffix followed by an apposition, i.e.

[Noun [*d-kl*+suffix [Noun <ap>] <sp>]]:

5:3 ܬܒܘܥܐ ܗܘ ܕܟܠܗܘܢ ܥܠܘ̈ܒܐ '(The Lord is) an avenger of all oppressed'.
18:24 ܒܚܪܬܐ ܗܘ ܕܟܠܗܘܢ ܚܛ̈ܗܐ '(Anger is) in the end of all sins'.
39:1 ܐܝܟ ܚܟܡܬܐ ܕܟܠܗܘܢ ܩܕ̈ܡܝܐ 'like the wisdom of all who were before him'.

With [Noun [*d-kl*+suffix [CstrNoun–Noun <ap>] <sp>]] we find

7:17 ܚܪܬܐ ܕܟܠܗܘܢ ܒܢ̈ܝܢܫܐ 'the end of men' (similarly 41:4).
16:17 ܒܝܬ ܪ̈ܘܚܬܐ ܕܟܠܗܘܢ ܒܢ̈ܝܢܫܐ 'among the spirits of all men'.
17:20 ܘܚܛ̈ܗܐ ܕܟܠܗܘܢ ܒܢ̈ܝܢܫܐ 'and the sins of all men'.
17:22a ܙܕܩܘܬܐ ܕܟܠܗܘܢ ܒܢ̈ܝܢܫܐ 'the justification of all men'.
17:22b ܛܝܒܘܬܐ ܕܟܠܗܘܢ ܒܢ̈ܝܢܫܐ 'the goodness of all men'.

In 16:17, 39:1 and 41:40 'all' also occurs in Heb and/or G, but in 5:3, 7:7, 17:22a, 22b and 18:24 ܟܠܗܘܢ is a plus in Syr. In 17:20 Syr has 'the sins of all people' instead of Gr 'all the sins of the people'. ܟܠܗܘܢ ܒܢ̈ܝܢܫܐ also occurs in 7:7, 16:17, 17:22a, 22b. The emphasis on '*all* people' may be part of a universalizing tendency in Syr.[67]

More complex patterns occur when the apposition is extended by further specifications. Thus the apposition is specified by a relative clause in

---

[65] Compare the combination of a construct chain with an apposition in the pattern [Prep–CstrNoun–ProperNoun [Noun <ap>]] in 48:20 ܒܐܝܕ ܐܫܥܝܐ ܢܒܝܐ; see below, § 10.3.1.
[66] In this case the apposition ܐܝܣܪܝܠ is a plus compared with Heb (MS B קרן עמו) and Gr (κέρας λαοῦ αὐτοῦ).
[67] Cf. above, note 62.

36:20 ܢܒܝܘܬܐ ܕܢܒܝܝܟ ܐܝܠܝܢ ܕܡܡܠܠܝܢ ܒܫܡܟ ‘the prophecies of your prophets who speak in your name’.[68]

2. Adjective. The basic pattern is

[Noun [*d*-Noun [Adjective <sp>] <sp>]]

This pattern is attested fifteen times. Two examples:

16:1 ܠܣܘܓܐ ܕܒܢܝܐ ܚܛܝܐ ‘for a multitude of sinful sons’.[69]
26:16 ܫܘܦܪܗ ܕܐܢܬܬܐ ܛܒܬܐ ‘the beauty of a good woman’.[70]

This pattern often corresponds to the Hebrew pattern

[CstrNoun–Noun [Adjective <sp>]]:

13:26 ܥܩܒܬܗ ܕܠܒܐ ܛܒܐ ‘the marks of a good heart’; A עקבת לב טוב.

But sometimes the adjective is a plus in Syr. Compare

25:17 ܒܝܫܘܬܗ ܕܐܢܬܬܐ ܒܝܫܬܐ ‘the evil of an evil woman’; C רע אשה; Gr πονηρία γυναικός.
25:21 ܠܫܘܦܪܗ ܕܐܢܬܬܐ ܒܝܫܬܐ ‘the beauty of an evil woman’; C אש[ה]; Gr ἐπὶ κάλλος γυναικός.[71]

In other cases ܕ is followed by a general word such as ܐܢܫܐ or ܓܒܪܐ with an adjective, corresponding to a substantivized adjective in Heb and/or Gr,[72] e.g.:

4:3 ܡܥܘܗܝ ܕܐܢܫܐ ܡܣܟܢܐ ‘the inner parts of the poor man’; A קרב עני; cf. Gr καρδίαν παρωργισμένην.
16:4 ܡܢ ܣܘܓܐ ܕܒܢܝܢܫܐ ܥܘܠܐ ‘from a multitude of wicked men’; A ממשפחת בגדים; B[1] ממשפחות בוגדים; B[2] ממשפחת בוגדים; Gr φυλὴ δὲ ἀνόμων.

---

[68] Cf. Heb (B) חזון דבר בשמך; Gr προφητείας τὰς ἐπ’ ὀνόματί σου; Syr expands on the succinct style of Heb (cf. § 3.2 [k]).

[69] Heb (A) has תואר נערי שוא. Accordingly, Syr has ܣܘܓܐ where A has תואר, but the meaning of the two words is different. The absence of an equivalent for תואר in Syr may be a simplification and the addition of ܣܘܓܐ may be inspired by the context; cf. Ryssel, ‘Fragmente’, II, 523: ‘Das Textwort “Menge” in G und S braucht nicht auf ein entsprechendes Textwort im Urtexte (תַּרְבּוּת “Brut” nach S.–T.?) zurückzugehen, sondern kann Hinzufügung sein, um den in dem Plural נערי liegenden Sinn unzweideutig zum Ausdruck zu bringen’; *pace* Schechter–Taylor, *Wisdom of Ben Sira*, 52.

[70] Syr ‘so is the beauty of a good woman’ corresponds to Gr κάλλος ἀγαθῆς γυναικός. Heb (C) is damaged; it seems to contain a predicative adjective: יפה א]שה] ‘A wife is beautiful…’.

[71] In these verses the addition of the adjective in Syr weakens their misogynist tone, see § 4.1 (2).

[72] Cf. above, § 10.1.1.

25:20 ܒܝܬ ܪ̈ܓܠܘܗܝ ܕܓܒܪܐ ܩܫܝܫܐ 'at the feet of an old man'; Gr ἐν ποσὶν πρεσβυτέρου.
31:12 ܥܠ ܦܬܘܪܗ ܕܓܒܪܐ ܥܬܝܪܐ 'at the table of a rich man'; Gr ἐπὶ τραπέζης μεγάλης ἐκάθισας.[73]

3. ܕ + Noun. The basic pattern is

[Noun [*d*-Noun [*d*-Noun <sp>] <sp>]]

This pattern occurs sixteen times in Syr. Some examples:

35:20 ܡܪܝܪܐ ܕܢܦܫܗ ܕܡܣܟܢܐ 'the bitterness of the soul of a poor man'.[74]
43:8 ܡܐܢܐ ܕܡܫܪܝܬܐ ܕܪܘܡܐ 'a vessel of the host of heaven'.[75]
44:5 ܒܟܬܒܐ ܕܐ̈ܢܫܐ ܕܬܘܩܦܐ 'in the book of men of strength'.[76]

Like the patterns [Noun [*d*-CstrNoun–Noun <sp>]] and [CstrNoun–Noun [*d*-Noun <sp>]], discussed in § 10.2.1, the construction with two *d*-phrases occurs often where Heb has two construct nouns, i.e. [CstrNoun–CstrNoun–Noun], e.g.:

41:12 ܡܢ ܐ̈ܠܦܐ ܕܣܝ̈ܡܬܐ ܕܕܗܒܐ 'than thousands of treasures of gold'; B מאלפי אוצרות חכמה; B^mg סומות חמדה.
44:19 ܐܒܐ ܕܟܢ̈ܘܫܬܐ ܕܥ̈ܡܡܐ 'the father of the communities of the people; B אב המון גוים.

In other cases the Syriac construction corresponds to [CstrNoun–Noun] in Heb or Gr, one of the two *d*-phrases in Syr being a plus, e.g.:

16:8 ܥܠ ܥܡܘܪ̈ܐ ܕܡܕܝܢܬܗ ܕܠܘܛ 'on the inhabitants of the city of Lot'; A מגורי לוט; cf. Gr τῆς παροικίας Λωτ.
47:16 ܘܒܪܘܡܐ ܕܐܝܩܪܐ ܕܡ̈ܠܟܐ 'and with the height of the honour of kings'; B במרום שירה.

There is also one example with CstrNoun–Noun in the first specification, i.e.

[Noun [*d*-CstrNoun–Noun [*d*-Noun <sp>] <sp>]]:

39:2 ܫܘ̈ܥܝܬܐ ܕܟܠ ܐ̈ܢܫܐ ܕܥܠܡܐ 'the discourses of all men of the world'.[77]

---

[73] Heb (B) has שלחן גדול, with איש added in the margin.
[74] ܕܡܣܟܢܐ is a plus compared with B and comes from 35:21; cf. § 3.7.1.
[75] Heb (B+M) has כלי צבא נבלי מרום, i.e. [CstrNoun–Noun [CstrNoun–Noun <ap>]]. Neither Syr nor Gr has an equivalent for the Hebrew נבלי.
[76] In Heb (B[+M]) we find at the end of 44:5 נושאי משל בכתב and in 44:6 אנשי חיל. The addition of ܕ between ܒܟܬܒܐ and ܐ̈ܢܫܐ ܕܬܘܩܦܐ results in a completely different arrangement of the clauses in this section.

In this example the second *d*-phrase specifies the *nomen rectum* of the first specification, which agrees with our observations in § 10.2.1 (2).

4. ܕ + Adjective. This would result in the pattern

[Noun [*d*-Noun [*d*-{[Adjective <PC>]} <sp>]]

But in the only possible example of this pattern, 4:2 ܪܘܚܗ ܕܐܢܫܐ ܕܡܬܒܪܐ, it is preferable to consider ܕܡܬܒܪܐ as a specification of ܪܘܚܗ rather than to ܐܢܫܐ.[78]

5. ܕ + Clause. In these cases ܕ introduces a relative clause. The basic pattern is

[Noun [*d*-Noun [*d*-{Clause} <sp>]]

Compare the following examples:[79]

44:23 ܥܠ ܪܝܫܗ ܕܐܝܣܪܝܠ ܕܩܪܝܗܝ ܒܪܝ ܒܘܟܪܝ ܐܝܣܪܝܠ
[<L RJCH [D->JSRJL
[D-{[QRJHJ <PO>] [BRJ [BWKRJ <ap>] [>JSRJL <ap>] <Ob>]} <sp>] <sp>]]
'on the head of Israel, whom He called my son, my first-born, Israel'.

47:18 ܒܫܡܗ ܕܐܠܗܐ ܕܕܝܠܗ ܗܘ ܐܝܩܪܐ
[B-CMH [D->LH>
[D-{[DJLH <PC>] [HW <Ep>] [>JQR> <Su>]} <sp>] <sp>]]
'by the name of God, whose is the honour'.[80]

With a construct chain in the first specification we find the pattern

[Noun [*d*-CstrNoun–Noun [*d*-{Clause} <sp>] <sp>]:

31:27 ܚܝܘܗܝ ܕܚܣܝܪ ܚܡܪܐ ܕܗܘ ܡܢ ܒܪܫܝܬ ܠܚܕܘܬܐ ܐܬܒܪܝ
[XJWHJ [D-XSJR XMR>
[D-{[HW <Su>] [MN B-RCJT <Ti>] [L-XDWT> <Aj>] [>TBRJ <Pr>]} <sp>] <sp>]]
'the life of him who lacks wine, which from the beginning was created for joy'.

---

[77] ܥܠ is a plus compared with Gr; cf. above, § 10.2.1.
[78] Cf. §§ 11.5, 20.1 (end). On ܕ + Adjective see further below, § 10.2.3.
[79] There are no formal syntactic criteria for distinguishing between restrictive relative clauses (embedding) and non-restrictive relative clauses (hypotaxis). The examples quoted in this section include non-restrictive relative clauses and hence the encoding with <sp> can be challenged. However, it suffices in the present discussion, in which we focus on the relation between *d*-Noun and *d*-Clause; cf. §§ 10.2.4 and 26.2.
[80] Corresponding to בשם הנכבד in MS B; cf. § 3.2 (g), (k).

Note that in this example the relative clause modifies the *nomen rectum*.[81]

6. Prepositional Phrase. The basic pattern is

[Noun [*d*-Noun [Preposition–Noun <sp>] <sp>]]:[82]

    47:11 ܡܠܟܘܬܐ ܕܡܠܟܘܬܐ ܥܠ ܐܝܣܪܐܝܠ 'the throne of the kingship over Israel'.

    50:9 ܐܝܟ ܪܝܚܐ ܕܠܒܘܢܬܐ ܥܠ ܦܝܪܡܐ 'like the odour of frankincense upon the censer'.[83]

The prepositional phrase follows an interrogative pronoun in

    34:29 ܩܠܐ ܕܝܢ ܡܢ ܬܪܝܗܘܢ 'to which of their two voices?'

7. Parallel Element. Two patterns are attested: one with and another without repetition of ܕ before the parallel element:

[Noun [*d*-Noun <sp>] [*w*-<cj>] [*d*-Noun <PA>] <sp>]]]
[Noun [*d*-Noun [*w*-<cj>] [Noun <PA>] <sp>]

The first pattern occurs twice, in

    44:10 ܓܒܪܐ ܕܛܒܘܬܐ ܘܕܙܕܝܩܘܬܐ 'men of goodness and of righteousness'.

    47:8 ܒܡܠܐ ܕܬܘܕܝܬܐ ܘܕܐܝܩܪܐ 'with words of thanksgiving and honour'.

In 44:10 B and M read אנשׁי חסד; Gr has ἄνδρες ἐλέους; in 47:8 B has [כ]בוד ...] and Gr ῥήματι δόξης. Accordingly, in both cases Syr has a longer phrase and the first *d*-phrase can be considered a plus compared with Heb and Gr. An extended form of this pattern with two parallel elements occurs in

    38:27 ܒܥܒܕܐ ܕܓܠܦܐ ܘܕܛܒܥܐ ܘܕܡܪܓܢܝܬܐ 'on the work of engraving and of seals and of pearls'.

The second pattern occurs once, in

    14:18 ܬܠܕܬܐ ܕܒܣܪܐ ܘܕܡܐ 'the generations of flesh and blood'.

---

[81] Cf. above, § 10.2.1 (2) and above, under (3).

[82] In Classical Syriac the construction in which ܕ precedes the prepositional phrase is more common; see the discussion in § 10.5.1.

[83] On this example see also § 7.2.3.

The use of this pattern, rather than that with repetition of ܕ is possibly related to the fact that 'flesh and blood' is a fixed expression.[84] One may compare here another construction, namely

[CstrNoun [Noun *w*-Noun]].

This construction occurs in

1:19 ܘܒܝܬ ܡܣܡܟ ܬܫܒܘܚܬܐ ܘܐܝܩܪܐ ܕܠܥܠܡ 'a house of support of praise and eternal honour'.[85]
24:16 ܣܘ̈ܟܝ ܬܫܒܘܚܬܐ ܘܐܝܩܪܐ 'branches of praise and honour'.
40:3 ܘܥܕܡܐ ܠܝܬ̈ܒܝ ܥܦܪܐ ܘܩܛܡܐ 'till those who sit in dust and ashes'.
45:18 ܐ̈ܢܫܝ ܕܕܬܢ ܘܐܒܝܪܡ 'the men of Dathan and Abiram'.

And perhaps also with ܟܠ in[86]

10:6 ܡܢ ܟܠ ܣܘܪ̈ܚܢܐ ܘܕܓܠܘܬܐ 'from all sins and falsehood'.
15:13 ܟܠ ܒܝܫܬܐ ܘܡܪܚܘܬܐ 'all evil and insolence'.
36:11 ܟܠ ܪ̈ܘܪܒܢܐ ܘܫ̈ܠܝܛܢܐ ܕܥܡ̈ܡܐ 'all leaders and rules of the people'.

Compare the more complex structures with ܟܠ + Noun *w*-Noun *w*-Noun in

34:5 ܟܠ ܢܚ̈ܫܐ ܘܩܣ̈ܡܐ ܘܚ̈ܠܡܐ 'all divinations and oracles and dreams'.

In Biblical Hebrew this construction is attested as well.[87] In other words: a *nomen regens* can govern several juxtaposed genitives. This occurs especially in a later phase of the language, e.g.:

1 Chr 18:10 כלי זהב וכסף ונחשת 'vessels of gold and silver and brass' //
2 Sam 8:10 כלי כסף וכלי זהב וכלי נחשת.[88]

It is also attested in earlier literature, e.g.:

1 Kgs 18:36 אלהי אברהם יצחק וישראל 'the God of Abraham, Isaac and Israel', instead of
Exod 3:15 and others אלהי אברהם אלהי יצחק ואלהי יעקב.

Also in the Hebrew text of Sirach:

4:21 (A[+C]) בשת כבוד וחן '(there is) a shame of honour and mercy'.[89]

---

[84] Cf. 17:31 and Bauer, *Wörterbuch*, 1488 (on σὰρξ καὶ αἷμα); Strack–Billerbeck I, 730–731.
[85] For the analysis of ܡܣܡܟ as a construct noun rather than a Pael participle see § 9.2.
[86] But according to J.W. Dyk and P.S.F. van Keulen, it is more likely that ܟܠ governs only the first element; see their 'Words and Phrases', 53–55.
[87] Cf. Verheij, 'Genitive Construction with Two *Nomina Recta*'.
[88] Joüon–Muraoka, *Grammar*, § 129*b*; Kropat, *Syntax*, 55.

In Biblical Hebrew the usual construction is that with repetition of the construct noun. In Syr there are no examples with repetition of the first word, neither with a construct noun, nor with a noun specified by *d*-Noun. In other words, the patterns

[CstrNoun$_A$–Noun$_B$ [*w*-<cj>] [CstrNoun$_A$–Noun$_C$ <PA>]]
[Noun$_A$ [*d*-Noun$_B$ <sp>] [*w*-<cj>] [Noun$_A$ [*d*-Noun$_C$ <sp>] <PA>]]

do not occur. Apparently Syr could dispense with them because of the flexibility of the patterns with ܕ mentioned above, at the beginning of (7).[90]

10.2.3 ܕ + *Adjective*

ܕ may also be followed by an adjective. In this construction the adjectival *d*-phrase constitutes a clause in itself,[91] e.g.:

8:6 ܥܠ ܐܢܫܐ ܕܣܐܒ ‘at an old person (a person who is old)’.

Accordingly, there are two patterns in which an adjective modifies a noun,[92] namely

[Noun [Adjective <sp>]]
[Noun [*d*-{[Adjective <PC>]} <sp>]].

Compare e.g.

32:6 ܡ̈ܠܐ ܫܦܝܪ̈ܬܐ [ML> [CPJRT> <sp>]] ‘beautiful words’, but
23:5 ܡܕܡ ܕܫܦܝܪ [MDM [D-{[CPJR <PC>]} <sp>]] ‘something that is beautiful’.

and the alternation of ܚܟܝܡܐ and ܕܚܟܝܡ (both corresponding to חכם in Heb [B+D]) in

37:20–24 ܐܝܬ ܓܒܪ ܕܚܟܝܡ (...) ܐܝܬ ܚܟܝܡܐ ܕܒܟܠ ܙܒܢ ܚܟܝܡ (...) ܘܐܝܬ ܚܟܝܡܐ ܕܠܢܦܫܗ ܚܟܝܡ (...) ܘܕܚܟܝܡ ܠܢܦܫܗ ‘There is one who is wise (…) There is a wise man who is always wise (…) There is a wise man who is wise for himself (…) And he who is wise for himself…’.

---

89 Syr has ܒܗܬܬܐ ܕܐܝܩܪܗ ܛܝܒܘܬܐ ‘a shame the honour of which is goodness’; cf. § 1.2.

90 Cf. Williams, ‘Peshitta to Jeremiah’, 290.

91 With ellipsis of the subject pronoun; cf. § 17.3 (1).

92 Cf. Muraoka, *Classical Syriac for Hebraists*, § 94; Muraoka calls the construction with ܕ a ‘pseudo-relative clause’.

We do not find examples such as *ܗ ܪܘܫܒܐܪ ܐܬܠܘܐ, that is, of the pattern

[Noun [*d*-{[Adjective <PC>] [Pronoun <Su>]} <sp>]].

It is hard to establish a functional difference between Noun + Adjective and Noun + *d*-Adjective, although it seems that the construction with ܕ is especially frequent in the following contexts.

1. The adjective is followed by an extension. This may be a prepositional phrase, as in

8:1 ܥܡ ܓܒܪܐ ܕܥܫܝܢ ܡܢܟ 'with a man who is stronger than you'.[93]

or a preposition + infinitive as in

14:16 ܟܠ ܡܕܡ ܕܫܦܝܪ ܠܡܥܒܕ 'everything that is beautiful to do'.[94]

or a parallel element as in

30:14 ܡܣܟܢܐ ܕܚܝ ܘܚܠܝܡ ܒܓܘܫܡܗ 'a poor man who is alive and sound in his body'.

41:2 ܠܓܒܪܐ ܕܬܒܝܪ ܘܚܣܝܪ ܢܦܫ 'to the man who is broken and lacks (strength of) life'.

2. The adjective does not follow a nominal head, e.g. ܕܫܦܝܪ 'what is beautiful, something beautiful', as in

3:31 ܕܥܒܕ ܕܫܦܝܪ 'he who does what is beautiful'.

13:22 ܘܐܢ ܐܡܪ ܕܫܦܝܪ 'and if he says what is beautiful'.[95]

37:11 ܠܡܥܒܕ ܕܫܦܝܪ 'to do what is beautiful'.

But compare the use of ܒܝܫ without ܕ as subject in

7:1 ܠܐ ܬܥܒܕ ܒܝܫ ܘܠܐ ܢܕܪܟܟ ܒܝܫ 'do not do what is evil and evil will not find you'.

3. The head is a *Leitwort allgemeiner Bedeutung* such as ܟܠ, ܡܕܡ or ܐܢܫ.[96]

---

[93] The reading in Syr is a combination of איש גדול (A¹; cf. Gr ἀνθρώπου δυνάστου) and קשה ממך (A²).

[94] In this verse Heb (A) too has a relative particle before the adjective: וכל דבר שיפה לעשות. For this example see also the third category, discussed below.

[95] Similarly 35:7.

[96] § 10.1.1. See also the example from 8:1, quoted above.

14:16 ܕܫܦܝܪ ܟܠ ܡܕܡ ‮ܗܘ‬ 'everything that is beautiful'.

18:28 ܕܚܟܝܡ ܠܟܠ 'to everyone who is wise'.

As to their syntactic behaviour it should further be noted that both the Adjective and *d*-Adjective function as specifications of the phrase atom. Both can, for example, be separated from the head by an intervening element such as ܐܝܟ, ܗܘ or the enclitic pronoun (§13.2). However, ܕ + Adjective functions as a relative clause, which has some impact on its position within the phrase (§12.6).

10.2.4 *Other* d-*phrases*

ܕ is also used to introduce other extensions in which predication occurs.[97] The basic pattern is

[Noun [*d*-{Clause} <sp>]]:

7:27 ܕܝܠܕܬܟ ܠܐܡܟ 'your mother who bore you'.

If the relative clause with ܕ follows a construct chain, it modifies the *nomen rectum*, e.g.:

49:6–7 ܒܝܘܡܝ ܐܪܡܝܐ ܕܗܘܐ ܢܒܝܐ ܡܢ ܟܪܣܐ ܕܐܡܗ 'in the days of Jeremiah, who was a prophet from his mother's womb'.

The relative clause introduced by ܕ functions as a specification of the *nomen rectum* ܐܪܡܝܐ. In this respect *d*-Clause agrees with *d*-Noun.[98]

Sometimes Noun + Relative Clause in Syr corresponds to CstrNoun–Noun in Heb:[99]

3:17 ܡܢ ܓܒܪܐ ܕܝܗܒ ܡܘܗܒܬܐ '(you will be loved) more than a giver of gifts'; A מנותן מתנות; C מאיש מתן.

37:11 ܥܡ ܐܓܝܪܐ ܕܡܕܓܠ ܥܠ ܥܒܕܗ '(Do not take counsel) with a hireling who lies about his work'; B[txt] פועל שוא; B[mg]+D פועל שכיר.[100]

---

[97] Admittedly, it is questionable to call these structures 'extensions', because they include non-restrictive relative clauses. See the refinement in § 26.2, where we distinguish between embedding (including restrictive relative clauses) and hypotaxis (including non-restrictive relative clauses); see also § 10.2.2 (5), note 79.

[98] On the comparison between *d*-Noun and *d*-Clause see further § 12.6.

[99] Cf. Avinery, *Syntaxe*, 189–191; cf. § 3.2 (k) ('Syr expands on the succinct style of the Heb').

[100] According to Smend, *Jesus Sirach*, 331, ܕܡܕܓܠ reflects שקר instead of שכיר (= Bmg+D); Ryssel, 'Fragmente', V, 563, thinks that the Syriac translator interpreted שוא in the sense of 'deceit'.

48:8 ܕܡܫܚ ܡܠܟ̈ܐ ܠܬܘܡܒܐ ܦܬܟܠܐ 'he who anointed kings for retribution'; B המושח מלא תשלומות.[101]

51:8 ܡܢ ܚܝ ܕܥܫܝܢ ܡܢܗܘܢ 'from him who is stronger than they'; B מכל
רע.[102]

10.3 APPOSITION

10.3.1 *Basic patterns*

The basic pattern for constructions with an apposition is

[Noun [Noun <ap>]]:[103]

51:1 ܡܪܝܐ ܡܠܟܐ 'Lord, King'.

Sometimes [Noun [Noun <ap>]] corresponds to a single noun in
Heb,[104] e.g.:

47:1 ܢܬܢ ܢܒܝܐ 'Nathan, the prophet'; B נתן (cf. Gr).
48:20 ܒܝܕ ܐܫܥܝܐ ܢܒܝܐ 'through Isaiah, the prophet'; B ביד ישעיהו.[105]

It corresponds to a single noun in Gr (Heb not extant) in

24:12 ܒܝܢܬ ܝܪܬܘܬܗ ܐܝܣܪܐܝܠ 'in His inheritance, Israel'; Gr κληρονο-
μίας αὐτοῦ.
24:25 ܐܝܟ ܢܗܪܐ ܦܝܫܘܢ 'like the river Pishon'; Gr ὡς Φισων.

The opposite phenomenon, i.e. an apposition in Heb has no equivalent
in Syr, is attested as well, e.g.:

50:16 ܒܢܝ ܐܗܪܘܢ 'the sons of Aaron' (= Gr); B בני אהרון הכהנים.

The apposition may contain a construct chain, i.e.

---

[101] It has been suggested that the Syriac (and Greek) translator read מלכי instead of
מלא; thus e.g. Smend, *Jesus Sirach*, 460; Lévi, *L'Ecclésiastique* I, 134.
[102] Perhaps the Syriac translator read מכל עז (or מעז מהם) in his source text;
Ryssel, 'Fragmente', VI, 219.
[103] Accordingly, we take the second noun as the noun in apposition; similarly
Waltke–O'Connor, *Biblical Hebrew Syntax*, §§ 12.1c, 12.3a on Biblical Hebrew;
differently Nöldeke, *Grammatik*, § 212; Avinery, *Syntaxe*, 201–204. Thus Avinery
analyses Gen 4:1 ܐܢܬܬܗ ܠܚܘܐ as [Noun [Noun <ap>]] but Gen 4:17 ܚܢܘܟ ܒܪܗ as
[Noun <ap> [Noun]].
[104] For some examples from other parts of the Peshitta where 'P provides names
with their standard epithets, even when these are lacking in the Hebrew' see Weitzman, *Syriac Version*, 24; idem, *From Judaism to Christianity*, 58–59; Greenberg,
Jeremiah, 43–44.
[105] On the semi-preposition ܒܝܕ see below.

[Noun [CstrNoun–Noun <ap>]]:

26:28 ܥܠ ܐܢܫܐ ܡܪܝ ܫܡܐ 'over men, lords of fame'.

The construction in which the apposition follows CstrNoun–Noun, i.e.

[CstrNoun–Noun [Noun <ap>]],

occurs only with the semi-prepositions ܓܘ and ܒܝܕ in[106]

24:12 ܓܘ ܝܪܬܘܬܗ ܐܝܣܪܐܝܠ 'in his inheritance, Israel'.
48:20 ܒܝܕ ܐܫܥܝܐ ܢܒܝܐ 'through Isaiah, the prophet'.

Other examples with a construct chain in the head of the apposition contain ܟܠ or ܒܪ:

[Noun [*br*-Noun <ap>]]:

45:23 ܦܝܢܚܣ ܒܪ ܐܠܝܥܙܪ 'Phinehas, the son of Eleazar'.
45:25 ܕܘܝܕ ܒܪ ܐܝܫܝ 'David, the son of Jesse'.

[*kl*+suffix [*bny*-Noun <ap>]]:

14:17 ܟܠܗܘܢ ܒܢܝܢܫܐ 'all men'.[107]
40:8 ܥܡ ܟܠܗܘܢ ܒܢܝ ܒܣܪܐ 'with all men of flesh'.
50:13 ܟܠܗܘܢ ܒܢܝ ܐܗܪܘܢ 'all the sons of Aaron'.

[CstrNoun–*kl*+suffix [Noun <ap>]]:

39:26 ܪܝܫ ܟܠܗܘܢ ܨܘܪܟܬܐ 'the most important of all things'.
44:23 ܒܥܝܢܝ ܟܠܗܘܢ ܚܝܐ 'in the eyes of all the living'.

[*bny*-Noun [*kl*+suffix <ap>]]:[108]

33:10 ܒܢܝܢܫܐ ܟܠܗܘܢ 'all men'.

[Noun [*br*-Noun <ap>]]

26:28 ܥܠ ܓܒܪܐ ܒܪ ܚܐܪܐ 'over a free-born man'.
46:1 ܓܒܪܐ ܒܪ ܚܝܠܐ 'a man, a warrior'.

If the first noun is preceded by a preposition, it may be repeated, as in

24:12 ܒܥܡܐ ܝܩܝܪܐ ܒܡܢܬܗ ܕܡܪܝܐ 'in the honourable people, in the Lord's portion'.
44:1 ܐܢܫܐ ܕܛܒܘܬܐ ܐܒܗܝܢ 'the men of goodness, our fathers'.

---

[106] In these cases the apposition modifies the *nomen rectum*.

[107] Similarly in a *d*-phrase in 7:17; 16:17; 17:20; 17:22 (*bis*); 41:4; 45:4, see § 10.2.2. The word order with suffixed ܟܠ preceding the noun phrase agrees with the rules formulated by Avinery, 'Position of the declined KL', 333.

[108] This is an exception to the rule formulated by Avinery, 'Position of the declined KL'.

It is not repeated in,[109] e.g.

24:25 ܐܝܟ ܢܗܪܐ ܦܝܫܘܢ 'like the river Pishon'.
26:28 ܥܠ ܐܢܫܐ ܡܪܝ ܫܡܐ 'over men, lords of fame'.
44:22 ܡܛܠ ܐܒܪܗܡ ܐܒܘܗܝ 'because of Abraham, his father'.

Note the repetition of ܥܠ before ܐܘܪܫܠܡ, but not before ܐܬܪܐ, in[110]

36:18 ܥܠ ܩܪܝܬܐ ܕܩܘܕܫܟ ܥܠ ܐܘܪܫܠܡ ܐܬܪܐ ܕܫܟܝܢܬܟ
[<L QRJT> [D-QWDCK <sp>] [<L >WRCLM [>TR> [D-CKJNTK <sp>] <ap>] <ap>]]
'on Your holy city, on Jerusalem, the place of Your habitation'.

10.3.2 *Apposition extended*

The apposition may be extended by the following elements.

1. An adjective, i.e.

[Noun [Noun [Adjective <sp>] <ap>]]:

46:6 ܟܠܗܘܢ ܥܡܡܐ ܚܪܡܐ 'all the doomed peoples'.

2. *d*-Noun, i.e.

[Noun [Noun [*d*-Noun <sp>] <ap>]]:

43:2 ܡܐܢܐ ܕܬܕܡܘܪܬܐ ܥܒܕܗ ܕܡܪܝܡܐ 'a marvellous vessel, a work of the Most High'.[111]
45:20 ܝܪܬܘܬܗ ܪܫܝܬܐ ܕܩܘܕܫܐ 'his inheritance, the holy first-fruits'.

With the apposition following ܟܠ + suffix we find the following patterns:

[*kl*+suffix [Noun (st. emph.) [*d*-Noun <sp>] <ap>]]:[112]

---

[109] According to Muraoka, *Basic Grammar*, § 95.3, the construction without repetition of the preposition is the norm; similarly Avinery, *Syntaxe* 204–209. Compare e.g. Gen 4:2 MT: ותסף ללדת את אחיו את הבל 'Again, she gave birth to his brother Abel'; Pesh: ܘܐܘܣܦܬ ܠܡܐܠܕ ܠܐܚܘܗܝ ܗܒܝܠ.

[110] Contrast Heb (B) על קרית קדשך ירושלם מכון שבתיך without repetition of the preposition. Since the preposition is repeated before ܐܘܪܫܠܡ and not before ܐܬܪܐ ܕܫܟܝܢܬܟ, we prefer to analyse ܐܬܪܐ ܕܫܟܝܢܬܟ as an extension of ܐܘܪܫܠܡ, rather than one of ܩܪܝܬܐ ܕܩܘܕܫܟ. Accordingly, we consider this verse as an example of 'apposition extended by another apposition' (§ 10.3.2 [5]), rather than 'phrase atom expanded by two appositions' (§ 11.3).

[111] For the first *d*-phrase preceding the apposition see § 11.4.

4:16 ܠܟܠܗܘܢ ܕܪ̈ܐ ܕܥܠܡܐ 'for all the generations of the world'.
36:13 ܟܠܗܘܢ ܫܒܛܘ̈ܗܝ ܕܝܥܩܘܒ 'all the tribes of Jacob'.
44:21 ܟܠܗܘܢ ܥܡ̈ܡܐ ܕܐܪܥܐ 'all the peoples of the earth'.
46:18 ܟܠܗܘܢ ܪܘܪܒܢܐ ܕܦܠܫ̈ܬܝܐ 'all the lords of the Philistines'.
50:13 ܠܘܩܒܠ ܟܠܗ ܥܡܐ ܕܐܝܣܪܝܠ 'before all the people of Israel'.

[*kl*+suffix [Noun+suffix [*d*-Noun <sp>] <ap>]]:

23:27 ܟܠܗܘܢ ܥܡܘܪ̈ܝܗ ܕܐܪܥܐ 'all the inhabitants of the world'.
47:4 ܟܠܗ ܫܘܒܗܪܬܗ ܕܓܘܠܝܕ 'all the boastfulness of Goliath'.

[*kl*+suffix [Noun+suffix [*d*-CstrNoun–Noun <sp>] <ap>]]:

15:19 ܟܠܗܝܢ ܬܪ̈ܥܝܬܗܘܢ ܕܒܢܝ̈ܢܫܐ 'all the reflections of men' (similarly 42:18).

In 44:21, 46:18a and 47:4 ܟܠ is a plus vis-à-vis Heb and/or Gr.[113] In 42:18 it is also found in MS B, but not in M. In 4:16 Syr is very different from A and Gr, but neither of the latter witnesses has 'all'. In 23:27 ܟܠܗܘܢ ܥܡܘܪ̈ܝܗ ܕܐܪܥܐ is part of a plus. Where Heb has 'all' (כל) as well, it occurs most often in a chain with two construct nouns, e.g. 15:19 (A[+B]) כל מפעל איש; 36:13 (B) כל שבטי יעקב; 46:18 (B) כל סרני פלשתים; 50:13 (B) נגד כל קהל ישראל.[114]

3. A relative clause, i.e.

[Noun [Noun [*d*-{Clause} <sp>] <ap>]]:

46:8 ܠܝܪܬܘܬܗܘܢ ܠܐܪܥܐ ܕܡܪܕܝܐ ܚܠܒܐ ܘܕܒܫܐ 'their inheritance, the land flowing with milk and honey'.

[CstrNoun–*kl*+suffix [Noun [*d*-{Clause} <sp>] <ap>]]:

39:26 ܪܫ ܟܠܗܝܢ ܣܘܢ̈ܩܬܐ ܕܡܬܒܥܝܢ ܠܚܝܐ ܕܒܢܝ̈ܢܫܐ 'the chief of all things that are necessary for the life of the people'.

4. A parallel element, i.e.[115]

[Noun [Noun [*w*-<cj>] [Noun <PA>] <ap>]]:

17:4 ܥܠ ܟܠ ܒܣܪ ܥܠ ܚܝܘܬܐ ܘܥܠ ܦܪܚܬܐ 'upon all flesh, upon the beasts and the birds'.

---

[112] Again, the position of ܟܠ in this pattern agrees with the rules formulated by Avinery, 'Position of the declined KL'; idem, *Syntaxe*, 228.
[113] See above, note 62.
[114] Also 39:19 (B) מעשה כל בשר 'the works of all flesh' (§ 10.2.1 [1]; Syr ܥܒ̈ܕܘܗܝ ܕܟܠ ܒܪ ܒܣܪܐ).
[115] Contrast the construction with two appositions, discussed in § 11.3.

45:20 ܝܪܬܘܬܗ ܪ̈ܫܝܬܐ ܕܩܘܕܫܐ ܘܣ̈ܕܪܐ ܕܠܚܡܐ 'his inheritance, the holy first-fruits and the rows of the shewbread'.[116]
46:13 ܫܡܘܐܝܠ ܕܝܢܐ ܘܟܗܢܐ 'Samuel, the judge and the priest'.
51:10 ܡܪܝܐ ܓܢܒܪܐ ܘܦܪܘܩܐ 'Lord, warrior and saviour'.

[*kl*+suffix [Noun [*w*-<cj>] [Noun <PA>] <ap>]]:[117]

24:6 ܒܟܠܗܘܢ ܥܡ̈ܡܐ ܘܐܘܡ̈ܘܬܐ 'over all the peoples and nations'.

5. Another apposition, i.e.

[Noun [Noun [Noun <ap>] <ap>]]:

36:18 ܥܠ ܩܪܝܬܐ ܕܩܘܕܫܟ ܥܠ ܐܘܪܫܠܡ ܐܬܪܐ ܕܡܫܪܝܬܟ 'on Your holy city, on Jerusalem, the place of Your habitation'.[118]

10.3.3 *Numerals*

Cardinal numbers usually take a construction with an apposition. Either the object counted stands in apposition to the cardinal, or, less frequently, the cardinal is an apposition to the object counted.[119] On the basis of a comparison of the Old Syriac Versions of Matthew and the Peshitta, Joosten argues that the order Numeral–Noun is common in earlier texts, while the reverse order becomes more frequent in later texts.[120] In Syr the order Numeral–Noun is attested in

1:28 ܒܬܪܝܢ ܠܒ̈ܝܢ 'double-hearted'.
16:10 ܫܬܡܐܐ ܐ̈ܠܦܝܢ ܪ̈ܓܠܝܢ 'six hundred thousand footmen'.
18:9 ܡܐܐ ܫ̈ܢܝܢ 'a hundred years'.
18:10 ܐܠܦ ܫ̈ܢܝܢ 'thousand years'.
22:12 ܫܒܥܐ ܝܘ̈ܡܝܢ 'seven days'.
23:16 ܬܪܝܢ ܙܢ̈ܝܢ 'two sorts'.
25:1 ܬܠܬ ܨܒ̈ܘܢ 'three things'.
25:2 ܬܠܬܐ ܓܢ̈ܣܝܢ 'three types'.
32:20 ܕܬܪܬܝܢ ܙܒ̈ܢܝܢ 'twice'.[121]
44:23 ܠܬܪܬܥܣܪ ܫܒ̈ܛܝܢ 'into twelve tribes'.

---

[116] For the *d*-phrase after the noun in apposition see above, (2).
[117] But see Dyk–Van Keulen, 'Words and Phrases', 53–55 (cf. above, n. 86).
[118] We consider ܐܬܪܐ ܕܡܫܪܝܬܟ as an apposition to the apposition ܥܠ ܐܘܪܫܠܡ; see above, § 10.3.1 (end).
[119] Nöldeke, *Grammatik*, § 237: 'Das Zahlwort steht als Apposition vor oder nach dem Gezählten. (…) Die Voranstellung des Zahlworts ist häufiger'.
[120] Joosten, *Syriac Language*, 61–63, 145.
[121] On the Dalath see § 14.2.

45:23 ܬܠܬܐ ܐܝܩܪܝܢ 'three honours'.
46:4 ܬܪܝܢ ܝܘܡ̈ܝܢ 'two days'.
47:21 ܠܬܪܬܝܢ ܡ̈ܠܟܘܢ 'into two kingdoms'.
48:3 ܬܠܬ ܙܒ̈ܢܝܢ 'three times'.
49:10 ܬܪܥܣܪ ܢܒ̈ܝܝܢ 'the Twelve Prophets'.
50:25 ܒܬܪܝܢ ܥܡ̈ܡܝܢ 'at two people'.

In all these cases the object numbered occurs in the absolute state. In most cases the expression is indefinite, but in 49:10 it is definite.[122] The ample use of the absolute state agrees with the situation in the Old Syriac Gospels compared with the Peshitta. Thus in the Peshitta of Matthew, unlike the Old Syriac versions, the cardinal number is sometimes followed by a noun in the emphatic state, which reflects an increased use of the emphatic state in later texts.[123]

In one case, however, the noun indicating the object counted has a suffix. In this example the cardinal has a suffix as well:[124]

20:25 ܬܪ̈ܬܝܗܝܢ ܐܘܪ̈ܚܬܗ 'both his ways'.

The construction

[Numeral–[*d*-Noun (thing numbered) <sp>]]

is attested once, namely in

---

[122] Perhaps also the reference to the 'six hundred thousand footmen' in 16:10 (cf. Exod 12:37, 38:26, Num 1:46, 2:32, 11:21, 26:51, 31:32). On the use of the absolute state see Nöldeke, *Grammatik*, § 202D: 'Sogar bei entschiedener Determination kann neben dem Zahlwort der St. abs. bleiben'.

[123] Cf. Joosten, *Syriac Language*, 61. In Pesh-Pentateuch the noun following the cardinal number is nearly always in the absolute state, while the noun preceding the cardinal number takes the emphatic state; Avinery, *Syntaxe*, 69–72.

[124] Cf. Nöldeke, *Grammatik*, § 149 ('Die Zahlen von 2–9 bilden besondere Formen mit Suffixen zur Bezeichnung der Determination'); Avinery, *Syntaxe*, 85–95; Muraoka, *Classical Syriac for Hebraists*, § 83; idem, *Basic Grammar*, § 91*c* (end); Joosten, *Syriac Language*, 63; about the type Numeral-suffix X Joosten remarks: 'This type is extremely rare in our corpus. It is used only with known entities of a set number'. Avinery (*Syntaxe*, 85–89) argues that this construction is used for 'more determinate' (מיודע יותר) constructions. In his view a distinction can be made between 'determinate' and 'more determinate', comparable to that between 'determinate' and 'indeterminate'. Compare e.g.

Gen 48:1 MT: את שני בניו 'his two sons'; Pesh: ܬܪܝܢ ܒܢܘ̈ܗܝ ('determinate');
Gen 48:13 MT: את שניהם 'both of them'; Pesh: ܬܪܝܗܘܢ ܒܢܘ̈ܗܝ ('more determinate');

If this explanation is also valid for Sir 20:25 this would mean that the construction with the suffix is used because the 'two ways' in question (i.e. ܠܡܗܝܡܢ and ܠܡܢ ܕܠܗ) are mentioned in the preceding lines.

41:12 ܡܢ ܐܠܦ̈ܐ ܘܣܝ̈ܡܬܐ ܕܥܘܠܐ 'than thousands of treasures of villainy'.[125]

With the numeral for 'one', ܚܕ, ܚܕܐ, the situation is different. Muraoka has demonstrated that 'in the case of ܚܕ, the position in relation to the counted substantive is of functional significance (...) The rule is that when the numeral precedes, it somehow stresses the concept of oneness, "only one, even one", while the numeral following the substantive is equal to the simple "one".'[126] The two attestations of ܚܕ + Noun in Syr conform with this rule. Thus ܚܕ – Noun occurs in

18:10 ܐܝܟ ܚܕ ܝܘܡܐ ܒܥܠܡܐ ܕܙܕܝܩ̈ܐ 'like one day in the world of the righteous'.

and Noun – ܚܕ in

46:4 ܘܗܘܐ ܝܘܡܐ ܚܕ ܗܘ̈ܝ ܠܗܘܢ ܬܪ̈ܝܢ 'and one day became two days'.

This example is exceptional not only for the order Noun–Numeral, but also for the use of the emphatic state for the thing numbered. While in all the examples of Numeral–Noun, the noun is in the absolute state, the present example, the only example of the reverse order, uses the emphatic state. This agrees with the rule formulated by Muraoka that the emphatic state becomes rather frequent when the numeral follows.[127]

On the basis of our observations we can draw the following conclusions about the numerals in Syr.

1. With ܚܕ there is one example of ܚܕ – Noun and one of Noun – ܚܕ. The distribution of these two word orders agrees with the rules formulated by Muraoka and Joosten.
2. With the other numerals there occur only examples of the order Numeral–Noun. This is the usual order in Classical Syriac.

---

[125] Cf. Nöldeke, *Grammatik*, § 237: 'Der pl. von ܐܠܦ regiert zuweilen einen Genitiv mit ܕ: ܫܬ ܐܠܦ̈ܝ ܫܢ̈ܝܐ "6 Tausende von Jahren"= 6000 J.'; see also Avinery, *Syntaxe*, 75–79. Heb (B) has the numeral in the construct state: מאלפי אוצרות חכמה (Bmg: חמדה, סומות).

[126] Muraoka, 'Noun Modifier', 192; idem, *Classical Syriac for Hebraists*, § 78; idem, *Basic Grammar*, § 91c; see also Joosten, *Syriac Language*, 60–61.

[127] Muraoka, 'Noun Modifier', 193; idem, *Classical Syriac for Hebraists*, § 78; idem, *Basic Grammar*, § 91c; this is a refinement of Nöldeke's observation (*Grammatik*, § 237) that the numbered object takes either the absolute or the emphatic state, and that the absolute state is more frequent. See also Joosten, *Syriac Language*, 59: in all the examples of Noun – ܚܕ in Joosten's corpus, the noun is in the emphatic state.

As far as a diachronic development is concerned, it agrees with earlier texts (Joosten).

3. In all examples of Numeral–Noun, the noun is in the absolute state. This agrees with the rule that the absolute state is more frequent (Nöldeke), especially when the numeral precedes the noun (Muraoka). As far as a diachronic development is concerned, it agrees with earlier texts (Joosten).

4. In the example of Noun – ܚܕ (46:4) the noun is in the emphatic state.

5. In the constructions with Numeral + Noun, there are no examples of discontinuous phrases such as ܫܢܝܢ ܗܘܐ ܡܐܐ ܒܪ 'he was a hundred years old'.[128]

6. ܚܕ functions only as real ordinal number, not as indeterminate article.[129]

10.4 DEMONSTRATIVE

Cases in which a noun is modified by a demonstrative are remarkably rare. Except for constructions with ܟܠ, there are only four examples. Two times we find

[[Demonstrative <sp>] Noun]]:

1:20f ܗܢܐ ܟܬܒܐ 'this book'.
16:10 ܗܘܡ ܙܒܢܐ 'in that time'.

and two times

[Noun [Demonstrative <sp>]]:

18:10 ܡܢ ܥܠܡܐ ܗܢܐ 'from this world'.
50:27 ܒܟܬܒܐ ܗܢܐ 'in this book'.[130]

---

[128] For this and other examples see Nöldeke, *Grammatik*, § 237. In fact, in Syr there are no cases at all where an element intervenes between a head and an apposition, see § 13.2.

[129] Cf. Muraoka, *Basic Grammar*, § 72: 'The addition of a form of the numeral "one" may have the effect of weakening the emphatic to that of the primitive, absolute state'. See e.g. Mark 9:36 ܛܠܝܐ ܚܕ 'a child' (παιδίον); Falla, *Key* II, 69b; Williams, *Early Syriac Translation Technique*, 133–141.

[130] For the expression ܥܠܡܐ ܗܢܐ cf. Joosten, *Syriac Language*, 35; In 18:10 ܡܢ ܥܠܡܐ ܗܢܐ is a specification of ܐܠ ܐܢܫ.

According to Muraoka the position of the demonstrative in relation to
its head seems to have no functional significance.[131] Nöldeke too
claims that there is no functional difference, but he observes a diachronic development: the earlier authors such as Aphrahat prefer the
order Demonstrative–Noun.[132] Avinery has investigated the position
of the demonstrative in Pesh-Pentateuch.[133] He improves on the general statements made by Muraoka and Nöldeke. According to Avinery
the usual order is Noun–Demonstrative. He defines seven conditions
for deviations from this order: only if one of these conditions is met,
does the reverse order occur.

> The seven conditions formulated by Avinery are the following: The
> demonstrative follows the noun, unless one of the following condi-
> tions is met.[134]
> 1. The qualified noun appears at the end of a verse.
> 2. The demonstrative qualifies a numeral.
> 3. The demonstrative qualifies ܟܠ.
> 4. The demonstrative qualifies a proper name.
> 5. The demonstrative denotes reciprocity.
> 6. The order Demonstrative–Noun avoids uniformity where similar
>   syntactical structures are to be found in the same vicinity.
> 7. The Syriac is a translation of a Hebrew construction where the
>   demonstrative precedes (usually as a predicate).
> It seems that the two examples in Syr where the demonstrative pre-
> cedes the noun do not meet any of these criteria.[135] Admittedly, we
> cannot be sure whether the seventh condition was met in the *Vorlage*
> of Syr, but we have no indication that it was. For 1:20 we do not have
> a Hebrew text; in 16:10 Heb (B) has כן corresponding to ܘܗܟܢܐ ܗܘܐ in
> Syr.

Examples with ܟܠ + Demonstrative are more frequent. There are thirteen examples of ܟܠܗܘܢ ܗܠܝܢ, with the order *kl*–Demonstrative: 1:4;
18:26; 24:23; 25:11; 32:13; 37:15; 38:31; 39:27; 39:29; 39:32; 44:7;
48:15; 49:16. But in 24:23 and 32:13 7a1 has ܗܠܝܢ ܟܠܗܘܢ as opposed to
all other manuscripts consulted for the Leiden edition and in 37:15 it
has only ܟܠܗܘܢ, without demonstrative. In four of these cases the He-

---

[131] Muraoka, 'Noun Modifier', 197 n. 16.
[132] Nöldeke, *Grammatik*, § 226.
[133] Avinery, 'Position of the Demonstrative Pronoun'; idem, *Syntaxe*, 255–260.
[134] Avinery, 'Position of the Demonstrative Pronoun', 124–125; idem, *Syntaxe*,
256–260.
[135] Cases that meet the third criteria will be discussed below.

brew text is extant as well. In 32:13; 37:15 and 44:7 Heb has כל אלה; in 48:15 it has כל זאת.

The order Demonstrative–*kl* occurs four times, in 18:27; 24:7; 26:27; 34:20. In none of these cases has the Hebrew text been preserved. As noted above, the order Demonstrative–*kl* is also attested elsewhere in the Old Testament Peshitta.[136] The Hebrew כל אלה is translated 18 times with ܟܠܗܘܢ ܗܠܝܢ and 25 times with ܗܠܝܢ ܟܠܗܘܢ.[137] According to Avinery the occasional order Demonstrative–*kl* is due to the influence of the type ܗܢܐ ܟܠܗ ܥܡܐ, which is quite frequent (e.g. Num 5:30 ܗܢܐ ܟܠܗ ܢܡܘܣܐ).[138]

In our corpus we do not find discontinuous phrases in which the demonstrative is separated from its head as in Luke 12:56 ܙܒܢܐ ܕܝܢ ܗܢܐ; Hebrews 7:1 ܗܢܐ ܕܝܢ ܡܠܟܝܙܕܩ.[139]

In all the examples quoted the demonstrative has a deictic function. We find no cases where it merely indicates that the noun is definite.[140]

10.5 PREPOSITIONAL PHRASE

10.5.1 *Basic patterns*

The basic pattern for constructions with a prepositional phase is

[Noun [Preposition–Noun <sp>]]:

27:16 ܪܚܡܐ ܐܝܟ ܢܦܫܗ 'a friend like himself' (or: 'a friend as he desires'[141]).
36:29 ܥܕܪܐ ܗܝ ܒܪ ܐܟܘܬܟ 'for she is a help like you'.[142]

---

[136] See Avinery's third condition for the order Demonstrative–Noun, and Avinery, 'Position of the Demonstrative Pronoun', 124.

[137] See Williams, 'Early Syriac Versions', 540.

[138] Avinery, 'Position of declined KL'; idem, *Syntaxe*, 231. There are no examples of this type in Syr. For a doubtful example of the pattern ܗܢܐ ܥܡܐ ܟܠܗ in 1:20f see § 11.8.

[139] Kuty, 'Particle *dên*', 188.

[140] Cf. Joosten, *Syriac Language*, 31: 'Under certain conditions we find that the Syriac is fond of using a demonstrative pronoun where the Greek has merely the definite article. In these cases it seems that the Syriac pronoun does not express deixis but is used to indicate that the noun is definite'; see also Nöldeke, *Grammatik*, § 228; Duval, *Traité*, §§ 288–289; Muraoka, *Basic Grammar*, § 72; Avinery, *Syntaxe*, 250; Falla, *Key* II, 4a.

[141] Cf. Smend, *Jesus Sirach*, 246: 'Syr: wie seine Seele (d. h. wie er ihn sich wünscht)'.

[142] On the possibility that Syr is influenced by Pesh-Gen 2:20 see § 5.2.

42:11 ܪܘܩܒܠܐ ܒܥܡܐ 'gainsaying among the people'.

We can compare here the construction with ܕ + Prepositional Phrase,[143] i.e.

[Noun [*d*-{[Preposition–Noun <PC>]} <sp>]][144]

However, in Syr this use is rather restricted. We have found the following cases.

13:19 ܥܪ̈ܕܐ ܕܒܡܕܒܪܐ 'the wild asses that are in the desert'.
46:2 ܢܝܙܟܐ ܕܒܐܝܕܗ 'the javelin that was in his hand'.

There are also some examples with ܡܐ and ܟܠ, e.g.:

8:19 ܡܐ ܕܒܠܒܟ 'what is in your heart'.
36:22 ܟܠ ܕܒܣܘܦ̈ܝܗ ܕܐܪܥܐ 'all who are at the end of the world'.

And further with ܠܥܠܡ, e.g.:

2:9 ܚܕܘܬܐ ܕܠܥܠܡ 'eternal joy'.

The construction with ܕ is idiomatic Syriac,[145] whereas the construction with the prepositional phrase seems to mirror Hebrew syntax. In the Peshitta we find both the construction without ܕ, as Gen 3:6 ܠܒܥܠܗ ܥܡܗ 'to her husband (who was) with her' (MT לאישה עמה) and the construction with ܕ, as in Gen 1:9 ܡܝܐ ܕܠܬܚܬ ܡܢ ܫܡܝܐ 'the waters that are under the sky' (MT המים מתחת השמים).[146] We have seen three other examples of a prepositional phrase in § 10.2.2 (6) ('*d*-phrase extended') and will see another nine cases in § 11.6 ('*d*-phrase and preposition phrase'). This evidence is too much to be ignored, and although in some cases an adverbial interpretation of the prepositional deserves consideration,[147] this alternative explanation does not account for all the examples. Our preliminary conclusion can be that the

---

[143] Cf. Wertheimer, 'Functions', 270.

[144] Our use of decorative brackets implies that we consider the prepositional phrase introduced by ܕ as a predication structure. Compare § 10.2.3 (end) on ܕ + Adjective; for the ellipsis of the subject pronoun in this construction see § 17.3.

[145] Thus according to Muraoka the construction with ܕ is used 'regularly' (*Classical Syriac for Hebraists*, § 94) or 'often' (*Basic Grammar*, § 91*h* [end]); cf. Duval, *Traité*, § 406.

[146] Muraoka, *Classical Syriac for Hebraists*, § 94; idem, *Basic Grammar*, § 91*h*. Sometimes the construction with ܕ corresponds to one with אשר in the Hebrew, e.g. Gen 44:15 MT: איש אשר כמני; Pesh: ܓܒܪܐ ܕܐܟܘܬܝ; note the variation in Gen 3:1–3 MT: (1) עץ הגן 'the trees of the garden'; (2) עץ הגן; (3) העץ אשר בתוך הגן; Pesh: (1) ܐܝ̈ܠܢܐ ܦܪܕܝܣܐ; (2) ܐܝ̈ܠܢܐ ܕܒܦܪܕܝܣܐ; (3) ܐܝܠܢܐ ܕܒܡܨܥܬܗ ܕܦܪܕܝܣܐ.

[147] Thus Professor Jan Joosten, personal communication.

construction without ܘ alternates with the more idiomatic construction with ܘ. It is likely that the former mirrors the syntax of a Hebrew source text, but a systematic investigation of a large non-translated corpus of Classical Syriac is necessary to validate this claim.

The construction with a prepositional phrase corresponds to [CstrNoun–Noun] in Heb in 13:19 (A) פראי מדבר; 36:29 (B[mg]+D) עיר מבצר[148] and 41:11 (B+M) וקהלת עם. This pattern of correspondence is also attested elsewhere in the Old Testament.[149] There is no reason to assume that the Syriac translator read a prepositional phrase in his Hebrew source.[150] Note also the succinct style of the Hebrew in 8:19 (A only לבך) and 36:22 (B כל אפסי ארץ).

10.5.2 *Prepositional phrase extended*

The prepositional phrase too can be extended. Thus we find with *d*-Noun, i.e.

[Noun [Preposition–Noun [*d*-Noun <sp>] <sp>]]:

18:10 ܪܬܘܢܬܐ ܕܥܠܡܐ ܐܝܟ ܚܕ ܝܘܡܐ 'like one day in the world of the righteous'.

32:5 ܕܕܗܒܐ ܟܝܣܐ ܥܠ ܕܚܬܡܐ ܐܝܟ 'like a seal upon a golden purse'.

and with a relative clause, i.e.

[Noun [Preposition–Noun [*d*-{Clause} <sp>] <sp>]]:

22:18 ܪܡܬܐ ܕܐܝܬܝܗ ܟܐܦܐ ܥܠ ܕܪܡܐ ܓܘܪܐ 'a small bundle on a stone that is high'.

The prepositional phrase may also be extended by an apposition, i.e.

[Noun [Preposition–Noun [Noun <ap>] <sp>]]

This is the case with the prepositional phrase ܒܚܪܡܘܢ in

24:13 ܘܐܝܟ ܐܠܘܐ ܕܣܚܘܦ ܒܚܪܡܘܢ ܛܘܪܐ ܕܬܠܓܐ 'and like an oleaster on the Senir, the mountain of snow'.[151]

---

[148] But B[txt] has ומבצר עזר. In this verse Syr may have been influenced by Pesh-Gen 2:20; cf. § 5.2.

[149] Cf. Avinery, *Syntaxe*, 191–193, for examples from the Pentateuch.

[150] *Pace* Bacher, 'Notes on the Cambridge Fragments', 283 (on 13:19).

[151] Cf. § 7.2.3.

In the present chapter we have focused on phrases in which the head takes one extension. We have seen that more complex structures occur if the extension itself takes further specifications. The consequences of our findings in the present chapter for our over-all view of phrase structure will be presented in Chapter 15. First we will address cases where the head takes two or more extensions.

CHAPTER ELEVEN

PHRASES WITH TWO EXTENSIONS

11.1 ADJECTIVE AND APPOSITION

This chapter will be concerned with cases in which a phrase atom is modified by two extensions. This construction should not be confused with that in which an extension takes another extension.[1] With an adjective and apposition the basic pattern is

[Noun [Adjective <sp>] [Noun <ap>]]:

24:12 ܪܡܝܢ ܕܡܪܝܐ ܣܘܬܐ ܒܚܫܒ 'in the honourable people, in the Lord's portion'.[2]

In § 10.3.2 (1) we have discussed the pattern [Noun [Noun [Adjective <sp>] <ap>]] in which the adjective functions as a specification of the apposition. We can conclude that there is a functional opposition between the orders Noun–Adjective–Apposition and Noun–Apposition–Adjective. The first order occurs when the adjective modifies the head, the second when it modifies the noun in apposition.[3]

11.2 ADJECTIVE AND *d*-PHRASE

If both an adjective and a *d*-phrase modify the same head, the adjective appears immediately after the noun.[4] According to the nature of

---

[1] See above, §§ 10.1.3, 10.2.2, 10.3.2, 10.5.2.

[2] For the repetition of the preposition see § 10.3.1.

[3] Elsewhere in the Peshitta exceptions to this rule occur with the cardinal ܚܕ and other numerals. When a noun is qualified by both an adjective and ܚܕ the latter comes immediately before or after it. Compare e.g. 1 Sam 6:7 MT: עגלה חדשה אחת; Pesh: ܥܓܠܬܐ ܚܕܐ ܚܕܬܐ. This indicates that 'the substantive and the numeral constitute a nucleus, which is further qualified by an adjective'; see Muraoka, 'Noun Modifier', 193; idem, *Basic Grammar*, § 91c; idem, *Classical Syriac for Hebraists*, § 79; cf. *ibid.* § 81: 'it appears that similar cohesion exists between other numerals and the nucleus noun, an additional modifier such as an adjective, demonstrative pronoun, and ܐܚܪܝܢ being prevented from intervening'; see also Avinery, *Syntaxe*, 262.

the element following the Dalath we can distinguish the following three patterns:

[Noun [Adjective <sp>] [*d*-Noun <sp>]]
[Noun [Adjective <sp>] [*d*-{[Adjective <PC>]} <sp>]]
[Noun [Adjective <sp>] [*d*-{Clause} <sp>]][5]

The first construction occurs three times:

16:3 ܒܢ̈ܝܐ ܣܓܝ̈ܐܐ ܕܥܘܠܐ 'many wicked sons'.[6]
26:27 ܐܝܟ ܩܪܢܐ ܡܠܗܒܬܐ ܕܩܪܒܐ 'like a horn instigating for the battle'.
28:14 ܠܐܢܫ̈ܐ ܡܝܩ̈ܪܐ ܕܡܕ̈ܝܢܬܐ 'honourable men of the cities'.

The second construction occurs in

10:22 ܬܘܬܒܐ ܐܟܣܢܝܐ ܕܡܣܟܝܢ ܘܥܩܐ ܠܗ 'a foreign sojourner who is poor and distressed'.

In this example the construction with ܕ enables the extension with a parallel element.

The third construction occurs in, e.g.:

16:7 ܠܡ̈ܠܟܐ ܩܕ̈ܡܝܐ ܕܡܠܘ ܚܠܕܐ ܒܓܢܒܪܘܬܗܘܢ 'the kings of old, who filled the earth with their strength'.
30:8 ܒܪܐ ܡܪܘܕܐ ܕܠܐ ܫܡܥ ܠܐܒܘܗܝ 'a rebellious son who does not listen to his father'.
41:2 ܓܒܪܐ ܣܒܐ ܕܡܬܬܩܠ ܒܟܠܙܒܢ 'the old man who stumbles always'.

In § 10.2.2 (2) we have discussed the pattern [Noun [*d*-Noun [Adjective <sp>] <sp>]], in which the adjective modifies the *d*-phrase. Here too there appears to be a functional opposition between the orders Noun–Adjective–*d*-phrase and Noun–*d*-phrase–Adjective. The first order is used if the adjective modifies the noun, the second if it modifies the *d*-phrase.[7] This observation is important for the interpretation

---

[4] On cases where the adjective precedes the noun, see above, § 10.1.2.

[5] In fact the pattern with *d*-{[Adjective <PC>]} is a subcategory of that with *d*-{Clause}; see § 10.2.3.

[6] Heb has בנים רבים עולה (MS A) and בנים רבים בני עולה (MS B). These constructions are odd. One would rather expect something like בני עולה רבים. For this reason it has been argued that Heb reflects a retroversion from Syr; cf. Van Peursen, 'Retroversions', 77; see also below, at the end of this paragraph.

[7] Elsewhere in the Peshitta and other Classical Syriac corpora there are exceptional cases where the adjective following *d*-Noun modifies the head, rather than the *d*-phrase, e.g. Exod 14:21 ܪܘܚܐ ܕܫܘܒܐ ܚܣܝܢܬܐ 'a fierce wind of blight' (MT רוח קדים

of phrases that are at first sight ambiguous, such as 1 Kgs 9:9 ܐܠܗܐ
ܕܥܡ̈ܡܐ ܐܚܪ̈ܢܐ (MT אלהים אחרים). From our investigation it follows
that this phrase should be translated with 'gods of other nations' rather
than 'other gods of the nations'.[8]

In this respect the Noun *d*-Noun behaves differently from
CstrNoun–Noun in Syriac and Hebrew. If in Biblical Hebrew an adjective modifies a noun that governs a 'genitive', the adjective follows
the *nomen rectum*, e.g. Esth 8:15 עטרת זהב גדולה 'a great crown of
gold'.[9] The only example of a discontinuous construction occurs in
Ezek 6:11 תועבות רעות בית ישראל 'the evil abominations of the house
of Israel'.[10] In Classical Syriac construct chains are occasionally broken up by short words such as the particles ܗܘ, ܕܝܢ and ܐܦ.[11] The
adjective always follows the *nomen rectum*.[12]

11.3 TWO APPOSITIONS

The basic pattern is[13]

[Noun [Noun <ap>] [Noun <ap>]]:

44:23 ܒܪܝ، ܒܘܟܪܝ، ܐܝܣܪܐܝܠ 'my son, my first-born, Israel'.

Variation in this pattern occurs when one of the appositions takes another extension, e.g.:

[ProperNoun [Noun <ap>] [Noun [*d*-Noun <sp>] <ap>]:

48:22 ܐܫܥܝܐ ܢܒܝܐ ܡܫܒܚܐ ܕܢܒܝ̈ܐ 'Isaiah, the prophet, the most praise-
worthy of the prophets'.[14]

עזה; cf. Payne Smith; *Thesaurus* II, 1085); see Muraoka, *Classical Syriac for Hebraists*, § 90; idem, *Basic Grammar*, § 91g.

[8] Note that our observations concern the rules we can establish in Syr. Although
these rules agree with strong tendencies in other Classical Syriac corpora, the exceptional cases collected by Muraoka mentioned in the preceding footnote demonstrate
that we cannot assume that the rules apply unequivocally and consistently in all cases.

[9] Cf. Gesenius–Kautzsch–Cowley, *Hebrew Grammar*, § 132a.

[10] Cf. Joüon–Muraoka, *Grammar*, § 129a, n. 4; Van Peursen, 'Retroversions', 78.

[11] In these cases the phrase atom is split up into two elements. Cf. Nöldeke,
Grammatik, § 208 and see the example from *Joseph and Asenath*, quoted in § 13.2
(end). In Syr there is no example of a discontinuous phrase atom.

[12] Compare the examples with CstrNoun–Noun–Adjective given in § 10.1.1 (end).

[13] Compare the construction in which an apposition is extended by another apposition in 36:18, discussed in §§ 10.3.1 (end), 10.3.2 (5).

[ProperNoun [CstrNoun–Noun <ap>] [Noun [Adjective <sp>] <ap>]]:

50:1 ܫܡܥܘܢ ܒܪ ܢܬܢܝܐ ܟܗܢܐ ܪܒܐ ‘Simeon the son of Netanya the high priest’.[15]

It is hard to discern a functional difference between the construction in which two appositions are juxtaposed asyndetically and that in which an apposition is followed by a parallel element (i.e. *w*-Noun) as in

46:13 ܫܡܘܐܝܠ ܕܝܢܐ ܘܟܗܢܐ ‘Samuel, the judge and the priest’.

Although we have analysed the latter construction under ‘apposition extended’ in § 10.3.2 (4), one may be inclined to view it as a syndetic alternative to the construction discussed in the present paragraph.

11.4 APPOSITION AND *d*-PHRASE

The basic pattern is

[Noun [*d*-Noun <sp>] [Noun <ap>]]

Wth repetition of the preposition before the apposition, this pattern occurs in e.g.

44:1 ܠܐܢܫܐ ܕܛܝܒܘܬܐ ܠܐܒܗܬܢ ‘the men of goodness, our fathers’.

More complex structures are created when the *d*-phrase and/or the apposition take further extensions. The apposition is extended in, e.g.

36:18 ܥܠ ܩܪܝܬܐ ܕܩܘܕܫܟ ܥܠ ܐܘܪܫܠܡ ܐܬܪܐ ܕܫܟܝܢܬܟ ‘on your holy city, on Jerusalem, the place of your habitation’.[16]

43:2 ܡܐܢܐ ܕܬܕܡܘܪܬܐ ܥܒܕܗ ܕܡܪܝܡܐ ‘a marvellous vessel, a work of the Most High’.

If the *d*-phrase contains predication, it comes after the apposition, i.e.

[Noun [Noun <ap>] [*d*-{Clause} <sp>]]:

26:28 ܥܠ ܓܒܪܐ ܒܪܚܐܪܐ ܕܐܬܡܣܟܢ ܘܐܣܬܢܩ ‘over a free-born man, who is impoverished and becomes needy’.

---

[14] Cf. Gr Ἠσαΐας ὁ προφήτης ὁ μέγας καὶ πιστὸς ἐν ὁράσει αὐτοῦ. Our categorization of this example implies that we interpret ܡܗܝܡܢܐ as a substantivized participle, rather than an adjectival specification of ܢܒܝܐ.

[15] See the discussion of this verse in § 10.1.

[16] See the discussion of this verse in § 10.3.1 (end).

30:8 ܐܝܟ ܣܘܣܝܐ ܥܠܐ ܕܠܐ ܡܬܟܒܫ 'like an horsefoal that is not subdued'.

47:23 ܠܝܘܪܒܥܡ ܒܪ ܢܒܛ ܕܚܛܐ ܘܐܚܛܝ ܠܐܝܣܪܝܠ 'Jeroboam the son of Nebat, who sinned and caused Israel to sin'.

A possible exception occurs in

36:17 ܘܚܕܝ، ܥܠ ܥܡܟ ܕܐܬܩܪܝ، ܫܡܟ ܥܠܘܗܝ، ܥܠ ܐܝܣܪܝܠ ܕܩܪܝܬܝܗܝ، ܒܘܟܪܟ 'And rejoice in Your people, who are called by Your name, in Israel, whom you called your first-born'.

But it is also possible to analyse ܥܠ ܐܝܣܪܝܠ ܕܩܪܝܬܝܗܝ، ܒܘܟܪܟ as an elliptical clause, rather than an apposition to ܥܠ ܥܡܟ. In other words, to analyse it as

[W-<Cj>] [XDJ <Pr>] [<L <MK
  [D-{[>TQRJ <Pr>] [CMK <Su>] [<LWHJ <Co>]} <sp>] <Co>]
[<L >JSRJL
  [D-{[QRJTJHJ <PO>] [BWKRK <Ob>]} <sp>] <Co>]

with ellipsis of the verb in the second clause, rather than

[W-<Cj>] [XDJ <Pr>] [<L <MK [D-{[>TQRJ <Pr>] [CMK <Su>] [<LWHJ <Co>]} <sp>] [<L >JSRJL [D-{[QRJTJHJ <PO>] [BWKRK <Ob>]} <sp>] <ap>]]

In § 10.2.2 (1) we have discussed the pattern [Noun [*d*-Noun [Noun <ap>] <sp>]] in which the apposition is an extension of the *d*-phrase. In this paragraph we have seen that the order *d*-phrase–Apposition also occurs in cases where the *d*-phrase and the apposition are both extensions of the same phrase atom. A distinction between the two constructions can be made if the head of the phrase contains a preposition that is repeated before the apposition, such as ܥܠ in 36:18 and ܠ in 44:1. The order Noun–Apposition–*d*-Noun is only used if the *d*-phrase modifies the apposition, that is the pattern [Noun [Noun [*d*-Noun <sp>] <ap>]]. We have seen examples of this pattern in § 10.3.2 (2).

With relative clauses the situation is different. The relative clause always follows the apposition, both in cases where it modifies the apposition, that is the pattern [Noun [Noun [*d*-{Clause} <sp>] <ap>]], discussed in § 10.3.2 (3), and in cases where it modifies the main noun, that is the pattern [Noun [Noun <ap>] [*d*-{Clause} <sp>]], discussed in the present paragraph.

11.5 TWO *d*-PHRASES

If two *d*-phrases modify the same noun, the basic pattern is

[Noun [*d*-phrase <sp>] [*d*-phrase <sp>]]

'*d*-phrase' stands for *d*-Noun, *d*-Adjective or *d*-Clause. However, the number of patterns attested in our corpus is limited. The only two patterns are

[Noun [*d*-Noun <sp>] [*d*-{[Adjective <PC>]} <sp>]]:

4:2 ܪܘܚܗ ܕܐܢܫܐ ܕܬܒܝܪܐ 'the spirit of the person which is broken'.[17]
19:22 ܬܪܥܝܬܐ ܕܚܛܝ̈ܐ ܕܡܣܬܟܠܢܐ '(there is no) reflection of the sinners that is prudent'

[Noun [*d*-Noun <sp>] [*d*-{Clause} <sp>]:[18]

8:9 ܫܘܥܝ̈ܬܐ ܕܣܒ̈ܐ ܕܫܡܥܘ ܡܢ ܐܒ̈ܗܝܗܘܢ 'the discourse of the elders, which they have heard from their fathers'.
22:16 ܐܝܟ ܥܪܘܬܐ ܕܩܝܣܐ ܕܐܣܝܪܐ ܒܐܣ̈ܐ ܕܙܘ̈ܝܬܐ ܕܒܝܬܐ 'like a wooden thwart that is fastened in the walls of the corners of a house'.
38:21 ܐܝܟ ܦܪܚܬܐ ܕܫܡܝܐ ܕܦܪܚܐ ܘܫܟܢܐ 'like a bird of heaven that flies and settles'.

In the following examples the first *d*-Noun specification is extended by another *d*-phrase, after which follows the second specification of the head:

16:8 ܥܠ ܥܡܘܪ̈ܐ ܕܡܕܝܢܬܗ ܕܠܘܛ ܕܐܪܫܥܘ ܡܛܠ ܫܘܒܗܪܗܘܢ 'on the inhabitants of the city of Lot, who acted impiously because of their pride'.
47:18 ܒܫܡܗ ܕܐܠܗܐ ܕܕܝܠܗ ܗܘ ܐܝܩܪܐ ܕܐܬܩܪܝ ܥܠ ܐܝܣܪܝܠ 'by the name of God, whose is the honour'.

These examples display the following patterns:

[Noun [*d*-Noun [*d*-Noun <sp>] <sp>] [*d*-{Clause} <sp>] (16:8)
[Noun [*d*-Noun [*d*-{Clause} <sp>] <sp>] [*d*-{Clause}] (47:18)

In Syr there are no examples of the type

[Noun [*d*-Noun <sp>] [*d*-Noun <sp>]]

---

[17] Cf. § 20.1 (end).
[18] Again, it should be noted that the previous pattern is a subcategory of this pattern; cf. § 10.2.3.

which is attested, for example, in

> Aphrahat, *Dem.* 21:21 ܢܟܘܒܘܪ ܕܩܘܕܫܐ ܪܘܚܐ 'the Holy Spirit of your Father'.[19]

This means that in all cases of Noun–*d*-Noun–*d*-Noun in our corpus the second *d*-Noun modifies the first *d*-Noun. Accordingly, their pattern is

[Noun [*d*-Noun [*d*-Noun <sp>] <sp>]]:

> 18:9 ܒܪܢܫܐ ܕܝܘܡܘܗܝ ܡܢܝܢܐ 'the number of the days of man'.[20]

In Syr, when two *d*-Noun specifications modify the same head, the second is added as a parallel element, with or without repetition of ܕ. The resulting patterns are[21]

[Noun [*d*-Noun <sp>] [*w*-<cj>] [*d*-Noun <PA>]]:

> 44:10 ܟܐܢܘ ܕܟܐܢܘܬܐ ܕܛܒܘܬܐ 'men of goodness and of righteousness'.

[Noun [*d*-Noun [*w*-<cj>] [Noun <PA>] <sp>]]:

> 14:18 ܕܡܐ ܘ ܕܒܣܪܐ ܕܪܐ 'the generations of flesh and blood'.

The reason for the construction with ܘ may be that in these examples the two *d*-phrases express the same type of relation, which is not the case in the example from Aphrahat, where ܪܘܚܐ and ܕܩܘܕܫܐ reflect two different types of genitive: a genitive of quality and a genitive of author/source.

11.6 *d*-PHRASE AND PREPOSITIONAL PHRASE

If both *d*-Noun and a prepositional phrase modify the same noun, the basic structure is:

[Noun [*d*-Noun <sp>] [Prep-Noun <sp>]]

Variation in this pattern occurs when the prepositional phrase is further extended by a *d*-phrase, an adjective or an apposition. Some examples:

---

[19] Ed. Parisot, 1.984, lines 8–9; Nöldeke, *Grammatik*, § 206E.
[20] For more examples of this pattern see § 10.2.2 (3).
[21] For further details see § 10.2.2 (7).

21:9 (= 25:20) ܐܝܟ ܡܣܩܬܐ ܕܚܠܐ ܒܪ̈ܓܠܘܗܝ ܕܓܒܪܐ ܣܒܐ 'like an ascent of sand at the feet of an old man'.

24:13 ܘܐܝܟ ܐܝܠܢܐ ܕܡܫܚܐ ܒܣܢܝܪ ܠܛܘܪܐ ܕܬܠܓܐ 'and like an oleaster on the Senir, the mountain of snow'.

26:18 ܐܝܟ ܣܘ̈ܡܟܐ ܕܕܗܒܐ ܥܠ ܐܣܛܘܢܐ ܕܣܐܡܐ 'like golden sockets on a column of silver'.[22]

33:13 ܐܝܟ ܛܝܢܐ ܕܓܒܝܠ ܒܐܝܕܐ ܕܦܚܪܐ 'like clay of the earth in the hand of the potter'.

35:26 ܐܝܟ ܥܢܢܐ ܕܡܛܪܐ ܒܥܕܢܐ ܕܣܢܝܩܘܬܐ 'like a cloud of rain in the time it is needed'.

39:14 ܐܝܟ ܪܝܚܐ ܕܠܒܢܢ ܒܐܪ̈ܙܘܗܝ 'like the odour of Lebanon in its cedars'.

50:8 ܘܐܝܟ ܐܝܠܢܐ ܕܠܒܢܢ ܒܝܘ̈ܡܝ ܩܛܦܐ 'and like a tree of the Lebanon in the days of the vintage'.

These examples support our claim in § 10.5.1 that the pattern [Noun [Prep–Noun] is attested in Syr, although the construction with ܕ may be more idiomatic Syriac.

In § 10.2.2 (6) we have discussed the pattern [Noun [*d*-Noun [Prep-Noun <sp>] <sp>]] in which the prepositional phrase modifies the *d*-phrase rather than the head. It appears that the structure Noun–*d*-Noun–Prep-Noun is used both if the prepositional phrase modifies the preceding *d*-phrase and when it modifies the head. The reverse order, i.e. Noun–Prep-Noun–*d*-Noun is used only if the *d*-phrase modifies the prepositional phrase (see § 10.5.2).

If the *d*-phrase consists of ܕ + relative clause, it follows the prepositional phrase, i.e.

[Noun [Prep-Noun <sp>] [*d*-{Clause} <sp>]:

33:7 ܝܘܡܐ ܒܫܢܬܐ ܕܡܢ ܝܘܡܐ ܦܪܝܫ 'a day in the year that differs from the other'.

Here we see again that the relative clause introduced by ܕ behaves differently from ܕ + Noun.[23]

[22] 7a1 has ܣܘܡܟܐ, without *seyame*.

[23] On the differences between *d*-Noun and *d*-Relative Clause see further § 12.6.

11.7 ADJECTIVE AND PREPOSITIONAL PHRASE

If both an adjective and a prepositional phrase modify the same noun, the basic pattern is

[Noun [Adjective <sp>] [Prep-Noun <sp>]]:

> 22:18 ܟܐܦܐ ܪܡܐ ܕܥܠ ܟܪܟܐ ܙܥܘܪܐ 'a small bundle on a stone that is high'.

11.8 DEMONSTRATIVE AND APPOSITION

There is one possible example where the head of the phrase is specified by both a demonstrative and an apposition in 1:20f ܗܢܐ ܟܬܒܐ ܟܠܗ ܡܠܐ ܚܝܐ 'This book is entirely full of life', if we analyse this as

> [[HN> <sp>] KTB> [KLH <ap>] <Su>]] [ML> <Pr>] [XJ> <Ob>][24]

However, it is also possible to apply a different analysis, in which ܗܢܐ ܟܬܒܐ is an element in extraposition that is resumed by the suffix in ܟܠܗ.

> [HN> KTB> <Ex>] ‖ [KLH <Su>] [ML> <Pr>] [XJ> <Ob>]

There are no other examples where a phrase atom is specified by both a demonstrative and another extension. Elsewhere in the Peshitta we do find such constructions. It appears that in those cases the demonstrative comes either immediately before or after the noun, thus differing from the usual word order in Hebrew, e.g. Deut 4:6 Pesh: ܥܡܐ ܗܢܐ ܪܒܐ 'this great people'; MT הגוי הגדול הזה.[25]

---

[24] Cf. § 10.4 (end) for the pattern *ܗܢܐ ܗܠ ܟܬܒܐ.

[25] See Muraoka, 'Noun Modifier', 194; idem, *Classical Syriac for Hebraists*, § 80; Avinery, 'Position of Demonstrative Pronoun', 125; idem, *Syntaxe*, 260–270. If, however, the phrase atom is extended by both a numeral and a demonstrative, the noun displays closer cohesion with the numeral (Muraoka, *Classical Syriac for Hebraists*, § 82; idem, *Basic Grammar*, § 91c; Avinery, *ibid.*); cf. above, footnote 3.

CHAPTER TWELVE

PHRASES WITH MORE THAN TWO EXTENSIONS AND OTHER COMPLEX PHRASE STRUCTURES

12.1 INTRODUCTION

In Chapter Ten we discussed phrases consisting of a phrase atom and one specification. For most types of specification we discovered examples in which the specification was expanded by another specification. In Chapter Eleven we discovered another way in which a phrase may be enlarged, namely by the addition of another specification of the head. In several cases we have seen that parallel elements also occur as extensions of a phrase. In § 9.1 we have indicated that the parallel element constitutes a separate category, because it concerns the addition of another element (phrase atom), rather than a modification of the head of the phrase. Accordingly, there are three types of expansions:

1. Specifications of the head of the phrase.
2. Specifications of another specification.
3. Parallel elements.

The question arises as to what extent these extensions are employed. One could speculate that theoretically the language system allows these extensions to be used *ad infinitem* and that a noun could take, for example, an endless number of adjectives. The present study, however, deals with corpus linguistics. We can register the maximum number of building blocks constituting a phrase attested in our corpus. Thus in Syr the highest number of parallel elements added to a single head is twelve (see below, § 12.4). It may be that other corpora of Classical Syriac contain longer chains, but for our corpus-linguistic study it will suffice to register the patterns that are attested in the text under investigation.[1]

12.2 PHRASE ATOM WITH THREE SPECIFICATIONS

The pattern in which a phrase atom takes three specifications is very rare. It is only attested with relative clauses. The following patterns are attested.

1. Two appositions and a relative clause:

50:1 ܫܡܥܘܢ ܒܪ ܢܬܢܝܐ ܟܗܢܐ ܪܒܐ ܕܒܝܘܡܘܗܝ ܐܬܒܢܝ ܒܝܬܐ
[CM<WN [BR NTNJ> <ap>] [KHN> RB> <ap>]
[D-{[B-JWMWHJ <Ti>] [>TBNJ <Pr>] [BJT> <Su>]} <sp>]]
'Simeon, the son of Netanya, the high priest, in whose days the house was built'.

2. Three relative clauses:

14:20–26 ܛܘܒܘܗܝ ܠܓܒܪܐ ܕܒܚܟܡܬܐ ܢܗܘܐ ܪܢܐ (...) ܕܢܦܢܐ ܥܠ ܐܘܪܚܬܗ
ܠܒܗ (...) ܕܢܪܡܐ ܐܝܕܘܗܝ ܥܠ ܣܘܟܝܗ
[VWBWHJ <Su>] [L-GBR> <sp>]
[D-<Re>] [B-XKMT> <Co>] [NHW> <Pr>] [RN> <PC>] (...)
[D-<Re>] [NPN> <Pr>] [<L >WRXTH <Co>] [LBH <Ob>] (...)
[D-<Re>] [NRM> <Pr>] [>JDWHJ <Ob>] [<L SWKJH <Aj>] (...)
'Blessed is the man who is reflecting upon wisdom (...); who directs his heart to her ways (...); and lays his hands on her boughs (...)'.

This is the only example where the head takes three relative clauses with ܕ. The clauses introduced by ܕ alternate with parallel clauses introduced by ܘ (one after the first *d*-phrase, eight after the second, and three after the third; cf. below, § 12.5). This is also the case in, e.g.:

51:2 ܬܘܟܠܢܝ ܕܡܢ ܥܠܡ ܡܪܝܡܐ ܕܦܪܩܬ ܢܦܫܝ ܡܢ ܡܘܬܐ ܘܚܣܟܬ ܒܣܪܝ ܡܢ
ܚܒܠܐ
[TWKLNJ <Vo>]
[D-<Re>] [MN <LM <Aj>] [MRJM> <PC>]
[D-<Re>] [PRQT <Pr>] [NPCJ <Ob>] [MN MWT> <Co>]
[W-<Cj>] [XSKT <Pr>] [BSRJ <Ob>] [MN XBL> <Co>]
'My Confidence, who is exalted from eternity, who saved my soul from death, and spared my flesh from corruption.'

---

[1] This is not only a consequence of our corpus-linguistic approach, but also the result of the fact that in the study of ancient texts, for which we do not have a native speaker, we can describe *la langue* only on the basis of *la parole*; cf. § 7.4.1 (end).

Compare further *w*-... *d*-... *w*-... in 42:19; 50:19–22 and 51:2; *d*-...
w-... *w*-...: in 30:19; and *d*-... *w*-... *w*-... *w*-... *w*-... in 38:25 and
38:26.

12.3 EXTENSIONS EXTENDED

Another way in which phrases are extended is by the addition of extensions that specify other extensions. In §§ 10.1.3, 10.2.2, 10.3.2 and
10.5.2 we have seen examples of the pattern

Head – <sp$_1$> – <sp$_2$>

in which <sp$_2$> modifies <sp$_1$>. This pattern can be extended to the
third degree. That is to say: a specification is specified by a second
specification, which in turn is specified by a third specification, as in

21:9 (= 25:20) ܐܝܟ ܡܫܩܠܐ ܕܚܠܐ ܕܒܪܓܠܘܗܝ ܕܓܒܪܐ ܣܒܐ
[>JK MSQT> [D-XL> <sp>] [B-RGLWHJ [D-GBR> [QCJC> <sp>] <sp>] <sp>]]
'Like a slope of sand at the feet of an old man'.[2]

Here we can also mention the examples with embedded relative
clauses, e.g.:

10:24 ܘܠܝܬ ܗܘ ܕܝܬܝܪ ܡܢ ܡܢ ܕܡܝܩܪ ܠܡܢ ܕܕܚܠ ܠܠܗ ܐܠܗܐ
[W-<Cj>] [L-<Ng>] [JT <PC>]
   [D- {[RB <PC>] [MN MN
      [D- {[MJQR <PC>] [L-MN
         [D- {[DXL <Pr>] [L->LH> <Co>]} <Co>]} <sp>] <Co>]} <Su>]
'And there is no one greater than he who honours someone who fears
God'.

In this example the subject of the ܐܝܬ clause is a so-called independent relative clause (beginning with ܡܢ). This subject clause contains
an embedded relative clause, which itself contains another embedded
clause. Another example is

---

[2] In this case the three-step specification is preceded by another specification of
the head: ܚܠܐ; cf. § 11.6; see also § 15.4.

1:20h ܡܢܘ ܕܨܒܐ ܕܢܐܪܬ ܚܝܐ ܝܘܪܬܢܐ ܕܠܥܠܡ ܘܚܕܘܬܐ ܪܒܬܐ
[MN-<Qp>] [W <Ep>]
[D-{[YB> <PC>]
[D-{[N>RT <Pr>] [XJ> [JWRTN>
[D-{[L-<LM <PC>]} <sp>] <ap>]
[W-<cj>] [XDWT> [RBT> <sp>] <PA>] <Ob>]} <Ob>]} <Su>]
'Who wants to inherit life, an eternal heritage and great joy?'

The subject clause with ܕܨܒܐ contains an object clause (ܕܢܐܪܬ etc.). The object of this object clause contains a specification consisting of ܕ + Clause (ܕܠܥܠܡ). Within the object clause there occur some other specifications: the apposition ܝܘܪܬܢܐ, the parallel element ܘܚܕܘܬܐ ܪܒܬܐ, and in that parallel element the adjective ܪܒܬܐ.

The moment we include relative clauses in our analysis, we encounter some complex structures which can hardly be handled with our usual annotation. In such cases it is preferable to apply a clause-hierarchical model of description, as we will see in § 12.5.[3]

12.4 PARALLEL ELEMENTS

A head may be followed by a parallel element. Thus we find with one parallel element:

6:28 ܢܝܚܐ ܘܬܦܢܝܩܐ 'rest and good cheer'.

With two parallel elements:

33:25 ܡܪܕܘܬܐ ܘܠܚܡܐ ܘܦܘܠܚܢܐ 'chastisement, bread and service'.

And with three parallel elements:

24:15 ܐܝܟ ܠܒܘܢܬܐ ܘܚܠܒܢܝܬܐ ܘܛܦܪܐ ܘܦܘܪܣܡܐ 'like incense and galbanum and onyx-spice and balsam'.

There seems to be no limit to the number of elements that can be paralleled, but in our corpus-linguistic approach we define the maximum number of elements in terms of the longest chain actually attested in our corpus. This chain consists of a head followed by twelve parallel elements, all coordinated syndetically.

39:26 ܡܝܐ ܘܢܘܪܐ ܘܦܪܙܠܐ ܘܡܠܚܐ ܘܬܪܒܐ ܘܚܠܒܐ ܘܕܒܫܐ ܘܚܢܛܐ ܘܚܡܪܐ ܘܡܫܚܐ ܘܬܟܣܝܬܐ ܘܠܒܘܫܐ 'water and fire, iron and salt, fat

[3] See also § 26.2 on the distinction between restrictive and non-restrictive relative clauses.

and[4] wheat, milk and honey, grapes and wine and oil, and covering and clothing'.

Sometimes [(Prep) Noun [*w*-<cj>] [(Prep) Noun <PA>]] in Syr corresponds to [(Prep) Noun] in Heb:

6:28 ܢܝܚܐ ܘܦܨܝܚܘܬܐ 'rest and good cheer'; A מנוחתה.
20:7 ܓܒܪܐ ܚܨܝܦܐ ܘܡܪܘܕܐ 'an insolent and unrighteous man'; C כסיל.[5]
37:3 ܒܝܫܐ ܘܣܢܐܐ 'the enemy and the wicked one'; B+D רע.[6]
39:26 (end; see above) ܘܬܟܣܝܬܐ ܘܠܒܘܫܐ 'and covering and clothing'; B ובגד.
46:13 ܫܠܝܛܢܐ ܘܡܠܟܐ 'rulers and kings'; B נגידים.

Four parallel nouns in Syr correspond to two in Heb in

18:33 ܡܣܟܝܢ ܘܪܘܝ، ܘܙܠܝܠ ܘܦܩܦܩ '(do not become) poor and a drunkard and licentious and gossip'; C זולל וסובא.[7]

Similar phenomena occur in cases where Heb is not extant, e.g.:

18:29 ܡܠܐ ܕܡܬܠܐ ܘܡܠܐ ܕܚܟܡܬܐ ܘܡܪܕܘܬܐ ܕܢܦܫܐ 'words of proverbs and words of wisdom and instruction of the soul'; Gr παροιμίας ἀκριβεῖς.[8]

Sometimes the Hebrew evidence is divided:

4:30 ܘܡܚܡܬ ܘܕܚܝܠ 'flaring up and fearsome'; A ומוזר ומתירא; C ומתפחז.

Vice versa there are cases in which a single noun in Syr corresponds to Noun *w*-Noun in Heb:

31:29 ܒܚܪܝܢܐ 'with contention'; B בתחרה וכעס.
40:4 ܡܢ ܡܠܟܐ، ܬ ܟܠܝܠܐ 'from those who put on a crown'; B מעוטה צניף וציץ.

A single noun corresponds to Noun–καί–Noun in Gr (Heb not extant) in

---

[4] Cf. below, note 12.

[5] For the addition of ܓܒܪܐ see § 10.1.1. Cf. Ryssel, 'Fragmente', VII, 399, 'S "der Freche und Missethäter", was wohl erläuternder Zusatz (von einer Randglosse her?) zu H ist'.

[6] This is not a compelling reason to assume that the Syriac translator had a Hebrew source reading צר ורע; *pace* Taylor, 'Wisdom of Ben Sira', 579; for the confusion of רֵעַ and רַע in this verse cf. § 3.4 (c).

[7] For the plus ܡܣܟܝܢ see § 2.3.3 ('Patterns of agreement between Syr and Gr'), (2) and § 3.7.1 ('Influence of adjacent lines').

[8] ܕܢܦܫܐ not in 7a1. Peters, *Ben Sirach*, 154, seems to take παροιμίας ἀκριβεῖς as corresponding to ܡܠܐ ܕܡܬܠܐ, because he calls the rest of the text in Syr an explanatory addition ('erläuternde Ergänzung'), but that is a simplification of the complex relationship between the two phrases.

23:8 ܘܣܟܠܐ 'and the fool'; Gr καὶ λοίδορος καὶ ὑπερήφανος.

In all these cases where [(Prep) Noun [*w*-<cj>] [(Prep) Noun <PA>]] in Syr corresponds to [(Prep) Noun] in Heb or *vice versa*, it is incorrect to consider the parallel element as a plus in Syr or Heb respectively. We should rather describe the phrase containing the single word and the one containing the parallel element as two corresponding phrases with different internal phrase structure.[9]

The same analysis is useful in the case of transpositions, i.e. $Noun_A$ *w*-$Noun_B$ in Syr corresponds to $Noun_B$ *w*-$Noun_A$ in Heb,[10] as in

37:8 ܚܝܐ ܘܡܘܬܐ 'life and death'; B חיים ומות; D מות וחיים.

In his study of Sir 44:16–45:26 Reiterer concludes that this phenomenon is infrequent in Syr. For this reason Reiterer thinks that in those few cases where it does occur it can be accounted for by assuming a variant in the translator's Hebrew source text.[11]

In other examples the pattern of correspondence is more complicated.[12] Thus [Noun [*w*-<cj>] [Noun <PA>]] in Syr corresponds to [CstrNoun–Noun] in Heb in

10:7 ܚܛܘܦܝܐ ܘܛܠܘܡܝܐ 'force and deceit'; A מעל עשק.[13]
11:12 ܡܢ ܥܦܪܐ ܘܡܢ ܩܛܡܐ 'from dust and ashes'; A מעפר צחנה.
31:29 ܟܐܒܐ ܘܡܣܟܢܘܬܐ ܘܟܐܒ ܪܫܐ 'pain and poverty and headache'; B+F כאב ראש.[14]

---

[9] Cf. Smend, *Jesus Sirach*, 364, on ܘܬܫܡܫܬܐ ܘܠܒܘܫܐ in 39:26: 'Aber בגד ist beides'.

[10] For this phenomenon see e.g. Shepherd, 'Flesh and Bones'; Taylor, *Daniel*, 320–321; Greenberg, *Jeremiah*, 53–54; Gelston, *Twelve Prophets*, 135–136; Williams, *Peshitta of 1 Kings*, 155; idem, *Early Syriac Translation Technique*, 204–235.

[11] Reiterer, *Urtext*, 51, 147; note the variation in the Hebrew witnesses in the example quoted; contrast Taylor, *Daniel*, 320: 'It is not likely, on either external or internal grounds, that this tendency is due to textual causes. Rather, the translator himself seems to have had a propensity for reversal of order in such phrases.'

[12] Compare also 39:26, quoted above, where Bacher ('Hebrew Text of Ecclesiasticus', 544), Peters (*Ben Sirach*, 332) and Lévi (*L'Ecclésiastique* I, 9) reconstruct וחלב חטים corresponding to Syr ܘܬܪܒܐ ܘܚܛܐ. This implies the correspondence of Noun *w*-Noun in Syr with CstrNoun–Noun in Heb. Bacher suggests that confusion of ܘ and ܕ took place in the Syriac transmission, i.e. ܘܬܪܒܐ ܘܚܛܐ → ܘܬܪܒܐ ܕܚܛܐ; Lévi thinks that the Syriac translator missed the figurative meaning of חלב; see also Elwolde, 'Ben Sira 39:27 (32)', n. 23. For the opposite phenomenon, i.e. Noun *d*-Noun corresponding to Noun *w*-Noun in Heb, see § 10.2.1. For inner-Syriac variation between Noun *w*-Noun and Noun *d*-Noun compare 16:18, where 7h3, 9c1 and 10c2 read ܘܬܗܘܡܐ ܕܐܪܥܐ instead of ܘܬܗܘܡܐ ܘܐܪܥܐ in the other manuscripts consulted for the Leiden edition (A ותהום וארץ).

[13] According to Lévi, *L'Ecclesiastique* II, 63, Syr reflects מעל ועשק.

39:26 ܘܥܢܒܐ ܘܚܡܪܐ 'and grapes and wine'; B דם ענב.[15]

The observations presented here support our argument in Chapter Seven (§ 7.7.2) that in the study of the Ancient Versions a comparison at phrase level may be more fruitful than a word-by-word comparison. However, as we have indicated there, the comparison should also be made at the higher linguistic levels. In the following example the phenomenon under discussion leads to divergences not only in phrase structure but also in clause structure. Heb reads

48:5 B המקים גוע ממות ומשאול כרצון ייי 'who raised a dead person from death and from Sheol according to the Lord's will'.

This verse can be analysed as two coordinate clauses, namely המקים גוע ממות and ומשאול כרצון ייי with ellipsis of המקים in the second one. Where Heb has ממות ומשאול Syr has only ܡܢ ܫܝܘܠ. This affects not only the phrase structure, but also the clause structure, because the result is a reading that can hardly be split up into two distinct clauses:

48:5 ܕܐܚܝ ܡܝܬܐ ܡܢ ܫܝܘܠ ܐܝܟ ܨܒܝܢܗ ܕܐܠܗܐ 'who gave life to a dead person from Sheol according to the will of God'

In the preceding examples the parallel element consists of a single word. However, both the head of a phrase and the parallel elements are capable of taking further extensions, which may lead to rather complex constructions. The following structures are attested.

1. Both the head and the parallel element take one or more specifications:

16:19 ܥܩܪܐ ܕܛܘܪܐ ܘܫܬܐܣܬܐ ܕܬܒܝܠ 'the roots of the mountains and the foundations of the earth'.

2. The head takes two specifications, the parallel element takes one:

39:14 ܐܝܟ ܪܝܚܐ ܕܠܒܢܢ ܒܐܪ̈ܙܘܗܝ ܘܐܝܟ ܥܩܪܐ ܕܫܘܫܢܬ ܡܠܟܐ 'like the odour of the Lebanon in its cedars and like the root of the lily of the king'.

---

[14] Syr contains a double rendering of the Hebrew phrase כאב ראש reflecting the interpretation of ראש both as 'head' and as 'poverty'.

[15] According to Peters, *Ben Sirach*, 332, ܘܥܢܒܐ ܘܚܡܪܐ is a corruption of ܘܥܢܒܐ ܕܚܡܪܐ; Lévi, *L'Ecclésiastique* I, 9, calls it 'une sorte de commentaire'; see also Elwolde, 'Ben Sira 39:27 (32)', n. 23 and above, note 12.

3. The head is followed by two parallel elements. The head takes a specification:

> 32:6 ܐܝܟ ܩܠܐ ܕܕܗܒܐ ܘܟܐܦܐ ܘܒܪ̈ܘܠܚܐ 'as a golden necklace and gems and emeralds'.

4. The head is followed by two parallel elements. The second parallel element takes a specification:

> 1:12 ܘܪܘܙܐ ܘܕܝܨܐ ܘܚܝܐ ܕܠܥܠܡ 'gladness and exultation and eternal life'.

5. The head is followed by two parallel elements, both of which take a specification:

> 40:2 ܬܫܒܘܚܬܗܘܢ ܘܗ̈ܪܓܐ ܕܠܒܗܘܢ ܘܚ̈ܘܫܒܐ ܕܡܠܝܗܘܢ 'their praise and the reflections of their heart, and the end of their words'.

6. Both the head and the second parallel element take a specification:

> 31:28 ܚܕܘܬܐ ܕܠܒܐ ܘܒܘܣܡܐ ܘܙ̈ܒܢܐ ܛ̈ܒܐ 'joy of the heart and good cheer and good seasons'.

7. Both the head and the two specifications take a parallel element:

> 1:2 ܚܠܐ ܕܝܡܐ ܘܢܘܛ̈ܦܬܐ ܕܡܛܪܐ ܘܝ̈ܘܡܬܐ ܕܥܠܡܐ 'The sand of the sea, the drops of the rain and the days of eternity'.

8. Various other constructions with three parallel elements:

> 1:11 ܫܘܒܚܐ ܘܐܝܩܪܐ ܘܪܒܘܬܐ ܘܟܠܝܠܐ ܕܬܫܒܘܚܬܐ 'glory, honour, majesty and a crown of praise'.
>
> 16:18 ܫܡܝܐ ܘܫܡܝ ܫܡܝܐ ܘܬܗܘܡܐ ܘܐܪܥܐ 'the heaven and the heavens of the heaven and the abyss and the earth'.
>
> 24:6 ܘܐܫܬܠܛܬ ܒ̈ܢܒܥܐ ܕܡ̈ܝܐ ܘܒܫ̈ܬܐܣܝ ܐܪܥܐ ܘܒܟܠܗܘܢ ܥܡ̈ܡܐ ܘܐܡ̈ܘܬܐ '(I ruled) over the springs of water and over the foundations of the earth, and over all the peoples and nations'.
>
> 25:2 ܡܣܟܢܐ ܓܐܝܐ ܘܥܬܝܪܐ ܕܓܠܐ ܘܣܒܐ ܣܟܠܐ ܘܚܣܝܪ ܪܥܝܢܐ 'the proud poor man and the false rich man and the old man who is foolish and lacking understanding'
>
> 34:20 ܚܕܘܬܐ ܕܠܒܐ ܘܢܘܗܪܐ ܕܥ̈ܝܢܐ ܘܐܣܝܘܬܐ ܕܚ̈ܝܐ ܘܒܘܪ̈ܟܬܐ 'joy of the heart and light of the eyes and cure of life and blessings'.

12.5 THE NEED FOR A HIERARCHICAL ANALYSIS OF PHRASES

A text is a composition of linguistic elements on several levels. Each
level provides the building blocks of the elements at a subsequent
level: morphemes make up words, words constitute phrases, phrases
are combined to build clauses, clauses are the building blocks of sentences, and sentences are combined to form textual units.[16] Graphi-
cally this could be rendered as follows:

Text	[	]
Sentences	[ ][ ][ ]
Clauses	[ ][ ][ ][ ][ ]
Phrases	[ ][ ][ ][ ][ ][ ][ ][ ][ ]
Words	[ ][ ][][][ ][][ ][ ][][ ][][][ ][ ]
Morphemes	[ ][]

Very often, however, a text is far more complex than the situation reflected in this table. On the one hand linguistic elements may be
smaller than the table above suggests:[17] Sentences may consist of one
word (e.g. a finite verb), phrases of one morpheme (e.g. an object suffix), etc. On the other hand linguistic elements may be enlarged extremely. The number of words that constitute one phrase or the number of phrases that constitute one clause may become very high. In
39:26 (quoted in §12.4) there is a phrase consisting of twelve parallel
elements and in 50:6–10 the sequence of eleven parallel prepositional
phrases with ܥܠ covers no fewer than five verses.[18]

Even more complex structures can be given if we include relative
clauses in our analysis. Thus in 14:20–27 ܟܗܢܐ ܠܡܘܫܐ is followed
by fifteen clauses, three of which are relative clauses introduced by ܕ,
the others parallel clauses introduced by ܘ. Should we consider these
relative clauses and parallel clauses specifications that are part of the
first phrase, this would mean that 14:20–27 is a single phrase covering
eight verses.[19] Such an approach, which is in line with traditional
grammar, is not very helpful in a case like this. Such a complex struc-

---

[16] Cf. § 7.6 (end).

[17] Cf. Talstra–Sikkel, 'WIVU-Datenbank', 36–38.

[18] For the literary structure of this passage see Mulder, *High Priest*, 119–121.

[19] We consider ܟܗܢܐ as a specification of ܠܡܘܫܐ, which implies that ܠܡܘܫܐ
ܟܗܢܐ is a one-member clause; cf. Van Peursen, 'Clause Hierarchy and Discourse
Structure', 138.

ture requires rather a hierarchical approach that takes into account the various relationships that exist between predication structures and applies a more sophisticated model of grammatical analysis and discourse segmentation, taking into account the distinction between restrictive relative clauses (embedding) and non-restrictive relative clauses (hypotaxis). This will be discussed in Part Five.

12.6 ADDITIONAL REMARKS ON RELATIVE CLAUSES

Logically relative clauses can be analysed as specifications of their head. In some respects d-phrases in which predication occurs function like specifications consisting of ז + Noun. Thus if d-Noun or d-Clause follows a construct chain, both modify the *nomen rectum* (§ 10.2). However, there are also some differences:

1. With nominal, adjectival and prepositional phrase extensions we did not find any examples of more than two extensions modifying the same head. The pattern with three specifications is only attested with relative clauses (§ 12.2).

2. Unlike the d-Noun extensions, the relative clauses are very apt to take a large number of parallel elements (d-... w-... w-... etc.) (§ 12.2). The structures with relative and parallel clauses are often too complex and too long to be described in a linear model in which all these elements are considered as parallel elements and specifications within the same sentence. A hierarchical analysis that takes into account the distinction between embedding and hypotaxis is more apt to describe such constructions (§ 12.5).

3. In the case of three- and four-step specifications too the most complex structures contain relative clauses (compare the examples from 10:24 and 1:20h quoted in § 12.3).

4. In the 'maximum matrix of phrase structure',[20] d-Noun and d-Clause take different positions. Thus if the head of a phrase is specified by a prepositional phrase, d-Noun precedes the prepositional phrase, but the relative clause comes after it (§ 11.6).

---

[20] On this concept see § 15.1.

5. *d*-Noun and *d*-Clause behave differently in the case of discontinuous phrases.[21] In the case of the *d*-Noun only some well-defined elements can intervene between the phrase atom and the *d*-phrase. Relative clauses with ܕ, however, can be further removed from the head. In our *Verbal System* we have argued that in the Hebrew text of Sirach this is a characteristic of poetic style.[22] In these cases too a hierarchical analysis is necessary.

Our last point can be illustrated by the following examples:

44:19–20 ܐܒܪܗܡ ܐܒܐ ܕܟܢܘܫܬܐ ܕܥܡܡܐ ܘܠܐ ܐܬܝܗܒ ܡܘܡܐ ܒܐܝܩܪܗ
ܕܥܒܕ ܦܬܓܡܘܗܝ ܕܥܠܝܐ ܘܥܠ ܒܩܝܡܐ ܥܡܗ

[>BRHM <Su>] [>B> [D-KNWCT> [D-<MM> <sp>] <sp>] <PC>]
[W-<Cj>] [L> <Ng>] [>TJHB <Pr>] [MWM> <Su>] [B->JQRH <Aj>]
[D-<Re>] [<BD <Pr>] [PTGMWHJ [D-<LJ> <sp>] <Ob>]
[W-<Cj>] [<L <Pr>] [B-QJM> <Co>] [<MH <Aj>]

‘Abraham was the father of the communities of the peoples, and no blemish was given on his honour, who did the words of the Most High and entered in a covenant with Him.’

48:4–5 ܡܐ ܕܚܝܠ ܐܢܬ ܐܠܝܐ ܘܡܢ ܕܐܟܘܬܟ ܗܘ ܢܫܬܒܚ ܕܐܚܝ ܡܝܬܐ ܡܢ
ܫܝܘܠ ܐܝܟ ܨܒܝܢܗ ܕܡܪܝܐ

[M> DXJL <Qp>] [>NT <Su>]
[>LJ> <Vo>]
[W-<Cj>] [MN <Ex>]
[D-<Re>] [>KWTK <PC>]
[HW <Su>] [NCTBX <PC>]
[D-<Re>] [>XJ <Pr>] [MJT> <PC>] [MN CJWL <Aj>] [>JK YBJNH [D-MRJ> <sp><Aj>]]

‘How awesome you were, Elijah, and he who is like you will be praised, who gave life to a dead person from Sheol according to the will of God.’

49:10 ܘܐܦ ܬܪܥܣܪ ܢܒܝܝܢ ܢܗܘܘܢ ܓܪܡܝܗܘܢ ܡܙܗܪܝܢ ܬܚܘܬܝܗܘܢ ܕܐܣܝܘ
ܠܐܝܣܪܝܠ ܘܐܬܟܠܘ ܐܢܘܢ ܕܡܬܦܪܩܝܢ

[W-<Cj>] [>P <Cj>] [TR<SR NBJJN <Ex>]
[NHWWN <Pr>] [GRMJHWN <Su>] [MZHRJN <PC>] [TXWTJHWN <Aj>]
[D-<Re>] [>SJW <Pr>] [L->JSRJL <Co>]
[W-<Cj>] [>TKLW <Pr>] [>NWN <Ob>]
[D-<Re>] [MTPRQJN <Pr>]

[21] See the following chapter.
[22] Cf. Van Peursen, *Verbal System*, 320–321.

‘And also the Twelve Prophets, may their bones shine beneath them, who cured Israel, and they caused those who were broken off to have confidence.’

49:13 ܢܚܡܝܐ ܢܣܓܐ ܕܘܟܪܢܗ ܕܐܩܝܡ ܚܪܒܬܢ ܘܒܢܝ ܡܣܚܦܬܢ ܘܥܒܕ ܬܪܥܝܢ ܘܣܘܟܪܝܢ

[NXMJ> <Ex>]
    [NSG> <Pr>] [DWKRNH <Su>]
  [D-<Re>] [>QJM <Pr>] [XRBTN <Ob>]
    [W-<Cj>] [BNJ <Pr>] [MSXPTN <Ob>]
    [W-<Cj>] [<BD <Pr>] [TR<JN W-SWKRJN <Ob>]

‘Nehemiah, let his memory be abundant, who raised up our ruins and restored our overthrown places and made our gates and our bars.’

51:8 ܘܐܬܕܟܪܬ ܚܣܕܘܗܝ ܕܡܪܝܐ ܘܛܝܒܘܬܗ ܕܡܢ ܥܠܡ ܕܡܫܘܙܒ ܠܟܠ ܕܬܟܝܠܝܢ ܥܠܘܗܝ ܘܦܪܩ ܠܗܘܢ ܡܢ ܡܢ ܕܬܩܝܦ ܡܢܗܘܢ

[W-<Cj>] [>TDKRT <Pr>] [XSDWHJ [D-MRJ> <sp>] [W-<cj> VJBWTH <PA>] <Ob>]
    [D-<Re>] [MN <LM <PC>]
  [D-<Re>] [MCWZB <PC>] [L-KL <Co>]
      [D-<Re>] [TKJLJN <PC>] [<LWHJ <Co>]
    [W-<Cj>] [PRQ <PC>] [LHWN <Co>] [MN MN <Co>]
      [D-<Re>] [TQJP <PC>] [MNHWN <Aj>]

‘And I remembered the mercies of the Lord, and His good things from eternity, who redeems all who rely upon Him and saves them from him who is stronger than they.’

In 44:19–20 and 49:10 Heb has אשר. In 48:4–5, 49:13 and 51:8 Heb has *ha-qotel*, also separated from the antecedent. In Heb the separation of the relative clause from the antecedent also occurs in 46:1 (where Syr has a completely different structure) and 47:13 (where Syr has ܡܛܠ ܕ corresponding to B אשר).[23]

To these observations we can add two remarks about ܕ + Adjective (cf. § 10.2.3).

1. If we compare *d*-Adjective with *d*-Noun and *d*-Clause, we can observe that in those cases where *d*-Clause and *d*-Noun behave differently, *d*-Adjective follows the former. This observation supports the analysis of *d*-Adjective as a relative clause, rather than an equivalent of *d*-Noun.

[23] Gr has a relative conjunction in 44:19–20, 46:1, 47:13 and 48:4–5. It does not have one in 49:10, 51:8 (ὅτι). In 49:13 (καὶ Νεεμιου ἐπὶ πολὺ τὸ μνημόσυνον τοῦ ἐγείραντος etc.) it uses the article.

2. If we compare *d*-Adjective with a single adjective the two behave differently, just as the single adjective and *d*-Clause do.
   Thus a single adjective precedes *d*-Noun or an apposition
   modifying the same head, but *d*-Adjective follows these extensions. Accordingly, there is a notable syntactical difference
   between the adjective alone and *d*-Adjective, even though it is
   difficult to establish a functional difference between them.

CHAPTER THIRTEEN

DISCONTINUOUS PHRASES

13.1 THE ELEMENT BREAKING UP A PHRASE

Some elements may break up phrases by taking a position within the phrase. The result is a discontinuous phrase. The elements that may break up a phrase are the following.

1. Enclitic pronouns:[1]

   1:19 ܫܒܛܐ ܗܝ ܕܬܘܩܦܐ 'She is a sceptre of strength'.
   6:14 ܪܚܡܐ ܗܘ ܕܬܘܩܦܐ '(A true friend is) a strong friend'.

2. The connective particles ܓܝܪ and ܕܝܢ:[2]

   40:15 ܥܩܪܗܘܢ ܓܝܪ ܕܚܛܗܐ 'For the root of sins (is like a spike)'.
   26:23 ܐܢܬܬܐ ܕܝܢ ܪܫܝܥܬܐ 'For a wicked woman (is given in the portion of the unrighteous man)'.

Two intervening elements are combined in[3]

36:29 ܥܕܪܐ ܗܝ ܓܝܪ ܐܟܘܬܟ 'For she is a help like you'.

In Sirach the enclitic pronouns and the connective particles are the only intervening elements. We do not find intervening prepositional phrases or noun phrases as in

Martyrium Theclae ܐܬܐܟܠܘ ܩܪ̈ܨܐ ܩܕܡ ܢܪܣܝ ܬܡܫܒܘܪ ܕܓܒܪܐ ܚܕ 'Accusations were brought against a man before Narsi Tamshabor'.[4]
Life of Rabbula ܫܡܗ̈ܝܗܘܢ ܠܗܝܢ ܒܥܕܬܐ ܟܠܗ ܡܟܪܙ ܗܘܐ ܕܟܠ ܐܝܠܝܢ ܕ 'He proclaimed before the whole Church the names of all those who…'.[5]

---

[1] This happens both in cases where the pronoun is the subject of a bipartite nominal clause of the type Pr–Su_{pron} (§ 17.1 [C]) and where it occurs in a tripartite nominal clause of the type Pr–Ep–Su (§ 18.2 [B]).

[2] Cf. Falla–Van Peursen, 'Particles ܓܝܪ and ܕܝܢ', § 3.1.2; for the designation 'connective particles' see ibid., § 3 (introduction).

[3] Cf. outside our corpus: *Laws* 539 (ed. Drijvers 6, line 5) ܨܒܘܬܐ ܗܘ ܓܝܪ ܫܦܝܪܐ 'it is a beautiful thing'.

[4] Ed. Assemani I, 123, line 1–2; Nöldeke, *Grammatik*, § 208B.

13.2 THE POSITION OF THE INTERVENING ELEMENT

If there is a discontinuous phrase, the break comes always after the first phrase atom.[6] Thus the intervening elements occupy the following slots.

1. Between the first phrase atom and a *d*-phrase, e.g.:

9:8 ܒܫܘܦܪܗ ܓܝܪ ܕܐܢܬܬܐ 'For through the beauty of a woman (many have been destroyed)'.
5:3 ܡܬܒܥܢܐ ܗܘ ܕܟܠܗܘܢ ܥܠܘܒܐ '(For the Lord is) an avenger of all the oppressed'.

Also with ܕ + Adjective:

7:25 ܠܓܒܪܐ ܕܝܢ ܕܚܟܝܡ '(And give her) to a wise man'.

And with ܕ + Verb:

10:27 ܛܒ ܗܘ ܓܝܪ ܕܦܠܚ 'For (better is) he who labours'.
16:4 ܡܢ ܚܕ ܓܝܪ ܕܕܚܠ ܠܐܠܗܐ 'For from one who fears God (the whole city can be filled)'.

2. Between the first phrase atom and a parallel element, e.g.:

2:11 ܡܛܠ ܕܚܢܢܐ ܗܘ ܘܡܪܚܡܢܐ 'Because (the Lord is) compassionate and merciful'.
17:31 ܡܛܠ ܕܒܣܪܐ ܗܘ ܘܕܡܐ 'Because he is flesh and blood'.

3. Between the first phrase atom and an adjective, e.g.:

21:10 ܓܘܡܐ ܗܘ ܥܡܝܩܐ '(Its end is) a deep pit'.
26:23 ܐܢܬܬܐ ܕܝܢ ܪܫܝܥܬܐ 'For a wicked woman (is given in the portion of the unrighteous man)'.

4. Between the adjective ܣܓܝ and the noun it modifies, e.g.:

29:4 ܣܓܝܐܐ ܓܝܪ ܝܙܦܐ ܕܫܐܠܘ ܝܙܦܬܐ 'For there are many borrowers who have asked for a loan'.

---

[5] Ed. Overbeck 176, line 2; Nöldeke, *Grammatik*, § 208B.
[6] Cf. Kuty, 'Particle *dên*', 189; see also Talstra–Sikkel, 'WIVU-Datenbank', 48: 'Während Atome stets lineare, ununterbrochene Wortfolgen sind, lassen die aus ihnen zusammengesetzten funktionale Einheiten Lücken bzw. Einschübe zu'. For an example in which the break comes in rather than after the first phrase atom, see below, at the end of this paragraph.

When the first phrase atom of the clause contains a construct chain, the intervening element comes after the *nomen rectum*:

> 26:22 ܐܢܬܬ ܓܒܪܐ ܕܝܢ ܐܝܟ ܡܓܕܠܐ ܗܝ ܕܡܘܬܐ 'But a man's wife is like a tower of death'.
> 30:22 ܚܕܘܬ ܠܒܐ ܐܝܟ ܓܝܪ ܚܝܘܗܝ ܕܒܪܢܫܐ 'Joy of the heart is man's life'.
> 38:5 ܠܘ ܡܩܝܣܐ ܓܝܪ ܚܠܝܘ ܡ̈ܝܐ ܡܪܝܪܐ 'For through the wood the bitter water became sweet'.

Accordingly, in our corpus there are no examples where the intervening element comes after a construct noun, i.e. inside a phrase atom, as in

> *Joseph and Asenath* 22:13 ܒܢ̈ܝ ܕܝܢ ܕܒܠܗܐ ܒܢ̈ܝ ܘܠܝܐ ܐܡܗܬܐ ܕܠܝܐ ܘܪܚܝܠ 'Now the sons of Bilha and the sons of Leah, the maidservants of Leah and Rachel'.[7]

13.3 ADDITIONAL OBSERVATIONS ON THE 'CONNECTIVE PARTICLES'

In the preceding paragraph we have seen that the connective particles ܓܝܪ and ܕܝܢ may break up a phrase. This enables them to occupy the slot after the first phrase atom in the clause.[8] In the following cases however there are exceptions to the rule that ܓܝܪ and ܕܝܢ follow the first phrase atom.[9]

---

[7] Ed. Brooks, 47, line 8 = Land, *Anecdota Syriaca* III, 39, line 16; quoted in Nöldeke, *Grammatik*, § 208. See also the examples in Nöldeke, *Grammatik*, § 246 (intervening elements between preposition and 'genitive' noun, e.g. ܚܠܦ ܕܝܢ ܟܘܣܒܝ 'but instead of Kosbi') and § 327 (between preposition and relative clause, e.g. ܡܛܠ ܕܝܢ ܕ); see also Muraoka, *Basic Grammar*, § 73*e*. On Biblical Hebrew see Waltke–O'Connor, *Biblical Hebrew Syntax*, § 9.3*d*; Freedman, 'Broken Construct Chain'.

[8] This agrees to a great extent with the behaviour of the Greek particles γάρ and δέ. These particles too follow the first word of the clause, unless that word constitutes an indivisible unit with the following word(s); cf. Denniston, *Greek Particles*, 56–114, 162–203; cf. Falla–Van Peursen, 'Particles ܓܝܪ and ܕܝܢ', § 3.2.

[9] In Greek too enclitic pronominal elements prefer the second position in the clause; see Wackernagel, 'Gesetz', 342. The general tendency of enclitics to take the second position in the clause is also attested in other Indo-European languages, see *ibid.* 402–403; cf. Denniston, *Greek Particles*, lix. The Greek particles γάρ and δέ too are moved to the right if the preceding words 'coalesce closely enough with the following word to be regarded as forming a unity with it'; (Denniston, *Particles*, 95; see also the preceding footnote).

1. If the enclitic pronoun and ܓܝܪ or ܕܝܢ occur together, the former comes first. This is easy understandable from the enclitic nature of the Ep. Nine times ܓܝܪ follows an Ep in a tripartite nominal clause and two times it comes after a subject pronoun, e.g.:

> 22:11 ܚ̈ܝܐ ܐܢܘܢ ܓܝܪ ܡܢ ܡܘܬܐ ܒܝܫܐ ܒ̈ܝܫܐ 'For an evil life is worse than death'.
> 30:14 ܛܒ ܗܘ ܓܝܪ ܡܣܟܢܐ ܕܚܝ 'For better is a poor man who is living'.
> 30:22 ܚܕܘܬ ܠܒܐ ܐܢܘܢ ܓܝܪ ܚ̈ܝܘܗܝ ܕܒܪܢܫܐ 'Joy of the heart is man's life'.[10]
> 36:29 ܥܕܪܐ ܗܝ ܓܝܪ ܐܟܘܬܟ 'For she is a help like you'.

In our corpus there occur only examples with the third person pronoun (singular or plural). Compare with the first and second person pronoun:

> *Laws* 568 ܐܡܪ ܐܢܐ ܕܝܢ ܕ 'Now I say that'.[11]
> *Laws* 602 ܥܗܕܝܢ ܐܢܬܘܢ ܓܝܪ ܕܐܡܪܬ ܗܘܝܬ ܠܟܘܢ 'You surely remember I told you'.[12]

In Syr we do not find any cases where ܓܝܪ or ܕܝܢ follows enclitic ܗܘܐ as in

> *Laws* 536 ܥܝܕܗ ܗܘܐ ܓܝܪ ܕܐܡܬܝ، ܕܡܪܓܫ ܗܘܐ ܠܢ ܕܡܡܠܠܝܢ ܗܘܝܢ ܡܕܡ 'It was his habit, when he noticed that we were discussing something…'.[13]
> *Laws* 547 ܡܿܢ ܕܠܐ ܗܘܐ ܓܝܪ ܡܢ ܨܒܝܢܗ ܥܒܕ ܕܛܒ ܐܘ ܕܒܝܫ 'He who does no good or evil out of his own will'.[14]

2. In three cases where the connective particle follows ܐܝܬ + ܠܗ:

> 15:12 ܠܝܬ ܠܗ ܓܝܪ ܗܢܝܢܐ ܒܒܪ ܐܢܫܐ ܥܘܠܐ 'For there is no profit to Him in the unrighteous man'.
> 22:21 ܐܝܬ ܠܗ ܓܝܪ ܡܦܩܢܐ 'For there is a way out for him'.
> 22:22 ܡܛܠ ܕܐܝܬ ܠܗ ܓܝܪ ܬܪܥܘܬܐ 'Because there is reconciliation for him'.

There are no counter-examples where a conjunction or another element occurs between ܐܝܬ and the Lamadh phrase.[15] Although in our

[10] On the uninterrupted construct chain ܚܕܘܬ ܠܒܐ, see above, § 13.2.
[11] Ed. Drijvers 28, line 20.
[12] Ed. Drijvers 54, line 20.
[13] Ed. Drijvers 4, line 5.
[14] Ed. Drijvers 12, lines 18–19.
[15] See further § 22.4.

corpus the phenomenon that ܠ + suffix precedes ܓܝܪ or ܕܝܢ is restricted to ܐܝܬ clauses, elsewhere it is attested in other contexts as well, e.g.:

> *Laws* 603 ܕܩܪܝܒܐ ܠܟܘܢ ܕܝܢ ܕܬܚܙܘܢܗ ܗܕܐ 'For this is close to you so that you can see it'.[16]
>
> Matt 7:29 ܦܩܚ ܠܟ ܓܝܪ ܕܢܐܒܕ ܚܕ ܗܕܡܝܟ 'It is better for you that one member of you is lost'.

In the cases discussed under 1 and 2, we see that besides ܓܝܪ and ܕܝܢ there are other elements that tend to occupy the second position in the clause. When these elements come together, there is a striking regularity in the order of the elements. In our corpus there are no cases where three second-position-elements occur together, as in

> Matt 7:29 ܡܠܦ ܗܘܐ ܠܗܘܢ ܓܝܪ ܐܝܟ ܫܠܝܛܐ 'For he was teaching them as one who had authority'.
>
> Matt 14:4 ܐܡܪ ܗܘܐ ܠܗ ܓܝܪ ܝܘܚܢܢ 'For John had been saying to him'.

3. In one case ܓܝܪ seems to follow the second phrase atom, in

> 35:12 ܡܢ ܕܝܗܒ ܓܝܪ ܠܡܣܟܢܐ 'For he who gives to the poor man (lends to God)'.

But in the relative clause itself ܓܝܪ takes the second slot, that is, after ܕܝܗܒ.[17]

4. In three other cases the particle seems to take the initial position in the clause. In the first one, the particle follows the conjunction ܐܢ:

> 18:31 (7a1) ܐܢ ܓܝܪ ܬܥܒܕ ܨܒܝܢܐ ܕܢܦܫܟ 'For if you do your own will (you are like one who does the will of his enemy)'.

R. Kuty has demonstrated that in the Syriac New Testament there is a tendency that ܕܝܢ takes the second slot when the preceding word is short (monosyllabic), whereas it is liable to take the slot directly after the conjunction when a longer word follows.[18] In the example from Syr the textual evidence is divided. Some witnesses, including 7a1, have ܐܢ ܓܝܪ, which agrees with the tendency that Kuty has established for ܕܝܢ, while others, including 7h3 read ܐܢ ܬܥܒܕ ܓܝܪ.[19]

---

[16] Ed. Drijvers 56, line 16.

[17] The same analysis applies to e.g. *Laws* 543 ܡܢ ܕܒܨܝܪܐ ܕܚܠܬܗ ܓܝܪ ܕܐܠܗܐ ܠܘܬ ܗܘ 'He who lacks the fear of God' (ed. Drijvers 8, line 20); cf. *Laws* 547, quoted above, under (1); see also Falla–Van Peursen, 'Particles ܓܝܪ and ܕܝܢ', § 3.1.3.

[18] Kuty, 'Particle *dên*', 194–195; Falla–Van Peursen, 'Particles ܓܝܪ and ܕܝܢ', § 3.1.4 (end).

ܓܝܪ or ܕܝܢ may also follow other conjunctions such as ܒܪܡ or the compound conjunction ܐܠܘ and ܐܦ as in

Laws 539 ܒܪܡ ܕܝܢ ܕܥ 'But know…'.[20]
Laws 547 ܐܠܘ ܓܝܪ ܟܠ ܡܕܡ ܡܫܥܒܕ ܗܘܐ 'For if everything be altogether subservient'.[21]
Laws 551 ܐܦ ܓܝܪ ܗܘܐ ܐܝܬ ܡܣܟܢ 'Even if someone is poor'.[22]

In our corpus ܒܪܡ ܕܝܢ occurs in a variant reading in

48:11 ܒܪܡ ܕܝܢ ܠܐ ܢܡܘܬ 'But he will not die'.[23]

Two other apparent cases of ܕܝܢ and ܓܝܪ in initial position occur in

3:1 ܒܢܝ ܕܝܢ ܠܐܒܗܐ ܫܡܥܘ 'Sons, listen to the fathers'.
41:11 ܪܫܝܥܐ ܓܝܪ ܚܪܬܗ ܠܐܒܕܢܐ ܗܝ 'For the wicked man's end is for destruction'.

However, in both cases one can argue that the clause boundary comes after the particle, rather than after respectively the vocative and the extraposition, i.e.

3:1 [BNJ> <Vo>] [DJN <Cj>]
    [L->BH> <Co>] [CM<W <PC>]
41:11 [RCJ<> <Ex>] [GJR <Cj>]
    [XRTH <Su>] [L->BDN <PC>] [HJ <Ep>]

We can conclude that for the description of discontinuous phrases the notion of 'phrase atoms' is very helpful. Nöldeke says in his grammar about particles such as ܓܝܪ and ܕܝܢ that 'their proper place is immediately after the first word, yet they may also take a place farther on'.[24] Studies that try to improve on such general statements often provide lists of exceptions in which ܓܝܪ and ܕܝܢ do not follow the second word.[25] Although such lists may be very helpful and accurate,

---

[19] Here too we can notice a parallel with the behaviour of Greek γάρ and δέ, since both εἰ γάρ and εἰ δέ are well-attested. Although many scholars refer to the parallel usage with γάρ and δέ for the position of ܓܝܪ and ܕܝܢ in second position, the fact that a parallelism with the Greek usage can also be established in cases where these Syriac particles do not occur after the first word (either more to the right if the words in first position are closely connected or more to the left, that is in first position after a conditional particle) receives little or no attention.

[20] Ed. Drijvers 6, lines 10–11.
[21] Ed. Drijvers 12, lines 4–5.
[22] Ed. Drijvers 16, lines 8–9.
[23] Thus 8a1ᶜ 9c1 10c1.2 11c1 12a1fam →; 7a1, 7h3 and 8a1* have ܒܪܡ ܠܐ ܢܡܘܬ.
[24] Nöldeke, Grammatik, § 327 (quotation from Crichton's translation).
[25] Thus, e.g., Kuty, 'Particle dên', 186.

we think that the notion of 'phrase atoms' enables us to give a more precise description of the position of ܐܝܟ and ܕܝܢ and to reduce the number of exceptions. Thus cases such as 26:22 ܕܝܢ ܐܝܟ ܐܬܐ and 38:5 ܐܝܟ ܘܡܢ ܡܢ are covered by the rule that ܐܝܟ and ܕܝܢ follow the first phrase atom, even though they do not come after the first word.

In the present chapter we have seen at least two elements that prefer the position in the clause after the first phrase atom: the Ep and the particles ܐܝܟ and ܕܝܢ. If both elements occur together, the Ep comes before the connective particle. This is easily understandable in the light of the tight connection between the Ep and the preceding element due to its enclitic nature. If our point of departure is the question 'In what cases do ܐܝܟ and ܕܝܢ not come in second position?' such cases belong to the exceptions. However, in a broader approach, starting from the question: 'What elements prefer to occupy the second position in the clause, and what happens if more than one of them occur together?' there is little need to label cases such as 36:29 ܐܝܟ ܗܘ ܐܝܬ ܘܗܘܐ as exceptions.[26]

It is worth noting that ܠ + suffix behaves similarly to the Ep in that it precedes ܐܝܟ or ܕܝܢ. This observation is relevant to the study of Syriac clause structure, because it demonstrates the strong tendency to put the ܠ + suffix as far to the left as possible (cf. § 21.3.1 B [1,3]).

---

[26] This shows that the formulation of the research question influences the results of the investigations in terms of 'regularities' and 'exceptions'.

CHAPTER FOURTEEN

INDEPENDENT USE OF ܕ

14.1 INDEPENDENT USE OF ܕ WITH THE MEANING 'THAT OF…' / 'THOSE OF…'

In the preceding chapters we have seen two usages of ܕ. In the first usage it is followed by a noun that specifies the preceding word. In this case ܕ shares many syntactic characteristics with prepositions.[1] In the second usage it is followed by a predication structure. A. Wertheimer has argued that these two usages are related because in both cases ܕ serves as a *translatif*, which marks the 'syntactic operation which transfers a word from one grammatical category to another'. Thus in the so-called genitive construction it marks the translation from a noun to the function of an attribute, and in relative clauses it marks the translation from a predication structure to a noun.[2] Her attempt to explain the relationship between the various usages of ܕ is attractive, but her analysis of relative ܕ applies only to structures with embedding, whereas ܕ is also used for hypotaxis.[3] From a diachronic perspective, both usages are related in that ܕ derives from the Semitic determinative-relative *tu/ḏu*. In his *Semitic Languages* E. Lipiński describes the relationship as follows:

> The determinative-relative *tu / ḏu* introduces a determination which can consist either in a noun or proper name (…) or in a relative clause (…). In the first case, it functions in a genitival structure; in the second, it acts as a pronominal or adjectival antecedent of a relative clause (…) In Aramaic, the determinative-relative *ḏi* in the genitive case is used in its original function and as element of demonstratives.[4]

---

[1] Thus Dyk, 'Desiderata', 147–148. Note however, that *d*-Noun and Prep-Noun occupy different positions in the phrase; see §§ 11.6, 15.4.

[2] Cf. Wertheimer, 'Functions' (quotation from p. 261).

[3] For the distinction between embedding and hypotaxis see § 26.2.

[4] Lipiński, *Semitic Languages*, 332 and 334. The relation of the ܕܡܕܡ pattern to the ܒܝܬ ܕܡܕ construction is disputed. According to Goldenberg the 'head-less' con-

According to Nöldeke, *Grammatik*, § 209A the 'superior independence' of the 'Demonstrative-(Relative-)Pronoun ܕ ("that of")' is shown in those cases where *d*-Noun is separated from the governing noun. But it 'becomes still more conspicuous when no governing word is expressed'.[5] In Syr there occur the following examples.[6]

14:9 ܕܚܒܪܗ '(he who takes) what belongs to his neighbour' (MS A חלק רעהו).
25:15 ܡܢ ܕܐܢܬܬܐ '(there is no enmity more bitter) than that of a wife' (Heb not extant).
45:5 ܠܒܝܬ ܐܝܣܪܝܠ 'to those of the House of Israel' (MS B לישראל).
47:21 ܡܢ ܕܒܝܬ ܐܦܪܝܡ 'from those of the House of Ephraim' (MS B מאפרים).
47:23 ܠܒܝܬ ܐܦܪܝܡ 'to those of the House of Ephraim' (MS B לאפרים).
48:15 ܠܒܝܬ ܕܘܝܕ 'to those of the house of David' (MS B לבית דוד).

The construction with independent ܕ + (proper) noun occurs parallel to constructions without ܕ. Thus in 45:5 ܠܒܝܬ ܐܝܣܪܝܠ occurs parallel to ܠܝܥܩܘܒ 'to Jacob' and in 47:23 ܠܒܝܬ ܐܦܪܝܡ stands in parallelism to ܠܐܝܣܪܝܠ 'Israel'. In 48:15 ܝܗܘܕܐ 'Judah' is attested besides ܠܒܝܬ ܕܘܝܕ. In 25:15 ܘܠܝܬ ܒܥܠܕܒܒܘܬܐ ܕܡܪܝܪܐ ܡܢ ܕܐܢܬܬܐ 'And there is no enmity more bitter than that of a wife' (without repetition of ܒܥܠܕܒܒܘܬܐ) occurs parallel to ܠܝܬ ܪܫܐ ܡܪܝܪܐ ܡܢ ܪܫܗ ܕܚܘܝܐ 'There is no head more bitter than the head of a serpent' (with repetition of ܪܫ). Sometimes there is variation in the textual witnesses. Thus in 48:15 most manuscripts have ܠܒܝܬ ܕܘܝܕ, but 7a1 has the construction without ܕ. Where Syr has ܕ and Heb is extant, ܕ is a plus vis-à-vis Heb.

14.2 ܕ + CARDINAL NUMBER

To the demonstrative-relative use of ܕ discussed in § 14.1 also belongs the use of ܕ + cardinal number in the sense of 'the first, the second, etc.'[7] This use is attested two times in a numerical proverb with ܕܬܠܬܐ, in 23:16 and 50:25:

---

struction has priority, but Wertheimer explains it as elliptical; cf. Goldenberg, 'Attribution' 4–5, 12–13; Wertheimer, 'Functions', 264–266.

[5] Nöldeke, *Grammatik*, § 209A (quotation from Crichton's translation); see also Muraoka, *Basic Grammar*, § 91*e*; Beck, 'Sprache Ephräms', II, 12–14.

[6] Compare also 47:22, where 7h3 and 8a1* read ܠܒܝܬ ܕܘܝܕ instead of ܘܠܕܘܝܕ (Heb [B]: [לב]ית).

23:16 ܬܪܝܢ ܐܢܘܢ ܣܢܝܐ ܢܦܫܝ ܘܬܠܬܐ ܡܓܪܓ ܪܘܓܙܝ 'Two sorts my soul hates, and a third arouses my anger'.

50:25 ܕܬܪܝܢ ܥܡܡܝܢ ܐܬܬܥܝܩܬ ܢܦܫܝ ܘܬܠܬܐ ܠܐ ܗܘܐ ܥܡܐ 'Of two people my soul becomes wearied, and the third one is not a people'.

In Syr there are no examples where ܕ + cardinal number functions as an extension of a noun, in which case the construction with ܕ is an alternative for the construction with an ordinal number, as in ܝܘܡܐ ܕܬܪܝܢ = ܝܘܡܐ ܬܪܝܢܐ.[8] The construction with an ordinal number is rare as well, it occurs only three times in the expression ܠܫܢܐ ܬܠܝܬܝܐ 'the triple tongue', in 28:13–15. In numerical proverbs we find besides 'two... the third' also 'two... and three', etc., e.g.:

26:28 ܥܠ ܬܪܬܝܢ ܨܒܘܢ ܕܚܠ ܠܒܝ ܘܕܡ ܬܠܬ ܐܬܪܗܒ ܐܢܝܢ ܥܠܝ 'At two things my heart is shocked, and three displease me'.

26:5 ܡܢ ܬܠܬ ܨܒܘܢ ܕܚܠ ܠܒܝ ܘܡܢ ܐܪܒܥ ܐܢܐ ܕܚܠ ܪܘܪܒܐܝܬ 'Because of three things my heart trembles, and because of four I fear much'.

25:7 ܬܫܥ ܨܒܘܢ ܕܠܐ ܥܠ ܠܒܝ ܫܒܚܬ ܘܥܣܪ ܕܠܐ ܐܡܪܬ 'Nine things that I had not thought of I have praised, and ten that I have not said'.

Compare also ܕܬܪܬܝܢ ܙܒܢܝܢ 'twice' in

32:20 ܕܠܡܐ ܬܬܩܠ ܒܟܐܦܐ ܕܬܪܬܝܢ ܙܒܢܝܢ 'Lest you stumble against a stone twice'.[9]

We can conclude that for 'the first, the second, etc.' two constructions are used in Syr: one with an ordinal number, which occurs as specification of a noun, and one with ܕ + cardinal number, which is used independently. However, since the construction with the ordinal number is attested only in a frozen idiom ('the triple tongue'), the material does not allow us to conclude that there is a complementary distribution of the two constructions (i.e. dependent use of ordinal number and independent use of ܕ + cardinal number).[10]

ܕ + cardinal number is also used in adverbial expressions.[11] This occurs twice in

---

[7] Cf. Nöldeke, *Grammatik*, § 209; Nöldeke quotes Luke 20:30 ܘܢܣܒܗ ܕܬܪܝܢ ܐܢܬܬܐ 'And the second one took his wife'. In Pesh-Exodus the preference for the ordinal instead of ܕ + Cardinal is overwhelming; see Weitzman, *Syriac Version*, 167–168.

[8] Nöldeke, *Grammatik*, § 239; Wertheimer, 'Functions', 267.

[9] 7a1 omits the Dalath before ܬܪܬܝܢ.

[10] In Pesh-Pentateuch too the type ܝܘܡܐ ܕܬܪܝܢ is much more frequent than ܝܘܡܐ ܬܪܝܢܐ; Avinery, *Syntaxe*, 271–274.

[11] Cf. Nöldeke, *Grammatik*, § 209B on 'adverbiale Anwendungen' of ܕ.

23:23 ܚܕܐ ܕܒܓܠܬ ܒܢܡܘܣܐ ܕܐܠܗܐ ܘܕܬܪܬܝܢ ܒܒܥܠ ܛܠܝܘܬܗ ܘܕܬܠܬ ܒܙܢܝܘܬܐ ܕܓܘܪܐ ܕܡܢ ܢܘܟܪܝܐ ܐܩܝܡܬ ܝܠܕܐ

[XD> <Aj>]
  [D-<Cj>] [DGLT <Pr>] [B-NMWS> [D->LH> <sp>] <Co>]
 [W-<cj> D-TRTJN <PA><Aj>]
  [B-B<L VLJWTH <Co>]
 [W-<cj> D-TLT <PA><Aj>]
  [B-ZNJWT> [D-GWR> <sp>] <Fa>]
   [D-<Cj>] [MN NWKRJ> <Aj>] [>QJMT <Pr>] [JLD> <Ob>]

'Firstly, that she has acted treacherously against the Law of God, and secondly, against the husband of her youth, and thirdly, in the fornication of adultery, that she has established a child from a stranger.'

14.3 ܕܠܐ 'WITHOUT' IN ADVERBIAL EXPRESSIONS

A number of times there occur adverbial expressions with the pattern ܕܠܐ + Noun: 13:12 ܕܠܐ ܪܚܡܐ 'without mercy'; 13:24 ܕܠܐ ܣܘܪܚܢܐ 'without transgressions'; 16:3 ܕܠܐ ܒܢܝܐ 'without sons'; 20:16 ܕܠܐ ܡܠܚܐ 'without salt'; 32:19 ܕܠܐ ܡܠܟܐ 'without counsel'; 51:25 ܕܠܐ ܟܣܦܐ 'without money'. In all these cases the noun occurs in the emphatic state, but constructions with the absolute state are attested as well, cf. Isa 55:1 ܕܠܐ ܟܣܦܐ (as in Sir 51:25), but Exod 21:11 ܕܠܐ ܟܣܦ.[12] In § 14.1 we have distinguished two usages of ܕ: ܕ + Noun and ܕ + Clause. If we regard the construction with ܕܠܐ as belonging to the first category, ܕܠܐ ܪܚܡܐ is the negative equivalent of ܕܪܚܡܐ (syntactically rather than semantically). In this context it should be remembered that ܠܐ frequently mirrors the α-*privativum* in Greek, e.g.: ܕܠܐ ܐܠܗ 'godless' (ἄθεος).[13]

Alternatively one could argue that the construction with ܕܠܐ + Noun belongs to the second category, which implies that it is analysed as an elliptical predication structure.[14] In this analysis the use of simple ܠܐ, rather than *ܕܠܐ ܗܘܐ ܪܚܡܐ or *ܕܠܐ ܗܘ ܪܚܡܐ, agrees with Nöldeke's observation that simple ܠܐ is retained in elliptical constructions.[15]

---

[12] Cf. Nöldeke, *Grammatik*, § 202F; see also the examples in Joosten, *Syriac Language*, 70–71 and Joosten's discussion on p. 73.

[13] Muraoka, *Basic Grammar*, § 93.1; see also Wertheimer, 'Functions', 287.

[14] Beck, 'Sprache Ephräms', II, 25 prefers this analysis; he considers ܕܠܐ ܪܚܡܐ as elliptical for ܕܠܐ ܪܚܡܐ ܠܗ.

[15] Nöldeke, *Grammatik*, § 328.

The advantage of the latter interpretation is that it can also be applied to constructions with a prepositional phrase,[16] as in

> 22:6 ܡܠܬܐ ܕܠܐ ܒܙܒܢܗ 'unseasonable talk'; cf. Gr ἄκαιρος.
> 25:18 ܕܠܐ ܒܨܒܝܢܗ 'against his will'.
> 33:30 ܕܠܐ ܒܡܘܥܕܗ 'unseasonably'.

---

[16] Cf. Beck, 'Sprache Ephräms', II, 27, and see § 10.5.1.

CHAPTER FIFTEEN

TOWARDS A MAXIMUM MATRIX OF PHRASES

15.1 INTRODUCTION

In the preceding chapters we have investigated the structure of phrases and the order of phrase atoms and expansions. The regularities we have discovered enable us to define a 'maximum matrix of phrase structure'. Such a matrix is a linear model that indicates the order of all slots that are present within a phrase. In the present chapter we define the maximum matrix of phrase atoms (§ 15.2), summarize our observations on the ways in which phrase atoms can be extended (§ 15.3), and suggest a maximum matrix of phrase structure (§ 15.4). We will end this chapter with some remarks about the interrelationship of phrase structure and clause structure. The latter will be the subject of Part Four. In the present paragraph we will make some general remarks on the notion of a 'maximum matrix'.

The 'maximum matrix' is a tool to describe the internal structure of phrases. Each phrase contains a head (phrase atom). If this head consists of more than one word, the word order is well-defined (e.g. Preposition–Noun). The head may take a number of extensions (Adjective, *d*-Noun etc.). Each type of extension has its own slot in the maximum matrix. That is to say: the slot may be empty, but if it is filled, the place of the extension in relation to the head and other extensions follows a fixed pattern.

The model of a *maximum* matrix indicates not only the constituents of a clause, but also its boundaries. Elements that have a position outside the maximum matrix do not belong to the phrase. At first sight this suggests that the size of phrases is rather limited: the maximum matrix contains a number of slots, and when all the slots are filled, the maximum has been reached. We will see, however, that the maximum matrix contains a recursive element which enables long strings of words to occupy a single slot in it.[1]

We are not aware of any attempt in Hebrew or Aramaic/Syriac studies to describe phrase structure with the help of a maximum matrix. But we can compare models of syntactic analysis at sentence level in which sentences are described as a sequence of positions. The position that a word occupies depends on its grammatical function and the information structure of the clause.

A number of scholars have used such a model to describe clause structure in Biblical Hebrew. W. Gross, for example, uses the *Stellungsfeldermodell* that has been developed by German linguists in his description of word order in Biblical Hebrew verbal clauses.[2] He argues that this model is useful to describe complete sentences in contrast to one-sided approaches that restrict themselves to the relative order of the subject and the verb.[3] Gross distinguishes between (a) the *Vorfeld*, the part of the sentence that comes before the verb, (b) the verbal predicate, and (c) the *Hauptfeld*, containing all constituents following the verbal predicate.

The *Stellungsfeldermodell* has been criticized because it concerns a linear rather than a hierarchical description.[4] However, the validity of this criticism is limited because the description of regularities of surface phenomena is an integrated part of linguistic analysis. Gross argues that word order is such a surface phenomenon *par excellence*, and that the *Stellungsfeldermodell* is very helpful to describe the linear order of the elements in a sentence.[5]

In his 2001 publication (*Vorfeld*) Gross also uses concepts that play an important role in Functional Grammar, such as Topic and Comment, Theme and Rheme, and Focus and Background. In Functional Grammar it is assumed that these functions, if present, each occupy their own slot in the sentence pattern. In this context mention should

---

[1] For examples see below, § 15.4.

[2] Gross, *Satzteilfolge*, 43–48; idem, *Vorfeld*, 5–6; cf. Van der Merwe–Naudé–Kroeze, *Reference Grammar*, 336–343.

[3] Gross, *Satzteilfolge*, 46. In the field of phrase structure we see a comparable one-sided focus on the relation between the head and one specification (e.g. the 'genitive') rather than complete clause constituents (§ 9.1, end).

[4] Cf. Dürscheid, *Modelle der Satzanalyse*, 11–18.

[5] Gross, *Satzteilfolge*, 43–48. For the role of 'surface structure' in the study of Syriac word order, compare Kuty, 'Particle *dēn*', 196.

be made of an important contribution by R. Buth, who has applied this view to the analysis of Biblical Hebrew nominal clauses.[6] Buth distinguishes the following positions:[6]

[Contextualizing Constituent (Topic)] [Focus] [Subject] [Predicate]

Thus in the clause יהוה אלהיך אש אכלה הוא 'The Lord your God is a consuming fire' (Deut 4:24) the contextualizing constituent is יהוה אלהיך and הוא is the subject. The predicate אש אכלה has not its unmarked position after the subject, but the focus position between the contextualizing constituent and the subject.

The appropriateness of these and other approaches to grasping Biblical Hebrew sentence structure with a *Stellungsfeldermodell* will not be our concern here. We have adduced these examples to illustrate how the notion of *Stellungsfelder* or slots has been applied to the study of sentence structure in a North-West Semitic language.[7] The situation with our maximum matrix of phrase structure is different in the following respects.

1. At phrase level the positions of the elements and the rules that govern their order are much more transparent and consistently applied than at clause or sentence level: at the lower level of phrase structure there is less freedom and variation than at the higher levels of clauses and sentences.
2. Pragmatic deviations from the 'default' word order to created marked constructions, which play an important role at clause level, do not occur at phrase level.
3. The maximum matrix of phrase structure is recursive: within a phrase one of the extensions can itself function as a head and take its own extensions. This phenomenon is accounted for in our model (see below, § 15.4). Accordingly, the objection to the *Stellungsfeldermodell* that it is linear rather than hierarchical does not apply to our model of phrase structure analysis.

---

[6] Buth, 'Generative-Functional Approach'; for a critical evaluation see Van Hecke, *Job 12–14*, 100–107; for a different view see Shimasaki, *Focus Structure*, 120–130.

[7] In this context it should be mentioned that the model of a maximum matrix is also very useful for the morphological analysis; cf. Dyk 'Data Preparation', 135.

15.2 THE MAXIMUM MATRIX OF PHRASE ATOMS

The distinction between phrases and phrase atoms appeared to be very useful for the analysis of phrase structure. Phrases consist of an obligatory head and optional extensions. Phrase atoms are the smallest groups of words that can constitute a clause constituent. Accordingly, obligatory expansions of a noun, such as the genitive noun following a noun in the construct state, are regarded as part of the head, not as extensions. This definition of phrase atoms, which does not automatically equate a phrase atom with something such as the 'most important word of the phrase', implies that phrase atoms may have a complex internal structure. They may contain a construct noun followed by a *nomen rectum* and sometimes even two construct nouns. These nouns may be preceded by a preposition, which results in the following maximal matrix:[8]

> [Preposition–CstrNoun–CstrNoun–Noun]

15.3 PHRASE ATOMS AND THEIR EXTENSIONS

In the preceding chapters we have seen many ways in which phrase atoms take extensions to build up phrases. To come to an appropriate analysis of phrase structure it is necessary to distinguish carefully between phrase atoms and extensions, to describe in an accurate manner the types of extensions, the relationship between the phrase atom and the extensions, as well as the interrelationship between the extensions.

1. *Distinguishing between phrase atom and extensions.* A construct chain of the type CstrNoun–Noun is a phrase atom, whereas a construction of the type Noun *d*-Noun in a phrase atom with an extension. In studies on Classical Syriac these constructions are often treated together as 'genitive constructions'.[9] From a functional perspective this may be justified,

---

[8] The final noun may be in the absolute or emphatic state or take a suffix pronoun; see § 9.2, note 21. The question of whether the language system would also allow for longer chains of construct nouns, unattested in our corpus, will not concern us here.
[9] E.g., Muraoka, *Basic Grammar*, § 73; Williams, *Peshitta of 1 Kings*, 7–37.

but syntactically they behave differently in the following respects.

a. They take different positions in the maximum matrix of phrase structure. Thus if the head of the phrase is specified by an adjective, the adjective will come after a *nomen rectum*, but before *d*-Noun.[10]

b. They take different position when an intervening element such as ܪܝ, ܐܝܟ or the Ep breaks up a phrase. Such intervening elements come directly after the first phrase atom and hence after a *nomen rectum* but before *d*-Noun.

2. *Different types of extensions.* Extensions can be subdivided according to their form: Adjective, *d*-phrase, prepositional phrase, noun, demonstrative. In the case of *d*-phrases a distinction should be made between *d*-Noun and *d*-Clause (including *d*-Adjective). In § 12.6 we have mentioned some differences between these constructions, including their position in the maximum matrix.

3. *Relation between phrase atom and extensions.* If the phrase atom is followed by a specification, this specification may modify the whole phrase atom or part of it. In our corpus in all examples of [CstrNoun–Noun [Adjective <sp>]] the specification modifies the phrase as a whole, whereas in the examples of [CstrNoun–Noun [*d*-Noun <sp>]] and [CstrNoun–Noun [Apposition <sp>]], the extension modifies the *nomen rectum*.

4. *Relationship between extensions.* Extensions can be modified in the same way as the head is modified. This leads to some contrasting pairs that display functional oppositions. For example, the order is Noun–Adjective–*d*-Noun if the adjective modifies the head, but Noun–*d*-Noun–Adjective if the adjective modifies the *d*-phrase. In other cases such a functional opposition cannot be established. Thus with an adjective and a *d*-phrase in which predication occurs the order is Noun–Apposition–*d*-Clause, irrespective of the question of whether the *d*-phrase modifies the Apposition or the Noun.[11]

---

[10] Cf. Nöldeke, *Grammatik*, § 208B.
[11] See the 'Table of Phrase Patterns' in the appendix to this chapter.

15.4 THE MAXIMUM MATRIX OF PHRASES

Examples of phrase atoms with one extension are abundantly attested. The extensions nearly always follow the head, but there are some exceptions with the adjective ܩܡ. Examples of phrase atoms with two extensions are frequent as well. Some rules can be established for the order of the elements.

1. Adjective precedes *d*-phrase.
2. *d*-Noun precedes *d*-Adjective or *d*-Clause.
3. *d*-Noun precedes prepositional phrase.
4. Prepositional phrase precedes *d*-Clause.
5. *d*-Noun precedes apposition.
6. Apposition precedes *d*-Adjective and *d*-Clause.
7. Adjective precedes prepositional phrase.
8. Adjective precedes apposition.

Accordingly the relative order of the extensions follows a fixed pattern, which can be rendered with the following maximum matrix.

[Phrase atom] [Demonstrative] [Adjective] [Apposition] [*d*-Noun] [Prep–Noun] [*d*-{Clause}] [Parallel Element]

Combined with the maximum matrix for phrase atoms (above, § 15.2) this leads to the following *maximum matrix of phrase structure*.

[Prep–CstrNoun–CstrNoun–Noun] | [Dem.] [Adj.] [App.] [*d*-Noun] [Prep–Noun] [*d*-{Clause}] [Parallel Element]

Some comments:

1. The place of the demonstrative directly after the phrase atom is based on material outside Syr (cf. § 11.8).
2. Sometimes a specification may precede the phrase atom. In our corpus this occurs with the adjective ܩܡ and the demonstrative (§§ 10.1.2, 10.4).[12]

---

[12] In our definition of 'apposition', there are no cases where an apposition precedes the phrase atom; cf. § 10.3.1, note 103, on our definition of 'apposition'.

3. If the phrase is split up in two parts, the intervening element comes always directly after the first phrase atom. In the maximum matrix we have indicated this by a vertical stroke. There are no examples where it comes, for example, between the first and the second extension.

4. This is a first attempt to grasp word order at phrase level with a maximum matrix, mainly based on Syr. In other Classical Syriac corpora occasional exceptions do occur, such as the patterns

[Noun [Numeral <ap>] [Adjective <sp>]]][13]
[Noun [d-Noun <sp>] [Adjective <sp>]]][14]

In our corpus there are no examples where, in addition to the phrase atom, more than two slots are filled. If the phrase contains more extensions, this concerns extensions of extensions (e.g. a d-phrase modifying an apposition). This may lead to complex patterns such as

21:9 (= 25:20) ܪܡܟܐ ܐܝܟ ܕ ,ܪܓܠܘ̈ ܒܗ ܕܓܒܪ ܩܨܝܨܐ ܐܝܟ
[>JK MSQT> [D-XL> <sp>] [B-RGLWHJ [D-GBR> [QCJC> <sp>] <sp>] <sp>]]
'Like an ascent of sand at the feet of an old man'.

1st level: [>JK MSQT> [D-XL> <sp>] [B-RGLWHJ D-GBR>]]
2nd level: [B-RGLWHJ [D-GBR><sp>]]
3rd level: [D-GBR> [QCJC> <sp>]]
1st level: [Phrase atom [d-Noun] [Prepositional phrase]]
2nd level: [Phrase atom [d-Noun]]
3rd level: [Phrase atom [Adjective]]

ܪܓܠܘܗܝ ܐܝܟ is a phrase atom followed by two specifications: d-Noun and Prep-Noun. These two specifications follow the order of the maximum matrix. At a second level the prepositional phrase functions as a phrase atom that is modified by a d-phrase. The latter specification is further specified by an adjective.

1:2 ܚܠܐ ܕܝܡܐ ܘܢܘ̈ܦܬ ܕܡܛܪ ܘܝܘ̈ܡܬ ܕܥܠܡ
[XL> [D-JM> <sp>] [W-<cj> NWVPT> [D-MVR> <sp>] <PA>] [W-<cj> JWMT> [D-
<LM> <sp>] <PA>]]
'The sand of the sea, the drops of the rain and the days of eternity'.

1st level: [XL>[D-JM> <sp>] [W-<cj> NWVPT> <PA>]
2nd level: [NWVPT> [D-MVR> <sp>]] [W-<cj> JWMT> <PA>]
3rd level: [JWMT> [D-<LM> <sp>]]

---

¹³ See § 11.1, note 4.
¹⁴ See § 11.2 (3), note 7.

1st level: [Phrase atom] [*d*-Noun]   [Paral. El.]
2nd level: [Phrase atom] [*d*-Noun] [Parallel element]
3rd level: [Phrase atom] [*d*-Noun]

In this example we see how parallel elements are chained with preceding elements. This may result in rather long chains of parallel elements (§ 12.4).

These two examples illustrate how rather complex phrases fit into the maximum matrix defined in the present chapter. It is noteworthy that even the most complex phrase structures discussed in Chapter 12 fit into the maximum matrix.

Like the chains of parallel elements discussed in § 12.4, the phenomenon that specifications can be further specified by other extensions raises the question as to the limits to the maximum size of phrases. Is it possible to form phrases *ad infinitum* ('the frame of the window of the house of the neighbours of the mother of the friend of...)'? Here we have to repeat that our concern is not in theoretical speculation, but in the actual forms attested in our corpus. Some phrases may indeed be very long, extending over a number of verses (e.g. 50:6–10, see § 12.5).

15.5 PHRASE STRUCTURE AND CLAUSE STRUCTURE

Anticipating Part Four, which will deal with clause structure, we conclude this chapter with some remarks on the relationship between phrase structure and clause structure.

1. According to our definitions phrases are the building blocks of clauses. However, the relationship between phrases and clauses is complicated because the 'nominalizer' ‎ enables clauses (i.e. constructions in which predication occurs) to function as phrases or even part of phrases (e.g. specifications).

2. At times these 'phrase-internal clauses' show some particularities such as the frequent ellipsis of the subject pronoun in relative clauses (§ 17.3; compare also the examples of *d*-Adjective in § 10.2.3).

3. To describe the phenomena mentioned under (1) and (2) properly, a distinction should be made between embedding and hypotaxis (§§ 12.5; 26.2).
4. The analysis of phrase structure sheds light on some syntactic phenomena at clause level. The fact that the connective adverb ܓܝܪ follows ܠ ܐܝܬ + suffix indicates the close connection between ܐܝܬ and the prepositional phrase. It functions as an indivisible, 'a-tomic' constituent. (§ 13.3 [2])
5. A careful analysis of phrases may play a role in the ongoing debate on Syriac clause structure.

The last point is related to the fact that discontinuous phrases are split off after the first atom (§ 13.2) and that the Ep and the connective adverbs are preferably placed after the first phrase atom of the clause (§ 13.3). Thus in 1:15 ܥܡ ܐܢܫܐ ܗܝ ܩܘܫܬܐ 'She is with the people of truth' the predicate of the bipartite nominal clause is split up and the Ep comes immediately after the first phrase atom (cf. § 17.1 [C], end). These observations support the view that also in a clause such as

> 18:24 ܕܪܘܓܙܐ ܒܚܪܬܐ ܗܘ ܕܟܠܗܘܢ ܚܛܗܐ '(remember) that anger is in the end of all sins'.

the element preceding ܗܘ, that is ܒܚܪܬܐ, is the first phrase of the clause and hence that the tripartite nominal clause should be analysed as a construction with extraposition, namely

[D-<Cj>] [RWGZ> <Ex>]
[B-XRT> <PC>] [HW <Su>] [D-KLHWN [XVH> <ap>]<sp>]

Also illuminating is a case such as

> 3:11 ܐܝܩܪܗ ܗܘ ܕܐܒܘܗܝ ܕܓܒܪܐ ܓܝܪ ܐܝܩܪܗ 'For the honour of a man is the honour of his father'.

ܓܝܪ follows the phrase atom of the element in extraposition; ܗܘ occupies the second slot in the main clause. This observation argues for the analysis of this nominal clause as Su ‖ Pr–s rather than Su–Pr–Ep.[15] But note that we also find examples of the type

> 14:15 ܠܐܚܪܢܐ ܓܝܪ ܫܒܩ ܐܢܬ ܩܢܝܢܝܟܘܢ 'Because you leave behind your possessions to others'.

Apparently ܐܢܬ functions here differently from the Ep in 3:11.

---

[15] See further § 21.4 (A).

APPENDIX: TABLE OF PHRASE PATTERNS

A. PHRASE ATOMS

Maximum matrix (§ 9.2)   [Preposition–CstrNoun–CstrNoun–Noun]

B. PHRASES WITH ONE EXTENSIONS

1. Extension = adjective (§ 10.1)

   a. Basic pattern, abundantly attested: [Noun [Adjective <sp>]]
   b. Exception: adjective preceding head (with ܡ):   [[Adjective <sp>] Noun]
   c. Head is construct chain, adjective modifies head as a whole: [CstrNoun–Noun [Adjective <sp>]][1]
   d. Adjective extended by parallel element: [Noun [Adjective [w-<cj>] [Adjective <PA>] <sp>]][2]

2. Extension = d-phrase (§ 10.2)

   a. Basic pattern, abundantly attested: [Noun [d-Noun <sp>]]
   b. If d-phrase modifies two nouns: [Noun [d-Noun [w-<cj>] [Noun+suffix <PA>] <sp>]][3]
   c. d-phrase contains construct chain ('A of B of C'):   [Noun [d-CstrNoun–Noun <sp>]]
   d. With ܠ and ܥܠ even with two construct nouns: [Noun [d-CstrNoun–CstrNoun–Noun <sp>]]

---

[1] There no are examples of * ܪܚܡܬܐ ܐܢܬܬ ܛܒܬܐ 'the beauty of a good woman' with the adjective modifying the *nomen rectum*.
[2] There are other examples of extended adjectival phrases, but not with attributive adjectives.
[3] There are no examples of the pattern Noun w-Noun d-Noun in which d-Noun modifies both preceding nouns.

e. Head contains construct chain, *d*-phrase modifies *nomen rectum*   [CstrNoun–Noun [*d*-Noun <sp>]]
   ('A of B of C')
f. *d*-Adjective: [Noun [*d*-{[Adjective]} <sp>]][4]
g. Other cases of ז + extension in which predication occurs: [Noun [*d*-{Clause} <sp>]]
h. *d*-phrase extended by   Apposition: [Noun [*d*-Noun [Noun <ap>] <sp>]]
                                            Noun [*d*-Noun [CstrNoun–Noun <ap>] <sp>]]
                  Adjective: [Noun [*d*-Noun [Adjective <sp>] <sp>]]
                  d-Noun: [Noun [*d*-Noun [*d*-Noun <sp>] <sp>]]
                               [Noun [*d*-CstrNoun–Noun [*d*-Noun <sp>]][5]
                  d-Adjective: [Noun [*d*-Noun [*d*-{[Adjective <PC>]} <sp>]]
                  d-Clause: [Noun [*d*-Noun [*d*-{Clause} <sp>]]
                  Parallel element: [Noun [*d*-Noun [*w*-<cj>] [Noun <PA>] <sp>]]
                                       Noun [*d*-Noun [*w*-<cj>] [*d*-Noun <PA>] <sp>]]

3. Extension = apposition (§ 10.3)

a. Basic pattern: [Noun [Noun <ap>]]
b. Apposition contains construct chain: [Noun [CstrNoun–Noun <ap>]]
c. Head contains construct chain, apposition modifies *nomen rectum*:   [CstrNoun–Noun [Noun <ap>]]
d. Repetition of preposition: [Prep–Noun [Prep–Noun <ap>]]

---

[4] Contrast [Noun [Noun [Adjective <sp>]] (above, B 1). There is no functional or semantic difference between the two constructions, but syntactically they differ (word order, following specifications; *d*-Adjective behaves like the relative *d*-).
[5] In this pattern the second *d*-phrase specifies the *nomen rectum* of the first *d*-phrase.

e. Apposition extended by   Adjective: [Noun [Noun [Adjective <sp>] <ap>]]
                        d-Noun: [Noun [Noun [*d*-Noun <sp>] <ap>]]
                        d-CstrNoun–Noun: [Noun [Noun [*d*-CstrNoun–Noun <sp>] <ap>]]
                        d-Clause: [Noun [Noun [*d*-{Clause} <sp>] <ap>]]
                        Prepositional phrase: [Noun [Noun [Prep–Noun <sp>] <ap>]]
                        Parallel element: [Noun [Noun [*w*-<cj>] [Noun <PA>] <ap>]]
                        Other apposition: [Noun [Noun [Noun <ap>] <ap>]]

4. Constructions with numerals (§ 10.3.3)

a. Thing numbered in apposition to the numeral: [Number [Noun <ap>]]
b. With 'one' same pattern, but also: [Noun [Number <ap>]]
c. Object numbered is preceded by ן (one example):   [Number [*d*-Noun <sp>]]

5. Extension = demonstrative (§ 10.4)

a. Demonstrative precedes noun: [Demonstrative <sp> [Noun]]
b. Demonstrative follows noun: [Noun [Demonstrative <sp>]]

6. Extension = prepositional phrase (§ 10.5)

a. Basic pattern: [Noun [Prep–Noun <sp>]]
b. Prepositional phrase extended by   *d*-Noun: [Noun [Prep–Noun [*d*-Noun <sp>] <sp>]]
                        d-Clause: [Noun [Prep–Noun [*d*-{Clause} <sp>] <sp>]]
                        Apposition: [Noun [Prep–Noun [Noun <ap>] <sp>]]

C. PHRASES WITH TWO EXTENSIONS

1. Adjective and apposition (§ 11.1)

    [Noun [Adjective <sp>] [Noun <ap>]]

2. Adjective and *d*-phrase (§ 11.2)

    [Noun [Adjective <sp>] [*d*-Noun <sp>]]
    [Noun [Adjective <sp>] [*d*-{[Adjective <PC>]} <sp>]]
    [Noun [Adjective <sp>] [*d*-{Clause} <sp>]]

3. Two appositions (§ 11.3)

    [Noun [Noun <ap>] [Noun <ap>]][6]

4. *d*-phrase and apposition (§ 11.4)

   a. Basic pattern with *d*-Noun:

    [Noun [*d*-Noun <sp>] [Noun <ap>]]

   b. Reverse order with *d*-Clause:

    [Noun [Noun <ap>] [*d*-{Clause} <sp>]]

5. Two *d*-phrases (§ 11.5)

   Basic pattern, only with *d*-Noun + *d*-Clause (or *d*-Adjective)

    [Noun [*d*-Noun <sp>] [*d*-{[Adjective <PC>]} <sp>]]
    [Noun [*d*-Noun <sp>] [*d*-{Clause} <sp>]]

6. *d*-phrase and prepositional phrase (§ 11.6)

   a. Basic pattern with *d*-Noun:

    [Noun [*d*-Noun <sp>] [Prep–Noun <sp>]]

   b. Reverse order with *d*-Clause:

    [Noun [Prep–Noun <sp>] [*d*-{Clause} <sp>]]

---

[6] Compare [Noun [Noun [*w*-<cj>] [Noun <PA>] <ap>]] with two appositions coordinated by *w*- (above, B 3e).

7. Adjective and prepositional phrase (§ 11.7)

a. Basic pattern:

[Noun [Adjective <sp>] [Prep–Noun <sp>]]

D. CONTRASTING PAIRS

1. Noun–Adjective–*d*-Noun if the adjective modifies the head,
   Noun–*d*-Noun–Adjective if the adjective modifies the *d*-phrase:

   [Noun [Adjective <sp>] [*d*-Noun <sp>]]   versus   [Noun [*d*-Noun [Adjective <sp>] <sp>]]

2. Noun–*d*-Noun *w*-*d*-Noun or Noun *d*-Noun *w*-Noun if the second *d*-phrase modifies head,
   Noun–*d*-Noun–*d*-Noun if the second *d*-phrase modifies the first *d*-phrase:[7]

   [Noun [*d*-Noun <sp>] [*w*-<cj>] [*d*-Noun <PA>]][8]   versus   [Noun [*d*-Noun [*d*-Noun <sp>] <sp>]]
   [Noun [*d*-Noun [*w*-<cj>] [Noun <PA>] <sp>]

3. Noun–*d*-Noun–Prep–Noun if the *d*-phrase modifies the head,
   Noun–Prep–Noun–*d*-Noun if the *d*-phrase modifies the prepositional phrase:

   [Noun [*d*-Noun <sp>] [Prep–Noun <sp>]]   versus   [Noun [Prep–Noun [*d*-Noun <sp>] <sp>]]

---

[7] But see § 11.5 on an example of [Noun [*d*-Noun] [*d*-Noun]] outside our corpus (Aphrahat, *Dem.* 21:21).
[8] Compare [CstrNoun–(Noun *w*-Noun)]: There are no examples with repetition of the first word, i.e. *[Noun$_A$ [*d*-Noun$_B$ <sp>] [*w*-<cj>] [Noun$_A$ [*d*-Noun$_B$ <sp>]] <PA>].

4. Noun *d*-Noun–Apposition if the *d*-phrase modifies the head,
   Noun–Apposition–*d*-Noun if the *d*-phrase modifies the apposition:

   [Noun [*d*-Noun <sp>] [Noun <ap>]]   versus   [Noun [Noun [*d*-Noun <sp>] <ap>]]

5. Noun–Adjective–Apposition if the adjective modifies the head,
   Noun–Apposition–Adjective if the adjective modifies the apposition:

   [Noun [Adjective <sp>] [Noun <ap>]]   versus   [Noun [Noun [Adjective <sp>] <ap>]]

E. 'HOMONYMOUS' PAIRS

1. Noun–*d*-Noun–*d*-Clause:
   d-Clause modifies the head or the preceding *d*-Noun:

   [Noun [*d*-Noun <sp>] [*d*-{[Adjective <Pr>]} <sp>]]   and   [Noun [*d*-Noun [*d*-{[Adjective <Pr>]} <sp>] <sp>]]
   [Noun [*d*-Noun <sp>] [*d*-{Clause} <sp>]]   and   [Noun [*d*-Noun [*d*-{Clause} <sp>] <sp>]]

2. Noun–Noun–*d*-Clause:
   d-Clause modifies the head or the preceding apposition:

   [Noun [Noun <ap>] [*d*-{Clause} <sp>]]   and   [Noun [Noun [*d*-{Clause} <sp>] <ap>]]

3. Noun–*d*-Noun–Prep–Noun:
   Prepositional phrase modifies the head or the preceding *d*-phrase:

   [Noun [*d*-Noun <sp>] [Prep–Noun <sp>]]   and   [Noun [*d*-Noun [Prep–Noun <sp>] <sp>]

4. Noun–*d*-Noun–Noun:
   The third noun is an apposition to the head or to the preceding *d*-Noun:

   [Noun [*d*-Noun <sp>] [Noun <ap>]]   and   [Noun [*d*-Noun [Noun <ap>] <sp>]]

F. MAXIMUM MATRIX OF PHRASE STRUCTURE (§ 15.4)

[Prep–CstrNoun–CstrNoun–Noun] | [Demonstrative] [Adjective] [Apposition] [*d*-Noun] [Prep–Noun] [*d*-{Clause}] [Parallel Elem.]

PART FOUR

CLAUSE STRUCTURE

CHAPTER SIXTEEN

PRELIMINARY REMARKS ON CLAUSE STRUCTURE

16.1 NOMINAL AND VERBAL CLAUSES

A clause is a construction in which predication occurs. Traditionally the construction of two or more clauses that are coordinated in one grammatical unit is called a compound sentence. A sentence made up of a main clause and one or more dependent clauses is called a complex sentence.[1] In the study of clause structure in Classical Syriac these distinctions are highly important, since some of the most common types of clauses (the tripartite nominal clauses and the so-called cleft sentences) are interpreted by some as simple clauses and by others as complex sentences.[2]

We can distinguish between verbal clauses, in which the predication is expressed by means of a finite verb, and nominal or non-verbal clauses, in which the predicate is a non-verbal element. In Syriac, the predicate of a non-verbal clause may be an adjectival phrase, an indefinite substantive phrase, a definite substantive phrase, a pronoun, an adverb or a prepositional phrase.[3]

Clauses containing a participle are included in our description of nominal clause patterns, but we shall see that the syntactic behaviour of participles differs from that of other predicative elements due to their verbal character. Since predicative adjectives show the same syntactic behaviour as participles, it is preferable to examine the participles and adjectives together in the category of 'participials'.[4]

---

[1] Thus e.g. Waltke–O'Connor, *Biblical Hebrew Syntax*, 690; see, however, § 8.8 for the problems involved in applying the notion of 'sentence' to Classical Syriac and § 26.2 for the refinement of the definition of dependency.

[2] See §§ 18.1, 24.1–2.

[3] Joosten, *Syriac Language*, 78. Neither Nöldeke nor Goldenberg distinguishes between definite and indefinite substantive phrases; ibid., 86. When the predicate is an adverb or a prepositional phrase, Joosten speaks of an adverbial clause, rather than a nominal clause (ibid., 77).

[4] Cf. Goldenberg, 'Syriac Sentence Structure', 115–117; see also Chapter 20.

16.2 SUBJECT AND PREDICATE, TOPIC AND COMMENT

It is common usage to call the verb in a verbal clause the predicate, and the element agreeing with it in gender, number and person the subject. Since, however, the verb contains both elements that express the predicate (the lexeme of the verb) and elements that indicate the subject (inflectional elements), it is preferable to consider the verb as an expression of predication, containing both the subject and the predicate, and the element agreeing with the subject in gender, number and person as an extraposed or modifying element.[5]

The basic core of a nominal clause (NC) consists of a subject (Su) and a predicate (Pr). In Syriac and general Semitic studies two approaches to the definition of Su and Pr are prevalent:

1. A logical or grammatical definition: Su is the more particular/definite constituent; Pr is the more universal/indefinite constituent.
2. A psychological or pragmatic definition: Pr is the contextually new information.

Elsewhere we have argued that this double use of the terms 'subject' and 'predicate' is confusing, and therefore it is preferable to use distinct pairs of terms for on the one hand the logical or grammatical Su and Pr and on the other hand the psychological or pragmatic Su and Pr.[6] Therefore we reserve the terms 'subject' and 'predicate' to the first pair, and call the second set 'topic' and 'comment'.

A subject is the grammatical point of reference for what is talked about in a clause, the predicate is the semantic communication about the subject. Sometimes it is possible to describe the relationship between Su and Pr from the perspective of agreement (in the case of participles and adjectives, cf. § 20.1) and determination (Su is the more definite element, § 16.3).

---

[5] Cf. Hoftijzer, 'Preliminary Remark', 647 n. 8 (on Biblical Hebrew): 'I do not agree with those authors who consider finite verbal forms as the predicate of a verbal clause (...). I consider the noun (phrase)/pronoun/pronominal phrase which mostly is described as subject of the verbal clause as a (often contextually necessary) modifier of the subject marked by the grammatical morpheme(s) of the finite verbal form'. See also Hoftijzer's comments on Classical Arabic in idem, 'Particle 't', 3.

[6] Van Peursen, 'Three Approaches', 163–165; see also Baasten, *Non-Verbal Clause in Qumran Hebrew*, 28–34.

A topic presents the entity *about* which the clause predicates something in the given setting. It is the constituent that relates the clause to the larger context. Hence it may also be called a contextualizing constituent. The rest of the clause gives a 'comment' on the topic.[7] 'Topic' should not be confused with 'focus'. The latter is the constituent that contains the salient *new* information.[8]

16.3 DEFINITENESS

If we identify Su and Pr on the basis of definiteness—Su is more definite than Pr—we should define definiteness not in absolute but in relative terms.[9] Thus the determinate noun phrase 'the king' is the subject in the clause 'the king is old', but the predicate in 'David is the king', because a proper noun phrase has a higher degree of definiteness than a determined noun phrase.[10]

In the present study we will rely heavily on a study by J.W. Dyk and E. Talstra on relative definiteness in Biblical Hebrew.[11] Dyk and Talstra elaborate on the pioneering work done by F.I. Andersen.[12] For the computer-assisted parsing of NCs in Biblical Hebrew Dyk and Talstra developed a matrix for identifying Su and Pr on the basis of phrase type and determination. This matrix is built on two assumptions: (1) there is a hierarchical order of phrase types that can receive the label Su, and (2) determination is defined in terms of 'referred to

---

[7] See also Khan, *Studies in Semitic Syntax*, xxxv.

[8] Cf. Pennacchietti's criticism of Moshe Azar (on Modern Hebrew) and Goldenberg (on Syriac) in his 'Frase nominale tripartita', 159–160, and the reaction in Goldenberg, 'Comments on "Three Approaches" by Wido van Peursen', 178–179; see further Dik, *Theory of Functional Grammar*, 266, and (on Biblical Hebrew) Buth, 'Generative-Functional Approach', 81; Gross, *Satzteilfolge*, 53–72.

[9] For the identification of Su and Pr a definition in terms of 'universal' and 'particular' (Niccacci, 'Simple Nominal Clause', 216–217; cf. Lyons, *Theoretical Linguistics*, 337–338) is not satisfactory, because it suggests too much a dichotomy between words that indicate universals and words that are used for particulars.

[10] Cf. Van Peursen, 'Three Approaches', 165, and the discussion in Joosten, 'Response to Wido van Peursen', 186–187; Van Peursen, 'Response to the Responses', 200–201.

[11] One of the major differences between Hebrew and Syriac concerns the use of the emphatic state in Syriac, which cannot be taken simply as the equivalent of the article in Hebrew; cf. below, note 20; on definiteness in Syriac see Khan, 'Object Markers and Agreement Pronouns', esp. 470.

[12] Andersen, *Verbless Clause*; see also Lowery, 'Relative Definiteness'.

or not yet referred to in the situation of communication'.[13] The matrix
contains in hierarchical order the following phrase types: suffix on יֵשׁ,
הִנֵּה, אַיִן etc.; demonstrative pronoun; personal pronoun; definite noun
phrase; proper noun; indefinite noun phrase; interrogative pronoun;
adjective; prepositional phrase; locatives.[14]

This approach helps us identify Su and Pr in cases where one element has the emphatic state and another the absolute state, such as

> 11:30 ܡܐ ܡܓܝܐܝܢ ܣܘܟܠܝܗܘܢ ܕܥܘܠܐ How many are the transgressions
> of the unrighteous!'

Or in cases where Pr is a prepositional phrase, such as

> 5:6 ܪܚܡܐ ܘܪܘܓܙܐ ܥܡܗ 'Mercy and anger are with Him'.

But this approach enables us also to identify Su and Pr in cases such
as

> 1:14, 16 ܪܝܫ ܚܟܡܬܐ ܕܚܠܬܗ ܕܡܪܝܐ 'The beginning of wisdom is fear of
> the Lord'.
> 10:11 ܒܡܘܬܗ ܕܒܪ ܐܢܫܐ ܪܡܬܐ ܡܢܬܗ 'When a man dies, maggots are
> his share'.

In 1:14, 16 the proper noun ܡܪܝܐ is more definite than the common
noun ܕܚܠܬܐ and in 10:11 the suffixed noun ܡܢܬܗ is more definite
than the emphatic state ܪܡܬܐ.

16.4 STRUCTURAL MEANING

We can distinguish three structural meanings: descriptive, identificatory and contrastive. In a semantic sense, the clause 'David is my master' is

1. descriptive if it is a reply to 'What is David?',[15]

---

[13] Dyk's and Talstra's definition of definiteness includes both grammatical criteria
(state, agreement) and pragmatic criteria (known versus new referent). From a methodological view this means a concession from a strictly formal approach, but from a
practical perspective it has great advantages because it renders it possible to combine
deixis, phrase type, grammatical features, syntactic features and lexical features into
the one category of determination; cf. Dyk–Talstra, 'Paradigmatic and Syntagmatic',
150–152; Van Peursen, 'Three Approaches', 166.

[14] Dyk–Talstra, 'Paradigmatic and Syntagmatic', 150–152; cf. Andersen, Verbless
Clause, 22, on which see Dyk–Talstra, ibid., 145–146.

[15] Some scholars use 'classifying' or 'classificatory' instead of 'descriptive'.

2. identificatory if it is a reply to 'Who among you is David?',
3. contrastive if it is contrasted with, say, 'and John is my servant'.

These three concepts have a long history in Semitic linguistics. The distinction between 'descriptive' and 'identificatory' was introduced into Semitic studies by F. Praetorius and S.R. Driver.[16] It plays an important role in studies on the NCs in Biblical Hebrew by Andersen, Waltke–O'Connor and Muraoka.[17] To our best knowledge, Muraoka was the first to use the concepts descriptive, identificatory and contrastive in Syriac studies.[18]

There are two ways in which 'identification' and 'description' can be defined. Muraoka defines them in the contextual or semantic terms given above.[19] This differs from a strictly logical approach, which defines identification in terms of total semantic overlap. Joosten is an advocate of such a logical approach. He considers all clauses in which both Su and Pr are definite to be identificatory. Thus a clause such as 'David is my master' is identificatory under all circumstances, in contrast to a descriptive clause such as 'David is a shepherd'.[20]

The difference between the two approaches is evident. From a strictly formal perspective 'my master' is determinate and has exactly the same referent as 'David', which for Joosten is enough reason to call the clause 'David is my master' identificatory. However, 'David is my master' does not necessarily presuppose some shared knowl-

---

[16] Driver, *Tenses*, § 199 (on Biblical Hebrew); Praetorius, *Äthiopische Grammatik*, 159–160 (on Geʿez); idem, Review of Stern, *Koptische Grammatik*, 755.

[17] Andersen, *Verbless Clause*, 32; Waltke–O'Connor, *Biblical Hebrew Syntax*, 130; Muraoka, *Emphatic*, 6–46, esp. 7–8; Joüon–Muraoka, *Grammar*, § 154*ea*; Muraoka, refers to Lyons, *Semantics* II, 471–473; Lyons speaks of 'equative' and 'ascriptive' clauses. In Hebrew too Muraoka recognizes a third notion, namely that of contrast, see his *Emphatic*, 12–13, 16; cf. Hoftijzer, 'Nominal Clause Reconsidered', esp. 488–493.

[18] Muraoka, *Classical Syriac for Hebraists*, § 105; idem, 'Nominal Clause in Old Syriac Gospels', 30.

[19] Similarly for Hebrew, see Muraoka, *Emphatic*, 7–8; Joüon–Muraoka, *Grammar*, § 154*ea* n. 3.

[20] Joosten, *Syriac Language*, 78: 'A clause with as predicate a definite noun (or pronoun) phrase is an identificatory non-verbal clause'; ibid. 85–86 (esp. n. 14); similarly idem, 'Negation', 585–586 (esp. n. 14). Note that for Syriac the emphatic state does not necessarily indicate definiteness. Thus ܐܢ̱ܬ ܢܒܝܐ can mean both 'Are you the prophet?' (John 1:21) or 'You are a prophet' (John 4:19); see Joosten, ibid., 88. Others, including Goldenberg and Buth, do not consider these categories useful for describing clause structure in Semitic languages, see Goldenberg, 'Syriac Sentence Structure', 105; Buth, 'Generative-Functional Approach', 94–95.

edge that the speaker has a master. If this is not the case and 'my master' is purely new information, Muraoka would call the clause descriptive. Accordingly, Muraoka analyses 'I am the good shepherd' (John 10:11) as descriptive, because it does not necessarily presuppose some common knowledge that there is a good shepherd.

CHAPTER SEVENTEEN

BIPARTITE NOMINAL CLAUSES

17.1 BASIC PATTERNS

According to the nature of the subject (Noun or Pronoun) and the relative order of the clause constituents we can distinguish four types of bipartite NCs.[1]

A. Type 1: Pr–Su$_{noun}$

This pattern is attested about 130 times. In 50% of the examples the Pr is participial:

> 6:20 ܟܡܐ ܥܣܩܐ ܗܝ ܚܟܡܬܐ 'How difficult is Wisdom for a fool'.[2]
> 13:22 ܘܣܓܝܐܝܢ ܥܕܘܪܘܗܝ, 'And his helpers are many'.

In about 25% of the cases the Pr is a noun:

> 1:14, 16, 18 ܪܝܫ ܚܟܡܬܐ ܕܚܠܬܗ ܕܡܪܝܐ 'The beginning of wisdom is fear of the Lord'.[3]

In about 14 % of the cases the Pr is the adverbial ܗܟܢܐ, which resumes a fronted element introduced by ܐܝܟ:

> 2:18 (= 6:17), ܘܐܝܟ ܫܡܗ ܗܟܢܐ ܥܒܕܘܗܝ 'and like His name so are His works'.

In other cases the Pr is a prepositional phrase, a numeral or an interrogative:

> 10:4 ܒܐܝܕܘܗܝ, ܕܡܪܝܐ ܫܘܠܛܢܐ ܕܐܪܥܐ 'In the hands of the Lord is the authority over the world'.
> 21:3 ܕܬܪܝܢ ܦܘܡܝܗ, '(a) two-edged (sword)'.

---

[1] Cf. Muraoka, 'Nominal Clause in Old Syriac Gospels', 29.
[2] Heb (A) has a NC of the type P–S$_{pron}$ but the Syriac translator has replaced the pronoun by a noun; cf. § 3.2 (h).
[3] For our identification of Su and Pr see § 16.3.

18:8 ܘܡܢܐ ܚܘܣܪܢܗܘܢ 'And what is their loss?'

B. Type 2: Su_{noun}–Pr

This type is the most frequent bipartite pattern. It occurs about 220 times. In 65% of the cases the Pr is a participial:

1:12 ܕܚܠܬܗ ܕܡܪܝܐ ܡܚܕܝܐ ܠܒܐ 'Fear of the Lord gladdens the heart'.

In more than 20% of the cases the Pr is a prepositional phrase:

5:6 ܪ̈ܚܡܐ ܘܪܘܓܙܐ ܥܡܗ 'Mercy and anger are with Him'.
20:16 ܐܟ̈ܠܝ ܠܚܡܝ ܐܝܟ ܫܘܥܐ ܕܟܐܦܐ 'Those who eat my bread are like a rock of stone'.

And in more than 10% of the cases the Pr is a noun:

4:14 ܡܫܡܫܢܝܗ̇ ܡܫ̈ܡܫܢܝ ܩܘܕܫܐ 'Her servants are servants of holiness'.
44:19 ܐܒܪܗܡ ܐܒܐ ܕܟܢ̈ܘܫܬܐ ܕܥܡ̈ܡܐ 'Abraham was the father of the communities of the peoples'.

In five cases the Pr is an infinitive:

25:12 ܪܫ ܕܚܠܬܗ ܕܡܪܝܐ ܠܡܪܚܡܗ 'The beginning of fear of the Lord is to love Him'.

C. Type 3: Pr–Su_{pron}

This pattern is attested about 50 times. In half of the cases the subject is a pronoun of the third person. In about 70% of the cases the Pr is a participial:

18:17 ܕܝܢ ܡܘܗܒܬܐ ܛܒܐ ܗܝ '(A good word) that is better than a gift'.
29:28 ܘܐܢ ܥܪܛܠܝ ܗܘ 'And if he is naked'.

The participial predicate occurs more often with the subject pronoun of the 1st or 2nd person (65%) than with the participial of the third person (35%).[4] In eight cases the Pr is a noun:

29:25, 26 ܐܟܣܢܝܐ ܐܢܬ 'You are a foreigner'.

Six times it is a prepositional phrase:

1:15 ܥܡ ܐܢܫܐ ܗܝ ܕܩܘܫܬܐ 'She is with the people of truth'.

And once it is the adverbial ܗܪܟܐ (in a relative clause):

[4] This is related to the fact that the third person subject pronoun was more easily omitted; cf. §§ 17.3 (end), 20.2.

32:23 ܟܠ ܕܐܟܘܬܗ ܗܘ 'Everyone who is like this'.

If the Pr consists of more than one word, it is idiomatic for the enclitic to be placed immediately after the first phrase atom:[5]

6:21 ܐܝܟ ܟܐܦܐ ܗܘ ܝܩܝܪܬܐ ܠܘܬܗ 'She is to him like a heavy stone'.[6]

D. Type 4: Su_{pron}–Pr

This pattern is attested 45 times. In almost all cases the Pr is a participial:

1:20 ܕܗܝ ܛܒܐ ܠܗ ܡܢ ܟܠ ܣܝܡܬܐ 'To whom she is better than all treasures'.

Two times it is a prepositional phrase:

24:30 ܐܦ ܐܢܐ ܐܝܟ ܢܗܪܐ ܕܡܫܩܐ 'And also I am like an irrigating river'.

45:15 ܘܗܘܐ ܠܗ ܠܩܝܡܐ ܕܠܥܠܡ 'And it became for him an eternal covenant'.

And once it is a noun (in a relative clause):

17:32 ܕܗܢܘܢ ܥܦܪܐ ܘܩܛܡܐ 'Who are dust and ashes'.

According to Muraoka this type is contrastive if the subject pronoun is in the first or second person.[7]

E. Other patterns

In the discussion above we have distinguished cases where the subject is a noun and cases in which it is a personal pronoun. There are also

---

[5] See § 13.2; cf. Nöldeke, *Grammatik*, § 312A: 'Ist das Subj. ein Personalpronomen, so genügt seine einmalige Setzung, und zwar steht es meist enclitisch nach dem wichtigsten Wort des Präd.'; see also § 324E; Muraoka, *Classical Syriac for Hebraists*, 64 n. 130; idem *Basic Grammar*, § 104; Avinery, 'Nominal Clause in the Peshitta', 48; Goldenberg, 'Syriac Sentence Structure', § 2 (pp. 100–102); Joosten, *Syriac Language*, 78; cf. Andersen, *Verbless Clause*, 23, 29–30, 36–37 on discontinuous predicates in Biblical Hebrew. See also the example from 1:15, quoted above.

[6] But when the subject is a noun (above, Type A) it does not intervene between the first phrase atom of the Pr and its extensions. Compare 6:21, quoted above (with S_{pron}), with 21:21 ܐܝܟ ܚܠܩܐ ܕܕܗܒܐ ܚܟܡܬܐ ܠܓܒܪܐ ܕܝܕܥ 'Like a golden bracelet is wisdom to the prudent man' (with S_{noun}).

[7] Muraoka, 'Nominal Clause in Old Syriac Gospels', 30–32; similarly Avinery, 'Nominal Clause in the Peshitta', 48–49. According to Nöldeke (*Grammatik*, § 312B) and Duval (*Traité*, § 375b) the subject pronoun precedes the Pr when it is emphasized ('ein gewisser Nachdruk'). Muraoka's 'contrast' is a refinement of Nöldeke's and Duval's 'emphasis'.

about twenty cases in which the subject is an independent relative clause, or a relative clause preceded by a 'dummy antecedent'[8] such as ܡܢ or ܡܕܡ. With the pattern Pr–Su there occur six examples: three in which the Pr is a participial, two in which it is a noun, and one in which it is the adverbial ܗܟܢܐ:

3:4 ܘܣܐܡ ܣܝܡܬܐ ܡܢ ܕܡܝܩܪ ܠܐܡܗ 'And storing up treasures is he who honours his mother'.
22:22 ܒܪ ܡܣܩܕܐ ܡܢ ܕܓܠܐ ܐܪܙܐ 'A reproachful man is he who reveals a secret'.
30:19 ܗܟܢܐ ܡܢ ܕܐܝܬ ܠܗ ܥܘܬܪܐ ܘܠܐ ܡܫܬܡܫ ܒܗ 'So is one who has riches, but does not make use of it'.

With the pattern Su–Pr there occur fifteen examples: thirteen with a participial and two with a prepositional phrase:

30:3 ܕܡܠܦ ܒܪܗ ܡܛܢ ܠܒܥܠܕܒܒܗ 'He who teaches his son provokes his enemy to jealousy'.
40:17 ܘܕܡܬܩܪܒ ܠܗܘܢ ܐܝܟ ܐܢܫ ܕܡܫܟܚ ܣܝܡܬܐ 'And he who draws near to them is like a man who finds a treasure'.

There are also some cases in which the subject is a demonstrative pronoun. Five times the Pr is a participial, twice it is a noun and once a prepositional phrase. All cases have the pattern Pr–Su:

39:17 ܕܗܢܐ ܒܝܫ ܘܗܢܐ ܛܒ 'This is evil and this is good'.
44:10 ܒܪܡ ܗܠܝܢ ܐܢܫܐ ܕܛܝܒܘܬܐ ܘܙܕܝܩܘܬܐ 'But these were people of goodness and of righteousness'.

In one case the subject is a prepositional phrase:

8:6 ܕܡܢܢ ܡܣܐܒܝܢ 'That some of us will become old'.[9]

17.2 BIPARTITE PATTERNS AND SYRIAC CLAUSE STRUCTURE

The interpretation of the bipartite NC patterns presented in the preceding paragraph is a much-debated issue. There are basically two ap-

---

[8] Muraoka uses this terminology in his *Basic Grammar*, § 111.
[9] The interpretation of the prepositional phrase as a subject agrees with that put forward by Joüon–Muraoka and Waltke–O'Connor for similar examples in Biblical Hebrew; cf. Joüon–Muraoka, *Grammar*, § 154*b*; Waltke–O'Connor, *Biblical Hebrew Syntax*, § 4.4.1*b*; alternatively we could consider the prepositional phrase a specification of a subject that has been omitted; see also Van Peursen, *Verbal System*, 312–313 on partitive מן in Heb.

proaches, one represented by T. Muraoka, the other by G. Goldenberg. According to Muraoka there are four basic patterns corresponding to our Types 1 to 4.[10] Although Muraoka does not explicitly deal with cases in which the subject is an independent relative clause or a demonstrative, we can safely assume that he considers them subsets of these basic patterns.

According to Goldenberg the basic pattern of any NC is our Type 3: Pr–Su$_{pron}$. He does not recognize bipartite NCs in which the subject is a noun (our Types 1 and 2) or in which the subject pronoun precedes the Pr (our Type 4). In his view these clauses are basically elliptical clauses wanting an enclitic pronominal subject, because the core of a non-verbal clause is 'a minimal nexus-complex where the subject is expressed in the form of an enclitic personal pronoun'.[11] In other words, the patterns Su$_{noun}$–Pr and Su$_{pron}$–Pr (our Types 1 and 3) are elliptical representatives of the patterns Su ∥ Pr–s, and Pr–Su$_{noun}$ (our Type 2) is elliptical for Pr–s ∥ Su (cf. § 18.1). According to Goldenberg, 'the examples adduced in the grammars as evidence of such a construction [i.e. a bipartite NC 'without a copula'] are in fact special cases of diverse types'.[12] He mentions four categories.

1. Sentences with participial predicates.

This category is well attested in Syr. Ellipsis of the 3rd person pronoun after a participial is a widespread phenomenon. It agrees with the rule that a participial, because of its verbal nature, does not need the enclitic pronoun.[13] But the examples in Syr include ten cases with a subject pronoun of the first or second person. Since ellipsis is uncommon with the 1st or 2nd person, it is problematic to analyse an example such as

9:13 ܘܥܠ ܡܨܝܕܬܐ ܐܢܬ ܡܗܠܟ 'and you walk over nets'.

---

[10] Muraoka, 'Nominal Clause in Old Syriac Gospels', 29.

[11] Goldenberg, 'Syriac Sentence Structure', 99; Wertheimer, *Problems*, 39–40; idem, 'Syriac Nominal Sentences', 3; contrast Muraoka, *Classical Syriac for Hebraists*, § 103, and especially 60 n. 119: 'A nominal predicate may form a sentence by just being juxtaposed with any nominal subject'; similarly Nöldeke, *Grammatik*, § 310; Duval, *Traité*, § 375a; Costaz, *Grammaire*, § 737; Brockelmann, *Grammatik*, § 218; see also Muraoka, *Basic Grammar*, § 103; Joosten, *Syriac Language*, 78–79, 93 (following Goldenberg).

[12] Goldenberg, 'Syriac Sentence Structure', 132.

[13] See § 20.3; cf. Goldenberg, 'Syriac Sentence Structure', 116; Joosten, *Syriac Language*, 78–81; idem, 'Negation', 585.

as elliptical for the tripartite constructions *ܘܟܠ ܢܒ̈ܝܐ ܐܝܬ ܡܗܠܟܝܢ ܐܝܬ.[14]

2. Sentences with a prepositional phrase introduced by ܒ, in which ܐܝܬ is omitted.

In Syr there are about 60 cases in which the Pr is a prepositional phrase, but only some of them belongs to Goldenberg's second category. There are eleven examples with ܒ, e.g.:

> 21:26 ܘܦܘܡܗ ܕܚܟܝܡܐ ܒܠܒܗ 'And the mouth of the wise is in his heart'.[15]

But sometimes the locative function of ܒ is questionable, as in

> 38:29 ܥܝܢܘܗܝ ܒܡܐ̈ܢܝ ܟܠ ܥܒܕܗ 'And his eyes are upon the vessels of all his work'.

Sometimes another preposition has a locative function:

> 5:6 ܡܛܠ ܕܪ̈ܚܡܐ ܘܪܘܓܙܐ ܥܡܗ 'For mercy and anger are with Him'.

But this is obviously not the case when the Pr is introduced by ܐܝܟ (20×):

> 20:16 ܐܟ̈ܠܝ ܠܚܡܝ ܐܝܟ ܫܘܥܐ ܕܟܐܦܐ 'Those who eat my bread are like a rock of stone'.

This means that at least 20 bipartite NCs with a prepositional Pr are not locative and hence are not covered by this category of ellipsis.

3. Expressions for telling what one's name is.

Expressions for 'and his name is/was N' or 'whose name is/was N' may take the bipartite construction. This construction is attested once in Syr:

> 37:1 ܕܫܡܗ ܪܚܡܐ '(A friend) whose name is friend'.

Also sentences for asking what one's name is may take the bipartite pattern (besides the 'normally expected' tripartite pattern). In Syr there is only one example of such a question, and it takes the tripartite structure:

---

14 For more details see § 20.3.

15 Parallel to ܘܦܘܡܗ ܕܣܟܠܐ ܗܘܝܘ ܠܒܗ 'The mouth of the fool is his heart' in the first part of this verse.

22:14 ܘܡܢܘ ܫܡܗ ܐܠܐ ܣܟܠܐ ‘And what is his name but “Fool”?’

4. Sentences rendering ‘This is…’, ‘This is the..’ and the like.

In this category too the bipartite pattern alternates with the more usual tripartite pattern. In Syr the bipartite pattern is attested once, in

44:10 ܒܪܡ ܗܠܝܢ ܐܢܫܐ ܕܛܝܒܘܬܐ ܘܙܕܝܩܘܬܐ ‘But these were people of goodness and of righteousness’.

The tripartite pattern occurs in

16:11 ܗܘ ܬܡܗܐ ܐܢ ܙܟܐ ‘It were amazing if he were to be unpunished’.

41:4 ܡܛܠ ܕܗܢܐ ܗܝ ܚܪܬܐ ܕܟܠܗܘܢ ܒܢܝܢܫܐ ܩܕܡ ܐܠܗܐ ‘Because this is the end of all people before God’.

Altogether Syr contains about 480 bipartite clauses. 50 of them belong to the pattern P–S_{pron}. Of the remaining 430 cases, ca. 290 belong to the categories of ellipsis identified by Goldenberg: 280 examples contain a participial, and about ten examples belong to one of the other types. If we disregard another 30 examples of prepositional predicates with ܡܢ, ܥܠ, ܠ and others (but not ܐܝܟ), 110 cases remain that do not belong to Goldenberg’s categories. This high number suggests that at least in the Syriac language as reflected in Syr the bipartite pattern was accepted. This does not by itself deny that Goldenberg’s description of clause patterns holds true for Classical Syriac. The situation in Syr may be enhanced by a factor of language development (i.e. Syr reflects an early phase in the history of Classical Syriac[16]) or translation technique (i.e. Syr has been influenced by the Hebrew source text).[17]

---

[16] Cf. Joosten, ‘Negation’, 586; ‘A large number of exceptions are found which simply juxtapose Su and Pr without an EPP. These clauses are of different kinds, and it is probably impossible to determine the rules that regulate their structure’; similarly idem, *Syriac Language*, 79, 93: ‘These cases (…) are sufficiently numerous to show that the mere juxtaposition of Su and Pr was recognized as a possible clause structure in the Syriac of our corpus’. In the Old Syriac Version of the Gospel of Matthew the bipartite structure is more frequent than in the Peshitta.

[17] Cf. Van Peursen, ‘Response to Responses’, 198–200; idem, ‘Language Variation and Textual History’, § 9.

17.3 ELLIPSIS

The pronominal subject of a bipartite NC has been omitted many times. Ellipsis is extremely rare with the first and second persons. It is frequent with participles, which indicates their verbalization.[18] Some special contexts in which ellipsis occurs are recognized in the scholarly literature:

1. Relative clauses (including the so-called independent relative clauses).[19]

The Pr is most often a participial:

13:22 ܕܫܦܝܪ 'What is beautiful'.
41:1 ܠܓܒܪܐ ܕܚܣܝܢ 'A man who is strong'.

In other cases the Pr is a prepositional phrase (9×), a phrase with ܕܝܠ (1×) or the adverbial ܗܟܢܐ (1×):

8:19 ܡܐ ܕܒܠܒܟ 'What is in your heart'.
9:8 ܫܘܦܪܐ ܕܠܐ ܕܝܠܟ 'A beauty that is not yours'.
20:15 ܐܝܠܝܢ ܕܗܟܢܐ 'Those who are like this'.

2. Circumstantial or conditional clauses introduced by ܟܕ, ܥܕ or ܐܢ:[20]

3:5 ܘܟܕ ܡܨܠܐ 'And when he prays'.
13:6 ܥܕ ܥܒܕ ܨܒܝܢܗ ܥܡܟ 'As long as he is doing his will with you'.

Another special category, not explicitly identified as such in the literature consists of clauses introduced by ܘ in which the Pr is a participial. This pattern is attested almost ninety times:

6:8 ܘܠܐ ܩܐܡ ܒܝܘܡܐ ܕܐܘܠܨܢܐ 'but he will not stand (with you) in the time of affliction'.
29:6 ܘܩܢܐ ܠܗ ܣܢܐܐ 'And he acquires an enemy'.

Eight times two clauses with ellipsis of the subject pronoun are coordinated, the second clause being introduced by ܘ:

---

[18] Goldenberg, 'Syriac Sentence Structure', 116; similarly Joosten, *Syriac Language*, 78, 81; see further §§ 20.3–4. Ellipsis of the subject pronoun in NCs with a participial Pr is also well attested in Heb; see Van Peursen, *Verbal System*, 222–223; cf. Joüon–Muraoka, *Grammar*, § 154*c* on Biblical Hebrew.
[19] Cf. § 10.2.3 on ܕ + Adjective and § 10.5.1 on ܕ + Prepositional Phrase.
[20] Cf. Muraoka, 'Nominal Clause in Old Syriac Gospels', 30; *Classical Syriac for Hebraists*, § 105; Nöldeke, *Grammatik*, §§ 310, 314 (see also § 275).

38:21 ܠܟ ܡܗܢܐ ܘܠܐܚܪܢܐ ܡܒܐܫ 'It gladdens you, but it does evil to someone else'.

A sequence of several coordinated clauses with ellipsis occurs in, e.g.

16:27 ܠܐ ܟܦܢܝܢ ܘܠܐ ܨܗܝܢ ܘܠܐ ܥܡܠܝܢ ܘܠܐ ܠܐܝܢ ܘܠܐ ܚܣܝܪܝܢ ܡܢ ܓܢܒܪܘܬܗܘܢ 'And they do not hunger, nor thirst, nor labour, nor weary themselves and they do not lack strength'.

Compare the following case where two clauses with a subject pronoun and three clauses with ellipsis of the subject pronoun occur together:

34:19 ܘܬܘܟܠܢܐ ܗܘ ܪܒܐ ܘܡܣܬܪܢܐ ܡܢ ܣܢܐܐ ܘܦܪܘܩܐ ܡܢ ܒܥܠܕܒܒܐ ܘܡܦܪܩܢܐ ܗܘ ܡܢ ܡܚܘܬܐ ܘܣܡܟ ܡܢ ܕܠܡܦܠ 'And He is a great confidence and a shelter against the enemies, a saviour from adversaries and He is a redeemer from the wound and He supports from falling'.

However, ellipsis of the subject is not restricted to these special contexts. It also occurs more than twenty-five times in independent clauses. In all cases the Pr is a participle:

12:18 ܒܪܝܫܗ ܡܢܝܕ 'He shakes his head'.

The pronouns of the first and second persons are usually retained.[21] Note especially

15:16 ܒܐܝܢܐ ܕܨܒܐ ܐܢܬ '(stretch out your hand) to that what you want'.

Here the pronoun of the second person occurs in a relative clause with a participle, a syntactical context where we frequently find ellipsis of the third person pronoun.

17.4 REFERENCE TO THE PAST

Most examples of bipartite NCs occur in statements expressing a general truth (general present), but sometimes the reference is to the past. This applies to some circumstantial clauses introduced by ܟܕ + participle (with ellipsis of the subject pronoun), such as

46:2 ܟܕ ܡܪܝܡ ܪܘܡܚܐ ܕܐܝܕܗ ܘܟܕ ܡܢܝܦ ܥܠ ܡܕܝܢܬܐ 'When he raised the spear which was in his hand, and when he waved it against the city'.

---

21 In Heb there is one example of ellipsis of a pronoun of the second person singular in 12:15. In this place Syr has an imperfect. In Biblical Hebrew there are some examples where the personal pronoun of the 1st person has been omitted. Joüon–Muraoka, *Grammar*, § 154*c*, mentions Hab 1:5, Zech 9:12.

50:5 ܕܟ ܡܕܟܘܬܐ ܡܢ ܬܚܝܬ ܦܪܣܐ 'When he appeared from under the veil'.

But also with the pattern *w*-Su$_{noun}$–Pr (Type 1):

44:23 ܘܒܘܪܟܬܐ ܕܟܠ ܕܩܕܡܘܗܝ ܢܚܬ ܥܠ ܪܝܫ ܐܝܣܪܐܝܠ 'And the blessing of all who were before him rested on the head of Israel'.

48:1 ܘܡܠܬܗ ܝܩܕܐ ܐܝܟ ܐܬܘܢܐ ܕܢܘܪ 'And his word was burning like a glowing furnace'.

And even in clauses not introduced by a conjunction, such as

51:21 ܓܘܝ ܕܝܠܝ ܝܩܕ ܐܝܟ ܐܬܘܢܐ 'My inner parts were burning like a furnace'.

17.5 CONCLUSION

Bipartite clauses are well attested in Syr. Each of the four types discussed in § 17.1 occurs frequently. According to Goldenberg the basic pattern of each NC is Pr–Su$_{pron}$ and other patterns should be explained in terms of ellipsis. There are some syntactic contexts that account for the omission of the subject pronoun. Thus if the Pr is a participial, the verbalization of the participial accounts for the omission of the subject pronoun of the 3rd person. There remain more than 110 examples, however, that neither belong to one of the categories of ellipsis identified by Goldenberg, nor to the 'undisputed' pattern Pr–Su$_{pron}$. These examples cannot be dismissed as exceptions or errors.

We suggested above that the large number of the exceptions to the pattern Pr–Su$_{pron}$ may reflect an early phase of the Syriac language or the influence of the Hebrew source text. In that case Goldenberg's theory could still hold true for non-translated 'standard' Classical Syriac. To establish whether this is the case or not, a comparison of our corpus and other Biblical Syriac texts with non-translated Syriac texts is required, but such a comparison is beyond the scope of the present study.[22]

---

[22] Such a study will be undertaken in the research project 'TURGAMA: Computer-Assisted Analysis of the Peshitta and the Targum: Text, Language and Interpretation'. This project involves both an analysis of the Peshitta and Targum of Judges and Bardaiṣan's *Book of the Law of the Countries*. For more information, see the website www.leidenuniv.nl/gg/turgama.

CHAPTER EIGHTEEN

TRIPARTITE NOMINAL CLAUSES

18.1 INTRODUCTION

The tripartite NC contains three members, one of which is an enclitic personal pronoun (Ep). As to its syntactic analysis there are basically two views:

1. The tripartite NC is an extension of the bipartite NC by the addition of the pronoun. The bipartite patterns Su–Pr and Pr–Su are expanded to four types, namely Su–Pr–Ep, Su–Ep–Pr, Pr–Su–Ep and Pr–Ep–Su. This view is represented by T. Muraoka in various publications.[1]

2. The tripartite NC is an extension of a bipartite clause core of the pattern Pr–s. The subject is added in fronted or rear extraposition. The Ep is the lesser subject in the clause core. It always follows the Pr. Accordingly, there are only two patterns of tripartite NCs: Su ‖ Pr–s and Pr–s ‖ Su. The main representative of this approach is G. Goldenberg.[2]

Elsewhere we have argued that the difference between these two approaches concerns not so much the interpretation of Syriac NCs as such, but rather the model employed to describe them and the termi-

---

[1] Muraoka, *Classical Syriac for Hebraists*, § 103. In his description of patterns Muraoka uses a lower case s (for 'lesser subject'), e.g. Pr–s–Su, but apparently he considers it equivalent to E (for 'enclitic'), because he adds in a footnote (p. 62 n. 124): 'Goldenberg uses lower cases [read: lower case s?] for our E, which stands for Enclitic'. In his *Basic Grammar* he used both s (§ 105) and E (§ 108) in the first edition, but has corrected s to E in the second edition. Recently Muraoka has changed his view. He no longer recognizes the pattern Su–Ep–Pr (see the discussion in § 18.2 [C]), but the controversial pattern Pr–Su–Ep is still a hallmark of his model (see § 18.2 [D]). See Muraoka, 'Response to Wido van Peursen', 189; Van Peursen, 'Response to Responses', 202–203.

[2] In this approach the term 'tripartite nominal clause' is imprecise, because the construction as a whole is regarded as a clause + an element in extraposition; cf. Goldenberg, 'Comments on "Three Approaches" by Wido van Peursen', 177 n. 3.

nology used. Thus in the first model a clause such as ܐܢܐ ܗܘ ܐܒܪܗܡ
'I am Abraham' is an identificatory clause of the type Su–Ep–Pr; in
the second approach it is a Pr–s ‖ Su clause, in which ܐܢܐ is the new
information and hence the Pr.[3] In both interpretations ܐܢܐ is the most
important or salient information of the clause, be it as a rhematized
subject (the first approach) or as the 'rheme/comment = predicate' (the
second approach).

In our computer-assisted analysis we have used the labels <Su>
and <Pr> on the basis of the criteria of definiteness given in § 16.3. As
a consequence of our *form-to-function* approach, we considered this
preferable to a psychological definition of Su and Pr.[4] For the Ep we
have introduced the label <Ep>.[5] We use this encoding only for the
formal registration of the data, but this does not imply an *a priori*
preference for the first approach. The computer programs allow for a
reanalysis of the data in terms of extraposition if our analysis gives us
reason to do so.

18.2 BASIC PATTERNS

On the basis of two formal criteria, namely the relative order of Su
and Pr and the position of the Ep, four basic patterns of NCs can be
distinguished.

A. Type 1: Su–Pr–Ep

This pattern is attested about forty times. The subject is most often a
noun and sometimes an independent relative clause or a relative clause
with a 'dummy antecedent'.[6] Two times the subject is a personal pronoun of the 3rd person singular:

1:1 ܘܗܝ ܠܥܠܡ ܥܡܗ ܗܝ ܡܢ ܠܥܠܡ 'And she is with Him from eternity'.

---

[3] Cf. Goldenberg, 'Syriac Sentence Structure', 104–105: 'Analysing Pattern-C sentences such as ܐܢܐ ܗܘ ܒܪܝ or ܐܢܐ ܐܢܐ ܒܪܝܐ as if their initial ܐܢܐ should be the
subject and the enclitic pronoun a "copula" (Nöldeke § 312C-D, Duval § 375*d-e*) is
totally wrong'; see also Goldenberg, 'Niceties', 337. For more details see Van
Peursen, 'Three Approaches', 166–172 (= § 4 'Syntactic Analysis of the Enclitic').
[4] Van Peursen, 'Three Approaches', 163–166 (= § 3 'The Identification of S and P
in a Nominal Clause').
[5] This was a new category to be added to the WIVU system (§§ 8.1–2).
[6] Cf. § 17.1 (E).

37:13 ܘܐܦ ܗܘ ܡܗܝܡܢ ܗܘ ܐܟܘܬܟ 'And also he is faithful like you'.

The subject is an infinitive in

27:21 ܠܓܠܐ ܕܝܢ ܐܪܙܐ ܦܣܩ ܣܒܪܐ ܗܘ 'But to reveal secrets is despair'.

And a numeral in

28:12 ܘܬܪܝܗܘܢ ܡܢܟ ܐܢܝܢ 'And both come from you'.

The Pr is a noun, a participial or a prepositional phrase:

3:11 ܐܝܩܪܗ ܓܝܪ ܕܓܒܪܐ ܗܘ ܐܝܩܪܗ ܕܐܒܘܗܝ, 'For a man's honour is the honour of his father'.

1:1 ܟܠ ܚܟܡܬܐ ܡܢ ܡܪܝܐ ܗܝ, 'All wisdom comes from the Lord'.

5:4 ܡܛܠ ܕܐܠܗܐ ܢܓܝܪ ܪܘܚܐ ܗܘ 'Because God is patient'.

The Pr consists of ܕ followed by a noun in

34:21 ܕܒܚܝܗܘܢ ܕܥܘܠܐ ܕܥܘܠܐ ܐܢܘܢ 'The sacrifices of the unrighteous are of iniquity'.[7]

If the Pr takes one or more specifications, the Ep is placed after the first phrase atom:[8]

6:16 ܪܚܡܐ ܡܗܝܡܢܐ ܗܘ ܣܡܐ ܕܚܝܐ 'A faithful friend is a medicine of life'.

The Su–Pr–Ep pattern is well attested. The identification of Su and Pr is the same in the two approaches of Goldenberg and Muraoka discussed in § 18.1. The syntactic analysis differs in that in Muraoka's model the subject is part of the main clause, whereas in Goldenberg's analysis it stands in extraposition.[9]

In about 25 cases the tripartite NC in Syr corresponds to a bipartite NC in Heb. Compare e.g.

3:11 (A) ‏כבוד איש כבוד אביו.
6:16 (A) ‏צרור חיים אוהב אמונה.

---

[7] Peters, *Ben Sirach*, 286, reconstructs the translator's Hebrew source text as ‏עולות עול מעולה.

[8] Cf. § 17.1 (C) on the same phenomenon in bipartite clauses of the type Pr–Su$_{pron}$ and below, B, for its appearance in the pattern Pr–Ep–Su. The position of the Ep argues for the interpretation of the tripartite pattern Su–Pr–Ep as an extraposition construction, see § 15.5.

[9] On the relationship between extraposition and tripartite NCs see the preceding footnote and further § 21.4.

In 6:16 there is also a difference in constituent order: where Syr has Su–Pr–Ep, Heb has Pr–Su. If the Syriac tripartite NC is analysed as an extraposition construction (cf. above, § 18.1), one could argue that this construction enabled the Syriac translator to put ܪ̈ܚܡܘܗܝ ܗܘ in topic position, while at the same time retaining the Pr–Su pattern of the main clause. However, if this explanation is correct, it is hard to explain why this pattern of correspondence occurs only once in Syr.

The phenomenon that a tripartite NC in the Syriac text corresponds to a bipartite NC in the Hebrew is well attested in other books of the Old Testament as well. Where, however, early manuscripts such as 5b1 are available, these manuscripts have often a bipartite structure. We have discussed this phenomenon elsewhere.[10] In Syr we can observe the patterns of correspondence, but the material available is insufficient to establish whether we should explain them in terms of translation technique (the translator rendered Hebrew bipartite NCs with the tripartite pattern because that was more idiomatic Syriac) or textual transmission (in an earlier, unattainable, phase of the textual history there were more bipartite patterns; the tripartite patterns in Syr are later adaptations to idiomatic Syriac).[11]

B. Type 2: Pr–Ep–Su

This pattern too is attested almost fifty times. In most cases the subject is a noun. Three times it is an independent relative clause. It is an infinitive in

11:21 ܡܛܠ ܕܦܫܝܩ ܗܘ ܩܕܡ ܡܪܢ ܚܠܝܐ ܠܡܥܬܪ ܠܡܣܟܢܐ ܒܕܠܝܠ ܡܢ ܫܠܝ 'For it is in the Lord's power to make the poor one rich suddenly'.

The subject consists of the numeral ܚܕ followed by a relative clause in

16:3 ܡܛܠ ܕܛܒ ܗܘ ܚܕ ܕܥܒܕ ܨܒܝܢܐ ܡܢ ܐܠܦ 'Because better is one who does the will (of God) than a thousand'.

---

[10] Cf. Van Peursen, 'Response to Responses', 199–200.

[11] It is remarkable that earlier scholars who assumed that the Hebrew Geniza manuscripts contained retranslations from Syr ignored the difference between a bipartite clause in Heb against a tripartite clause in Syr. This is the more remarkable since these scholars often assumed that such a retroversion was made almost slavishly (cf. Van Peursen, 'Retroversions'; idem, 'Sir 51:13–30'; idem, Verbal System, 19–23). Thus Lévi, L'Ecclesiastique II, 32, calls 6:14 (A) אוהב אמונה אוהב תקוף a calque of ܪܚܡܐ ܕܡܗܝܡܢ ܪܚܡܐ ܗܘ ܬܩܝܦܐ, but apparently he assumed that the Hebrew translator ignored the Ep and that there was a shift from a tripartite clause (Syriac) to a bipartite clause (Hebrew).

The Pr is a participial in about 50% of the cases:

3:24 ܡܚ̈ܫܒ̈ܬܐ ܕܓ̈ܒܪܐ ܣܓ̈ܝܐܢ ܐܢܝܢ ܕܒܢ̈ܝܢܫܐ 'For many are the thoughts of men'.

5:6 ܡܪܚܡܢܐ ܗܘ ܡܪܝܐ 'The Lord is merciful'.

Nine times it is the adverbial ܗܟܢܐ:[12]

26:12 ܗܟܢܐ ܗܝ ܐܢܬܬܐ ܓܝܪܬܐ 'So is the adulterous wife'.

Five times the Pr is a noun:

31:7 ܡܛܠ ܕܬܘܩܠܬܐ ܗܘ ܡܡܘܢܐ ܠܣܟܠܐ 'Because Mammon is a stumbling-block for the fool'.

Three times it is a prepositional phrase:

21:2 ܐܝܟ ܫܢܐ ܕܐܪܝܐ ܗܝ ܢܟܠܐ 'Deceit is like the teeth of a lion'.

The Pr is a numeral in

33:31 (bis) ܐܢ ܚܕ ܗܘ ܥܒܕܟ 'If you have but one slave'.

In one case the Pr consists of ܕܝܠ with suffix:

47:18 ܕܝܠܗ ܗܘ ܐܝܩܪܐ '(By the name of God) whose is the honour'.

Five times the Pr is an interrogative:

22:14 ܘܡܢܘ ܫܡܗ 'And what is his name?'

31:9, 10 ܡܢܘ ܗܢܐ 'Who is this?'

When the element preceding the enclitic consists of more than one word, it is idiomatic for the enclitic to be placed immediately after the first component:[13]

2:11 ܡܛܠ ܕܪܚܘܡ ܗܘ ܡܪܝܐ ܘܡܪܚܡܢܐ 'Because the Lord is compassionate and merciful'.

The pattern Pr–Ep–Su occurs a number of times where Heb has a bipartite NC of the type Pr–Su.[14] Compare e.g.

---

[12] In 28:10 8a1 has ܡܢܘ ܗܘ ܪܓܗ against the bipartite construction in all other manuscripts.

[13] See § 17.1 (C) on the same phenomenon in bipartite clauses of the type Pr–Su$_{pron}$ and above, A, for its appearance in the pattern Su–Pr–Ep and further Muraoka, *Classical Syriac for Hebraists*, 64 n. 130; idem *Basic Grammar* § 104; Avinery 'Nominal Clause in the Peshitta', 48; Goldenberg, 'Syriac Sentence Structure', § 2 (pp. 100–102); Joosten, *Syriac Language*, 78.

[14] An exception is 31:9, 10 where ܡܢܘ corresponds to מי הוא זה in Heb (B); cf. § 21.2 (end) on ܡܢܘ corresponding to מי.

‏כי רבים עשתוני בני אדם‎ (A) 3:24
‏רחום יי‎ (A) 5:6

C. Type 3: Su–Ep–Pr

This pattern is attested ten times. Typical examples are those in which
the subject is a personal or demonstrative pronoun:

16:11 ܬܗܪܐ ܗܘ 'It would be amazing'.
36:22 ܕܐܢܬ ܗܘ ܐܠܗܐ ܒܠܚܘܕܝܟ 'That you alone are God'.
41:4 ܡܛܠ ܕܗܢܐ ܗܘ ܗܘ ܫܘܠܡܐ ܕܟܠܗܘܢ ܒܢܝܢܫܐ ܩܕܡ ܐܠܗܐ 'Because this is
  the end of all people before God'.

When the subject is ܗܘ, it is most often contracted with the enclitic to
ܗܘܝܘ:[15]

1:8 ܕܗܘܝܘ ܫܠܝܛ ܥܠ ܟܠ ܒܝܬ ܓܙܝܗ 'Who is the ruler over all her store-
  houses'.
21:27 ܗܘܝܘ ܠܝܛ ܠܢܦܫܗ 'He curses himself bitterly'.
38:9 ܕܗܘܝܘ ܢܐܣܝܟ '(Pray) that he will heal you'.
41:3 ܡܛܠ ܕܗܘܝܘ ܡܢܬܟ 'Because it is your portion'.

This structure is also common in interrogative clauses with ܡܢܘ (< ܡܢ
ܗܘ) 'who is it that…'.[16] In Syr there are two examples:

1:2 ܡܢܘ ܡܫܟܚ ܠܡܡܢܐ 'who can count?'
16:21 ܡܢܘ ܝܕܥ 'who knows?'

Also this pattern corresponds fairly often with a bipartite structure in
Heb, e.g.:

‏תמה זה‎ (A) 16:11
‏מי יודע‎ (A) 16:21
‏כי אתה אל [עו]ל[ם]‎ (B) 36:22
‏זה חלק כל בשר מאל‎ (B) 41:4

The interpretation of this type of clauses is a debated issue. The main
question concerns the identification of Su and Pr. In Goldenberg's
approach the element preceding the Ep is by definition the predicate
and hence these clauses belong to the pattern Pr–s ‖ Su. A clause like
that in 1:8 can be rendered as 'It is He who rules over all her store-

---

[15] Nöldeke, *Grammatik*, § 38; Duval, *Traité*, § 375*f*. In Syr ܗܘܝܘ is attested seven
times, but note that in 37:19 7h3 has ܗܘ ܗܘ where the other manuscripts have ܗܘܝܘ
(in a quadripartite NC, see § 19.1). For contraction of a demonstrative pronoun and
the Ep see the example from 16:11, quoted above; in this case 7a1 has ܗܘ ܗܢܐ.
[16] Cf. Cohen, *Phrase nominale*, 200–201 on Ethiopic.

houses'. The Ep functions as a rhematizer that turns the preceding element into the predicate. Muraoka, on the other hand, used to analyse clauses of this type as identificatory clauses of the type Su–Ep–Pr, but now he too adheres to the view that the Ep can never follow the subject.[17] According to Joosten we should not assign all clauses of the type NP–Ep–NP to either the Pr–Ep–Su or the Su–Ep–Pr pattern. If the noun phrase preceding the Ep contains the new information, the clause reflects the pattern Pr–Ep–Su.[18] This happens, for example, in

> Matt 24:5 ܡܫܝܚܐ ܐܢܐ ܐܢܐ 'I am the Messiah' (i.e. 'I and no one else').

But if the second noun phrase contains the new information, the pattern is Su–Ep–Pr, e.g.:

> Matt 16:16 ܡܫܝܚܐ ܗܘ ܐܢܬ 'You are the Messiah' (an answer to the question 'Who do you say that I am?').[19]

Matt 24:5 and 16:16 are often quoted in the debate about the tripartite NC in Syriac, but they cannot be adduced as support for either Goldenberg's or Muraoka's view. The pattern used in Matt 16:16 is exceptional both in Goldenberg's approach (because it is difficult to consider ܐܢܬ as the Pr) and in Muraoka's model (because it is problematic to consider this clause identificatory rather than descriptive) and hence it does not argue for either them.

We agree with Joosten that clauses of the type NP–Ep–NP may be either Pr–Ep–Su or Su–Ep–Pr, but in our parsing the identification of Su and Pr is primarily based on criteria of definiteness. Accordingly, in cases where the element preceding the Ep is a pronoun and the element following it is a noun or a substantivized adjective, we analyse these clauses as Su–Ep–Pr, because the first noun phrase is more definite than the second.[20]

The role that we assign to contextual factors does not go beyond what we have said in § 16.3: Determination is defined not only on the

---

[17] Muraoka, 'Response to Wido van Peursen', 190 n. 4. (Our remarks in this chapter were originally based on a version of Muraoka's paper where he stated that the Ep *never* follows the Su, but in the final version he has formulated it more carefully in that it does so *only rarely*. However, this correction seems to be intended to allow for the pattern Pr–Su–Ep [below, D], rather than for exceptional cases of Su–Ep–Pr.)

[18] Joosten uses a pragmatic definition of Su and Pr, cf. § 16.2 and Joosten, *Syriac Language*, 77.

[19] Joosten 'Negation', 586; idem, *Syriac Language*, 87.

[20] See § 16.3. For examples that we analyse as Pr–Ep–Su see above, on Type 2.

basis of phrase types, but also in terms of 'referred to or not yet referred to in the situation of communication'.[21] This helps us identify Su and Pr in

> 30:22 ܚܕܘܬ ܠܒܐ ܐܢܘܢ ܚܝܝܢ ܫ̈ܢܘܗܝ ܕܓܒܪܐ 'Joy of the heart is a man's life'.

In this example contextual arguments support the analysis of ܚܕܘܬ ܠܒܐ as the subject and ܫ̈ܢܘܗܝ ܕܓܒܪܐ as the Pr (cf. ܕܘܘܢܐ 'grief' in the preceding verse and note the parallelism with ܘܬܪܥܝܬܗ ܕܓܒܪܐ ܗܝ ܬܘܪܟܐ ܫ̈ܢܘܗܝ 'And a man's reflections make his life long'[22]). It follows that this clause has the pattern Su–Ep–Pr in which the Ep agrees with the Pr.[23]

As to the structural meaning of the clauses under discussion we agree with Joosten that no one structural meaning can be assigned to them; some are identificatory (in which case the tripartite pattern is obligatory[24]), others are descriptive (in which case it is hard to establish a functional difference from the bipartite pattern[25]).

D. Type 4: Pr–Su–Ep

We have found one example of this pattern in

> 6:16 ܘܐܝܢܐ ܕܕܚܠ ܠܐܠܗܐ ܗܘܝܘ '(A faithful friend is a medicine of life) and he who fears God is one'.[26]

This type too is much debated. Muraoka has strongly defended its existence. It deviates from Goldenberg's two basic patterns of tripartite NCs and hence supports Muraoka's own model against that of

---

[21] Thus Dyk and Talstra, quoted in § 16.3.

[22] With the pattern Su–Ep–Verb = *Vedette* – pronominal subject – *glose*, see § 24.4.

[23] See below, § 18.3.

[24] Unlike description and contrast, identification cannot be expressed by bipartite NCs; cf. Joosten, *Syriac Language*, 88.

[25] Thus in Matt 16:16 ܐܢܬ ܡܫܝܚܐ instead of ܐܢܬ ܗܘ ܡܫܝܚܐ could have been possible as well.

[26] Heb (A) ירא אל ישיגם 'He who fears God will obtain them'; Ginzberg, 'Randglossen', 615 emends ישיגו in Heb and suggests that the Syriac translator had the defective spelling ישגו in his source text, which he misread as ישנו and hence translated it with ܗܘܝܘ (similarly Peters, *Ben Sirach*, 59 and others), but this implies that the Syriac translator misread an unproblematic Hebrew verb into a construction that is uncommon in Classical Hebrew. In the Hebrew Bible there are only five occurrences of copulaic יש; cf. Joüon–Muraoka, *Grammar*, 154*l*; Muraoka, *Emphatic*, 78.

Goldenberg. Even in his recent article, in which he argues that the Ep only rarely follows the subject, he recognizes the Pr–Su–Ep pattern.[27]

Joosten suggests an alternative interpretation, in which the Ep is not directly related to the preceding constituent, but rather to the preceding clause as a whole, i.e. [[Pr–Su]–Ep].[28] Since, however, one of the basic principles of our computer-assisted analysis is that we start from a formal registration of the clause patterns attested (cf. § 7.2.3), we prefer to follow the same parsing procedure that we use for other patterns, and hence to use the designation Pr–Su–Ep.[29] That we have found only one example of this pattern, prevents us from giving it too much weight in the general discussion about NC patterns in Syr.

18.3 AGREEMENT

If the two noun phrases in the pattern NP–Ep–NP (Su–Ep–Pr or Pr–Ep–Su) differ in gender and/or number, the Ep agrees with either the preceding or the following component. Usually it agrees with the grammatical subject, but there are some deviating instances.[30] In Syr the enclitic agrees with the subject in

> 22:3 ܣܟܠܐ ܒܪܐ ܠܐܒܐ ܗܘ ܒܗܬܬܐ 'A foolish son is a shame for his father'.

The enclitic does not agree with the subject in

> 30:22 ܚܕܘܬܐ ܠܒܐ ܐܝܢ ܚܝܘܗܝ, ܚܝܐ ܕܓܒܪܐ 'Joy of the heart is a man's life'.[31]

When the first element of the clause is a pronoun the enclitic agrees in gender and number with this pronoun.[32] Sometimes it also agrees in

---

[27] Muraoka, 'Response to Wido van Peursen', 190; cf. Van Peursen, 'Response to Responses', 202.

[28] Joosten, Review of Muraoka, *Basic Grammar*, § 5; idem, 'Response to Wido van Peursen', 187.

[29] Van Peursen, 'Response to Responses', 202–203.

[30] Goldenberg, 'Syriac Sentence Structure', 107–110; Khan, *Studies in Semitic Syntax*, 143. Khan observes a similar phenomenon in substandard Middle Arabic. He compares further Spanish *el probleme eres tú* 'the problem is you' (ibid. 50 n. 75). For the same phenomenon in Biblical Hebrew see Muraoka, 'Tripartite Nominal Clause', 206–208.

[31] Note that Heb (B) has הם; cf. Lévi, *L'Ecclésiastique* II, 133: 'Plus correct serait איה; même singularité en S'. For the identification of Su and Pr in this clause see above, § 18.2 (C).

person.[33] Thus for 'I am the Messiah' one could use ܡܫܝܚܐ ܐܢܐ ܗܘ,[34] but also Matt 24:5 ܐܢܐ ܐܢܐ ܡܫܝܚܐ.[35] There is no discernible difference in structural meaning between the two patterns. Muraoka has argued that they reflect two ways in which the notion of identification was expressed: (1) by repetition of the subject pronoun, or (2) by means of the fossilized ܗܘ, which can be attached to any emphasized element. The type with ܐܢܐ ܐܢܐ is probably secondary. Either ܐܢܐ ܐܢܐ originated from ܗܘ ܐܢܐ as a result of 'attraction'[36] or 'assimilation',[37] or ܐܢܘܢ (< ܗܘ ܗܘ), originally the subject pronoun ܗܘ with the emphasizing enclitic ܗܘ, was reinterpreted as a repetition of one and the same pronoun and ܐܢܐ ܐܢܐ was formed by analogy.[38] In Syr there is one example of ܗܘ ܐܢܬ in

36:22 ܒܠܚܘܕܝܟ ܐܠܗܐ ܗܘ ܐܢܬ 'That you alone are God'.

In the pattern Su–Pr–Ep the Ep agrees either with the immediately preceding or with the clause-initial element. Cases of disagreement between the subject and the Ep support Muraoka's claim that the Ep is an emphatic particle rather than a copula or a lesser subject of a bipartite clause core.[39] But in Syr no examples of disagreement can be identified. In those few cases where the Su and the Pr differ in gender or number, the Ep agrees with the Su, as in

---

[32] Joosten, *Syriac Language*, 87; compare the examples given above.

[33] Muraoka, 'Nominal Clause in Old Syriac Gospels', 34–35; *Classical Syriac for Hebraists*, § 103 (esp. p. 61 n. 122), § 105; Goldenberg, 'Syriac Sentence Structure', 108; Joosten, *Syriac Language*, 67.

[34] Cf. Nöldeke, *Grammatik*, § 312D: 'Oft tritt aber das Pronomen der 3. Person enclitisch auch als Copula neben der 1. und 2. auf'; similarly Duval, *Traité*, § 375d.

[35] Cf. Nöldeke, *Grammatik*, § 312C: 'Sehr gern wird das Personalpronomen als Subject vorangestellt und vor oder hinter dem Hauptwort des Präd. enclitisch wiederholt, so dass diese 2. Form die Copula bildet'; similarly Duval, *Traité*, § 375e. For examples see also Falla, *Key* I, 47b, 49a.

[36] Muraoka, *Classical Syriac for Hebraists*, § 103.

[37] Cf. Muraoka, *Basic Grammar*, § 104.

[38] The type ܗܘ ܐܢܐ has parallels in other Semitic languages. Compare e.g. Biblical Hebrew 2 Sam 7:28 אתה הוא האלהים 'It is you who are the (true) God' (Joüon–Muraoka, *Grammar*, § 154j: 'Pr-pron–Su'; Peshitta: ܐܢܬ ܗܘ ܐܠܗܐ) and Ethiopic Matt 5:14 ʾantəmu wəʾətu bərhānu la-ʿālam 'You are the light of the world'; Ps 80:9 ʾana wəʾətu ʾəgziʾabḥer 'I am the Lord' (Cohen, *Phrase nominale*, 198–199).

[39] Note that in Goldenberg's approach it is not in the type ܐܢܐ ܗܘ ܡܫܝܚܐ that the Ep does not agree with the subject, but in the type ܐܢܐ ܐܢܐ ܡܫܝܚܐ, since in his model both types have the pattern Pr–s ‖ Su; Goldenberg explains the latter type in terms of attraction; see Goldenberg, 'Comments on "Three Approaches" by Wido van Peursen', 183.

26:26 ܘܗ ܪ̈ܚܐܡܣܗ ܪ̈ܐܒܘܪܐ ܝܘܝܚ 'The dispute of a woman is in humility'.

This is even the case when Heb has an undeclined הוא that is co-referential with a plural or feminine subject.[40]

18.4 CONCLUSION

There are more than a hundred tripartite NCs in Syr. Most frequent are the patterns Su–Pr–Ep (Goldenberg: Su ‖ Pr–s) and Pr–Ep–Su (Goldenberg: Pr–s ‖ Su). There are ten examples of the pattern Su–Ep–Pr. Our parsing of these clauses is based on our grammatical definition of Su and Pr, but even in a pragmatic definition, it is problematic to analyse the first element in the examples of this third type as the Pr (i.e. Pr–Ep–Su or Pr–s ‖ Su). There is one example of the pattern Pr–Su–Ep (Joosten: [Pr–Su]–Ep).

Where Su and Pr differ in gender or number the Ep agrees with either of them. However, the examples in which this is the case are few in number, so that no firm conclusions can be based on it. Clauses of the type *ܪ̈ܡܠܐ ܐܘܪ ܐܘܪ (cf. ܪ̈ܡܠܐ ܘܗ ܐܘܪ in 36:22) are not attested in Syr.

There is some overlap in the functions of bipartite and tripartite NCs. Especially in the case of participles and adjectives. For identification tripartite NCs of the pattern Su–Ep–Pr are employed, but description and contrast can be expressed by both bipartite and tripartite clauses. When the subject of a descriptive clause is a personal pronoun, the bipartite construction is the norm.[41] In the preceding chapter we have seen that the presence of a participial Pr may enhance the bipartite pattern. But there are also a large number of participial predicates in tripartite clauses of the patterns Pr–Ep–Su and Su–Pr–Ep.

Fairly often the tripartite NC in Syr corresponds to a bipartite NC in Heb. Whether this is due to a translator who rendered Hebrew bipartite clauses with more idiomatic tripartite clauses in Syriac, or to later scribes who changed bipartite clauses into tripartite clauses by adding the Ep cannot be established.

---

[40] See § 21.4 (A), where we give three examples from 11:14–15 that we prefer to analyse as extraposition constructions of the type Su ‖ Pr–s or Ex ‖ Pr-Su$_{pron}$.

[41] Muraoka, *Basic Grammar*, § 107. Possible exceptions occur in 1:1 and 37:13, quoted in § 18.2 (A).

CHAPTER NINETEEN

QUADRIPARTITE NOMINAL CLAUSES

19.1 BASIC PATTERNS

Quadripartite NCs are extensions of tripartite NCs. In Muraoka's model they are extensions of the tripartite patterns Pr–Ep–Su and Su–Ep–Pr. The first pattern is extended to Pr–pron–Ep–Su, the second to Su–pron–Ep–Pr.[1] Both the Su and the Pr are definite.[2] Compare the following two examples.

Type 1: Pr–pron–Ep–Su

Deut 7:9 ܐܠܗܐ ܗܘ ܡܪܝܐ ܐܠܗܟ 'The Lord your God is God'.[3]

Type 2: Su–pron–Ep–Pr

Matt 13:39 (Curet.) ܙܪܘܥܐ ܗܘ ܒܝܫܐ 'The sower is the evil one'.

The second pattern is disputed. Goldenberg, who does not acknowledge the tripartite pattern Su–Ep–Pr, does not acknowledge its quadripartite extension Su–pron–Ep–Pr either. In his approach there is only one quadripartite pattern, namely Pr ‖ p – s | Su, which is an extension

---

[1] Muraoka, *Classical Syriac for Hebraists*, § 106; similarly Joosten, 'Negation', 586. Nöldeke (*Grammatik*, § 317) analyses these clauses as cases of 'nominativus absolutus'.

[2] Joosten, *Syriac Language*, 79, 86; idem, 'Negation', 586; Goldenberg, 'Syriac Sentence Structure', 106–107.

[3] Thus both Goldenberg and Muraoka (unlike Pennacchietti, 'Frase nominale tripartita', 163, 167); Goldenberg, 'Syriac Sentence Structure', 106, analyses this clause as Pr–p–s–Su. According to Muraoka, *Classical Syriac for Hebraists*, § 106, the p in this construction is originally a resumptive element, just as in a verbal clause such as Matt 24:13 ܡܢ ܕܢܣܝܒܪ ܕܝܢ ܥܕܡܐ ܠܚܪܬܐ ܗܘ ܢܚܐ 'One who endures till the end shall be saved'. Compare in Syr:

> 31:7 ܘܟܠ ܡܢ ܕܛܥܐ ܒܗ ܗܘ ܡܬܬܩܠ 'And everyone who goes astray through it will stumble'.
> 48:4 ܘܡܢ ܕܐܟܘܬܟ ܗܘ ܢܫܬܒܚ 'And he who is like you will be praised'.

of the tripartite pattern Pr–s || Su.[4] However, in our view this interpretation of Pr and Su is sometimes difficult to maintain. Thus in the example quoted ܙܪܘܥܐ is the symbol and ܣܛܢܐ its referent in the explanation of a parable. It is preferable therefore to take ܙܪܘܥܐ as the Su and ܣܛܢܐ as the Pr.[5]

In Syr there are no examples of the first pattern. The second pattern is attested three times:

> 19:20 ܘܕܚܠܬܗ ܕܐܠܗܐ ܗܝ ܗܝ ܚܟܡܬܐ 'And fear of God is wisdom'.
> 21:26 ܦܘܡܗ ܕܣܟܠܐ ܗܘܝܘ ܠܒܗ 'The mouth of the fool is his heart'.
> 37:19 ܟܠ ܡܢ ܕܚܟܝܡ ܒܪܥܝܢܗ ܗܘܝܘ ܣܟܠܐ 'Everyone who is wise in his own opinion is a fool'.[6]

19.2 FUNCTION

The following functions have been ascribed to the quadripartite NC.

1. To avoid clumsiness or misunderstanding, especially when the predicate is long or when it consists of a relative clause.[7]
2. To indicate that the predicate is determinate.[8]
3. To turn a word (the initial Pr) into the theme ('logical subject') of the sentence.[9]

The first function can explain its use in 37:19, although it is difficult to see a functional difference from tripartite NCs of the type

> 31:7 ܘܟܠ ܡܢ ܕܛܥܐ ܒܗ ܗܘ ܡܬܬܩܠ 'And everyone who goes astray through it will stumble'.

In 19:20 and 21:26 the function of the quadripartite construction is hard to establish. It is remarkable, however, that in almost all examples of the corresponding tripartite pattern (i.e. Su–Ep–Pr) the Su is a pronoun, whereas in these two examples of the quadripartite pattern the Su is a noun.

---

[4] Goldenberg, 'Syriac Sentence Structure', 106–107.

[5] Accordingly, Joosten (*Syriac Language*, 89) analyses it as Su–pron–Ep–Pr. The Sinaiticus has ܙܪܘܥܗܘܢ instead of ܙܪܘܥܐ, which makes it even a more likely candidate to be the Su; cf. § 16.3.

[6] 7h3 has ܗܘ ܗܘ instead of ܗܘܝܘ; cf. § 18.2 (C), n. 16.

[7] Muraoka, *Classical Syriac for Hebraists*, § 106; Joosten, *Syriac Language*, 89.

[8] Cf. Matt 13:39 (Curet.), quoted above, where the Greek text has ὁ διάβολος; Joosten, *Syriac Language*, 89.

[9] Goldenberg, 'Syriac Sentence Structure', 106–107.

In 19:20 and 21:26 no Hebrew text is available and in 37:19 Heb
has a reading completely different from Syr. It is possible that the
Syriac translator's Hebrew source text contained a tripartite NC in
these places, since this pattern of correspondence (i.e. a quadripartite
NC in the Syriac corresponds with a tripartite NC in the Hebrew text)
also occurs in other parts of the Peshitta. Compare e.g.

Gen 42:6 ܐܪܥܐ ܥܠ ܫܠܝܛ ܗܘܐ ܘܝܘܣܦ 'And Joseph was the governor
of the land'; MT ויוסף הוא השליט על הארץ.

CHAPTER TWENTY

PARTICIPIALS

20.1 FORM: ABSOLUTE STATE AND EMPHATIC STATE

The category of 'participials' includes both participles and adjectives (§ 16.1). In some respects the syntactic behaviour of participials differs from that of other predicative elements. In the present paragraph we will deal with the use of the absolute and emphatic state, in the following paragraph we will deal with the clause patterns in which participials occur. Whereas predicate nouns usually take the emphatic state, participials prefer the absolute state.[1] Compare the following pairs in which the Pr is a noun (emphatic state) and a participial (absolute state) respectively:

1:11 ܕܚܠܬܗ ܕܡܪܝܐ ܗܕܪܐ ܘܐܝܩܪܐ ܘܪܒܘܬܐ ܘܟܠܝܠܐ ܕܬܫܒܘܚܬܐ 'The fear of the Lord is glory, honour, majesty and a crown of praise'.
1:12 ܕܚܠܬܗ ܕܡܪܝܐ ܡܚܕܝܐ ܠܠܒܐ 'Fear of the Lord gladdens the heart'.

5:3 ܡܛܠ ܕܡܪܝܐ ܬܒܘܥܐ ܗܘ ܕܥܠܘܒܝܗܘܢ ܠܥܠܝܒܐ 'For the Lord is an avenger of all who are oppressed'.
18:2 ܘܡܪܝܐ ܒܠܚܘܕܘܗܝ ܙܕܩ 'And the Lord alone is just'.

29:25, 26 ܐܟܣܢܝܐ ܐܢܬ 'You are a foreigner'.
48:4 ܡܐ ܕܚܝܠ ܐܢܬ 'How awesome you were!'

In other Syriac literature predicative participials occasionally take the emphatic state. Joosten points out that this is especially the case when the Pr is an essential, inherent characteristic of the subject, rather than an accidental attribute. Compare

1 Cor 7:22 ܡܚܪܪܐ ܗܘ ܕܐܠܗܐ '(He who was called as a slave in the Lord) is a free man of God'.[2]

---

[1] Nöldeke, *Grammatik*, § 204A-B; Muraoka, *Classical Syriac for Hebraists*, § 58; *Basic Grammar*, § 71*e*; cf. Joosten, *Syriac Language*, 80.

[2] Joosten, 'Predicative Adjective', 19–21; idem, *Syriac Language*, 67–73; cf. Nöldeke, *Grammatik*, § 204B: 'Dieser Gebrauch geht wohl von substantivischer Auffassung der Adjectiva aus'. The *status emphaticus* is also employed when the predi-

This analysis comes close to the traditional explanation that in such cases the adjective is substantivized.[3] *Vice versa*, the use of substantival predicates in the absolute state can be considered cases of 'adjectivization' of the substantive.[4] Compare e.g.

Ps 82:6 ⲟⲏⲣ ⲡⲙⲗⲣ 'You are gods'.

In Syr there are no cases of a predicative noun in the absolute state or a predicative participial in the emphatic state.[5] An exception would be

4:2 ⲣⲓⲏⲏⲁ ⲣⲧⲣⲁ ⲟⲏⲟⲓ 'The spirit of the person which is broken'.

If we analyse ⲣⲓⲏⲏⲁ as a specification of the masculine ⲣⲧⲣⲁ (§ 10.2.2 [4]) it would be an emphatic masculine form. But if we take it as a specification of ⲟⲏⲟⲓ (§ 11.5) it can be analysed as an absolute feminine form.

20.2 STRUCTURES OF CLAUSES CONTAINING A PARTICIPLE

If we investigate the distribution of participial predicates over the types of NCs described in Chapters 16–19 we can distinguish the following patterns.[6]

(1) $Pr_{ptcp} - Su_{noun}$

13:22 ⲱⲟⲓⲟⲁⲗ ⲡⲣⲧⲝⲟⲟ 'And his helpers are many'.

This pattern is attested seventy times. Goldenberg considers it elliptical for Pr–s ‖ Su.

(2) $Su_{noun} - Pr_{ptcp}$

1:12 ⲣⲁⲗ ⲣⲧⲁⲩⲟ ⲣⲓⲟⲁ ⲟⲁⲗⲩⲁ 'Fear of the Lord gladdens the heart'.

---

cate expresses the superlative, e.g. Luke 1:42 ⲣⲧⲟ ⲁⲏⲣ ⲣⲁⲁⲁⲟ 'You are the most blessed among women' and with ⲣⲁⲟ when it expresses '(the) many' as opposed to 'one'; cf. Joosten, 'Predicative Adjective', 21–23.

[3] Goldenberg, 'Predicative Adjectives', 718–721; compare the expression 'a free man' rather than 'free' in Joosten's translation of 1 Cor 7:22 quoted here.

[4] Cf. also Goldenberg, 'Syriac Sentence Structure', 115 and 99 n. 5.

[5] The same distribution occurs if the clause contains a form of the verb ⲣⲟⲟ. But in this category there are some exceptions in which a participial as a predicative complement takes the emphatic state or a predicative noun occurs in the absolute state; see § 23.5.

[6] But quadripartite NCs with a participial predicate (Chapter 19) are not attested.

This pattern is even more frequent: it is attested almost 150 times. Goldenberg analyses it as elliptical for Su || Pr–s.

(3) $Pr_{ptcp} - Su_{pron\ 3rd\ pers}$

> 34:19 ܪܚܘܡܐ ܡܢ ܗܘ ܡܣܘܙܢܐ 'And He is a redeemer from the wound'.

This pattern is attested eleven times, against fourteen examples with a non-participial Pr. A functional difference from the pattern without the subject pronoun (below, Pattern 10) is difficult to establish.

(4) $Pr_{ptcp} - Su_{pron\ 2nd/1st\ pers}$

> 14:15 ܠܐܚܪ̈ܢܐ ܝܬ ܥܬܪ ܐܢܬ ܡܫܒܩ 'Because you leave behind your possessions to others'.

This pattern is attested 21 times. Whereas the subject pronoun of the 3rd person is often omitted (see below, Pattern 10), ellipsis of the subject pronoun of the 1st or 2nd person does not occur.

(5) $Su_{pron\ 3rd\ pers} - Pr_{ptcp}$

> 14:6 ܘܗܘ ܡܩܒܠ ܦܘܪܥܢܐ ܒܝܫܐ 'And he receives an evil recompense'.

This pattern is attested 35 times. In Goldenberg's approach the analysis mentioned under (2) applies here as well.

(6) $Su_{pron\ 2nd/1st\ pers} - Pr_{ptcp}$

> 9:13 ܕܒܝܢܬ ܦܚ̈ܐ ܐܢܬ ܦܣܥ 'That you step between snares'.

This pattern is attested eight times. It is especially this pattern that argues against the interpretation of bipartite NCs of the type Su–Pr as elliptical representatives of Su || Pr–s (see the discussion below).

(7) $Pr_{ptcp} - Su_{indep.\ rel.\ clause}$

> 3:4 ܘܡܣܡ ܣܝ̈ܡܬܐ ܗܘ ܕܡܝܩܪ ܠܐܡܗ 'And storing up treasures is he who honours his mother'.

(8) $Su_{indep.\ rel.\ clause} - Pr_{ptcp}$

> 30:3 ܘܕܡܠܦ ܒܪܗ ܡܛܢ ܠܒܥܠܕܒܒܗ 'He who teaches his son provokes his enemy to jealousy'.

Patterns 7 and 8 are two subsets of Pattern 1 and 2 respectively. Pattern 7 is attested three times, Pattern 8 thirteen times, including those cases where the relative clause is preceded by a 'dummy' antecedent such as ܡܐ.

(9) Su$_{demonstrative}$ – Pr$_{ptcp}$

39:34 ܗܢܐ ܒܝܫ ܡܢ ܗܢܐ 'This is worse than that'.

This pattern is attested five times. It can be considered as a subset of Pattern 5.

(10) Pr$_{ptcp}$ (without Su being expressed)

3:5 ܘܡܐ ܕܡܨܠܐ 'And when he prays'.

This pattern is the elliptical equivalent of Pattern 3. It is attested about 200 times, against a relatively small number of cases in which the Pr is not a participial. It is especially frequent in relative clauses, circumstantial clauses, and clauses introduced by ܘ, but it is not restricted to these contexts (cf. § 17.3).

(11) Su$_{noun}$ – Pr$_{ptcp}$ – Ep

18:26 ܘܟܠܗܘܢ ܗܠܝܢ ܫܦܝܪܝܢ ܐܢܘܢ ܩܕܡ ܐܠܗܐ 'And they are all beautiful before God'.

(12) Su$_{indep. rel. clause}$ – Pr$_{ptcp}$ – Ep

10:20 ܘܡܝܩܪ ܠܐܠܗܐ ܕܚܠ ܗܘ ܝܬܝܪ ܡܢܗ 'And he who fears God is honoured more than him'.

(13) Su$_{pron 3rd pers}$ – Pr$_{ptcp}$ – Ep

37:13 ܘܐܦ ܗܘ ܡܗܝܡܢ ܗܘ ܐܟܘܬܟ 'And also he is faithful like you'.

Patterns 11–13 all belong to the type Su–Pr–Ep (Goldenberg: Su ‖ Pr–s). Pattern 11 is attested eight times, Pattern 12 five times, and Pattern 13 once. They show that, even though bipartite Su–Pr clauses with participial predicates are frequent, their tripartite counterpart with the Ep is attested as well.

(14) $\mathrm{Pr}_{\text{ptcp}}$ – Ep – $\mathrm{Su}_{\text{noun}}$

28:18 ܣܓܝܐܝܢ ܐܢܘܢ ܩܛܝܠܝ ܚܪܒܐ ‘Many are those who have been killed by the sword’.

(15) $\mathrm{Pr}_{\text{ptcp}}$ – Ep – $\mathrm{Su}_{\text{ܡܢ + relative clause}}$

16:3 ܡܛܠ ܕܛܒ ܗܘ ܕܥܒܕ ܨܒܝܢܐ ܡܢ ܐܠܦܐ ‘Because better is one who does the will (of God) than a thousand’.

(16) $\mathrm{Pr}_{\text{ptcp}}$ – Ep – $\mathrm{Su}_{\text{infinitive}}$

11:21 ܡܛܠ ܕܦܫܝܩ ܗܘ ܩܕܡ ܡܪܝܐ ܠܡܥܬܪܘ ܠܡܣܟܢܐ ܡܢ ܫܠܝ ‘Because it is in the Lord’s power to make the poor one rich suddenly’.

(17) $\mathrm{Pr}_{\text{ptcp}}$ – Ep – $\mathrm{Su}_{\text{indep. rel. clause}}$

33:22 ܡܛܠ ܕܛܒ ܗܘ ܕܢܒܥܘܢ ܒܢܝܟ ܡܢܟ ܡܢ ܕܬܒܥܐ ܐܢܬ ܡܢܗܘܢ ‘Because it is better that your sons beseech you than that you beseech them’.

Patterns 14–17 belong to the type Pr–Ep–Su (Goldenberg: Pr–s || Su). Pattern 14 is attested almost twenty times; each of the other three patterns is attested once. Again we see that participial predicates may occur with the Ep in the tripartite pattern.

(18) $\mathrm{Su}_{\text{pron}}$ – Ep – $\mathrm{Pr}_{\text{ptcp}}$

37:8 ܡܛܠ ܕܐܦ ܗܘ ܢܦܫܗ ܗܘ ܡܬܪܥܐ ‘Because he too has himself in mind’.
38:9 ܕܗܘܝܘ ܡܐܣܐ ‘(Pray) that He will heal you’.

(19) $\mathrm{Su}_{\text{indep. rel. clause with ‘dummy antecedent’}}$ – Ep – $\mathrm{Pr}_{\text{ptcp}}$

31:7 ܘܟܠ ܡܢ ܕܛܥܐ ܒܗ ܗܘ ܡܬܬܩܠ ‘And everyone who goes astray through it will stumble’.

Patterns 18–19 belong to the type Su–Ep–Pr. This type is used for identification, rather than description. Consequently, the Pr is most often a determinate noun. However, in the three examples quoted the Pr is a participial. In 37:8 and 38:9 the reason for the pattern Su–Ep–Pr is probably the fact that the subject contains the new information and is therefore rhematized by the Ep. In 31:7 it may be a desire to clarify the syntactic structure of the clause.

20.3 PATTERNS WITH A PARTICIPIAL
AND SYRIAC CLAUSE STRUCTURE

We have seen in § 17.2 that Goldenberg considers sentences with participial predicates as 'special cases' that show ellipsis of the s in the Pr–s nucleus. There seems to be a paradigm consisting of participial + ∅ for the third person and participial + pronoun for the first and second person:

	Singular	Plural
3m	ܩܛܠ	ܩܛܠܝܢ
3f	ܩܛܠܐ	ܩܛܠܢ
2m	ܩܛܠ ܐܢܬ	ܩܛܠܝܢ ܐܢܬܘܢ
2f	ܩܛܠܐ ܐܢܬܝ	ܩܛܠܢ ܐܢܬܝܢ
1m	ܩܛܠ ܐܢܐ	ܩܛܠܝܢ ܚܢܢ
1f	ܩܛܠܐ ܐܢܐ	ܩܛܠܢ ܚܢܢ

The observation that the participial can dispense with the 3rd person pronoun explains the frequency of bipartite patterns in which the subject is a noun (Patterns 1, 2) or an independent relative clause (Patterns 7, 8) and in which it is a 3rd person pronoun or demonstrative preceding the Pr (Pattern 5, 9). Clauses in which the participial is followed by a subject pronoun of the 2nd or 1st person (Pattern 4) fit this paradigm as well. In some cases the subject pronoun of the third person in the P–Su pattern is retained as well (Pattern 3), but the pattern with ellipsis of the 3rd person subject pronoun (Pattern 10) is about twenty times as frequent.

The phenomenon of ellipsis does not account for the eight examples in which a subject pronoun of the 2nd or 1st person precedes the participle, i.e. $Su_{\text{pron 2nd/1st pers}}$ – Pr_{ptcp} (Pattern 6). If we follow Goldenberg in analysing clauses of the pattern Su–Pr as elliptical for Su ‖ Pr–s, we have to assume that in these cases the subject pronoun of the 2nd or 1st person is omitted, which does not agree with the paradigm outlined above.[7]

---

[7] Cf. Goldenberg, 'Syriac Sentence Structure', 114–115: 'In such constructions the independent pronoun and the participle appear actually to form an analytic verbal expression, where the "non-conjugated" participle proves capable of occupying the predicate position with no need for marked agreement in person with the subject.'

The bipartite patterns without an Ep can be compared with their tripartite counterparts. Thus in addition to Su_{noun} − Pr_{ptcp} (Pattern 2) there is Su_{noun} − Pr_{ptcp} − Ep (Pattern 11), although the former is far more frequent. In Goldenberg's analysis both types reflect the basic pattern Su ‖ Pr–s, the only difference being that Pattern 2 shows ellipsis of the s. Similarly, besides the pattern Pr_{ptcp} − Su_{noun} (Pattern 1) there is Pr_{ptcp} − Ep − Su_{noun} (Pattern 14), again with a higher frequency of the bipartite pattern. Altogether there occur in Syr about forty examples in which the Ep after a participial Pr is retained, be it in tripartite patterns or in bipartite patterns of the type Pr–Su (Pattern 3 mentioned above). Accordingly, it appears that in a small number of cases the Ep has been retained (the number of occurrences is less than 10% of those that can be analysed in terms of ellipsis).

20.4 VERBALIZATION

In Goldenberg's view the high frequency of participials in bipartite NCs is a consequence of their verbalization: The bare participial can function as a nexus-complex implying the 3rd person pronominal subject.[8] Goldenberg elaborates on David Cohen's monumental work on the NC in Semitic languages. Cohen distinguishes three degrees of verbalization, related to the following three characteristics of verbal status:

A. The predicative function is marked syntactically.
B. Conjugation: there is a morphological connection between the pronominal subject and the Pr.
C. Entering into the system of aspectual-temporal oppositions.

In the first degree of verbalization only A is the case, in the second degree B or C is the case as well in the third degree each of the characteristics of verbal status is present.[9] According to Goldenberg all Syriac constructions built on the nucleus complex Pr–s fulfil the conditions A and B, and those in which the Pr is a participial enter the third degree of verbalization.[10]

---

[8] Goldenberg, 'Syriac Sentence Structure', 113.
[9] Cohen, *Phrase nominale*, 89.
[10] Goldenberg, 'Syriac Sentence Structure', 113; see also Duval, *Traité*, §§ 324, 350–351.

The background of this analysis is Goldenberg's assumption that the Pr in the Syriac NC needs to be followed by an enclitic subject pronoun and that this construction is syntactically equivalent to finite verbs.[11]

In Syr, however, the participial constructions have not developed thus far. The examples of the construction with a participle + pronoun 3rd person singular show that the paradigm outlined above was not fully developed.

20.5 CONCLUSION

In some respects participials behave differently from other nominal predicates. They occur in the absolute state rather than the emphatic state and take the Ep less frequently than non-participial predicates. As a consequence, clauses containing a participial differ regarding the distribution and frequency of the clause patterns attested. The phenomena described here arc related to the verbalization of participles that took place in Classical Syriac. Syr reflects a stage in which this development had not been completed.

---

[11] Goldenberg, 'Syriac Sentence Structure', 112. According to Muraoka this interpretation goes too far, because there are still considerable differences between the so-called conjugated nouns and conjugated verbs; see his 'Response to Wido van Peursen'.

CHAPTER TWENTY-ONE

EXTRAPOSITION AND PRONOMINAL AGREEMENT

21.1 TERMINOLOGY

In his *Studies in Semitic Syntax* G. Khan distinguishes between 'extraposition' and 'pronominal agreement'. Extraposition is 'the syntactic construction in which a noun or nominal phrase stands isolated at the front of a clause without any immediate formal connection to the predication (...) The grammatical relation of nominal in the predication is usually indicated vicariously by means of a coreferential resumptive pronoun.'[1] Pronominal agreement is 'a construction where a noun or nominal phrase whose grammatical relation is indicated by its case inflection or by an adjoining relational particle is accompanied in the same clause by a coreferential pronoun agreeing with it in number, gender, person, and grammatical relation (...) Unlike extraposed nominals, nominals which are accompanied by such "agreement pronouns" are not restricted to initial position but may occur anywhere in the clause – the front, the interior, or the end.'[2]

Accordingly, pronominal agreement differs from extraposition in that the nominal stands inside the predication whereas in extraposition it is isolated from the predication and is referred to by the coreferential pronoun. In traditional grammars the extraposition construction is often called 'casus pendens' or 'nominative absolute'.[3] In

---

[1] Khan, *Studies in Semitic Syntax*, xxvi; cf. Muraoka, *Emphatic*, 93 on Biblical Hebrew: 'Quite frequently a noun or a pronoun, or its equivalent, is placed at the head of a sentence, syntactically independent of the sentence which follows (...) The extraposed or fronted sentence part is usually resumed later by means of a pronominal element.' See also Nöldeke, *Grammatik*, § 317; Duval, *Traité*, § 376 ('Il est rare que le nom, mis ainsi en tête de la phrase, ne soit pas repris par le suffixe'); Goldenberg, 'Tautological Infinitive', 37.

[2] Khan, *Studies in Semitic Syntax*, xxvi-xxvii; see also idem, 'Object Markers and Agreement Pronouns', 468.

[3] Cf. Joüon–Muraoka, *Grammar*, § 156a: 'A noun or a pronoun is often placed at the head of a clause in such a way as to stand aloof from what follows, and then *resumed* by means of a retrospective pronoun. The noun is thus *suspended*, so to speak,

extraposition the co-referential pronoun is always resumptive, while in pronominal agreement it may be either resumptive or anticipatory.

21.2 EXTRAPOSITION

Extraposition is well attested in Syr. A classification can be made according to the form of the extraposed element or according to the grammatical function of the resumptive element.

A. Form of the extraposed element[4]

(a) Pronoun:[5]

> 37:8 ܡܛܠ ܕܐܦ ܗܘ ܒܢܦܫܗ ܗܘ ܡܬܪܥܐ 'Because he too[6]—he has himself in mind'.[7]

---

hence it is termed *casus pendens*' and ibid., 552 n. 1: 'In contemporary general linguistics it is customary to discuss these issues in terms of "topic" and "comment" or similar ideas'. For the 'nominative absolute', see e.g. Brockelmann, *Grammatik*, § 220: 'Die dominierende Vorstellung tritt als sog. absoluter Nominativ oft an die Spitze des Satzes und erhält ihre grammatische Beziehung durch ein rückweisendes Pron. (…) seltener fehlt die Rückweisung'.

[4] For other Syriac examples see Khan, *Studies in Semitic Syntax*, 123–124.

[5] Cf. Muraoka, *Emphatic*, 97–98 on Biblical Hebrew.

[6] In other structures too ܐܦ is used to introduce a fronted element, e.g.

> 16:11 ܘܐܦ ܚܕ ܐܢ ܢܩܫܐ ܩܕܠܗ ܗܘܐ ܬܕܡܘܪܬܐ 'And as to one—if he were to harden his neck, it would be amazing'.
> 38:1 ܡܛܠ ܕܐܦ ܠܗ ܐܠܗܐ ܒܪܝܗ، 'Because also him—God has created him'.
> 49:10 ܘܐܦ ܬܪܬܥܣܪ ܢܒܝܐ ܢܗܘܘܢ ܓܪ̈ܡܝܗܘܢ ܡܢܗܪܝܢ ܬܚܝܬܗܘܢ ܕܐܣܝܘ ܠܐܝܣܪܐܝܠ 'And also the Twelve Prophets—may their bones shine beneath them—who cured Israel'.

[7] The analysis of this example is difficult. If we take the second ܗܘ as a subject pronoun, we can parse this clause as:

> [MVL D-<Cj>] [>P <Cj>] [HW <Ex>] || [B-NPCH <Co>] [HW <Su>] [MTR<> <PC>]

If, however, we take it as a rhematizing or emphatic particle (cf. § 24.3), the first ܗܘ is not resumed by an element in the main clause, and its interpretation as a fronted element can be questioned. In that case the analysis

> [MVL D-<Cj>] [>P <Cj>] [HW <Su>] [B-NPCH <Co>] [HW <Ep>] [MTR<> <PC>]

is possible as well. The second ܗܘ is absent from 7a1.

(b) Construction with *kl*-suffix + demonstrative:

44:7 ܟܠܗܘܢ ܗܠܝܢ ܒܕܪ̈ܝܗܘܢ ܗܘܐ ܠܗܘܢ ܐܝܩܪܐ 'And all these—in their generation they had honour'.

(c) Noun phrase:

16:18 ܗܐ ܫܡܝܐ ܘܫܡܝ̈ ܫܡܝܐ ܘܬܗܘܡܐ ܘܐܪܥܐ ܒܓܠܝܢܗ ܕܥܠܝܗܘܢ ܡܩܘܝܢ 'Behold the heaven and the heavens of the heaven and the abyss and the earth, at His revelation upon them, they stand firm'.

16:19 ܥܩܪܐ ܕܛܘܪ̈ܐ ܘܫܬܐܣ̈ܐ ܕܬܒܝܠ ܟܕ ܡܬܚܙܐ ܠܗܘܢ ܙܝܥܝܢ 'The roots of the mountains and the foundations of the earth—they tremble when He appears to them'.

43:8 ܝܪܚܐ ܐܝܟ ܫܡܗ ܐܝܬܘܗܝ 'The (new) moon—it is like its name'.

Also with a generic sense:

3:26 ܠܒܐ ܩܫܝܐ ܬܒܐܫ ܚܪܬܗ 'A stubborn heart—its end will be bad'.

3:27 ܠܒܐ ܩܫܝܐ ܢܣܓܘܢ ܟܐܒ̈ܘܗܝ 'A stubborn heart—its pains will be many'.

7:21 ܥܒܕܐ ܚܟܝܡܐ ܐܚܒܝܗܝ ܐܝܟ ܢܦܫܟ 'A wise servant—love him as yourself'.

The noun phrase may be followed by a relative clause:

4:2 ܢܦܫܐ ܕܚܣܝܪܐ ܠܗ̇ ܠܐ ܬܟܐܒ ܪܘܚܗ̇ 'The soul that is in want—do not grieve its spirit'.

(d) Independent relative clause (generic):

13:1 ܕܩܪܒ ܠܙܦܬܐ ܕܒܩܐ ܒܐܝܕܗ 'He who approaches pitch—it cleaves to his hand'.

14:6 ܕܒܝܫ ܠܢܦܫܗ ܠܝܬ ܕܒܝܫ ܡܢܗ 'He who is evil to himself—there is no-one more evil than him'.

34:17 ܕܕܚܠ ܠܐܠܗܐ ܛܘܒܝܗ̇ ܠܪܘܚܗ 'He who fears God—blessed is his spirit'.

35:2 ܘܕܢܛܪ ܦܘܩܕܢܐ ܛܘܒܝܗ̇ ܠܪܘܚܗ 'And he who keeps the command—blessed is his spirit'.

B. Grammatical functions of the resumptive element[8]

(a) Subject:

16:18 ܗܐ ܫܡܝܐ ܘܫܡܝ ܫܡܝܐ ܘܬܗܘܡܐ ܘܐܪܥܐ ܒܓܠܝܢܗ ܕܥܠܝܗܘܢ ܩܝܡܝܢ ‘Behold the heaven and the heavens of the heaven and the abyss and the earth, at His revelation upon them, they stand firm’.

16:19 ܥܩܪܐ ܕܛܘܪܐ ܘܫܬܐܣܬܐ ܕܬܒܝܠ ܟܕ ܡܬܚܙܐ ܠܗܘܢ ܙܝܥܝܢ ‘The roots of the mountains and the foundations of the earth—they tremble when He appears to them’.

18:29 ܚܟܝܡܝܢ ܒܡܠܦܢܐ ܐܦ ܗܢܘܢ ܡܬܚܟܡܝܢ ‘Those who are wise in instruction—they too, prove themselves wise’.

27:29 ܦܚܐ ܘܡܨܝ̈ܕܬܐ ܗܠܝܢ ܠܝܕܘܥܝܗܘܢ ‘Snares and nets—they are for those who know them’.

27:30 ܡܐܟܬܐ ܘܪܘܓܙܐ ܐܦ ܗ̈ܢܝܢ ܛܡܐܢ ‘Indignation and anger—they, too, are unclean’.[9]

37:8 ܡܛܠ ܕܐܦ ܗܘ ܒܢܦܫܗ ܗܘ ܡܬܪܥܐ ‘Because he too—he has himself in mind’.

40:12 ܘܡܟܫܪܝ ܥܠܡܐ ܐܦ ܗܢܘܢ ܢܬܩܝܡܘܢ ‘But the diligent of the world—they too will be established’.[10]

Also with ܐܝܬ:

43:8 ܣܗܪܐ ܐܝܟ ܫܡܗ ܐܝܬܘܗܝ ‘The (new) moon—it is like its name’.

(b) Object:

4:2 ܢܦܫܐ ܕܚܣܝܪܐ ܠܗ ܠܐ ܬܟܐܒ ܪܘܚܗ ‘The soul that is in want—do not grieve its spirit’.

7:21 ܥܒܕܐ ܚܟܝܡܐ ܐܚܒܝܗܝ ܐܝܟ ܢܦܫܟ ‘A wise servant—love him as yourself’.

16:12 ܘܐܢܫ ܐܝܟ ܥܒ̈ܕܘܗܝ ܕܐܢ ܠܗ ‘And a man (absolute state!)—He judges him according to his works’.

(c) Prepositional complement:[11]

14:6 ܕܒܝܫ ܠܢܦܫܗ ܠܝܬ ܕܒܝܫ ܡܢܗ ‘He who is evil to himself—there is noone more evil than him’.

26:25 ܘܐܝܕܐ ܕܕܚܠܐ ܡܢ ܡܪܝܐ ܐܝܬ ܒܗ̇ ܒܗܬܬܐ ‘And she who fears the Lord—there is shame in her’.

---

[8] For other Syriac examples see Khan, *Studies in Semitic Syntax*, 125–126.

[9] 7a1 has ܘܐܦ.

[10] Note the use of ܐܦ before the fronted element in 37:8 (cf. above, note 6) and in the main clause in 18:29, 27:30, 40:12.

[11] Contrast the construction with repetition of the preposition, which will be discussed in the following paragraph.

44:7 ܟܠܗܘܢ ܗܠܝܢ ܒܕܪܝܗܘܢ ܗܘܐ ܠܗܘܢ ܐܝܩܪܐ 'And all these—in their generation they had honour'.

(d) Noun complement ('genitive'):

3:26 ܠܒܐ ܩܫܝܐ ܬܒܐܫ ܚܪܬܗ 'A stubborn heart—its end will be bad'.
3:27 ܠܒܐ ܩܫܝܐ ܢܣܓܘܢ ܟܐܒܘܗܝ 'A stubborn heart—its pains will be many'.
4:2 ܢܦܫܐ ܕܚܣܝܪܐ ܠܗ ܠܐ ܬܟܐܒ ܪܘܚܗ 'The soul that is in want—do not grieve its spirit'.
13:1 ܕܩܪܒ ܠܙܦܬܐ ܕܒܩܐ ܒܐܝܕܗ 'He who approaches pitch—it cleaves to his hand'.
26:26 ܐܢܬܬܐ ܛܒܬܐ ܛܘܒܘܗܝ ܠܒܥܠܗ 'A good wife—blessed is her husband'.
30:25 ܠܒܐ ܛܒܐ ܣܓܝܐܝܢ ܡܐܟܘܠܬܗ 'A good heart—its foods are many'.
34:17 ܕܕܚܠ ܠܐܠܗܐ ܛܘܒܘܗܝ ܠܪܘܚܗ 'He who fears God—blessed is his spirit'.
35:2 ܘܕܢܛܪ ܦܘܩܕܢܐ ܛܘܒܘܗܝ ܠܪܘܚܗ 'And he who keeps the command—blessed is his spirit'.

Also as a complement to ܟܠ:

39:29 ܢܘܪܐ ܘܒܪܕܐ ܘܟܐܦܐ ܕܡܘܬܐ ܟܠܗܘܢ ܗܠܝܢ ܠܕܝܢܐ ܐܬܒܪܝ 'Fire and hail and stones of death—all these are created for judgment'.

The main function of extraposition seems to be topicalization or rather thematization.[12] According to Khan extraposition characteristically occurs at some kind of boundary or reorientation in the discourse. Thus it may occur at the beginning or closure of a discourse unit or signal a shift in topic or theme.[13] From the examples given above there are four cases in which it occurs at the beginning of a new discourse unit: 13:1, 34:17 and 35:2 (also 19:4, quoted below).

Sometimes the extraposition is also found in the parallel Hebrew text, e.g. 3:26 (A) לב כבד תבאש אחריתו; 14:6 (A) רע לפשו אין רע ממנו. In other cases Heb does not contain a resumptive element. Thus in 7:21 (A[+C]) עבד משכיל חבב כנפש the Hebrew verb, unlike the Syriac one, has no resumptive object suffix and an analysis in terms of extraposition is inappropriate. In 4:2 Heb (A) reads דווח נפש חסירה אל תפוח 'Do not blow against the trouble of the soul that is in want'. If we emend with most commentators דווח to רוח and consider the suffix of

[12] Compare the quotation from Joüon–Muraoka, *Grammar*, § 156*a*, n. 1, given above, in note 3, and below, § 21.4.

[13] Khan, *Studies in Semitic Syntax*, 132–139.

ܪܘܚܗ in Syr as referring to ܢܦܫܐ ܕܡܣܬܢܩ ܠܗ, the relation between the words רוח / ܪܘܚܗ, נפש / ܢܦܫܐ and חסירה / ܕܡܣܬܢܩ ܠܗ (i.e. 'the spirit of the soul that is in want') has been retained in Syr, although the syntactic structure of the clause has been 'reorganized' in that 'the soul that is in want' has been put in extraposition. Heb has been explained as the result of a marginal gloss נפש or רוח, which became part of the main text.[14]

There occur quite a lot sentences with ܡܢܘ preceded by an element in extraposition, whether ܡܢܘ is followed by a nominal Pr (tripartite NC; see § 18.2 [C]), or by a verbal Pr (cleft sentence, see § 24.3):

10:29 ܡܢ ܕܡܚܝܒ ܢܦܫܗ ܡܢܘ ܢܙܟܝܘܗܝ 'He who condemns himself—who will acquit him?'

28:5 ܗܘ ܕܒܪܢܫܐ ܗܘ ܠܐ ܨܒܐ ܠܡܫܒܩ ܠܗ ܡܢܘ ܢܫܒܘܩ ܠܗ ܚܛܗ̈ܘܗܝ 'He whom a human being does not want to forgive—who will forgive him his sins?'

In the following cases there is no resumptive pronoun, but the absence of a ܠ before the fronted element supports their categorization as extraposition rather than pronominal agreement:

1:2 ܚܠܐ ܕܝܡܐ ܘܢܛܘ̈ܦܬܐ ܕܡܛܪܐ ܘܝܘܡ̈ܬܐ ܕܥܠܡܐ ܡܢܘ ܡܨܐ ܠܡܡܢܐ 'The sand of the sea, the drops of the rain and the days of eternity—who can count (them)?'

1:3 ܪܘܡܐ ܕܫܡܝܐ ܘܦܬܝܐ ܕܐܪܥܐ ܘܬܗܘܡܐ ܪܒܐ ܡܢܘ ܢܥܩܘܒ 'The height of the heaven, the breadth of the earth and the great abyss—who can measure (them)?'

1:6 ܘܪ̈ܙܝ ܣܘܟܠܬܢܘܬܐ ܡܢܘ ܝܕܥ 'And the secrets of understanding—who knows (them)?'

16:20 ܘܐܘܪ̈ܚܬܝ ܡܢܘ ܢܬܒܝܢ 'And my ways—who takes notice (of them)?'

We prefer to analyse the following examples also as extraposition because of the position of the interrogative pronoun:

1:6 ܥܩ̈ܪܝ ܚܟܡܬܐ ܠܡܢ ܐܬܓܠܝܘ 'The roots of wisdom—to whom have they been revealed?'

14:5 ܕܒܝܫ ܠܢܦܫܗ ܠܡܢ ܢܛܐܒ 'He who is evil to himself—to whom will he do good?

16:17 ܘܒܪܘܡܐ ܕܫܡܝܐ ܡܢܘ ܢܬܕܟܪܢܝ 'And in the height of heaven—who will remember me?'

[14] Cf. Bacher, 'Notes on the Cambridge Fragments', 275. It is also possible to consider רוח (emendation of רווח) as belonging to the end of the preceding line; this solution is mentioned but rejected in Ginzberg, 'Randglossen', 611–612.

Where Heb is available (A and B in 10:29; B in 16:17) it has מי corresponding to ܥܠܡ in Syr.[15]

21.3 PRONOMINAL AGREEMENT

21.3.1 *Anticipatory pronominal agreement*

We can distinguish between anticipatory pronominal agreement and resumptive pronominal agreement. The first is also called 'prolepsis'. With 'prolepsis' ('taking-in-advance') we mean that a pronoun refers to a person or thing that is later specified by a noun. This device occurs frequently in Syriac and may be applied to various syntactic relations both on phrase level and on clause level.[16]

A. Phrase level

(1) Periphrastic genitive constructions:[17]

>   1:20j ܕܡܪܝܐ ܕܚܠܬܗ 'the fear of the Lord' (similarly 1:28 and elsewhere).
>   2:1 ܕܐܠܗܐ ܠܕܚܠܬܗ 'to the fear of God'.
>   2:7 ܕܡܪܝܐ ܕܚܠܬܗ, 'those who fear the Lord'.

Several scholars have studied the way in which the so-called genitive relation is expressed in Syriac.[18] In his study on Pesh-1 Kings P.J. Williams concludes that the construction with the proleptic suffix 'occurs most frequently with masculine singular form first members and masculine singular second members'.[19] The second member is usually

---

[15] Contrast 31:9, 10 where ܗܘ ܥܠܡ corresponds to מי זה הוא in Heb (B) (§ 18.2 [B], n. 14)

[16] See the lists in Muraoka, *Classical Syriac for Hebraists*, § 109; *Basic Grammar*, § 112. See also Nöldeke, *Grammatik*, § 222; Duval, *Traité*, §§ 304–306; Khan, *Studies in Semitic Syntax*, 128–130 ('anticipatory pronominal agreement').

[17] In Syr there are no constructions with ܕ in prepositional adjuncts of the type ܥܡ ܒܢ̈ܬܗ 'with his daughters' (cf. Khan, *Studies in Semitic Syntax*, 129; Goldenberg, 'Syriac Idiom', 30; Wertheimer, 'Functions', 364–265). Constructions with possessive ܕܝܠ of the type ܒܝܬܐ ܕܝܠܢ 'our place', which Muraoka also categorizes as prolepsis, are not attested either; see Muraoka, *Classical Syriac for Hebraists*, § 87; Nöldeke, *Grammatik*, § 225; Joosten, *Syriac Language*, 57–58.

[18] See Khan, *Studies in Semitic Syntax*, 129; Muraoka, *Classical Syriac for Hebraists*, § 88; Nöldeke, *Grammatik*, § 205C and the literature mentioned in the following footnotes.

[19] Williams, *Peshitta of 1 Kings*, 37.

a known individual,[20] most often a personal proper noun.[21] According to J. Joosten the distinction between alienable and inalienable plays a role as well: The construction with the proleptic suffix 'is regular when the first member is of the class of "inalienable" words: parts of the body, members of the family etc.'[22]

In Syr there are many examples in which the second member is ܐܠܗܐ or ܒܝܬ. Compare with the examples given above with ܕܠܘܬܗ the absence of a proleptic suffix in 9:13 ܕܠܘܬܗ ܩܘܡܬܐ 'the fear of death'.

(2) With ܟܠ:[23]

> 1:3 ܗܠܝܢ ܟܠܗܘܢ 'all these'.
> 15:5 ܚܒܖܘܗܝ، ܟܠܗܘܢ 'all his fellows'.
> 15:19 ܕܥܡܐ ܨܘܖܬܗܘܢ ܟܠܗܝܢ 'all the reflections of the people'.
> 16:4 ܡܕܝܢܬܐ ܟܠܗ 'the whole city'.

In all examples noun or pronoun following ܟܠ + suffix is determined.[24] In the following example the suffix attached to ܟܠ is coreferential with the subject pronoun:

> 25:24 ܡܢ ܟܠܢ ܚܢܢ 'we all will die'.

In Syr we do not find pronominal agreement of adverbial phrases of the type ܒܗ ܒܠܠܝܐ 'in that night'.[25]

---

[20] Joosten, *Syriac Language*, 50–51.

[21] Williams, *Peshitta of 1 Kings*, 37; cf. Khan, 'Object Markers and Agreement Pronouns', 473–474.

[22] Joosten, *Syriac Language*, 50. Compare Khan's scale of individuation and salience hierarchies in his 'Object Markers and Agreement Pronouns', 470. See further Khan, *Studies in Semitic Syntax*, 129; Muraoka, *Classical Syriac for Hebraists*, § 88; Nöldeke, *Grammatik*, § 205C. In the Hebrew Bible this construction is found in Songs 3:7 מטתו שלשלמה 'the litter of Solomon'; cf. Polzin, *Late Biblical Hebrew*, 39; Khan, *Studies in Semitic Syntax*, 77.

[23] The suffix attached to ܟܠ is co-referential with the following noun or pronoun.

[24] This agrees with Williams' conclusions regarding the Peshitta of 1 Kings; Williams, *Peshitta of 1 Kings*, 46; similarly Khan, *Studies in Semitic Syntax*, 129; see also Muraoka, *Classical Syriac for Hebraists*, § 83; Joosten, *Syriac Language*, 65–66; Nöldeke, *Grammatik*, §§ 217–218.

[25] On this construction see Khan, 'Object Markers and Agreement Pronouns', 475; Baasten, 'Anticipatory Pronominal Agreement'.

B. Clause level

(1) Direct object:

> 7:31 ܫܒܚܝܗܝ ܠܗ 'Praise Him'.
> 17:1 ܐܠܗܐ ܡܢ ܐܪܥܐ ܒܪܝܗܝ ܠܐܕܡ 'God created man (or: Adam) from dust'.
> 24:28 ܠܐ ܢܫܡܠܘܢܗ̇ ܩܕܡܝ̈ܐ ܠܚܟܡܬܐ 'The first ones will not accomplish wisdom'.
> 25:17 ܒܝܫܘܬܗ̇ ܕܐܢܬܬܐ ܒܝܫܬܐ ܬܘܪܩ ܐܝܟ ܐܦܘ̈ܗܝ ܕܒܥܠܗ̇ 'The evil of an evil wife makes pale the face of her husband'.[26]
> 36:1 ܦܪܘܩܝܢ ܐܠܗܐ ܠܟܠܢ 'Save us, O God, all of us'.[27]
> 43:3 ܒܡܨܥܬܗ ܕܛܗܪܐ ܡܘܩܕ ܠܗ̇ ܠܐܪܥܐ 'At noon it causes the earth to burn'.

This construction is infrequent compared with other object constructions.[28] Some rules or tendencies determining its distribution are mentioned in the literature.[29] Thus it is particularly used if the object is definite,[30] especially if it is a human proper noun,[31] although even if the object is a proper noun or a definite animate it occurs less consistently than the construction without the proleptic suffix.[32] It does not tend to occur with compound objects or with plural objects.[33] It tends to be used in double accusative constructions.[34] Most often the object is an element that has been mentioned in the preceding context.[35]

In the examples from Syr all objects are definite, but they do not always refer to an element that has been mentioned in the preceding context. In 7:31 the suffix attached to the Lamadh refers back to ܒܪܝܟ 'your creator' in 7:30; in 24:28 it refers to ܚܟܡܬܐ 'wisdom' in 24:25

---

[26] The claim that ܐܝܟ should be omitted is unfounded; *pace* Ryssel, 'Fragmente', VII, 392.

[27] Heb (B): הושיענו אלהי הכל. According to Lévi, *L'Ecclésiastique* II, 168, the Syriac translator took הכל as the object because he did not understand the expression אלהי הכל.

[28] Similarly in the Peshitta of 1 Kings, see Williams, *Peshitta of 1 Kings*, 78.

[29] Nöldeke, *Grammatik*, § 288 and the literature mentioned in the following footnotes.

[30] Joosten, *Syriac Language*, 40–41.

[31] Khan, 'Object Markers and Agreement Pronouns', 473.

[32] Williams, *Peshitta or 1 Kings*, 78.

[33] Williams, *Peshitta of 1 Kings*, 78.

[34] Williams, *Peshitta of 1 Kings*, 78.

[35] Joosten, *Syriac Language*, 40–41; cf. Khan, 'Object Markers and Agreement Pronouns', 473: 'In Syriac (…) A[greement] P[ronoun]s occur predominantly either with human referents (…) or with inanimate referents which are textually prominent, e.g. those which have been referred to in the immediately preceding discourse'.

ܕܢܗܘܐ ܐܝܟ ܗܘܢ ܕܡܠܐ 'Which is full like the river Pishon with wisdom'. (Note the difference in object marking between the first occurrence in 24:25 and the second occurrence in 24:28.) ܐܕܡ 'Adam' or 'man' in 17:1, the 'we' in 36:1 and ܐܪܥܐ 'the earth' in 43:3 are new participants in the context. The evil wife's husband in 25:17 has not been mentioned in the preceding context either, but in this latter example the suffix in ܕܒܥܠܗ refers to a known participant (i.e. the evil wife). The example from 25:17 is further remarkable because of the absence of the Lamadh before ܐܒܗܝ̈ܗ[36] and because of the use of a proleptic suffix for a plural object.

G. Khan has argued that the use of the proleptic object suffix also depends on the status of the clause in the discourse. Anticipatory pronouns are sometimes used to mark the endpoint or climax of a sequence of closely related clauses.[37] We did not find unequivocal examples of this tendency in Syr.

Another aspect that should be taken into account—besides the nature of the object (definite, animate, etc.) and the larger discourse context—is the relation between pronominal agreement and Syriac clause building. In many cases pronominal agreement functions as a means to keep clause nuclei intact. There is a tendency to put small pronominal elements close to the verb or, in other words, to complete the valency of the verb before the agents and patients are specified.[38] In 24:28, for example, the addition of the object pronoun makes the valency of ܠܐ ܢܬܒܥܝܘܗܝ complete. The subject ܡܪܝܐ and the object specification ܠܟܫܠܬܐ are related to this nucleus as a type of satellites. Similarly in 36:1 the valency of ܢܥܒܕ is completed before the vocative ܐܠܗܐ occurs. After this vocative the object is further specified. Even in those cases where the object directly follows the verb, the use of the object suffix may be ascribed to the same tendency to fill, so to speak, the valency of the verb, which creates a clause nucleus to which other specifications are related as satellites.[39]

---

[36] Cf. Muraoka, *Classical Syriac for Hebraists*, § 95D; idem, *Basic Grammar*, § 97g.

[37] Khan, 'Object Markers and Agreement Pronouns', 482–484; idem, *Studies in Semitic Syntax*, 139–140.

[38] This was suggested by Janet Dyk in a CALAP meeting on 5 September 2002. Similar phenomena occur in other language families, such as the Bantu languages; cf. § 13.3 (end) on a similar phenomenon with ܐܝܬ ܠ.

[39] The construction with object suffixes incorporated in the verbal complex has reached generalization in Eastern Neo-Aramaic; see Goldenberg, 'Syriac Idiom', 30.

The proleptic object suffix is also attested in Biblical Hebrew, e.g.
Exod 2:6 ותראהו את הילד 'And she saw the child'. It is very common
in Mishnaic Hebrew.[40] There are no indications, however, that the influence of the translator's Hebrew source did play a role in any of the
examples quoted. In 7:31 (A) and 43:3 (B[+M]) Heb has a single object noun without an object marker (אל and תבל respectively). In 25:17
(C) the object marker את can be reconstructed in רע אשה ישחיר [את]
מראה איש. In 17:1 and 24:28 Heb is not extant; and in 36:1 Heb (MS
B) has a reading different from Syr: הושיענו אלהי הכל (similarly Gr).

(2) Prepositional verbal complement:

> 45:20 ܘܡܒ ܠܗ ܡܢܬܗ ܩܘܕܫܐ ܘܪܫܝܬܐ ܘܣܕܪܐ ܕܠܚܡܐ ܠܗ ܘܠܙܪܥܗ 'And
> He gave him his inheritance, the holy first-fruits and the rows of the
> shewbread—to him and his descendants'.
> 47:23 ܘܠܐ ܢܗܘܐ ܠܗ ܕܘܟܪܢܐ ܠܝܘܪܒܥܡ ܒܪ ܢܒܛ 'And let there be no
> memory to him, to Jeroboam the son of Nebat'.[41]

This category is related to the preceding one.[42] The use of the pronominal agreement construction seems to be motivated by factors of
clause structure: it enables the formation of a nucleus clause with
complete valency. In both cases the proleptic verbal complement is
resumed at the end of the clause. Especially in 45:20 the difference in
size between the small nucleus ܘܡܒ ܠܗ and the complete clause is
striking.

The comparison with Heb is complicated because of text-historical
problems. In 45:20 Heb (MS B) has a different order of the cola and
repeats 'to give', which results in a syntactic structure completely different from that in Syr. In 47:23 MS B reads עד אשר קם אל יהו לו זכר
ירבעם בן נבט 'Until there arose—let there be no memory to him—
Jeroboam, the son of Nebat'. Heb, unlike Syr, does not repeat the
preposition before the name of Jeroboam, which renders it difficult to

---

[40] Khan, 'Object Markers and Agreement Pronouns', 481; Joüon–Muraoka,
Grammar, § 146e; Waltke–O'Connor, *Biblical Hebrew Syntax*, § 12.4; see also Muraoka, 'Morphosyntax and Syntax of Qumran Hebrew', 199–200. The use of the proleptic object suffix increases in Late Biblical Hebrew; cf. Polzin, *Late Biblical Hebrew*, 38; Kropat, *Syntax*, 49.

[41] After ܠܐ ܢܗܘܐ ܠܗ ܕܘܟܪܢܐ we do not expect the mention of Jeroboam's name.
But if it is an addition, it was probably also in the translator's source text; cf. Smend,
Jesus Sirach, 458.

[42] Cf. Joosten, *Syriac Language*, 45–47; Khan, 'Object Markers and Agreement
Pronouns', 474.

assign ירבעם בן נבט the same syntactic status as ܠܝܘܪܒܥܡ ܒܪ ܢܒܛ in Syr. The addition עד אשר קם comes from 48:1. Pronominal agreement with a verbal complement occurs occasionally in Biblical Hebrew, e.g. Josh 1:2 הארץ אשר אנכי נתן להם לבני ישראל 'The land that I will give to the sons of Israel'.[43]

(3) ܠ-phrase in ܐܝܬ clauses:[44]

> 17:27 ܡܛܠ ܕܡܢܐ ܗܢܝܐ ܐܝܬ ܠܗ ܠܐܠܗܐ ܒܟܠ ܗ̈ܢ ܕܐܒܕܘ ܒܥܠܡܐ 'Because what profit is there for God in all those who perish in the world'.
>
> 20:2 ܠܝܬ ܠܗ ܛܝܒܘܬܐ ܠܡܢ ܕܡܟܣ ܠܥܘܠܐ 'There is no goodness for the one who reproves the unrighteous one'.

In this category too the use of the pronominal agreement construction can be explained from a tendency to build a clause nucleus, to which the other constituents are added as a kind of satellite.[45] In this category the basic structure of the nucleus is ܐܝܬ + preposition + suffix pronoun. Compare the ܠ-phrase in 'Woe'-clauses:

> 2:13 ܘܝ ܠܗ ܠܠܒܐ ܕܠܐ ܡܗܝܡܢ 'Woe to the heart that does not trust'.
> 41:8 ܘܝ ܠܗܘܢ ܠܐܢܫܐ ܥܘ̈ܠܐ 'Woe to the unrighteous men'.

(4) An independent pronoun precedes a subject nominal:

> 23:2 ܕܗܘ ܡܪܝܐ ܢܚܘܣ ܥܠ ܫܘܥܪܝ 'That the Lord forbid that I would transgress'.

The addition of a personal pronoun before the subject has been explained in terms of emphasis,[46] but more than once it seems to have lost its emphatic function.[47] Joosten refines the traditional explanation in terms of emphasis with the terms topicalization and focus: 'The personal pronoun "topicalizes" the NP: the NP is referred to in a more

---

[43] Cf. Joüon–Muraoka, *Grammar*, § 146*e*.

[44] In this pattern we analyse the ܠ-phrase as the Pr, see § 22.4.

[45] See § 22.4 on the tight connection between ܐܝܬ and ܠ.

[46] Nöldeke, *Grammatik*, § 227: 'Das immer substantivische Personalpronomen der 3. Person dient, vorangestellt, oft zur stärkeren Hervorhebung eines Substantivs'; Brockelmann *Grammatik*, § 194: 'Zur Hervorhebung eines Nomens oder Demonstrativpron. kann das Pron. der 3. Ps. auch voranstehn und stimmt dann in Genus und Numerus mit diesem überein'.

[47] Brockelmann *Grammatik*, § 194: 'Wie nun aber ein vorausweisendes Possessiv- und Objektsuffix meist schon ohne besonderen Nachdruck steht, so auch das selbständige Pron. der 3. Ps. beim Subj.'; Khan, 'Object Markers and Agreement Pronouns', 475.

general way in what precedes, and the construction pers. pron-NP fo-
cuses on the NP much in the way of French *quant à*.[48] Joosten further
observes that this use of the pronoun occurs especially with proper
nouns.[49] This construction is attested in Biblical Hebrew as well. See
e.g. Exod 7:11 ויעשו גם הם חרטמי מצרים בלהטיהם כן 'The Egyptian
magicians, they also did in like manner with their enchantments'.[50]

(5) The subject of ܐܝܬ clauses:

22:1 ܣܟܠܐ ܐܝܬܘܗܝ, ܗܟܢܐ 'Similar is the fool'.

This category is related to the preceding one because the subject is a
proleptic pronoun, this time attached to ܐܝܬ. As in the preceding category, the use of the proleptic construction is related to the determination of the subject. *ܗܟܢܐ ܐܝܬ ܣܟܠܐ would have meant 'Similarly
there is a fool'. In this category there is a functional difference between clauses in which ܐܝܬ takes the suffix (descriptive) and in which
it does not (existential).[51] Note that in this category too there is a nucleus ܗܟܢܐ ܐܝܬܘܗܝ, to which ܣܟܠܐ is a satellite.

21.3.2 *Resumptive pronominal agreement*

Resumptive pronominal agreement occurs with the following grammatical elements.[52]

(a) Prepositional adjunct:

11:16 ܘܥܡ ܐܝܠܝܢ ܕܡܬܪܒܝܢ ܒܒܝܫܬܐ ܒܝܫܬܐ ܣܐܒܬ ܥܡܗܘܢ ܣܝܒܘܬܐ 'And evil
grows old with those who are brought up in evil'.
29:8 ܒܪܡ ܠܡܣܟܢܐ ܐܝܟ ܢܣ ܐܓܪ ܪܘܚܐ ܥܡܗ 'But have patience with the
poor man'.

---

[48] Joosten, *Syriac Language*, 36.
[49] Joosten, *Syriac Language*, 36; See further Khan, *Studies in Semitic Syntax*, 130;
Duval, *Traité*, §§ 299–230 (According to Duval the pronoun functions as an article in
these cases).
[50] Joüon–Muraoka, *Grammar*, § 146e; Waltke–O'Connor, *Biblical Hebrew Syntax*, § 12.4 On its increased used in Late Biblical Hebrew see Kropat, *Syntax*, 49;
Khan, *Studies in Semitic Syntax*, 77.
[51] For details see §§ 22.1–2.
[52] Cf. Khan, *Studies in Semitic Syntax*, 130–131.

(b) Prepositional predicate:

40:8 ܡܥ ܠܟܠܗܘܢ ܩܨ ܒܣܪܐ ܨܝܕܘܗܝ ܨܝܘܬܐ 'Care is with all the men of flesh'.

(c) Prepositional phrase in ܐܝܬ clauses:[53]

3:28 ܠܡܚܘܬܗ ܕܡܒܙܚܢܐ ܠܝܬ ܐܣܝܘܬܐ 'To the wound of the scorner there is no cure'.

6:15 ܠܪܚܡܐ ܡܗܝܡܢܐ ܠܝܬ ܛܝܡܝܢ 'To a faithful friend there is no price'.

16:14 ܠܟܠ ܡܢ ܕܥܒܕ ܙܕܝܩܘܬܐ ܐܝܬ ܠܗ ܦܘܪܥܢܐ 'For everyone who does righteousness there is a reward'.

23:13 ܕܐܦ ܐܝܬ ܒܗ ܡܠܐ ܕܫܘܩܪܐ 'Because also there are words of falsehood in it'.

38:12 ܡܛܠ ܕܐܦ ܒܗ ܐܝܬ ܒܗ ܝܘܬܪܢܐ 'Because also in him there is profit'.

(d) Direct object:

38:1 ܡܛܠ ܕܐܦ ܠܗ ܐܠܗܐ ܒܪܝܗܝ 'Because also him God has created'.[54]

In these cases the resumptive pronominal agreement makes it possible to put a clause constituent to the front, without disturbing the basic structure of the clause, or, in other words, to retain the clause nucleus.[55] Thus we see again a number of examples with ܐܝܬ in which the basic core ܐܝܬ + preposition + suffix pronoun has been retained. Note that pronominal agreement is even used if the element agreed with consists itself of a preposition + pronoun (as in 23:13 and 38:12). Pronominal agreement constructions with resumptive pronouns are 'by and large functionally equivalent' to extraposition constructions.[56] The main difference is a formal one, because it concerns the questions as to whether the fronted element is part of the predication structure. A functional difference can be observed, however, in that the element in extraposition is always topicalized, whereas the fronted element in a pronominal agreement construction sometimes receives focus. This is especially the cases where this constituent is preceded by ܐܦ

---

[53] In these cases we analyse the prepositional phrase as the Pr, see § 22.4.

[54] On the use of ܐܦ see above, note 6.

[55] Cf. Khan, *Studies in Semitic Syntax*, 130: 'In constructions in which the agreement pronoun is resumptive the "agreed with" nominal generally stands at the front of the nuclear clause'.

[56] Khan, *Studies in Semitic Syntax*, 132.

(23:13, 38:12, 38:2, 33:10). Like extraposition, pronominal agreement is sometimes related to the status of the clause in the discourse. Thus it occurs at the beginning of a discourse unit in 29:8 and at span closure in 16:14.

The agreement pronoun is often an addition vis-à-vis Heb. Compare e.g. 6:15 (A) כי גם אותו חלק (B[txt+]mg) 38:2 ;לאוהב אמונה אין מחיר אל. In other cases Heb has a resumptive pronoun, but the coreferential element does not take the prepositions or object marker of the agreement pronoun. Compare 11:16 (A) ומרעים רעה עמם (not ועם מרעים) 16:14 (A) כל העושה צדקה יש לו שכר (not לכל העושה) However, that the pronominal agreement construction is not foreign to Classical Hebrew appears from examples such as

> 2 Sam 6:22 ועם האמהות אשר אמרת עמם אכבדה 'I shall be honoured with the handmaids about whom you spoke'.
> 2 Sam 6:23 ולמיכל בת שאול לא היה לה ילד 'Mikal, the daughter of Saul, had no child'.[57]

21.4 EXTRAPOSITION, PRONOMINAL AGREEMENT AND CLAUSE STRUCTURE

There are a number of similarities between the constructions discussed in the preceding paragraphs and some patterns of the NC. Especially if one analyses the tripartite and quadripartite NCs as extraposition constructions, the phenomena discussed in the present chapter and those that have been addressed in the preceding chapters (especially Chapter 18–19) are basically the same.

A. The type Su–Pr–Ep (Goldenberg: Su ‖ Pr–s)

According to Goldenberg clauses of the type Su–Pr–Ep have the pattern Su ‖ Pr–s and can be considered as cases of extraposition.[58] Since Goldenberg defines Su and Pr in pragmatic terms, his analysis implies

---

[57] Cf. Khan, *Studies in Semitic Syntax*, 75–76.
[58] See § 18.1; compare also the examples of topicalization discussed in § 22.4; cf. Nöldeke, *Grammatik*, § 317 on the *nominativus absolutus*: 'ferner beruht hierauf die Verwendung von ܘܗ als Copula'; and § 311: '…die Anwendung einer Copula. Als solche dient zunächst das Pron. der 3. Pers., eigentlich eine Hin- oder Rückweisung auf das Subj.' ; cf. Khan, *Studies in Semitic Syntax*, 142: 'An enclitic subject resumptive pronoun in a verbless clause functions as a copula.'

that in this type of NCs the topic is placed in first position and is resumed by an Ep. The same topicalizing function can be discerned in
the examples of extraposition discussed in the present chapter (§21.2).
Even if one disagrees with Goldenberg's analysis, one has to agree
that in both the tripartite NCs and the extraposition structures the topic
is placed in first position.[59]

An argument in favour of Goldenberg's interpretation is the position of the enclitic and other particles that prefer the second position in
the clause. To this category belongs the Ep, particles such as ܓܝܪ and
ܕܝܢ and prepositional phrases with a pronoun (§ 15.5). Compare e.g.

> 3:11 ܐܝܩܪܗ ܓܝܪ ܕܓܒܪ ܗܘ ܐܝܩܪܗ ܕܐܒܘܗܝ 'For the honour of a man is
> the honour of his father'.
> 14:17 (8a1) ܡܒܠ ܕܟܠܗܘܢ ܒܢܝܢܫܐ ܡܒܠܐ ܒܠܝܢ ܢܒܠܘܢ 'Because all people
> will certainly wear away'.

If we consider these NCs as extraposition constructions of the type Su
‖ P–s, we can say that in both cases the Ep takes the second slot of the
main clause, and that in 3:11 ܓܝܪ occupies the second slot after the
head of the extraposed element. This argues for the following analysis:

> 3:11 [>JQRH <Ex>] [GJR <Cj>] [D-GBR> <sp><Ex>]
>   [>JQRH <PC>] [HW <Su>] [D->BWHJ <sp><PC>]
> 14:17 [MVL D-<Cj>] [KLHWN [BNJ-NC> <sp>] <Ex>]
>   [MBL> <Mo>] [>NWN <Su>] [BLJN <PC>]

This argument would be weakened if we were to find examples where
the tripartite clause is preceded by another extraposed element, because an analysis with two elements in extraposition, such as X ‖ Su ‖
Pr–s is odd.[60] In Syr the only tripartite NCs that are preceded by another extraposed element are interrogative clauses,[61] but in Golden-

---

[59] The thematizing function of extraposition has also been noticed by Pennacchietti in his study of the identificatory tripartite nominal clause in Hebrew and
Syriac. He makes a sharp distinction between (a) the theme, which is represented in
the basic clause by a co-referential pronoun and (b) the focus, which is not represented in the basic clause. See his 'Frase nominale tripartita' and Chapter 16, note 8.
On Biblical Hebrew see also Muraoka, 'Tripartite Nominal Clause', 201–203. Muraoka discusses the function of the pronoun in clauses of the type NP–Pron–NP, such as
Gen 9:18 וחם הוא אבי כנען 'And Ham was the father of Canaan'. In Muraoka's view 'a
greater or lesser degree of prominence of some sort appears to be conferred by a third-
person person pronoun on the preceding constituent' (p. 201), but at the same time the
pronoun has a 'topicalizing function' (p. 202). At first sight this seems to be contradictory, but see our remarks on 'topical prominence' in 'Three Approaches', 162–163.

berg's definition the interrogative is the Pr, which means that a clause such as 1:6 ܘܚ ܐܝܢ ܟܣ̈ܝܬܐ ܕ̈ ,ܘܠܝܬ can be analysed as Ex ‖ Pr–s ‖ Su: 'And the secrets of understanding—who is it that knows (them)?

If one prefers to distinguish between tripartite NCs and 'real' extraposition, there are some cases in which it is difficult to decide whether we are dealing with a tripartite NC or a case of extraposition. Note especially the following examples with a long phrase in the first slot:[62]

> 11:14 ܚ̈ܝܐ ܘܡܘܬܐ ܥܘܬܪܐ ܘܡܣܟܢܘܬܐ ܛܒܬܐ ܘܒ̈ܝܫܬܐ ܐܝܬ ܐܢܘܢ 'Good and evil, life and death, the rich one and the poor one—they are equal before the Lord'.
>
> 11:15 ܚܟܡܬܐ ܘܣܘܟܠܐ ܘܝܕܥܬܐ ܕ̈ܢܡܘܣܐ ܡܢ ܠܘܬ ܡܪܝܐ ܗܝ 'Wisdom, prudence and knowledge of the law are from the Lord'.
>
> 11:15 ܚܘܒܐ ܘܐܘܪ̈ܚܬܐ ܕ̈ܥܒܕܐ ܛ̈ܒܐ ܡܢ ܠܘܬ ܐܠܗܐ ܐܢܝܢ 'Love and the ways of good works are from the Lord'.

In these three examples the subject pronoun of the main clause agrees with the element in extraposition, whereas in Heb (A) the pronoun is הוא. Such cases of disagreement play an important role in Muraoka's argument that the pronoun in such cases should be understood as a fossilized emphatic particle, rather than a 'real' pronoun that is coreferential with the subject in extraposition.[63]

B. The type Pr–Ep–Su (Goldenberg: Pr–s ‖ Su)

Goldenberg also sees extraposition in clauses of the type Pr–Ep–Su. These are cases of rear extraposition with the pattern Pr–s ‖ Su. Accordingly, in both Pr–Ep–Su and Su–Pr–Ep Goldenberg takes the pronoun as referring to the subject.[64]

---

[60] W. Gross has put forward a somewhat similar argument against the notion of the 'compound nominal clause' in Biblical Hebrew, see Gross, 'Ein verdrängter Bibelhebräischer Satztyp', 17; idem, 'Compound Nominal Clause', 45–49.

[61] See above, § 21.2 (end).

[62] Cf. Joüon–Muraoka, *Grammar*, § 154*i* on Biblical Hebrew; compare the examples from 16:18, 19, quoted in § 21.2 A (c), but note that in these cases there is no resumptive pronoun.

[63] See § 18.3 (end). But whereas for Muraoka the fossilized Ep in Syriac provided the occasion to apply this view also to Hebrew, in our example it is Heb rather than Syr that shows 'fossilization'.

[64] Unlike Muraoka, who regards the Ep as a particle rather than a pronoun, in which case there is no question of taking-in-advance or resumption; cf. § 18.1.

C. The type Su–Ep–Pr (Goldenberg: Pr–s ‖ Su)

Another NC type is Su–Ep–Pr. It seems that Duval considers clauses of the type as cases of the phenomenon that Khan calls Pronominal Agreement. Duval translates John 15:1 ܐܢܐ ܐܢܐ ܓܦܬܐ ܕܫܪܪܐ with 'moi, je suis la vigne de vérité' and John 17:3 ܐܢܬ ܐܢܬ ܐܠܗܐ ܕܫܪܪܐ with 'toi, tu es le Dieu de vérité' and comments: 'Un pronom intensif se rencontre souvent à côté d'un autre pronom personnel, à forme affaiblie, qui exprime le verbe substantif dans les phrases nominales, ou le sujet après un participe'.[65] This formulation suggests that Duval considers the first rather than the second pronoun as an added element.[66] Unlike Duval, who analyses these clauses as topic constructions, Goldenberg takes them as focus constructions of the type Pr–s ‖ Su: '*I* am the true vine'.[67]

---

[65] Duval, *Traité*, § 298*f.*

[66] Note also the broader context of Duval's § 298.

[67] Goldenberg's criticism of Duval is also valid in Muraoka's analysis of these clauses. According to Muraoka these are identificatory clauses, in which the Ep emphasizes the preceding subject, which also means that the initial pronoun is focalized.

CHAPTER TWENTY-TWO

EXISTENTIAL CLAUSES

22.1 INTRODUCTION

Clauses containing ܐܝܬ[1] can be classified according to a number of formal, semantic and functional criteria.[2] As to the form we can classify the clauses according to

1. The form of ܐܝܬ: suffixed or unsuffixed.
2. In the case of suffixed ܐܝܬ: the presence or absence of a NP making the Su explicit.[3]
3. The presence and form of other clause constituents.
4. Word order.

The function of clauses with unsuffixed ܐܝܬ is to indicate that something that is new in the context exists. Goldenberg distinguishes between 'statements of absolute existence' (clauses with ܐܝܬ and a NP) and 'situated existence' (clauses that have a constituent besides ܐܝܬ and the NP).[4] Clauses of this latter type are most frequent with the preposition ܠ of possession.

Clauses with suffixed ܐܝܬ fulfil two functions: a locative and a copulaic function.[5] Muraoka introduced the semantic category 'locative' in his article 'On the Syriac Particle ܐܝܬ'. Taking Nöldeke's division between the existential and the copulaic function of ܐܝܬ as a starting-point, Muraoka subdivides Nöldeke's 'existential' into 'exis-

---

[1] Throughout this chapter ܐܝܬ stands for both ܐܝܬ and its negative counterpart ܠܝܬ (or ܐܝܬ ܠܐ; cf. Nöldeke, *Grammatik*, § 199).

[2] Nöldeke, *Grammatik*, §§ 301–308; Duval, *Traité*, §§ 220 (end), 339–341; Muraoka, *Classical Syriac for Hebraists*, § 107; idem, *Basic Grammar*, § 109; Falla, *Key* I, 20–24; Joosten, *Syriac Language*, 97–107; Muraoka, 'Syriac Particle ܐܝܬ'; Goldenberg, 'Syriac Sentence Structure', 117–131; Jenner, 'Particle ܐܝܬ'.

[3] This implies that with suffixed ܐܝܬ we consider the suffix as the Su; cf. Joosten, *Syriac Language*, 103 and see § 21.3 B (5).

[4] Goldenberg, 'Syriac Sentence Structure', 117. Situated existence ('There are slaves in the house') should not be confused with location ('David is in the house').

[5] Muraoka, 'Syriac Particle ܐܝܬ', 21; Joosten, *Syriac Language*, 103.

tential' and 'locative'.[6] Locative clauses differ from existential clauses in that they indicate where something that is already known in the context is to be located.[7]

> There are exceptional cases of suffixed ܐܝܬ with an indefinite Su,[8] as well as examples of unsuffixed ܐܝܬ with a definite Su, particularly in the construction with ܐܝܬ + possessive ܠ.[9] It seems that at an early stage the bare ܐܝܬ or ܠܝܬ was also capable of indicating (non-)existence of something definite. This appears from examples where ܐܝܬ is followed by an independent pronoun, as in Jer 31:15 ܡܛܠ ܕܠܝܬ ܐܢܘܢ 'because they are no more'.[10]

Locative clauses without ܐܝܬ do occur as well, e.g. Matt 1:23 (Sinaiticus) ܐܠܗܐ ܥܡܢ.[11] However, whereas these clauses are common in other Semitic languages, they are infrequent in Syriac.[12] According to Goldenberg they are elliptical and should not be regarded as real bipartite NCs.[13]

In copulaic clauses ܐܝܬ indicates the predicative relationship between the Su and the Pr. Copulaic ܐܝܬ clauses are normally descriptive, occasionally identificatory. The origin of copulaic ܐܝܬ lies in its asseverative use as in Ezra 5:17 הן איתי די 'if it is really the case that...', but Biblical Aramaic already shows the beginning of the weakening of אית to a copula.[14]

---

[6] Nöldeke, *Grammatik*, § 303; Muraoka, 'Syriac Particle *iṯ*', 21.

[7] Accordingly, the difference between existential and locative clauses has to do mainly with the question as to which portion of the clause is the topic and which is the comment. Compare the observations on Modern Hebrew in Berman–Grosu, 'Copula', 272–274 and 283 n. 5.

[8] For examples see Muraoka, 'Syriac Particle *iṯ*', 21; Goldenberg, 'Syriac Sentence Structure', 124–125; Joosten, *Syriac Language*, 105 n. 7.

[9] See Muraoka, *Classical Syriac for Hebraists*, § 107; Falla, *Key* I, 20–21; Joosten, *Syriac Language*, 99, 102 (Sections 1.2.1.4, 1.3.1.8); Jenner, 'Particle ܐܝܬ', 297. In the case of ܐܝܬ + possessive ܠ this may be due to the fact that ܠ ܐܝܬ was on its way to becoming a frozen expression indicating possession; Joosten, *Syriac Language*, 101, 103.

[10] Similarly in the quotation of this verse in Matt 2:18 in the Curetonian, but the Sinaiticus and the Peshitta have ܐܝܬܝܗܘܢ. See further Van Rompay, 'Standard Language', 82; Goldenberg, 'Syriac Sentence Structure', 111; cf. Nöldeke, *Grammatik*, § 302; Costaz, *Grammaire*, § 681.

[11] For more examples see Muraoka, *Basic Grammar*, § 109.

[12] Cf. Joosten, *Syriac Language*, 97: 'To express that something or some person exists, or exists in a certain place, the particle *it* must be used'; ibid. n. 2: 'It is only exceptionally that we find in our corpus clauses of the structure indefinite NP–adverbial phrase. In other Semitic languages this structure is very common'. It seems that at an earlier stage of the Syriac language this pattern was allowed; see below, § 22.5.4.

[13] See the discussion in § 17.2 (2).

If the Ep is interpreted as a copula as well,[15] the copulaic ܐܝܬ is a free variant of the Ep.[16] Compare e.g.

> Matt 12:8 Sinaiticus: ܡܪܗ ܓܝܪ ܕܫܒܬܐ ܒܪܗ ܗܘ ܕܐܢܫܐ 'The Son of Man is the Lord of the Sabbath'; Peshitta: ܡܪܗ ܓܝܪ ܕܫܒܬܐ ܐܝܬܘܗܝ ܒܪܗ ܕܐܢܫܐ.

It is hard to perceive a functional distinction between the construction with ܐܝܬ and that with an enclitic pronoun, except that the construction with ܐܝܬ is rare for identificatory clauses.[17] From a diachronic perspective we can see a gradual increase in the use of copulaic ܐܝܬ, perhaps due to Greek influence.[18] In Syriac texts translated from Greek an aspect of translation technique also seems to play a role: the use of ܐܝܬ served as a translational device that made it possible to adhere more closely to the form of the Greek text.[19]

22.2 STRUCTURAL PATTERNS

Muraoka's distinction between existential and locative enables him to define rules that determine the choice between suffixed and unsuffixed ܐܝܬ and to relate three formally different clause patterns to three different structural meanings:

---

14 See Muraoka, *Emphatic*, 80–81.

15 On this question see Van Peursen, 'Three Approaches', 159–160.

16 But note that even Muraoka, who considers the Ep to be more than a mere copula, regards copulaic ܐܝܬ as 'a substitute for a pronominal enclitic of tripartite nominal clauses'; Muraoka, *Classical Syriac*, § 107; idem, *Basic Grammar*, § 109; idem, 'Syriac Particle *iṯ*', 22.

17 Muraoka, 'Syriac Particle *iṯ*', 22; cf. Joosten, *Syriac Language*, 105. To the infrequent examples of identificatory ܐܝܬ belong John 8:50, 54.

18 Joosten, *Syriac Language*, 150–151; idem, 'Materials', 213. In the Gospel of Matthew copulaic ܐܝܬ occurs twenty-two times in the Peshitta, four times in the Curetonian and four times in the Sinaiticus. On the low frequency of ܐܝܬ in the works of Ephrem see Beck, 'Sprache Ephräms', II, 10. See also Muraoka, *Classical Syriac for Hebraists*, § 107: 'No doubt the exposure to the Greek culture has a great deal to do with the development of the copulaic ܐܝܬ, as is suggested by its relative infrequency in the Old Syriac Gospels (esp. S[inaiticus]) compared with the Peshitta version'. On the very few instances of the alleged copulaic use of יש and אין in Biblical Hebrew see Muraoka, *Emphatic*, 77–79. It should be noted, however, that the Greek influence cannot be the only factor that triggered the extensive copulaic use, since copulaic אית is already attested in Bibical Aramaic (cf. Muraoka, *Emphatic*, 81). Copulaic אית is not attested in Egyptian Aramaic, see Muraoka–Porten, *Egyptian Aramaic*, 290–291, esp. n. 1141.

19 Joosten, *Syriac Language*, 175; Wertheimer, *Problems*, 52–53; cf. Jenner, 'Nominal Clause', 53–56; idem, 'Particle ܐܝܬ', 307.

1. Existential: Su is indefinite; ܐܝܬ is unsuffixed.
2. Locative: Su is definite; ܐܝܬ is suffixed; Pr is an adverbial of place.
3. Copulaic: Su is definite; ܐܝܬ is suffixed; Pr is another adverbial or a nominal.

We can expand this scheme if we take into account Goldenberg's distinction between absolute and situated existence (§ 22.1) and the distinction between descriptive and identificatory clauses (§ 16.4). This results in the following table:

ܐܝܬ	Subject	Other elements	Function
Unsuffixed	Indefinite NP[20]	Ø	absolute existence
		adverb or equivalent	situated existence
Suffixed	Definite NP (optional)	adverb of place or equivalent	locative
		other adverb or equivalent	copulaic/descriptive
		indefinite NP	
		definite NP	copulaic/identificatory

22.3 ܐܝܬ CLAUSES INDICATING ABSOLUTE EXISTENCE

Clauses that indicate the existence of something that is new in the context are abundantly attested in Syr. The clauses contain the existential particle ܐܝܬ and a Su, e.g.:

> 6:8 ܐܝܬ ܪܚܡܐ ܒܐܦܝ ܙܒܢܐ 'There is a friend in the face of the time (i.e. just for the occasion)'.
> 20:9 ܘܐܝܬ ܡܡܠܠܐ ܕܠܚܘܣܪܢܗ 'And there is discourse that is to his damage'.

Also frequent are those cases where the Su is an 'independent relative clause'. The Su gives a certain qualification rather than denoting a single entity, e.g.:[21]

---

[20] I.e. something that is new in the context.

11:18 ‎ܡܗܘܐܥܬܪ ‎ܡܢ ‎ܕܚܣܝܪ ‎ܐܝܬ 'There is one who becomes rich from his poverty'.

20:12 ‎ܝܨܦ ‎ܐܝܟ ‎ܣܓܝ ‎ܕܝܙܦ ‎ܐܝܬ 'There is one who borrows much like little'.

One could argue that in these clauses ‎ܐܝܬ is the Pr: It is the new information about the person indicated by the Su, namely that he exists. However, we prefer to analyse these clauses as 'subject-only' clauses expanded by ‎ܐܝܬ. Compare Joosten's description of the function of ‎ܐܝܬ:

> Non-suffixed *it* is purely a grammatical element, with no semantic expression of itself. Its general function is to indicate predication: where we find *it* we know there is a clause. More specifically, its function can be described as that of a 'two-place' predicator. The first place is to be occupied by an indefinite nominal phrase, the second by an adverbial phrase. Either place can be empty.[22]

In all cases in Syr ‎ܐܝܬ precedes the Su, but in other corpora the reverse order is attested as well, apparently without different meaning.[23] If the Su is a noun, it is most often followed by a specification. This may be either a prepositional phrase or a relative clause introduced by ‎ܕ. In all the examples the specification has a limiting function, i.e. it serves to distinguish between the members of the class denoted by the antecedent.[24] This means that the antecedent does not denote a single entity, but a class or group, in which a further distinction can be made.

Sometimes an ‎ܐܝܬ clause indicates the absolute existence of something that is already known in the context.[25] Examples mentioned in the scholarly literature include[26]

---

[21] Cf. Beck, 'Sprache Ephräms', II, 1–2 on ‎ܕ ‎ܐܝܬ in the works of Ephrem.

[22] Joosten, *Syriac Language*, 97–98; see also Dyk–Talstra, 'Paradigmatic and Syntagmatic', 168–171. According to Dyk and Talstra the treatment of Hebrew ‎יש and ‎אין as expansions of the NC 'allows for a simple and elegant analysis of the constructions in which they occur' (p. 169). See also their discussion on pp. 159–160 about subject-only clauses indicating existence without ‎יש or ‎אין. To their example from Qoh 3:2 we can add its Syriac translation: ‎ܠܡܡܬ ‎ܘܙܒܢܐ ‎ܠܡܐܠܕ ‎ܙܒܢܐ ‎ܘܐܝܬ '(there is) a time to be born and a time to die'.

[23] Joosten, *Syriac Language*, 100; Muraoka, *Basic Grammar*, § 109.

[24] Cf. Joüon-Muraoka, *Grammar*, § 158a*.

[25] This phenomenon is not covered by the table in § 22.2.

[26] Examples taken from Goldenberg, 'Syriac Sentence Structure', 123–124, 131. For more examples see Joosten, *Syriac Language*, 103–104; Beck, 'Sprache Ephräms', II, 6–9. In Gen 42:36 the second clause may be elliptical for *‎ܠܝܬܘܗܝ ‎ܘܫܡܥܘܢ, ‎ܥܡܝ 'Simeon is not with me'; cf. MT ‎יוסף ‎איננו ‎ושמעון ‎איננו; Targum Onqelos ‎יוסף ‎ליתוהי ‎ושמעון ‎לא ‎הוה ‎כא.

Aphrahat, *Dem.* 23:58 ܐܢ ܨܒܐ ܐܝܬܝܢ 'if You wish, we exist'.[27]

Meliton, *Apology to Antonius Caesar* ܘܫܪܝܪܐܝܬ ܐܝܬܘܗܝ 'and he really exists'.[28]

Gen 42:36 ܝܘܣܦ ܠܝܬܘܗܝ ܘܫܡܥܘܢ ܠܝܬܘܗܝ 'Joseph is not and Simeon is not'.

There is one example in Syr:

7:28 ܕܐܠܘ ܠܐ ܗܢܘܢ ܠܐ ܐܝܬܝܟܘܢ '(Remember) that without them you would not have existed'.

Goldenberg prefers to categorize these cases under Muraoka's second group ('locative clauses') and replace the term 'locative' by 'existential'.[29] In the examples he gives, however, the adverbial phrase, which in Muraoka's definition is essential for locative clauses, is absent. Therefore we prefer to take these cases apart as a distinct category— i.e. absolute existence of something that is already known in the context—and retain the name 'locative' for the category defined by Muraoka.

22.4 ܐܝܬ CLAUSES INDICATING SITUATED EXISTENCE

Unlike clauses indicating absolute existence, clauses expressing situated existence contain in addition to ܐܝܬ and the Su another clause constituent. Clauses of this type are most frequent with the preposition Lamadh of possession (cf. § 22.1), e.g.:

5:1 ܣܓܝ ܐܝܬ ܠܝ 'I have much'.

5:12 ܐܢ ܐܝܬ ܠܟ ܡܠܬܐ 'If you have a word'.[30]

11:9 ܐܢ ܐܝܬ ܒܟ ܚܝܠܐ 'If you have strength'.

18:33 ܒܕ ܡܕܡ ܕܠܝܬ ܒܟܝܣܟ ܠܟ 'When nothing is in your purse'.

With ellipsis of the Su:

13:5 ܐܢ ܐܝܬ ܠܟ 'If you have something'.

With the Su in the absolute state (all examples are with ܠܝܬ):[31]

---

[27] Ed. Parisot 2.117, lines 20–21.

[28] Ed. Cureton 22, line 20.

[29] Goldenberg, 'Syriac Sentence Structure', 131.

[30] ܡܠܬܐ is a plus compared with Heb (A+C) אם יש אתך.

[31] Also elsewhere in the Peshitta, e.g. Prov 10:2 ܠܝܬ ܝܘܬܪܢ 'There is no profit'; cf. with ܐܠ + ܗܘܐ: Sir 47:23 7h3 ܠܡܕܥܠܐ ܘܠܐ ܗܘܐ ܠܗܘܢ 'And let there be no

12:1 ⟨Syriac⟩ 'Also is there no goodness in his goodness'.

12:3 ⟨Syriac⟩ 'There is no goodness for him who honours the evil person'.

20:16 ⟨Syriac⟩ 'And there is no goodness in return of my goodness'.

The parsing of the constituent besides ܐܝܬ and the Su depends on the interpretation of ܐܝܬ. If ܐܝܬ is considered the Pr, the prepositional phrase is a complement. However, we prefer to interpret the prepositional phrase as the Pr and to regard ܐܝܬ as a particle that indicates the predicative relationship between the Su and the Pr.[32]

In the majority of cases ܐܝܬ takes the initial position in the clause, but sometimes the Su precedes, e.g.:[33]

5:1 ⟨Syriac⟩ 'I have much'.
7:22 ⟨Syriac⟩ 'If you have cattle'.

This is also the case when the Su is an interrogative, e.g.:[34]

20:30 ⟨Syriac⟩ 'What profit is in either of them?'
30:19 ⟨Syriac⟩ 'What profit is there to the idols of the nations?'

Four times the Pr precedes ܐܝܬ:

21:3 ⟨Syriac⟩ 'And to her wound there is no cure'.
27:21a ⟨Syriac⟩ 'Because there is a bandage for a bruise'.
27:21b ⟨Syriac⟩ 'And there is a reconciliation for a strife'.
33:7 ⟨Syriac⟩ 'Why is one day in the year distinguished from the other?'

In 21:3, 27:21a, 21b the word order serves to topicalize the Pr. In § 21.2 we have seen that a device that is frequently used to mark an element as the topic is extraposition (i.e. placing it at the front of the clause, outside the predication structure). Since in the examples from Syr it is the topic that precedes ܐܝܬ, we prefer to analyse them as ex-

memory for Jeroboam' (other witnesses: ⟨Syriac⟩!); Nöldeke, *Grammatik*, § 330; see also Nöldeke, *Grammatik*, §§ 202F, 202I.

[32] Cf. Dyk–Talstra, 'Paradigmatic and Syntagmatic', 168–171, and above, § 22.3.

[33] See above, § 22.3, and the examples from 18:33, quoted below, and 7:22, 23, 24, 26 quoted in § 22.5.4.

[34] See also the example from 17:27, quoted in § 21.3.1 B (2).

traposition as well, even though they lack the resumptive pronoun that is typical of extraposition constructions. This implies that the resumption of the Pr is an optional device, that is sometimes used (in the examples quoted in § 21.2[35]) and sometimes not (in the examples under discussion). The alternative would be that we analyse them as cases of fronting (i.e. placing an element in the first slot inside the predication structure) and conclude that fronting can be used for topicalization as well, but the disadvantage of that analysis is that it implies that one and the same structure, namely fronting, has two completely different functions, namely topic and focus.[36] Compare the fronting of the interrogative Pr in 33:7. An unequivocal example of extraposition (with resumptive pronoun) of the topic of an ܐܝܬ clause occurs in an explanation of a parable in

> Matt 13:38 ܘܩܪܝܬܐ ܐܝܬܝܗ ܥܠܡܐ 'And the field is the world'.

An example in which an element that receives focus is fronted occurs in

> Matt 6:30 ܥܡܒܪܐ ܕܚܩܠܐ ܕܝܘܡܢܐ ܐܝܬܘܗܝ, 'The grass of the field which today is'.

ܕܝܘܡܢܐ makes up a contrast with the following ܘܡܚܪ ܢܦܠ ܒܬܢܘܪܐ 'and (which) tomorrow will fall into the fire'.[37]

There is one example in which both the Su and the Pr precede ܐܝܬ:

> 18:33 ܟܕ ܡܕܡ ܒܟܝܣܟ ܠܝܬ 'When nothing is in your purse'.

If both the Su and the Pr follow ܐܝܬ, the Pr comes directly after ܐܝܬ if it consists of preposition + suffix pronoun,[38] e.g.:

> 19:8 ܘܐܢ ܐܝܬ ܠܟ ܚܛܗܐ 'And if you have sin'.

If the prepositional phrase contains a noun instead of the pronoun, the Pr usually comes after the Su,[39] e.g.:

> 12:1 ܐܦܠܐ ܐܝܬ ܛܝܒܘ ܠܛܝܒܘܬܟ 'Also is there no goodness in his goodness'.

---

[35] See also the discussion below, after the quotation of 40:26.

[36] On the importance to distinguish between topic and focus see § 16.2 (end) and Chapter 21, n. 59.

[37] Examples taken from Falla, *Key* I, 23*b*.

[38] Cf. Joosten, *Syriac Language*, 100.

[39] Cf. Joosten *Syriac Language*, 99–100.

But the reverse order is attested in

40:26 ܠܝܬ ܒܕܚܠܬܗ ܕܐܠܗܐ ܣܘܢܩܢܐ 'In the fear of God there is no need'.

Although there are a number of cases where the Pr consists of preposition + noun, there seems to be a tendency to retain the basic structure of ܐܝܬ + preposition + suffix. Thus if the Pr precedes ܐܝܬ, it is sometimes resumed by preposition + suffix pronoun,[40] even if the Pr itself consists of preposition + suffix pronoun.[41] In addition, there are cases where ܐܝܬ is followed by a preposition with a proleptic suffix pronoun that is later resumed by preposition + noun (20:2), even with the specification directly following the preposition + pronoun (17:27).[42] Especially with the possessive ܠ it seems that the combination ܐܝܬ ܠ was on its way to becoming a stereotyped expression meaning 'to have'.[43] The connection between ܐܝܬ and the prepositional phrase is so strong that even the connective particles ܓܝܪ and ܕܝܢ do not intervene (§ 13.3 [2]):

15:12 ܠܝܬ ܠܗ ܓܝܪ ܗܢܝܢܐ ܒܒܪ ܐܢܫܐ ܥܘܠܐ 'For there is no profit to Him in the unrighteous man'.
22:21 ܐܝܬ ܠܗ ܓܝܪ ܡܦܩܢܐ 'For there is a way out for him'.
22:22 ܡܛܠ ܕܐܝܬ ܠܗ ܓܝܪ ܬܪܥܘܬܐ 'Because there is reconciliation for him'.

Four times the predicative complement consists of ܡܢ + Pronoun (ܡܢܗܘܢ):

44:8 ܐܝܬ ܡܢܗܘܢ ܕܫܒܩܘ ܫܡܐ 'Some of them have left behind a name'.
44:9 ܘܐܝܬ ܡܢܗܘܢ ܕܠܝܬ ܠܗܘܢ ܕܘܟܪܢܐ 'And some of them have no memory'.
48:16a ܐܝܬ ܡܢܗܘܢ ܕܥܒܕܘ ܛܝܒܘܬܐ 'Some of them did goodness'.
48:16b ܘܐܝܬ ܡܢܗܘܢ ܕܐܘܣܦܘ ܚܛܗܐ 'And some of them increased sins upon sins'.

In these four cases Heb has יש מהם.[44]

---

[40] This happens in 3:28; 6:15; 16:14, quoted in § 21.3.2 (c) (pronominal agreement) and in 26:25, quoted in § 21.2 B (c) (extraposition).

[41] This happens in 23:13 and 38:12, quoted in § 21.3.2 (c).

[42] 17:27 and 20:2 are quoted in § 21.3.1 B (3).

[43] Joosten, *Syriac Language*, 101–103; cf. Beck, 'Sprache Ephräms', II, 2–3 on ܐܝܬ ܠ 'to belong to' in the works of Ephrem.

[44] The use of מן with the meaning 'some of' is frequent in Late Biblical Hebrew; cf. Van Peursen, *Verbal System*, 312.

A construction that at first sight also belongs to this category, is that
with the preposition *ܐܟܘܬܗ, which is attested in

> 25:12 ܡܟܘܬܗ ܠܝܬ ܕܡܐ 'Because there is nothing like it' (= 40:26).
> 36:12 ܐܟܘܬܝ، ܠܝܬ 'There is no-one like me'.

However, it is problematic to consider the prepositional phrase in this
construction the Pr. It is rather a subject-orientated adjunct.[45] Compare
the following passage from Kings, where the function of ܐܟܘܬܟ as a
subject-orientated adjunct rather than the Pr is obvious from the presence of other elements that function as the Pr (ܗܘܐ ܠܐ and ܠܐ
ܢܩܘܡ).[46]

> 1 Kgs 3:12–13 ܐܟܘܬܟ، ܢܩܘܡ ܠܐ ܘܡܢ ܒܬܪܟ ܗܘܐ ܠܐ ܐܟܘܬܟܕ
> 'That anyone like you have been before and after you will not arise'.

22.5 ܐܝܬ CLAUSES AND OTHER PATTERNS
INDICATING SITUATED EXISTENCE

22.5.1 *The predicative complement is a*
prepositional phrase with ܒ

In § 22.3 we have indicated that we regard ܐܝܬ as a third element
added to a bipartite structure. This raises the question of how this pattern relates to other NCs. If we take, for example, all clauses in which
the Pr consists of a phrase introduced by the preposition ܒ, we can
make the following observations.[47]

A. The construction with ܐܝܬ is attested fourteen times. See e.g. 18:33
quoted above, in § 22.4.

---

[45] Cf. Dyk–Talstra, 'Paradigmatic and Syntagmatic', 170: 'At times the particles
of existence can occur without an explicit S but with further specifications referring to
an impersonal S.'

[46] Since the clause refers to the past, we prefer to analyse ܗܘܐ here as a verb
rather than a mere fossilized element added to the negation; cf. § 23.2.4

[47] According to Goldenberg, 'Syriac Sentence Structure', 129, a bare prepositional
phrase with ܒ standing for 'there is in...' etc. is a 'special construction that should be
regarded as involving the omission of *it*'.

B. In main clauses the bipartite construction is attested almost as frequently as the construction with ܐܝܬ: thirteen times. Compare especially such pairs as

29:26 ܘܐܟܘܠ ܡܕܡ ܕܐܝܬ ܒܐܝܕܝܟ 'And eat what is in your hands'.
29:28 ܘܣܥܘܪ ܡܢ ܕܐܝܬܝ ܒܐܝܕܟ, 'And nourish him from what is in your hand'.

Clauses that have a modal function are preferably considered cases of 'ellipsis of a form of the verb ܗܘܐ' rather than of 'ellipsis of ܐܝܬ', e.g.:

6:6 ܣܓܝܐܐ ܢܗܘܘܢ ܫܠܡܝܟ ܘܡܠܟܐ ܕܝܢ ܚܕ ܡܢ ܐܠܦ 'Let those who greet you be many, but your confidant one in a thousand'.
9:15 ܥܡ ܡܢ ܕܕܚܠ ܠܐܠܗܐ ܢܗܘܘܢ ܚܘܫܒܢܝܟ ܘܡܠܟ ܟܠܗ ܒܐܘܪܚܬܗ ܕܡܪܝܐ 'Let your reckonings be with him who fears God, and all your discourse in the ways of the Lord'.

The simple bipartite structure is also used in relative clauses (eight occurrences), often with ellipsis of the Su,[48] e.g.:

8:19 ܡܐ ܕܒܠܒܟ 'What is in your heart'.
13:19 ܥܪܕܐ ܕܒܡܕܒܪܐ 'The wild asses that are in the desert'.[49]

Also in constructions with ܕܠܐ (four attestations),[50] e.g.:

51:30 ܥܒܕܘ ܥܒܕܟܘܢ ܕܠܐ ܒܙܒܢܗ 'Do your work unseasonably'.

C. The tripartite NC with the Ep occurs twice:

18:24 ܥܗܝ ܕܪܘܓܙܐ ܒܚܪܬܐ ܗܘ ܕܟܠܗܘܢ ܚܛܗܐ '(Remember) that anger is in the end of all sins'.
27:11 ܡܡܠܠܗܘܢ ܕܚܟܝܡܐ ܒܚܟܡܬܐ ܐܝܬ ܟܠܗ 'The discourse of the wise is always with wisdom'.

D. There are five examples of a clause with the verb ܗܘܐ. Three times the reference is to the past, e.g.:

24:11 ܘܒܐܘܪܫܠܡ ܫܘܠܛܢܝ ܗܘܐ 'And in Jerusalem was my authority'.
44:1 ܠܐܒܗܝܢ ܕܗܘܘ ܒܕܪܝܗܘܢ 'Our fathers who were in their generations'.

In one case the verb ܗܘܐ has a modal nuance:

---

[48] On the existential clause with the bipartite pattern see § 17.2; on ellipsis of the Su see § 17.3.
[49] Heb (B) has פראי מדבר; cf. § 10.5.1
[50] Cf. § 14.3.

9:16 ܡܚܝܠܝܘ ܒܕܚܠܬܐ ܕܐܠܗܐ ܬܗܘܐ ܬܫܒܘܚܬܟ 'And let your praise be in the fear of God'.

And in one case a participle of ܗܘܐ occurs:

12:9 ܒܛܒܬܗ ܓܝܪ ܕܓܒܪܐ ܒܥܠܕܒܒܘܗܝ, ܒܟܪܝܘܬܐ ܗܘܘ 'For in a man's prosperity his adversaries are in sadness'.

22.5.2 *The predicative complement is a prepositional phrase with ܥܡ*

With the preposition ܥܡ the situation is as follows. Ten times the predicative complement is a prepositional phrase with ܥܡ.

A. There are no examples of patterns with ܐܝܬ.

B. The bipartite pattern occurs with ellipsis of the Su in an embedded structure in

25:23 ܘܠܒܐ ܕܥܡܗ 'And the heart that is with her'.

In another case the Su is a pronoun:

1:15 ܥܡ ܐܢܫܐ ܗܝ ܩܘܫܬܐ 'She is with the people of truth'.

There are six other attestations of the bipartite construction, e.g.:

5:6 (= 16:11) ܡܛܠ ܕܪܚܡܐ ܘܪܘܓܙܐ ܥܡܗ 'For mercy and anger are with Him'.
31:20 ܟܐܒܐ ܘܫܗܪܐ ܘܡܪܪܐ ܘܢܟܝܢܐ ܘܗܦܟܐ ܕܓܘܐ ܥܡ ܓܒܪܐ ܝܥܢܐ 'Pain, watching, vexation, suffering and turning of the inner parts are with the greedy man'.

C. There is one example of a tripartite NC. In this case too the Su is a pronoun (cf. the example from 1:15 quoted under B):

1:1 ܘܗܝ ܥܡܗ ܗܝ, ܡܢ ܥܠܡ 'And she is with Him from eternity'.

D. In 9:15 there is one example with the verb ܗܘܐ. This example is quoted above, in § 22.5.1 (B).

The general tendency that appears from the patterns with ܒ and ܥܡ is that the bipartite NCs, the tripartite NCs and ܐܝܬ clauses are more or less free variants. If the verb ܗܘܐ is used, it most often expresses past or future tense or modality. However, the example with the participle of ܗܘܐ (12:9) shows that this verb is also employed when there is no need to add a temporal or modal nuance.

22.5.3 *The predicative complement is a prepositional phrase with* ܠ

A. If the predicative complement consists of a prepositional phrase with ܠ, the construction with ܐܝܬ is most frequent. It occurs thirty-eight times. For examples see § 22.4.

B. The bipartite construction occurs ten times, e.g.:

27:29 ܦܚܐ ܘܡܨܝܕܬܐ ܗܠܝܢ ܠܝܕܘܥܘܗܝ 'Snares and nets—they are for those who know them'.

41:9 ܐܢܬܬܐ ܕܝܠܕܐ ܠܚܕܘܬܐ ܠܥܡܗ 'A woman who gives birth is to the joy of her people'.

And further in a relative clause in

20:9a ܡܕܡ ܕܐܝܬܘܗܝ ܗܘ ܠܒܝܫܬܐ '(There is) something that is to a man's evil'.

Also with ellipsis of the Su:

20:9b ܡܡܠܠܐ ܕܠܢܟܝܢܘܬܗ '(There is) discourse that is to his damage'.

C. There is only one example of a tripartite NC:

41:11 ܪܫܝܥܐ ܠܐܒܕܢܐ ܚܪܬܗ ܕܝܠܗ 'The wicked man—his end is for destruction'.

D. With the perfect of ܗܘܐ we find:[51]

24:31 ܘܗܘܐ ܐܦ ܠܝ ܢܚܠܐ 'And behold, I had also a torrent'.

31:10 ܘܗܘܐ ܠܗ ܫܠܡܐ ܘܗܘܐ ܠܗ ܠܬܫܒܘܚܬܐ 'And he has peace and it is for him to a praise'.

And with ܠܐ + the perfect of ܗܘܐ:[52]

5:4 ܘܠܐ ܗܘܐ ܠܝ ܡܕܡ 'And nothing happened to me'.

---

[51] Different in structure and function are cases with ܗܘܐ + ܠ (beneficiary) + ܠ (predicative complement), discussed in § 23.2.6.

[52] But note that we interpret ܗܘܐ here as a full verb, see § 23.2.4.

With the participle of ܗܘܐ:

7:17 ܡܛܠ ܕܚܪܬܐ ܕܟܠܗܘܢ ܒܢܝ̈ܢܫܐ ܠܬܘܠܥܬܐ ܗܘܝܐ 'Because the end of all the sons of men is to the maggots'.
16:3 ܕܗܘܝܐ ܠܗܘܢ ܚܪܬܐ ܛܒܬܐ 'That they will have a good end'.
16:3 ܡܢ ܗܘ ܕܗܘܝܢ ܠܗ ܒܢ̈ܝܐ ܣܓܝ̈ܐܐ ܕܥܘܠܐ '(Better) than he who has many unrighteous sons'.

To some extent the data of the predicates with ܠ corroborate the conclusions based on the patterns with ܒ and ܥܡ. A difference is that in the case of predicates with ܠ the clauses with ܐܝܬ outnumber the bipartite NCs.

22.5.4 *Conclusion*

In comparing the three classes discussed in §§ 22.5.1–22.5.3, we can conclude the following.

1. Clauses with ܐܝܬ are frequently employed to indicate 'situated existence'.
2. The ܐܝܬ clauses and the bipartite constructions seem to be free variants, but in the patterns with ܠ the ܐܝܬ clauses are more frequent.
3. Tripartite NCs with an Ep indicating 'situated existence' are rare.
4. ܗܘܐ + predicative complement most often serves to express past or future tense or modality. Sometimes the participle of ܗܘܐ is used.

The assessment of these data depends on one's basic assumptions about the Syriac NC. Muraoka has claimed that the bipartite construction is a genuine pattern in itself, while Goldenberg has argued that bipartite clauses should be understood as elliptical constructions. Joosten has argued that a diachronic factor is involved as well: It seems that in an earlier stage of the Syriac language the pattern without ܐܝܬ was more common.[53] Compare especially such pairs as

Luke 1:66 Sinaiticus ܐܝܕܗ ܕܡܪܝܐ ܥܡܗ 'The Lord's hand was with him'; Peshitta ܐܝܕܗ ܕܡܪܝܐ ܐܝܬ ܗܘܬ ܥܡܗ.[54]

[53] Joosten, *Syriac Language*, 93, 149.

In this respect Syr represents an early phase: There is a strong tendency to use ܐܝܬ, but the bipartite clauses are more than mere exceptions to the rule.

The preference for the construction with ܐܝܬ also appears from those cases where ܐܝܬ occurs in Syr without a corresponding יש in Heb. Craig Morrison has discussed this phenomenon in his PhD dissertation on the Syriac version of Samuel.[55] Compare e.g.

7:22 ܐܝܬ ܠܟ ܒܥܝܪܐ 'If you have cattle'; A+C בהמה לך.
7:23 ܐܝܬ ܠܟ ܒܢܬ 'If you have sons'; A+C בנים לך.
7:24 ܐܝܬ ܠܟ ܒܢܬܐ 'If you have daughters'; A בנות לך (C בנים לך).
7:26 ܐܝܬ ܠܟ ܐܢܬܬܐ 'If you have a wife'; A אשה לך 'If you have a wife'.

Sometimes the Hebrew evidence is divided, e.g.:

10:30 ܐܝܬ ܡܣܟܢܐ ܕܡܬܝܩܪ 'There is a poor man who is honoured'; A יש
דל נכבד; B דל נכבד.

Although in the case of Sirach the relation between the source text of the Syriac translator and the extant Hebrew manuscripts is complicated, the fact that a tendency that appears in the Peshitta of Samuel is also visible in Syr when compared with Heb, strongly supports the view that the Syriac translator used ܐܝܬ in his translation even in those cases where there was no יש in his source text. Accordingly, if ܐܝܬ occurs in Syr, we cannot conclude that the translator's Hebrew source contained יש.

Correspondences between ܠܝܬ and אין are more frequent, but in these cases too we cannot automatically assume that the source text of the Syriac translator had אין where Syr has ܠܝܬ. Sometimes ܠܝܬ corresponds to a word in Heb other than אין. It occurs, for example, in 3:25, 11:9 and 36:30, where Heb has באין.[56] In other cases the Hebrew evidence is divided: In 39:34 B^mg has אין לאמר corresponding to ܠܝܬ

<hr>

[54] Muraoka, *Classical Syriac for Hebraists*, § 107; idem, *Basic Grammar*, § 119. For the construction with ܐܝܬ and an enclitic form of the verb ܗܘܐ see Nöldeke, *Grammatik*, §§ 301, 304; Duval, *Traité*, § 339*b*; cf. Costaz, *Grammaire*, § 682; Muraoka, *Classical Syriac for Hebraists*, § 107; idem, *Basic Grammar*, § 109; Goldenberg, 'Syriac Sentence Structure', 118, 122–123; Falla, *Key* I, 21*a*. This construction does not occur in Syr.
[55] Morrison, *First Book of Samuel* (1995), 146–148; this section of Morrison's PhD dissertation has not been included in the revised version that appeared in the MPIL series.
[56] On באין 'without' in Heb see Van Peursen, 'Negation', 235.

ܓܠܝ in Syr, but B^{txt} has אל לאמר, and in 36:31 B^{mg}+C+D have אשר
אין לו קן, but B^{txt} has לא instead of אין.[57]

22.6 LOCATIVE ܐܝܬ CLAUSES

'Locative clauses' indicate where something that is already known in
the context is to be located. Like clauses expressing 'situated existence', they contain three constituents: the existential particle, a Su
and a Pr; the latter is an adverbial. The difference from 'situated existence' is that in locative clauses the Su is definite.[58] In Syr there is at
most one example of a locative ܐܝܬ clause:

> 16:2 ܡܛܠ ܕܠܝܬ ܐܝܬܝܗܘܢ ܒܕܚܠܬܗ ܕܐܠܗܐ 'Because they are not in the
> fear of God'.

However, since ܒܕܚܠܬܗ ܕܐܠܗܐ can hardly be considered an adverb of
place, this is rather an example of the class of copulaic ܐܝܬ clauses, to
be discussed in the following paragraph.

22.7 COPULAIC ܐܝܬ CLAUSES

There are some cases where ܐܝܬ functions as a copula.[59] In all cases
this concerns descriptive NCs. Copulaic/identificatory ܐܝܬ clauses are
not attested in our corpus.

A. The Pr is a prepositional phrase in

> 16:2 ܡܛܠ ܕܠܝܬ ܐܝܬܝܗܘܢ ܒܕܚܠܬܗ ܕܐܠܗܐ 'Because they are not in the
> fear of God'.[60]
> 18:10 ܠܐ ܐܝܬܝܗܘܢ ܐܝܟ ܚܕ ܝܘܡܐ ܒܥܠܡܐ ܕܙܕܝܩܐ 'They are not like
> one day in the world of the righteous'.
> 43:8 ܣܗܪܐ ܐܝܟ ܫܡܗ ܐܝܬܘܗܝ 'The (new) moon is like its name'.

---

[57] Cf. Van Peursen, 'Negation', 229. In these cases Syr cannot be taken as supporting the reading with אין; *pace* Peters, *Ben Sirach*, 300 (on 36:31), 333 (on 39:34).

[58] A formal indication that the Su is semantically determinate is its co-referen-
tiality with elements mentioned earlier or deictic elements. The use of the emphatic
state as such does not indicate that the Su is 'already known'.

[59] The low frequency of this construction agrees with the situation in other early
Syriac texts; see above, § 22.1.

[60] See above, § 22.6.

In the last example ܪܘܝܬ takes topic position and ܡܬܐ ܐܝܟ can be analysed as a focalized Pr.[61]

B. The Pr is the adverb ܗܟܢ in

> 20:15 ܕܐܝܬܝܗܘܢ ܗܟܢܐ 'Those who are like this'.
> 22:1 ܣܟܠܐ ܐܝܬܘܗܝ, ܗܟܢ 'Thus is the fool'.

In these two cases ܗܟܢ precedes ܐܝܬ, probably because it is the topic (see above, § 22.4).

C. The Pr is an adjective in

> 28:21 ܒܫܝܘܠ ܡܢ ܛܒ ܠܡܢܚ ܐܝܬ ܘܢܝܚܐ 'And rest is in Sheol better than with it'.[62]

D. The Pr is a participle in

> 25:26 ܒܐܬܪܟ ܐܙܠܐ ܐܝܬܝܗ ܘܐܢ 'And if she is not following you'.

In this case the use of the particle ܐܝܬ is remarkable, because the participle usually takes the bipartite construction.

For only two of the seven verses quoted is Heb extant. In both cases it reflects a different syntactic structure. In 16:2 Heb ([A+]B) has כי אין אתם יראת ייי and in 43:8 M has [חד]ש כשמו הוא מת[חדש]; Bᵗˣᵗ חדש בחדשו הוא מתחדש; Bᵐᵍ כשמו והוא.

22.8 CONCLUSION

In §§ 22.1–22.2 we have made a classification of ܐܝܬ clauses according to a number of formal, semantic and functional criteria. Important distinctions for making such a classification are those between existential and copulaic (Nöldeke), between existential and locative (Muraoka), and between absolute and situated existence (Goldenberg).

In our discussion of ܐܝܬ clauses indicating absolute existence (§ 22.3) and those indicating situated existence (§ 22.4) we could ob-

---

[61] Cf. above, § 22.4.

[62] The precise analysis of this clause is difficult. Copulaic ܐܝܬ without the suffix is exceptional, but an existential interpretation of ܐܝܬ (something like 'And there is rest in Sheol that is better than [that] with it') is not satisfactory either; cf. Calduch-Benages–Ferrer–Liesen, *Sabiduria del Escriba*, 180: 'And the rest in Sheol is better than (the rest) at its side'.

serve a number of phenomena that we had also noticed in earlier chapters, such as the topicalizing function of extraposition, the use of pronominal agreement, supporting the tendency to retain the basic structure of ܐܝܬ + preposition + suffix pronoun, and the strong connection between ܐܝܬ and ܠ + pronoun, in which even the connective particles ܓܝܪ and ܕ do not intervene.

In § 22.5 we compared ܐܝܬ clause with other patterns indicating situated existence. There is a strong tendency to use ܐܝܬ, but bipartite NCs also occur fairly often and cannot be considered mere exceptions to the rule. In this respect Syr represents an early phase of Classical Syriac. Locative ܐܝܬ clauses (§ 22.6) and copulaic ܐܝܬ clauses (§ 22.7) are rare.

CHAPTER TWENTY-THREE

CLAUSES CONTAINING THE VERB ܗܘܐ

23.1 INTRODUCTION

Constructions with the verb ܗܘܐ display a large variety. We can categorize them according to the following parameters:

1. The conjugation of the verb ܗܘܐ.
2. The form of the predicative complement.
3. The position of ܗܘܐ vis-à-vis the predicative complement.

The first parameter is related to more general questions about the Tense-Aspect-Mood system in Classical Syriac. Whereas it can be argued, for example, that the perfect of ܗܘܐ serves to add past tense reference to a NC, the expression of tense is clearly not the function of ܗܘܐ if it occurs in the participle or the imperative.

The second parameter concerns the part of speech of the predicative complement and, if applicable, its state. Thus a distinction can be made between participials and other elements. The combination ܗܘܐ + participle functions as a compound tense and can be contrasted with non-periphrastic constructions, while constructions with other predicative complements constitute contrasting pairs with bi- or tripartite NCs or ܐܝܬ clauses.

The third parameter is related to the fact that in some contexts there is a functional difference between pre-predicative ܗܘܐ and post-predicative ܗܘܐ. While the pre-predicative ܗܘܐ functions as a full verb, the post-predicative ܗܘܐ may appear in its reduced state (e.g. *qātel (h)wā*) and serve as an enclitic to mark past tense.[1]

---

[1] Van Rompay, 'Post-Predicative *hwā*', 211.

23.2 THE PERFECT OF ܗܘܐ

23.2.1 *General survey*

According to the parameters mentioned in § 23.1, we can distinguish four constructions in which the perfect of ܗܘܐ is used:

1. The predicative complement is a participial; ܗܘܐ precedes it (*hwā qātel*).
2. The predicative complement is a participial; ܗܘܐ follows it (*qātel (h)wā*).
3. The predicative complement is not a participial; ܗܘܐ precedes it.
4. The predicative complement is not a participial; ܗܘܐ follows it.

The first construction is used to express a wish or advice of general applicability. In our corpus this usage is only attested with the perfect of the 2nd pers. masc. sing.[2] Joosten has drawn attention to another function of this construction, namely the expression of iterative actions in the past.[3] This use is not attested in Syr. The second construction is mainly used for an ongoing action in the past. It stands in opposition to the simple perfect. The third and fourth constructions are the past equivalents of the NC. The third category also contains examples where ܗܘܐ functions as a full verb in the meaning 'to become'. Sometimes ܗܘܐ does not take a predicative complement. This is the case in

17:30 ܡܛܠ ܕܠܐ ܗܘܐ ܐܝܟ ܗܢܐ ܒܪܢܫܐ 'Because in man is not like this' (i.e. 'Because the like of this is not found in a human being'[4]).

23:20 ܥܕ ܠܐ ܗܘܐ ܠܡܕܡ 'Before something exists'.

In these examples ܗܘܐ indicates absolute existence.[5]

---

[2] The same is true for the Old Syriac and Peshitta versions of Matthew; see Joosten, *Syriac Language*, 129. For examples of *hwā qātel* with the perfect of the 3rd person see Nöldeke, *Grammatik*, § 260; Duval, *Traité*, § 334c.

[3] Joosten, 'Repetition in the Past', esp. 9–12; idem, 'Materials', 214; Williams, *Peshitta of 1 Kings*, 113.

[4] Thus Calduch-Benages–Ferrer–Liesen, *Sabiduria del Escriba*, 132. We interpret the prepositional phrase ܐܝܟ ܗܢܐ ܒܪܢܫܐ as a subject-oriented adjunct, see our comment on 25:12 (= 40:26) ܡܛܠ ܕܠܝܬ ܐܟܘܬܗ 'Because there is nothing like it' in § 22.4 (end).

[5] On the notion of absolute existence see § 22.1.

23.2.2 *hwayt qātel*

In some Aramaic dialects the construction with the imperative of 'to be' + participle is attested. J.C. Greenfield has investigated this periphrastic imperative in Hebrew and Aramaic dialects. He concludes that the periphrastic imperative, unlike other periphrastic tenses, is rare in Aramaic. It is not attested in Biblical Aramaic or Qumran Aramaic and it is only rarely found in some Egyptian Aramaic documents. It is employed several times in the Hermopolis Letters and in Galilaean Aramaic and Christian Palestinian Aramaic. Greenfield suggests that these occurrences may be traces of a much wider use in Western Aramaic.[6] In Syriac, however, the imperatival use of the perfect of the 2nd pers. masc. sing. of ܗܘܐ + participle is more frequent.[7] In Syr there are a number of cases of this 'imperatival' *hwayt qātel*, e.g.:

5:11a ܗܘܝܬ ܡܣܪܗܒ ܠܡܫܡܥ 'Be quick to hear'.
5:11b ܘܒܡܬܝܢܘܬܐ ܗܘܝܬ ܡܦܢ ܦܬܓܡܐ 'And answer slowly'.
6:34 ܒܟܢܘܫܬܐ ܕܩܫܝܫܐ ܗܘܝܬ ܩܐܡ 'Take your stand in the community of the elders'.
6:35 ܠܟܠ ܫܘܥܝܬܐ ܗܘܝܬ ܪܓܝܓ ܠܡܫܡܥ 'Be eager to hear every discourse'.
6:37 ܘܒܦܘܩܕܢܘܗܝ ܗܘܝܬ ܪܢܐ ܒܟܠܝܘܡ 'And reflect upon His commands every day'.
7:34 ܘܥܡ ܟܠ ܐܒܝܠܐ ܗܘܝܬ ܡܬܐܒܠ 'And mourn with all who mourn'.
7:36 ܒܟܠ ܥܒܕܝܟ ܗܘܝܬ ܕܟܝܪ ܚܪܬܐ 'In all your works remember your end'.
8:8 ܘܒܡܬܠܝܗܘܢ ܗܘܝܬ ܕܪܫ 'And train yourself in their proverbs'.
9:14 ܘܥܡ ܚܟܝܡܐ ܗܘܝܬ ܡܡܠܟ ܐܪܙܐ 'And take secret council with the wise'.
13:9 ܗܘܝܬ ܡܬܪܚܩ ܡܢܗ 'Keep your distance from him'.
21:2 ܣܓܝ ܗܘܝܬ ܥܪܩ ܡܢ ܚܛܗܐ 'Flee much from sin'.
37:12 ܥܡ ܐܢܫܐ ܙܕܝܩܐ ܗܘܝܬ ܥܡܪ 'Dwell with righteous people'.
37:15 ܘܥܡ ܟܠܗܝܢ ܗܠܝܢ ܗܘܝܬ ܡܨܠܐ ܠܐܠܗܐ 'And with all this pray to God'.

---

[6] Greenfield, 'Periphrastic Imperative'.

[7] The origin of this construction may be the precative use of the suffix-conjugation, which is also attested in other Semitic languages; Joosten, *Syriac Language*, 130; cf. Brockelmann, *Grundriss* II, 29–30; Lipiński, *Semitic Languages*, 514; for Syriac see Nöldeke, *Grammatik*, § 259; on the alleged precative use of the suffix-conjugation in Biblical Hebrew see Waltke–O'Connor, *Biblical Hebrew Syntax*, § 30.5.4*c*-*d*.

Hwayt qātel indicates a wish, advice or obligation of general and universal applicability, but not an order for an immediate action, for which one uses the imperative.[8] In some cases the conditional-frequentative character of the command is also expressed by another element in the clause, such as ܒܟܠܝܘܡ in 6:37, ܥܡ ܟܠ ܐܒ̈ܝܠܐ in 7:34, ܒܟܘܠ ܥܒ̈ܕܝܟ in 7:36 and ܥܡ ܟܠܗܘܢ ܗܠܝܢ in 37:12.[9] In seven cases Heb has an imperative, e.g. 6:35 (A+C) חפוץ.[10] Only in 5:11 does Heb have a periphrastic imperative: היה ממהר (thus MS A; C has נכון היה). In 13:9 MS A has היה רחוק (parallel to התרחק in the following line). In the remaining cases Heb is not extant or has a completely different reading.

In the opposition *hwayt qātel – qtol*, the former is the marked term.[11] That means that an order for some immediate action is always expressed by the simple imperative, while for the expression of a general wish or advice either the unmarked simple imperative or the marked periphrastic imperative are employed. Compare e.g.[12]

> Matt 7:12 Curetonian ܗܘܝܬܘܢ ܥܒܕܝܢ ܠܗܘܢ '(Everything that you wish others to do to you), do it to them'; Pesh ܐܦ ܐܢܬܘܢ ܥܒܕܘ ܠܗܘܢ.
> Matt 10:11 Sinaiticus ܗܘܝܬܘܢ ܫܐܠܝܢ ܡܢܘ ܫܘܐ '(Whatever village you enter) search for someone who is worthy'; Pesh ܫܐܠܘ ܡܢܘ ܫܘܐ ܒܗ.

With the verbs used in the examples of the periphrastic construction quoted above, the non-periphrastic imperative is attested as well, e.g.:

> ܩܘܡ 11:20 ܒܪܝ ܩܘܡ ܥܠ ܐܘܪܚܟ 'My son, stand on your way'.
> ܕܟܪ 28:7 ܐܬܕܟܪ ܦܘܩܕܢܐ 'Remember the command'.
> ܪܚܩ 6:13 ܘܡܢ ܣܢܐܟ ܐܬܪܚܩ 'And keep away from your enemy'.
> ܗܒ 12:11 ܗܒ ܠܒܟ ܠܡܕܚܠ ܡܢܗ 'Take care to fear him'.
> ܨܠܝ 18:20 ܥܕ ܠܐ ܬܡܛܝܟ ܥܩܬܐ ܨܠܝ 'And before distress reaches you, pray'.

Compare also the following prohibitives with these verbs:

> ܣܪܗܒ 6:7 ܘܠܐ ܬܣܪܗܒ ܠܡܬܬܟܠܘ ܥܠܘܗܝ 'And do not make haste to rely on him'.

---

[8] Nöldeke, *Grammatik*, § 260; Duval, *Traité*, § 334*c-d*; Muraoka, *Classical Syriac for Hebraists*, § 72; idem, *Basic Grammar*, § 87; Joosten, 'Repetition in the Past', 9.

[9] Cf. Joosten, *Syriac Language*, 129–130.

[10] In the Peshitta of 1 Kings *hwayt qātel* twice translates *tiqtol* (1 Kgs 17:4, 22:25); see Williams, *Peshitta of 1 Kings*, 112.

[11] Joosten, *Syriac Language*, 129.

[12] For more examples see Joosten, *Syriac Language*, 129–130; Muraoka, *Classical Syriac for Hebraists*, § 72.

ܩܘܡ 8:11 ܠܐ ܬܩܘܡ ܥܡ ܩܕܡ ܥܘܠܐ 'Do not stand up against an unrighteous person'.

ܨܒܐ 7:13 ܠܐ ܬܨܒܐ ܠܡܕܓܠܘ ܟܘܠ ܕܓܠܘܬܐ 'Do not desire to tell any lie'.

There are also cases where *hwayt* is followed by an adjective:[13]

5:10 ܗܘܝܬ ܣܡܝܟ ܥܠ ܡܕܥܟ 'Be steadfast in your discernment'.
6:13 ܘܡܢ ܪܚܡܟ ܗܘܝܬ ܙܗܝܪ 'And be on your guard for your friend'.
13:13 ܘܗܘܝܬ ܙܗܝܪ 'Be careful'.
18:25 ܗܘܝܬ ܕܟܝܪ ܠܟܦܢܐ ܒܝܘܡ̈ܝ ܣܒܥܐ 'Be mindful of hunger in the days of plenty'.
31:22 ܒܟܠ ܥܒܕ̈ܝܟ ܗܘܝܬ ܡܟܝܟ 'In all your works, be humble'.
32:22 ܘܒܐܘܪ̈ܚܬܟ ܗܘܝܬ ܙܗܝܪ 'And be careful on your way'.
33:23 ܒܟܠ ܥܒܕ̈ܝܟ ܗܘܝܬ ܡܥܠ 'In all your works be lofty'.
40:28 (7a1) ܐܠܐ ܗܘܝܬ ܛܒ ܠܡܚܝܘ 'but be good to keep alive'.

In 40:28 other manuscripts have ܗܘܝ. This variant reading is the only example in Syr of an imperative of ܗܘܝ with a participial.[14]

23.2.3 *qātel (h)wā*

Qātel (h)wā is used for ongoing repeated or habitual actions in the past.[15] According to Joosten the main function of this construction is the expression of durativity in the past; subsidiary functions are the expression of (a) cursive aspect, (b) actions that form the background of the narrative and (c) durativity anterior to the moment of speaking.[16] At first sight *qātel (h)wā* designates an ongoing situation anterior to the moment of speaking in

11:5 ܕܠܐ ܣܠܩܝܢ ܗܘܘ ܥܠ ܠܒܐ ܠܒܫܘ ܠܒܘ̈ܫܐ ܕܐܝܩܪܐ 'Those never thought of have clothed themselves with clothes of honour'.

But the combination of imperfective aspect and negation is logically problematic, because it is odd to indicate the internal temporal constituency of an event. that has not taken place. In the Praise of the Fathers, a section that contains many verb forms referring to past events,

---

13 Cf. Muraoka, *Basic Grammar*, § 87.

14 On the imperative of ܗܘܝ followed by another type of predicative complement, see below, § 23.4.3.

15 Nöldeke, *Grammatik*, §§ 277, 299; Muraoka, *Classical Syriac for Hebraists*, § 71; Van Rompay, 'Post-Predicative *hwā*', 212; Joosten, *Syriac Language*, 115–129; Williams, *Peshitta of 1 Kings*, 111 and 114–116 (on *w-qātel (h)wā*).

16 Joosten, *Syriac Lanugage*, 115–129, esp. 129.

there are only two examples of *qātel (h)wā*. In both cases it expresses a frequentative aspect in the past:

47:8 ‭ܡܛܠ ܗܢܐ ܗܘܐ ܡܪܝܡ ܩܠܗ ܒܡܠܬܐ ܕܬܘܕܝܬܐ ܘܕܐܝܩܪܐ‬ 'Therefore he raised his voice with words of thanksgiving and honour'.

47:9 ‭ܘܒܟܠ ܝܘܡ ܐܡܝܢܐܝܬ ܐܡܪ ܗܘܐ ܬܫܒܚܬܐ ܩܕܡ ܡܕܒܚܐ‬ 'And every day, assiduously, he said praises before the altar'.

Qātel (h)wā and *qtal* constitute 'the main axis of opposition in narrative'.[17] Each of the three verbs used in the *qātel (h)wā* construction also takes the non-periphrastic perfect, e.g.:

‭ܣܠܩ‬ 48:18 ‭ܒܝܘܡܬܗ ܣܠܩ ܥܠܝܗܘܢ ܣܢܚܪܝܒ‬ 'In his days Sennacherib came up against them'.

‭ܝܗܒ‬ 50:18 ‭ܘܝܗܒܘ ܬܘܕܝܬܐ ܩܠܗܘܢ‬ 'And they gave their voices to thanksgiving'.

47:10 ‭ܝܗܒ ܬܫܒܚܬܐ ܪܘܪܒܬܐ ܥܠ ܟܠ ܫܢܐ ܒܫܢܐ‬ 'He gave great praises every year by year'.

‭ܐܡܪ‬ 22:10 ‭ܡܢܐ ܐܡܪܬ‬ 'What did you say?'

36:16 ‭ܐܝܟܢܐ ܕܐܡܪܬ ܡܢ ܩܕܝܡ ܡܬܘܡ‬ 'As You have said from the days of old'.

49:9 ‭ܘܐܦ ܥܠ ܐܝܘܒ ܐܡܪ‬ 'And he spoke also about Job'.[18]

There is no reason to assume that the *qātel (h)wā* forms are due to the influence of a Hebrew source text. In 47:8 Heb (B) has נתן in 47:8 (B), which for orthographic reasons is most likely to be interpreted as a perfect[19] and in 47:9 Heb (B) is damaged. In 11:5 Heb (A+B) has ובל על לב, without a verb at all.

23.2.4 *Constructions with* ‭ܠܐ ܗܘܐ‬

‭ܠܐ ܗܘܐ‬ is used for the negation of a NC or an element other than the verb in a verbal clause.[20] It is placed immediately before the word or phrase that is negated. Joosten has convincingly argued that in ‭ܠܐ‬

---

[17] Joosten, *Syriac Language*, 114. The construction with *hwā* is the marked form in the opposition, cf. Van Rompay, 'Post-Predicative *hwā*', 211 n. 10.

[18] In other cases the perfect of ‭ܐܡܪ‬ is followed by direct speech: 15:20; 17:14; 19:14; 24:8; 36:12.

[19] The defective spelling of participles does occur in MS B, but infrequently; cf. Van Peursen, *Verbal System*, 38. For some cases in 1 Kings where *qātel (h)wā* translates Hebrew *qātal* see Williams, *Peshitta of 1 Kings*, 11.

[20] Cf. Nöldeke, *Grammatik*, § 328B; Duval, *Traité*, § 380*b*; Muraoka, *Basic Grammar*, § 93.9; Falla, *Key* II, 21–22.

ܗܘܐ the use of the verb does not imply past tense, but simply the negation of the NC.[21] The construction with ܗܘܐ ܠܐ corresponds to the positive type of NC constructed with an Ep. An important argument in favour of his position is the observation that ܗܘܐ ܠܐ excludes the use of the Ep. Thus the negative counterpart of ܗܝ ܐܢܬܬܝ is ܐܢܬܬܝ ܗܘܬ ܠܐ, and not *ܗܝ ܐܢܬܬܝ ܗܘܬ ܠܐ.

> In later literature, however, this rule is no longer followed and the type ܗܝ ܐܢܬܬܝ ܗܘܬ ܠܐ occurs as well.[22] Goldenberg analyses clauses of this latter type as cleft sentences ('it is not my wife [that] she is'). The element directly following ܗܘܐ ܠܐ (or ܗܘ ܠܐ) is rhematized, the rest of the sentence is 'virtually nominalized and anyway dislodged from the position of main predication'.[23] It should be noted, however, that in the other Syriac 'cleft sentences' the element *preceding* the enclitic is rhematized.[24]

ܗܘܐ ܠܐ is declined and agrees with the Su. It immediately precedes the element that in the positive clause would be followed by the Ep. Whereas ܗܘܐ ܠܐ is used to negate clauses that in their positive form have an Ep, simple ܠܐ corresponds to the positive types that dispense with an Ep. Simple ܠܐ always immediately precedes the predicate.

In Syr the following patterns are attested:

(1) ܗܘܐ ܠܐ + Su + Pr

The pattern Su–*lā (h)wā*–Pr occurs in

---

[21] Joosten 'Negation', 586–587; idem, *Syriac Language*, 95; idem, 'Materials', 210; see also Goldenberg, 'Syriac Idiom', 31. For two examples where ܗܘܐ following ܠܐ functions as a full verb see § 23.2.1 (end).

[22] Joosten, 'Negation', 588. The early construction is attested in Syriac sources up to the fourth century. The development of the later construction may be prompted by the ambiguity that could arise with the earlier one; see Muraoka, 'Response to Goldenberg', 45.

[23] Cf. Goldenberg, 'Syriac Idiom' 27: 'In the negative (...) the rhematization of the specifically negatived constituent is expressed in Syriac more explicitly than in Hebrew or Greek, by employing the special constructions with *lā (h)wā* or *lā-w*, not merely by placing the negative particle immediately before the negatived nominal. The rest of the sentence is thus implicitly nominalized to become the "glose" of a cleft sentence'; ibid. 32–33: 'The new grammatical predicate of the *lā-w X* or the *lā (h)wā X* nuclear construction is obviously the *X*; its subject is the virtually nominalized rest of the sentence, which will mostly be represented by "it" in a literal English translation.'

[24] See § 24.3; cf. Muraoka, 'Response to Goldenberg', 45–46 on the alternation between *lā (h)wā X* and *lā X (h)wā*.

7:13 ܡܛܠ ܕܚܪܬܗ ܠܐ ܗܘܬ ܛܒܐ 'Because its end will not be good'.
50:25 ܘܬܠܝܬܝܐ ܠܐ ܗܘܐ ܥܡܐ 'And the third one is not a people'.

This pattern is the negative equivalent of the tripartite NC of the type Su–Pr–Ep. Thus 7:13 contains the negative counterpart of *ܚܪܬܗ ܛܒܐ ܗܝ.

The pattern *lā (h)wā*–Su–Pr occurs in

37:28 ܡܛܠ ܕܠܐ ܗܘܐ ܟܠ ܡܐܟܘܠܬܐ ܛܒܐ 'Because not every food is good'.

According to the rule that '*lā (h)wā* immediately precedes the element which, in the positive clause, is followed by EPP',[25] this would be the negative equivalent of Su–Ep–Pr. But since this is a descriptive clause, we consider it rather the negative counterpart of *ܟܠ ܡܐܟܘܠܬܐ ܛܒܐ ܗܝ (Su–Pr–Ep).

ܗܘܐ is a full verb in

5:4 ܘܠܐ ܗܘܐ ܠܝ ܡܕܡ '(I have sinned) and nothing happened to me' (rather than: 'And I have nothing').

(2) ܠܐ ܗܘܐ + Pr

15:9 ܠܐ ܗܘܬ ܝܐܝܐ ܒܦܘܡܐ ܕܥܘܠܐ 'She is not fitting in the mouth of the unrighteous'.[26]
19:10 ܠܐ ܗܘܬ ܐܝܟ ܓܐܪܐ ܕܬܒܙܥܟ 'Let it not be[27] like an arrow that pierces you'.

This pattern constitutes the negative equivalent of the bipartite NC with a subject pronoun. Thus 15:9 contains the negative counterpart of *ܝܐܝܐ ܗܝ ܒܦܘܡܐ ܕܥܘܠܐ.

A NC that in its positive form would be constructed without the Ep is negated by ܠܐ without ܗܘܐ. This applies, for example, to the various categories of bipartite clauses identified in § 17.2 and the elliptical clauses in § 17.3:

---

[25] Joosten, 'Negation', 586; see also the discussion above.
[26] But 7h3 adds ܚܟܡܬܐ 'wisdom' at the end of the clause, which results in the pattern *lā (h)wā*–Pr–Su.
[27] The modal interpretation is required by the context.

1. Participial clauses:

16:27 ܠܐ ܟܦܢܝܢ ܘܠܐ ܨܗܝܢ ܘܠܐ ܠܐܝܢ ܘܠܐ ܡܬܛܪܦܝܢ ܘܠܐ ܡܣܬܘܚܪܝܢ ܚܝܠܗܘܢ 'And they do not hunger, nor thirst, nor labour, nor weary themselves and they do not lack strength'.

30:19 ܡܢܐ ܗܢܝܢ ܐܝܬ ܠܦܬܟܪܐ ܕܥܡܡܐ ܐܝܠܝܢ ܕܠܐ ܐܟܠܝܢ ܘܠܐ ܫܬܝܢ ܘܠܐ ܡܪܝܚܝܢ 'What profit is there to the idols of the nations, who cannot eat, nor drink, nor smell'.

With a subject pronoun of the 2nd pers. sing.:

12:15 ܠܐ ܡܨܐ ܐܢܬ ܠܩܘܒܠܗ 'You will be no match for him'.

This is the negative counterpart of the bipartite construction *ܡܨܐ ܐܢܬ ܠܩܘܒܠܗ; cf. § 17.2 (1). The other participial clauses are the negative counterpart of either the Pr–Su$_{pron}$ or its equivalent with ellipsis of the subject pronoun.

2. Circumstantial clauses containing a prepositional phrase:

19:16 ܐܝܬ ܓܝܪ ܕܡܫܬܪܥ ܘܠܐ ܡܢ ܠܒܗ ܘܐܝܬܘ ܕܡܬܬܩܠ ܘܠܐ ܒܠܫܢܗ 'For there is one who sins unintentionally, and there is one who has stumbled, but not with his tongue'.

3. Relative clauses:

9:8 ܒܫܘܦܪܐ ܕܠܐ ܕܝܠܟ 'By a beauty that is not yours'.

Since the distribution of bipartite and tripartite NCs does not always follow strict rules, it is not surprising that the use of ܠܐ and ܠܐ ܗܘܐ does not follow strict rules either. Compare the use of ܗܘܐ in ܠܐ ܗܘܐ ܪܓܝܓ in 15:9 quoted above with the absence of ܗܘܐ in

14:3 ܠܐ ܪܓܝܓ ܥܘܬܪܐ '(To the feeble heart) riches are not fitting'.

Heb has ܠܐ corresponding to ܠܐ ܗܘܐ in Syr in 7:13 (A), 15:9 (A+B), 37:28 (B). In 50:25 Heb (B) has איננו. In 5:4 Heb (C) has ומה יהיה לו (A ומה יעשה לי).[28] That only in this case Heb has a form of היה corresponding to ܗܘܐ in Syr supports our analysis of ܗܘܐ as a full verb in this verse (see above).

---

[28] The use of מה as a negation is well-attested in Classical Hebrew; cf. Van Peursen, 'Negation', 231–232.

23.2.5 ܠܐ ܗܘܐ *in verbal clauses*

In negative verbal clauses ܠܐ usually comes directly before the verb.[29] If, however, an element other than the verb is negated, this element follows ܠܐ immediately. In Syr there is one example in

> 34:23 ܘܐܦ ܠܐ ܒܣܓܝܐܘܬ ܩܘܪܒܢܝܗܘܢ ܫܒܩ ܠܗܘܢ 'And He does not forgive them because of the multitude of offerings'.

More common is the construction with ܠܐ ܗܘܐ.[30] It is placed immediately before the word or phrase that is negated. This happens four times in Syr:

> 3:10 ܡܛܠ ܕܠܐ ܗܘܐ ܐܝܩܪܐ ܗܘܐ ܠܟ 'Because it is no honour to you'.
> 12:1 ܠܐ ܗܘܐ ܡܕܡ ܥܒܕ ܐܢܬ 'You are doing nothing at all'.
> 15:9 ܡܛܠ ܕܠܐ ܗܘܐ ܡܢ ܩܕܡ ܐܠܗܐ ܐܬܝܗܒܬ ܠܗܘܢ 'Because not from God is it given to him'.
> 29:7 ܕܠܐ ܗܘܐ ܡܢ ܒܝܫܘܬܐ ܐܬܟܠܝܘ ܠܡܘܙܦܘ '(There are many) who refrained from lending, (but) not out of wickedness'.

29:7 contains the negative counterpart of *ܕܡܢ ܒܝܫܘܬܐ ܐܬܟܠܝܘ ܠܡܘܙܦܘ or perhaps even better: *ܕܡܢ ܒܝܫܘܬܐ ܗܘ ܐܬܟܠܝܘ ܠܡܘܙܦܘ.[31] The example from 3:10 is remarkable because the main verb in the clause is a verb of ܗܘܐ as well. This shows that the first ܗܘܐ does not function as a full verb. Heb has לא corresponding to ܠܐ ܗܘܐ in Syr in 3:10 (A) and 15:9 (A). In 12:1 it has a completely different reading.

23.2.6 *Other constructions with the perfect of* ܗܘܐ

There are four examples of post-predicative ܗܘܐ following a prepositional phrase:

> 2:10 ܠܡܕܡ ܕܡܢ ܠܩܕܡܝܢ ܗܘܐ '(Consider closely) that which was before'
> 24:11 ܘܒܐܘܪܫܠܡ ܫܘܠܛܢܝ ܗܘܐ 'And in Jerusalem was my authority'.
> 37:30 ܡܛܠ ܕܡܢ ܣܓܝܐܘܬܐ ܕܡܐܟܘܠܬܐ ܗܘܐ ܡܪܥܐ 'Because from the abundance of food comes disease'.
> 48:25 ܘܟܕ ܒܥܠܡܐ ܗܘܐ 'And when he was in the world'.

In 37:30 ܗܘܐ functions as a full verb with the meaning 'to become'. The three other clauses express situated existence,[32] and the function

---

[29] Nöldeke, *Grammatik*, § 328.
[30] Cf. Nöldeke, *Grammatik*, § 328B; Duval, *Traité*, § 380*b*.
[31] See Chapter 24 on cleft sentences.

of ܗܘܐ is to mark the past tense of the NC. Thus 24:11 contains the past equivalent of e.g. *ܘܒܐܘܪܫܠܡ ܫܘܠܛܢܝ or *ܘܐܝܬ ܒܐܘܪܫܠܡ ܫܘܠܛܢܝ.[33] In his PhD dissertation Morrison has demonstrated that Pesh-Samuel frequently uses ܗܘܐ where the Masoretic Text has a NC.[34]

In addition to the cases of imperatival *hwayt qātel* discussed in § 23.2.2, there are four examples where the perfect of ܗܘܐ precedes a participial:

20:21 ܕܗܘܐ ܙܕܝܩܐ ܘܥܠ ܥܘܬܪܗ ܡܬܬܟܝܠ '(Who is it) who is righteous and rests on riches?'
31:6 ܕܗܘܘ ܥܬܝܪܐ ܘܐܬܬܟܠܘ ܥܠ ܢܟܣܝܗܘܢ 'Who were rich and who relied upon their possessions'.
41:7 ܕܒܡܛܠܬܗ ܗܘܘ ܡܒܣܪܐ ܒܥܠܡܐ 'For because of him they are scorned in the world'.
47:14 ܟܡܐ ܚܟܝܡ ܗܘܝܬ ܒܛܠܝܘܬܟ 'How wise you were in your youth'.

Sometimes the perfect of ܗܘܐ precedes a prepositional phrase, e.g.:[35]

6:11 ܒܛܒܬܟ ܗܘܐ ܐܟܘܬܟ 'In your prosperity he will be like you'.
44:7 ܒܕܪܝܗܘܢ ܗܘܐ ܠܗܘܢ ܐܝܩܪܐ 'All these had honour in their generations'.

Compare also the pattern with ܗܘܐ + ܠ (beneficiary) + ܠ (predicative complement), e.g.:

31:10 ܘܗܘܐ ܠܗ ܠܬܫܒܘܚܬܐ 'And it is for him to a praise'.
45:15 ܘܗܘܬ ܠܗ ܠܩܝܡܐ ܕܠܥܠܡ 'And it became for him an eternal covenant'.
51:17 ܢܝܪܗ ܗܘܐ ܠܝ ܠܐܝܩܪܐ 'Her yoke was to me an honour'.

ܗܘܐ followed by a noun as predicative complement is attested as well, e.g.:[36]

44:17 ܒܙܒܢܐ ܕܛܘܦܢܐ ܗܘܐ ܚܠܘܦܬܐ ܠܥܠܡܐ 'In the time of the flood he became a substitute'.[37]
46:4 ܘܗܘܐ ܝܘܡܐ ܚܕ ܬܪܝܢ ܝܘܡܝܢ 'And one day became two days'.

---

[32] For the concept of situated existence see § 22.1; for clauses with ܐܝܬ and other constructions indicating situated existence see §§ 22.4–22.5.
[33] See § 22.5.1 (D); cf. Van Rompay, 'Post-Predicative *hwā*', 211: 'In its reduced status, as a perfect form and placed after the predicate, *hwā* is used to mark the past tense in the nominal sentence'; similarly Wertheimer, 'Syriac Nominal Sentences', 15.
[34] Morrison, *First Book of Samuel* (1995), 147. This section has not been included in the revised version of this dissertation, which appeared in the MPIL series.
[35] See also the examples in Nöldeke, *Grammatik*, § 299.
[36] See also the examples in Nöldeke, *Grammatik*, § 299.
[37] Instead of ܗܘܐ 7a1 reads ܗܘܬ; see Owens, 'Early Syriac Text of Ben Sira', 68.

49:7 ܡ ܟܐܢ ܟܐܢ ܡ ܟܐ ܟ ܟ ܟ 'Who was a prophet from his mother's womb'.

In these cases ܟܐ is used as a full verb with the meaning 'to be, to become'.[38]

Heb has a form of היה corresponding to ܟܐ in Syr in 31:10 (B), 44:17 (B), 45:15 (B), 51:17 (B+M). It has a NC with הוא in 6:11 (A) and 49:7 (B). In 44:7 Heb (B^mg+M) has נכבדו corresponding to ܟܐ ܟ ܟܐ ܟ in Syr. In 37:30 B(+D) has יקנן חולי corresponding to ܟ ܟܐ in Syr, and in 48:25 B has עד עולם corresponding to ܟ ܟ ܟܐ ܟ ܟ in Syr (cf. § 3.5).

23.3 THE IMPERFECT OF ܟܐ

23.3.1 *General survey*

As with the perfect of ܟܐ we can make a distinction between cases where the predicative complement is a participial and cases where it is another element. A frequent usage of the imperfect concerns the negative imperative. The construction with the imperfect of ܟܐ expresses durative or repeated actions.[39] Sometimes ܟܐ is used as a verb of existence, without a predicative complement. This happens in

29:9 ܟ ܟ ܟܐ ܟ ܟ 'If there is a loss'.
44:17 ܟ ܟ ܟܐ ܟ ܟ 'That there would be no flood again'.

23.3.2 *ܟܐ + participial*

The imperfect of ܟܐ followed by a participle is sometimes used for the expression of a negative command, e.g.:

3:25 ܟ ܟ ܟܐ ܟ ܟ 'Do not counsel to persuade' (i.e. 'Do not give persuasive advice').[40]

---

[38] Cf. Van Rompay, 'Post-Predicative *hwā*', 211.

[39] Cf. Nöldeke, *Grammatik*, § 300: 'Das Impf. ܟܐ wird gern dem Participium vorangestellt, um das Impf. zu umschreiben (...) Diese Verbindung steht besonders, um dauernde oder sich wiederholende oder doch gesetzlich bestimmte Handlungen auszudrücken.'

[40] However Calduch-Benages–Ferrer–Liesen, *Sabiduria del Escriba*, 76: 'And he (...) will not be a persuasive counsellor'.

5:9 ܠܐ ܬܗܘܐ ܕܪܝ ܠܟܠ ܪܘܚ 'Do not winnow [= ܬܕܪܐ] in every wind'.
23:9 ܘܥܡ ܕܝܢܐ ܠܐ ܬܗܘܐ ܝܬܒ 'And do not sit among judges'.

This use can be contrasted with that of the non-periphrastic prohibitive (also with the verb ܝܬܒ, as in 23:9) in

8:14 ܠܐ ܬܬܒ ܥܡ ܕܝܢܐ ܥܘܠܐ ܒܕܝܢܐ 'Do not sit together with an unrighteous judge in judgment'.
27:15 ܥܡ ܪܫܝܥܐ ܠܐ ܬܬܒ 'Do not sit among the wicked'.

ܗܘܐ + adjective occurs in e.g.

4:29 ܠܐ ܬܗܘܐ ܫܒܗܪܢ ܒܠܫܢܟ 'Be not boastful with your tongue'.
40:28 ܘܠܐ ܬܗܘܐ ܛܒ ܠܡܩܛܠ 'And be not good to kill'.

The imperfect 2nd pers. masc. sing. of ܗܘܐ + participial is also used in other contexts. An example with a participle:

1:201 ܘܡܐ ܬܗܘܐ ܩܪܒ 'And when you draw near'.

And with an adjective:

13:4 ܐܢ ܬܗܘܐ ܚܫܚ ܠܗ 'If you are profitable to him'.
18:32 ܕܠܐ ܬܗܘܐ ܡܣܟܢ 'Lest you become twofold poor'.

Here too we can contrast *tehwē qātel* with the non-periphrastic construction (also with ܩܪܒ as in 1:201) in

13:9 ܘܡܐ ܕܩܪܒ ܗܘ ܥܬܝܪܐ 'If a rich man draws near to you'.

Compare also the construction with participle + pronoun in a conditional clause in

9:13 ܘܐܢ ܩܪܒ ܐܢܬ 'And if you draw near'.

The periphrastic construction is also used with the imperfect of the 3rd person:

4:31 ܠܐ ܬܗܘܐ ܦܫܝܛܐ ܐܝܕܟ ܠܡܣܒ 'Let not your hand be stretched out to take'.
14:20 ܕܡܬܗܓܐ ܗܘܐ ܒܚ̈ܟܡܬܐ '(Blessed is the man) who reflects upon wisdom'.
14:26 ܘܥܡ ܣܘ̈ܟܝܗ ܗܘܐ ܫܪܐ 'And he dwells among her branches'.
17:9 ܕܢܗܘܘܢ ܡܫܬܥܝܢ ܕܚܠܬܗ ܒܥܠܡܐ 'That they would tell His fear in the world'.
17:10 ܘܠܫܡܗ ܩܕܝܫܐ ܢܗܘܘܢ ܡܫܒܚܝܢ 'And they will praise His holy name'.
25:1 ܟܕ ܢܗܘܘܢ ܫܠܝܢ 'When they are at peace'.
49:10 ܢܗܘܘܢ ܓܪ̈ܡܝܗܘܢ ܡܙܗܪܝܢ ܬܚܘܬܝܗܘܢ 'May their bones shine beneath them'.

51:24 ܘܢܦܫܟܘܢ ܬܗܘܐ ܨܗܝܐ ܠܚܕܐ ‘And (how long) will your soul be very thirsty?’.[41]

A number of the verbs used in the examples above are also employed in the non-periphrastic construction:

ܪܢܐ 50:28 ܕܒܗܠܝܢ ܪܢܐ ‘(Blessed is the man) who reflects upon these things’.
ܫܥܐ 44:15 ܘܬܫܒܘܚܬܗܘܢ ܬܫܬܥܐ ܥܡܐ ‘The people will talk about their praise’.
ܫܒܚ 37:24 ܘܡܫܒܚܝܢ ܠܗ ܟܠܗܘܢ ܚܙܝܘܗܝ ‘And all who see him will praise him’.
ܫܠܡ 13:18 ܡܢܐ ܬܫܠܡ ܐܦܥܐ ܠܟܠܒܐ ‘How can a hyena have peace with a dog’.
ܢܗܪ 46:12 ܘܢܗܪܘܢ ܓܪܡܝܗܘܢ ܐܝܟ ܫܘܫܢܐ ‘May their bones be clear like lilies’.
ܨܗܐ 24:21 ܘܫܬܝܢܝ ܬܘܒ ܢܨܗܘܢ ܠܝ ‘And those who drink me will still thirst for me’.

Nehwē + adjective is attested in e.g.

6:6 ܫܐܠܝ ܫܠܡܟ ܢܗܘܘܢ ܣܓܝܐܝܢ ‘Let those who greet you be many’.
28:13 ܘܐܦ ܠܫܢܐ ܬܠܝܬܝܐ ܠܝܛ ܢܗܘܐ ‘And also the triple tongue will be cursed’.[42]
35:11 ܒܟܠ ܡܘܗܒܬܟ ܢܗܘܘܢ ܢܗܝܪܝܢ ܐܦܝܟ ‘With all your gifts, let your face be shining’.

Six times Heb has a form of היה corresponding to ܗܘܐ in Syr, in 4:29 (A), 4:31 (A+C), 5:9 (A+C), 6:6 (A), 49:10 (B) and 51:24 (B). In four cases it has a non-periphrastic construction: לא תשב in 8:14 (A); אם תכשר in 13:4 (A); יתלונן in 14:26 (A); and האר פנים in 35:11 (B).

23.3.3 *nehwē + noun or prepositional phrase*

Whereas *nehwē qātel* constitutes a contrastive pair with the non-periphrastic construction, *nehwē* + noun or prepositional phrase forms a contrastive pair with the simple NC and its complex equivalents. Most often the verb serves to express future tense or to add a modal nuance. The modal nuance is clear when *la tehwē* + predicative complement expresses a negative command, e.g.:

---

[41] For our translation of ܠܚܕܐ see Joosten, ‘Eléments d’araméen occidental’.
[42] This is the only example in Syr where the finite verb follows the predicative complement.

4:30 ܠܐ ܬܗܘܐ ܟܠܒ ܒܒܝܬܟ ‘Do not behave like a dog in your house’.
8:10 ܠܐ ܬܗܘܐ ܫܘܬܦܐ ܠܪܫܝܥܐ ܓܡܝܪܐ ‘Be not an associate for the wicked one who is complete’.[43]
37:11 ܠܐ ܬܗܘܐ ܠܗ ܒܥܠ ܡܠܟܐ ‘Be not a counsellor for him’.

Other examples with the imperfect of the 2nd person (without ܠܐ):

4:10 ܘܬܗܘܐ ܠܐܠܗܐ ܐܝܟ ܒܪܐ ‘And you will be to God like a son’.
50:23 ܘܢܗܘܐ ܫܠܡܐ ܒܝܢܬܗܘܢ ‘And He will be (or: there will be) peace among them’.

Examples with the imperfect of the 3rd person:

2:6 ܘܗܘ ܢܗܘܐ ܠܟ ܡܥܕܪܢܐ ‘And He will be a helper to you’.
6:29 ܘܢܗܘܘܢ ܠܟ ܡܨܝܕܬܗ ܡܘܬܒܐ ܥܫܝܢܐ ‘Her snares will be for you a stronghold’.
8:11 ܕܠܡܐ ܢܗܘܐ ܒܟܡܐܢܐ ܘܢܟܡܢܟ ‘Lest he will be an ambush against you’.
37:2 ܪܚܡܐ ܕܫܪܪܐ ܐܝܟ ܢܦܫܟ ܢܗܘܐ ‘Let a true friend be to you like your own soul’.

Examples with post-predicative *nehwē*:

5:10 ܘܡܠܬܟ ܚܕܐ ܬܗܘܐ ‘And let your word be one’.
9:16 ܘܒܕܚܠܬܗ ܕܐܠܗܐ ܬܗܘܐ ܬܫܒܘܚܬܟ ‘And let your praise be in the fear of God’.

Heb has a form of היה corresponding to ܗܘܐ in Syr in 4:30 (A), 5:10 (A), 6:29 (A) and 50:23 (B). Where it does not have one, in 8:10, 11 (A), this may be related to other differences between Heb and Syr. In 9:16 Heb (A) has a bipartite NC: וביראת אלהים תפארתך.

23.4 OTHER FORMS OF ܗܘܐ

23.4.1 *Participle*

The construction with the participle of ܗܘܐ is only found in combination with a prepositional phrase, interrogative or adverb as predicative complement. A prepositional phrase occurs in

7:17 ܡܛܠ ܕܣܘܪܬܐ ܕܟܠܗܘܢ ܒܢܝܢܫܐ ܠܪܡܬܐ ܗܘܝܐ ‘Because the end of all the sons of men is to the maggots’.

---

43 Compare 11:7 ܠܐ ܬܫܬܘܬܦ (similarly 13:2; 22:23).

12:9 ܩܘܡ ... 'For in a man's prosperity his adversaries are in sadness'.

16:3b ... 'That they will have a good end'.

16:3e ... 'Who has many unrighteous sons'.

The predicative complement is an interrogative in

9:11 (= 11:19) ... 'What his end will be'.

It is an adverb in

26:21 ... 'And thus will be your harvest'.

In these cases the construction with ܗܘܐ is an alternative for the bi- or tripartite NC or the construction with ܐܝܬ. The reason for the use of ܗܘܐ is not always clear. Thus in 7:17 the natural construction would be ... and in 16:3 the more usual constructions would be ... and ... .

In 26:21 Heb is not extant. In all the other cases the participle of ܗܘܐ in Syr is a plus compared with Heb.

23.4.2 *Infinitive*

There are only two examples with the infinitive of ܗܘܐ. In neither case is the predicative complement a participial. It is a prepositional phrase in

46:1 ... 'Through the prophecy he was preserved to be like the great Moses'.

The predicative complement is a noun in

7:6 ... 'Do not seek to be a judge'.

In both cases Heb has להיות.

23.4.3 *Imperative*

There are only a few examples with the imperative of ܗܘܐ. More frequent is the construction with the perfect of ܗܘܐ with imperatival force (see above, § 23.2.2). If the predicative complement is a participial, *hwayt qāṭel* is used.[44] The imperative of ܗܘܐ is attested in

4:10 ܗܘܝ ܐܝܟ ܐܒܐ ܠܝܬܡܐ 'Be like a father for the orphans'.
8:13 ܗܘܝ ܐܝܟ ܦܪܘܥ '(And if you become surety), be as someone who has to pay'.
12:11 ܗܘܝ ܠܗ ܐܝܟ ܓܠܐ ܐܪܙܐ 'Be to him as a revealer of a secret'.
22:23 ܒܥܕܢ ܥܩܬܗ ܗܘܝ ܠܗ ܚܒܪܐ 'In the time of his distress be a friend to him'.
32:1 ܗܘܝ ܠܟ ܐܝܟ ܚܕ ܡܢܗܘܢ 'Be as one of them'.

Heb has an imperative of היה in 4:10 (A), 8:13 (A) and 32:1 (B+F). In 8:12 (A) it has an elliptical construction without a form of היה. Whereas ܗܘܐ + participial functions as a free variant of the non-periphrastic construction, and often corresponds with a non-periphrastic construction in Heb, in these cases where the predicative complement is a noun or prepositional phrase such alternation is impossible. Likewise, whereas clauses with the perfect, imperfect or participle of ܗܘܐ and a nominal or prepositional predicative complement may correspond to NCs in Heb, such a free alternation is impossible with the imperative.

23.5 THE STATE OF THE PREDICATIVE COMPLEMENTS

In the present chapter we have seen several types of predicative complements. Where the predicative complement is a participial, it is most often in the absolute state, e.g.:

5:11 ܗܘܝܬ ܡܣܪܗܒ ܠܡܫܡܥ 'Be quick to hear'.
6:13 ܘܡܢ ܪܚܡܟ ܗܘܝܬ ܙܗܝܪ 'And be on your guard for your friend'.
47:14 ܟܡܐ ܚܟܝܡ ܗܘܝܬ ܒܛܠܝܘܬܟ 'How wise you were in your youth'.

There are some exceptions:

20:21 ܕܗܘܐ ܙܕܝܩܐ 'Who is righteous'.
31:6 ܕܗܘܘ ܥܬܝܪܐ 'Who were rich'.
41:7 ܕܡܛܠܬܗ ܗܘܘ ܒܨܝܪܐ ܒܥܠܡܐ 'For because of him they are scorned in the world'.

If the predicative complement is a noun, it usually takes the emphatic state, e.g.:

[44] An exception is the variant reading in 40:28; see above, § 23.2.2 (end). For other examples with ܗܘܝ + participial see Duval, *Traité*, § 334*c*.

2:6 ܪܝܫܐ ܠܟ ܗܘܐ ܘܗܘ 'And He will be a helper to you'.

8:10 ܪܫܝܥܐ ܠܚܒܪܐ ܬܫܬܘܬܦ ܗܘܝܬ ܠܐ 'Be not an associate for the wicked one who is complete'.

An exception occurs in

4:30 ܒܒܝܬܟ ܠܟܠܒ ܗܘܝܬ ܠܐ 'Do not behave like a dog in your house'.

The use of the absolute state indicates an 'adjectivization' of the noun.[45] In bipartite and tripartite NCs too the predicative complement is usually in the absolute state when it is a participial and in the emphatic state when it is a noun (§ 20.1).

23.6 CONCLUSION

In Syr there are thirteen cases of *hwayt qātel* with imperatival force. *Hwayt qātel* indicates a wish, advice or obligation of general and universal applicability. In most cases it corresponds to a simple imperative in Heb. The construction with the imperative of ܗܘܐ + participial (*hwi qātel*) occurs only once in a variant reading. *Hwayt qātel* constitutes a functional opposition with *qtol*, in which the former is the marked term.

Qātel (h)wā is used for frequentative aspect in the past or an ongoing situation anterior to the moment of speaking. The number of occurrences is low compared with the large number of verbs referring to past events. As with *hwayt qātel*, there is no reason to assume that the *qātel (h)wā* forms are due to the influence of a Hebrew source text. There is a functional opposition between *Qātel (h)wā* and *qtal* in which the former is the marked term. If the predicative complement is not a participial, ܗܘܐ serves to mark the past tense of the NC.

With the imperfect of ܗܘܐ too *nehwē qātel* constitutes a contrastive pair with the non-periphrastic construction, and *nehwē* + noun or prepositional phrase forms a contrastive pair with the simple NC and its complex equivalents. Most often the verb serves to express future tense or to add a modal nuance.

ܠܐ ܗܘܐ is used for the negation of a NC. It is placed immediately before the word or phrase that is being negated. The verb in ܠܐ ܗܘܐ does not imply past tense, but simply the negation of the NC. ܠܐ

---

[45] Cf. § 20.1 on NCs without ܗܘܐ.

ܟܘܡ + Su + Pr is the negative equivalent of the tripartite NC and ܠܐ ܟܘܡ + Pr that of the bipartite NC with a subject pronoun. In verbal clauses ܟܘܡ ܠܐ is used if an element other than the verb is negated.

The construction with the participle of ܟܘܡ is only found in combination with a prepositional phrase, interrogative or adverb as predicative complement. In these cases the construction with ܟܘܡ is an alternative for the bi- or tripartite NC or the construction with ܐܝܬ. The reason for the use of ܟܘܡ is not always clear.

If the predicative complement is a participle or adjective, it is most often in the absolute state; if it is a noun, it usually takes the emphatic state. These and other observations support Goldenberg's thesis that in the domain of syntax the category of participials should be considered as also comprising the participial adjectives.

CHAPTER TWENTY-FOUR

CLEFT SENTENCES

24.1 INTRODUCTION

In Chapter 18 we have seen that in tripartite NCs of the type Su–Ep–Pr the Ep serves to rhematize or focalize the preceding Su. If one follows a pragmatic definition of Su and Pr, this means that it marks the preceding element as the Pr (§ 18.2 [C]). But the rhematizing function of the Ep is not restricted to NCs. Also in verbal clauses the Ep is used to mark an element other that the verb as the comment or most salient information, in a pragmatic definition: to mark any preceding element as the Pr, as in 46:6 ܩܘܡܠܐ ܐܬܘܪ ܗܘ ܐܠܗܐܕ 'that *God* joined the battle with them' or 'that it was God who joined the battle with them'.

Clauses of this type have been called 'cleft sentences',[1] because of their similarities with this category in other languages. The term 'cleft sentence' was introduced by O. Jespersen for sentences such as *it is... who, c'est lui, qui...* The sentences are cleft in order 'to single out one particular element of the sentence and very often, by directing attention to it and bringing it, as it were, into focus'.[2] In these sentences the logical Pr is turned into the formal Pr of a nominal or copular sentence and the rest of the utterance is nominalized so as to become a subject clause of that sentence.[3] The focalized logical Pr is designated with the French term *vedette*, the rest of the utterance with the term *glose*. Thus cleaving the sentence 'you broke the window' results in 'it is you who broke the window' (or 'it is the window that you broke'); 'you' is the *vedette* and 'who broke the window' the *glose*, which serves as an explanation or gloss to 'it':[4]

---

[1] More precisely, 'imperfectly-transformed cleft sentences', see below, § 24.2.
[2] Wertheimer, 'Cleft Sentences', 222, quoting Jespersen; idem, 'More Thoughts', 22; see also Jespersen, *Analytical Syntax* 73–74.
[3] Cf. Goldenberg, 'Cleft Sentences', 128.
[4] Goldenberg, 'Cleft Sentences', 128; cf. Wertheimer, 'Cleft Sentences', 223.

It is	you	who broke the window
pronominal subject	*vedette*	*glose*

24.2 CLEFT SENTENCES IN SYRIAC LINGUISTICS

In Syriac studies 'cleft sentence' is employed to designate clauses of the type ܐܝܬܘܪ ܗܘ ܐܢܬ 'it is you who said'. Here the enclitic ܗܘ 'cleaves' the sentence into two parts. Schematically it can be analysed as X – Ep – (verbal) clause, in which X (in the example: ܐܢܬ) is the *vedette* and the clause following the enclitic (ܐܝܬܘܪ) the *glose*. The enclitic can be considered as a pronominal Su with a function similar to 'it' in English cleft sentences:[5]

ܐܢܬ	ܗܘ	ܐܝܬܘܪ
X	Ep	clause
vedette	pronominal subject	*glose*

The Syriac cleft sentences disagree with the usual definition of cleft sentences in three respects:

1. The *glose* is not marked formally as nominalized. We do not find *ܐܝܬܘܪܐ ܗܘ ܐܢܬ (or *ܐܝܬܘܪܐ ܗܘ ܐܢܬ).[6]
2. When the clause is the transformation of a clause in which the X was the grammatical Su of the clause (e.g. ܐܝܬܘܪ ܗܘ ܐܢܬ as a transformation of ܐܝܬܘܪ 'you said') the *glose* still agrees with it, i.e. we do not find *ܐܝܬܪ ܗܘ ܐܢܬ.[7]
3. The *vedette* precedes the pronominal Su.[8]

For Goldenberg these differences between the Syriac sentences under discussion and the 'standard' cleft sentences are reason to call the

---

[5] Cf. Wertheimer, 'Cleft Sentences', 223.

[6] The only exception is ܐ ܗܘ ܐ, ܐ ܐܡܪ 'if it is that...'; Goldenberg, 'Cleft Sentences', 130 n. 9; Nöldeke, *Grammatik*, § 374B; Duval, *Traité*, § 414; see also Bravmann, *Arabic and General Syntax*, 55. Compare the absence of a subordinate particle in English sentences of the type 'It is she I so admire'; (ibid., 53; Goldenberg, 'Niceties', 340). Contrast the presence of the Dalath in Babylonian Aramaic, on which see Goldenberg, 'Cleft Sentences', 128; idem, 'Niceties', 340.

[7] Cf. Goldenberg, 'Cleft Sentences', 129: 'But in Syriac, the finite verb that follows the enclitic ܗܘ in this construction is never marked formally as nominal to fit into the position it actually occupies, namely that of an extraposed topic.' See also idem, 'Tautological Infinitive', 50–57.

[8] Wertheimer, 'Cleft Sentences', 223.

former 'imperfectly-transformed cleft sentences'.[9] For Muraoka they are reason to abandon the term 'cleft sentences' altogether.[10]

24.3 CLEFT SENTENCES AND RHEMATIZATION

In § 24.1 we have seen that the main function of the so-called cleft sentences is rhematization. In verbal clauses the verb usually is or contains the new information. If another element in the clause contains the salient information, a device is needed to turn the verb into the topic and that other element into the comment.[11] The rhematization is achieved by the enclitic element, either because it 'cleaves' the sentence and turns the preceding element into the predicate (Goldenberg) or because it is a particle that gives prominence or focus to the preceding element (Muraoka). Here too Goldenberg and Muraoka differ in their syntactic analysis of the construction, but agree in the evaluation of its function.[12]

As in the case of tripartite NCs we prefer to keep apart the syntactic and the pragmatic analysis. We agree with Goldenberg and Muraoka that the enclitic in the so-called cleft sentences functions as a rhematizer, turning the preceding element into the comment, but we think that there is not sufficient evidence for the claim that it is a device to turn the 'logical Pr' into the *grammatical* Pr.

In Syr the Ep follows the grammatical Su in

    28:5 ܡܠ ܠܡܐ ܪܨܘ ܪܠ ܗܘ ܪܐܝܗ ܗܘ 'He whom a human being does not want to forgive (who will forgive him his sins?)

    30:22 ܡܘܥܝܝ ܪܥܘܐ ܝܡ ܪܐܝܗ ܡܚܝܐܗ 'And a man's reflections make his life long'.

    37:13 ܡܥܝܝܗ ܝܡ ܡܗܢܡܘܡ ܠܐܝ 'Because his faithfulness makes him live'.[13]

---

[9] For the sake of brevity we will use the term 'cleft sentences' for Goldenberg's 'imperfectly-transformed cleft sentences'.

[10] Muraoka, 'Response to Wido van Peursen', 195.

[11] In the case of tripartite NCs, the discussion about the rhematizing function of the Ep is confused by different definitions of Su and Pr: Is the element preceding the Ep by definition the Pr, or may the Ep also mark the grammatical Su as the comment, thus marking a deviation from its 'default' pragmatic function? See §§ 18.2 (C), 24.1.

[12] Cf. Goldenberg, 'Cleft Sentences', esp. 116; idem, 'Niceties', 337–340; idem, 'Syriac Idiom', 26–28; idem, 'Tautological Infinitive', 50–51; Muraoka, *Classical Syriac for Hebraists*, § 103; idem, *Basic Grammar*, § 104.

46:6 ܕܐܠܗܐ ܗܘ ܐܬܩܪܒ ܥܡܗܘܢ 'That God joined the battle with them'.

The Ep follows a prepositional verbal complement in[14]

13:16 ܘܠܓܢܣܗ ܗܘ ܡܬܕܒܩ ܒܪܢܫܐ 'And a man clings to his own kind'.
29:28 ܘܠܐܠܗܐ ܗܘ ܡܘܙܦ ܐܢܬ 'And you lend to God'.
37:8 ܡܛܠ ܕܐܦ ܗܘ ܒܢܦܫܗ ܗܘ ܡܬܪܢܐ 'Because he too has himself in mind'.[15]

The Ep follows an adjunct in

4:24 ܡܛܠ ܕܒܡܐܡܪܐ ܗܘ ܡܬܝܕܥܐ ܚܟܡܬܐ 'Because wisdom becomes known through speech'.
11:28 ܡܛܠ ܕܒܚܪܬܗ ܗܘ ܡܫܬܒܚ ܒܪܢܫܐ 'Because in his end a man will be praised'.
51:27 ܡܛܠ ܕܙܥܘܪ ܗܘ ܥܡܠܬ ܒܗ 'Because I laboured for her a little'.

In a number of cases a cleft sentence is preceded by an extraposed element. In this construction the topicalizing function of extraposition (§ 21.2) and the rhematizing function of the Ep in cleft sentences is clearly visible, e.g.:

38:27b ܘܠܠܝܐ ܘܐܝܡܡܐ ܒܗܘܢ ܗܘ ܪܢܝܢ 'And night and day—on these things they reflect'.
38:27d (7h3) ܘܐܦ ܡܚܫܒܬܗܘܢ ܠܥܒܕܐ ܗܘ ܕܐܘܡܢܘܬܗܘܢ ܡܬܒܥܝܢ 'And also their thoughts—they are needed for the work of their craftsmanship'.[16]

Interrogative clauses take the form of a cleft sentence very frequently, e.g.:

12:13 ܡܢܘ ܓܝܪ ܢܪܚܡ ܥܠ ܐܫܘܦܐ 'For who will have mercy on a charmer (whom a serpent has bitten)?'

Since interrogative pro-words are by definition logical predicates, they are especially apt to enter the position of the *vedette* of a cleft sentence.[17] Clauses of this type too are often preceded by an element in extraposition, e.g.:

---

13 The word that is focalized here plays a prominent role in Syr and other witnesses of SirII, see § 2.4.1.

14 See also 38:27b, 27d, quoted below.

15 For an alternative analysis see § 21.2 (A), n. 7. The second ܗܘ does not occur in 7a1.

16 ܗܘ does not occur in the other textual witnesses.

17 Goldenberg, 'Cleft Sentences', 130. Cf. French *qu'est-ce que*... On Syriac ܡܢܘ (= ܡܢ ܗܘ) see Nöldeke, *Grammatik*, §§ 233, 311 (end).

1:2 ܐܠܘ ܘܐ̈ܒܠܐ ܕܝܡܐ ܘܢ̈ܛܘ̈ܦܐ ܕܡܛܪܐ ܘ̈ܝܘܡܬܐ ܕܥܠܡܐ ܡܢܘ ܡܫܟܚ ܠܡܡܢܐ
'The sand of the sea, the drops of the rain and the days of eternity—
who can count (them)?'[18]

As far as Heb is available, it does not have an element corresponding
to the Ep.[19] In 46:6 Syr differs from Heb not only in the use of the Ep,
but also in word order:

46:6 ܕܐܠܗܐ ܗܘ ܐܩܪܒ ܥܡܗܘܢ 'That God joined the battle with them';
B כי צופה יי' מלחמתם.

24.4 CLEFT SENTENCES AND NOMINAL CLAUSES

The analysis of the so-called cleft sentences shows similarities with
that of tripartite NCs of the type Su–Ep–Pr. The two patterns can be
represented by e.g.

ܐܢܬ ܗܘ ܐܚܝ 'You are my brother' or 'It is you who are my brother'
(tripartite NC) and
ܐܢܬ ܗܘ ܐܡܪܬ 'You said' or 'It is you who said' (cleft sentence).

The two types occur in parallelism in

30:22 ܚܕܘܬ ܠܒܐ ܐܢܘܢ ܚ̈ܝܘܗܝ ܕܓܒܪܐ, ܘܡܚ̈ܫܒܬܗ ܕܓܒܪܐ ܡܢ̈ܓܪܢ
ܚ̈ܝܘܗܝ 'Joy of the heart is a man's life and a man's reflections make
his life long'.

The function of the Ep seems to be the same in both patterns. In Muraoka's view it is a rhematizer, which adds prominence to the preceding element.[20] Goldenberg analyses both patterns as P–s ‖ Su. In his
view the *vedette* and the Ep in cleft sentences make up a nuclear

---

[18] More examples in § 21.2 (end).

[19] Cf. Goldenberg, 'Syriac Idiom', 26: 'Here Syriac idiom, perfectly represented
in the translated texts of all levels, offers means of expression more explicit than those
usually available in Hebrew or in Greek. What Hebrew and Greek in their written
forms express by word-order only, is made explicit in idiomatic Syriac'; see also
Weitzman, *Syriac Version*, 24 and idem, *From Judaism to Christianity*, 58.

[20] Muraoka, 'Response to Goldenberg', 44; idem, *Classical Syriac for Hebraists*,
§ 103: The basic function of the enclitic is 'to extrapose or underline the immediately
preceding clause component, mostly in the manner of a cleft sentence'. But in a later
publication ('Response to Wido van Peursen', 195) Muraoka says: 'In some of my
past studies I myself entertained the notion of cleft sentences as one of several possible analyses of the structure under discussion, alongside alternatives such as *casus
pendens*, extraposition, and emphasis. I now believe that that we should abandon the
category of cleft sentence as applicable at all to classical Semitic languages'.

nominal sentence that is comparable to the nucleus of Pr + Ep in tripartite NCs.[21]

---

[21] Cf. Goldenberg, 'Cleft Sentences', 129–130; idem, 'Syriac Sentence Structure',
135; idem, 'Niceties', 338–339; Wertheimer, *Problems*, 46–47. Compare also our
remarks on pronominal agreement as a means of keeping clause nuclei intact in
§ 21.3.1.

CHAPTER TWENTY-FIVE

FUNCTIONS OF THE PRONOUN

25.1 CLAUSE PATTERNS WITH THE ENCLITIC OR THE INDEPENDENT PERSONAL PRONOUN

In the preceding chapters we have seen a number of clause patterns containing the Ep or the independent personal pronoun. In the present chapter we will put them together and make a comparative analysis. We have seen the following constructions.

Bipartite nominal clauses

Pr–Su$_{pron}$ (§ 17.1 [C])

15:18 ܘܡ ܪܚܘܬ̈ܐ ܚܝܠܬ̄ܢ ܗܘ 'And He is strong in miracles'.

With a discontinuous Pr:

1:15 ܥܡ ܐܢܫ̈ܐ ,ܗ ܩܘܫܬ̈ܐ 'She is with the people of truth'.

With ellipsis of the Su (§ 17.3):

3:4 ܘܟܕ ܡܨ ܠܗ 'And when he prays'.

Su$_{pron}$–Pr (§ 17.1 [D])

Only examples in which the Pr is a participial:

1:20 ܕܗܝ̈, ܛܒ̄ܐ ܠܗ ܡܢ ܟܠ ܣܝܡ̈ܬܐ 'To whom she is better than all treasures'.

Another element precedes the Su:

13:13 ܕܥܡ ܡܚܒ̈ܠܢܐ ܐܢܬ ܡܗܠܟ 'That you walk with despoilers'.

Tripartite nominal clauses

Su–Pr–Ep (§ 18.2 [A])

1:1 ܠܟ ܫܘܒܚܬܐ ܡܢ ܡܪܡ ܡܪܝܐ ܗܝ, 'All wisdom comes from the Lord'.

The Su is a pronoun:

1:1 ܘܡܗ ܥܡܗ ܗܝ, ܡܢ ܠܥܠܡ 'And she is with Him from eternity'.

The Su is an infinitive:

27:21 ܠܡܓܠܐ ܪܙܐ ܕܐܝܬ ܦܘܡ ܣܘܡܐ ܗܘ ܡܒܕܐ 'But to reveal secrets is despair'.

Pr–Ep–Su (§ 18.2 [B])

5:6 ܕܡܪܚܡܢܐ ܗܘ ܡܪܝܐ 'The Lord is merciful'.

The Su is an infinitive:

11:21 ܡܛܠ ܕܣܘܢ ܗܘ ܡܪܡ ܡܪܝܐ ܠܡܥܬܪܘ ܠܡܣܟܢܐ ܡܢ ܫܠܝܐ 'For it is in the Lord's power to make the poor one rich suddenly'.

With a discontinuous Pr:

2:11 ܡܛܠ ܕܚܢܢܐ ܗܘ ܘܡܪܚܡܢܐ ܡܪܝܐ 'Because the Lord is compassionate and merciful'.

The Pr is an interrogative:

18:8 ܡܢܐ ܐܢܘܢ ܒܢܝܢܫܐ 'What are the sons of man?'

Su–Ep–Pr (§ 18.2 [C])

16:11 ܗܘܝܘ ܬܗܪܐ 'It would be amazing'.

The Su is a personal pronoun of the 2nd pers. masc. (§ 18.3):

36:22 ܕܐܢܬ ܗܘ ܐܠܗܐ ܒܠܚܘܕܝܟ 'That you alone are God'.

The Su is a personal pronoun of the 3rd pers. masc.; contraction with the Ep:

41:3 ܡܛܠ ܕܡܢܬܟ ܗܝ 'Because it is your portion'.

The Su is an interrogative pronoun; with extraposition (§ 21.2, end):

1:2 ܚܠܐ ܕܝܡܐ ܘܢܘܛܦܬܐ ܕܡܛܪܐ ܘܝܘܡܬܐ ܕܥܠܡܐ ܡܢܘ ܡܫܟܚ ܠܡܡܢܐ 'The sand of the sea, the drops of the rain and the days of eternity—who can count (them)?'

Pr–Su–Ep (§ 18.2 [D])

6:16 ܘܐܝܟܢܐ ܕܕܚܠ ܠܐܠܗܐ ܗܘܝܘ '(A faithful friend is a medicine of life) and he who fears God is one'.

Quadripartite nominal clauses

Su–pron–Ep–Pr (§ 19.1)

19:20 ܘܕܚܠܬܗ ܕܐܠܗܐ ܗܝ ܗܝ ܚܟܡܬܐ 'And fear of God is wisdom'.

Not attested in Syr: Pr–pron–Ep–Su.

'Cleft sentences'

Su–Ep–Verb (§ 24.3)

46:6 ܕܐܠܗܐ ܗܘ ܐܩܪܒ ܥܡܗܘܢ 'That God joined the battle with them'.

The Su is an interrogative pronoun:

12:13 ܡܢܘ ܓܝܪ ܢܚܘܣ ܥܠ ܐܫܘܦܐ 'For who will have mercy on a charmer (whom a serpent has bitten)?'

The Su is an interrogative pronoun; the object stands in extraposition:

10:29 ܡܢ ܕܡܚܝܒ ܢܦܫܗ ܡܢܘ ܢܙܕܩܝܘܗܝ 'He who condemns himself—who will acquit him?'

Complement–Ep–Verb (§ 24.3)

29:28c ܘܠܐܠܗܐ ܗܘ ܡܘܙܦ ܐܢܬ 'And you lend to God'.

Preceded by an element in extraposition:

38:27 ܘܠܠܝܐ ܘܐܝܡܡܐ ܒܗܘܢ ܗܘ ܪܢܐ 'And night and day they reflect upon these things'.

Adjunct–Ep–Verb (§ 24.3)

51:27 ܡܛܠ ܕܙܥܘܪ ܗܘ ܥܡܠܬ ܒܗ 'Because I laboured for her a little'.

In Syr we do not find cases where the Ep follows a verb as in

Laws 539 ܐܢ ܬܐܠܦ ܗܘ ܨܒܝܬ 'If it is learning that you desire'.[1]

---

[1] Ed. Drijvers, 4, line 19; cf. Nöldeke, *Grammatik,* § 221.

Extraposition

Personal pronoun in extrapostion (§ 21.2 A [a]):

37:8 ܪܨܝܗܘ ܗܘ ܡܪܐܝܢ ܗܘ ܐܦ݁ܢ ܡܛܠ 'Because he too—he has himself in mind'.

Pronominal agreement

An independent pronoun precedes a nominal subject (§ 21.3 B [4]).

23:2 ܢܦܫܝ ܠܝ ܢܣܟܘܗ ܡܪܝܐ ܗܘܢ 'That the Lord forbid that I would transgress'.

25.2 DISCUSSION

In many tripartite NCs, as well as in the so-called imperfectly trans-formed cleft sentences, the enclitic ܗܘ serves to indicate focus on the immediately preceding clause constituent. This observation is valid regardless of the question as to whether we describe the Ep as an em-phatic particle that gives prominence to the preceding element (Mura-oka) or as a rhematizer, which turn the preceding element into the predicate (Goldenberg). A similar function can be identified where the preceding constituent is other than a noun or noun phrase. In fact, the enclitic pronoun may follow any part of speech, even a verb.[2]

The usages discussed in the present and preceding chapters differ from that of the independent personal pronoun in verbal clauses, al-though there is some overlap in the functions. Thus in a clause such as

15:12 ܐܬܘܠܝ ܗܘܢ '(Do not say) He caused me to stumble'.

the independent personal pronoun in first position turns the Su of ܐܬܘܠܝ into the rheme: 'It is due to Him that I stumble'. Also ܐܦ +
pronoun is frequently found in verbal clauses,[3] e.g.:

23:24 ܬܦܘܩ ܩܘܝܬܐ ܡܢ ܗܝ ܐܦ 'And also she will go out from the community'.[4]

---

[2] Muraoka, *Classical Syriac for Hebraists*, 60–61 n. 121; in his *Basic Grammar* Muraoka devotes a separate paragraph to the focusing function of the Ep (§ 110); Nöldeke, *Grammatik*, § 221; Duval, *Traité*, § 302; Brockelmann, *Grammatik*, § 194.

[3] Cf. Chapter 21, n. 6, and Nöldeke, *Grammatik*, § 220A.

In other verbal clauses the independent personal pronoun is a resumptive element, e.g.:

31:7 ܟܠܗܘܢ ܗܘ ܒܗ ܕܛܥܐ ܓܝܪ ܘܡܢ 'And everyone who goes astray through it will stumble'.

According to Muraoka the pronoun in quadripartite NCs is originally a similar resumptive element.[5]

A full discussion of these other usages is beyond the scope of the present study. The usages that have been treated show an interesting interrelatedness, even though they are often treated separately and have received different labels. The subtle ways in which the Ep can clarify the syntactic and pragmatic structure in various clause types can rightly be called a 'nicety of Syriac syntax'.[6]

---

[4] Compare also 46:6 ܐܠܗܐ ܒܬܪ ܫܠܡ ܗܘ ܘܐܦ 'And also he wholly followed God'; B: וגם כי מלא אחרי אל.

[5] See above, Chapter 19, n. 3.

[6] This designation is taken from Goldenberg's famous article 'Niceties'.

PART FIVE

TEXT HIERARCHY

CHAPTER TWENTY-SIX

PRELIMINARY REMARKS ON CLAUSE HIERARCHY

26.1 INTRODUCTION

The present chapter deals with the question of how clauses combine to constitute texts. A text differs from a collection of unrelated sentences in that it can be defined as a unified whole.[1] But what makes a text a unified whole? In what respect does a text differ from a collection of random sentences? And how is a text recognized as text? In answering these questions one can focus on logical or conceptual *coherence* relations between the individual discourse units, or concentrate on the *cohesion* of a text, brought about by the formal linguistic signals marking the interrelatedness of its units. Before we address the question of how discourse units are connected to constitute a coherent and cohesive text, we should discuss briefly the concept of 'discourse units' and its relation to the grammatical category of 'clauses' (§§ 26.2–26.3).

26.2 EMBEDDING AND HYPOTAXIS

Traditional Semitic grammars usually distinguish two types of clause relations: coordination and subordination. Coordination refers to asyndetic clause connections or constructions with a coordinating conjunction (such as the Syriac ܘ); subordination covers subject and complement clauses, relative clauses, and other clauses introduced by a subordinating conjunction.[2] This distinction between coordination

---

[1] Cf. e.g., Halliday–Hasan, *Cohesion in English*, 1–2.

[2] Thus, e.g. Costaz, *Grammaire*, 201–216; Wertheimer, 'Functions', 267–286; Waltke–O'Connor, *Biblical Hebrew Syntax*, Ch. 38–39; Von Soden, *Grundriss*, Ch. 6 (§§ 163–180); Tropper, *Altäthiopische Grammatik*, Ch. 65 (pp. 233–253). Costaz, *Grammaire*, 201–214, discusses under 'subordinate clauses' ('propositions subordonnées') (a) subject clauses and attributive clauses; (b) complement clauses; (c) circumstantial clauses'.

and subordination is part of a long grammatical tradition and is not restricted to Semitic linguistics. However, in their influential 1988 article C. Matthiessen and S.A. Thompson have questioned the usefulness of the label 'subordination',[3] because it refers to two distinct phenomena: embedding and hypotaxis. Embedding is the phenomenon that one clause functions as a constituent within another clause. Hypotaxis is a phenomenon that concerns the way in which clauses are connected. It is the grammaticalization of rhetorical relations of the so-called Nucleus-Satellite kind.[4] To the best of our knowledge there are no studies that apply Matthiessen's and Thompson's insights to Syriac or other Semitic languages, except for Winther-Nielsen's study on Biblical Hebrew.[5]

In traditional Semitic grammars one can find more than once the remark that a 'subordinate clause' functions as a clause constituent in a main clause, be it as subject, as complement, as attribute (in the case of relative clauses) or as adjunct (in the case of all kinds of adverbial clauses).[6] This view too is widespread and not restricted to Semitic studies.[7] Matthiessen and Thompson have argued that it should also be abandoned, because it is impossible to define or even characterize 'subordinate clauses' in strictly sentence-level terms.[8] The main argument that supports their view is that one clause may combine with a combination of clauses rather than a single clause. In such cases it is quite clear that there is no single clause of which the 'subordinate clause' could be an embedded constituent.[9] Matthiessen and Thompson's English examples can be supplemented with an example from Syr:

---

[3] Cf. esp. Matthiessen–Thompson, 'Structure of Discourse', 317: 'There is no advantage to postulating a grammatical category of "subordinate" clause'.

[4] Matthiessen–Thompson, 'Structure of Discourse', 275, 301.

[5] Winther-Nielsen, *Functional Discourse Grammar*, 55–56. Winther-Nielsen discusses the distinction between 'embedding' and 'cosubordination by dependency' in his § 2.3.1.

[6] Thus e.g. Costaz, *Grammaire*, 201; Richter, *Grundlagen* III, 193; Von Soden, *Grundriss*, § 163.

[7] Cf. e.g. Jespersen, *Philosophy of Grammar*, 103–106. It is also found in more recent English grammars; see the references in Matthiessen–Thompson, 'Structure of Discourse', 279–280.

[8] Matthiessen–Thompson, 'Structure of Discourse', 275.

[9] Matthiessen–Thompson, 'Structure of Discourse', 281.

37:12–13 ,ܣ ܡܐܐܘܒܘܡܐ ܕܠܗܘ ܒܕܠܗܘ ܗܘ ܡܐܒܐ ܠܗ ܒܕܠܗܘ ܘܪܐܘ
,ܣܐܘܐܗ
[W-<Cj>] [>N <Cj>] [MV>B <PC>] [LK <Co>]
   [L-NPCH <Co>] [HW <Su>] [MV>B <PC>]
   [MVWL D-<Cj>] [HJMNWTH <Su>] [HJ <Ep>] [TXJWHJ <PO>]
And if he does evil to you, he does evil to his own soul,
and if he does good to you, he does good to his own soul.
Because his faithfulness makes him live.

It will be evident that the clause in the final line relates to the preceding *clause combination* rather than only to the simple clause in the second line.

According to Matthiessen and Thompson the traditional argument for the interpretation of 'adverbial clauses' as 'adverbials', the so-called substitution test, is invalid. If we paraphrase hypotactic clauses with a prepositional phrase (e.g. 'before he left the city' > 'before his leaving the city') the result is a grammatical metaphor in which the complement of the metaphor is a nominalization that is rather different from an adverbial (e.g. 'before noon').[10]

J. Schilperoord and A. Verhagen have elaborated Matthiessen's and Thompson's theory by providing an explanation for the exceptional status of embedded clauses (subject clauses, complement clauses and restrictive relative clauses). They argue that this status is related to the 'condition of discourse segmentation': 'If a constituent of a matrix-clause A is conceptually dependent on the contents of a subordinate clause B, then B is not a separate discourse segment'.[11] In other words: the exceptional status of embedded clauses is not due to their dependency on the matrix clause, but rather to the dependency of the matrix clause on the embedded clause for its conceptual realization. Compare e.g.

3:21 ܪܒܘܐܗ ܪܠ ܡܝܗ ܦܐܡܬ ܘ 'Do not seek what is too difficult for you'.

The clause ܪܒܘܐܗ ܪܠ 'do not seek' is not conceptually independent without the object clause ܡܝܗ ܦܐܡܬ ܘ 'what is too difficult for you'. In other words, it depends for its conceptual realization on the embedded clause. As we shall see in the following paragraph, this turning upside-down of the notion of dependency has important consequences for the delimitation of discourse segments.

---

[10] Matthiessen–Thompson, 'Structure of Discourse', 280–281.
[11] Schilperoord–Verhagen, 'Conceptual Dependency', 150; quotation from Verhagen, 'Subordination and Discourse Segmentation', 340.

26.3 CLAUSES AND DISCOURSE SEGMENTS

In § 16.1 we have defined 'clause' as any construction in which predication occurs. In many cases clauses function as discourse segments, that is, the minimum building blocks that constitute a discourse. This is not only true for simple main clauses, but also for hypotactic clauses. Thus adverbial clauses introduced by a subordinating conjunction function as separate discourse segments. Compare e.g.

23:16 ܪܝܫ ܡܢ ܝܩܪܗܝ ܪܥܘܬܐ ܡܘܬܒܗܝ ܠܐ

[L> <sp><Aj>] [NTTNJX <PC>]

[<DM> D-<Cj>] [T>QD <Pr>] [BH <Aj>] [NWR> <Su>]

He does not rest till a fire burns in him.

In this case the second clause is a separate discourse segment.[12] The clause combination with the temporal conjunction ܂ ܥܘܬܐ can be regarded as a grammaticalization of the discourse relation between the two segments.

There are cases, however, where a clause does not coincide with a separate discourse segment. Whereas 'clause' is a syntactical category, the identification of 'discourse segments' is based on conceptual considerations.[13] The segmentation of a text into clauses may result in incomprehensible units that cannot be regarded as discourse segments because they do not have an 'independent functional integrity'.[14] Thus in the case of embedding it is preferable to take the embedded clause and its host clause together as a single discourse unit (§ 8.8). Compare e.g.[15]

4:21 ܡܝܘܪܐܝ ܪܚܕܡܘ ܐܘܪܐܘ ܪܥܠܝܘ ܪܝܘܝ ܪܚܕܡܘ ܐܘܪܐܝ ܠܩܠܝ ܪܚܐܘܠܒ

[MVWL D-<Cj>] [>JT <eX>] [BHTT> <Su>]

[D-<Re>] [BRJ> <PC>] [XVH> <Ob>]

[W-<Cj>] [>JT <eX>] [BHTT> <Su>]

[D-<Re>] [>JQRH <Su>] [VJBWT> <PC>]

---

[12] We could describe the first clause as the nucleus and the second as the satellite; cf. Matthiessen–Thompson, 'Structure of Discourse', 289–290; Mann–Thompson, 'Rhetorical Structure Theory', 265–271.

[13] Cf. Schilperoord–Verhagen, 'Conceptual Dependency'; *pace* Mann–Thompson, 'Rhetorical Structure Theory', 248, and Sanders–Van Wijk, 'PISA', 97, 126.

[14] Mann–Thompson, 'Rhetorical Structure Theory', 248.

[15] See also the example from 3:21 at the end of § 26.2.

For there is a shame that creates sins,
and there is a shame the honour of which is goodness. [16]

Although from a syntactic viewpoint we can distinguish four predication structures, in an analysis of the discourse structure the second and fourth clauses should be taken as embedded clause constituents to their respective host clauses. Defining embedding structures in terms of the conceptual dependence of the matrix-clause on the embedded clause, rather than the other way round, [17] we can regard the matrix-clauses in the first and the third lines as dependent for their conceptualization on the embedded clauses in the second and the fourth lines.[18]

This procedure of segmentation of discourse units can also be applied to more complex structures such as

14:20–26 ܡ̈ܒܘܝܐ ܠܕ ܓܒܪܐ (...) ܕܗܝ ܢܗܘܐ ܕܒܚܟܡܬܐ ܪܢܐ, ܠܒܗ
ܡ̈ܣܟܝܢ ܠܕ, ܡܘܪ̈ܚ ܕܒܝܕ (...) ܡܠ

[VWBWHJ <Su>] [L-GBR> <PC>]
[D-<Re>] [B-XKMT> <Co>] [NHW> <Pr>] [RN> <PC>] (...)
[D-<Re>] [NPN> <Pr>] [<L >WRXTH <Co>] [LBH <Ob>] (...)
[D-<Re>] [NRM> <Pr>] [>JDWHJ <Ob>] [<L SWKJH <Aj>]

Blessed is the man who is reflecting upon wisdom (...)
who directs his heart to her ways (...)
and who lays his children[19] on her boughs (...).[20]

In the traditional notion of dependent clauses, all the *d*-clauses are dependent on the first line. If it comes to the segmentation of this passage into minimal discourse units, however, we should take only the matrix clause (the first line) and the first subordinate clause together. While the matrix needs the first subordinate clause for its conceptualization, it can dispense with the others.[21]

Our observations on restrictive relative clauses do not apply to non-restrictive relative clauses. Compare e.g.

---

[16] Perhaps we should read ܪ̈ܚܒܝ̈ܐ ܘ ܪ̈ܝܐܪܐ; see § 1.2.

[17] Cf. the quotation from Schilperoord–Verhagen, 'Conceptual Dependency', 150 in § 26.2.

[18] Verhagen, 'Subordination and Discourse Segmentation', 340.

[19] Reading ܡܘ̈ܪܠ instead of ܡܘܪ̈ܚ; cf. Chapter 3, n. 102.

[20] Note that we have quoted here only three lines from a passage consisting of sixteen lines.

[21] Cf. Verhagen, 'Subordination and Discourse Segmentation', 342. Van Peursen, 'Clause Hierarchy and Discourse Structure'.

47:18 ܠܝܣܪ ܠ ܝܘܐܪܐ ܪܝܘܪ ܘܘ ܘܠܝܐ ܪܘܠܪܐ ܘܬܟܪ ܬܘܝܘܐܪܘ
[W-<Cj>] [>TQRJT <Pr>] [B-CMH [D->LH> <sp>] <Co>]
   [D-<Re>] [DJLH <PC>] [HW <Ep>] [>JQR <Su>]
   [D-<Re>] [>TQRJ <Pr>] [<L >JSRJL <Aj>]
You were called by the name of God, whose is the honour, which was
called over Israel.

The second line is a relative clause to ܪܘܠܪ 'God', the third line a
relative clause to ܪܘܠܪܐ ܘܬܟ 'the name of God'. However, the first
line is not dependent on the second and the third lines. The conceptual
realization of ܪܘܠܪ and ܪܘܠܪܐ ܘܬܟ is independent of the following
relative clauses, which rather provide additional information.[22]

26.4 COHERENCE AND COHESION

The way in which discourse units are connected to form a text can be
described in terms of 'coherence' and in terms of 'cohesion'. 'Coherence' refers to the conceptual organization of a text. If the focus is on
the content this concerns referential or topical continuity.[23] Coherence
can also be described in terms of the conceptual relations between discourse segments. The relations between discourse segments, called
'relational propositions'[24] or 'coherence relations',[25] have attracted a
lot of attention in the past few decades. The basic insight underlying
various approaches in this field is the fact that 'in addition to the
propositions represented explicitly by independent clauses in a text,
there are almost as many propositions (...) which arise (often implicitly) out of combinations of these clauses. (...) Often unsignalled,
these relational propositions can be shown to be the basis for various
kinds of inferences and to function as elements of communicative
acts.'[26] Compare e.g.

---

[22] Cf. Verhagen, 'Subordination and Discourse Segmentation', 339, 341; Schilperoord–Verhagen, 'Conceptual Dependency' 149. See also some variant readings
involving the relative ܁ and ܘ given below, in § 26.7.2.

[23] Sanders–Spooren–Noordman, 'Coherence Relations', 2.

[24] Mann–Thompson, 'Relational Propositions'.

[25] Sanders–Spooren–Noordman, 'Coherence Relations'. Rather than assuming that
all 'relational propositions' or 'coherence relations' are cognitively based (cf. Mann–
Thompson), Sanders, Spooren and Noordman argue that the set of coherence relations
is ordered and that there are a few 'cognitive primitives' from which the coherence
relations derive; cf. ibid. 4–5.

43:4–5 ܘܡܫܒܚ ܠܗ ܗܢ ܕܪ ܡܪܝܐ ܠܥܝܢܐ ܡܗܪ ,ܘܫܒܝܠܗܘ ܡܢܗܪ[27]
[W-<Cj>] [MNHR <PC>] [ZLJQWHJ <Ob>]
    [W-<Cj>] [MCRG <PC>] [<JN> <Ob>]
        [RB <PC>] [HW <Ep>] [MRJ> <Su>]
And it enlightens its rays and dazzles the eyes. Great is the Lord who
    made it.

What is the conceptual relation between the description of the breath-
taking appearance of the sun in 43:4 and the remark about the Lord, its
Maker, in 43:5? The lines quoted are part of a hymn on God's glory in
creation. One could reasonably argue that the main focus is on God's
greatness and that the manifestations described in 43:4 serve as arguments to support the claim about God's greatness in 43:5; in other
words: that there is an Argument-Claim relation between the two
verses.[28] Conceptual relationships such as, for example, this one make
the hymn what it is: a coherent textual unit. These coherence relations
can be established almost independently of the linguistic markers of
clause relations. Thus in the present example there is no signal that
these clauses are connected, except for the object suffix attached to the
verb in 43:5. The nature of the conceptual relation between the two
clauses is not signalled at all. The coherence arises, so to speak, from
the fact that the two lines are put together.[29]

While 'coherence' concerns the conceptual relations between discourse segments, 'cohesion' relates to the explicit markers of underlying conceptual relations.[30] Compare the following two passages:

---

[26] Mann–Thompson, 'Relational Propositions', 57; see also Mann–Thompson,
'Rhetorical Structure Theory' 244: 'RST provides a general way to describe the relations among clauses in a text, whether or not they are grammatically or lexically signalled'; ibid., 260–261: 'Relational propositions, therefore, challenge theories of language that equate the communication effect of a text with the "meanings" of its sentences and compose those meanings from the meanings of its syntactic structures and
lexical items.'

[27] 12a1fam reads ܡܫܒܚ; cf. above, § 26.3, on non-restrictive relative clauses and
below, § 26.7.2.

[28] Following the taxonomy of Sanders, Spooren, and Noordman, 'Coherence Relations', 13.

[29] But note that Heb (B+M) has the conjunction כי; see below, § 26.7.3.

[30] Sanders–Spooren–Noordman, 'Coherence Relations', 2–3. The linguistic surface cues play an important role in the Procedure for Incremental Structure Analysis
(PISA); cf. Sanders–Van Wijk, 'PISA', 122; on the concept of 'cohesion' see also Halliday–Hasan, *Cohesion in English*.

4:20–21 ܐܝܟ ܗܘ ... (Syriac)
... (Syriac)

[<DN> <Ob>] [VR <Pr>]
  [W-<Cj>] [DXL <Pr>] [MN BJC> <Co>]
    [W-<Cj>] [MN NPCK <Co>] [L> <Ng>] [TBHT <Pr>]
      [MVWL D-<Cj>] [>JT <eX>] [BHTT> <Su>]
        [D-<Re>] [BRJ> <PC>] [XVH> <Ob>]
        [W-<Cj>] [>JT <eX>] [BHTT> <Su>]
          [D-<Re>] [>JQRH <Su>] [VJBWT> <PC>]

Observe the time and fear what is wrong,
and do not be ashamed of yourself.
For there is a shame that creates sin
and there is a shame the honour of which is goodness.

6:7–8 ... (Syriac)
... (Syriac)

[>N <Cj>] [QN> <PC>] [>NT <Su>] [RXM> <Ob>]
  [B-NSJN> <Aj>] [QNJWHJ <PO>]
    [W-<Cj>] [L> <Ng>] [TSTRHB <Pr>] [L-MTTKLW <Pr>] [<LWHJ <Co>]
      [>JT <eX>] [RXM> [B->PJ C<T> <sp>] <Su>]
        [W-<Cj>] [L> <Ng>] [Q>M <PC>] [B-<DN> [D->WLYN> <sp>] <Ti>]

If you acquire a friend, acquire him with testing,
and do not make haste to rely on him.
There is a friend 'in the face of the time'
and he will not stand in the time of affliction.

In both cases a recommendation is followed by a clause indicating the reason for the recommendation, and in both cases the coherence relation between the imperative clause and the following ܐܝܟ clause can be described as a Claim-Argument relation.[31] The two examples differ, however, in that in the first example the ܐܝܟ clause is introduced by the causal conjunction ... , while in the second example it is juxtaposed asyndetically. In other words, the first example has an explicit linguistic marker of the coherence relation, while the second has not.[32] Many pairs like this one can be collected to show that coherence relations are sometimes marked explicitly, while in other case they remain implicit. They show that the linguistic signals of the conceptual relations between clauses are optional grammaticalizations of these relations.

---

[31] According to the taxonomy of Sanders, Spooren and Noordman ('Coherence Relations' 13); Claim-Argument is a subcategory of the Causal-Pragmatic relationship.

[32] In Heb (A) such a linguistic signal is present: 6:8 opens with the causal conjunction כי.

Taking into account that linguistic signals of clause connections can be regarded as optional grammaticalizations or 'occasional manifestations'[33] of underlying conceptual relations, it will be evident that an analysis of these signals will not cover all aspects of the organization of discourse. In the study of ancient texts, however, it is the best thing to start with. An approach that proceeds in the other direction, that is, from the conceptual relations between discourse segments to their optional linguistic markers is only possible if one knows the conceptual relations. In their presentation of the Rhetorical Structure Theory, Mann and Thompson state explicitly that one of the basic requirements to apply their theory is that 'the analyst has access to the text, has knowledge of the context in which it was written, and shares the cultural conventions of the writer and the expected readers'.[34] This is not the case when we are dealing with ancient texts.[35]

The examples given above concern the use or non-use of conjunctions. However, there are a number of other signals or 'ties' that give a text cohesion.[36] These will be discussed in the following paragraph.

26.5 COHESIVE ELEMENTS

Having said that we give priority to the analysis of linguistic signals of coherence relations, we should address the question as to what these signals or ties are that give a text cohesion. In the present paragraph we give a preliminary survey of the parameters that have been used in the computer-assisted interactive text-hierarchical analysis of the CALAP project.[37]

> The parameters are used by the computer program syn05 to calculate relations between clauses (§ 8.9). At the present stage the computer-assisted analysis has to cope with some shortcomings. One problem concerns the importance attached to the parameters. While there will be little discussion that the parameters listed below play a role as cohesive elements, it is very difficult to set up general rules about the weight given to the parameters. The human researcher may wish to re-

---

[33] Mann–Thompson, 'Relational Propositions', 89.
[34] Mann–Thompson, 'Rhetorical Structure Theory', 245–246.
[35] See also our arguments for a form-to-function approach in § 7.2.1.
[36] For the concept of 'ties' see Halliday–Hasan, *Cohesion in English*, 3–4.
[37] Cf. Talstra, 'Hierarchy of Clauses'; Den Exter Blokland, *Text Syntax*, 143–152; Bosman, 'Lamentations 3 and 5'; idem, 'Deuteronomy 8'; Dyk, '2 Kings 18 and 19'.

ject a suggestion of the program as to which clauses are related because he or she attaches different weight to them. Another problem is
that the computer can register formal data, but that these data may differ in their relevance. For example, not every repetition of a morpheme is a real correspondence. However, even if the human researcher rejects the suggestion made by the computer, he or she
should do so on the basis of grammatical arguments as much as possible.

1. Clause opening type. An important indication for the relation of
one clause with a preceding clause is its clause opening type: asyndetic or syndetic; parataxis (e.g. ο) or hypotaxis (e.g. ℩).

2. Grammatical clause type. Sequences of clauses of the same type
generally have a higher degree of cohesion. A basic distinction is that
between nominal and verbal clauses. In the case of verbal clauses we
can discern different patterns on the basis of the verb form used.

3. Grammatical and lexical correspondences. Morphological correspondences between clause constituents in two clauses generally mark
a higher degree of cohesion. The computer program calculates the
number of identical morphemes and can register parameters such as
identical person-number-gender of the verb, a suffix attached to a verb
or a suffix attached to a noun. Lexical correspondences contribute to
or confirm the clause connections established with the help of syntactic data.

4. Distance. For each clause a preceding clause is sought to which it
can be matched according to the above-mentioned parameters, such as
morphological and lexical correspondences and clause type. The computer gives a score to each preceding clause on the basis of the parameters and the weight attached to them. The distance to the preceding clauses is also taken into account in establishing the score. This
implies that if on the basis of the listed parameters two clauses have an
equal score, the computer will suggest a connection between clauses
that have a smaller distance.

5. Set of participants. This relates to the set of participants that are
present in the text and the way in which they are referred to. Continuity of the set of participants contributes to the cohesion of the text. In

the case of subject or object continuity, pronominal reference (e.g. 'Abraham said... and he went') is more cohesive than nominal reference (e.g. 'Abraham said... and Abraham went'). Subject change can be an important marker of discontinuity, but the discontinuity is weaker if the new subject is not expressed.[38]

6. Syntactic marking of paragraphs. This is somewhat different from the other 'ties', in that the opening of a new paragraph marks discontinuity rather than continuity. Nevertheless, syntactic paragraph markers are important to analyse the cohesion of a text and to establish which discourse units are closely connected and which are not. Some special clause types may function as paragraph markers. This has been claimed for the types [*wayyiqtol* Subject] and [*w*-Subject *qatal*] in Biblical Hebrew prose.[39] As to Biblical Syriac prose, J.W. Dyk has suggested that absolute specifications of time introduced by the preposition ـد mark more or less independent paragraphs.[40] In Syr the vocative functions as a syntactical devices to mark the opening of a new textual unit (ܪܒܝ in 3:1; ـܒ in 3:8; 3:12 etc.). There are also some interjections that come preferably at the opening of a textual unit, such as ܪܟ (41:1) or ـܘ (2:13; 41:8).

26.6 BOTTOM-UP AND TOP-DOWN ANALYSIS

In § 7.6 we have characterized the CALAP method as a bottom-up approach. This means that the analysis proceeds from the lower linguistic levels to the higher ones: The analysis of words precedes the analysis of phrases, the analysis of phrases comes before that of clauses, etc. In the text level analysis, the bottom-up approach implies that the analysis proceeds from the individual text segments to the text as a whole, rather than the other way round.

The procedure of our computer-assisted analysis is also incremental. That is to say, the analysis starts with the first clause of the text. As we have indicated in § 8.9, the basic assumption in the analysis is that each clause is connected to a preceding clause. Accordingly,

---

[38] For further details about Biblical Hebrew see De Regt, 'Paricipant Reference', 156–158; idem, *Participants*, 13–23.

[39] Cf. Talstra, 'Hierarchy of Clauses', 96.

[40] Dyk, '2 Kings 18 and 19', 532.

the second clause is taken as parallel to or dependent on the first clause. The third clause is connected either to the first or the second clause. In the interactive analysis the computer program calculates which of the two preceding clauses is the best candidate to be the mother clause. This calculation is based on the parameters presented in the preceding paragraph. The procedure continues till the end of the text. For each clause it is established to which preceding clause it is connected and what the type of the connection is.

The alternative procedure, a descendent or top-down analysis, starts from the text as a whole and attempts to identify the units of which it consists in a top-down analysis. Such a descendent analysis may be useful in a thematic or stylistic discourse analysis, but for the present study, with its main focus on the linguistic organization of texts, we prefer an ascendant analysis.[41]

26.7 TEXT-CRITICAL AND TRANSLATIONAL ASPECTS

26.7.1 *Markers of clause relations as optional grammaticalizations*

As we have seen above, the linguistic signals of clause relations can be regarded as optional manifestations of conceptual relations. This implies that one conceptual relation between two clauses in the text (e.g. temporal, causal) can correspond to various types of clause connections in the surface structure of the text, some that mark the conceptual relation between the two clauses, others that do not. We have seen an example of this in § 26.4: A causal relationship is indicated by ܐ ܡܛܠ in 4:21, whereas the same coherence relation is not overtly marked in 6:8.[42]

---

[41] For the reasons behind this choice see also § 7.6 and cf. Den Exter Blokland, *Text Syntax*, 14, 136–137.

[42] We can also refer here to the situation in Heb. In our study on the verbal system in Heb, we have seen that for various kinds of clauses (causal, temporal, final, consecutive, explicative, conditional and comparative) a wide range of constructions (syndetic and asyndetic; paratactic and hypotactic) is used; see Van Peursen, *Verbal System*, Part Three.

26.7.2 *Inner-Syriac variants*

Variation in the use of the linguistic signals of clause relations is visible if we compare different passages in the same corpus, but also if we compare different textual witnesses of the same passage. Compare e.g.

28:1 ܘܦܘܪܥܢܐ ܡܢ ܩܕܡ ܐܠܗܐ ܢܫܟܚ ܡܛܠ ܕܟܠ ܚܛܗܘ̈ܗܝ ܡܛܪ ܢܛܝܪܝܢ ܠܗ
[W-<Cj>] [PWR<N> <Ob>] [MN QDM >LH> <Aj>] [NCKX <Pr>]
[MVL D-<Cj>] [KL XVHWHJ <Su>] [MVR <Mo>] [NVJRJN <PC>] [LH <Aj>]
And he will find vengeance from God,
because all his sins will certainly be preserved for him.

In this verse 7h3 has ܘ 'and' instead of ܡܛܠ ܕ 'because'. The difference between 7h3 and the other manuscripts does not pertain to the rhetorical structure of this verse, but to the use of a linguistic marker of the coherence relation between the two lines. Compare also

21:28 ܥܝܩܐ ܢܦܫܗ ܕܚܟܝܡܐ ܥܠ ܣܟܠܐ ܕܠܐ ܝܕܥ ܡܢܐ ܢܐܡܪ ܠܗ
[<JJQ> <PC>] [NPCH [D-XKJM> <sp>] <Su>] [<L SKL> <Co>]
[D-<Re>] [L> <Ng>] [JD< <Pr>]
[MN> <Qo>] [N>MR <Pr>] [LH <Co>]
The soul of the wise man is grieved at the fool,
because he does not know what to say to him.

In this verse some manuscripts[43] have ܡܛܠ ܕ instead of ܕ. Both ܡܛܠ ܕ and ܕ are well-attested as conjunctions introducing a causal clause, but the range of functions of ܕ is much wider than that of ܡܛܠ ܕ. Accordingly, ܡܛܠ ܕ narrows down the range of possible interpretations of the coherence relation between the two clauses.

The claim of Verhagen *et al.* that in the case of non-restrictive relative clauses the antecedent is conceptually independent and that the relative clause gives additional information is corroborated by variant readings involving relative ܕ, e.g.:

22:1 ܐܝܟ ܟܐܦܐ ܝܚܢܬܐ ܕܪܡܝܐ ܒܫܘܩܐ ܘܟܠܢܫ ܥܪܩ ܡܢ ܪܝܚܗ ܗܟܢܐ
ܐܝܬܘܗܝ ܣܟܠܐ ܘܟܠ ܐܢܫ ܡܬܪܚܩ ܡܢܗ
[>JK K>P> YXNT> <Fa>]
[D-<Re>] [RMJ> <PC>] [B-CWQ> <Aj>]
[W-<Cj>] [KL-NC <Su>] [<RQ <PC>] [MN RJXH <Co>]
[HKN> <PC>] [>JTWHJ <Xs>] [SKL> <Su>]
[W-<Cj>] [KL >NC <Su>] [MTRXQ <PC>] [MNH <Co>]

---

43 8a1$^{c/mg}$ 9c1 10c1.2 11c1 12a1*fam* → according to the preliminary critical apparatus in the forthcoming volume of the Leiden Peshitta edition.

Like a filthy stone which is thrown in the street
and everyone flees from its smell,
so is the fool, and everyone turns afar from him.

In the last line MS 8a1 has a non-restrictive relative clause with ܒܗ
instead of the parallel clause with ܘܒܗ in the other manuscripts.

37:1–2 ܩܕܡ ܐܝܬ ܚܒܪܐ ܕܫܡܗ ܚܒܪܐ ܕܠܐ ܢܛܐ ܠܡܘܬܐ
[BRM <Cj>] [>JT <eX>] [RXM> <Su>]
    [D-<Re>] [CMH <Su>] [RXM> <PC>]
    [D-<Re>] [L> <Ng>] [MV> <PC>] [<DM> L-MWT> <Co>]
But there is a friend, whose name is friend, who does not arrive to
death.

In this example ܚܒܪܐ is followed by two relative clauses. The denotation of ܚܒܪܐ is dependent on the first relative clause, but not on
the second one. In the second one MSS 7h3 and 8a1 read ܘܠܐ instead
of ܕܠܐ.[44]

26.7.3 *Multilingual comparison*

The preceding examples concern inner-Syriac variants pertaining to
hypotaxis. In the case of Syr, however, we are dealing with a translation from Hebrew and the question arises regarding the extent to
which the cohesion markers in Syr correspond to those in Heb. If
clause combining is regarded as a grammaticalization of conceptual
relations, one expects considerable variation, because the grammaticalization of conceptual relations is a language-internal phenomenon.[45] Variant readings in the field of clause combining are indeed
abundantly attested.[46] A number of times conceptual relations that remain implicit in Heb have been made explicit in Syr, e.g.:

---

[44] See also the example from 43:5 quoted in § 26.4 (cf. n. 27); other examples occur in 14:26; 17:15; 17:29; 26:8; 29:11; 31:20; 38:32; 39:1; 38:5.

[45] Cf. Matthiessen–Thompson, 'Structure of Discourse', 317, in their conclusions,
mainly based on hypotaxis and discourse relations in English: 'There is an interesting
consequence of these suggestions for attempts to consider clause combining from a
cross-linguistic perspective: if hypotaxis in English is a grammaticalization of rhetorical relations, then it follows that the grammar of clause combining may differ
radically from one language to another.'

[46] See the examples mentioned in the present paragraph and further the examples
given in the 'Systematisch-formale Darstellung von Sir 44,16a–45,26d' in Reiterer,
Urtext, 34–50.

38:17–18 ܘܥܒܕ ܐܒܠܐ ܒܙܕܩܗ ܝܘܡܐ ܘܬܪܝܢ ܡܛܠ ܒܢܝ ܐܢܫܐ ܘܐܬܒܝܐ ܡܛܠ
ܚܝܐ ܡܛܠ ܕܡܢ ܟܪܝܘܬܐ ܡܬܝܠܕܐ ܥܩܬܐ
[W-<Cj>] [<BD <Pr>] [>BL> <Ob>] [B-ZDQH <Aj>]
[JWM> W-TRJN <Aj>] [MVL BNJ >NC> <Aj>]
[W-<Cj>] [>TBJ> <Pr>] [MVL XJ> <Aj>]
[MVL D-<Cj>] [MN KRJWT> <Aj>] [MTJLD> <Pr>] [<QT> <Su>]
And make mourning as is his due,
a day or two because of the people,
and be consoled because of life
Because from pressure comes forth distress.

In Heb (B) 38:18 opens with an asyndetic clause where Syr has ܡܛܠ ܕ.[47] A similar example occurs in 15:18, where Syr has ܡܛܠ ܕ, without a corresponding conjunction in Heb (A+B).[48]

The opposite phenomenon, i.e. Heb has a linguistic signal of the conceptual relation between two clauses that is not recorded in Syr, is attested as well. In § 26.4 we have seen two examples in 6:8 and 43:5: Heb has the conjunction כי, whereas Syr has an asyndetic construction.

In the comparison of sources in different languages, we find further support for the claim that the non-restrictive relative clause gives additional information, which can also be added in other ways, e.g.:

47:13 ܫܪܐ ܒܫܠܝܐ ܫܠܝܡܘܢ ܘܐܠܗܐ ܐܢܝܚ ܠܗ ܡܢ ܟܠܗܘܢ ܚܕܪܘܗܝ ܡܛܠ ܕܢܒܢܐ
ܒܝܬܐ ܠܫܡܗ ܠܥܠܡ
[CR> <PC>] [B-CLJ> <Aj>] [CLJMWN <Su>]
[W-<Cj>] [>LH> <Su>] [>NJX <Pr>] [LH <Co>] [MN KLHWN [XDRWHJ <ap>] <Aj>]
[MVL D-<Cj>] [NBN> <Pr>] [BJT> <Ob>] [L-CMH <Aj>] [L-<LM <Ti>]
Solomon dwelt in peace and God gave him rest on all his sides, so that he would build a house for His name for ever.

Syr has the conjunction ܡܛܠ ܕ corresponding to אשר in Heb (B), which introduces a non-restrictive relative clause.

In rendering a Hebrew text into Syriac, the Syriac translator could —within the restraints of the target language—use linguistic signals of clause relations and cohesion where they were already present in the

[47] From our general observations in this paragraph it will be obvious that there is no reason to emend an additional כי on the basis of Gr γάρ or Syr ܡܛܠ ܕ; cf. Van Peursen, *Verbal System*, 377 (*pace* Smend, *Jesus Sirach*, 343).

[48] According to the edition of the Hebrew Academy there are traces of an added כי in MS A, but it is hard to discern them in the manuscript. Here too it is imprecise to say that Syr and Gr add כי, because this suggests that the translators added or read it in their Hebrew source. If one wants to describe the relationship between the textual witnesses in terms of an addition, one can say no more than that Gr adds ὅτι and Syr ܡܛܠ ܕ; *pace* Peters, *Ben Sirach*, 131.

Hebrew text, omit them if they occurred in the Hebrew, or add them if
they did not occur in the Hebrew. It follows that we cannot draw firm
conclusions from the presence or absence of such a linguistic marker
in Syr about its *Vorlage*, unless there are reasons to assume that the
translator tried to mirror every word and particle of the source text.[49]

> The differences between the source text and the target text are even
> stronger in early translations from Greek into Syriac.[50] Syriac has a
> stronger tendency to parataxis than Greek, which has led to frequent
> restructuring of entire sentences, especially in the Old Syriac Gos-
> pels.[51] Even cohesion markers that at first sight seem to have exact
> correspondences in the two languages such as the particles ܓܝܪ – γάρ
> and ܕܝܢ – δέ do not have complete overlap in the Old Syriac Gospels
> or the NT Peshitta.[52]

The variation in the textual witnesses relates not only to the choice of
conjunctions, but also to other parameters that influence the hierarchical structure of a text. Compare e.g.

> 6:20 ܒܡܐ ܥܣܩܐ ܗܝ ܚܟܡܬܐ ܠܣܟܠܐ 'How difficult is Wisdom for the
> fool'

---

[49] Accordingly, we do not agree with Reiterer's conclusion that 'Syr, der relativ
korrekt mit Konj[unktionen] umzugehen scheint, im Zusammenhang des Fehlens
einer Konj den Rückschluß zuläßt, in seiner Vorlage habe er auch keine gelesen' (Reiterer, *Urtext*, 53). Thus it is incorrect to say that the presence or absence of a Waw in
Syr reflects the presence or absence of a Waw in its Hebrew source text; *pace* Reiterer, ibid., 95 (on 44:19), 229 (on 45:25) and elsewhere; Peters, *Ben Sirach* 251
(31:1), 259 (31:23), 294 (36:9), 305 (37:11), 309 (37:22, 28), 375 (44:1), 396 (48:5),
423 (49:16), 430 (50:14), 436 (50:28) and elsewhere; Ryssel, 'Fragmente', V, 575
(37:27); nor is it correct to regard ܓܝܪ or ܕ ܡܛܠ as reflecting Hebrew כי or אשר;
pace Lévi, *L'Ecclésiastique* I, 23 (ܓܝܪ in 40:15); Ryssel, 'Fragmente', V, 579 and
Schechter–Taylor, *Wisdom of Ben Sira*, 61 (ܕ ܡܛܠ in 38:1); Peters, *Ben Sirach*, 390
and Reiterer, *Urtext*, 213 (emending אשי to אשר in 45:22 where Syr has ܕ ܡܛܠ); cf.
above, notes 47, 48; see also Williams, *Peshitta of 1 Kings*, 42–99, on 'and' in the
Peshitta of Kings. As Williams points out, even a standard edition such as the *BHS*
sometimes erroneously draws conclusions about the presence or absence of a Waw on
the basis of its presence or absence in the Peshitta, ignoring linguistic or stylistic factors that influence its use and non-use in Hebrew and Syriac. The use of a Waw in the
Peshitta where there is no equivalent in the Hebrew is also well-attested in Lamentations, see Albrektson, *Lamentations*, 210. For variation in the use of Waw and other
conjunctions in the Aramaic versions of Job see Shepherd, *Targum and Translation*,
Ch. 11 (pp. 227–258) and Szpek, *Peshitta to Job*, 117–131; on the use of ܘ in the New
Testament, whether or not corresponding to καί see Brock, 'Limitations', 84; Williams, *Early Syriac Translation Technique*, 149–160.

[50] For the situation in later Syriac texts, cf. Brock, 'History of Syriac Translation
Technique'.

[51] Cf. Brock, 'Limitations', 83.

[52] Cf. Brock, 'Treatment of Greek Particles'; Falla–Van Peursen, 'Particles ܓܝܪ
and ܕܝܢ'.

Here Syr has ܣܘܼܟ݂ܬ݂ܐ where Heb (A) has the pronoun היא 'she'. The noun ܣܘܼܟ݂ܬ݂ܐ also occurs in 6:18. In 6:19 it is the referent of the suffix pronoun in the verbal complement ܠܗ݁ܿ '(draw near) to her' and the objects ܣܘ ܐܟ݂ܠ ܣܓܝܐܘܼܬ݂ܗ݁ܿ 'the multitude of her harvest' and ܐܒܗ݁ܿ 'her fruit'. In 6:20 there is a subject change, although the subject is not a new participant in the context. Heb uses a pronoun and is therefore more cohesive than Syr.[53]

We conclude this section with an example of participant reference in which both inner-Syriac and inner-Hebrew variants are involved:

> 15:14 ܐܠܗܐ ܡܢ ܒܪܫܝܬ݂ ܒܪܐ ܒܪܢܫܐ 'God from the beginning created the human beings'.

Instead of ܐܠܗܐ a number of manuscripts read ܗܘ.[54] The word ܐܠܗܐ occurs in a prepositional adjunct in 15:11. It is one of the implied participants in the following lines, in various syntactic functions (subject, complement) and it is the implied grammatical subject of the two clauses in 15:13. Accordingly, the explicit subject noun ܐܠܗܐ does not mark a subject change, but rather makes the connection with the preceding lines somewhat looser. The Hebrew evidence is divided as well: MS A and the margin of MS B read אלהים, while the main text of MS B has הוא. The reading 'God' can be explained as a harmonization towards Gen 1:1.[55]

26.8 CONCLUSION

In his main paper presented at the IOSOT Congress at Basel in 2001, M. O'Connor, argued that a barrier should be maintained between 'linguistics' and 'biblical exegesis' or 'reading'. One of his arguments is that in some subfields of biblical studies, such as textual criticism, linguistic factors play a very minor role.[56] At the end of this chapter

---

[53] Cf. above, § 26.5 (5). For the 'targumic' tendency to make explicit the referents of pronominal elements in Heb, see further § 3.2 (h); for cross-linguistic variation in participant reference as it appears from Bible translations, see De Regt, 'Participant Reference' and *Participants*.

[54] According to the preliminary apparatus in the Leiden edition these are 8a1^C 9c1 10c1.2 11c1 12a1*fam*.

[55] Van Peursen, 'Retroversions', 63.

[56] O'Connor, 'Discourse Linguistics', 40–41.

we can conclude that textual criticism and linguistics are much more
interrelated than O'Connor suggests.

The examples from § 26.7 show that what from a linguistic perspective can be described as optional manifestations of underlying
rhetorical structures, appears from a text-critical viewpoint an area in
which many inner-Syriac variants are attested. This means that the
text-critical evidence supports the view that the linguistic markers of
clause relations are optional, while the linguistic considerations warn
the text-critical scholar not to attach too much weight to this 'optional'
variation.

Moreover, from a linguistic perspective markers of clause relations
can be described as the grammaticalization of rhetorical structures,
and hence a language-internal phenomenon. This linguistic view is
corroborated by the text-critical observation that a comparison of two
sources in different languages (in our case Hebrew and Syriac) shows
a lot of variation in the field of clause combining. From a text-critical
perspective we have emphasized that we cannot draw firm conclusions
about the presence or absence of linguistic markers of clause relations
in the Hebrew *Vorlage* of the Syriac translator on the basis of their use
or non-use in Syr. This view is supported by the linguistic observations that these markers are language-internal phenomena.[57]

Taking into account linguistic and cross-linguistic aspects of cohesion markers, the question arises as to whether any analysis of these
markers in terms of translation technique or textual history is possible
at all. We think it is. In the examples discussed so far the pattern is
clear: both Heb and Syr contain two clauses and there is little doubt
about the coherence relation between the two clauses. In such cases it
appears that the linguistic marker of this signal is optional. It does not
change the coherence relations.

In some cases, however, the coherence relation between two
clauses is not evident if it is not made explicit. This applies, for example, to the introduction of 'a prophet like fire' in 48:1. The relation
with the preceding clause signalled by 'until' (עד אשר in MS B and
ܥܕܡܐ ܠ in Syr) would not have been self-evident if it was left implicit. In Gr, which opens with καὶ ἀνέστη the coherence relation
with the preceding clause is rather different. From a text-critical view-

---

[57] Unless, of course, there are strong reasons to assume that the Syriac translator
attempted to mirror every word from his source text in the translation; cf. above, note
49.

point, the reading in Heb and Syr, being the *lectio difficilior*, is preferable to Gr.[58] Accordingly, there is an essential difference between Syr, which has preserved the coherence relation present in Heb, and Gr, which has not.

---

[58] See further § 27.3.

CHAPTER TWENTY-SEVEN

CLAUSE HIERARCHY IN THE PRAISE OF THE FATHERS

27.1 INTRODUCTION: THE GENRE OF THE
PRAISE OF THE FATHERS

In an article on the verbal system in the Hebrew text of the Praise of the Fathers we have given a short survey of opinions about the aim and genre of this section.[1] According to some it is a representative of 'didactic narrative', which is also attested in Proverbs,[2] while others relate these chapters to the historical outlines that are found in some psalms and in Deuteronomistic literature.[3] However, the Praise of the Fathers displays many differences from these biblical genres. For this reason T.R. Lee has argued that the closest parallels do not occur in the Hebrew Bible, but in Classical Greek literature. In his view the genre of the Praise of the Fathers can best be described with the Greek ἐγκώμιον.[4] As in the Greek parallels of this genre, someone (in this case Simon the High Priest) is praised for his achievements and virtues. For this purpose other examples of honourable people are adduced. The form in which Ben Sira organizes the examples is that of the *Beispielreihe*, a genre well-known in biblical and post-biblical Jewish literature. In the present chapter we will test the hypothesis that Sirach 44–49 is a *Beispielreihe* (preparing the way, so to speak, for Chapter 50 about Simon the High Priest) from a linguistic perspective.

---

[1] Van Peursen, 'Praise of the Fathers'.
[2] Skehan–Di Lella, *Wisdom of Ben Sira*, 30.
[3] Box–Oesterley, 'Sirach', 479; Peters *Ben Sirach*, 372.
[4] Lee, *Sirach 44–50*.

27.2 CLAUSE HIERARCHY IN 44:17–23 (THE PATRIARCHS)

We will start with an analysis of Sir 44:17–23. After the introduction in 44:1–16, which praises the fathers of old, Ben Sira goes on to discuss the hero's of the past, beginning with Noah, followed by Abraham, Isaac, Jacob.[5]

44:17–18 ܢܘܚ ܙܕܝܩܐ ܐܫܬܟܚ ܒܕܪܗ ܫܠܡ ܒܙܒܢܐ ܕܛܘܦܢܐ ܗܘܐ ܚܠܦܬܐ ܠܥܠܡܐ
ܘܡܛܠܬܗ ܗܘܬ ܡܫܘܙܒܘܬܐ ܘܝܡܐ ܠܗ ܐܠܗܐ ܕܠܐ ܢܗܘܐ ܬܘܒ ܛܘܦܢܐ ܡܘܡܬܐ
ܕܝܡܐ ܠܗ ܒܫܪܪܐ ܕܠܐ ܢܐܒܕ ܟܠ ܒܣܪ

1 [NWX ZDJQ> <Su>] [>CTKX <Pr>] [B-DRH <Aj>] [CLM <Ob>]
2 [B-ZBN> [D-VWPN> <sp>] <Ti>] [HW> <Pr>] [XLPT> <PC>] [L-<LM> <Aj>]
3 [W-<Cj>] [MVLTH <Aj>] [HWT <Pr>] [MCWZBWT> <Su>]
4 　[W-<Cj>] [JM> <Pr>] [LH <Co>] [>LH> <Su>]
5 　　　[D-<Cj>] [L> <Ng>] [NHW> <Pr>] [TWB <Mo>] [VWPN> <Su>]
6 　　[MWMT> <Aj>]
7 　　　　[D-<Re>] [JM> <Pr>] [LH <Co>] [B-CRR> <Aj>]
8 　　　[D-<Cj>] [L> <Ng>] [N>BD <Pr>] [KL BSR <Su>]

1 Noah the righteous one was found perfect in his generation.
2 At the time of the flood he was a substitute.
3 And for his sake there was redemption.
4 　and God swore to him
5 　　　that there would be no flood again.
6 　　Oaths
7 　　　　which He swore to him in truth
8 　　　that He would not destroy all flesh.

44:17–18 is a paragraph concerning Noah. It can be identified as a coherent textual unit on the basis of the following observations:

1. There is no connective element (such as the conjunction ܘ) that connects the first line of this paragraph to the preceding paragraph.
2. The opening clause, containing an explicit subject noun phrase referring to a new participant, marks the beginning of the paragraph.

[5] In the Masada manuscript too the first biblical hero mentioned is Noah, but in Gr and MS B the passage on Noah is preceded by a remark on Enoch. For the secondary character of the reference to Enoch in this place see Van Peursen, *Verbal System*, 163–164.

3. There is a limited set of actors: Noah and God. In the present paragraph Noah appears in almost all the lines, but in the following paragraph he is absent. God appears as an actor in the subsequent paragraph as well, but is then introduced anew with the noun phrase 'the Most High'.

4. The following paragraph is marked as a new textual unit by the same means: an asyndetic clause in which a new participant appears as the explicit subject.

The status of ܥܘܒܬܐ in 44:18 is not clear. Perhaps we should regard it as an object to ܥܒܕ in line 4. The hierarchical structure presented above reflects this interpretation, in which both line 5 and ܥܘܒܬܐ in line 6 depend on line 4. Otherwise we can consider it as an element that is loosely related to the preceding line, or as a one-member clause in itself.

44:19–21 *[Syriac text, five lines]*

9	[>BRHM <Su>] [>B] [D-KNWCT] [D-<MM> <sp>] <sp>] <PC>]
10	[W-<Cj>] [L> <Ng>] [>TJHB <Pr>] [MWM> <Su>] [B->JQRH <Aj>]
11	[D-<Re>] [<BD <Pr>] [PTGMWHJ [D-<LJ> <sp>] <Ob>]
12	[W-<Cj>] [<L <Pr>] [B-QJM <Co>] [<MH <Aj>] [B-BSRH <Aj>]
13	[>TQJM <Pr>] [LH <Aj>] [QJM> <Su>]
14	[W-<Cj>] [B-NSJWNH <Aj>] [>CTKX <PC>] [MHJMN <Ob>]
15	[MVL HN> <Aj>] [B-MWMT> <Aj>] [JM> <Pr>] [LH <Co>] [>LH> <Su>]
16	[D-<Cj>] [NTBRKWN <Pr>] [B-ZR<H <Aj>] [KLHWN [<MM>
	[D->R<> <sp>] <ap>] <Ob>]
17	[W-<Cj>] [L-MSGJW <Pr>] [ZR<H <Ob>] [>JK XL> [D-JM> <sp>] <Aj>]
18	[W-<Cj>] [L-MTL <Pr>] [ZR<H <Ob>] [L-<L MN KLHWN
	[<MM> <ap>] <Ob>]
19	[L-MWRTW <Pr>] [>NWN <Ob>] [MN JM> [L-JM> <sp>] [W-<cj>]
	[MN PRT [<DM> L-SWPJH [D>R<> <sp>] <sp>] <PA>] <Aj>]

9	Abraham was the father of the communities of the peoples,
10	and no blemish was given on his honour,
11	who did the words of the Most High
12	and entered into a covenant with Him.
13	In his flesh the covenant was established,
14	and in temptation he was found faithful.

15	Therefore God swore to him with oaths
16	that in his descendants all nations of the world would be blessed,
17	and to multiply his descendants like the sand of the sea,
18	and to appoint his descendants above all peoples,
19	giving them inheritance from sea to sea
	and from the Euphrates to the ends of the world.

Line 9 introduces a new hero, Abraham. He appears as the explicit grammatical subject of an asyndetic main clause. As in the section on Noah, some lines on the hero in question are followed by some clauses in which God is the actor and the hero the recipient.

20   [W-<Cj>] [>P <Cj>] [L->JSXQ <Co>] [JM> <Pr>] [MVL >BRHM
                                                          [>BWHJ <ap>] <Aj>]
21   [W-<Cj> [BWRKT> [D-KL QDMJ> <sp>] <Su>] [MTNJX> <Pr>] [<L RJCH
                                                          [D->JSRJL <sp>] <Co>]
22   [D-<Re>] [QRJHJ <Pr>] [BRJ [BWKRJ <ap>] [>JSRJL <ap>] <Ob>]
23   [W-<Cj>] [JHB <Pr>] [LH <Co>] [JWRTN> <Ob>]
24   [W-<Cj>] [>QJMH <PO>] [>B <Ob>] [L-CBV> <Aj>]
25   [W-<Cj>] [NPQ <Pr>]
26   [W-<Cj>] [>TPLG <Pr>] [L-TR<SR CBVJN <Aj>]

20	And also to Isaac He swore for the sake of Abraham his father.
21	And the blessing of those before him rested on the head of Israel,
22	whom He called My son, My first-born, Israel.
23	And He gave him an inheritance
24	and made him the father of the tribes,
25	but they went out
26	and were divided into twelve tribes.

Unlike Noah and Abraham, Isaac and Israel do not receive their own paragraph. A comparison of the sections about Isaac and Israel with that on Noah and Abraham reveals some striking differences. Firstly, the ways in which the new participants are introduced differs considerably. Whereas Noah and Abraham were the grammatical subject of the line in which they appear for the first time, the first occurrence of Isaac is part of a verb complement, and Jacob appears in a specification of a complement. Secondly, a number of linguistic elements that

are commonly understood as markers of linguistic cohesion connect
44:22–23 with the preceding lines:

1. Conjunctions. Whereas the first occurrences of Noah and
   Abraham are marked as the beginning of a new paragraph
   with an asyndetic main clause, the first occurrences of Isaac
   and Jacob occur in clauses that are syndetically coordinated to
   the preceding lines by the conjunction ‌ܘ.
2. Grammatical correspondences. 44:22 shares with its antecedent clause (line 15) the person-number-gender and lexeme of
   the verb ܚܝܐ.
3. Lexical correspondences. All lexemes in line 20 occur in the
   previous lines, except for ܐܠܘܗܐ ܐܪ: ܐܠܗܐ and ܚܝܐ in line
   15 (the antecedent clause), ܐܒܪܗܡ and ܐܠܗܐ in line 9 (the first
   line about Abraham).
4. The absence of an explicit subject. In 44:22 the subject is not
   mentioned; it has to be understood from the preceding lines.

If we compare this passage about Noah, Abraham, Isaac and Jacob
with representatives of the *Beispielreihe*, the differences are striking.
In Hebrews 11, for example, each hero is introduced with the ana-
phoric πίστει, followed by a clause in which the new hero occurs as
the explicit subject. In 1 Macc 2:52–60 each hero that is put forward
as an example is introduced as the grammatical subject of an asyndetic
clause. Moreover, all these subject proper nouns occur in first
position:

Ἀβραὰμ οὐχὶ ἐν πειρασμῷ εὑρέθη πιστός, καὶ ἐλογίσθη αὐτῷ εἰς
    δικαιοσύνην;
Ἰωσὴφ ἐν καιρῷ στενοχωρίας αὐτοῦ ἐφύλαξεν ἐντολὴν καὶ ἐγένετο
    κύριος Αἰγύπτου.
Φινεὲς ὁ πατὴρ ἡμῶν ἐν τῷ ζηλῶσαι ζῆλον ἔλαβεν διαθήκην ἱερωσύνης
    αἰωνίας.
Ἰησοῦς ἐν τῷ πληρῶσαι λόγον ἐγένετο κριτὴς ἐν Ἰσραήλ.
Χαλὲβ ἐν τῷ μαρτύρασθαι ἐν τῇ ἐκκλησίᾳ ἔλαβεν γῆς κληρονομίαν.
Δαυὶδ ἐν τῷ ἐλέει αὐτοῦ ἐκληρονόμησεν θρόνον βασιλείας εἰς αἰῶνας.
Ἠλίας ἐν τῷ ζηλῶσαι ζῆλον νόμου ἀνελήμφθη εἰς τὸν οὐρανόν.
Ἀνανίας, Ἀζαρίας, Μισαὴλ πιστεύσαντες ἐσώθησαν ἐκ φλογός.
Δανιὴλ ἐν τῇ ἁπλότητι αὐτοῦ ἐρρύσθη ἐκ στόματος λεόντων.

> Was not Abraham found faithful when tested, and it was reckoned to him as righteousness?
> Joseph in the time of his distress kept the commandment, and became lord of Egypt.
> Phinehas our father, because he was deeply zealous, received the covenant of everlasting priesthood. Joshua, because he fulfilled the command, became a judge in Israel.
> Caleb, because he testified in the assembly, received an inheritance in the land.
> David, because he was merciful, inherited the throne of the kingdom for ever.
> Elijah because of great zeal for the law was taken up into heaven.
> Hannaniah, Azariah, and Mishael believed and were saved from the flame.
> Daniel because of his innocence was delivered from the mouth of the lions.
> (RSV)

Thus from a syntactical perspective the passages that we have analysed thus far do not constitute a 'list of examples'. The syntactic structure argues against this view. It seems that the author is more concerned with describing the line of history, than with presenting these heroes as individual separate examples.

27.3 CLAUSE HIERARCHY IN 47:23–48:15 (ELIJAH AND ELISHA)

In the preceding paragraph we saw some examples that argue against the interpretation of the Praise of the Fathers as a *Beispielreihe*. The presentation of the heros of the past does not consist of more or less disconnected 'examples' but of a chain of closely connected references to people and events. Another case may illustrate this further, namely the introduction of Elijah in 48:1.

```
1   [W-<Cj>] [L> <Ng>] [NHW> <Pr>] [LH <PC>] [DWKRN> <Su>] [L-JWRB<M
                                              [BR NBV <ap>] <sp><PC>]
2       [D-<Re>] [XV> <Pr>]
3           [W-<Cj>] [>XVJ <Pr>] [L->JSRJL <Ob>]
4           [W-<Cj>] [JHB <Pr>] [L-D-BJT >PRJM <Co>] [TWQLT> <Ob>]
5             [L-MGLJW <Pr>] [>NWN <Ob>] [MN >TRHWN <Co>]
6           [W-<Cj>] [>SGJ <Pr>] [XVHJHWN <Ob>] [VB <Mo>]
7           [W-<Cj>] [<L KL BJCT> <Aj>] [>TMLK <Pr>]
8       [<DM> D-<Cj>] [QM <Pr>] [NBJ> <Su>]
9         [D-<Re>] [DM> <Pr>] [L-NWR> <Co>]
10            [W-<Cj>] [MLTH <Su>] [JQD> <PC>]
                                        [>JK TNWR> <Aj>]
11                  [D-<Re>] [MCTGR <Pr>]
12              [W-<Cj>] [>JTJ <Pr>] [<LJHWN <Co>] [KPN> <Ob>]
13            [W-<Cj>] [B-VNNH <Aj>] [BZ< <Pr>] [>NWN <Ob>]
14  [B-MLTH [D-MRJ> <sp>] <Aj>] [KL> <Pr>] [CMJ> <Ob>]
15  [W-<Cj>] [>XT <Pr>] [TLT ZBNJN <Aj>] [NWR> <Ob>] [MN CMJ> <Co>]
                              [<L MDBX> W-<L >NC> RCJ<> <Aj>]
16  [M> DXJL <Qp>] [>NT <Su>]
17  [>LJ> <Vo>]
18  [W-<Cj>] [MN <Ex>]
19      [D-<Re>] [>KWTK <PC>]
20  [HW <Su>] [NCTBX <PC>]
```

```
1   And let there be no memory to him, to Jeroboam the son of Nebat,
2   who sinned
3           and caused Israel to sin
4           and put a stumbling-block before Ephraim
5                   to cause them to be exiled from their place
6           and multiplied their sins abundantly
7           and took counsel about all evil things;
8       until there arose a prophet
9           who was like fire
10                  and whose word was burning like a furnace
11                          that glows.
12                  and he brought upon them famine,
13              and in his zeal he rent them.
14  By the word of the Lord he shut up the heaven
15      and three times he brought fire down from heaven,
                                upon the altar and upon the wicked people.
16  How awesome you were,
17      Elijah,
18  and he
19          who is like you
20      will be praised.
```

Many modern Bible translations insert a break between 47:25 and 48:1 and give the passage starting in 48:1 the heading 'Elijah' or 'Elijah and Elisha'. As far as these translations are based on Gr, this is understandable because Gr opens with καὶ ἀνέστη 'Ηλίας. In Heb and Syr, however, the line in which Elijah enters the scene starts with a subordinating conjunction and the name of Elijah is mentioned not earlier than in 48:4.[6] Claiming that in Heb and Syr a new paragraph starts in 48:1 would overrule this syntactic observation.

In Gr some of the difficulties raised by the text in Heb (B) and Syr have been resolved by the introduction of the name of Elijah in 48:1 and the change of 'until' into 'and'. As to the name of Elijah, it is likely that it has been added in Gr or its Hebrew source text to make explicit who was the 'prophet like fire' and to resolve the tension caused by the delay of the mention of the prophet's name.

The reading 'and' in Gr instead of 'until' in MS B and Syr also seems a means to resolve a difficult reading. It is more reasonable to assume that 'until' has been changed into 'and' than the other way round, because the reading 'until' is enigmatic. If understood in a temporal sense, it suggests that the ministry of Elijah and Elisha took place *after* the deportation of the Northern Kingdom. And even if 'until' is understood as relating to Israel's sins rather than to its going into exile, Ben Sira's presentation does not agree with the book of Kings, which makes clear that Elijah's and Elisha's activities did not mark the end of 'the sins of Jeroboam'.

If we agree that the reading 'until' is the best candidate to be the original reading, the questions arises as to how this enigmatic *lectio difficilior* should be understood in the context of the Praise of the Fathers in Heb (B) and Syr. Apparently, the relation expressed by עד אשר / ג ܟܡܐ between on the one hand Israel's sin and its going into exile and on the other hand Elijah's and Elisha's activities as prophets, is logical (or, if one prefers, theological) rather than temporal.[7] After

---

[6] Other heroes too are first characterized before their name appears in the text, cf. 44:23 (Moses), 46:13 (Samuel) and 47:23 (Jeroboam); *pace* Beentjes, 'Stammen van Israël', 149.

[7] *Pace* Beentjes, 'Stammen van Israël', 149. See the examples where עד אשר expresses degree rather than time in BDB 725 ('to the point that, so that even') and compare our *Verbal System*, 330: 'In the Bible עד אשר occasionally marks the climax or culmination of a certain situation, rather than the temporal limit or continuation of an action or state'.

the description of the two prophets, there is again a reference to the exile, and again עַד אֲשֶׁר / ܕ ܫܒܝܐ is used:[8]

> 48:15 ܘܥܡ ܟܠܗܘܢ ܗܠܝܢ ܠܐ ܬܒ ܥܡܐ ܘܠܐ ܦܪܩܘ ܡܢ ܒܕܝܗܘܢ ܒܝܫܐ ܥܕܡܐ ܕܓܠܝܘ ܡܢ ܐܬܪܗܘܢ ܘܐܬܒܕܪܘ ܒܟܠ ܡܕܝܢܬ܂
>
> [W-<Cj>] [B-KLHJN [HLJN <ap>] <Aj>] [L> <Ng>] [TB <Pr>] [<M> <Su>]
>   [W-<Cj>] [L> <Ng>] [PRQW <Pr>] [MN <BDJHWN BJC> <Co>]
>   [<DM> D-<Cj>] [GLJW <Pr>] [MN >TRHWN <Co>]
>   [W-<Cj>] [>TBDRW <Pr>] [B-KL MDJNT> <Aj>]
>
> Despite all these things the people did not return,
>   and they did not abandon their evil deeds,
>   until they were exiled from their place
>   and were scattered over all cities.

We can conclude that the depiction of Elijah and Elisha is strongly rooted in the account of the people's sin, their refusal to return from their evil deeds and the final outcome of their transgressions: the exile. This entrenchment is marked both syntactically (the subordinating conjunction in 48:15) and by literary means (the parallelism of 'until' in 48:1 and 48:15 and the inclusio of 47:25–27 and 48:15). For this reason it is incorrect to consider 48:1–15 as two episodes of a *Beispielreihe*.

It is worth noting that the delimitation markers in the Syriac manuscripts corroborate this view. Thus there is no Peshitta manuscript that has a delimitation marker before 48:1. 7a1 has one before 47:23; 7h3 before 47:14; 9c1 has a delimitation marker before 47:12 and one between vv. 3 and 4. Further, 7a1, 8a1, 9c1, 10c1 and 10c2 have a delimitation marker after 48:16.[9] Only the Syro-Hexapla has a delimitation marker between 47:25 and 48:1, which is easily understandable because it is a translation from Gr. In this version 48:1 does not open with ܫܒܝܐ ܗܘܐ but with ܩܡ.

---

[8] Beentjes, 'Stammen van Israël', 149–150; note also the reference to the remnant that is left for David in 47:25 // 48:15.

[9] Jenner–Van Peursen, 'Unit Delimitation and the Text of Ben Sira', 163.

27.4 CONCLUDING REMARKS ABOUT THE PRAISE OF THE FATHERS

In § 27.1 we referred to our article about the Praise of the Fathers in which we expressed our sympathy with Lee's view, who argues that the genre of this section can best be described with the Greek ἐγκώμιον and that Sirach 44–49 can be considered as a *Beispielreihe*. After our syntactic analysis, we have to reformulate our standpoint. In both Syr and Heb (and partly also in Gr) the heroes of the past are not presented as individual examples, but as part of a long chain of history. The passages we have discussed in the present chapter are representative of the whole section. From this perspective, the interpretation of the Praise of the Fathers should be reconsidered. Ben Sira is deeply concerned with the flow of history as an ongoing chain of interrelated events rather than with the individual heroes who played a role in it.

PART SIX

CONCLUSIONS

CHAPTER TWENTY-EIGHT

CONCLUSIONS

28.1 THE FRAMEWORK OF THE PRESENT STUDY

The subjects addressed in the present study are at first sight very het-
erogeneous: Quotations from Syr in early Syriac literature, the question of whether the translator of Syr used a Greek version, the eschatological outlook of Syr, the computer programs that have been used in
the analysis of which the present monograph is the result, a new
model for the analysis of Syriac phrase patterns with a 'maximum matrix of phrase structure', a discussion of the debate between Muraoka
and Goldenberg about the nominal clause in Classical Syriac and an
attempt to apply insights from general linguistics regarding text linguistics to a North-West Semitic language. All these issues, however,
served the larger aim of establishing how *Language and Interpretation* interact in Syr: What elements are the results of the requirements
of the target language? What is the linguistic profile of Syr? How does
this profile relate to the linguistic profile of the Hebrew witnesses?
What elements in the translation are not required by the target language, and how can we account for them? Where did the Syriac language allow various alternative renderings of a construction in the
source text and what are the motivations behind the translator's
choices?

For the linguistic analysis that is necessary to address these questions we have followed a computer-assisted approach. This decision
was based on the insight that a systematic and consistent analysis of
the language system is a *conditio sine qua non* for addressing the
questions mentioned above and that a computer-assisted approach can
contribute considerably to such a linguistic analysis. This was an experiment in itself, because the application of corpus-based computer
linguistics to Syriac is still in its infancy. The experiment concerned
not only technical and linguistic aspects, but also the methodological
challenge to find a balance between the new possibilities provided by

computer-assisted research and the honourable traditions of philological scholarship. Computer-assisted approaches cannot replace traditional philological approaches, but they can complement and enrich them.

Our view of the role of computer-assisted research in relation to traditional philology is reflected in the table of contents of the present study. Part One contains a discussion about the text of Syr, its place in the textual history of Sirach, its character as a translation and its relationship to other texts and traditions. It concludes with a discussion of its religious profile. To some extent Part One can be regarded as a study in itself. It shows where the traditional philological analysis of Syr can bring us. We had to reject, question or modify some results of previous research, but to a large extent our critical evaluation of these results took place within the same framework of traditional philological and exegetical approaches in which this research has been carried out. In the present study, however, Part One functions as a preamble to Parts Two to Five, in which we present the method (Part Two) and results (Parts Three to Five) of the computer-assisted analysis.

28.2 SYR AND THE TEXTUAL HISTORY OF SIRACH

The textual basis for the present study is the text of Syr that will appear in the Leiden Peshitta edition. The earliest extant biblical manuscripts containing Sirach, which date from the seventh or maybe the sixth century, show many traces of textual corruption. The quotations in early Syriac literature reflect perhaps an earlier stage in the textual history of Syr, in which Syr was closer to Heb, but the evidence is too scant to draw any firm conclusion. Winter's thesis that they show traces of a Vetus Syra should be abandoned.

The relation of Syr to the other textual witnesses of Sirach, especially Heb and Gr, is complex. Syr shares many tendencies with the so-called expanded text of Sirach (SirII), some of which also occur elsewhere in the Peshitta. This made it extremely difficult to determine which tendencies should be ascribed to the translator's 'expanded' source text, and for which he himself is responsible. The arguments put forward in scholarly literature for the commonly held view that the Syriac translator consulted Gr, are unconvincing.

Syr appears to be a free, sometimes imprecise translation from a Hebrew source text. The characteristics of Syr include a number of 'targumic features', such as the creation of repetitive parallelism and the avoidance of anthropomorphisms.

28.3 THE RELIGIOUS PROFILE OF SYR

We should distinguish between the religious profile of Syr as a text, and the religious profile of the Syriac translator. The original book of Ben Sira, the considerable changes that took place in the textual transmission, including those that gave shape to SirII, and the way in which the Syriac translator did his work, all contributed to the religious profile of Syr. However, a study of the translator's religious profile should in the first place focus on those features for which the translator is responsible. Good candidates to belong to this category are the features that are not attested in the other textual witnesses of Sirach. These include the indifferent, if not hostile attitude towards sacrifices, the priesthood, the temple and the Law, and a high esteem for poverty. The claim that they also involve a preference for vegetarianism, an attempt to avoid references to the creation of Wisdom (reflecting an anti-Arian revision of the text), and a negative attitude towards the Prophets is unfounded (*pace* Winter).

Syr contains many borrowings from Old Testament passages, parallels with rabbinic literature, and rabbinic concepts and idioms. They may be due to the rabbinic flavour of the translator's source text and cannot be adduced as evidence of the translator's religious background. The parallels with New Testament passages may indicate a Christian or Jewish-Christian background, but the evidence is scarce.

The characteristics of the translator's religious profile give some indications as to where he should be located in the Jewish-Christian spectrum in the first centuries of the Common Era. His negative attitude towards sacrifices, priesthood and temple suggest that he should not be located in the 'rabbinic-Jewish' part of the spectrum. If the parallels with the New Testament are original, he can be located at the Jewish-Christian or Christian side of the spectrum. However, attempts to establish the translator's religious background more precisely and to identify it, for example, with the Ebionite movement, have proved impossible (*pace* Winter).

28.4 THE MODEL OF THE COMPUTER-ASSISTED ANALYSIS

Part Two contains a description of the CALAP model of the computer-assisted analysis that has been the basis for Parts Three to Five. It constitutes the bridge between Part One and the other parts. Part One presented the results of a traditional philological approach to Syr. A computer-assisted formal description of linguistic structures and the analysis of corresponding patterns in the Ancient Versions approach the texts from a different angle. A crucial point in this analysis is the principle that the formal description of structures and the systematic registration of corresponding patterns in parallel texts is distinct from and should receive priority over the functional or rhetorical explanation of these structures and parallels.

The CALAP model follows a distributional form-to-function approach; it gives the linguistic analysis priority over the literary and rhetorical analysis, and includes syntactical structures beyond sentence level. The text-hierarchical analysis of separate witnesses follows a bottom-up analysis. This means that it starts with the smaller textual units from which larger patterns are constructed. In this way we try to avoid the arbitrariness that is often involved in attempts to interpret smaller elements by positing them into larger, more abstract textual units that have been defined in advance on the basis of rhetorical or literary considerations.

The bottom-up analysis of the separate witnesses constitutes the point of departure for the subsequent comparative analysis of parallel texts. This comparative analysis follows a top-down approach: Within parallel texts we search for parallel paragraphs, within parallel paragraphs we look for parallel clauses, within parallel clauses we try to establish parallel phrases, and within parallel phrases we look for parallel words. The motivation behind this top-down comparison is that it cannot be decided *a priori* on which linguistic level the correspondences between parallel texts can be established. The comparison of parallel texts at various linguistic levels is an enrichment vis-à-vis approaches that are restricted to comparison at word level (compare J. Lust's complaint about the role of the computer in Septuagint studies).

28.5 PHRASE STRUCTURE

28.5.1 *Phrase atoms*

In our discussion of phrase structure the notion of 'phrase atoms' or 'minimal units' played an important role. In scholarly literature the distinction between optional specifications and obligatory parts of phrase atoms receives little attention. We see, for example, that grammars combine cases of [CstrNoun–Noun] and [Noun [*d*-Noun <sp>]] together under a heading such as 'noun expanded', but syntactically they represent quite different phenomena, namely the obligatory 'genitive' after a CstrNoun and the optional specification consisting of ܕ + Noun. The text-critical evidence illuminates this distinction since the optional specifications can be added or omitted in variant readings, whereas with the obligatory elements this is hardly ever the case.

The concept of phrase atoms also helps describe discontinuous phrases more accurately than in many traditional grammars. Thus Nöldeke's remark that the proper place of ܐܦ and ܕܝܢ is immediately after the first word can be refined if we replace 'word' with 'phrase atom'. Compare e.g. the position of ܕܝܢ in 26:23 ܐܢܬܬܐ ܕܝܢ ܙܢܝܬܐ 'For a wicked woman...' and 26:22 ܕܝܢ ܐܢܬܬ ܓܒܪܐ 'But a man's wife...'. In both cases ܕܝܢ follows the first phrase atom, but in 26:22 it does not come directly after the first word. Other elements that prefer the second position in the clause, such as the Ep, also follow the first phrase atom of the clause, rather than the first word.

Prepositions and construct nouns may give the phrase atom a complex internal structure. Some nouns, such as ܟܠ and ܒܝܬ, lend themselves more easily to construct chains. The maximum matrix that we could establish for phrase atoms is

[Preposition–CstrNoun–CstrNoun–Noun]

There are seven examples in Syr where all slots of the matrix are filled, e.g. 1:29 ܒܥܝܢܝ ܒܢܝ ܐܢܫܐ 'in the eyes of men'. In Heb longer chains of construct nouns are attested. Apparently the Syriac construction with ܕ offered an appropriate means to avoid long chains of construct nouns.

28.5.2 *Extensions*

A phrase atom can take several types of extensions: adjectives, phrases with ܕ, nouns, demonstratives, prepositional phrases and parallel elements. The basic pattern of an extended phrase is that in which a head consisting of a single word takes one extension, e.g. 7:21 ܚܟܝܡܐ ܥܒܕܐ 'a wise servant'. In traditional grammars the patterns consisting of a noun with one extension receive due attention. In many cases, however, more complex structures occur because of the following phenomena:

1. The extensions themselves can be extended by other specifications, as in 13:26 ܛܒܐ ܕܠܒܐ ܢܝܫܗܐ 'the marks of a good heart', where ܛܒܐ modifies the extension ܕܠܒܐ.
2. A phrase atom can take more than one extension, as in 16:3 ܕܒܝܫܐ ܣܓܝܐܐ ܒܢܝܐ 'many wicked sons', where both ܣܓܝܐܐ and ܕܒܝܫܐ modify ܒܢܝܐ.
3. Phrase atoms can have a complex internal structure. This applies both to phrase atoms that function as the head of a phrase (cf. the construct chain in 49:4 ܕܝܗܘܕܐ ܕܒܝܬ ܡܠܟܐ 'the kings of the house of Judah'), and to phrase atoms that function as a specification of another phrase atom (cf. the construct chain in the *d*-phrase in 39:19 ܒܣܪܐ ܕܒܢܝ ܥܒܕܐ ܟܠܗܘܢ 'all the works of the men of flesh').
4. A specification may be separated from its head. The result is a discontinuous phrase. The 'breakpoint' in a phrase is the slot between its head and the first specification. A phrase is not broken up, for example, between the first and the second specification.

We have tried to grasp the complex structures that may arise due to these phenomena with the 'maximum matrix of phrase structure':

[Prep–CstrNoun–CstrNoun–Noun] | [Dem.] [Adj.] [App.] [*d*-Noun] [Prep–Noun] [*d*-{Clause}] [Parallel Element]

If the phrase atom contains one or more construct nouns the specifications modify the *nomen regens* rather than the *nomen rectum*.

The maximum matrix enables us to establish a number of functional oppositions between e.g. the orders Noun–Adjective–*d*-phrase (the adjective modifies the noun) and Noun–*d*-phrase–Adjective (the adjective modifies the *d*-phrase) and to determine what is the most likely interpretation in patterns that are at first sight ambiguous, such as 1 Kgs 9:9 ܐ‍ܚܪ‍ܢ‍ܐ ܕ‍ܥܡܡ‍ܐ ܐܠ‍ܗ‍ܐ 'gods of other nations' rather than 'other gods of the nations'.

28.5.3 *Corresponding phrase patterns in Syr and Heb*

There are some corresponding patterns that occur fairly often in Heb and Syr, such as that in which [CstrNoun–Noun] in Heb corresponds to [Noun [Adjective <sp>]] in Syr, as in 15:12 ܒ‍ܢ‍ܐ ܐ‍ܢ‍ܫ‍ܐ ܥܘ‍ܠ‍ܐ 'in a wicked man' corresponding to Heb (A+B) חמס באנשי. Although we cannot equate the extant Hebrew manuscripts with the Syriac translator's Hebrew source text, the large frequency of these patterns of regular correspondences as well as, more generally, the large number of differences in internal phrase structure between Heb and Syr strongly suggest that Syr is a translation at phrase level. Consequently, we should be very hesitant to reconstruct the source text of the Syriac translator below phrase level. For the same reason, to account for the many differences between Heb and Syr below word level by explanations that apply only to individual cases would be methodologically unsound because it would ignore the frequency and general character of the phenomena described here.

As to the possibilities of reconstructing the source text of the Syriac translator, we have seen many examples where earlier scholars, especially up to the first decades of the twentieth century, reconstructed the translator's Hebrew source up to the internal structure of a phrase. Our study of corresponding phrase patterns argues against such reconstructions. Thus because of the frequency of the correspondence of a noun in Heb with Noun–Adjective in Syr (and *vice versa*) the view that in 13:17 ܕ‍ܝ‍ܩ‍ܐ ܠ‍ܓ‍ܒ‍ܪ‍ܐ 'with a righteous man' reflects איש צדיק instead of A's לצדיק (Bacher) or that in 20:7 ܚ‍ܟ‍ܝ‍ܡ‍ܐ ܓ‍ܒ‍ܪ‍ܐ 'a wise man' reflects איש חכם instead of C's חכם (Lévi) should be abandoned.

Also the view that in 15:18 ܡ̇ܢ ܕܡܡܠܠ ܒܝܫܬܐ 'and those who speak evil'
the translator's source text had a reading different from A's אנשי כזב
(Ginzberg) or in 37:3 ܗܘ ܣܢܐܐ 'the enemy and the wicked' a reading different from רע in B+D (C. Taylor) is unfounded. The same applies to reconstructions of the translator's Hebrew source pertaining to
the internal structure of phrase atoms, such as the claim that 36:3
ܐܝܕܟ 'your hand' reflects ידך instead of B's ביד (Ryssel) or that 47:22
ܠܛܒܘܬܗ 'his goodness' reflects חסדו instead of B's חסד (Lévi).

Theses observations imply that we are more pessimistic about the
possibilities of reconstructing the Hebrew source of the Syriac translator than Reiterer, who in his valuable study *'Urtext' und Übersetzungen* considers it possible to reconstruct it even on the level of words or
their equivalents such as object suffixes or possessive suffixes. He
ascribes many differences between Syr and Heb to the translator's
Hebrew source text, which we are inclined to explain as translational
features. Reiterer's approach may be valid for the corpus he investigated (44:16–45:26), but if we take into account the complete book of
Sirach, the frequency and regularity of the correspondences of different patterns argues for an explanation in terms of translation rather
than one in terms of many individual variants in the translator's Hebrew source text.[1]

Other explanations that are doubtful because of their atomistic and
incidental character concern the emendation of Syr on the basis of
Heb, such as the suggestion to delete ܕܣܟܠܬܐ in 25:18 ܒܥܠܗ ܕܣܟܠܬܐ
'the husband of a foolish woman' on the basis of C בעלה (Ryssel); the
assumption that the Syriac translator misread or misunderstand his
Hebrew source in 38:10 ܟܕܒܘ 'falsehood'; B מהכר פנים (Ryssel); and
the assumption of influence of Gr in 7:7 ܒܟܢܘܫܬܐ ܕܡܕܝܢܬܐ 'in the
community of the city'; A בעדת שערי אל (Smend).

Our systematic registration of all correspondences led us to attach
more weight to processes of translation than to incidental textual corruption for explaining the differences between the textual witnesses.
The acknowledgment of the importance of translation technique or
translation strategy is in itself not new. In general one sees that the
tendency to explain differences between Heb and Syr in terms of tex-

---

[1] It was precisely the infrequency of certain phenomena that led Reiterer to a text-
critical explanation, but the enlargement of the corpus tips the balance towards a more
general explanation in terms of a translational phenomenon.

tual corruption was especially strong at the end of the nineteenth century and the early decades of the twentieth century, but that in the second half of the twentieth century there is a tendency to attach more weight to translation technique. We have seen that an exhaustive registration of corresponding phrase patterns is very helpful to describe more precisely the various phenomena that are generally covered by terms such as 'translation technique'.

A complete registration of the corresponding phrase patterns is also helpful to give a formal description of the relation between witnesses without taking resort to designations that imply both description and explanation. Thus a formal registration of the pattern Noun *d*-Noun in Syr corresponding to a single noun in Heb covers examples that in Part One received various labels, such as 'Syr adds an explanatory word or phase' (e.g. 13:2 ܡܐܢܐ ܕܦܚܪܐ 'a pot of earthenware'; A פרור), 'avoidance of anthropomorphisms' (e.g. 32:13 ܫܡܗ ܕܐܠܗܐ 'the name of God'; B+F עושך), and 'targumic features' (e.g. 11:5 ܟܘܪܣܝܐ ܕܡܠܟܘܬܐ 'a royal throne'; A כסא). Likewise, examples where Noun–Adjective in Syr corresponds to a single noun in Heb include cases that belong to the categories 'Syr adds an explanatory word or phase' (e.g. 50:1 ܟܗܢܐ ܪܒܐ 'the High Priest'; B הכהן; 38:5 ܡܝܐ ܡܪܝܪܐ 'the bitter water'; B מים; this latter example could also receive the label 'Syr makes a reference to a biblical story more explicit'), 'adaptations to social and cultural conditions' (e.g. 25:21 ܠܫܘܦܪܗ ܕܐܢܬܬܐ ܒܝܫܬܐ 'the beauty of an evil woman'; C [אש]ה), 'influence of other parts of the Old Testament' (e.g. 49:5 ܠܥܡܐ ܢܘܟܪܝܐ 'to a foreign people'; B לגוי נבל נכרי; cf. Deut 32:11), and 'influence of the New Testament' (18:13 ܪܥܝܐ ܛܒܐ 'a good shepherd'; Gr ποιμήν; cf. John 10:11). Other corresponding phrase patterns account for phenomena that in Part One have been labelled 'Syr provides a free rendering of an idiomatic Hebrew expression' (e.g. 15:12 ܒܓܒܪ ܐܢܫܐ ܥܘܠܐ 'in a wicked man'; A+B באנשי חמס), 'Syr expands on the succinct style of the Hebrew' (e.g. 47:18 ܒܫܡܗ ܕܐܠܗܐ ܕܕܝܠܗ ܗܘ ܐܝܩܪܐ 'in the name of God whose is the honour'; B בשם הנכבד), 'Syr replaces a pronoun by a noun or proper noun' (e.g. 38:5 ܚܝܠܗ ܕܐܠܗܐ 'God's strength'; B^{txt} כחו; B^{mg} כוחם), 'Syr gives a shortened or imprecise rendering of sacrificial terminology' (e.g. 50:13 ܩܘܪ̈ܒܢܐ 'the offerings'; B אשי ייי), 'Syr reflects a feature or tendency that is typical of SirII' (e.g. 7:17 ܕܟܠܗܘܢ ܒܢܝܢܫܐ; A+C אנוש), and 'influence of adjacent lines' (e.g. 18:33 ܡܣܟܢ ܘܪܘܝ, ܘܙܠܝܠ ܘܡܦܩ 'poor and a drunkard and licentious and a gossip'; C: זולל וסובא); and further phenomena such as 'Syr provides

זולל וסובא‎ (‎); and further phenomena such as 'Syr provides names with their standard epithets even when these are lacking in the Hebrew' (e.g. 47:1 ܢܬܢ ܢܒܝܐ 'Nathan, the prophet'; B נתן‎) and 'transpositions' (37:8 ܚܝܐ ܘܡܘܬܐ 'life and death'; B חיים ומות‎; D מות וחיים‎).

The formal registration of the correspondences does not contradict the explanation or labels given to these examples in more traditional approaches, but they help us distinguish between the phenomena that can be registered formally and the explanations that can be given to them. A label such as 'explanatory addition' indicates both a plus in one of the textual witnesses, and its secondary character (implied by the word 'addition' rather than the neutral 'plus') and its function ('explanation' rather than, for example, changing the meaning of the text to bring into harmony with other passages). The formal registration of correspondences is also useful if it comes to their interpretation. Thus the designation of a number of examples as 'targumic' is of limited value if it is used for a set of examples that belong to a larger group of cases reflecting similar phenomena. And even one of the most convincing examples of a Christian background of Syr, namely the addition of 'good' in 18:13 partly loses its weight if one realizes that such additions of adjectives occur rather frequently in Syr.

Stressing the importance of linguistic and translational factors, we should at the same time not try not to press all variants into this strait-jacket. Inner-Hebrew as well as inner-Syriac variations show that in both the Hebrew and the Syriac transmission changes in internal phrase structure occurred. The methodological exigency that 'plurality should not be posited without necessity' (Occam's razor) should not be applied with such a stringency that any other explanation that applies to an individual case is *a priori* dismissed.[2] This warning is even more serious in areas where the Hebrew or Syriac witnesses show much variation and development.

In many cases a phrase in Syriac corresponds to a phrase in Hebrew, although both versions show a different internal phrase structure. This means that the translation unit is most often the phrase. This phenomenon, which is not restricted to Sirach, is often described in terms of translation technique, but other factors related to the process

---

[2] In this respect we disagree with Van der Louw, *Transformations*, who is very stringent in giving priority to translation technique in the explanation of differences between the Masoretic Text and the Septuagint.

of construal and interpretation may have played a role as well. Thus we cannot rule out the possibility that the cognitive processes involved in picking up a segment from the source text, its interpretation, the decision how to render it and the writing down of the translation has influenced the size of the translation units.[3] The differences from Targum Onkelos and Targum Jonathan, in which the translation unit is most often the word rather than the phrase, but in which we also find expansions of the size of a clause or even larger, may be explained by the different functions these translations have.

28.6 CLAUSE STRUCTURE

28.6.1 *Introduction*

In the history of research clause structure has received much more attention than phrase structure. Whereas in our analysis of phrase structure our main adventure was the development of a new model of analysis that takes into the account the complex structures that occur in the corpus instead of the simplified examples given in many grammars, in our chapter on clause structure the main challenge was to cope with competing theories and views that have been developed around much-debated issues such as the Syriac NC and the so-called cleft sentences.

28.6.2 *Nominal clauses*

In the field of bipartite NCs there are basically two views. According to Muraoka there are four patterns: Pr–Su_{noun}, Su_{noun}–Pr, Pr–Su_{pron}, Su_{pron}–Pr. Goldenberg acknowledges only one pattern, namely Pr–Su_{pron} (Pr–s) and explains the other patterns as exceptions to this basic pattern due to various factors. Syr contains many examples of each of the four types of bipartite NCs, including a number of examples not accounted for by Goldenberg's exceptions. This seems to argue against Goldenberg's view, but the character of our corpus (an early text,

---

[3] See Jenner–Van Peursen–Talstra 'Interdisciplinary Approach', 30–31; cf. Weitzman, *From Judaism to Christianity*, 56–57; idem, *Syriac Version*, 3–7.

translated from Hebrew) prevents us from expanding our observations
on Syr to Classical Syriac in general.

A similar disagreement between Goldenberg and Muraoka concerns the tripartite NC. Goldenberg also derives all tripartite NCs from
the basic pattern P–s: In a tripartite NC a subject is added in fronted or
rear extraposition (Su || Pr–s and Pr–s || Su). Muraoka distinguishes
four patterns: Su–Pr–Ep, Su–Ep–Pr, Pr–Su–Ep and Pr–Ep–Su. Joosten
takes an intermediate position: in most respects he follows Goldenberg but he also acknowledges the pattern Su–Ep–Pr. Accordingly, the
focus point of the debate are the two disputed patterns Su–Ep–Pr and
Pr–Su–Ep. In Syr these patterns are much less frequent than the two
undisputed patterns. Su–Ep–Pr is attested about ten times, e.g. 41:3
ܡܢܬܟ ܗܘܐܝ ܡܛܠ 'Because it is your portion'. We have tried to describe the differences between Muraoka's and Goldenberg's approach
to such clauses as being related to different levels of linguistic analysis, namely that of grammar and of information structure respectively.
Moreover, the differences between them are often not as great as they
seem. Thus the view that in 41:3 the first ܗܘ is the grammatical subject that has been rhematized or focalized (Muraoka) and the view that
it has been turned into the predicate (Goldenberg) reflect the same
interpretation of this clause as 'That is your portion'. Problematic examples, such as the often quoted Matt 16:16 ܡܫܝܚܐ ܗܘ ܐܢܬ as an
answer to the question 'Who do you say that I am?' pose problems to
both approaches and hence do not support either of them. We are
aware that Muraoka has recently changed his view, but prefer to follow the 'old Muraoka' in the acknowledgment of the pattern Su–Ep–
Pr. Our corpus does not contain material that would enable us to contribute to the discussion about the other disputed pattern, Pr–Su–Ep.
The only possible example in Syr of this pattern is 6:16 ܚܝܐ ܘܐܝܢܐ
ܕܐܠܗܐ ܗܘ '(A faithful friend is a medicine of life) and he who
fears God is one'.

Besides the NC there are other ways to express the notion of 'to
be'. In our case study for 'situated existence' we saw that this notion
can be expressed by bipartite NCs (e.g. 29:28 ܡܐ ܕܒܐܝܕܟ 'what is in
your hand'), tripartite NCs (e.g. 1:1 ܘܡܢ ܗܝ ܥܡܗ ܡܢ ܥܠܡ 'and she is
with Him from eternity'), clauses with ܐܝܬ (e.g. 29:26 ܡܕܡ ܕܐܝܬ
ܒܐܝܕܝܟ 'what is in your hands'), and clauses with ܗܘܐ (e.g. 24:11
ܘܒܐܘܪܫܠܡ ܗܘܐ ܫܘܠܛܢܝ 'and in Jerusalem was my authority'). The ܐܝܬ
clauses and the bipartite constructions seem to be free variants, but in

the patterns with ܠ the ܐܝܬ clauses are more frequent. Tripartite NCs to indicated situated existence are rare. The construction with ܗܘܐ most often serves to express past or future tense or modality.

The main function of ܐܝܬ is to indicate existence or location, but occasionally it is used in descriptive NCs. We made a classification of ܐܝܬ clauses in which we combined Nöldeke's distinction between 'existential' and 'copulaic', Muraoka's distinction between 'existential' and 'locative', and Goldenberg's distinction between 'absolute existence' and 'situated existence', and in which we took into account whether or not ܐܝܬ takes a suffix, whether the subject is definite or indefinite, and the presence and nature of other elements in the clause.

ܗܘܐ with a predicative complement is used as an alternative for the bipartite or tripartite NC and serves to express past or future tense or modality, but other usages are attested as well. Thus there occur a number of examples of the syntagm *hwayt qātel* with imperatival force and of *lā (h)wā* for the negation of a NC or a constituent other than the predicate in verbal clauses.

28.6.3 *Extraposition and pronominal agreement*

For an investigation of 'extraposition' and 'pronominal agreement', Khan's *Studies in Semitic Syntax* proved to be the best point of departure. Not only because he gives a precise and detailed analysis of these phenomena, but also because his *form-to-function* methodology fits in very well with our approach. Extraposition is often used to indicate the topic of a sentence. The use of a resumptive pronoun makes the analysis of clauses in terms of extraposition (rather than mere variation in word order) unequivocal, as in 7:21 ܥܒܕܐ ܚܟܝܡܐ ܐܚܒܘܗܝ, ܐܝܟ ܢܦܫܟ 'A wise servant—love him as yourself', corresponding to עבד משכיל חבב כנפש in Heb (A[+C]).

The issue of 'extraposition' is closely related to the scholarly debate about the syntactic structure of NCs, because Goldenberg and others analyse the most frequent patterns of tripartite NCs (Su–Pr–Ep and Pr–Ep–Su) in terms of extraposition. Although our analysis of extraposition does not give decisive arguments in the ongoing debate, the functional equivalence of 'real' extraposition in e.g. 10:29 ܡܢ ܕܡܚܝܒ ܢܦܫܗ ܡܢܘ ܢܙܟܝܘܗܝ, 'He who condemns himself—who will acquit him?' and NCs of the type Su–Pr–Ep, such as 1:1 ܠܟ ܫܘܒܚܐ ܗܘ

ܡܢ ܡܪܝܐ ܗܝ 'All wisdom—it comes from the Lord' and Pr–Ep–Su, such as 15:18 ܡܛܠ ܕܓܢܒܪܐ ܗܝ ܚܟܡܬܗ ܕܐܠܗܐ 'Because she is a warrior—God's wisdom', favours an interpretation of the these NCs in terms of extraposition (Su || Pr–s and, with rear extrapostion, Pr–s || Su). This analysis is also helpful to explain the difference in word order between Syr and Heb in 6:16 ܪܚܡܐ ܡܗܝܡܢܬܐ ܣܡܐ ܗܘ ܕܚܝܐ 'A faithful friend is a medicine of life'; A צרור חיים אוהב אמונה: The extraposition construction enabled the Syriac translator to put ܪܚܡܐ ܡܗܝܡܢܬܐ in topic position, while at the same time retaining the Pr–Su pattern of the main clause.

Pronominal agreement may take place at phrase level or at clause level. In the latter case one of its functions is to keep clause nuclei intact. Compare the nucleus ܠܐ ܢܓܡܪܘܢܗ̇ in 24:28 ܠܐ ܢܓܡܪܘܢܗ̇ ܩܕ̈ܡܝܐ ܠܚܟܡܬܐ 'The first ones will not accomplish wisdom'.

28.6.4 *Cleft Sentences*

Another phenomenon directly related to NCs are the so-called cleft sentences. This designation is used for clauses of the type X–Ep–Verb, such as 46:6 ܕܐܠܗܐ ܗܘ ܐܩܪܒ ܥܡܗܘܢ 'That God joined the battle with them'. This type of clause too has been the subject of a fierce debate between Goldenberg and Muraoka. Both scholars ascribe a rhematizing function to the Ep, but they differ in their description of this phenomenon. According to Goldenberg the Ep 'cleaves' the sentence and turns the preceding element into the predicate; according to Muraoka the Ep is an emphatic particle that gives the preceding element prominence or focus. Likewise, both scholars agree in observing some differences between the Syriac 'cleft sentences' and cleft sentences known from Indo-European languages. However, whereas for Goldenberg this is reason to speak of 'imperfectly-transformed sentences'; Muraoka concludes that the notion of 'cleft sentences' should be abandoned at all.

As in the case of the tripartite NC, we have tried to describe the differences between Muraoka's and Goldenberg's approach as related to different levels of linguistic analysis. Although we prefer, unlike Goldenberg, to distinguish between the grammatical level of analysis (i.e. ܐܠܗܐ in 46:6 is the subject) and the functional level (i.e. ܐܠܗܐ is the comment), our attempts to build a bridge between the two approaches imply that we do not share Muraoka's strong opposition against the application of the notion of 'cleft sentences'.[4]

28.6.5 *Comparison with the Hebrew*

Our discussion of phrase level in Part Three contains many references to reconstructions of the translator's Hebrew source text and other text-critical arguments found in the scholarly literature. As to the differences between Syr and Heb at clause level, however, only rarely are philological 'solutions' given for these differences. Exceptions include Ginzberg's assumption that in 6:16 ܘܡܢ ܐܠܗܐ ܚܝܐ ܐܣܝܐ ܕܚܝܐ '(A faithful friend is a medicine of life) and he who fears God is one', which corresponds to ירא אל ישיגם in Heb (A), the Syriac translator read ישנו and translated it with ܗܘܡ. However, this assumption is unconvincing, because the copulaic use of יש is very unusual in Classical Hebrew. Sometimes a scholar seems to have been puzzled by a pronominal agreement construction in Syr. This may be the background of Ryssel's claim that ܐܢܬ in 25:17 ܡܚܘܪܐ ܕܐܢܬܬܐ ܒܝܫܬܐ ܡܚܫܟܐ ܐܦܘܗܝ ܕܒܥܠܗ, ܘܐܢܬ 'The evil of an evil wife makes pale the face of her husband' should be omitted and of Lévi's comment on 36:1 ܦܨܢ ܐܠܗܐ ܠܟܠܢ 'Save us, O God, all of us' corresponding to B הושיענו אלהי הכל, that the Syriac translator did not understand the expression אלהי הכל. Differences between Syr and Heb at clause level have also been ignored by scholars who argued that the Geniza manuscripts of Heb reflect a retranslation from Syr. Thus Lévi's claim that 6:14 (A) אוהב אמונה אוהב תקיף is a calque of ܪܚܡܐ ܪܓܝܪܐ ܪܚܡܐ ܗܘ ܬܩܝܦܐ ignores that Heb has a bipartite NC and Syr the tripartite pattern.

   One should not conclude from the little attention paid in commentaries and other studies to the differences between Syr and Heb in clause structure that such differences are rare. Thus a tripartite NC in Syr corresponds frequently with a bipartite clause in Heb; a number of

---

[4] Muraoka expressed this opposition most explicitly in a response to my 'Three Approaches', in which I tried to build a bridge between Goldenberg's and Muraoka's approaches to the tripartite NC. Note especially the end of his response (p. 196): 'The fact that some of what Goldenberg and Wertheimer call cleft sentences, whether imperfectly transformed or pseudo, can be translated into English as cleft sentences does not mean that they can be analysed as such in terms of Syriac or Hebrew grammar. If one wishes to stay in touch with general linguistics, one had better stick to this fundamental of any linguistic analysis'.

times Syr has ܐܝܬ or ܗܘܐ where there is no equivalent in Heb; it uses
hwayt qātel where Heb has an imperative; and it has *qātel (h)wā*
where Heb has a perfect. Sometimes Syr and Heb display different
constituent orders in NCs. In other cases the Syriac translator used the
'niceties of Syriac syntax' (Goldenberg) to express certain nuances
that in Heb are only marked by word order. Thus he used ܠܐ ܗܘܐ
where his source text had in all likelihood only אל; he 'cleft' sentences
with the help of the Ep to make the information structure more explicit, and added resumptive pronouns referring to an element in extraposition as well as agreement pronouns.

This evidence strongly suggests that the Syriac translator did not
try to mirror the clause structure of his Hebrew source. However, interference from the source text is a complex process that may take
place even if there is no conscious attempt to mirror the source text.
For example, although the Syriac translator adds ܐܝܬ or the Ep in a
number of cases, the high frequency of bipartite NCs is still remarkable. To decide whether this phenomenon reflects the influence of a
Hebrew source text or rather an early stage in the Syriac language,
requires an analysis of non-translated sources that is beyond the scope
of the present study.

28.7 TEXT HIERARCHY

In Part Three (Phrase Structure) we investigated phenomena that have
received little attention in scholarly literature. In Part Four (Clause
Structure), on the contrary, we discussed issues that gave rise to fierce
scholarly debates and we had to determine which model we preferred
for our analysis of Syr and how our research into Syr, although a
translation, could contribute to the debate. In Part Five (Text Hierarchy) we covered an area that has received attention in Semitics, especially in Hebrew studies, but in which the research in Semitics does
not line up with insights in general linguistics that have been developed over the past few decades. Weinrich's *Tempus*, which appeared
in 1964, still seems to be the main reference point for the integration
of text linguistics in North-West Semitic studies. For this reason we
started Chapter 26 with a discussion of some basic concepts and the
distinctions between 'embedding' and 'hypotaxis', 'clause' and 'discourse segment', and 'coherence' and 'cohesion'. We observed that

phenomena that from a linguistic perspective can be labelled as *optional* manifestations of rhetorical relations show much more text-critical variation than other phenomena, both in the Syriac textual transmission and in the multilingual comparison of Syr, Heb and Gr. Thus in the case of relative ܕ we could observe variation between non-restrictive relative clauses and other types of hypotaxis, but such variation does not occur where ܕ introduces a restrictive relative clause. A number of times conceptual relations that remain implicit in one witness, are made explicit in another. Since the grammaticalization of conceptual relations is a language-internal phenomenon and since there are no indications that the Syriac translator tried to mirror each word and particle of his source text, it is impossible to determine the markers of clause relations in the translator's Hebrew source. For this reason we had to reject many reconstructions of the translator's source text, especially regarding the presence or absence of conjunctions, made in scholarly literature. The formal description of participant reference appeared to be helpful to grasp the 'targumic' tendency to replace a proper noun by a common noun.

In Chapter 27 we applied these insights to some sections of Sirach 44–50, the Praise of the Fathers. We concluded that the interpretation of this section as a *Beispielreihe* should be abandoned because of the syntactic and text-hierarchical structure of this passage. It presents the chain of events in the past and the role that the Fathers played in it, but it does not present the heroes of the past as individual separate examples. Although this conclusion is based on an analysis of these chapters in Syr, they apply to a large extent also to Heb and Gr.

28.8 THE LINGUISTIC PROFILE OF SYR

In the course of our investigation we discussed some phenomena that are well-known for the diachronic development that they underwent in Classical Syriac as appears, for example, from a comparison between the Old Syriac Gospels and the Peshitta. In these cases Syr reflects the early constructions. This applies to the position of ܣܓܝ and ܐܚܪܝܢ, the position of a number in relation to the thing numbered, the use of the absolute state for numbered objects, the rare use of copulaic ܐܝܬ and the high frequency of bipartite NCs.

To what extent interference of the Hebrew source text has shaped
the linguistic profile of Syr is hard to establish. The differences between Heb and Syr mentioned in the preceding paragraphs suggest
that this profile has hardly been influenced by the Hebrew source text.
Thus the translator uses fairly often the construction with ܕ instead of
the construct chain, or a tripartite NC where Heb has a bipartite construction. Moreover, the pattern of Hebrew influence that Avinery established for other parts of the Peshitta (i.e. a Hebrew construct chain
is translated with a Syriac construct chain at its first occurrence, after
which the translator shifts to a construction with ܕ) is not attested in
Syr. Nevertheless, we cannot rule out the possibility that the influence
of the Hebrew source text played a role in those cases where the
Syriac translator used the construct state or the bipartite construction.
As we noted above, the high frequency of bipartite NCs is striking and
requires an explanation, whether in terms of language development
(reflection of an early phase of Classical Syriac), or in terms of interference (influence of the Hebrew source text).

There are other phenomena that perhaps indicate the influence of
a Hebrew source text, because they reflect unidiomatic Syriac, such as
the modification of a noun by a prepositional phrase not preceded by
ܕ. However, for an overall assessment of the influence of the Hebrew
source text on the linguistic profile of Syr we should also take into
account the much larger number of phenomena that do not strike us as
unidiomatic and are more difficult to evaluate. Thus there are some
cases where the constituent order of a NC in Syr differs in Heb, but in
those many cases where the orders agree, the question as to whether
Syr has been influenced by its Hebrew source can only be answered
after a thorough investigation of constituent order in non-translated
Syriac texts. Such an investigation was beyond the scope of the
research project that resulted in the present study, but will be
addressed in a new research project, called 'TURGAMA: Computer-
Assisted Analysis of the Peshitta and the Targum: Text, Language and
Interpretation'.

BIBLIOGRAPHY

The abbrevaiations of series and periodicals conform with those in S.M. Schwertner, *Theologische Realenzyklopaedie Abkürzungsverzeichnis* (2nd ed.; Berlin/New York 1994). Other abbreviations used:

AS	*Aramaic Studies*
BIS	Biblical Interpretation Series
ELH	English Language Series
FGS	Functional Grammar Series
HCP	Human Cognitive Processing
JAB	*Journal for the Aramaic Bible*
JCPS	Jewish and Christian Perspectives Series
KLAG	Kölner Linguistische Arbeiten – Grammatik
LC	Language and Computers
LOAPL	*Langues Orientales Anciennes Philologie et Linguistique*
NHLS	North-Holland Linguistic Series
POSL	Perspectives on Syriac Linguistics
SAIS	Studies in the Aramaic Interpretation of Scripture
SBL.SBL	Society of Biblical Literature Studies in Biblical Literature
SNLP	Studies in Natural Language Processing

1. VERSIONS OF BEN SIRA

1.1 *Syriac*

Ceriani A.M., *Translatio syra pescitto veteris testamenti ex codice Ambrosiano sec. fere VI photolithographice edita* (2 vols.; Milan, 1876–83).

Lagarde, P.A de, *Libri veteris testamenti apocryphi syriace* (Leipzig–London, 1861).

'Sirach', in *The Old Testament in Syriac according to the Peshitta Version* IV, 1 (in preparation).

1.2 *Hebrew*

Beentjes, P.C., *The Book of Ben Sira in Hebrew: A Text Edition of All Extant Hebrew Manuscripts and a Synopsis of All Parallel Hebrew Ben Sira Texts* (VT.S 68; Leiden, 1997).

Ben Ḥayyim, Z., ספר בן סירא: המקור קונקורדנציה וניתוח אוצר המלים (*The Book of Ben Sira: Text, Concordance and an Analysis of the Vocabulary*) (Jerusalem, 1973).

1.3 *Greek*

Ziegler, J., *Sapientia Iesu Filii Sirach* (Septuaginta 12/2; 2nd ed.; Göttingen, 1980).

1.4 *The 'Prosodic Version of Ben Sira' (MS Adler 3053)*

Marcus, J., 'A Fifth MS of Ben Sira', *JQR* N.S. 21 (1930–31), 223–240.

Marcus, J., *The Newly Discovered Original Hebrew of Ben Sira (Ecclesiasticus xxxiii, 16–xxiv, 1): The Fifth Manuscript and a Prosodic Version of Ben Sira (Ecclesiasticus xxi, 22–xxiii, 9)* (Philadelphia, 1931).

2. SYRIAC LITERATURE

2.1 Aphrahat, *Demonstrations*

Parisot, I., *Aphraatis Sapientis Persae demonstrationes* (PS I/1–2; 1894–1907).

2.2 Bar Hebraeus, *Scholia on Bar Asira*

Kaatz, S., *Die Scholien des Gregorius Abulfaragius Bar Hebraeus zum Weisheitsbuch des Josua ben Sira nach vier Handschriften des Horreum Mysteriorum mit Einleitung, Übersetzung und Anmerkungen* (Halle, 1892).

2.3 Bardaiṣan, *Book of the Law of the Countries*

Drijvers, H.J.W., *The Book of the Laws of the Countries. Dialogue on Fate of Bardaiṣan of Edessa* (Assen, 1965).

2.4 *Catalogus Sinaiticus*

Smith Lewis, A., *Catalogue of the Syriac Mss. in the Convent of S. Catharine on Mount Sinai* (StSin 1; London–Cambridge, 1894).

2.5 Ephrem, *Testament of Ephrem*

Duval, R., 'Le testament de Saint Ephrem', *JA*, 9th series, 18 (1901), 234–239.

2.6 Ephrem, Pseudo-, *Sermo de admonitione et poenitentia*

Lamy, T.J., *Sancti Ephraem Syri hymni et sermones* (4 vols.; Mechelen, 1882–1902).

2.7 Ishoyahb III, *Letters*

Duval, R., *Īšōʿyahb III patriarchae. Liber epistularum* (CSCO 11–12, Syr. 11–12).

2.8 John Rufus, *Plerophories*

Nau, F., *Jean Rufus, évêque de Maïouma, Plérophories: témoignages et révélations contres le concile de Chalcédoine* (Recueil de monographies 4; PO 8/1; Paris–Freibourg, 1911).

2.9 *Joseph and Asenath*

Brooks, E.W., *Historia ecclesiastica Zachariae Rhetori vulgo adscripta* I (CSCO 83, 88, Syr. 38, 41; Leuven, 1924).

Land, J.P.N., *Zachariae episcopi Mitylenes aliorumque scripta historica graeca plerumque deperdita* (Anecdota Syriaca 3; Leiden, 1870).

2.10 *Liber Graduum*

Kmosko, M., *Liber graduum* (PS I/3; Paris, 1926).

2.11 *Life of Eulogius the Stone-Cutter*

Smith Lewis, A., *Life of Eulogius the Stone-Cutter, The Forty Martyrs of the Sinai Desert and the Story of Eulogius* from a Palestinian Syriac and Arabic Palimpsest transcribed by Agnes Smith Lewis (HSem 9; Cambridge, 1912), ܓܗ–ܓ (text), 17–23 (translation).

Müller-Kessler, C. and M. Sokoloff, *The Forty Martyrs of the Sinai Desert, Eulogius, the Stone-Cutter, and Anastasia* (A Corpus of Christian Palestinian Aramaic 3; Groningen, 1996), 69–97.

2.12 *Life of Rabbula*

Overbeck, J.J., *Opera selecta S. Ephraemi Syri Rabulae episcopi Edesseni, Balaei aliorumque* (Oxford, 1865), 212–248.

2.13 *Martyrium Theclae*

Assemani, S.E., *Acta sanctorum martyrum orientalium et occidentalium in duas partes distributa* (2 vols.; Rome, 1748), 123–128.

2.14 Meliton, *Apology to Antonius Caesar*

Cureton, W., *Spicilegium syriacum* (London, 1855), ܡܝܬܪܐ, 85–99.

2.15 Peshitta

The Old Testament in Syriac according to the Peshiṭta Version (Leiden, 1976–..).

2.16 Philoxenus of Mabbug, *Discourses*

Wallis Budge, E.A., *The Discourses of Philoxenus Bishop of Mabbôgh, AD 485–519* (2 vols.; London, 1893–94).

2.17 Philoxenus of Mabbug, *Letter to the Monks of Senun*

Halleux, A. de, *Philoxène de Mabbog, Lettre aux moines de Senoun* (CSCO 231–232, Syr. 98–99; Leuven, 1963).

3. OTHER SOURCES

3.1 *Aboth de Rabbi Nathan*

Schechter, S., אבות דרבי נתן (*Aboth de Rabbi Nathan*) (London–Vienna–Frankfurt, 1887).

3.2 *Amman Citadel Inscription*

Aufrecht, W.E., *A Corpus of Ammonite Inscriptions* (ANETS 4; Lewston–Queenston–Lampeter, 1989).

3.3 Aules Persius Flaccus, *Satires*

Kißel, W., *Aules Persius Flaccus Satiren* (Heidelberg, 1990).

3.4 Philo, *Quod omnis probus liber sit*

Petit, M., *Philon d'Alexandrie, Quod omnis probus liber sit* (Les œuvres de Philon d'Alexandrie 28; Paris, 1974).

4. OTHER LITERATURE

Ahituv, S., בית-שני ימי וראשית בית-ראשון מימי עבריות כתובות אסופות (*Handbook of Ancient Hebrew Inscriptions: From the First Temple Period and the Beginning of the Second Temple Period*) (Jerusalem, 1992).

Aland, B. and A. Juckel, *Das Neue Testament in syrischer Überlieferung* 1. *Die grossen Katholischen Briefe* (Berlin–New York, 1986).

Albrektson, B., *Studies in the Text and Theology of the Book of Lamentations* (Lund, 1963).

Andersen, F.I., *The Hebrew Verbless Clause in the Pentateuch* (JBL.MS 14; Nashville–New York, 1970).

Andersen, F.I. and A.D. Forbes, 'On Marking Clause Boundaries', in *Proceedings of the Third Interantional Colloquium Bible and Computer: Interpretation, Hermeneutics, Expertise, Tübingen, 26–30 August 1991* (Paris–Genève, 1992), 181–202.

Avinery, I., 'An Example of the Influence of Hebrew on the Peshitta Translation— The Status Constructus', *Textus* 9 (1981), 36–38.

——. 'On the Nominal Clause in the Peshitta', *JSSt* 22 (1977), 48–49.

——. הפשיטתא תרגום יד על הסורית הלשון תחביר (*Syntaxe de la Peshitta sur le Pentateuche*) (PhD diss., Jerusalem 1973).

——. 'The Position of Declined KL in Syriac', *JAOS* 104 (1984), 333.

——. 'The Position of the Demonstrative Pronoun in Syriac', *JNES* 34 (1975), 123–127.

Baasten, M.F.J., 'Anticipatory Pronominal Agreement and Qumran Hebrew Phraseology', in *Miscelánea de estudios árabes y hebraicos. Sección de hebreo* 53 (2004), 59–72.

——. *The Non-Verbal Clause in Qumran Hebrew* (PhD diss., Leiden University, 2006).

Baasten, M.F.J. and W.Th. van Peursen, *Hamlet on a Hill: Semitic and Greek Studies Presented to Professor T. Muraoka on the Occasion of his Sixty-Fifth Birthday* (OLA 118; Leuven, 2003).

Bacher, W., 'Notes on the Cambridge Fragments of Ecclesiasticus', *JQR* 12 (1899), 272–290.

——. Review of Lévi, *L'Ecclésiastique* I (Paris, 1989): *REJ* 37 (1898), 308–317.

——. 'The Hebrew Text of Ecclesiasticus', *JQR* 9 (1897), 543–562.

Baillet, M., J.T. Milik and R. de Vaux, *Les 'Petites Grottes' de Qumrân* (DJD 3; Oxford,1962).

Barnes, W.E., 'On the Influence of the Septuagint on the Peshitta', *JThS* 2 (1901), 186–197.

Barr, J., *The Typology of Literalism in Ancient Biblical Translations* (MSU XV; Göttingen, 1979).

Barthélemy, D., 'La qualité du texte massorétique de Samuel', in E. Tov (ed.), *The Hebrew and Greek Texts of Samuel* (Jerusalem, 1980), 1–44.

Barthélemy, D. and J.T. Milik, *Qumran Cave 1* (DJD 1; Oxford, 1955).

Barton, J., *Oracles of God. Perceptions of Ancient Prophecy in Israel after the Exile* (London, 1986).

Bauer, W., *Griechisch-deutsches Wörterbuch zu den Schriften des Neuen Testaments und der frühchristlichen Literatur* (6th ed. by K. Aland and B. Aland; Berlin, 1988).

Baumstark, A., *Nichtevangelische syrische Perikopenordnungen des ersten Jahrtausends* (2nd ed.; LWQF 15; Münster, 1972).

Beck, E., 'Die konditionale Periode in der Sprache Ephräms des Syrers', *OrChr* 64 (1980), 1–34.

Beckwith, R., *The Old Testament Canon of the New Testament Church and its Background in Early Judaism* (London, 1985).

Beentjes, P.C., 'De stammen van Israël herstellen. Het portret van Elia bij Jesus Sirach', *AmstCah* 5 (1984), 147–155.

——. 'Jesus Sirach 38:1–15: Problemen rondom een symbool', *Bijdr.* 41 (1980), 260–265.

——. 'Reading the Hebrew Ben Sira Manuscripts Synoptically: A New Hypothesis', in P.C. Beentjes (ed.), *The Book of Ben Sira in Modern Research: Proceedings of the First International Ben Sira Conference, 28–31 July 1996* (BZAW 255; Berlin–New York, 1997), 95–111.

Benveniste, E., 'Les niveaux de l'analyse linguistique', in H.G. Lunt (ed.), *Proceedings of the Ninth International Congress of Linguists, Cambridge, Mass., August 27–31, 1962* (The Hague, 1964), 266–275 (= idem, *Problèmes de linguistique générale* [2 vols.; Paris, 1966–74] I, 119–131).

Bergen, R.D. (ed.), *Biblical Hebrew and Discourse Linguistics* (Winona Lake, 1994).

Berman, R.A. and A. Grosu, 'Aspects of the Copula in Modern Hebrew', in P. Cole (ed.), *Studies in Modern Hebrew Syntax and Semantics. The Transformational-Generative Approach* (NHLS 32; Amsterdam–NewYork–Oxford, 1976), 265–285.

Boer, M.C. de, 'Elkesaites', in Schiffman–VanderKam, *Encyclopaedia of the Dead Sea Scrolls* I, 247–248.

Böhmisch, F., '"Haec omnia liber vitae": Zur Theologie der erweiterten Textformen des Sirachbuches', *SNTU* 22 (1997), 160–180.

——. 'Die Textformen des Sirachbuches und ihre Zielgruppen', *Protokolle zur Bibel* 6,2 (1997), 87–122.

Borbone, P.G., 'Response to "A Discourse on Method" by Hendrik Jan Bosman and Constantijn J. Sikkel', in Van Keulen–Van Peursen, *Corpus Linguistics and Textual History*, 115–117.

Borbone, P.G., K.D. Jenner et al., *The Old Testament in Syriac according to the Peshiṭta Version V. Concordance 1. The Pentateuch* (Leiden, 1997).

Bosman, H.J., 'Computer-Assisted Clause Description of Deuternomy 8', in *Proceedings of the Fourth International Colloquium Bible and Computer: Desk and Discipline: The Impact of Computers on Bible Studies* (Paris, 1995), 76–100.

——. 'Two Proposals for a Structural Analysis of Lamentations 3 and 5', in *Proceedings of the Third International Colloquium Bible and Computer: Interpretation, Hermeneutics, Expertise, Tübingen, 26–30 August 1991* (Paris–Genève, 1992), 77–98.

Bosman, H.J. and C.J. Sikkel, 'A Discourse on Method: Basic Parameters of Computer-Assisted Linguistic Analysis on Word Level', in Van Keulen–Van Peursen, *Corpus Linguistics and Textual History*, 85–113.

——. 'Reading Authors and Reading Documents', in Cook, *Bible and Computer*, 113–134.

——. 'Response to Pier G. Borbone', in Van Keulen–Van Peursen, *Corpus Linguis-
    tics and Textual History*, 119–121.
——. 'Worked Examples from 1 Kings 2:1–9: Word Level Analysis', in Van
    Keulen–Van Peursen, *Corpus Linguistics and Textual History*, 129–132.
Box, G.H. and W.O.E. Oesterley, 'Sirach', in R.H. Charles (ed.), *Apocrypha and
    Pseudepigrapha of the Old Testament* (Oxford, 1913), 268–517.
Bravmann, M.M., *Studies in Arabic and General Syntax* (TAEI 11; Cairo, 1953).
Brock, S.P., 'Bibelübersetzungen I, 4. Die Übersetzungen ins Syrische; 4.1. Altes
    Testament', *TRE* 6.181–196.
——. 'Limitations of Syriac in Representing Greek', in B.M. Metzger (ed.), *The
    Early Versions of the New Testament. Their Origin, Transmission, and Limita-
    tions* (Oxford, 1977), 83–98.
——. 'The Treatment of Greek Particles in the Old Syriac Gospels, with Special
    Reference to Luke', in J.K. Elliott (ed.), *Studies in New Testament Language and
    Text. Essays in Honour of George D. Kilpatrick on the Occasion of his Sixty-
    Fifth Birthday* (NT.S 44; Leiden, 1976), 80–86.
——. 'Toward a History of Syriac Translation Technique', in R. Lavenant (ed.), *III
    Symposium Syriacum 1980* (OCA 221; Rome, 1983), 1–14.
Brockelmann, C., *Grundriss der vergleichenden Grammatik der semitischen Sprachen*
    (2 vols.; Berlin, 1908–13).
——. *Hebräische Syntax* (Neukirchen, 1956).
——. *Syrische Grammatik* (12th ed.; Leipzig, 1976).
Bronznick, N.M., 'An Unrecognized Denotation of the Verb *ḥsr* in Ben-Sira and
    Rabbinic Hebrew', *HAR* 9 (1985), 91–105.
Brown, F., S.R. Driver and C.A. Briggs, *A Hebrew and English Lexicon of the Old
    Testament* (Oxford, 1907; repr. 1979) (= BDB).
Burkitt, F.C., 'The Early Syriac Lectionary System', *Proceedings of the British Acad-
    emy* 10 (1923), 301–338.
Buth, R., 'Word Order in the Verbless Clause: A Generative-Functional Approach', in
    Miller, *Verbless Clause in Biblical Hebrew*, 79–108.
Buttenwieser, M., 'Are there any Maccabean Psalms?', *JBL* 36 (1917), 225–248.
——. *The Psalms: Chronologically Treated with a New Translation* (New York,
    1969).
Calduch-Benages, N., 'Traducir-Interpretar: la versión siríaca de Sirácida 1', *EstB* 55
    (1997), 313–340.
Calduch-Benages, N., J. Ferrer and J. Liesen, *La Sabiduría del Escriba. Edición di-
    plomática de la versión siriaca del libro de Ben Sira según el Códice Ambro-
    siano, con traducción española e inglesa – Wisdom of the Scribe. Diplomatic
    Edition of the Syriac Version of the Book of Ben Sira according to Codex Am-
    brosianus, with Translations in Spanish and English* (Biblioteca Midrásica 26;
    Estella, 2003).
Carleton Paget, J., 'Jewish Christianity', in W. Horbury, W.D. Davies and J. Sturdy
    (eds.), *The Cambridge History of Judaism* 3. *The Early Roman Period* (Cam-
    bridge, 1999), 731–735.
Charlesworth, J.H., 'Secrecy', in Schiffman–VanderKam, *Encyclopaedia of the Dead
    Sea Scrolls* II, 852–853.
Chazon, E., 'Psalms, Hymns and Prayers', in Schiffman–VanderKam, *Encyclopaedia
    of the Dead Sea Scrolls* II, 710–715.
Clines, D.J.A. (ed.), *The Dictionary of Classical Hebrew* (Sheffield, 1993–....).
Cohen, A., *The Minor Tractates of the Talmud. Massektoth Ḳeṭannoth* (2 vols.; Lon-
    don, 1965).

Cohen, D., *La phrase nominale et l'évolution du système verbal en sémitique* (Leuven, 1984).

Cook, J. (ed.), *Bible and Computer: The Stellenbosch AIBI-6 Conference. Proceedings of the Association Internationale Bible et Informatique "From Alpha to Byte", University of Stellenbosch, 17–21 July 2000* (Leiden, 2002).

Costaz, L., *Grammaire syriaque* (Beirut, 1955).

Cowley, A.E. and A. Neubauer, *The Original Hebrew of a Portion of Ecclesiasticus* (Oxford, 1897).

Dalman, G., *Grammatik des jüdisch-palästinischen Aramäisch* (2nd ed.; Leipzig, 1905; repr. Darmstadt, 1960).

Daube, D., 'Direct and Indirect Causation in Biblical Law', *VT* 11 (1961), 246–269, esp. 265–266.

Déaut, R. le, *Introduction à la littérature targumique* (Rome, 1966).

Delitzsch, F., *Die Lese- und Schreibfehler im Alten Testament nebst den dem Schrifttexte einverleibten Randnoten klassifiziert. Ein Hilfsbuch für Lexicon und Grammatik, Exegese und Lektüre* (Berlin–Leipzig, 1920).

Denniston, J.D., *The Greek Particles* (2nd ed.; London, 1996).

Derrett, J.D.M., '2 Cor 6,14ff.: A Midrash on Dt 22,10', *Bib.* 59 (1978), 231–250.

Di Lella, A.A., 'Qumrân and the Geniza Fragments of Sirach', *CBQ* 24 (1962), 245–267.

——. *The Hebrew Text of Sirach: A Text-Critical and Historical Study* (SCL 1; The Hague, 1966).

Dik, S.C., *The Theory of Functional Grammar 1. The Structure of the Clause* (FGS 9; Dordrecht, 1994).

Dirksen, P.B., 'The Old Testament Peshitta', in M.J. Mulder (ed.), *Mikra: Text, Translation, Reading and Interpretation of the Hebrew Bible in Ancient Judaism and Early Christianity* (CRI 2/1; Assen–Maastricht, 1988), 255–297.

——. 'The Peshitta and Textual Criticism of the Old Testament' (PIC 22), *VT* 42 (1992), 376–390.

Dirksen, P.B. and A. van der Kooij (eds.), *The Peshitta as a Translation: Papers Read at the II Peshitta Symposium Held at Leiden 19–21 August 1993* (Leiden, 1995).

Dirksen, P.B. and M.J. Mulder, *The Peshitta: Its Early Text and History. Papers Read at the Peshitta Symposium held at Leiden 30–31 August 1985* (MPIL 4; Leiden, 1988).

Dodd, C.H., *According to the Scriptures. The Sub-Structure of New Testament Theology* (Londen, 1952).

Doedens, C.-J., *Text Databases: One Database Model and Several Retrieval Languages* (LC 14; Amsterdam–Atlanta, 1994).

Drijvers, H.J.W., 'The Peshitta of Sapientia Salomonis', in H.L.J. Vanstiphout *et al.* (eds.), *Scripta Signa Vocis: Studies about Scripts, Scriptures, Scribes and Languages in the Near East, presented to J.H. Hospers by his Pupils, Colleagues and Friends* (Groningen, 1986).

Driver, S.R., *Notes on the Hebrew Text and the Topography of the Books of Samuel* (2nd ed.; Oxford 1912; repr. Winona Lake, 1984).

——. *A Treatise on the Use of the Tenses in Hebrew and Some Other Syntactical Questions* (3rd ed.; Oxford 1892; repr. with an introductory essay by W.R. Garr; Grand Rapids, 1998).

Dürscheid, C., *Modelle der Satzanalyse. Überblick und Vergleich* (KLAG 26; Hürth-Efferen, 1991).

Duval, R., *Traité de grammaire syriaque* (Paris, 1881).

Dyk, J.W., '1 Kings 2:1–9: Some Results of a Structured Hierarchical Approach', in

Van Keulen–Van Peursen, *Corpus Linguistics and Textual History*, 277–309.
———. 'Data Preparation: What Are We Doing and Why Should We?' in Van Keulen–Van Peursen, *Corpus Linguistics and Textual History*, 133–154.
———. 'Desiderata for the Lexicon from a Syntactic Point of View', in A.D. Forbes and D.G.K. Taylor (eds.), *Foundations in Syriac Lexicography 1* (POSL 1; Piscataway, 2005), 141–156.
———. 'Lexical Correspondence and Translation Equivalents: Building an Electronic Concordance', in Van Keulen–Van Peursen, *Corpus Linguistics and Textual History*, 311–326.
———. 'Linguistic Aspects of the Peshitta Version of 2 Kings 18 and 19', in Cook, *Bible and Computer*, 519–554.
Dyk, J.W. and P.S.F. van Keulen, *Language System, Translation Technique and Textual Tradition in the Peshitta of Kings*, forthcoming in the MPIL series.
———. 'Of Words and Phrases: Syriac Versions of 2 Kings 24:14', in Van Peursen–Ter Haar Romeny, *Text, Translation, and Tradition*, 39–58.
Dyk, J.W. and E. Talstra, 'Paradigmatic and Syntagmatic Features in Identifying Subject and Predicate in Nominal Clauses', in Miller, *Verbless Clause in Biblical Hebrew*, 133–185.
Edersheim, A., 'Ecclesiasticus', in Henry Wace (ed.), *The Holy Bible according to the Authorised Version (A.D. 1611) with an Explanatory and Critical Commentary and a Revision of the Translation by the Clergy of the Anglican Church. Apocrypha* (2 vols.; London, 1888), II, 1–239.
Ehrlich, A.B., *Randglossen zur hebraischen Bibel* (7 vols.; Leipzig, 1908–14).
Elwolde, J.F., 'Ben Sira 39:27 (32): A Variant in the Hebrew Mss. and the Ancient Versions', in A. Zaborski *et al.* (eds.), *Proceedings of a Second International Conference, 'Oriental Languages in Translation'* (Cracow, forthcoming).
———. 'The Use of ʾēt in Non-Biblical Hebrew Texts', *VT* 44 (1994), 170–182.
Exter Blokland, A.F. den, *In Search of Text-Syntax: Towards a Syntactic Text-Segmentation Model for Biblical Hebrew* (PhD diss., Amsterdam, Vrije Universiteit, 1995).
Falla, T.C., *A Key to the Peshitta Gospels.* I *Ālaph-Dālath* (NTTS 14; Leiden, 1991).
———. *A Key to the Peshitta Gospels.* II *Hē-Yōdh* (NTTS 29; Leiden, 2000).
———. 'Questions Concerning the Content and Implications of the Lexical Work *A Key to the Peshitta Gospels*', in R. Lavenant (ed.), *VI Symposium Syriacum 1992* (OCA 247; Rome, 1994), 85–99.
Falla, T.C. and W.Th. van Peursen, 'The Particles ܐܝܟ and ܕ in Classical Syriac: Syntactic and Semantic Aspects', forthcoming in the Proceedings of Second Meeting of the International Syriac Language Project (Groningen, July 2005), edited by P.J. Williams, in the POSL series.
Flesher, P.V.M. (ed.), *Targum and Peshitta* (Targum Studies 2; Atlanta, 1998).
Fohrer, G., *et al.*, *Exegese des Alten Testaments* (UTB 267; 4th ed.; Heidelberg, 1983).
Folmer, M.L., *The Aramaic Language in the Achaemenid Period: A Study in Linguistic Variation* (OLA 68; Leuven, 1995).
Forcellini, A., *Lexicon Totius Latinitatis* (4th edition; Padua, 1864–1926).
Fraenkel, S., 'Die syrische Übersetzung zu den Büchern der Chronik', *JPTh* 5 (1879) 508–536 (Part I), 720–759 (Part II).
Freedman, D.N., 'The Broken Construct Chain', *Bib.* 53 (1972), 534–536. (= idem, *Pottery, Poetry and Prophecy. Studies in Early Hebrew Poetry* [Winona Lake, 1980], 339–341).

García Martínez, F. and E.J.C. Tigchelaar, *The Dead Sea Scrolls. Study Edition* (2 vols.; Leiden, 1997–98).
Gelston, A., 'Some Readings in the Peshiṭta of the Dodekapropheton', in Dirksen–Mulder, *Early Text and History*, 81–98.
——. *The Peshiṭta of the Twelve Prophets* (Oxford, 1987).
Gesenius, W. and F. Buhl, *Hebräisches und aramäisches Handwörterbuch über das Alte Testament* (17th ed.; Leipzig, 1921).
Gesenius, W., E. Kautzsch and A.E. Cowley, *Hebrew Grammar* (2nd ed.; Oxford, 1910).
Gilbert, M., 'Jesus Sirach', *RAC* XVII, 878–906.
Ginzberg, L., 'Randglossen zum hebräischen Ben Sira', in C. Bezold (ed.), *Orientalische Studien* (Fs. Th. Nöldeke; 2 vols.; Giessen, 1906), II, 609–625.
Gnan, M., *Nachklänge des Buches Jesus Sirach von synagogalen Gesängen bis zur Gegenwart: Beiträge zur Rezeptionsgeschichte insbesondere zu Sir 51, 12a-o, 50, 24–26 (Lutherbibel); 44, 16. 20 (Vulgata)* (PhD diss.; Passau, 1996).
Goldenberg, G., 'Attribution in Semitic Languages', *LOAPL* 5–6 (1995), 1–20. (= idem, *SSL*, 46–65).
——. 'Bible Translations and Syriac Idiom', in Dirksen–Van der Kooij, *Peshitta as a Translation*, 25–40 (= *SSL*, 591–604).
——. 'Comments on "Three Aproaches to the Tripartite Nominal Clause in Syriac" by Wido van Peursen', in Van Keulen–Van Peursen, *Corpus Linguistics and Textual History*, 175–184.
——. 'Imperfectly-Transformed Cleft Sentences', in *Proceedings of the Sixth World Congress of Jewish Studies* (Jerusalem, 1977), I, 127–133 (= *SSL*, 116–122).
——. 'On Predicative Adjectives in Syriac Syntax', *BiOr* 48 (1991), 716–726 (= *SSL*, 579–590).
——. 'On Some Niceties of Syriac Syntax', in R. Lavenant (ed.), *V Symposium Syriacum 1988* (OCA 236; Rome, 1990), 335–344 (= *SSL*, 569–578).
——. 'On Syriac Sentence Structure', in M. Sokoloff (ed.), *Arameans, Aramaic and the Aramaic Literary Tradition* (Ramat-Gan, 1983), 97–140 (= *SSL*, 525–568).
——. *Studies in Semitic Linguistics* (Jerusalem 1998) (= *SSL*)
——. 'Tautological Infinitive', *IOS* 1 (1971), 36–85 (= *SSL*, 66–115).
Greenfield, J.C., *'Al Kanfei Yonah. Collected Studies of Jonas C. Greenfield in Semitic Philology* edited by S.M. Paul, M.E. Stone and A. Pinnick (2 vols; Leiden, 2001).
——. 'Early Aramaic Poetry', *JANES* 11 (1979), 45–51 (= *'Al Kanfei Yonah* I, 167–173).
——. 'The "Periphrastic Imperative" in Aramaic and Hebrew', *IEJ* 19 (1969), 199–210 (= *'Al Kanfei Yonah* I, 56–67).
Greenberg, G., *Translation Technique in the Peshitta to Jeremiah* (MPIL 13; Leiden, 2002).
Gross, W., *Die Satzteilfolge im Verbalsatz alttestamentlicher Prosa* (FAT 17; Tübingen, 1996).
——. *Doppelt besetztes Vorfeld* (BZAW 305; Berlin–New York, 2001).
——. 'Ein verdrängter bibelhebräischer Satztyp: Sätze mit zwei oder mehr unterschiedlichen konstituenten vor dem verbum finitum', *JNSL* 23 (1997), 15–41.
——. 'Is There Really a Compound Nominal Clause in Biblical Hebrew?', in Miller, *Verbless Clause in Biblical Hebrew*, 19–49.
Gzella, H., 'New Ways in Textual Criticism. Isa 42,1–4 as a Paradigm Case', *ETL* 81 (2005), 387–423.
Haar Romeny, R.B. ter, 'Hypotheses on the Development of Judaism and Christianity

in Syria in the Period after 70 C.E.', in H. van de Sandt (ed.), *Matthew and the Didache. Two Documents from the Same Jewish-Christian Milieu?* (Assen, 2005), 13–33.

——. 'Techniques of Translation and Transmission in the Earliest Text Forms of the Syriac Version of Genesis', in Dirksen–Van der Kooij, *The Peshitta as a Translation*, 177–185.

——. 'The Syriac Versions of the Old Testament', in M. Atallah *et al.* (eds.). *Sources syriaques 1. Nos sources: arts et littérature syriaques* (Antélias, 2005), 75–105.

Haefeli, L., *Die Peshitta des Alten Testamentes mit Rücksicht auf ihre textkritische Bearbeitung und Herausgabe* (ATA XI,1; Münster, 1927)

Halévy, J., 'Étude sur la partie du texte hébreu de l'Ecclésiastique récemment découverte', *RSEHA* 5 (1897), 148–165 (= I), 193–255 (= II).

Halliday, M.A.K. and R. Hasan, *Cohesion in English* (ELS 9; London, 1976).

Heide, A. van der, *Aḥar samukh, aharei muflag*: On the Reception of a Linguistic Statement in the Midrash', in Baasten–Van Peursen, *Hamlet on a Hill*, 257–263.

Hoftijzer, J., 'A Preliminary Remark on the Study of the Verbal System in Classical Hebrew', in A.S. Kaye (ed.), *Semitic Studies in Honor of Wolf Leslau on the Occasion of his Eighty-Fifth Birthday, November 14th, 1991* (2 vols.; Wiesbaden, 1991), I, 645–651.

——. *A Search for Method. A Study in the Syntactic Use of the H-Locale in Classical Hebrew* (SSLL 12; Leiden, 1981).

——. 'Remarks Concerning the Use of the Particle *ʾt* in Classical Hebrew', in P.A.H. de Boer (ed.), כה *1940–1965* (OTS 14; Leiden, 1965), 1–99.

——. 'The Nominal Clause Reconsidered', *VT* 23 (1973), 446–510.

Hollander, H.W. and M. de Jonge, *The Testaments of the Twelve Patriarchs: A Commentary* (SVTP 8; Leiden, 1985).

Huber, K., 'Die Könige Israels: Saul, David und Salomo', in M. Öhler (ed.), *Alttestamentliche Gestalten im Neuen Testament. Beiträge zur biblischen Theologie* (Darmstadt, 1999), 161–183.

Jastrow, M., *Dictionary of the Targumim, Talmud Babli, Yerushalmi and Midrashic Literature* (2 vols.; New York, 1886–1903).

Jenkins, R.G., *The Old Testament Quotations of Philoxenus of Mabbug* (CSCO 514, Sub. 84; Leuven, 1989).

Jenner, K.D., 'A Review of the Methods by which Syriac Biblical and Related Manuscripts Have Been Described and Analysed: Some Preliminary Remarks', *Aram* 5 [Fs Brock] (1993), 255–266.

——. *De perikopentitels van de geïllustreerde Syrische kanselbijbel van Parijs (MS Paris, Bibliothèque Nationale, Syriaque 341): een vergelijkend onderzoek naar de oudste Syrische perikopenstelsels* (PhD diss., Leiden University, 1994).

——. 'La Peshitta: fille du texte massorétique', in Schenker–Hugo, *L'enfance de la Bible hébraïque*, 238–263.

——. 'Nominal Clauses in the Peshitta and Jacob of Edessa', in Dirksen–Van der Kooij, *The Peshitta as a Translation*, 47–62.

——. 'Petucha and Setuma: Tools for Interpretation or Simply a Matter of Lay-Out? A Study of the Relations between Layout, Arrangement, Reading and Interpretation of the Text in the Apocalypse of Isaiah (Isa. 24–27)', in H.J. Bosman and H. van Grol (eds.), *Studies in Isaiah 24–27* (OTS 43; Leiden, 2000), 157–182.

——. 'Some Introductory Remarks concerning the Study of 8a1', in Dirksen–Mulder, *Early Text and History*, 200–224.

——. 'The Development of Syriac Lectionary Systems. A Discussion of the Opinion of P. Kannookadan', *The Harp* 10 (1997), 9–24.

——. 'The Unit Delimitation in the Syriac Text of Daniel and its Consequences for the Interpretation', in Korpel–Oesch, *Delimitation Criticism*, 105–129.

——. 'The Use of the Particle ܗܘ in the Syro-Hexaplaric Psalter and the Peshitta', in Baasten–Van Peursen, *Hamlet on a Hill*, 287–308.

Jenner, K.D. and W.Th. van Peursen, 'Unit Delimitations and the Text of Ben Sira', in M. Korpel and J.M. Oesch (eds.), *Studies in Scriptural Unit Division* (Pericope 3; Assen, 2002), 144–201.

Jenner, K.D., W.Th. van Peursen and E. Talstra, 'CALAP: An Interdisciplinary Debate between Textual Criticism, Textual History and Computer-Assisted Linguistic Analysis', in Van Keulen–Van Peursen, *Corpus Linguistics and Textual History*, 13–44.

Jespersen, O., *Analytic Syntax* (Londen, 1937; repr. New York, 1969).

——. *The Philosophy of Grammar* (London–New York, 1924).

Jongeling, K., H.L. Murre-van den Berg and L. Van Rompay (eds.), *Studies in Hebrew and Aramaic Sytnax Presented to Professor J. Hoftijzer on the Occasion of his Sixty-Fifth Birthday* (SSLL 17; Leiden, 1991)

Jongman, R.W., *Het oog van de meester: een experimenteel psychologisch onderzoek naar waarnemingsprestaties van schaakmeesters en ongeoefende schakers* (Assen, 1968).

Joosten, J., 'Biblical Hebrew *wᵉqāṭal* and Syriac *hwā qāṭel* Expressing Repetition in the Past', *ZAH* 5 (1992), 1–14.

——. 'Comments on "Three Approaches to the Tripartite Nominal Clause in Syriac" by Wido vanPeursen', in Van Keulen–Van Peursen, *Corpus Linguistics and Textual History*, 185–188.

——. 'Eléments d'araméen occidental dans la version syriaque de Ben Sira', forthcoming in a Festschrift.

——. 'Materials for a Linguistic Approach to the Old Testament Peshiṭta', *JAB* 1 (1999), 203–218.

——. 'On Ante-Position of the Attributive Adjective in Classical Syriac and Biblical Hebrew', *ZAH* 6 (1993), 188–192.

——. 'On Aramaising Renderings in the Septuagint', in Baasten–Van Peursen, *Hamlet on a Hill*, 587–600.

——. Review of Muraoka, *Basic Grammar: Hugoye* 2/1 (1999).

——. 'The Indicative System of the Biblical Hebrew Verb and its Literary Exploitation', in Van Wolde, *Narrative Syntax*, 51–71.

——. 'The Negation of the Non-Verbal Clause in Early Syriac', *JAOS* 112 (1992), 585–588.

——. 'The Predicative Adjective in the *Status Emphaticus* in Syriac', *BiOr* 46 (1989), 18–24.

——. *The Syriac Language of the Peshitta and Old Syriac Versions of Matthew: Syntactic Structure, Translation Technique and Inner Syriac Developments* (SSLL 22; Leiden, 1996).

Joüon, P. and T. Muraoka, *A Grammar of Biblical Hebrew* (SubBi 27; rev. ed.; Rome, 2006).

Kahle, P.E., 'The Age of the Scrolls', *VT* 1 (1951), 38–48.

Kasher, R., 'Metaphor and Allegory in the Aramaic Translations of the Bible', *JAB* 1 (1999), 53–78.

Kasteren, J.P van, 'De Canon des Ouden Verbonds bij de Syrische Christenen', *Studien. Tijdschrift voor Godsdienst, Wetenschap en Letteren* N.S. 40 (1908), 385–403, 520–538.

Kearns, C., 'Ecclesiasticus, or the Wisdom of Jesus the Son of Sirach', in R.C. Fuller, L. Johnston and C. Kearns (eds.), *A New Catholic Commentary on Holy Scripture* (London, 1969), 541–462.

——. *The Expanded Text of Ecclesiasticus. its Teaching on the Future Life as a Clue to its Origin* (PhD diss., Pontificio Istituto Biblico, Rome, 1951).

Keulen, P.S.F. van, 'Nature et contexte des différences de la Peshitta des Rois par rapport au TM', in Schenker–Hugo, *L'enfance de la Bible hébraïque*, 264–285.

——. 'Points of Agreement between the Targum and Peshitta Versions of Kings against the MT: a Sounding', in Van Keulen–Van Peursen, *Corpus Linguistics and Textual History*, 205–235.

Keulen, P.S.F. van and W.Th. van Peursen (eds.), *Corpus Linguistics and Textual History. A Computer-Assisted Interdisciplinary Approach to the Peshitta* (SSN 48; Assen, 2006).

Khan, G., 'Object Markers and Agreement Pronouns in Semitic Languages', *BSOAS* 47 (1984), 468–500.

——. 'Response to "Data Preparation: What Are We Doing and Why Should We? by Janet W. Dyk', in Van Keulen–Van Peursen, *Corpus Linguistics and Textual History*, 155–156.

——. *Studies in Semitic Syntax* (Oxford, 1988).

——. *The Neo-Aramaic Dialect of Qaraqosh* (SSLL 36; Leiden, 2002).

Kiraz, G.A., *Computational Nonlinear Morphology with Emphasis on Semitic Languages* (SNLP; Cambridge, 2001).

Kister, M., בשולי ספר בן סירא (Notes on the Book of Ben Sira), *Leš.* 47 (1983), 125–146.

——. נוספות למאמר 'בשולי ספר בן סירא' (Additions to 'Notes on the Book of Ben Sira'), *Leš.* 53 (1989), 36–53.

——. לפירושו של ספר בן סירא (A Contribution to the Interpretation of Ben Sira), *Tarb.* 59 (1989–90), 303–378.

Klein, M., 'Converse Translation: A Targumic Technique', *Bib.* 57 (1976), 515–537.

——. 'The Preposition קדם ('before'): A Pseudo-Anti-Anthropomorphism in the Targums', *JThS* 30 (1979), 502–507.

Koehler, L., W. Baumgartner *et al.*, *The Hebrew and Aramaic Lexicon of the Old Testament* (translated and edited under the supervision of M.E.J. Richardson; 5 vols.; Leiden, 1994–2000). (= *HALOT*).

Kooij, A. van der, '*1QIsaᵃ* Col. VIII, 4–11 (Isa 8, 11–18): A Contextual Approach of its Variants', *RdQ* 13 (1988), 569–581.

——. 'Accident or Method? on "Analogical" Interpretation in the Old Greek of Isaiah and in 1QIsaᵃ', *BiOr* 43 (1986), 366–376.

——. 'The Old Greek of Isaiah in Relation to the Qumran Texts of Isaiah: Some General Comments', in G.J. Brooke and B. Lindars (eds.), *Septuagint, Scrolls and Cognate Writings* (SCSt 33; Atlanta, 1992), 195–213.

——. *The Oracle of Tyre. The Septuagint of Isaiah 23 as Version and Vision* (VT.S 71; Leiden, 1998).

Korpel, M.C.A., 'Introduction to the Series Pericope', in Korpel–Oesch, *Delimitation Criticism*, 1–50.

Korpel, M.C.A. and J.C. de Moor, *The Structure of Classical Hebrew Poetry: Isaiah 40–55* (OTS 41; Leiden, 1998), 7–8.

Korpel, M.C.A. and J.M. Oesch (eds.), *Delimitation Criticism. A New Tool in Biblical Scholarship* (Pericope 1; Assen, 2000).

Koster, M.D., 'The Copernican Revolution in the Study of the Origins of the Peshitta', in Flesher, *Targum and Peshitta*, 15–54.

——. *The Peshiṭta of Exodus. The Development of its Text in the Course of Fifteen Centuries* (Assen–Amsterdam, 1977).

——. '"Translation or Transmission? That is the Question". The Use of the Leiden O.T. Peshitta Edition', in M. Augustin and H.M. Niemann (eds.), *"Basel und Bibel". Collected Communications to the XVIIth Congress of the International Organization for the Study of the Old Testament, Basel 2001* (Frankfurt a.M., 2004), 297–312.

——. 'Which Came First? The Chicken or the Egg? The Development of the Text of the Peshiṭta of Genesis and Exodus in the Light of Recent Studies', in Dirksen–Mulder, *Early Text and History*, 99–126.

Kroeze, J.H., 'Towards a Multidimensional Linguistic Database of Biblical Hebrew', *JNSL* 30 (2004), 99–120.

Kropat, A., *Die Syntax des Autors der Chronik verglichen mit der seiner Quellen. Ein Beitrag zur historischen Syntax des Hebräischen* (BZAW 16; Giessen, 1909).

Kuhn, G., 'Beiträge zur Erklärung des Buches Jesus Sira', *ZAW* 47 (1929), 286–296 (Part I), *ZAW* 48 (1930), 100–121 (Part II).

Kutscher, E.Y., *The Language and Linguistic Background of the Isaiah Scroll (1QIsaᵃ)* (StTDJ 6; Leiden, 1974).

Kuty, R., 'The Position of the Particle *dēn* in New Testament Syriac', *ANES* 38 (2001), 186–199.

Lane, D.J., *The Peshiṭta of Leviticus* (MPIL 6; Leiden, 1994).

Lee, T.R., *Studies in the Form of Sirach 44–50* (SBL.DS 75; Atlanta, 1986).

Leiman, S.Z., *The Canonization of Hebrew Scripture: The Talmudic and Midrashic Evidence* (Hamden, 1976).

Lévi, I., *L'Ecclésiastique ou la Sagesse de Jésus, fils de Sira* (2 vol.; Paris, 1898, 1901).

——. Notes sur les Ch. VII. 29– XII. 1 de Ben Sira édités par M. Elkan N. Adler', *JQR* 13 (1901), 1–17.

Levy, J., *Neuhebräisches und Chaldäisches Wörterbuch über die Targumim und Midraschim* (4 vols.; Leipzig, 1876–89).

Lieberman, S., הוראות נשכחות (Forgotten Meanings), *Leš.* 32 (1968), 89–102.

Liesen, J., *Full of Praise. An Exegetical Study of Sir 39,12–35* (JSJ.S 64; Leiden, 2000).

Lipiński, E., *Semitic Languages: Outline of a Comparative Grammar* (OLA 80; Leuven, 1997).

Louw, Th. van der, *Transformations in the Septuagint* (PhD diss., Leiden University, 2006).

Lowery, K.E., 'Relative Definiteness and the Verbless Clause', in Miller, *Verbless Clause in Biblical Hebrew*, 251–272.

Lund, J.A., 'Grecisms in the Peshitta Psalms', in Dirksen–Van der Kooij, *The Peshitta as a Translation*, 85–102.

——. *The Influence of the Septuaginta on the Peshitta. A Re-evaluation of Criteria in light of Comparative Study of the Versions in Genesis and Psalms* (PhD diss., Hebrew University, Jerusalem, 1988).

Lust, J., 'The "Rekenaar" and the Septuagint – LXX Ezekiel. A Case Study', in Cook, *Bible and Computer*, 364–393.

Lyons, J., *Introduction to Theoretical Linguistics* (Cambridge, 1968).

——. *Semantics* (2 vols.; Cambridge, 1977).

Macholz, C., 'Das "Passivum Divinum", seine Anfänge im Alten Testament under "Hofstil",' *ZNW* 81 (1900), 247–253.

Macomber, W.F., 'The Chaldean Lectionary System of the Cathedral Church of

Kokhe', *OCP* 33 (1967), 483–516.

Mann, W.C. and S.A. Thompson, 'Rhetorical Structure Theory: Toward a Function Theory of Text Organization', *Text* 8 (1988), 243–281.

——. 'Relational Propositions in Discourse', *Discourse Processes* 9 (1986), 57–90.

Maori, Y., 'Methodological Criteria for Distinguishing between Variant *Vorlage* and Exegesis in the Peshitta Pentateuch', in Dirksen–Van der Kooij, *The Peshitta as a Translation*, 103–120.

——. 'The Relationship Between the Peshitta Pentateuch and the Pentateuchal Targums', in Flesher, *Targum and Peshitta*, 57–73.

Margoliouth, G., 'The Original Hebrew of Ecclesiasticus XXXI. 12–31, and XXXVI. 22–XXXVII. 26', *JQR* 12 (1899–1900), 1–33.

Matthes, J.C., 'Bemerkungen zu dem hebräischen Texte Jesus Sirachs und seiner neuesten Übersetzung', *ZAW* 29 (1909), 161–176.

Matthews, P.H., *Oxford Concise Dictionary of Linguistics* (Oxford, 1997).

Matthiessen, C. and S.A. Thompson, 'The Structure of Discourse and "Subordination",' in J. Haiman and S.A. Thompson (eds.), *Clause Combining in Grammar and Discourse* (Amsterdam–Phildelphia, 1988), 275–329.

McHardy, W.D., *A Critical Text of the Syriac Version of Ecclesiasticus* (PhD diss.; Oxford, *s.a.*).

Merwe, C.H.J. van der, 'A Critical Analysis of Narrative Syntactic Approaches, with Special Attention to their Relationship to Discourse Analysis', in Van Wolde, *Narrative Syntax*, 133–156.

——. 'An Overview of Hebrew Narrative Syntax', in Van Wolde, *Narrative Syntax*, 1–20.

——. 'Discourse Linguistics and Biblical Hebrew Grammar', in R.D. Bergen (ed.), *Biblical Hebrew and Discourse Linguistics* (Dallas, 1994), 13–49.

Merwe, C.H.J. van der, J.A. Naudé and J.H. Kroeze, *A Biblical Hebrew Reference Grammar* (Sheffield, 1999).

Milgrom, J., 'Sacrifice', in Schiffman–VanderKam, *Encyclopaedia of the Dead Sea Scrolls* II, 807–812.

Miller, C.L. (ed.), *The Verbless Clause in Biblical Hebrew: Linguistic Approaches* (Winona Lake, 1999)

Moor, J.C. de, 'Unit Division in the Peshiṭta of Micah', *JAB* 1 (1999), 225–248.

Moor, J.C. de and F. Sepmeijer, 'The Peshiṭta of the Targum of Joshua', in Dirksen–Van der Kooij, *The Peshitta as a Translation*, 129–176.

Morrison, C.E., *The Character of the Syriac Version of the First Book of Samuel and its Relationship to Other Biblical Versions* (PhD diss., Rome, Pontifical Biblical Institute, 1995).

——. *The Character of the Syriac Version of the First Book of Samuel* (MPIL 11; Leiden, 2001).

Mulder, O., *Simon the High Priest in Sirach 50. An Exegetical Study of the Significance of Simon the High Priest as Climax to the Praise of the Fathers in Ben Sira's Concept of the History of Israel* (JSJ.S 78; Leiden, 2003).

Muraoka, T., *A Greek-English Lexicon of the Septuagint Chiefly of the Pentateuch and the Twelve Prophets* (Leuven, 2002).

——. 'A Response to "Three Approaches to the Tripartite Nominal Clause in Syriac" by Wido van Peursen and a Bit More', in Van Keulen–Van Peursen, *Corpus Linguistics and Textual History*, 189–196.

——. 'An Approach to the Morphosyntax and Syntax of Qumran Hebrew', in T. Muraoka and J.F. Elwolde (eds.), *Diggers at the Well: Proceedings of a Third In-*

ternational Symposium on the Hebrew of the Dead Sea Scrolls and Ben Sira (StTDJ 36; Leiden, 2000), 193–214.

——. *Classical Syriac: A Basic Grammar with a Chrestomathy* (with a select bibliograpy compiled by S.P. Brock; PLO N.S. 19; Wiesbaden, 1997).

——. *Classical Syriac for Hebraists* (Wiesbaden, 1987).

——. *Emphatic Words and Structures in Biblical Hebrew* (Jerusalem–Leiden, 1985).

——. 'On the Nominal Clause in the Old Syriac Gospels', *JSSt* 20 (1975), 28–37.

——. 'On the Syriac Particle *it*', *BiOr* 34 (1977), 21–22.

——. 'Remarks on the Syntax of Some Types of Noun Modifier in Syriac', *JNES* 31 (1972), 192–194,

——. 'Response to G. Goldenberg, "Bible Translations and Syriac Idiom",' in Dirksen–Van der Kooij, *The Peshitta as a Translation*, 41–46.

——. 'The Tripartite Nominal Clause Revisited', in Miller, *Verbless Clause in Biblical Hebrew*, 187–213.

Muraoka, T. and B. Porten. *A Grammar of Egyptian Aramaic* (HdO 1/32; Leiden, 1998).

Nelson, M.D., *The Syriac Version of the Wisdom of Ben Sira Compared to the Greek and Hebrew Materials* (SBL.DS 107; Atlanta 1988).

Niccacci, A., 'Simple Nominal Clause (SNC) or Verbless Clause in Biblical Hebrew Prose', *ZAH* 6 (1993), 216–227.

——. *The Syntax of the Verb in Classical Hebrew Prose* (transl. by W.G.E. Watson; Sheffield).

Nöldeke, Th., *Die alttestamentliche Literatur in einer Reihe von Aufsätzen dargestellt* (Leipzig, 1868).

——. *Kurzgefasste syrische Grammatik* (2nd ed.; Leipzig 1898; repr. with additional materials: Darmstadt, 1966).

——. *Compendious Syriac Grammar* (transl. From the second improved German edition by J.A. Crichton; Winona Lake, 2001).

O'Connor, M., 'Discourse Linguistics and the Study of Biblical Hebrew', in A. Lemaire (ed.), *Congress Volume Basel 2001* (VT.S 92; Leiden 2002), 17–42.

Oeming, M., *Biblische Hermeneutik. Eine Einführung* (Darmstadt, 1998).

Owens, R.J., 'Aphrahat as a Witness to the Early Syriac Text of Leviticus', in Dirksen–Mulder, *Early Text and History*, 1–48.

——. Review of Nelson, *Syriac Version*: *JSSt* 36 (1991), 164–167.

——. 'The Early Syriac Text of Ben Sira in the Demonstrations of Aphrahat', *JSSt* 34 (1989), 39–75.

——. *The Genesis and Exodus Citations of Aphrahat the Persian Sage* (MPIL 3; Leiden, 1983).

Payne Smith, J., *A Compendious Syriac Dictionary Founded upon the Thesaurus Syriacus by R. Payne Smith* (Oxford, 1903; reprint Winona Lake, 1998).

Payne Smith, R., *Thesaurus Syriacus* (2 vol.; Oxford, 1897–1901) with *Supplement* by J.P. Margoliouth (Oxford, 1927).

Pennacchietti, F.A., "La struttura della frase nominale tripartita di identificazione in ebraico e in siriaco", in G. Bernini and V. Brugnatelli (eds.), *Atti della 4ª giornata di studi camito-semitici e indeuropei, Bergamo, Istituto Universitario, 29 novembre 1985* (Milan, 1987), 157–169.

Peters, N., *Das Buch Ben Sirach oder Ecclesiasticus* (EHAT 25; Münster, 1913).

Petersen, U., 'Emdros – A Text Database Engine for Analyzed or Annotated Text' (available at emdros.org/petersen-emdros-COLING-2004.pdf).

Peursen, W.Th. van, 'Clause Hierarchy and Discourse Structure in the Syriac Text of
    Sirach 14:20–27', in Van Peursen–Ter Haar Romeny, *Text, Translation, and
    Tradition*, 135–148.
——. 'Language Variation, Language Development and the Textual History of the
    Peshitta', forthcoming in the Proceedings of the congress *Aramaic in its Histori-
    cal and Linguistic Setting* (Leiden, August 2006), edited by H. Gzella, in the se-
    ries VOK.
——. 'Negation in the Hebrew of Ben Sira', in T. Muraoka and J.F. Elwolde (eds.),
    *Sirach, Scrolls, and Sages: Proceedings of a Second International Symposium on
    the Hebrew of the Dead Sea Scrolls, Ben Sira, and the Mishnah held at Leiden
    University, 15–17 December 1997* (StTDJ 33; Leiden, 1999), 223–243.
——. 'Progress Report: Three Leiden Projects on the Syriac Text of Ben Sira', in R.
    Egger-Wenzel (ed.), *Ben Sira's God. Proceedings of the Second International
    Ben Sira Conference, Durham, Ushaw College, 2001* (BZAW 321; Berlin,
    2002), 361–370.
——. 'Que vive celui qui fait vivre: le texte syriaque de Sirach 48:10–12', in Schen-
    ker–Hugo, *L'enfance de la Bible hébraïque*, 286–301.
——. 'Response to the Responses', in Van Keulen–Van Peursen, *Corpus Linguistics
    and Textual History*, 197–204.
——. Review of Calduch-Benages–Ferrer–Liesen, *La Sabiduría del Escriba*: *JSJ* 36
    (2005), 94–101.
——. 'Sirach 51:13–30 in Hebrew and Syriac', in Baasten–Van Peursen, *Hamlet on a
    Hill*, 357–374.
——. 'Sirach Quotations in the *Discourses* of Philoxenus of Mabbug: Text and Con-
    text', in R.B. ter Haar Romeny (ed.), *The Peshitta: Its Use in Literature and Lit-
    urgy. Proceedings of the Third Peshitta Symposium held at Leiden University,
    12–15 August 2001*, forthcoming in the MPIL series.
——. 'Some Issues in the Verbal System in the Hebrew Text of the Praise of the
    Fathers (Sir. 44–50)', *Proceedings of the Twelfth World Congress of Jewish
    Studies* (forthcoming).
——. 'The Alleged Retroversions from Syriac in the Hebrew Text of Ben Sira Revis-
    ited: Linguistic Perspectives', in R.G. Lehmann (ed.), *Kleine Untersuchungen
    zur Sprachen des Alten Testaments und seiner Umwelt* 2 (Waltrop, 2001), 47–95.
——. 'The Peshitta of Ben Sira: Jewish and/or Christian?', *AS* 2 (2004), 243–262.
——. *The Verbal System in the Hebrew Text of Ben Sira* (SSLL 41; Leiden, 2004).
——. 'Three Approaches to the Tripartite Nominal Clause in Classical Syriac', in
    Van Keulen–Van Peursen, *Corpus Linguistics and Textual History*, 157–173.
Peursen, W.Th. van and R.B. ter Haar Romeny, *Text, Translation, and Tradition.
    Studies on the Peshitta and its Use in the Syriac Tradition Presented to Konrad
    D. Jenner on the Occasion of his Sixty-Fifth Birthday* (MPIL 14; Leiden, 2006).
Peursen, W.Th. van and E. Talstra, 'Computer-Assisted Analysis of Parallel Texts in
    the Bible. The Case of 2 Kings xviii-xix and its Parallels in Isaiah and Chroni-
    cles', *VT* 57 (2007), 45–72.
Philonenko, M., 'Sur une interpolation esséniante dans le Siracide (16,15–16)', *Or-
    Suec* 33 (1986), 317–321.
Pinkerton, J., 'The Origin and the Early History of the Syriac Pentateuch', *JThS* 15
    (1914), 14–41.
Polak, F.H., 'Bottom-Up Structuring and Top-Down Analysis: Narratology and Com-
    puter Analysis of Biblical Texts', in Talstra, *Narrative and Comment*, 126–136.
Polzin, R., *Late Biblical Hebrew. Toward an Historical Typology of Biblical Hebrew
    Prose* (HSM 12; Missoula, 1976).

Praetorius, F., *Äthiopische Grammatik mit Paradigmen, Litteratur, Chrestomathie und Glossar* (PLO 7; Karlsruhe–Leipzig, 1886).
——. Review of L. Stern, *Koptische Grammatik* (Leipzig, 1880): *ZDMG* 35 (1881), 750–761.
Prato, G.L., 'La lumière interprète de la sagesse dans la tradition textuelle de Ben Sira', in M. Gilbert (ed.), *La sagesse de l'Ancien Textament* (BETL 51; 2nd ed.; Leuven, 1990), 317–346.
Regt, L.J. de, 'Participant Reference in Some Biblical Hebrew Texts', *JEOL* 32 (1991–92), 150–172.
——. *Participants in Old Testament Texts and the Translator. Reference Devices and their Rhetorical Impact* (SSN 39; Assen, 1999).
Reiterer, F.V., *'Urtext' und Übersetzungen: Sprachstudie über Sir 44,16–45,26 als Beitrag zur Siraforschung* (ATSAT 12; St. Ottilien, 1980).
Reymond, E.D., *Innovations in Hebrew Poetry. Parallelism and the Poems of Sirach* (SBL.SBL 9; Atlanta, 2004).
Richter, W., *Exegese als Literaturwissenschaft : Entwurf einer alttestamentlichen Literaturtheorie und Methodologie* (Göttingen, 1971).
——. *Grundlagen einer althebräischen Grammatik B. Die Beschreibungsebenen III. Der Satz (Satztheorie)* (ATST 13; St. Ottilien, 1980).
Rüger, H.P., *Text und Textform im hebräischen Sirach: Untersuchungen zur Textgeschichte und Textkritik der hebräischen Sirachfragmente aus der Kairoer Geniza* (BZAW 112; Berlin, 1970).
Ryssel, V., 'Die neuen hebräischen Fragmente des Buches Jesus Sirach und ihre Herkunft', *ThStKr* 73 (1900), 364–403 (Part I), 505–541 (Part II), 74 (1901), 75–109 (Part III), 269–294 (Part IV), 547–592 (Part V), 75 (1902), 205–261 (Part VI), 347–420 (Part VII).
——. 'Die Sprüche Jesus' des Sohnes Sirachs', in E. Kautzsch (ed.), *Die Apokryphen und Pseudepigraphen des Alten Testaments 1. Die Apokryphen des Alten Testaments* (Tübingen, 1900), 230–475.
Sanders, T. and C. van Wijk, 'PISA—A Procedure for Analyzing the Structure of Explanatory Texts', *Text* 16 (1996), 91–132.
Sanders, T.J.M., W.P.M. Spooren and L.G.M. Noordman, 'Toward a Taxonomy of Coherence Relations', *Discourse Processes* 15 (1992), 1–35.
Schechter, S., 'A Further Fragment of Ben Sira', *JQR* 12 (1899–1900), 456–465.
Schechter, S. and C. Taylor, *The Wisdom of Ben Sira: Portions of the Book Ecclesiasticus from Hebrew Manuscripts in the Cairo Geniza* (Cambridge, 1899; repr. Amsterdam, 1979).
Schenker, A. and Ph. Hugo, *L'enfance de la Bible hébraïque. Histoire du texte de l'Ancien Testament* (MoBi 52; Genève, 2005).
Schiffman, L.H. and J.C. VanderKam (eds.), *Encyclopaedia of the Dead Sea Scrolls* (2 vols.; Oxford, 2000).
Schilperoord, J. and A. Verhagen, 'Conceptual Dependency and the Clausal Structure of Discourse', in J.-P. Koenig (ed.), *Discourse and Cognition. Bridging the Gap* (Stanford, 1998), 141–163.
Schlatter, A., *Das neu gefundene hebräische Stück des Sirach. Der Glossator des griechischen Sirach und seine Stellung in der Geschichte der jüdischen Theologie* (BFChTh I,5–6; Gütersloh, 1897).
Schmidt, G., 'Die beiden syrischen Übersetzungen des I. Maccabäerbuches', *ZAW* 17 (1897), 1–47 (Part I), 233–262 (Part II).
Schneider, W., *Grammatik des Biblischen Hebräisch. Ein Lehrbuch* (München, 1974).

Schrader, L., *Verwandtschaft der Peschitta mit der (alt)lateinischen Übersetzung im Sirachbuch? Ein Beitrag zur Methodik textgeschichtlicher Forschung* (BN.B 11; München, 1998)

Schweizer, H., *Biblische Texte verstehen: Arbeitsbuch zur Hermeneutik und Methodik der Bibelinterpretation* (Stuttgart, 1986).

Sèd, N., 'La shekhinta et ses amis "Araméens",' in R.-G. Coquin (ed.), *Mélanges Antoine Guillaumont. Contributions à l'étude des christianismes orientaux* (Geneve, 1988), 233–242.

Segal, M.H., ‏ספר בן סירא בקומרן‎ (Ben Sira in Qumran), *Tarb.* 33 (1963–64), 243–246.

———. ‏ספר בן סירא השלם‎ (*The Complete Book of Ben Sira*) (2nd ed.; Jerusalem, 1958; repr. 1997).

———. 'The Evolution of the Hebrew Text of Ben Sira', *JQR* N.S. 25 (1934–35), 91–149.

Shepherd, D.J., 'Rendering "Flesh and Bones": Pair Reversal and the Peshitta of Job 2.5", *AS* 3 (2005), 205–213.

———. *Targum and Translation. A Reconsideration of the Qumran Aramaic Version of Job* (SSN 45; Assen, 2004).

Shimasaki, K., *Focus Structure in Biblical Hebrew* (Bethesda, 2002).

Skehan, P.W. and A.A. Di Lella, *The Wisdom of Ben Sira* (AncBi 39; New York, 1987).

Smelik, W.F., 'Orality, Manuscript Reproduction and the Targums', in A.A. den Hollander, U. Schmid and W. Smelik (eds.), *Paratext and Megatext as Channels of Jewish and Christian Traditions. The Textual Markers of Contextualization* (JCPS 6; Leiden, 2003), 49–81.

———. *The Targum of Judges* (OTS 36; Leiden, 1995).

Smend, R., *Die Weisheit des Jesus Sirach erklärt* (Berlin, 1906).

———. *Griechisch–syrisch–hebräischer Index zur Weisheit des Jesus Sirach* (Berlin, 1907).

———. *Weisheit des Jesus Sirach. Hebräisch und Deutsch* (Berlin, 1906).

Soden, W. von, *Grundriß der akkadischen Grammatik* (3rd ed.; AnOr 33; Rome, 1995).

Sörries, R., *Die syrische Bibel von Paris: Paris, Bibliothèque Nationale, syr. 341: eine frühchristliche Bilderhandschrift aus dem 6. Jahrhundert* (Wiesbaden, 1991).

Staalduine–Sulman, E. van, *The Targum of Samuel* (SAIS 1; Leiden, 2002).

Stanley Jones, F., 'Pseudo-Clementine Literature', in Schiffman–VanderKam, *Encyclopaedia of the Dead Sea Scrolls*, II, 717–719.

Strack, H.L. and P. Billerbeck, *Kommentar zum Neuen Testament aus Talmud und Midrasch* (6 vols.; München, 1922–61).

Strothmann, W., 'Jesus-Sirach-Zitate bei Afrahat, Ephraem und im Liber Graduum', in Robert H. Fischer (ed.), *A Tribute to Arthur Vööbus: Studies in Early Christian Literature and its Environment, Primarily in the Syrian East* (Chicago, 1977).

Szpek, H.M., *Translation Technique in the Peshitta to Job. A Model for Evaluating a Text with Documentation from the Peshitta to Job* (SBL.DS 137; Atlanta, 1992).

Talstra, E., 'A Hierarchy of Clauses in Biblical Hebrew Narrative', in Van Wolde, *Narrative Syntax*, 85–118.

———. 'Clause Types and Textual Structure. An Experiment in Narrative Syntax', in idem, *Narrative and Comment*, 166–180.

———. 'Hebrew Syntax: Clause Types and Clause Hierarchy', in Jongeling–Murre-van den Berg–Van Rompay, *Studies in Hebrew and Aramaic Syntax*, 180–193.

———. 'Singers and Syntax. On the Balance of Grammar and Poetry in Psalm 8', in J.W. Dyk (ed.), *Give Ear to My Words. Psalms and other Poetry in and around the Hebrew Bible. Essays in Honour of Professor N.A. van Uchelen* (Amsterdam, 1996), 11–22.

———. 'Text Grammar and Hebrew Bible. I: Elements of a Theory', *BiOr* 35 (1978), 168–175; 'II: Syntax and Semantics', *BiOr* 39 (1982), 26–38.

Talstra, E., *et al.* (eds.), *Narrative and Comment. Contributions Presented to Wofgang Schneider on the Occasion of his Retirement as a Lecturer of Biblical Hebrew at the Theologische Hochschule in Wuppertal* (Amsterdam, 1995).

Talstra, E. and J.W. Dyk, 'The Computer and Biblical Research: Are there Perspectives beyond the Imitation of Classical Instruments?', in Van Peursen–Ter Haar Romeny, *Text, Translation, and Tradition*, 189–203.

Talstra, E., K.D. Jenner and W.Th. van Peursen, 'How to Transfer the Research Questions into Linguistic Data Types and Analytical Instruments', in Van Keulen–Van Peursen, *Corpus Linguistics and Textual History*, 45–83.

Talstra, E. and C.H.J. van der Merwe, 'Analysis, Retrieval and the Demand for More Data. Integrating the Results of a Formal Textlinguistic and Cognitive Based Pragmatic Approach to the Analysis of Deut 4:1–40', in Cook, *Bible and Computer*, 43–78.

Talstra, E. and C.J. Sikkel, 'Genese und Kategorienentwicklung der WIVU-Datenbank oder: ein Versuch, dem Computer Hebräisch beizubringen', in C. Hardmeier *et al.* (eds.), *Ad Fontes! Quellen erfassen – lesen – deuten. Was ist Computerphilologie? Ansatzpunkte und Methodologie – Instrument und Praxis* (Applicatio 15; Amsterdam, 2000), 33–68.

Taylor, C., 'The Wisdom of Ben Sira', *JThS* 1 (1900), 571–583.

Taylor, R.A., *The Peshiṭta of Daniel* (MPIL 7; Leiden, 1994).

Thesaurus Linguae Latinae III (Leipzig, 1906–12).

Tov, E., *Textual Criticism of the Hebrew Bible* (2nd ed.; Assen, 2001).

Trask, R.L., *A Dictionary of Grammatical Terms in Linguistics* (Londen–New York, 1993).

Tropper, J., *Altäthiopische Grammatik des Ge'ez mit Übungstexten und Glossar* (ELO 2; Münster, 2002).

Vall, G., 'The Enigma of Job 1,21a', *Bib.* 76 (1995), 325–342.

Van Hecke, P.J.P., *Job 12–14. A Functional-Grammatical and Cognitive-Semantic Approach* (PhD diss., Tilburg University, 2005).

———. 'Searching for and Exploring Wisdom. A Cognitive-Semantic Approach to the Hebrew Verb *ḥāqar* in Job 28', in Van Wolde, *Cognition in Context*, 139–162.

Van Rompay, L., 'Some Preliminary Remarks on the Origins of Classical Syriac as a Standard Language. The Syriac Version of Eusebius of Caesarea's Ecclesiastical History', in G. Goldenberg and S. Raz (eds.), *Semitic and Cushittic Studies* (Wiesbaden, 1994), 70–89.

———. 'Some Reflections on the Use of the Post-Predicative *hwā* in Classical Syriac', in Jongeling–Murre-van den Berg–Van Rompay, *Studies in Hebrew and Aramaic Syntax*, 210–219.

Verhagen, A., 'Subordination and Discourse Segmentation Revisited, or: Why Matrix Clauses May Be More Dependent than Complements', in T. Sanders, J. Schilperoord and W. Spooren (eds.), *Text Representation. Linguistic and Psycholinguistic Aspects* (HCP 8; Amsterdam–Philadelphia, 2001).

Verheij, A.J.C., 'The Genitive Construction with Two *Nomina Recta*', *ZAH* 2 (1989), 210–212.

Wackernagel, J., 'Über ein Gesetz der indogermanische Wortstellung', *Indog. Forsch.* 1 (1891), 333–436.

Waltke, B.K. and M. O'Connor, *An Introduction to Biblical Hebrew Syntax* (Winona Lake, 1990).

Weber, K., 'Wisdom False and True (Sir 19,20–30)', *Bib.* 77 (1996), 330–348.

Weinrich, H., *Tempus. Besprochene und erzählte Welt* (Stuttgart, 1964; 3rd ed. 1977).

Weitzman, M.P., 'Is the Peshitta of Chronicles a Targum?' in Flesher, *Targum and Peshitta*, 159–193 (= *From Judaism to Christianity*, 217–264).

——. *From Judaism to Christianity. Studies in the Hebrew and Syriac Bibles by Michael P. Weitzman* edited by A. Rapoport-Albert and G. Greenberg (JSSt.S 8; Oxford, 1999).

——. תפילת הקדיש וה״פשיטתא" לדברי הימים (The Qaddish Prayer and the Peshitta of Chronicles), in H. Ben-Shammai (ed.), חקרי עבר וערב מוגשים ליהושע בלאו על ידי חבריו ותלמידיו במלאת לו שבעים (*Hebrew and Aramaic Studies in Honour of Joshua Blau Presented by Friends and Students on the Occasion of His Seventieth Birthday*) (Jerusalem 1993), 261–290.

——. *The Syriac Version of the Old Testament. An Introduction* (UCOP 56; Cambridge, 1999).

Wernberg-Møller, P., 'Some Scribal and Linguistic Features in the Genesis Part of the Oldest Peshiṭta Manuscript (B.M. Add. 14425)', *JSSt* 13 (1968), 136–161.

Wertheimer, A., עיונים נוספים במשפטים מבוקעים (More Thoughts about Cleft Sentences), *Hebrew Linguistics*, 49 (2000), 21–34.

——. *Selected Problems in Syriac Syntax: Fundamentals of Sentence Stucture* (PhD diss., Tel Aviv University, 1996).

——. 'Special Types of Cleft Sentences in Syriac', *JSSt* 46 (2001), 221–242.

——. 'Syriac Nominal Sentences', *JSSt* 47 (2002), 1–21.

——. 'The Functions of the Syriac Particle d-', *Muséon* 114 (2001), 259–289.

Wiegand, A., 'Die Gottesname צור und seine Deutung in dem Sinne Bildner oder Schöpfer in der alten jüdischen Litteratur', *ZAW* 10 (1890), 85–96.

Williams, P.J., 'A Study on Translation Technique in the Peshitta to Jeremiah', *AS* 1 (2003), 289–298.

——. '"According to All" in MT and the Peshitta', *ZAH* 12 (1999), 107–109.

——. 'Bread and the Peshitta in Matthew 16:11–12 and 12:4', *NT* 43 (2001), 331–333.

——. *Early Syriac Translation Technique and the Textual Criticism of the Greek Gospels* (Texts and Studies, Third Series 2; Piscataway, 2004).

——. 'Some Problems in Dertermining the *Vorlage* of Early Syriac Versions of the NT', *NTS* 47 (2001), 537–543.

——. *Studies in the Syntax of the Peshitta of I Kings* (MPIL 12; Leiden, 2001).

Winter, M.M., 'Ben Sira in Syriac: An Ebionite Translation?', in E.A. Livingstone (ed.), *Studia Patristica XVI: Papers Presented to the Seventh International Conference on Patristic Studies Held in Oxford 1975* (Berlin, 1975), 121–123.

——. *Ben Sira in Syriac* (PhD diss., Freiburg, 1974).

——. 'The Origins of Ben Sira in Syriac', *VT* 27 (1977), 237–253 (Part I), 494–507 (Part II).

——. *A Concordance to the Peshitta Version of Ben Sira* (MPIL 2; Leiden, 1976).

Winther-Nielsen, N., *A Functional Discourse Grammar of Joshua. A Computer-Assisted Rhetorical Structure Analysis* (Stockholm, 1995).

Wolde, E. van, 'Introduction', in idem, *Narrative Syntax*, vii-x.

Wolde, E. van (ed.), *Job 28. Cognition in Context* (BIS 64; Leiden, 2003).

——. *Narrative Syntax and the Hebrew Bible: Papers of the Tilburg Conference*

1996 (BIS 29; Leiden, 1997).

Wright, B.G., *No Small Difference: Sirach's Relationship to its Hebrew Parent Text* (SCSt 26; Atlanta, 1989).

Wright, W., *Catalogue of Syriac Manuscripts in the British Museum* (London, 1870–72).

Yadin, Y., *The Scroll of the War of the Sons of Light against the Sons of Darkness* (transl. by B. and Ch. Rabin; Oxford, 1962).

INDEX OF PASSAGES

1. BEN SIRA

3. NEW TESTAMENT

5. APOCRHYPA, DEAD SEA SCROLLS, RABBINIC LITERATURE

MONOGRAPHS
OF THE PESHITTA INSTITUTE
LEIDEN

1. DIRKSEN, P.B. *The Transmission of the Text in the Peshiṭta MSS of* The Book of Judges. 1972. ISBN 90 04 03452 8
2. WINTER, M.M. *A Concordance to the Peshiṭta Version of Ben Sira.* 1976. ISBN 90 04 04507 4
3. OWENS, R.J. *The Genesis and Exodus of Aphrahat the Persian Sage.* 1983. ISBN 90 04 06969 0
4. DIRKSEN, P.B. & M.J. MULDER. *The Peshiṭta.* Its Early Text and History. (Papers of Symposium, Leiden 1985). 1988. ISBN 90 04 08769 9
5. DIRKSEN, P.B. *An Annotated Bibliography of the Peshiṭta of the Old Testament.* 1989. ISBN 90 04 09017 7
6. LANE, D.J. *The Peshiṭta of Leviticus.* 1994. ISBN 90 04 10020 2
7. TAYLOR, R.A. *The Peshiṭta of Daniel.* 1994. ISBN 90 04 10148 9
8. DIRKSEN, P.B. & A. VAN DER KOOIJ (eds.). *The Peshiṭta as a Translation.* Papers Read at the II Peshiṭta Symposium Held at Leiden 19-21 August 1993. 1995. ISBN 90 04 10351 1
9. SALEY, R.J. *The Samuel Manuscript of Jacob of Edessa.* A Study in Its Underlying Textual Traditions. 1998. ISBN 90 04 11214 6
10. SALVESEN, A. *The Books of Samuel in the Syriac Version of Jacob of Edessa.* 1999. ISBN 90 04 11543 9
11. MORRISON, C.E. *The Character of the Syriac Version of the First Book of Samuel.* 2001. ISBN 90 04 11984 1
12. WILLIAMS, P.J. *Studies in the Syntax of the Peshitta of 1 Kings.* 2001. ISBN 90 04 11978 7
13. GREENBERG, G. *Translation Technique in the Peshitta to Jeremiah.* 2002. ISBN 978 90 04 11980 2
14. VAN PEURSEN, W.Th. & B. TER HAAR ROMENY, *Text, Translation, and Tradition.* Studies on the Peshitta and its Use in the Syriac Tradition Presented to Konrad D. Jenner on the Occasion of his Sixty-Fifth Birthday. 2006. ISBN 978 90 04 15300 4
15. TER HAAR ROMENY, B. (ed.). *The Peshitta: Its Use in Literature and Liturgy.* Papers Read at the Third Peshitta Symposium. 2006. ISBN 978 90 04 15658 6
16. VAN PEURSEN, W.Th. *Language and Interpretation in the Syriac Text of Ben Sira.* A Comparative Linguistic and Literary Study. 2007. ISBN 978 90 04 16394 2